THE WINE ATLAS OF

FRANCE

AND TRAVELLER'S GUIDE TO THE VINEYARDS

MITCHELL BEAZLEY

THE WINE ATLAS OF FRANCE

AND TRAVELLER'S GUIDE TO THE VINEYARDS

HUBRECHT DUIJKER & HUGH JOHNSON

The Wine Atlas of France
Hubrecht Duijker and Hugh Johnson

First published in Great Britain in 1987
Fourth edition printed in 1997 by Mitchell Beazley, an imprint of
Reed International Books Limited, Michelin House, 81 Fulham
Road, London SW3 6RB and Auckland and Melbourne

A CIP catalogue record of this book is available from the
British Library.

ISBN 1 85732 336 X

Commissioning Editor	Sue Jamieson
Executive Art Editor	Fiona Knowles
Editor	Diane Pengelly
Design	Watermark Communications
Cartographic Editor	Zoë Goodwin
Picture Research	Claire Gouldstone
Index	Marie Lorimer
Gazetteer	Sally Chorley
Production	Rachel Lynch
Cartography	Map Creation Ltd, Lovell Johns Ltd,
	Colin Earl Cartography
Typeset in	ITC Century Old Style and Gill Sans
Origination by	Mandarin Offset Singapore
Printed and bound	Cayfosa Industria Grafica, Spain

Contributors

The following revised and updated edition would not have been
possible without the significant contributions of the following
specialist wine writers, many of whom completely rewrote the
text from new research.

Wine Law and Vineyard Classification;
Grape Varieties; Vineyard Sites: Climate and Soil
Rosemary George MW
One of the first female Masters of Wine and author of eight wine
books including *French Country Wine* and *Wines of New Zealand*.

The Loire; The Rhône; Provence;
Languedoc-Roussillon Roger Voss
Author of the *Mitchell Beazley Pocket Guide to the Wines of Loire,
Alsace and the Rhône and other French Regional Wines*, and *France:
A Feast of Food and Wine*.

Champagne Michael Edwards
Wine writer specialising in Champagne and author of *The
Champagne Companion*.

Burgundy Jasper Morris MW
Author of *The White Wines of Burgundy*, regular contributor to
Decanter magazine and managing director of wine importer Morris
& Verdin.

Bordeaux James Lawther MW
Wine writer and contributing editor to *Decanter* magazine.

Cognac & Armagnac Nicholas Faith
Wine and spirits writer and author of the *Mitchell Beazley Pocket
Guide to Cognac and Brandy*.

The South-West Paul Strang
Wine writer and author of *Wines of South-West France*.

Contents

Introduction

France more than any other country is the wine-lover's Mecca. Almost all the wines we drink, even if they come from California or New Zealand, ultimately owe their fundamental identity, the aromas and flavours of their grapes, their method of making and ageing, their role in partnership with food, to the regions of France and their mature traditions. France's wine-growing landscapes, her terroirs, are part of the subconscious of every wine producer, and most wine-drinkers too.

This Atlas is a practical guide to the terroirs of France for visitors. Even if it is more consulted by the fireside than on the autoroute, it is designed as a way of tackling a vast and complex, incredibly varied, tempting and beguiling prospect: the Tour de France du Vin.

Why is the very thought of touring France so exciting? There are many answers, but all point in the same direction. France is the country that has perfected the art of living – public living, that is. She offers the world a polished front. French food is chosen and prepared with a care and seriousness that has no parallel. Surely it is the same gustatory genius that made France the creator of wine at the level of luxury.

What the French have done through history, almost it seems without knowing it, is to breed quality in wine. Just as a trainer and breeder produces faster and faster horses, wine-growers in certain privileged parts of France (and they are many) have acted to speed and direct the process of evolution. Long before technology had any meaning, owners of good land were seeking a premium for its products, reinvesting it in the land itself. From the fields in better heart they grew the best grapes they could find and studied the art of making their wine better and more distinct.

For distinction – individual character – is at the heart of the matter. Were wine one single beverage, however excellent, we should drink it gratefully, but it would lose its fascination. To teach the product of each region, even each vineyard, to taste like itself, and not precisely like any other wine, has been France's contribution.

To explain just what this means, and why the wine of this slope is lighter, more perfumed, more structured or leaves its flavour longer in the mouth than the wine from the slope across the way, France has coined the term 'terroir'. Terroir literally means soil, but it embraces far more. It includes shelter, drainage, angle of slope in relation to the sun, microclimate, incidence of frost, and even traditional or novel practices of cultivation. All these things constitute the terroir that gives identity and distinction to a wine. What English word can we offer as an equivalent? The hard-worked term 'environment' is perhaps the nearest.

How much of the environment that created and produces the world's favourite wines is due to the land, and how much to the people? Given the genius of the French for taking pains with what they eat and drink, would or could they have turned any other country – Spain, for example, or Italy – into the motherland of wine?

In historical terms the answer must be no. France makes great wine, and delicate, digestible, easily drinkable wine, because she has the ideal climate for it: above all, moderate summer heat, with nights growing cooler as vintage time approaches. More important even than the terroir, there are perfect natural conditions for wine's fermentation and cellaring. France did not need to wait for the invention of refrigeration and air-conditioning. Her grapes are picked at the moment when autumn chill takes over from summer heat. Spain or most of Italy without electricity for refrigeration would be back in the Dark Ages as far as fine wine is concerned – with the notable exception of sherry.

The north of France lies so close to the limit of practicable viticulture that it is touch and go whether in any year the grapes will reach full ripeness. To the west the mouth of Loire, to the east Champagne and the valley of the Moselle define the line beyond which grapes are no longer a satisfactory crop. The limit is farther north in the east than in the west because of the English Channel. Successive waves of clouds coming from the Atlantic cover the sun over Brittany and Normandy for too much of the summer. They roll inland to Paris and beyond and cover Picardy and the Pas de Calais. Champagne is the nearest point to the Channel that escapes this unwelcome cover. It even benefits marginally from the continental climate with its warmer summers to the east.

So much for the natural conditions. As for the people, enthusiasm for wine goes back to the inhabitants of France in Roman times and beyond. Three hundred years before Julius Caesar divided all Gaul into three parts, a substantial raiding party from what is now Burgundy headed south into Italy, sacked Rome, settled in Lombardy and occupied it for several generations. They returned home vignerons, so that by the time of Roman rule wine was already established as part of Gallic culture.

The factors that decided which should be the principal vineyards of Roman Gaul were reinforced by the growing power of bishops and, later, monasteries. Of these Cîteaux in Burgundy became, with the advent of the Cistercians in the 12th century, the most influential. Its great walled vineyard, the Clos de Vougeot, still remains as a reminder of the resources and technology at the disposal of the medieval church. But its location was a decision taken 1,000 years before that, when the traffic on the Saône Valley highway, passing through the territory of what later became (and still is) the diocese of Autun, suggested to the citizens a use for the scrubby hillside that we now call the Côte d'Or. There is scarcely an exception, indeed, to the rule that France's great vineyards began with the Romans.

If France's vineyards were established an astonishingly long time ago, so it seems were the families of grapes that were eventually to decide the flavour of the wines. According to the great historian of French wine-growing Roger Dion, the vines that helped to form the different characters of Burgundy and Bordeaux came from two widely different sources. Burgundy shares with the east of France right up to Champagne in the north the group of varieties that includes the Pinot Noir. Dion speculates that Pinot and its cousins are the result of centuries of selection from the wild grapes of the Alpine foothills of the Dauphiné by the Gallic tribe whose alliance with Julius Caesar assured the conquest of Gaul. The Romans referred to their hardy vine as Allobrogica, the plant of the Allobrogic people.

By contrast the Bordeaux group of grapes, the Cabernets, Merlot and Petit Verdot, have a common ancestor in the plant known as Biturica, which was probably brought to Bordeaux from the older Roman settlements of the Ebro Valley in Spain. The substantial remains of a Roman *cuvier* are still to be seen near Cenicero in Rioja. Perhaps its grapes formed the character of Bordeaux, and fashioned the style of winemaking that was to be re-exported to Rioja 1,800 years later.

What better proof can there be of the continuity of French wine-growing than the existence even today of two distinct stylistic traditions in eastern and western France, their headquarters respectively in Burgundy and Bordeaux? There is only one region where they meet and mingle, and that is along the valley of the Loire, presumably invaded with wine-growing ideas from both ends, from Burgundy near its headwaters and from Bordeaux via the Bay of Biscay.

Historians have argued the toss about why the progress of 2,000 years has not led to a more homogeneous pattern. Why have all French growers not settled for the same grapes, the same techniques, the same ideal of what a good wine should be? Terroir is part of the answer: the land itself chooses the crop that suits it best. Another, not to be underestimated, is local pride – even secrecy.

France up to the last century was, in practical terms, a bigger place than the entire world today. There was no hobnobbing between winemakers of different regions (unless it was among the Cistercians). There were no universities for winemakers. Tradition fed on itself. Grape varieties arose by continually taking cuttings from the best plants in your own vineyards. The date of the harvest was directed by the local authorities so that everyone in the district made the same sort of wine. These were the conditions that in the country backwaters bred some wonderfully individual and even eccentric traditions. They are also the reason why no wine traveller should stick solely to the 'classic' areas, or be condescending about a 'little' local wine that has 2,000 years of history behind it.

What is the best way, then, to turn a distant acquaintance with the wines of France to a full familiarity with the regions and their varied products? There is no substitute for travel. Much can be done by tasting the different wines at home, more with reading about them, but only by going there can you learn to associate a certain taste with a certain cut of the landscape, colour of roof-tile, grey river estuary or green-floored valley in view of the perpetual snow.

Sooner or later a keen wine-lover will be tempted to visit all the major wine regions of France. As this book amply illustrates, each has its own way of doing things, its own attractions and drawbacks. Champagne, at one extreme, is so highly organised to welcome visitors and dazzle them with its vast cellars and complex procedures that most tours are impersonal affairs in which you feel rather like one of the bottles being processed. Bordeaux, although infinitely fascinating and varied to its devotees, can be rather slow-going for casual visitors.

It is worth bearing in mind, certainly as a novice, that nearly all cellar tasting is of very young wines. Rarely is the crusted bottle broached, at least on first acquaintance. There is therefore more enjoyment to be had visiting and tasting in regions where the wines are delicious in their youth. It is what makes Germany a perfect land for wine tourism. The same principle applies to Alsace, the Loire Valley, the Alps, much of south-west France and indeed almost all 'minor' areas. With less monoculture of the vine, minor areas are also generally more varied and picturesque (if less rich in historical monuments).

The obvious time to plan a visit to a wine region is at vintage time, when there is most to see. Actually to see the pickers at work, the tumbrils trundling in laden with blue fruit, the fruit disappearing into hoppers; to see presses at work, to smell the heady, dangerous fumes of fermentation is the most vivid way to learn how wine is made. It is also, for equally obvious reasons, the time when the wine-grower has least time – probably, in fact, no time – for visitors. You will be tolerated, but you can scarcely expect a red carpet when every moment is full of action and anxiety.

You should see one vintage somewhere (my favourite spots at vintage time are Beaujolais and Alsace). But then consider the other seasons. Each has its charms: spring most of all, perhaps, while the leaves are still tender green, or mid-June when the vines are in flower over most of France, filling vineyards with a most haunting sweet perfume said to provoke young love like no other scent.

Late October, after the vintage, is an excellent time to go. Vineyards are golden and village streets still full of the scent of fermenting wine. Later still, although days are short, empty roads and busy towns decorated for Christmas make France a friendly, convivial place to be. Even the coldest months have their attractions and snow in the vineyards can be more beautiful than heavy summer leaves. There is only the pruning to be done outdoors, and plenty of time for tasting and talk in the cellar. Hotels are almost empty and even three-star restaurants become approachable.

To revisit a corner of France, especially one that is not in every guidebook, until you have a sense of belonging is (to some people) the most rewarding way of really entering into the spirit of the place. With only a little persistence, two to three visits perhaps, your face becomes familiar and the welcome warmer when you arrive.

VISITING WINE-GROWERS

This Atlas presupposes an independently minded traveller. Group travel offers the anonymity that glosses over ignorance of language or of the subject in hand. It is the way not to become involved; to look on as a bystander – but also to miss a great deal.

As an independent visitor you have some homework to do. First, in planning your itinerary. It is not normally essential to make reservations in French country hotels far in advance, unless there is some particular event drawing the crowds. Burgundy on the third weekend in November is full up for Les Trois Glorieuses. Bordeaux at VinExpo time is so full that a special express train shuttles back and forth to Biarritz to take advantage of that resort's hotels. The key weekends at the beginning and end of August when all France is on the roads are difficult – but then it is a time to avoid travelling in France at all.

Outside famous resort areas of three-star restaurant-hotels, outside special events, and outside of big cities (above all, Paris) a telephone call a few days in advance is usually enough to secure a reasonable hotel room. Hotels below the luxury category are notably good value: it is these that are principally featured in the travel information in this book.

If you plan to spend more than a night or two in one place it is worth doing more specific research, writing for brochures and confirming your reservation in writing. Famous restaurants are generally booked up for weeks in advance in the summer season; a reservation by letter is often essential.

As to announcing your arrival at a château or a wine estate, the general rule is simple enough. The grander and more prestigious the establishment the more notice (and indeed influence) you need to be made welcome, or sometimes even to be admitted at all. A first-growth Bordeaux château, or one of the grandest Burgundy domaines, rather reasonably likes to limit visits to those who are actual or potential customers for its very expensive wines. The conventional way of establishing your standing as a regular massive buyer of first-growth wines is to ask your supplier at home to write you a letter of introduction, which you then send in advance with a request for a visit, if possible giving a choice of dates. If your request is granted (which is normal, but not automatic) you can then expect to be received with some formality, punctually at the prearranged time, probably by the cellarmaster or *maître de chai*.

Courtesy on your part demands that you have done some homework about the château or domaine in question. At least be sure you know the appellation and its ground rules as to grape varieties. In Bordeaux this is straightforward. Most *chais* (the Bordeaux word for cellar, a building usually half-underground)

contain one kind of wine only – probably from two vintages, the newest and the previous year's, waiting for the appropriate moment to be bottled. By contrast, in Burgundy one cellar often contains barrels of wine from ten different appellations, red or white. It will certainly encourage the grower to confide in you if you have prepared yourself with a reference book and know in advance where he has plots of vines, and therefore which wines from among the long list of Nuits, Beaune, Corton, Pommard and the rest you can expect to find in his barrels. An honoured guest (certainly an established buyer) will be offered a tasting from every barrel in the cellar if time allows.

Far more common, and less demanding for all parties, is the unstructured casual visit to a less prestigious establishment. Most such visits are prompted by a sign by the roadside: 'Vente Directe' (direct sales) or 'Dégustation Gratuite' (free tasting). An ever-open door is, of course, unlikely to be attended by the proprietor himself. In a large establishment it will be an employee; in a small one a member of the family who will offer you a little routine visit. A growers' cooperative is also usually an excellent place to make acquaintance with the wine of the region and perhaps start a trail leading to friendship.

A casual visitor is often offered just one glass – and that from a bottle already open, perhaps kept in a refrigerator. This is the moment to size up the property and decide whether you would like to know more – perhaps based on what you are tasting, perhaps on a glimpse of something more interesting in the background.

If your host goes to the length of drawing a sample direct from a barrel for you, you have the right to feel flattered. He (or she) is taking trouble, and is trusting you to judge the wine in its pre-bottled state (which is almost always slightly different, for better or worse, from after it has been finally filtered into bottles). In these circumstances taste the wine with extreme care. This is not the place to start on a course of instruction in wine-tasting, but the following procedure both observes the proprieties and allows you to make up your own mind about what you are tasting.

Accept the glass you are offered with both your hands, taking the foot (not the stem) in your right hand and steadying the top with your left. Spend ten seconds looking at the wine before you do anything else. Take a piece of white paper from your pocket and tip the glass you are holding (still by the foot) against it so that the colour is shown up clearly against the paper. You need not comment on the colour, but if you are feeling loquacious the safe remark is "jolie robe".

Briefly swirl the wine in your glass so as to give it more contact with the air. This is much easier to do if you are holding the glass by the foot. There is no need to make your debut at this exercise in a cellar: practise at home, even with water if you like. It will soon become second nature and, more important, increase your enjoyment of every glass.

Having swirled, sniff. Two or three short sharp sniffs should be enough if you are concentrating on the matter in hand. I find it easier to concentrate on what I am smelling if I close my eyes. Being self-conscious I usually turn away or walk to one side at this moment. Vaguely to hold the glass under your nose while chattering about something else is pure futility; you can form no impression of an aroma while you are talking (or even listening).

While you are still concentrating, take a good-sized sip, hold it in your mouth, then chew the wine as though it were bread. In a cold cellar, and especially in winter, take a very small sip: a mouthful of icy wine can make your teeth protest. As soon as you have thoroughly soaked your palate in flavour, spit the wine out. Some cellars provide a spittoon or perhaps a box of sawdust.

Autoroute
Main road
Other road
Main railway
⊕ Principal airport
International boundary
Département boundary
■ Chief town of département

1:5,000,000

Km. 0   50   100   150 Km.
Miles 0   50   100 Miles

If there is no obvious provision, spit on the floor. It is perfectly good form. If there is a doorway leading outside, I often wander over to it and spit in the open air. The pause gives time to reflect.

Having tasted, what you say or do next is a more open question. A remark of some sort is clearly called for. If you liked what you tasted, and want to prolong the encounter, homework once again comes to the rescue. Anyone in a wine region will tell you when the normal bottling time is for each vintage. Before you risk a pronouncement on what you have tasted, you might draw out your host by asking him when he expects to 'faire la mise' (en bouteilles). His reply will often give you a hint of his opinion of the vintage.

It is prudent to keep your own pronouncement on a fairly general level. "Très prometteux" (very promising) is acceptably neutral. "Intéressant" is perhaps the minimum compliment within the bounds of courtesy. One remark that can lead to further conversation (and tasting) is to say that you would like to taste the wine again in six months' or a year's time. Does Monsieur sell his wine in London/Amsterdam/San Francisco? Does he have an agent whose address you might make a note of? (To take notes while you are tasting is not only a sign of serious purpose which will be duly noted, it is also by far the best way to add to your stock of accurate wine knowledge.)

One well-tried route to competent and welcoming producers, particularly in the less-frequented parts of France, is via the local hoteliers and restaurateurs. A conversation at your hotel may lead to a telephone call by the hotelier and a genuinely friendly reception. This approach has led me to many excellent producers whose market has been primarily local (and highly discriminating). To be realistic, I have had more than one thoroughly surly encounter too. Nor, I'm afraid, has a roadside Dégustation Gratuite ever yet led me to an Aladin's cave of unknown nectar.

But whoever said that to travel hopefully is better than to arrive must have had the byways of France in mind. Especially those in wine country.

HUGH JOHNSON

A WORD ABOUT THE MAPS...

The maps in this Atlas vary in scale, the level of detail depending on the complexity of the area mapped. There is a scale bar with each map. Contour intervals vary from map to map and are shown in each individual key.

Each map has a grid with letters down the side and numbers across the top and bottom. To locate a château or winery, look up the name in the index/gazetteer to find the page number followed by the grid reference.

AND TELEPHONE NUMBERS

In October 1996 a new numbering plan was introduced in France with the effect that all eight-digit numbers became nine-digit numbers (Paris numbers remained unchanged as they already had nine digits).

When calling France from Great Britain, dial the international prefix 00 followed by the country code 33, followed by the new nine-digit number as listed in this Atlas (that is, excluding the zero in parentheses which precedes each number).

If you are dialling from within France, dial the number as it is listed – including the '(0)'.

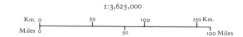

——·——International boundary

————·Département boundary

○ Chief town of département

● Centre of VDQS area

Côte Roannaise VDQS name

Champagne

Loire Valley

Burgundy

Savoie and Jura

Rhone

Southwest

Cognac

Bergerac

Bordeaux

Languedoc-Roussillon

Provence

Alsace

Massif Central

Other wine-producing areas

Calais

Lille

BELGIQUE

PAS-DE-CALAIS

NORD

LUXEMBOURG

ALLEMAGNE

Arras

SOMME

AISNE

Charleville-Mézières

ARDENNES

Metz
Vins de Moselle

MOSELLE

BAS-
RHIN

Strasbourg

Amiens

Laon

SEINE-MARITIME

le Havre

OISE

Beauvais

Reims

MARNE

MEUSE

MEURTHE-
ET- Nancy
MOSELLE

Rouen

Caen

EURE

CALVADOS

VAL-D'OISE
Pontoise

SEINE-ST-
DENIS

Châlons-en-
Champagne

Bar-le-Duc
Côtes de Toul

Toul

RHIN

Colmar

Evreux

HAUTS-DE-SEINE

PARIS

SEINE-
ET-MARNE

HAUTE-
MARNE

Épinal

VOSGES

HAUT-
RHIN

ORNE

Alençon

EURE-
ET-LOIR

Versailles

YVELINES

VAL-DE-
MARNE

Evry

Melun

ESSONNE

Troyes

AUBE

Chaumont

Belfort

Vesoul

HAUTE-
SAÔNE

BELFORT

MAYENNE

le Mans

SARTHE

Chartres

YONNE

Chablis

St-Bris-le-Vineux
Sauvignon
de St-Bris

CÔTE-D'OR

DOUBS

Besançon

Laval

LOIRET

Orléans
Vins de l'Orléanais

Auxerre

Dijon

Montoire-sur-le-Loir
Coteaux du Vendômois

Blois

Gien
Vins des Coteaux du Giennois

Beaune

LOIR-ET-
CHER

Angers

INDRE-
ET-
LOIRE

Tours

Valençay

NIÈVRE

CHER

le Creusot

JURA

Lons-le-
Saunier

SUISSE

Ancenis
Coteaux d'Ancenis

MAINE-ET-
LOIRE

INDRE

Bourges

Nevers

SAÔNE-ET-LOIRE

Thouars
Vins du Thouarsais

DEUX-
SÈVRES

Châteauroux

Châteaumeillant
Châteaumeillant

ALLIER

Moulins

Mâcon

Bourg-en-Bresse

Genève

HAUTE-
SAVOIE

Vins du
Haut Poitou

Poitiers

VIENNE

Guéret

St-Pourçain-
sur-Sioule
St-Pourçain

Roanne
Côte Roannaise

AIN

Annecy

Belley
Vins du Bugey

Niort

HAUTE-
VIENNE

CREUSE

PUY-DE-DÔME

LOIRE

Lyon

Chambéry

la Rochelle

Clermont-
Ferrand
Côtes d'Auvergne

Boën-sur-Lignon
Côtes du Forez

SAVOIE

CHARENTE-
MARITIME

Cognac

CHARENTE

Limoges

St-
Étienne

ISÈRE

Grenoble

ITALIE

Angoulême

CORRÈZE

le Puy

Tournon

Valence

Tulle

Périgueux

CANTAL

HAUTE-LOIRE

ARDÈCHE

Privas

HAUTES-ALPES

Gap

DORDOGNE

Aurillac

Mende

St-Remèze
Côtes du Vivarais

DRÔME

Haut-Comtat
Tulette

Bordeaux

GIRONDE

Libourne

Entraygues
Vins d'Entraygues et du Fel

LOT

Estaing
Vins d'Estaing

Rodez

LOZÈRE

ALPES-DE-
HAUTE-PROVENCE

Digne

ALPES-
MARITIMES

Nice

Marmande
Côtes du Marmandais

LOT-ET-
GARONNE

Cahors

AVEYRON

VAUCLUSE

Avignon

GARD

Pierrevert
Coteaux de Pierrevert

Buzet

Agen

TARN-ET-
GARONNE

Gorges et
Côte de Millau

Nîmes

Draguignan

LANDES

Côtes du Brulhois
la Villedieu-du-Temple
Vins de Lavilledieu

Montauban

Gaillac

Albi

TARN

BOUCHES-
DU-
RHÔNE

VAR

Mont-de-Marsan

GERS

Montpellier

Toulon

Vins du Tursan

Côtes de St-Mont

Auch

HÉRAULT

Marseille

Geaune

Toulouse

HAUTE-
GARONNE

Côtes du Cabardès
et de l'Orbiel
Carcassonne

Narbonne

PYRÉNÉES

Pau

Tarbes

Côtes de la
Malepère

Foix

AUDE

HAUTES-
PYRÉNÉES

ARIÈGE

Perpignan

ATLANTIQUES

ESPAÑA

PYRÉNÉES-
ORIENTALES

N

Wine Law and Vineyard Classification

French wines are controlled in a rigid hierarchy, with *appellation contrôlée* at the top of the pyramid, followed by VDQS, or *vin délimité de qualité supérieure*, which is a much smaller and slightly obscure category. Then come a growing number of vins de pays, or country wines, while at the broad base there is an anonymous mass of vin de table.

Appellation contrôlée, or to give its full name, *appellation d'origine contrôlée*, covers all the famous wine names and vineyards. It is a system that was developed in the 1930s following fears about fraud and the adulteration of wine at the beginning of the century. Baron le Roy of Château Fortia in Châteauneuf-du-Pape takes the credit for laying down in 1923 the basic concepts on which *appellation contrôlée* was modelled. His stipulations, initially for Châteauneuf-du-Pape, covered not only a geographical delimitation of the vineyard area but also specified which grape varieties were to be used, the method of pruning and training the vine and a minimum alcoholic strength. Also a *triage* or sorting of the grapes at harvest was imposed; a tasting panel (whose role was to maintain quality) was introduced and the production of pink wine in the area was forbidden. Thus the ground rules for *appellation contrôlée* were formulated.

The economic depression of the 1930s, combined with a wine surplus and the widespread cultivation of hybrids, gave an extra incentive for the creation of the Institut National des Appellations d'Origine (INAO), which had particular responsibility to lay down the guidelines for individual appellations in 1936. The first three appellations were Arbois in the Jura, Cassis in Provence and, appropriately, Châteauneuf-du-Pape.

The concept of quality in France depends upon geography, upon each appellation's specific 'terroir'. The term terroir is a peculiarly French concept, covering more than just the soil, for it also relates to climate, aspect, and the whole environment of the vineyard. Thus, in formal classifications, the area of production is carefully defined, a list of the various villages set out and the specific plots of land for higher classifications such as *grand* or *premier cru* mentioned by name. Often there are different categories within the same broad area. Chablis is the generic appellation, for example, Petit Chablis comes from the inferior sites, *premiers crus* from more favourable sites, and even better *grands crus* from the finest vineyards. The permitted grape varieties, with their minimum and maximum proportions, are laid down as well as the minimum or, in the case of Muscadet, maximum permitted alcoholic strengths.

Yields are an aspect of quality and are strictly controlled by means of a basic yield, which may then be adjusted according to annual conditions. Work in the vineyard is covered, such as the type of pruning and trellising, while irrigation is usually forbidden. Winemaking methods are also dealt with, specifying for example whole-bunch pressing in the production of Beaujolais and champagne, and the use or preclusion of chaptalization. Essentially *appellation contrôlée* aims to give a legal backing to the traditional practices of the region, the *usages locaux*.

Everything is carefully controlled by the INAO and checked by the Service de la Répression des Fraudes so that *appellation contrôlée* provides a reasonable guide to the quality wine of France. Of course much also depends upon individual producers and, especially in a large appellation such as Champagne or Bordeaux, the quality range can be very broad.

The serious disadvantage of the appellation system lies in its inflexibility and refusal to countenance the possibility of experimentation. As a wine producer within the delimited area of an appellation, you may grow only what the rules dictate if you are to produce the wine of that appellation, which seems stifling compared to the fluidity and flexibility of the New World system.

The other disadvantage from the consumers' point of view is the INAO's total antipathy to the mention of any grape variety on the label. Alsace is the principal exception to this, but normally one is expected to know that Chablis is made from Chardonnay, or red Hermitage from Syrah.

After *appellation contrôlée* comes VDQS (*vin délimité de qualité supérieur*) a category that covers a very small number of wines and which is often seen as a stepping stone to *appellation contrôlée* itself. The first VDQS were created in the early 1950s for areas that were not well known, or where the quality was still uncertain. For instance many of the appellations of the Midi started life as VDQS and were promoted to appellation status in the early 1980s. Occasionally a vin de pays may rise to VDQS, such as Vin de Pays des Gorges et Côtes de Millau, which became Côtes de Millau in 1993. Essentially the regulations for a VDQS are as strict as they are for an appellation wine and both are considered quality wine under European wine law categories.

Much more significant in quantity terms are the vins de pays, which were created in order to distinguish basic vin de table from those wines with some regional characteristics. The first tentative steps were taken in 1973 and vins de pays were defined by a government decree in 1979, since when they have evolved and grown in number and importance.

The criteria of production for vins de pays are much stricter than for vins de table and much more flexible than for any appellation or VDQS wines. Yields are limited to 90 hectolitres per hectare and the wine must attain a minimum alcohol level of 10 degrees. There are analytical and organoleptic tests, and in the Midi vin de pays may be chaptalized, but appellation wines may not. Most significant, however, is the flexibility as to which grape varieties may or may not be planted. There are two lists for each *département*: those that are recommended and those that are authorised. The latter are not as good as the former, but they are not bad enough to be disallowed altogether. Originally, if a grape variety was mentioned on the label, the wine had to be made from that variety alone, but since 1995 the regulations have allowed for the mention of two or possibly even three varieties.

There is no doubt that flexibility over grape varieties enables the more adventurous producers to plant unusual varieties in the name of experimentation, and this often has exciting results. This is why you can find examples of Viognier or Pinot Noir in the Midi, while Chardonnay and Cabernet Sauvignon are now well established there. If a grower produces both vin de pays and an appellation wine, the vin de pays may provide a way of disposing of inferior wine that is not suitable for the appellation, or may be an outlet for any experiments that incorporate grape varieties not permitted in the appellation.

There are three broad categories of vin de pays, covering the whole of viticultural France. The first comprises the four regional vins de pays, namely Vin de Pays d'Oc, incorporating the whole of the Midi; Vin de Pays du Comté Tolosan, which includes most of

The 'Bordeaux mixture', a bright blue blend of copper sulphate and slaked lime, is applied to guard against fungal disease as the vine buds swell and soften.

south-west France, Vin de Pays des Comtés Rhodaniens, for the Ardèche, Beaujolais, Jura, Savoie and the northern Rhône, and lastly Vin de Pays du Jardin de la France for the whole of the Loire Valley. The next vin de pays category includes those that are defined by the geographical boundaries of the *département* such as Vin de Pays de l'Hérault or Vin de Pays de l'Yonne; and then within a *département* there may be smaller, local areas, sometimes entailing stricter regulations about yield and alcohol. Some have wonderfully evocative names such Vin de Pays de la Vallée du Paradis while others, such as Vin de Pays des Terrasses et Coteaux de Montauban, may be less memorable. The only one that is really determined by a specific geological factor is the Vin de Pays des Sables du Golfe du Lion, where the vines must be planted on coastal sand dunes.

As well as experimentation with grape varieties, the vins de pays allow for innovation in the cellar and in winemaking practices that are not traditional to a region. For instance, fermentation in small barrels was unheard of in the south of France until the introduction of Chardonnay. The vins de pays have proved a great

source of inspiration for producers developing new wines in previously unappreciated areas and for establishing an individual reputation in a viticultural desert. The most obvious example of both is Mas de Daumas Gassac.

Finally at the bottom of the pyramid comes vin de table, the most basic level of wine, described as vin de consommation courante or vin ordinaire. This is the wine that has supplied the European wine lake. There are no regulations about yields and it is not impossible to attain an excessive 200 hectolitres per hectare from inferior grape varieties like Carignan, or even worse, Alicante Bouchet and Aramon. Although table wine is allowed no mention of any geographical origin more precise than France, most of it comes from the Midi. Its production is falling as the vins de pays are developed and vineyards in poorer sites on the fertile coastal plains are uprooted.

Vins de pays have meanwhile increased in number to the extent that there were over 140 at the last count. The success of the French wine laws has provided an example for other more recent legislation in other European countries such as Italy, Spain and Portugal.

Grape Varieties

ALIGOTÉ

Aligoté is Burgundian in origin, where it is seen as something of a poor relation to Chardonnay. Its chief characteristic is acidity, but in ripe years it produces good dry wine with slightly herbal, stony undertones. Oak does nothing for it.

On the Côte d'Or it is planted on less favourable sites for the simple appellation of Bourgogne Aligoté. However the Côte Chalonnaise village of Bouzeron, where some of the best examples are made, enjoys the individual appellation of Bourgogne Aligoté Bouzeron. Aligoté also performs well in the villages of St-Bris-le-Vineux and Chitry-le-Fort, close to Chablis.

CABERNET SAUVIGNON

Cabernet Sauvignon is the grape variety of Bordeaux, performing to the peak of its perfection in the vineyards of the Médoc and Graves. It is a tough, tannic variety, with small, thick-skinned

Above: Cabernet-Sauvignon, Chateau Clarke/Listrac. - The schizophrenic ticket.

berries and a high proportion of pips. Ageing in new-oak barrels softens the tannins and helps create wines which may benefit from several years of bottle age. Châteaux such as Mouton-Rothschild and Margaux have a very high proportion of Cabernet Sauvignon, while others prefer to blend it with more Cabernet Franc and Merlot, and perhaps Petit Verdot and Malbec. As it is a relatively late ripener, it performs better in Médoc, in the warm, well drained gravelly soil, than it does in the cooler clay of St-Émilion.

As well as in Bordeaux, the variety features in most of the appellations of the South-West, in Bergerac, Côtes de Duras, Buzet and Madiran; Cahors being the main exception. Although it is allowed in some of the red appellations of the Loire Valley, Cabernet Franc is the preferred variety there. In recent years Cabernet Sauvignon has grown in importance in the Languedoc for an infinite number of vins de pays, of which the most significant is Mas de Daumas Gassac. Provence too has succumbed to the appeal of Cabernet Sauvignon, allowing it in appellations such as Côtes de Provence and Coteaux d'Aix-en-Provence, where it is usually blended with Syrah and Grenache. It has also crossed the water to Corsica for the evocative Vin de Pays de l'Île de Beauté.

CABERNET FRANC

Cabernet Franc is a grape variety of western France. In Bordeaux it is often overshadowed by Cabernet Sauvignon, so that in the Médoc and Graves it usually accounts for about 15 per cent of a blend. In St. Emilion, it makes a much more significant contribution, at the expense of Cabernet Sauvignon. In comparison it buds and ripens earlier and tends to be less susceptible to bad weather at harvest. It tends to be lighter in colour and tannin and therefore earlier maturing as a wine. As well as Bordeaux, it features in many of the south-west appellations, including Bergerac, Buzet, Côtes de Duras and Madiran. Better examples are to be found in the Loire Valley in appellations such as Chinon, Saumur and Bourgeuil.

CARIGNAN

Carignan originated in Spain as Cariñena and has spread through all the mediterranean vineyards of France. It was widely planted in the 1960s as a substitute for the inferior Aramon and consequently features extensively in all the appellations of Languedoc-Roussillon, where it enjoys the warm, dry climate. Carignan is high in acidity, tannin and colour but short on finesse and fruit. However the development of the vinification process of carbonic maceration has successfully enhanced the fruit while removing some of the astringency. Generally, the sooner Carignan loses its importance the better, but with 150,000 hectares still in production, there is a long way to go.

CHARDONNAY

From its origins in Burgundy, Chardonnay has become the world's most fashionable white-grape variety, travelling not only to virtually every other part of France but also to other continents. Only in Bordeaux is it absent.

Above all, Chardonnay produces all the great white wines of Burgundy, from Chablis in the north to Pouilly-Fuissé in the south. The finest examples come from the vineyards of the Côte d'Or, and mainly the Côte de Beaune, with wines like Corton-Charlemagne, Meursault and Puligny-Montrachet which, in the best vintages and

Some growers leave vine cuttings to decompose between the vines and add structure to the soil – others burn them to avoid the risk of harbouring fungal disease.

from the best sites, develop considerable complexity with bottle-age. In the vineyard, Chardonnay is easy to grow. With an early bud-break, it is susceptible to spring frost but otherwise is reasonably resistant to other vineyard hazards. It is also capable of high yields and requires careful pruning.

In the cellar the variety is a winemaker's dream, responding well to a variety of techniques. The best examples of unoaked Chardonnay are found in Chablis: wines with a firm, flinty acidity, while in the Côte d'Or fermentation usually takes place in barrel, entailing a full malolactic fermentation and regular lees-stirring over several months. For humbler Mâcon, the process is more basic.

Further north, Chardonnay makes a significant contribution to Champagne, where it is planted extensively on the Côte des Blancs. Picked early, it retains the prerequisite high level of acidity that is essential for all good sparkling wine and adds finesse to the blend.

From Burgundy, Chardonnay has travelled to Alsace to become a minor ingredient of Crémant d'Alsace; to the Jura for both still and sparkling wine and to Savoie; in the Ardèche it is used for a varietal vin de pays and similarly in the Loire Valley for Vin de Pays du Jardin de la France. It has even reached down into Languedoc. The region has in recent years seen an enormous increase in plantings of Chardonnay for varietal vins de pays, which allow producers to experiment with Burgundian techniques. A small proportion is also included in Crémant de Limoux to enliven the otherwise somewhat dull Mauzac.

CHENIN BLANC

Chenin Blanc, also called Pineau de la Loire, is indisputably the most versatile grape variety of France. It originated in the Loire Valley where it makes an amazing diversity of wines, from the

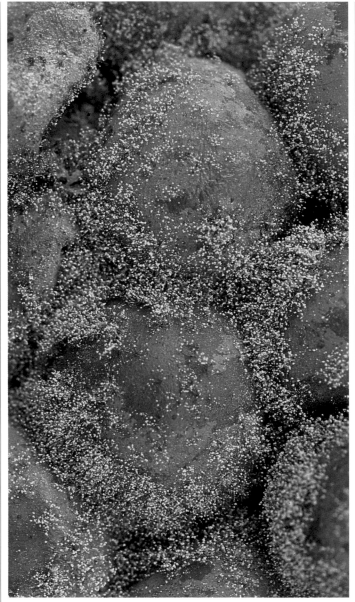

If conditions are right, Botrytis cinerea *(noble rot or* pourriture noble*) will strike. The fungus concentrates the sugar, raises the potential alcohol and the total acidity as well as adding an extraordinary vegetal honeyed flavour.*

firmly dry – and in unripe years searingly acidic – to the most intensely sweet, luscious wines capable of immense longevity. It also provides the base for most of the various sparkling-wine appellations of the Loire.

At its simplest Chenin Blanc is found in Anjou Blanc, while the finest dry wines come from Coulée de Serrant and Savennières. Vouvray and Montlouis vary in sweetness according to the quality of the vintage. In the best, when noble rot develops, Chenin Blanc makes the most wonderful Coteaux du Layon, Bonnezeaux and Quarts de Chaume.

The characteristic high acidity makes it eminently suitable for the various sparking wines of the Loire such as Crémant de Loire, Saumur Brut and so on, and for this reason it has also been included in Crémant de Limoux.

Outside the Loire Chenin Blanc may occasionally be found as a varietal vin de pays from an experimentally inclined producer in the Midi, but this is rare.

CINSAUT

Cinsaut, or Cinsault, often forms the basis of numerous red wines from the Midi, both vins de pays and appellation wines, in conjunction with Grenache and Carignan. It enjoyed a wave of planting in the 1970s, like Carignan as an improvement on Aramon, but now, again like Carignan, it is being extensively replaced by other varieties that really do enhance flavour. Cinsaut makes light, soft, fruity red wine with little depth and is therefore often appropriate for rosés.

As well as in Languedoc-Roussillon it features (insignificantly) as one of the 13 permitted varieties of Châteauneuf-du-Pape. It is also grown in Corsica and Provence.

GAMAY

Gamay, or Gamay Noir à Jus Blanc, to give the variety its full name and to distinguish it from inferior breeds of Gamay Teinturier which have coloured juice, is the grape of Beaujolais. Good Beaujolais illustrates the essential character of Gamay, the immediate appeal of a wine that is usually intended for early drinking. It is characterised by voluptuous ripe, easy fruit, acidity rather than tannin, and low alcohol. Most Beaujolais is vinified by a variation of carbonic maceration which emphasises its youthful charm and fruit.

In the Beaujolais region, Gamay grows well in granite soil and is pruned in short stubby, gobelet vines. It also features in other neighbouring appellations such as Côte Roannaise and Côtes du Forez. Elsewhere in Burgundy it is responsible for Mâcon rouge and may be blended with Pinot Noir to make Passe-Tout-Grains, for which its importance is declining.

Gamay is also grown all over the Loire Valley but not for any of the region's fine red-wine appellations. Gamay de Touraine is the variety at its best here.

GEWÜRZTRAMINER

Although the origins of Gewürztraminer lie in the Alto Adige of northern Italy, it is Alsace that produces the most characteristic examples of the variety. Many Alsace Gewürztraminers exude the heady spice and opulent perfume of lychees and other exotic fruit that make the grape so instantly recognisable.

Gewürztraminer is grown on the *grand cru* sites as well as for basic Gewürztraminer d'Alsace, and is also suitable for Vendange Tardive and Sélection des Grains Nobles wines. At its best it has an intense concentration of flavour accompanied by a heady alcohol level; at worst it can be flabby and overly sweet to compensate for the underlying bitterness on the finish. It is also a difficult variety to grow, producing a low yield of small bunches.

GRENACHE

Grenache is of Spanish origin but the variety spread around the Mediterranean in the Middle Ages and has since become the world's second most widely planted variety after the white Airén.

In France Grenache Noir is a vital ingredient of the appellations of the southern Rhône such as Côtes du Rhône, Gigondas, Tavel and, most significantly, Châteauneuf-du-Pape where it grows in bush vines in poor stony soil and hot dry conditions. It can achieve a heady level of alcohol but tends to lack colour pigment and oxidises easily, and for these reasons needs the support of other more tannic varieties.

In the Languedoc it is used extensively for blending, first with Carignan and Cinsaut, and now more commonly with Mourvèdre or Syrah. In Provence it plays an important role in most appellations. In Roussillon it makes delicious vins doux naturels

In France the well travelled Melon de Bourgogne is now almost exclusively used for the production of Muscadet at the mouth of the River Loire.

and responds well to lengthy maturation in appellations such as Vieux Rivesaltes and Banyuls, and Rasteau in the Rhône Valley.

Grenache Blanc is grown quite extensively for white Côtes du Roussillon and features in some of the white versions of the Languedoc appellation wines. Grenache Gris also appears in white and rosé from the Midi.

MALBEC / COT/ AUXERROIS
The most characteristic expression of Malbec is found in Cahors, where Auxerrois, as it is known locally, must account for a minimum of 70 per cent of the blend. Pure examples are not uncommon, but usually the somewhat rustic flavours of Auxerrois are enhanced by Tannat, or alternatively softened with a little Merlot. Increasingly Cahors is aged in small oak barrels.

Malbec still features in all the Bordeaux appellations but has declined in popularity due to its sensitivity to coulure and mildew. Its synonym in St-Émilion is Pressac, but it is in Entre-Deux-Mers and the vineyards of Bourg and Blaye that it is most widely grown. It also figures in other appellations of south west France, but more often in theory than in practice. Similarly in the Loire Valley, where it is known as Cot, it is allowed in various appellations of Touraine and Anjou, but there it has been increasingly replaced by Cabernet Franc and Cabernet Sauvignon.

MARSANNE
Marsanne is paired with Roussanne in the white versions of the northern Rhône's red appellations: Hermitage, Crozes-Hermitage, St-Joseph and St-Péray. Always the dominant partner, it is full bodied with good flavour but benefits from Roussanne's higher acidity and finer fruit. It is also favoured by producers for its yields which are more reliable than those of Roussanne.

Unlike Roussanne, Marsanne is not included in white Châteauneuf-du-Pape, but it does grow in Provence, notably in the appellation of Cassis, and is also included in Costières de Nîmes as well as featuring with increasing frequency in the Midi as a varietal vin de pays or in a blend with Roussanne.

MELON DE BOURGOGNE / MUSCADET
As its name implies, Melon de Bourgogne has its origins in Burgundy, but like Gamay it was outlawed from the region at various times in the 16th and 17th centuries, whereupon it travelled west to become the principal variety of the Loire Atlantique. It is now synonymous with Muscadet and produces crisp, dry white wine with few distinguishing features. It does not age well, although there are exceptions; nor does it respond well to oak, again with the occasional exception. Stony acidity and fairly neutral fruit are its key characteristics.

MERLOT

Merlot is one of the three principal red varieties of Bordeaux and, in terms of area, the most important. In the Médoc and Graves it plays second fiddle to Cabernet Sauvignon but in St-Émilion, Pomerol and Fronsac it really comes into its own, producing some wonderfully ripe, plummy wines. Compared to Cabernet Sauvignon, Merlot is generally lower in acidity and tannin, and it breaks bud and ripens earlier so that it performs better in the cool clay soils of the right bank. Its chief viticultural fault is coulure, which can reduce the crop in years when the weather is inclement at flowering. However the great wines of Pomerol and St-Émilion have as much as staying-power as the classed growths of the Médoc. Coufran is an example of a Médoc château that cultivates an unusually high proportion of Merlot.

Merlot also contributes to the more peripheral appellations of Bordeaux: Bourg, Blaye and the Premières Côtes de Bordeaux, and has travelled extensively throughout south-west France. It is used in Cahors to soften the rusticity of Auxerrois and in Madiran to provide balance for Tannat. It also plays a large part in Bergerac, Côtes de Duras and Buzet.

In the Languedoc Merlot has featured significantly among the so-called *cépages améliorateurs* (for 'improving vines'). It is not officially included in any appellations apart from Cabardès and Côtes de la Malepère, but is grown for countless vins de pays, for which it produces generous quantities of easy, fruity wine.

MUSCAT

Three varieties of Muscat grow in France, namely Muscat Blanc à Petits Grains and Muscat d'Alexandrie which are responsible for various Muscat-based vins doux naturels of the south, and Muscat Ottonel which features in Muscat d'Alsace.

Muscat Ottonel, though less pungent than the others, owes its success to its suitability to a cool climate. In Alsace Muscat (both Ottonel and à Petits Grains) is one of the four varieties permitted in *grand cru* sites.

Muscat à Petits Grains may be the very oldest grape variety grown in France, having been brought to the Narbonne area by the Romans, or even to Marseille by the Greeks. It also produces the finest flavour, redolent of ripe grapes, with hints of orange flowers, in wines such as Muscat de Frontignan, (also a synonym for the grape variety) as well as Muscat de Mireval, Muscat de Lunel, Muscat de St-Jean-de-Minervois and Muscat de Beaumes-de-Venise.

Muscat de Rivesaltes is a blend of both Muscat à Petits Grains and the less distinguished Muscat d'Alexandrie. The fall in popularity of these sweet dessert wines has resulted in the development of dry Muscat vin de pays as an alternative outlet.

NÉGRETTE

Négrette is the grape variety that gives Côtes du Frontonnais its original flavour for it must account for a minimum of 50 per cent of the blend – in some instances it accounts for much more. Although it has an appealing perfumed flavour it lacks tannin, so that it tends to oxidise easily and age quickly. Because of this it is often blended with other more substantial varieties, notably Cabernet Franc.

Négrette is also susceptible to disease and it dislikes humidity so requires a warm, dry climate. Small quantities are also found in the vineyards of Gaillac and Lavilledieu.

PETIT VERDOT

Petit Verdot is one of the classic grape varieties of Bordeaux. As a late ripener, it ripens fully only in the very best vintages and consequently fell from favour. However it is now enjoying something of a revival: there has been a recent increase in plantings as well as a renewed awareness and appreciation of its qualities. It is thick skinned, producing wines with immense colour and substance, and as such makes a small but valuable contribution (about five per cent) to a claret blend.

PINOT BLANC

Although Pinot Blanc originated in Burgundy and can in theory be used in the appellations of Bourgogne Blanc and Mâcon, the variety's most typical French examples are found in Alsace. There it is sometimes called Klevner or Clevner, and it may also be blended with white Auxerrois for Pinot Blanc d'Alsace. However it is regarded as something of a work-horse variety, producing soft, easy-to-drink, lightly flavoured wines with fresh acidity and a fleeting hint of spice. The particular clones used in Alsace are productive and relatively vigorous.

PINOT GRIS

Pinot Gris is a paler version of Pinot Noir, the ripe grapes being pink-skinned. It is still allowed in the vineyards of Burgundy where it is called Pinot Beurot and a small amount is grown in the Loire Valley where it is called Malvoisie. As with Pinot Blanc, however, it is in Alsace that it shows its true characteristics. Here it has traditionally been called Tokay and now, thanks to European bureaucracy, both names appear on the label. .

In Alsace it produces some highly distinctive, richly flavoured wines. It is permitted on the *grand cru* sites and in the ripest years makes spicily perfumed Vendange Tardive and Sélection des Grains Nobles as well as concentrated dry wines with an intense flavour that are more food-friendly than Gewürztraminer. Although plantings of Pinot Gris are gradually increasing, there is still insufficient production to meet demand.

PINOT MEUNIER

Pinot Meunier, or simply Meunier, is one of the three grape varieties of champagne and is the least highly rated but the most widely planted. It is probably an off-shoot of the Pinot family and takes its name from the fact that the undersides of its leaves look as though they have been dusted with flour (*meunier* is French for miller).

Pinot Meunier's advantage in the cool climate of Champagne is that it buds late and ripens earlier than Pinot Noir and therefore produces more reliable yields as well as wines with slightly higher acid levels. It is particularly popular in cooler sites. As an ingredient of champagne it is said to contribute youthful fruitiness to balance Pinot Noir and Chardonnay, but wines with a high proportion of Pinot Meunier tend to lack staying power and may taste prematurely aged.

PINOT NOIR

Pinot Noir provides one of the greatest of winemaking challenges. When it is good, it is sublime, but so often it can disappoint.

It is the grape variety of red Burgundy, grown in the Côte d'Or for wines ranging from Bourgogne Rouge to the best *grands crus*, and also grown further south in the Côte Chalonnaise for appellations such as Rully and Givry. Sometimes it is blended with Gamay for Passe-Tout-Grains. At its best Pinot Noir responds to refined vinification techniques, carefully controlled fermentations, possibly a pre-fermentation cold maceration, ageing in new oak and so on, to produce wonderfully subtle, silky, almost sweet fruit. It is lower in tannin and body than the other great red-grape varieties, notably Cabernet Sauvignon and Syrah, but nonetheless has ageing

The noble Pinot Noir mutates easily, is relatively short-lived and susceptible to viruses – and yet maintains a tantalising potential to yield top-class wine.

potential. Further north, near Chablis, it also makes the lighter appellation wines of Irancy and Coulanges-la-Vineuse and further north still accounts for a considerable area of the vineyards of Champagne, especially on the Montagne de Reims. In a champagne blend it provides body and structure.

Pinot Noir is the only red-grape variety of Alsace, where it makes rosés and light, fruity red wines which are occasionally aged in oak. In the Jura it features alongside the local varieties, Poulsard and Trousseau, and is often blended with them for Arbois and Côtes du Jura. At the eastern end of the Loire Valley it makes light, elegant Sancerre and Menetou-Salon, and also St-Pourçain-sur-Sioule further south. There are occasional examples from the Midi, where a curious or adventurous producer has tried his hand at this elusive variety and results can be good, if unusual. The variety is grown in increasing quantities on Corsica's Eastern Plain.

Clonal selection comes into play with Pinot Noir more than with any other variety; there are as many as 50 different recognised clones. These account for significant variations in performance since some are more suitable for producing quantity at the expense of quality. Pinot Noir buds early, so is susceptible to spring frosts and also to coulure. It also succumbs easily to rot but enjoys the relatively cool climate of Burgundy and performs at its best in the limestone soils of the Côte d'Or.

RIESLING

In France, this sadly underrated grape variety grows almost exclusively in Alsace, where it makes what are generally considered the finest wines of the region. The wines have firm slatey fruit, structure, backbone, and considerable ageing potential. Very young Riesling d'Alsace may seem thin and lean, but with a few years' bottle-age it develops into something magnificent, acquiring a wonderful depth of aroma and flavour and yet being bone-dry, almost to the point of steeliness, especially if it is grown on one of the better *grand cru* sites.

Riesling is a late ripener and, given the dry climate and long autumns of Alsace, the grapes can be left to ripen into Vendange Tardive or even richer Sélection des Grains Nobles wines in the richest vintages.

ROUSSANNE

Roussanne complements Marsanne in the still and sparkling white appellation of St-Péray in the northern Rhône, as well as in the white versions of the better known red appellations, Hermitage, Crozes-Hermitage and St-Joseph. Further south, it is one of the varieties allowed in white Châteauneuf-du-Pape and also grows in Provence as well as providing a source of experimentation for vin de pays in the Midi. Here too it may be blended with Marsanne. Curiously, Roussanne has also travelled to Savoie where it accounts for the little-known *cru* of Vin de Savoie, Chignin-Bergeron. Bergeron is the local name for Roussanne, which is grown in just one village of Chignin and produces a distinctive, aromatic wine.

Roussanne tends to be an irregular producer and for that reason is less widely planted than the more reliable Marsanne. But it supplies flavour and aroma to a blend as well as acidity, which enables it to age well, as it does for example in fine white Hermitage.

SAUVIGNON BLANC

The quintessence of elegant, subtle Sauvignon is to be found in the vineyards of the central Loire, notably in the appellations of Sancerre and Pouilly-Fumé, with a peripheral presence in Quincy, Reuilly and Menetou-Salon. Here Sauvignon thrives in mainly chalk vineyards, benefiting from the simplest vinification techniques to express its distinctive fruit and a dry flinty flavour, but it does not have the aromatic richness or aggression of some New World Sauvignon. In the Loire, however, oak rarely features in the vinification process.

From Sancerre, Sauvignon spreads west into Touraine for Sauvignon de Touraine, eastwards to the village of St-Bris near Chablis in the only Burgundian example of the grape, and south to the St-Pourçain region.

Far more significant is its contribution in Bordeaux, in most of the dry white appellation wines from Pessac-Léognan and Graves to basic Bordeaux Blanc and Entre-Deux-Mers. Usually it is blended with Sémillon, and the better wines are given some oak treatment. Similarly it features in the various white appellation wines of the South-West such as Buzet, Côtes de Duras and Bergerac, sometimes as a pure varietal and sometimes blended with Sémillon. Like Sémillon it is susceptible to noble rot, though not to the same extent, and is an important component of Sauternes and all the other sweet wines of Bordeaux as well as Monbazillac.

A little Sauvignon has been planted in the Midi for Vin de Pays d'Oc, but normally it prefers the cooler climate of the north. The variety also features occasionally in Cassis and Côtes de Provence.

SÉMILLON

Sémillon accounts for the great white wines of Bordeaux, both dry and sweet. However it is almost never found as a pure varietal, for it is usually blended with the livelier Sauvignon. It benefits from low yields and oak ageing. While a small proportion of Sauvignon adds acidity to the blend of a Pessac-Léognan or Graves, in Entre-Deux-Mers there is a tendency for Sauvignon to replace it entirely. Like Sauvignon it also contributes to the other white appellation wines of the South-West, notably those of Bergerac.

Sémillon is particularly susceptible to noble rot, hence its importance in Sauternes and the other lusciously sweet wines of Bordeaux, as well as in Monbazillac.

SILVANER

The origins of Silvaner are probably Austrian. In France it features only in the vineyards of Alsace as Sylvaner d'Alsace, where it tends to produce rather soft, grassy, fairly neutral wines. It is not considered one of the better varieties and is often included in a blend for Edelzwicker. However there are the occasional exceptions from warmer years which have a ripe, lightly spicy flavour.

SYRAH

Syrah is at its finest in the northern Rhône in the appellations of Côte Rôtie, Hermitage and Cornas, where it makes wonderful sturdy, intensely peppery, spicy, long-lived wines with great structure and immense concentration. Yields are usually small and the wines benefit from several months of oak ageing to bring out the flavour's full potential. Lighter appellation wines such as Crozes-Hermitage and St-Joseph make similar but more accessible, earlier maturing wines.

In the northern Rhône, apart from the addition of an occasional drop of Viognier to Côte Rôtie, Syrah is always vinified as a pure varietal. In contrast, further south in Châteauneuf-du-Pape and the Côtes du Rhône, Syrah is a vital ingredient in the blend as a support for Grenache, adding structure to the wines.

In Languedoc-Roussillon Syrah has been planted extensively as a *cépage améliorateur* and is now firmly established as a vital ingredient of the region's various appellations, thereby making a considerable impact on the quality of the wines of Midi, on both appellation wines and varietal vins de pays. Consequently total

Some estates still use osier, pliable water willow shoots, to tie young vines to stakes. Others favour jonc, *rush or cane, which is soaked in water before use to render it sufficiently supple.*

plantings have increased enormously, from 27,000 hectares in 1988 to 37,000 in 1994. Syrah is also significant in Provence where it is blended with Cabernet Sauvignon as well as Grenache in appellations such as Côtes de Provence and Coteaux d'Aix-en-Provence, and it is also grown in Corsica for vins de pays.

TANNAT

Tannat is the principal red-grape variety of the Pyrenees, featuring largely in the wines of Madiran, where it may be blended with Cabernet Franc, Cabernet Sauvignon and Fer, or produced as a pure varietal. Its deep colour and rugged tannic, indeed astringent, character is tempered by maturation in wood, and there is a growing trend towards the use of new oak in Madiran.

Tannat features in the other wines of the Pyrenees such as Irouléguy, Côtes de St-Mont, Tursan and Béarn, and also reaches as far north as Cahors, but only very small plantings are found there.

UGNI BLANC

Although of Italian origin as Trebbiano, this is France's most widely planted white-grape variety, far exceeding such popular varieties as Chardonnay and Sauvignon whose names appear on the label. In fact Ugni Blanc's principal role is to provide wine for

distillation in Cognac and Armagnac; consequently it also features in Vin de Pays Charentais and Vin de Pays des Côtes de Gascogne.

Throughout the south of France, Provence, the southern Rhône, and Languedoc-Roussillon, it is grown for its high yields and high acidity and is usually blended with other varieties such as Bourboulenc and Clairette. It has little flavour of its own.

VIOGNIER

After a somewhat limited existence in the vineyards of the northern Rhône producing Condrieu, Château Grillet and occasionally contributing to Côte Rôtie, Viognier has to some extent become the vogue, with a resulting dramatic increase in plantings from 82 hectares in 1988 to 1,500 in 1994.

Having mastered Chardonnay, producers in the south of France looking for another challenging alternative have opted for Viognier, and as a consequence several varietal vins de pays are being developed with differing degrees of success.

Viognier, which does not need the support of any wood, is identified by its intense and distinctive bouquet and a flavour of dried apricots. As the wine is low in acidity, with a deep colour and a high level of alcohol, it usually best drunk young. Neglected in the past because of its low yields, it now seems to be set for a revival.

Vineyard Sites: Climate and Soil

The vineyards of France may be divided into three broad regions according to climate, and these in turn determine which grape varieties will grow successfully where. This may seem simplistic, especially when set against the complexity of the French viticultural map, but the idea does have an underlying logic.

The western half of the country, comprising Bordeaux, the vineyards of the South-West and the Loire Valley, enjoys a maritime climate, benefiting from the moderating influence of the Atlantic Ocean. The grape varieties here are predominantly Cabernet Sauvignon, Cabernet Franc and Merlot for red wines and Sauvignon, Sémillon and Chenin Blanc for whites.

North-eastern France, particularly Champagne and Burgundy, is dominated by Chardonnay and Pinot Noir, as well as having some Gamay. The climate there is continental, which involves greater extremes of temperature including harsher winters and warmer summers. Alsace enjoys the same continental climate, but in some ways is quite separate from the rest of France, forming part of the viticultural map of the Rhine. It has more in common with Baden on the opposite riverbank. Several grape varieties are cultivated in Alsace that are grown nowhere else in France.

The third area comprises the Rhône Valley as well as all the vineyards of the Mediterranean, from the Spanish border round through the Languedoc and Provence to Nice, close to the Italian border. Corsica fits in here, having some similarities with the mainland. Vines flourish in the mediterranean climate, enjoying the hot dry summers and mild wet winters. Here red wines are more exciting than white, the finest flavours being provided by Syrah. Grenache and Mourvèdre are the other varieties used to supplement the blend.

All wines are the result of a unique combination of soil, climate, grape variety and winemaker. In the classic areas such as Bordeaux and Burgundy it has been determined over the centuries which grape varieties grow best where as a response to the particular combination of soil and climate. Consequently it would be inconceivable to plant Pinot Noir in the Gironde or Cabernet Sauvignon in the Côte d'Or. The climate and soil of each region would render success impossible, as each variety requires a combination of conditions that is not present in the other region. It is really only in the vineyards of Languedoc-Roussillon where, although there is a long tradition of viticulture, the search for

Low yields from gnarled, bush-like vines at Châteauneuf-du-Pape in southern Rhône produce big, alcoholic wines whose very essence is concentration.

quality is much more recent. This quest has resulted in a wave of experimentation as wine-growers strive to achieve the best (rather than the most) from their vineyards.

So let us look at the broader scheme in more detail, taking the western part of France first. Here there are two great river systems, that of the Loire with its various tributaries and that of the Gironde, which is the estuary through which the many rivers that flow into the Dordogne or the Garonne find their way to the Atlantic Ocean.

Rivers have an important impact on climate and on geology. A large expanse of water (the Loire and the Gironde are both very wide before they join the Atlantic) has a moderating effect, helping to temper frosts and other climatic extremes. Rivers also bring humidity, which helps to explain the development of Sauternes and Barsac, as well as the various appellations of the Loire Valley such as Bonnezeaux and Coteaux du Layon, where the quality of the wine depends upon noble rot.

The temperate climate of western France entails mild, damp springs which bring more than sufficient water for the growing season; a warm summer with occasional storms but little rainfall and then the risk of autumn rain before the vintage.

A maritime climate can be unpredictable. It makes for wines that are subtle and delicate and have not suffered the extremes of stress, but it means that vintages may vary considerably in quality. The weather at flowering, when rain or strong winds may prevail, can adversely affect the quantity, while rain at the harvest from mid-September can threaten potential quality. In years when all goes well, truly great wines are made; in other years the grapes may ripen adequately, but the results are far less satisfying. But for the consumer at least that is part of the charm and excitement of a region such as Bordeaux.

The vineyards of the South-West enjoy many similarities to those of Bordeaux. Geologically they share the same well drained gravel and varying degrees of clay. Climatically, the further they are from the ocean, the less they feel the effects of conditions generated by the Atlantic Gulf Stream, so that the vineyards further inland such as Cahors and Fronton tend to be warmer, while those further south such as Jurançon and Madiran are influenced by their proximity to the Pyrenees.

The grape varieties cultivated in these regions tend to be similar to those of Bordeaux, although there are local variations and unusual varieties peculiar to a particular appellation, such as Négrette in Fronton, Tannat in Madiran or Gros and Petit Manseng in Jurançon.

As the Loire Valley lies that little bit further north, the region generally tends to be cooler than Bordeaux. As a result Cabernet Franc is the principal grape variety for the best red wines of the valley, while Chenin Blanc accounts for most of the white wines in preference to Sauvignon and Sémillon in Bordeaux and the South-West. The red wines are rarely as tannic as those of Bordeaux, while one of the key characteristics of Chenin Blanc is acidity.

This is unfortunate in years when the grapes fail to ripen fully, but hot summers, followed by the appropriate autumnal mists and sunny days, can result in some fabulous sweet wines which retain their freshness and are capable of considerable longevity thanks to their acidity.

The maritime climate of western France meets the continental climate of the east in the vineyards of Sancerre, some 320 kilometres inland, soon after the river has turned south towards its source in the Massif Central. Here Sauvignon, a grape variety of western France, thrives in vineyards of chalk mixed with flint and gravel, while Pinot Noir, the red-grape variety of the east, makes delicate, fragrant red wines.

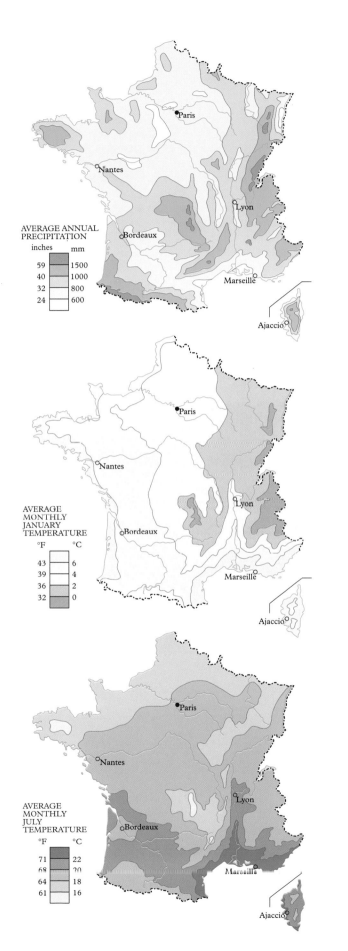

AVERAGE ANNUAL
PRECIPITATION

inches	mm
59	1500
40	1000
32	800
24	600

AVERAGE
MONTHLY
JANUARY
TEMPERATURE

°F	°C
43	6
39	4
36	2
32	0

AVERAGE
MONTHLY
JULY
TEMPERATURE

°F	°C
71	22
68	20
64	18
61	16

Burgundy and Champagne are firmly continental in climate. Winters can be bitter and spring frosts a problem, especially in the most northerly vineyards of Chablis and Champagne, while summers are shorter and more variable than in Bordeaux. As a result, the early-ripening Chardonnay and Pinot Noir are the traditional choices. They thrive on the limestone hills. Chardonnay, more forgiving of climatic vagaries, can produce sublimely subtle fine wines even in cooler years but Pinot Noir is far more temperamental and great red vintages on the Côte d'Or are uncertain indeed.

Beaujolais consists mainly of granite soil, on which Gamay thrives. Temperatures are warmer here in this southernmost part of Burgundy. Further east in the Jura, a hilly region close to the Swiss border, winters are extreme. The soil is based on limestone, which suits both Chardonnay and Pinot Noir as well as various indigenous varieties found nowhere else in France. Savoie enjoys some mountain isolation, where pockets of vines are able to survive the winter extremes.

The continental climate of Alsace is characterised by a particularly low rainfall. Colmar is one of the driest towns in France: prevailing easterly winds ensure that the rain falls mainly on the Vosges Mountains. Winters are cold and summers dry and hot, making for quite heady, alcoholic wines, while long autumns allow for the production of late-harvest wines. The soil of Alsace is immensely varied, a veritable geological jigsaw puzzle, which helps to explain the success of a such a diverse range of varieties.

Margaux, potentially the finest and most fragrant of all wines, is produced largely from Cabernet Sauvignon grown on deep gravel ridges in the Médoc.

The city of Lyons, where the Rhône and the Saône meet, provides a convenient landmark to separate the southernmost vineyards of Burgundy from the northernmost vineyards of the Rhône Valley. The Rhône Valley is distinctly hotter than Burgundy. At the northern end where viticulture is based above all on Syrah for red wine, it tends to be more continental in climate, with vineyards on steep hillsides of schist.

Travelling southward, the influence of the Mediterranean becomes more perceptible and the soils more varied. There is a distinct break between Valence and Montélimar: this area where there are no vines of significance separates the vineyards of the north, based on Syrah, from those of the south where Syrah is just part of a blend. The terrain changes quite dramatically from very steep hillsides to more gentle rolling countryside, then flattens out into the vast estuary.

Vines enjoy a mediterranean climate, explaining why viticulture is one of the key agricultural activities all around the mediterranean coast, and also on the island of Corsica. Vines and olive trees both thrive where little else will grow, especially on hillsides, which leaves the more fertile areas for other crops. Summers are warm and dry and the winters mild and wet enough to provide sufficient water for the summer months. Occasionally irrigation may be necessary, especially for young vines. The climatic risks are much smaller than elsewhere in France.

The wind too plays a significant part in the climate of the Mediterranean, not just the famous *Mistral*, but several other winds, depending on the season, bring a moderating influence of cooler air from the the mountains or the sea. The wind may also have a healthy drying effect, and with reduced humidity there is less danger of disease in the vineyard and often less risk of rain during the ripening period and at the harvest. However the superficially easy climate has allowed successful viticulture to be taken for granted, the traditional emphasis being on quantity rather than quality. Vines were planted on the alluvial coastal plain rather than in the rocky foothills of the Cévennes and the Pyrenees where the soil is predominately gravel and limestone. But things are now changing apace, with a definite shift in recent years away from the fertile plains and towards a viticultural objective based on quality and flavour.

Provence has the most mediterranean climate of all with some of the longest hours of sunshine and very little rain. Rain is usually concentrated in the spring and autumn months. Roussillon too has longer sunshine hours than the Languedoc, with some particularly arid conditions making for rugged warm wines, while the island of Corsica is even sunnier. Its viticulture has in some ways suffered from its island isolation, but that has also provided a note of originality with some unusual grape varieties.

The mediterranean climate of the South meets the maritime climate of the South-West in the little-known appellations of Cabardès and Côtes de la Malepère, to the north and south of the city of Carcassonne. What the French call the *partage des eaux*, the watershed, between the Atlantic and the Mediterranean is at Castelnaudary, some 40 kilometres west of Carcassonne. There is less sunshine here than on the coast, and adequate rainfall. The area's natural vegetation illustrates the climatic mix and the vineyards in both Cabardès and Côtes de Malepère contain a mosaic of grape varieties. Here Bordeaux mingles with the Midi. These wines may include Grenache and Cabernet Sauvignon, Syrah and Merlot, not to mention Malbec, Cabernet Franc, Cinsaut and Cot. They do not taste of the warm South, nor do they quite have the rigid structure of the South-West.

And so the circle is complete.

In the Côte Chalonnaise, 90 per cent of the production is of red wine. The Pinot Noir made here at Givry is somewhat akin to a good Côte de Beaune-Villages.

The Loire

For much of its course the River Loire runs through the essence of French countryside. The land may lack the high drama of the mountains or the austerity of the northern plains but it has been moulded over centuries into a region of quiet pastures, classic châteaux, cathedral cities and vineyards. The dappled reflections from the waters of the Loire and its many tributaries give a soft and diffuse style of light which inspired the Impressionist painters.

As with the landscape, so with the wines. Rarely do they indulge in bold gestures – they are more subtle, offering fragrance and fruit, lightness and pleasure rather than making too many intellectual demands. That is not to say that there are no great Loire wines, but even the finest can be enjoyed without the reverence demanded by, say, Bordeaux, or the hedonism associated with Burgundy.

Subtlety and fragrance are two aspects of Loire wines; others derive from the fact that this is, generally speaking, cool wine country. This means that the vines are susceptible both to adverse weather conditions – of which spring frosts are the most menacing – and to diseases such as mildew which arise in cool, wet weather in the summer. Some wine styles such as sweet whites, which depend on a warm, dry autumn, have to be written off completely in years when conditions are not favourable.

The positive side of the temperate Loire climate is that in good years the grapes can have a long, slow ripening season which brings them to ripeness but never super-ripeness. As a result the wines' fruit flavours are always more predominant than their alcohol. In an age where moderation in alcohol consumption is a mantra, the fact that Loire wines offer taste above power puts them in a strong position.

The Loire is France's longest river. It rises in the mountains of the Ardèche, close to the Rhône Valley and the city of Lyon, over 1,000 kilometres from its mouth in the Atlantic. The river system associated with the Loire itself is huge: together with its tributaries – the Allier, the Cher, the Indre, the Vienne, the Creuse, the Maine (and those of the Sarthe and the Loir) and the Sèvre Nantaise – it covers all the land north of Limoges, west of Vézelay, south of Le Mans and east of the ocean. It includes the mountains to the south

Left: The unhurried waters of the Loire stretch 1,020 kilometres from the mountainous heart of France to the Atlantic.

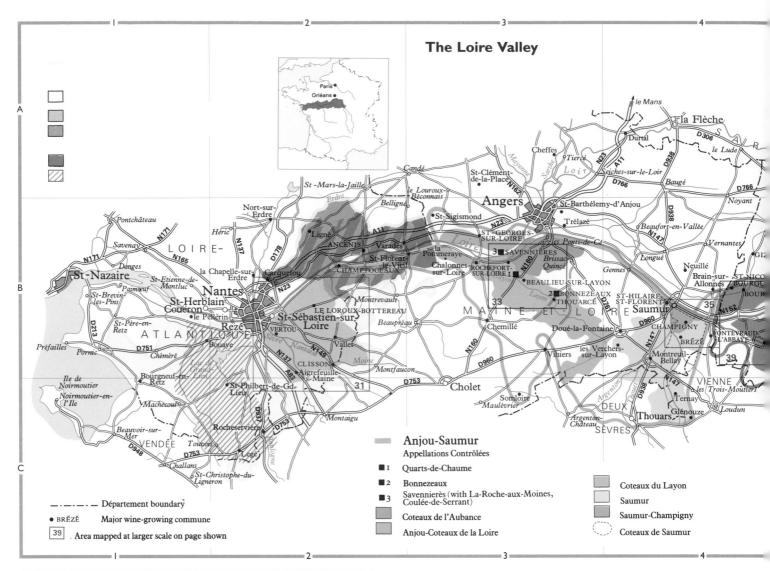

The Loire Valley

Anjou-Saumur
Appellations Contrôlées

■1 Quarts-de-Chaume

■2 Bonnezeaux

■3 Savennières (with La-Roche-aux-Moines, Coulée-de-Serrant)

Coteaux de l'Aubance

Anjou-Coteaux de la Loire

Coteaux du Layon

Saumur

Saumur-Champigny

Coteaux de Saumur

–––––– Département boundary

● BRÉZÉ Major wine-growing commune

39 . Area mapped at larger scale on page shown

La Sèvre Nantaise. The Loire and its tributaries are inclined to flood so towns, villages and vineyards are set back from the river or perched on the few points where high ground provides flood refuge and a bridging point.

of central France in the Auvergne and Limousin; the cereal-growing plains of the centre in Berry; the pasture lands of Touraine and Anjou and the flat lands of the Pays Nantais and the Vendée. The river flows through some of France's most ancient and beautiful cities – Nevers, Orléans, Blois, Tours, Saumur Angers – as well some of its poorest and most remote regions.

For much of its early course it is merely a mountain stream. Not until it reaches the town of Monbrison are the first vineyards seen, those of the Côtes du Forez. A few more are clustered around Roanne, the first large city on the river. To the west, the Allier passes through Clermont-Ferrand and the vineyards of the Auvergne. Further north the Sioule, a tributary of the Allier, links the vineyards of St-Pourçain-sur-Sioule. North and west, on the edge of the cereal fields of Berry, the tiny vineyards of Châteaumeillant struggle to survive. All these are small areas, remnants of vineyards which before phylloxera represented much greater wine industries. They are remote from the main stream of the wine business but that in itself – combined with the often beautiful countryside – makes them charming places to visit.

The first substantial vineyard area through which the Loire passes is the twin region of Sancerre and Pouilly-sur-Loire, famous for its Pouilly-Fumé wines. Downstream, at the city of Orléans only 100 kilometres or so from Paris, the river turns from being a south–north-flowing river and flows west to the Atlantic Ocean. From the great châteaux of Touraine – only one of which actually

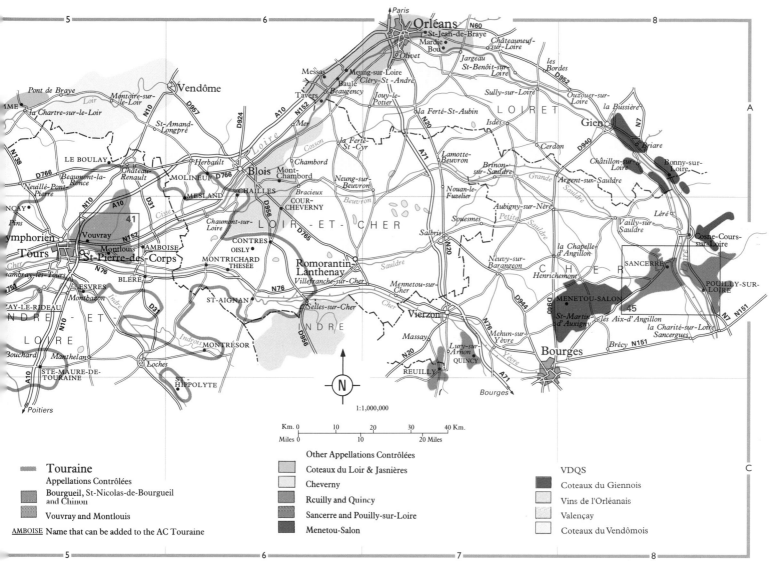

Touraine
Appellations Contrôlées
Bourgueil, St-Nicolas-de-Bourgueil and Chinon
Vouvray and Montlouis
AMBOISE Name that can be added to the AC Touraine

Other Appellations Contrôlées
Coteaux du Loir & Jasnières
Cheverny
Reuilly and Quincy
Sancerre and Pouilly-sur-Loire
Menetou-Salon

VDQS
Coteaux du Giennois
Vins de l'Orléanais
Valençay
Coteaux du Vendômois

1:1,000,000

possesses vineyards – the river and its tributaries pass through the vineyards of Touraine, Vouvray and Montlouis, Chinon and Bourgueil and so on into Anjou, to Saumur and to the Layon.

The sheer diversity of the wines from Anjou and Touraine amazes. Tiny appellations, Quarts de Chaume or Savennières for example, jostle with the huge swathes of land covered by the Touraine and Anjou appellations. Famous appellations such as Vouvray or Chinon are listed together with relatively obscure ones such as the northern Loir's Jasnières and Coteaux du Loir, or the Anjou's of Coteaux de l'Aubance. Some wines travel widely, others are seldom seen outside their home towns and villages. Away to the south is the developing region of Haut-Poitou.

The last stretch of the Loire vineyards is within sight and smell of the ocean. As the broad and slow-moving river drags itself past the city of Nantes it forms the northern boundary of the Muscadet vineyards, a concentrated region where vines dominate. Even here, however, small appellations hang from the main mass of vines: to the west the Fiefs-Vendéens produce racy whites and rosés which are drunk almost entirely at the beach-side resorts of the Vendée.

The Pays Nantais

The Muscadet region lies to the south of the Loire, across the river from the city of Nantes where the river widens to meet the ocean. There is a salty tang in the air which seems to imbue Pays Nantais wines with a freshness and zing that makes them perfect partners for the local seafood and fish dishes.

The vineyards lie in gently undulating countryside with wide open horizons. The deep, narrow gorge of the River Sèvre makes a dramatic contrast to the mono-cultural scenery of vines and more vines, broken only occasionally by a small copse of trees. The wine villages with their red-tiled roofs and tall-spired churches have a mix of atmospheres: part southern, part northern France. This is border country where the cool north, the land of dairy products, meets the south, the land of olive oil.

The heart of the Muscadet region lies between two small rivers, the Sèvre Nantaise and the Maine. Muscadet de Sèvre-et-Maine has always been seen as the finest of the Pays Nantais wines but there are other Muscadets: Muscadet des Coteaux de la Loire, which comes from vineyards on the banks of the Loire between Nantes and the castle-dominated town of Ancenis and, since 1994, Muscadet Côtes de Grand-Lieu, a wine from vineyards around the large expanse of the Lac du Grand-Lieu to the south-west of Nantes.

Above: An earthy appreciation of the wines is suggested by this carving at Château de Chasseloire.

Left: Dwarfed by the Château Église, the Pont de la Vallée spans the Sèvre Nantaise at Clisson.

Below: A vineyard procession of the Muscadet Confrérie Les Brevins.

The remaining vineyards in the more outlying regions are classified simply as Muscadet. While Muscadet is the main wine of the Pays Nantais region, however, there are three other wine areas and styles within the Loire Atlantique *département*. There is the 3,000-hectare VDQS zone of Gros Plant du Pays Nantais which covers much of the Muscadet region and produces high-acid wines from the Gros Plant grape. And there is the VDQS area of Coteaux d'Ancenis, a small area around Ancenis on both banks of the Loire which produces red wines from the Gamay grape, whites from the Chenin Blanc and some very rare sweet whites from the Malvoisie. Lastly, away near the coast, there is the small VDQS area of Fiefs-Vendéens which makes reds, whites and rosés from an extraordinary range of grape varieties. The main wine centre here is Mareuil-sur-Lay.

Muscadet was one of the mainstays of the wine bar and house-wine trade during the early 1980s. More recently it fell on hard times as the deadly frost of 1991 cut the harvest drastically and the wine's reputation and prices suffered by comparison with other uncomplicated whites. But the harvests of '94 and '95 changed much of that and revealed a new quality of Muscadet in which the regional characteristics are emphasised.

The light, delicate wines of south-western Sèvre-et-Maine, produced around the towns of St-Fiacre-sur-Maine, Haute-Goulaine, Gorges and Vertou, contrast with the weightier wines of the north-eastern area around Vallet, Le Pallet and La Chapelle-Heulin. Completing the range are the earthy-style Muscadets from Coteaux de la Loire and the fuller style of Grand-Lieu.

Greater emphasis is also being placed on the authenticity of one of Muscadet's more intriguing aspects – its bottling *sur lie*. This is a technique whereby wine is bottled directly from the cask or tank (in the spring following the vintage) without being racked or filtered. As a result the wine has an extra declicacy, a slight sparkle and a fuller body with a slightly yeasty character. But the system has been much abused: the wine can be moved from the tank in which it was fermented to the cellars of a *négociant* leaving the lees behind: the common practice of adding a little carbon dioxide to reproduce the sparkle might give a similar effect but it is hardly authentic. Now the rules have been tightened. While it was once permitted to move the wine from its fermentation tank at any time

up to February 15 following the harvest, it must now be moved before December 1 and it must be moved still on its lees.

Interest in estate Muscadets has also burgeoned in recent years. Where once most Muscadet was bottled by *négociants*, merchants whose premises might be well outside the region, today the focus is on an increasing number of high-quality domaines. Some have a long history, such as the 15th-century Château de Goulaine at Haute-Goulaine which has been in the same family for 1,000 years (and is well worth a visit) or the Château de Chasseloir near St-Fiacre-sur-Maine, which is a regional showplace. Others are younger firms, combining the business of making estate wines and acting as *négociants* but from a local base: Sauvion et Fils based at Château du Cléray is an example. There are also many more much smaller estates run from modest premises which, instead of sending their wine or grapes elsewhere, now make and bottle their own.

A leisurely visit to one or more of these estates makes an excellent introduction to the region, which is still largely dominated by small wine farms. Follow up with a bottle of Muscadet – or the greatly underrated Gros Plant – and a plate of shellfish or local oysters to experience one of the best food and wine marriages of all.

PRODUCERS OF SPECIAL INTEREST

PAYS NANTAIS

Donatien Bahuaud
44330 La Chapelle-Heulin
Négociant marketing the carefully
selected Le Master de Donatien,
Château de la Cassemichère and
other brands.

Guy Bossard 44430 Le Landreau
Produces estate Muscadets from
organic vineyards under the Domaine
de l'Écu label.

Claude Branger
44690 Maisdon-sur-Sèvre
Top-quality estate Muscadets including
Cuvée Excellence.

**Domaine de la Chaignée/
Mercier Frères** 85770 Vix
Fiefs-Vendéens.

Chereau-Carré
44690 St-Fiacre-sur-Maine
Distributes the estate wines from the
Chereau and Carré families. Among
them are Muscadets from Domaine
du Bois Bruley, Château de Chasseloir,
Château du Coing de St-Fiacre and
Grand Fief de la Cormeraie.

Michel Chiron 44330 Mouzillon
Excellent Clos de Roches Gaudinières.

Guilbaud Frères 44330 Mouzillon
Energetic medium-sized firm
producing a number of good wines
from its own estates.

Hardy-Luneau 44330 Mouzillon

Marquis de Goulaine
44115 Haute Goulaine
Top-quality producer established at
the historic Château de Goulaine.

Château de la Mercredière
44690 Le Pallet

Louis Métaireau
44690 St-Fiacre-sur-Maine
Métaireau has brought together a
group of like-minded growers who
select and sell their wines under the
Métaireau label.

Château la Noë 44330 Vallet
Jean de Malestroit produces attractive
wines at one of the few châteaux in
Muscadet. It was built in 1836.

Marcel Sautejeau 44690 Le Pallet
Négociant whose own Domaine de
l'Hyvernière is excellent.

**Sauvion et Fils, Château du
Cléray** 44330 Vallet
The Sauvion family produce their
own estate wine. They also market
pure, lively Muscadets from individual
estates, some under the name of
Les Découvertes.

FÊTES

Ancenis Wine fair on the first
Thursday in December.
Clisson Wine fair on Ascension Day.
Foire de **Nantes** in November.
St-Fiacre-sur-Maine Fête du
Muscadet on the second
Sunday in October.

The Pays Nantais

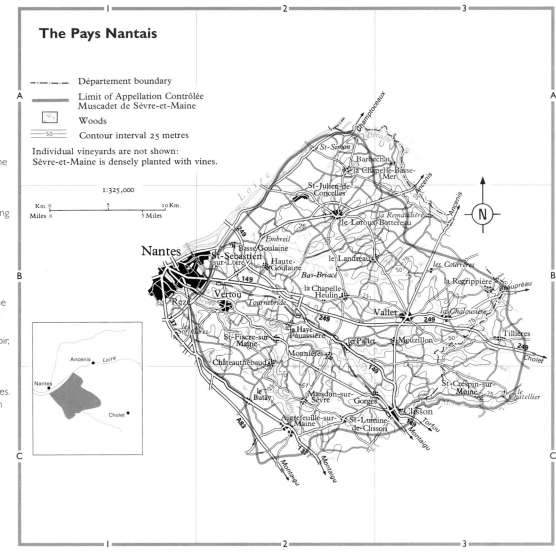

-·--·--·-- Département boundary

▬▬▬▬ Limit of Appellation Contrôlée
Muscadet de Sèvre-et-Maine

Woods

──50── Contour interval 25 metres

Individual vineyards are not shown:
Sèvre-et-Maine is densely planted with vines.

1:325,000

Vallet The region's largest fair takes
place on the third weekend in March.

WINE INFORMATION

Maison des Vins 44690 La Haye-
Fouassière (just south-east of Nantes
on the N149). Tel (0)240 36 90 10

HOTELS

Hôtel le Jules Verne 44000 Nantes
Tel (0)240 35 74 50
Comfortable city-centre hotel within
easy reach of the vineyards.

Abbaye de Villeneuve
44400 Les Sorinières
Tel (0)240 04 40 25
Luxurious hotel in an 18th-century
former abbey. Good cooking.
Swimming pool.

RESTAURANTS

Nantes is the capital of Brittany so it is
not surprising that the hotels and
restaurants provide an abundance of
fish and shellfish. Freshwater fish

(salmon, pike and perch) are also
served, often with beurre blanc, a
Nantes speciality. The region's whites
make an excellent accompaniment.

Auberge de Bel Air
44150 **Ancenis** Tel (0)240 83 02 87
On the main road to Ancenis (not the
autoroute). Old-fashioned, pleasant
surroundings.

Villa Mon Rêve 506 boulevard de la
Loire, 44115 **Basse-Goulaine**
Tel (0)240 03 55 50
Award-winning restaurant with a
garden. Fish a speciality.

Les Jardins de la Forge place
Piliers Champtoceaux, 49270
Champtoceaux Tel (0)240 83 56 23
Elegant restaurant in a small village
with excellent views of the Loire.

La Bonne Auberge 44190 **Clisson**
Tel (0)240 78 01 90
Inventive dishes and an inexpensive
weekday lunch menu.

Les Maraîchers 21 rue Fouré
44000 **Nantes** Tel (0)240 47 06 51
One of Nantes' best seafood
restaurants.

PLACES OF INTEREST

Ancenis An attractive little riverside
town dominated by castle ruins. Old
houses rise in tiers above the Loire.
An impressive suspension bridge.
The château is now a school and
tours are offered during school
holidays in the afternoon.

Clisson White walls and flat roofs
characterise many buildings in this
striking Italianate town at the
confluence of two rivers.

Nantes The centre of Nantes is
much more pleasant than the
outskirts. Many of the old streets are
now pedestrianised. In the cathedral
of St-Pierre-et-St-Paul lies the marble
tomb of Francis II and his wife Anne
of Brittany. The Château Ducal,
surrounded by a grassed moat, houses
three museums. The Musée Jules
Verne (3 rue de l'Hermitage)
documents the writer's life and work.

Le Pallet One of the Sèvre et Maine
wine villages housing a vineyard
museum at 82 rue Pierre Abélard
[tel (0)240 80 90 13].

31

Anjou

While vines can be found all over the ancient province of Anjou, there are two main concentrations. The one further west centres on the steep-sided valley of the Layon. Here Chenin Blanc reigns supreme in a wide variety of guises – bone-dry wines, soft medium-sweet wines and supremely, gloriously sweet wines. At the opposite end of the region around the town of Saumur, Chenin Blanc and Cabernet Franc jointly dominate the vineyards, the former making the base wine for Saumur's sparkling-wine industry, the latter creating some of the best Loire reds, those of Saumur-Champigny. Between these two areas, vines in any number of small vineyards produce the simple still wines of Anjou and Saumur.

The land is mainly agricultural. Villages are clusters of slate-roofed houses and tall-spired churches almost exclusively concerned with viticulture. Angers, home to Grand Marnier liqueur and to the greatest concentration of the population, is just outside the vineyard area to the north of the Loire. South of Angers and across the Loire on the south bank is a riverside road which leads, just to the west, to the town of Rochefort-sur-Loire. This is the best centre from which to explore the wines of the Layon Valley.

The climate of the Layon would be familiar to the wine producers of Sauternes. In the autumn, morning mists rise from the valley floor, clearing on fine days to leave a brilliant blue sky and warm afternoon. This – as in Sauternes – induces the noble rot in the Chenin Blanc grapes, concentrating the juice and producing classically sweet wines. The effects are felt to a greater or lesser extent along the valley and are reflected in the different appellations. The wines of Coteaux du Layon are only lightly affected; more deeply affected are those of Coteaux du Layon-Villages which sometimes, as in Chaume, have a village name attached. There is also a pair of tiny plots which produce some of the country's most luscious sweet wines: Quarts de Chaume and Bonnezeaux. With their balance of sweetness and acidity, these for many wine-lovers have a greater poise and lightness than Sauternes.

There is one other small area of vines at this western end of Anjou. It is, unusually, on the north bank of the Loire, centred around the village of Savennières. Here, on slopes so steep that tractors have to be abandoned in favour of horse-drawn ploughs, are more Chenin Blanc vines. These make bone-dry wines – searingly acid when young but developing extraordinary nutty flavours when mature after at least ten years. Two small vineyards within Savennières, Coulée de Serrant and Roches-aux-Moines, are entitled to their own appellations.

Moving eastwards, the next wine centre – hardly more than half an hour's drive from the Layon – is Brissac-Quincé, a small town surrounding a huge castle. Home to the Loire's biggest cooperative, this is where the main concentration of Anjou red and rosé wines is to be found. Much derogatory prose has been penned about the often dull, slightly sweet Anjou Rosé, a style of wine which is definitely losing out to drier rosés such as those under the appellation of Rosé de Loire. More interesting are the reds made from both Cabernet Franc and Gamay. While the more basic reds appear under the Anjou Rouge appellation, a superior appellation of Anjou-Villages created in 1991 has prompted the arrival of a new generation of reds. Never powerful, these have good tannins and plenty of chunky fruit and develop tobacco flavours when mature.

Saumur in eastern Anjou has many claims to fame. On one side of the town is the French cavalry's riding school where high-stepping horses give regular displays. Saumur also boasts France's

A splendid crenellated 14th-century affair complete with moat, Saumur's picture-book château stands high on a promontory above the Loire.

Anjou

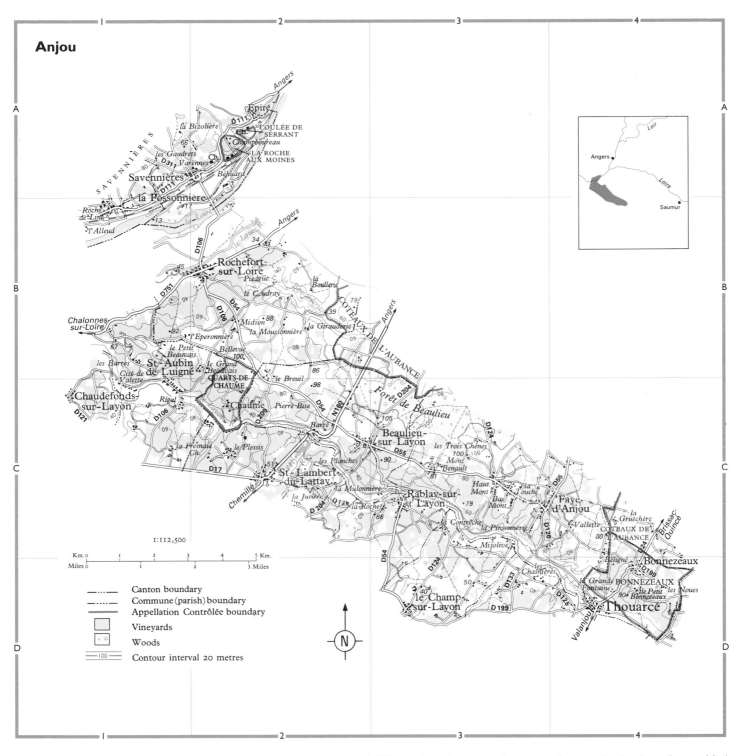

1:112,500

Km. 0   1   2   3   4   5 Km.

Miles 0   1   2   3 Miles

— · — · — Canton boundary

— · · — · · — Commune (parish) boundary

▭ Appellation Contrôlée boundary

▭ Vineyards

▭ Woods

— 100 — Contour interval 20 metres

N

most concentrated area of sparkling-wine production outside Champagne. In vast caves carved out of the local soft tufa rock are stocks of maturing bottles, laid on their sides, undergoing the same style of secondary fermentation as is found in Champagne. Visitors are welcome to join the tours and tastings offered at these cellars.

The vineyards for these wines were traditionally found on the plateau stretching to the south of the Loire where the Chenin Blanc grapes used in Saumur d'Origine sparkling wines were grown, but now non-traditional grapes, particularly Chardonnay, are increasingly being used. Grapes are brought into Saumur from other parts of the Loire to be used in the production of Crémant de Loire, which can often be superior to Saumur.

Where the vines stretch eastward towards the boundary with Touraine there is one further appellation which has assumed increasing importance: Cabernet Franc-based Saumur-Champigny. A concentration of vines on the plateau above little Loire-side villages – Dampierre-sur-Loire, Souzay-Champigny, Turquant and Parnay – produces reds which have recently become seriously fashionable among Parisian drinkers who want light, soft reds that can be drunk young. The wines of Saumur-Champigny fit this bill but they can also age well, particularly in warm years. Again, vinification takes place in cellars carved out of the rock beneath the vines, where modern stainless-steel tanks stand incongruously beneath roughly hewn ceilings.

The long-lived, intensely rich, golden wines of Quarts de Chaume are matured in cellars hewn out of rock beneath the vineyards.

PRODUCERS OF SPECIAL INTEREST

ANJOU AND ANJOU-VILLAGES

Domaine de Bablut
49320 Brissac-Quincé
Good-quality red Anjou-Villages, sweet Coteaux de l'Aubance and vin de pays.

Caves de la Loire
49320 Brissac-Quincé
Huge but well run cooperative cellar making all styles of Anjou wines.

Domaine Richou
49190 Rochefort-sur-Loire
White Anjou Blanc is the star here. There is also a red Cuvée de Printemps made for early consumption from young vines.

Les Vins Touchais
49700 Doué-la-Fontaine
Medium-sized merchant house whose main claim to fame is the legendary sweet Anjou Blanc.

COTEAUX DU LAYON

Domaine des Baumard
49190 Rochefort-sur-Loire
Family firm making good Quarts de Chaume and Savennières as well as Coteaux du Layon.

Domaine Beaujeau
49380 Thouarcé

Château de Belle-Rive
49190 Rochefort-sur-Loire
Jacques Lalanne makes Quarts de Chaume of great quality.

Château du Breuil
49190 Beaulieu-sur-Layon
Excellent red Anjou-Villages as well as sweet Coteaux du Layon. Experimental plantings of many grapes go into a wide range of wines.

Château de Fesles
49380 Thouarcé
Jacques Boivin remains in charge here despite changes in ownership. Fine Bonnezeaux.

Domaine de la Motte
49190 Rochefort-sur-Loire

Domaine de la Soucherie
49190 Beaulieu-sur-Layon
Coteaux du Layon and Coteaux du Layon Chaume, both sweet wines, are made as well as Anjou Blanc and Rouge and a sparkling wine.

Château de Suronde
49190 Rochefort-sur-Loire

SAVENNIÈRES

Domaine de Bizolière
49170 Savennières
One of the faster-developing Savennières.

Château de Chamboureau
49170 Savennières
One of the most technically advanced of the Anjou producers, yet one who contrives to make a Savennières that needs time in bottle.

Clos de la Coulée de Serrant
49170 Savennières
Mme Joly and her son Nicolas, who is in charge of production, are among the few owners in France who control an entire appellation with their Savennières Coulée de Serrant.

Château d'Épiré 49170 Savennières
Will last for up to 30 years, sometimes more.

Domaine aux Moines
49170 Savennières
Mme Laroche makes only Savennières Roche-aux-Moines from her small vineyard. Magnificent views of the Loire.

SAUMUR

Ackerman-Laurance
49400 St-Hilaire-St-Florent
Top Cuvée Privilège and Cuvée Privée. Considerable quantities of very good Crémant de Loire are also made.

Bouvet-Ladubay
49400 St-Hilaire-St-Florent
Generally regarded as the best producer of sparkling Saumur. Wood-fermented Cuvée Trésor.

Cave Coopérative
49260 St-Cyr-en-Bourg
A good-sized producer. Red Saumur-Champigny, Saumur Blanc (one of the better examples from the appellation) and sparkling Crémant de Loire.

Château de Chaintres
49400 Chaintres
A red-wine estate producing wine for the firm's classic Saumur-Champigny.

Paul Filliatreau 49400 Chaintres
This is the largest Saumur-Champigny producer. The wines are excellent examples of the appellation and have done much to promote its virtues.

Gratien et Meyer Château Gratien
49401 Saumur
Gratien et Meyer is the brand name for a range of sparkling Saumur wines – brut, demi-sec and rosé. A red sparkling wine from 100% Cabernet Franc is also made. The firm owns the champagne house of Alfred Gratien.

Château de Hureau
49400 Dampierre-sur-Loire
Based at the château, the Vatan family has been producing Saumur-Champigny for three generations.

Langlois-Chateau
49400 St-Hilaire-St-Florent
One of the famous names in sparkling Crémant de Loire, Langlois-Chateau also produces red and white still wines from the same AC.

Château de Targé 49730 Parnay
Top producer of Saumur-Champigny.

OTHER AREAS

Michel Gigon 79100 Oiron
The only producer of Vins du Thouarsais of any consequence. Good Chenin Blanc.

FÊTES

Martigné-Briand Festival des Fleurs et Vins on the first weekend in August.
St-Lambert-du-Lattay Fête de la Vinée the weekend before July 14.
Saumur Wine fair in the second week in February.
Thouarcé Alliance des Vins de Thouarcé et de Bonnezeaux avec le Fromage on the first Sunday in June.

WINE INFORMATION

Conseil Interprofessionel des Vins d'Anjou et de Saumur
73 rue Plantagenet, 49023 Angers
Tel (0)241 87 62 57
Maison du Vin 25 rue Beaurepaire 49400 Saumur

HOTELS

The two main tourist centres of Anjou (both convenient for the vineyards) are Angers, the region's capital, and Saumur.

Hôtel d'Anjou 1 boulevard Foch 49000 **Angers** Tel (0)241 88 99 55
Centrally located with modern comforts but a pleasant old-fashioned feel and a smart restaurant.
Hôtel de France 8 place de la Gare 49100 **Angers** Tel (0)241 88 49 42
Well appointed city-centre hotel near the main railway station.
Auberge de Thouet 49400 **Chacé** Tel (0)241 50 12 04
Rural simplicity in a wine village near Saumur. Restaurant.
La Prieuré
49350 **Chênehutte-lès-Tuffaux** Tel (0)241 50 15 31
Luxury hotel on a hill overlooking the Loire just west of Saumur. Elegant rooms in the main house. Swimming pool and excellent restaurant.
Relais du Bellay
49620 **Montreuil-Bellay** Tel (0)241 52 35 50
A comfortable hotel with a swimming pool.
Loire Hôtel rue du Vieux Pont 49400 **Saumur** Tel (0)241 67 22 42
Modern hotel on the banks of the Loire in central Saumur with splendid views of the town and château.

RESTAURANTS

Many regional dishes depend on the fruits of the Loire and its tributaries – freshwater fish such as chad, pike and salmon as well as crayfish – while there is also an abundance of delicious charcuterie, poultry and goats' cheese.

Le Toussaint 7 rue Toussaint, 49000 **Angers** Tel (0)241 87 46 20
Regional cooking with flair.

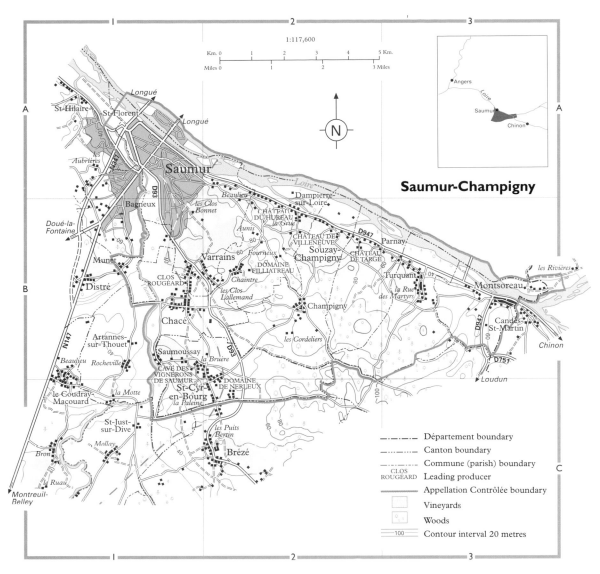

Saumur-Champigny

1:117,600

Km. 0   1   2   3   4   5 Km.

Miles 0   1   2   3 Miles

N

_.._.._ Département boundary

_.._.._ Canton boundary

_.._.._ Commune (parish) boundary

CLOS ROUGEARD   Leading producer

_____ Appellation Contrôlée boundary

Vineyards

Woods

100   Contour interval 20 metres

Restaurant du Grand Pont
Behuard 49190 **Rochefort-sur-Loire**
Tel (0)241 72 21 64
Good family restaurant with a sensibly priced menu.
Jeanne de Laval 49350 **Les Rosiers-sur-Loire** Tel (0)241 51 80 75
Excellent regional dishes and an expansive wine-list. Garden and terrace for summer dining.
Les Délices du Château Les Fouquières Château de Saumur 49400 **Saumur** Tel (0)241 67 65 60
Elegant restaurant, attractively set in the château courtyard.
Le Relais de Bonnezeaux 49380 **Thouarcé** Tel (0)241 54 08 33
Attractive, good-value restaurant with garden, set in the vineyards of Bonnezeaux.

PLACES OF INTEREST

Angers Despite its outwardly modern appearance, the centre of Angers is still full of ancient slate-fronted houses. The city's largest and most important monument is the forbidding Château du Roi René, a 13th-century fortress. It houses the richest collection of tapestries in the world and boasts a large garden and 15th-century chapel. The nearby Musée Jean Lurçat, (4 boulevard Arago) has a 12th-century cellar with a Musée du Vin.
Beaulieu-sur-Layon Beaulieu offers panoramic views of the Layon Valley as well as being home to many wine producers.
Brissac-Quincé The 17th-century Château de Brissac is one of the tallest in France. Many of the 150 rooms are furnished and wines can be tasted in the cellars.
Fontevraud-l'Abbaye This former abbey, now the cultural centre for western France, contains tombs of the English (and Angevin) Plantagenet monarchs including Eleanor of Aquitaine and Richard Lionheart. The octagonal kitchen is remarkable. There is a luxury hotel in the grounds.
Montreuil-Bellay A small town on the River Thouet with ancient houses and a magnificent castle.

St-Georges-sur-Loire The stately Château de Serrant (16th–18th-century) has a magnificent interior with Flemish tapestries and a library of 10,000 books.
St-Hilaire-St-Florent Twin village just west of Saumur which houses the cellars of many of the sparkling-wine houses including Ackerman-Laurance and Bouvet-Ladubay.
Saumur A magnificent 14th-century castle dominates the town and houses the Musée des Arts Décoratifs (tableware, tapestries, etc). The Musée du Cheval and the French national cavalry school are also in the town. In the centre are many half-timbered houses, a 16th-century town hall and two Romanesque churches.
Savennières Church with 10th-century side porch. On the nearby Île de Béhuard in the middle of the Loire there lies a hamlet with a 15th-century chapel.
Turquant The Moulin de la Herpinière, a restored windmill, houses a small wine museum.

The castle of Foulques at Angers, rebuilt by St Louis between 1228 and 1238, has 15th-century buildings inside its white-stone ramparts. The moats are now laid out as gardens.

Touraine

Touraine is the most diverse viticultural region of France. It produces wine in a wide range of styles – white, sweet white, red and sparkling. Within its borders are some of the most famous Loire appellations, and tucked away in corners are others that are as fascinating as they are curious. The fact that Touraine also contains some of the country's finest châteaux and most beautiful rivers and landscapes makes this a lovely part of France to visit.

The combination of charming scenery and viticulture is perhaps at its best where the vines slope down to the many rivers of Touraine. Near Chinon they cover the slopes above the River Vienne; around Vouvray they are planted on the plateau above the Loire. Vines cling to the precipitous slopes of the Cher near the villages of Meusnes and Oisly which have marvellous views of the river meandering through its valley. Occasionally, as at Chenonceaux, vines are planted close to the château.

Like many of the Loire regions Touraine is still essentially agricultural, although the larger towns such as Tours and Blois are more commercial than industrial. Many of the smaller market towns, Langeais, Chinon, Amboise and Montrichard for example, with their overbearing castles, narrow streets and timbered houses clustered along the river-front, still have a sense of the medieval spirit from which they originally sprang.

If you are coming from Anjou and the vineyards of Saumur, there is hardly a break: the vineyards of Chinon and Bourgueil start within a few kilometres. Bourgueil and St-Nicolas-de-Bourgueil are two of the few vineyards on the north bank of the Loire. Along most of the central section of the river, vines are planted principally on the low slopes (known as the coteaux) leading up to the plateau and on the plateau itself. Vines planted on the sandier soil of the river plain tend to produce lighter wines.

The heart of the Chinon vineyards is on the north bank of the Vienne just east of the town of Chinon. Here again vines are on the slopes, on the plateau and on the flatter land near the river. This is a particularly beautiful part of the country: the town is one of the prettiest in the Loire, while the gentle slopes of the hills alongside the Vienne have a summer mix of vineyard and cornfield. Little wonder that Rabelais, who was born near here in the 16th century, should see this as a land of plenty.

These two vineyard areas, along with neighbouring Saumur-Champigny in Anjou, produce by far the best reds of the Loire. In some years it is difficult for white wine grapes to ripen in the region, so it is not far short of miraculous that such fine reds can be produced – from the Cabernet Franc of St-Émilion in Bordeaux – so far north. It is a question of microclimate: the river valleys provide shelter and a few vital extra degrees of warmth. The red wines have a reputation for being lightweight, best drunk young and even chilled, but just a taste of the wines from the top producers of Chinon or Bourgueil reveals the opposite. These are serious reds

Above: Cabernet Franc matures into fine, delicate wine in this Chinon chais. The grape is ideally suited to the cool, inland climate of the middle-Loire.

Right: Leonardo da Vinci spent his last years in the Gothic château of Amboise, which dominates this pretty riverside town.

which in many years have the ability to age as well as any Bordeaux Cabernet Franc. Many producers now use wood as part of the vinification process and, in excellent years such as '89, '90 or '95, it can be difficult to distinguish some of the best Loire reds from those of Bordeaux.

Eastwards from Chinon and Bourgueil the appellation of Touraine is the most prominent. It covers a wide area and encompasses many styles – reds, whites and sparkling wines. Certain styles of wine such as the white Sauvignon de Touraine and the reds Gamay and Cabernet de Touraine have gained particular popularity. The names themselves are unusual in France where the labelling of wines by grape variety is generally frowned upon by the authorities. There are indeed moves to ban these names despite their obvious commercial success.

These varietal wines aside, the range of other grapes permitted for Touraine wines is pretty eclectic: Chenin Blanc, Menu Pineau, Chardonnay, Cabernet Sauvignon, Pinot Noir, Pinot Meunier, Pinot Gris, Pineau d'Aunis, Cot (the local name for Malbec) and Grolleau. Any of these grapes can turn up in any combination, although the general preference among producers is to stick to mono-varietal wines. A new style is Touraine Rouge Tradition, a blended red which was created in the 1980s as an antidote to the prevailing fashion for young Gamays. Traditional wines are meant to be aged and are a blend of around 50 per cent Gamay, 30 per cent Cabernet Franc and 20 per cent Cot.

Apart from the main Touraine appellations, three villages which historically have been considered to produce particularly fine wines are allowed to add their own name to the wine, so you may come across Touraine-Mesland, Touraine-Amboise and Touraine-Azay-le-Rideau.

On the fringes of Touraine there are other appellations, some of which are developing while others are only just surviving oblivion. To the east are the two appellations of Valençay in a 130-hectare region based around the hill-top town which also boasts a palace-like 16th-century château, acquired by the statesman Talleyrand in 1803. Valençay is a complicated appellation: red, white and rosé are produced and the grapes can be any one of the standard Touraine range. Many other Touraine producers also have vineyards in this

Tall and closely packed, the elegant buildings of Chinon cluster beneath the ruins of three fortresses which once afforded shelter to English monarchs Henry II and Richard Lionheart as well as Philippe Auguste.

Vines in Vouvray, a few kilometres east of Tours, grow on plateaux of limestone and tufa. Not only cellars, as here at Clos Baudouin, but three- and even four-storey dwellings have been carved out of this extraordinary rock.

appellation where whites are probably the most successful wines. Cheverny and Cour-Cheverny are twin appellations just to the north-east which were created amid much bureaucratic wrangling during the '93 harvest. The idea behind forming two appellations out of the one much simpler VDQS area of Cheverny was to give recognition to a peculiarly local grape, the Romorantin, which is now preserved in the Cour-Cheverny appellation as a single-varietal white wine – light, high in acid and crisp. An anachronistic quirk in the wine law of the Cheverny appellation, however, paradoxically requires that any Romorantin has to be blended with other varieties. This is just the sort of legalistic nonsense that makes New World wine producers laugh all the way to the bank.

There is an even more remote vineyard area away to the north of the main Loire vineyards. The River Loir (without a final 'e'), a tributary of the Sarthe which in turn reaches the Loire at Angers, is certainly at the limit of viticulture in France being on the edge of Normandy, where cider is the dominant drink. It is surprising – as it is with the reds of Chinon and Bourgueil – that anything as good as the Chenin Blanc-based wines of Jasnières can be produced here. But here they are: aromatic, floral and with a fleeting lightness that speaks for itself. The surrounding appellations of Coteaux du Loir and Coteaux du Vendômois produce wines in a similar but less sophisticated style as well as red and rosé wines from a mix of the traditional regional grape varieties.

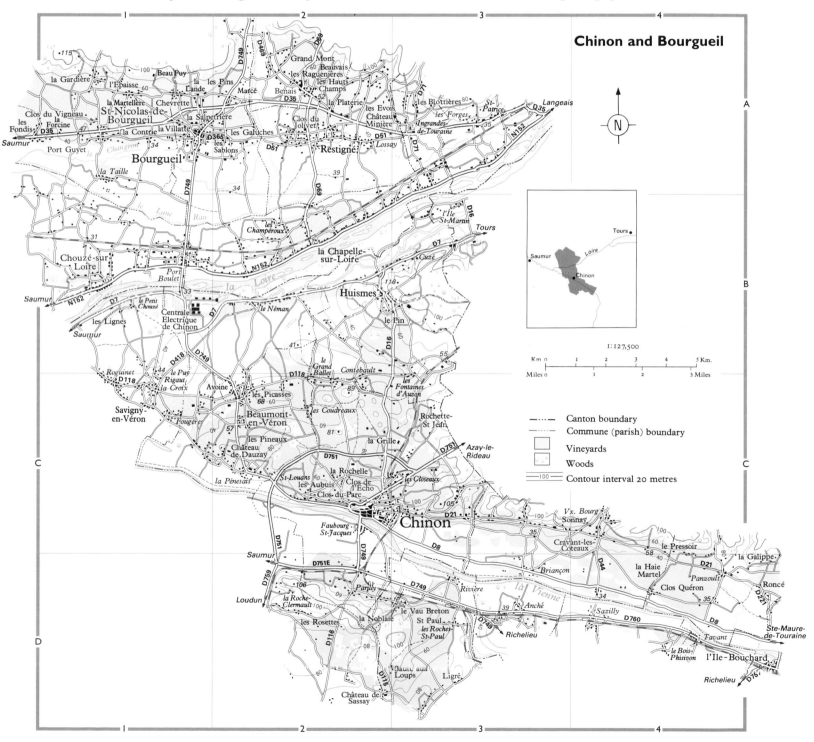

Chinon and Bourgueil

1:127,500

Km 0   1   2   3   4   5 Km.

Miles 0   1   2   3 Miles

–·–·– Canton boundary

–·–·– Commune (parish) boundary

☐ Vineyards

☐ Woods

═100═ Contour interval 20 metres

VOUVRAY AND MONTLOUIS

At the heart of the Touraine vineyards, almost within walking distance of Tours cathedral, are the twin vineyards of Vouvray and Montlouis, facing each other across the Loire – Vouvray on the north bank, Montlouis on the south.

Here the Chenin Blanc is king and appears in many guises, in bone-dry wines, medium-sweet wines, lusciously sweet and sparkling wines. The stylistic decision depends on the producer, on the year, on the market – almost, it seems, on a whim. In some years more still wine than sparkling is made, in others the proportions are reversed. It is confusing for the consumer, particularly as producers persist in giving no indication on the label of the style of wine inside the bottle.

Vouvray is certainly the more famous of the two appellations. At one time, indeed, Montlouis wines went under the Vouvray name until the granting of appellation in 1937 gave them their own separate identitiy.

Vouvray is the prettier area and it is also the more idiosyncratic. Here, people live literally in caves: houses may have normal façades but behind them the homes are carved out of the tufa cliff faces. Above on the plateau are the vineyards: from certain points you can enjoy the rather curious sensation of looking down on Vouvray's church spire. The appellation of Vouvray is a dynamic one, thanks to a young generation of growers who arrived at their maturity during the glory years of the late 1980s and 1990 when whatever they tried seemed to turn into luscious sweet wine. These growers now have the confidence – as well as the technology – to make drier and sparkling wines which enhance the apples-and-cream taste of Chenin while softening its sometimes hard edge.

Montlouis is still struggling to keep up with Vouvray. It never quite manages to achieve the intensity of flavours found in its northern neighbour yet these pleasant wines, less expensive than Vouvray, are well worth seeking out. Occasionally producers show flashes of inspiration which suggest that the potential is there.

Said to have inspired Charles Perrault to write The Sleeping Beauty (La Belle au Bois Dormant), *Château d'Ussé is indeed the stuff of fairy-tales. Towering above flowered terraces its numerous roofs, turrets, dormer windows and chimneys bristle before the dark forest of Chinon.*

Vouvray

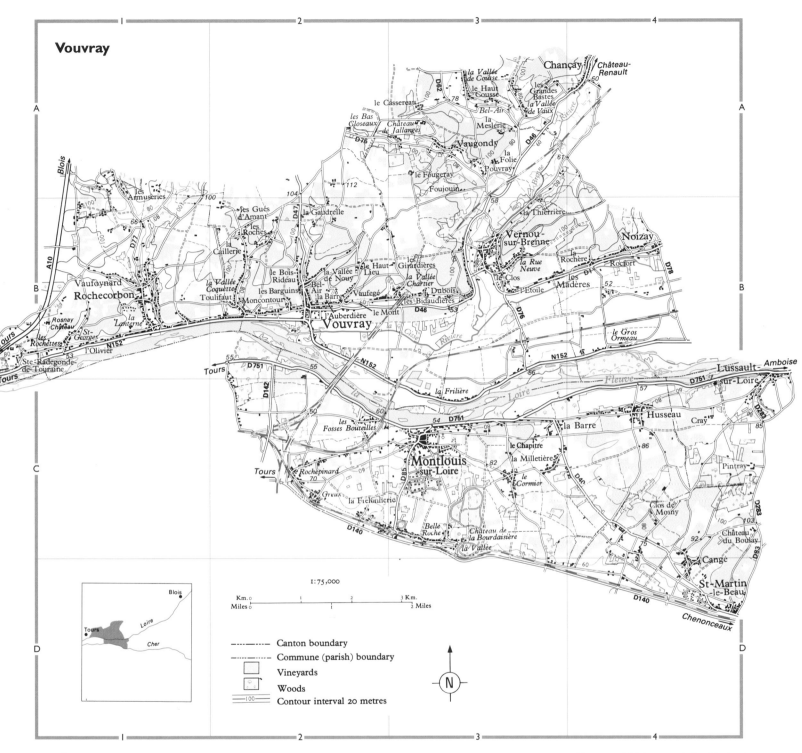

1:75,000

Km. 0 1 2 3 Km.
Miles 0 ½ 1 Miles

- – – – – – Canton boundary
- – – – – – Commune (parish) boundary
- Vineyards
- Woods
- —100— Contour interval 20 metres

N

CHÂTEAUX

The many châteaux along the banks of the Loire and its tributaries were built as fortresses but, from the late-15th century onward, their military role was superseded and increasingly they became sumptuous palaces for kings and nobility, along with their huge courts. Most of the châteaux and many of the medieval castles have been preserved in excellent condition and can be visited. Among the finest are some in the vineyard areas of

Touraine, where a visit to the château can be comfortably combined with one to the cellar. Others, such as Chambord and Blois, are outside the main vineyards but are well worth a detour. Some have summer *son et lumière* shows in the evenings; most are open in the morning and afternoon with a midday break. Some close on Mondays. Local tourist information offices give full details.

Azay-le-Rideau A brilliant example of Renaissance architecture.

Completed in 1529, it stands on an island in the Indre. It contains a museum devoted to the Renaissance.

Chenonceau Built out over the Cher and probably the most beautiful of all the Loire châteaux. Completed in 1521, it was given by Henri II to his mistress Diane de Poitiers in 1547. Many pieces of furniture date from the period. The ornamental gardens are based on de Poitiers' original designs. This is the only one of the châteaux that has its own vineyard producing Touraine wines.

Cheverny This luxuriously furnished 17th-century château is still owned by the founding family.

Chinon Famous as the castle where Joan of Arc first met Charles VII in 1429, this huge brooding fortification dominates the town.

Langeais This forbidding structure on the banks of the Loire near Bourgueil dates from 1467 and now houses a large collection of tapestries.

Ussé An ancient fortress and once the property of the great Bueils family of Touraine, this fairytale castle

The 16th-century Château de Chenonceau is known as 'The Château of Six Women' after the influences exerted by its colourful hostesses over 400 years. Today the château has its own vineyards, producing top quality wines.

overlooks both the Loire and the Indre. Rooms are beautifully furnished, there is a fine grand staircase and galleries are richly adorned with paintings and tapestries.
Valençay Built in the 16th century and enlarged during the 17th and 18th. A museum in the outbuildings details the life of of Prince Talleyrand.
Villandry The patiently reconstructed formal gardens, laid out on three levels, are unique in Europe.

PRODUCERS OF SPECIAL INTEREST

CHINON AND BOURGUEIL
Audebert et Fils 37140 Bourgueil
One of the area's largest family firms.
Bernard Baudry 37500 Chinon
Produces small quantities of top-class wines in Cravant-lès-Coteaux.
Cave des Vins de Rabelais 37500 Chinon
Good-quality, good-value wines.

Clos de l'Abbaye 37140 Bourgueil
The vineyard used to belong to the old abbey of Bourgueil.
Couly-Dutheil 37500 Chinon
Largest firm in Chinon, with spectacular cellars under the castle.
Pierre-Jacques Druet 37140 Benais
Enterprising producer of Bourgueil, trained in Bordeaux. Serious wines.
Château de la Grille 37500 Chinon
Elegant château producing equally elegant wines.
Pierre et Jean-Jacques Jamet 37140 Bourgueil
This company has been operating only since 1970 and makes wines that can be drunk young and fresh.
Charles Joguet 37500 Chinon
Poet and winemaker with vineyards in the south of the Chinon appellation.
Pascal Lorieux 37140 Bourgueil
Produces attractive St-Nicolas-de-Bourgueil.

VOUVRAY AND MONTLOUIS
Berger Frères 37270 Montlouis
Good sparkling wines as well as a range of still Montlouis.
Domaine Bourillon-d'Orléans 37210 Vouvray
Produces exciting examples of all styles of Vouvray.
Cave Coopérative de Montlouis 37270 Montlouis
Wine-tastings and a restaurant.
Deletang et Fils 37270 Montlouis
Huge underground cellars housing many old bottles of Montlouis.
Marc Brédif 37210 Vouvray
This large-scale producer makes sparkling wines.
Philippe Brisebarre 37210 Vouvray
One of the go-ahead younger generation of producers.
Cave des Producteurs de Vouvray 37210 Vouvray
The more enterprising of the two Vouvray cooperatives.
Gaston Huët 37210 Vouvray
Still one of the best producers in the appellation.
Clos Naudin 37210 Vouvray
Well established producer making wines of high quality.
Prince Poniatowski 37210 Vouvray
Specialist in the drier styles of Vouvray.

TOURAINE, CHEVERNY AND VALENÇAY
Jacky and Philippe Augis 41130 Meusnes
A small family concern making attractive Touraine wines.
Philippe Brossillon 41150 Mesland
A 200-year-old family firm which still relies on traditional practices.
Château de Chenonceau 37150 Chenonceaux
High-quality Touraine wines are made at the château.
Confrérie des Vignerons de Oisly et Thésée 41700 Oisly
Progressive and modern cooperative with a remarkable number of excellent wines. Superlative Sauvignon de Touraine.
Château Gaillard 41150 Mesland
Red wines of the Touraine-Mesland AC are the speciality. The best red is Vieilles Vignes Tradition.
Michel Gendrier, Domaine des Huards 41700 Cheverny
Romorantin Cour-Cheverny Cuvée François 1er is the star wine at this estate, which has been in the Gendrier family since 1846.
Patrice Hahusseau, Domaine du Salvard 41500 Muides-sur-Loire
Good whites from both Touraine and Cheverny.
J M Monmousseau 41400 Montrichard
Specialist in sparkling wines.
Domaine Octavie 41700 Oisly
Friendly, family-run domaine producing a full range of Touraine wines.

Jacky Preys 41130 Meusnes
Innovative producer of a wide range of wines, including reds from Cot.
Jean-François Roy 36600 Valençay
Attractive wines from a cellar in the town of Valençay.
Hubert Sinson 41130 Meusnes
Touraine producer also making Valençay.
Philippe Tessier 41700 Cheverny
Specialist in Cour-Cheverny wines from the Romorantin grape.
Les Vignerons des Coteaux Romanais 41140 St-Romain-sur-Cher
Reliable cooperative wines. Available in demi-john as well as in bottle.
Les Vignerons de Fontguenand 36600 Valençay
The main cooperative of Valençay.

JASNIÈRES AND COTEAUX DU LOIR
Martial Boutard 72340 La Chartre-sur-le-Loir
The Coteaux du Loir's biggest producer.
Joël Gigou 72340 La Chartre-sur-le-Loir
The most exciting producer of crisp, dry Jasnières.

COTEAUX DU VENDÔMOIS
Colin et Fils 41100 Thoré-la-Rochette
Patrice Colin makes excellent crisp rosé from Pineau d'Aunis.
Claude Norguet 41100 Thoré-la-Rochette
Tiny production of whites from Chenin Blanc.

WINE FÊTES

Amboise Wine fair on August 15.
Bourgueil Wine fair on the first weekend in February.
Chinon Wine fair on the third weekend in March; Medieval fair on August 15.
Cravant-lès-Coteaux Wine fair in early May.
Valençay Wine fair on the second weekend in May.
Vouvray Wine fair on the fourth weekend in January.

HOTELS

Le Choiseul quai Charles Guinot 37400 **Amboise**
Tel (0)247 30 45 45
River-front hotel in the town centre.
Le Chinon centre St-Jacques 37500 **Chinon** Tel (0)247 98 48 48
Modern hotel which has fine views of the town.
Hôtel de l'Espace parc des Bretonnières, 37300 **Joué-lès-Tours**
Tel (0)247 67 54 34
A modern hotel situated on the outskirts of Tours.

Domaine du Beauvois 37330 **Luynes** Tel (0)247 55 50 11 Château offering great comfort and excellent cooking. Has a park and swimming pool.

Château de Marçay 37500 Marçay Tel (0)247 93 03 47 Beautifully restored 15th-century castle. Luxurious rooms and fine, well presented cooking.

Domaine de la Tortinière 37250 **Monbazon** Tel (0)247 26 00 19 Small château on a hill overlooking the Indre. Swimming pool and park; restaurant in a converted orangery.

Relais des Landes 41120 **Les Montils** Tel (0)254 44 03 53 Attractive hotel set amid forested countryside to the south of Blois.

Les Hautes Roches 86 quai de la Loire, 37210 **Rochecorbon** Tel (0)247 52 88 88 Luxury hotel set in cliffs close to Vouvray with lovely views across the Loire to Tours.

Hôtel l'Espagne 9 rue du Château 36600 **Valençay** Tel (0)254 00 00 02 Comfortable town-centre hotel with an attractive courtyard restaurant.

RESTAURANTS

Le Mail St-Thomas 37400 **Amboise** Tel (0)247 47 22 52 Traditional cooking and excellent wine-list in a villa near the château of Amboise.

Au Plaisir Gourmand 37500 **Chinon** Tel (0)247 93 20 48 Top restaurant in the town centre with high-quality traditional cooking.

Auberge de l'Île 3 place Bouchard 37220 **l'Île-Bouchard** Tel (0)247 58 51 07 Modern cooking in a pretty restaurant with a terrace on the banks of the Vienne.

La Chancelière 37250 **Montbazon** Tel (0)247 26 00 67 Inspired cooking. A set lunch is available at lower prices.

L'Anguille Vagabonde place de l'Église, 37500 **St-Germain-sur-Vienne** Tel (0)247 95 96 48 Specialises in local dishes such as eels.

Auberge du Grand Vatel 37210 **Vouvray** Tel (0)247 52 70 32 Wide-ranging, traditional-style menu.

PLACES OF INTEREST

Amboise Town on the Loire with many attractive cafés and shops. Dominated by the huge château.

Blois Outside the wine area but full of interest with its medieval streets and central château.

Bourgueil A wine town with a 10th-century abbey and Gothic church.

Chinon Delightful town on the banks of the Vienne with many half-timbered houses and narrow streets. Overlooked by the castle.

Cravant-lès-Coteaux Chinon's most important wine village. In the Vieux Bourg there is a small church with Carolingian traces.

La Devinière The house near Chinon where the 16th-century satirist Rabelais was born.

Loches Medieval town centre with a castle, 12th-century church and museums.

Montlouis Comfortable, attractive town which faces Vouvray across the river.

Richelieu Built with a grid layout under the orders of Cardinal Richelieu, this is a textbook 17th-century town. La Fontaine called it "the most beautiful village in the universe".

Saché A museum in the town is dedicated to Honoré de Balzac.

Tours A large university city with many ancient buildings and a stunning Gothic cathedral. There is a museum of Touraine wines (16 rue Nationale) and many other interesting museums as well as good shops and a cosmopolitan air. The railway station at St-Pierre-des-Corps is on the TGV Paris-Bordeaux line.

Azay-le-Rideau's elegant château, completed in 1529, sits on the banks of the Indre and now houses a museum devoted to the Renaissance.

The matchless 16th-century formal gardens of Château de Villandry require teams of gardeners to maintain their immaculate order.

43

Upper Loire

The vineyards of the upper reaches of the Loire, lying along the part of the river that flows south–north rather than east–west, are scattered and much more isolated than those of Touraine, Anjou or the Pays Nantais. In few places do vines dominate the landscape. Many vineyard areas, particularly those at the southern end of the river, are much smaller than they once were: tiny pockets of vines where once there were swathes. The vineyards have been in decline since the devastating phylloxera epidemic, although the economic conditions governing their survival were already changing as the beetle arrived. Only small sections have been replanted.

Two areas have survived and prospered, however. Sancerre and Pouilly-Fumé are produced in a concentrated region south of Orléans: Sancerre on the western bank of the river, Pouilly facing it on the eastern bank. Having been borne along by fashion as much as by the quality of their product, the areas now make some of the best wines of the whole Loire Valley.

Sauvignon Blanc is what has made these vineyards famous: the aromas and perfumes of this fresh, sometimes flinty, sometimes overpoweringly exotic grape reach their French apogee here. Sancerre produces racy wines which can be drunk young, while Pouilly's wines are firmer, fuller, and need a year or two before they are opened, but in the long term are the finer.

Just as its wines are more showy, so the town of Sancerre is the more flamboyant. Perched on the top of a conical hill more like a Tuscan town than somewhere in central France, it has become a tourist Mecca. The central square is filled with pavement cafés, and wine shops ply a brisk trade at every strategic corner. Producers' cellars are buried deep beneath the medieval streets and from the Port César (yes, Julius Caesar is believed to have passed through here) there are magnificent views of the Loire as it meanders through the valley.

The main vineyards are spread on the slopes south and west of the town. In small side valleys are the principal villages of the appellation: Bué, Chavignol (home of a celebrated goats' cheese which pairs splendidly with the wine), Verdigny and Crézancy. The main street of Bué ends abruptly with the huge amphitheatre of vines that is the Clos de la Poussie, while in Chavignol the vineyard of Les Monts Damnés clings to an almost vertical slope.

Sancerre's production is mainly of white wines but small quantities of reds and rosés from Pinot Noir are popular locally and some producers make a speciality of them with justifiable success.

Across the river in Pouilly, white wine is everything. A tiny proportion is made from the Chasselas grape and is known by the name of the town, Pouilly-sur-Loire. By far the bulk of production and the area's claim to fame is Pouilly-Fumé, so called because of the smoky film that sometimes covers the berries, not because of any smokiness in the taste. A tightly concentrated area of vines spreads along the riverbank past Les Loges to Tracy, and then across the main N7 road and up the broad slope to St-Andelain where the church spire is a prominent landmark. The showpiece of Pouilly is the Château du Nozet, an elegant 19th-century fantasy of conical towers and steep-pitched turrets, where fine wines are made by the de Ladoucette family.

Abutting the northern end of the Pouilly vineyards are those of Coteaux du Giennois, centred on the town of Cosne-Cours-sur-Loire. Reds, rosés and whites are made but production is tiny and sustained as much by the joint efforts of the Pouilly cooperative,

Above: Sancerre and Pouilly-Fumé, the best known white wines of the entire valley, are grown along the upper reaches of the Loire.

Left: Sauvignon Blanc grows in few places as successfully as it does here in Sancerre, where it yields aromatic wines with a powerful perfume and an exhilarating fresh taste.

which vinifies the bulk of the grapes, as by the beneficent influence of the Institut National de la Recherche Agricole at Gien.

As the Loire turns to flow west to the Atlantic there is another patch of vineyards, the most northerly in the Loire, around the city of Orléans and only 145 kilometres from Paris. Five communes on the left bank of the river just downstream from Orléans provide the bulk of the vineyards from which some interesting light-red Pinot Meunier wines are produced in addition to whites and rosés.

There is more Sauvignon in isolated pockets to the west of Sancerre. Menetou-Salon makes whites from this grape as well as reds and rosés from Pinot Noir. This is a pretty region but its wines seem to stay under the shadow of neighbouring Sancerre; indeed Sancerre's producers tend to regard them as a secondary product.

Further west still, almost in the centre of France near the city of Bourges, are the two tiny areas of Reuilly and Quincy. Again Sauvignon Blanc is the dominant grape, although Reuilly also specialises in rosé wines from either Pinot Noir or Pinot Gris and lightweight reds from Pinot Noir.

If those two areas are tiny – even though they are finding some success on export markets – then by comparison the vineyards of Châteaumeillant are minute. They occupy a small slope just outside the town in empty country west of La Châtre in the *département* of the Cher. Red and rosé wines only are made under the dispensation of the local VDQS. There are just 75 hectares under vine and the

number of vignerons seems to be declining, so it is hardly surprising that the wines are seldom encountered outside the local area.

Further south the Loire and its tributaries support a rare mixture of tiny viticultural areas. Grapes include Gamay, Sauvignon and Chardonnay of St-Pourçain-sur-Sioule, an area which makes some high-quality wines. A local curiosity is Tressalier, the local name for Sacy, which is supposed to have been brought from Italy in the 13th century and was once found in the Chablis region. A difficult grape, it barely ripens in some years but it can form the base of some attractive sparkling wines.

Gamay is also found in the vineyards of Roanne. Since at this point the Loire is not too far from Beaujolais it is hardly surprising that the grape is cultivated in this area and in the even more southerly area of Côtes du Forez. Côte Roannaise wines are really only of local importance. The production is almost entirely of red, although a little rosé is also produced. Côtes du Forez wines have been exported thanks to an enterprising cooperative, the style of the wines being recognisable as an alternative to Beaujolais.

Further west, the Massif Central was once an enormous wine-producing area. Although the advent of phylloxera ended that monopoly, the vineyards of the Côtes d'Auvergne, centred on hilltop villages near the town of Clermont-Ferrand, still exist. Gamay, Pinot Noir and Chardonnay are planted. A few producers are having some success and there is a lively cooperative.

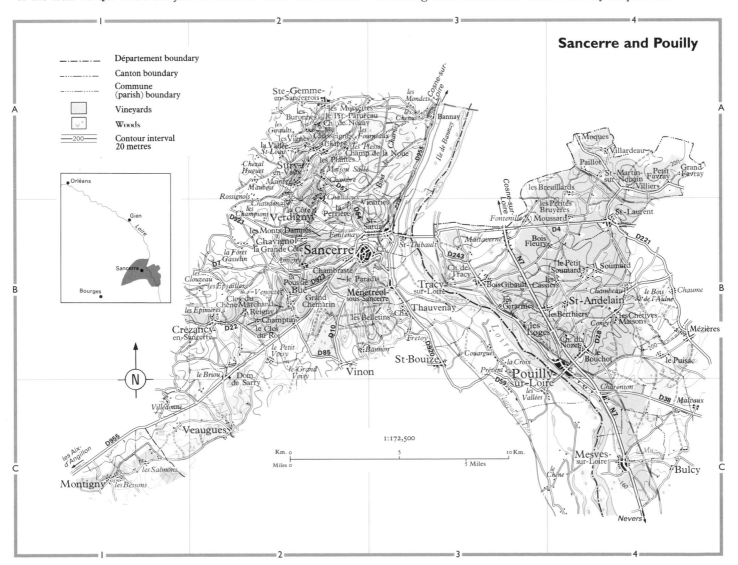

45

Intricately patterned glazed roof-tiles flank an octagonal belfry in Ambierle.

Renaissance Château du Nozet, which has been owned since 1787 by the de Ladoucette family, is the impressive source of some of the area's best Pouilly-Fumé.

PRODUCERS OF SPECIAL INTEREST

SANCERRE
Domaine Henri Bourgeois
18300 Chavignol
This rapidly growing firm also owns Domaine Laporte.
Clos de la Poussie 18300 Bué
Single-vineyard wine.
Lucien Crochet 18300 Bué
Producer of wines from the Clos du Chêne Marchand.
Vincent Delaporte
18300 Chavignol
Gitton Père et Fils
18300 Ménétréol-sous-Sancerre
Domaine wines from both Sancerre and Pouilly.
Alphonse Mellot 18300 Sancerre
Quality-minded merchant.
Jean-Max Roger 18300 Bué
Energetic producer making elegant wines; also Menetou-Salon.
Domaine Vacheron
18300 Sancerre
Some of the best reds in the area.

POUILLY
Michel Bailly 58150 Les Loges
Les Caves de Pouilly-sur-Loire
58150 Pouilly-sur-Loire
Didier Dagueneau
58150 St-Andelain
Producing some of the most exciting wines in the appellation.
Paul Figeat 58150 Les Loges

Pascal Jolivet
58150 Pouilly-sur-Loire
Impeccable wines, including Sancerre, from this *négociant*.
Domaine J Masson-Blondelet
58150 Pouilly-sur-Loire
Small family estate producing expertly made wines.
Château du Nozet
58150 Pouilly-sur-Loire
The region's show-piece, owned by the de Ladoucette family, also produces Sancerre (Comtes Lafon).
Michel Redde et Fils
58150 Pouilly-sur-Loire
Domaine Guy Saget
58150 Pouilly-sur-Loire
Large-scale *négociant* making wines from throughout the Loire.

MENETOU-SALON
Bernard Clément et Fils
18510 Menetou-Salon
Family firm dating back to 1560. The red is more interesting than the white.
Domaine Henri Pellé
18220 Morogues
The firm remains one of the best known producers in Menetou-Salon. It also owns vineyards in the Sancerre appellation.

QUINCY AND REUILLY
Claude Lafond
36360 Reuilly
One of the most dynamic producers in the Reuilly area.

Domaine de la Maison Blanche
18120 Quincy
Largest producer of good-quality Quincy.
Jean Mardon 18120 Quincy
Attractive Quincy.
Jean-Michel Sorbe 18120 Quincy
Produces both Reuilly and Quincy to a high standard.

CÔTES D'AUVERGNE
Cave Coopérative St-Verny
63960 Veyre-Monton
The Auvergne's major cooperative. Recently modernised.
Paul Champroux 63730 Corent
Good-quality wines from Corent.
M & R Rougeyron
63960 Châteaugay
One Auvergne's few producers to have gone entirely into stainless steel.

CÔTES DU FOREZ
Les Vignerons Foreziens 42130
Boën-sur-Lignon
Dominates production in the area with good-quality wines.

CÔTE ROANNAISE
Pierre Gaume 42155 Lentigny
A red and rosé from the VDQS Côte Roannaise and also a Gamay rosé and a Chardonnay Vin de Pays d'Urfé.
GIE des Producteurs
42370 Villemontais
Old-fashioned winemaking.
Paul Lapandry et Fils
42370 St-Haôn-le-Vieux
Simple, attractive wines.
Maurice Lutz 42820 Ambierle
A Gamay wine, made using semi-carbonic maceration techniques to give plenty of strawberry fruit flavour and colour, is the bulk of M Lutz' production.

ST-POURÇAIN-SUR-SIOULE
André et Yves Gallas
03500 Saulcet
Attractive small-scale producer.
Guy et Serge Nebout
03500 St-Pourçain-sur-Sioule

Particularly proud of the red from Gamay and Pinot Noir.
Ray Père et Fils 03500 Saulcet
The area's best known private producer.
Union des Vignerons
03500 St-Pourçain-sur-Sioule
This is St-Pourçain's biggest production unit by far. Methods are good and the wines reliable.

FÊTES

Bué Foire aux Sorciers (magicians) on the first Sunday in August.
Pouilly Wine fair on August 15.
St-Pourçain-sur-Sioule Foire des Vins at the end of February.
Roanne Foire des Vins et Fromages in May.
Sancerre Fête du Crottin du Chavignol (the local goats' cheese) held in the Caves de la Mignonne on the weekend after May 1; Foire aux Vins de France also held in the Caves de la Mignonne on the last weekend of August.

HOTELS

SANCERRE AND POUILLY
Le Relais Fleuri 42 avenue de la Tuilerie, 58150 **Pouilly-sur-Loire**
Tel (0)386 39 12 99
Comfortable hotel with good river views and the best restaurant in Pouilly, Le Coq Hardi.
Le St-Martin 10 rue St-Martin
18300 **Sancerre** Tel (0)248 54 21 11
A simple hotel conveniently placed in the centre of town.

OTHER REGIONS
Auberge de la Ferme 58200
Cosne-Cours-sur-Loire
Tel (0)388 28 15 85
Quiet hotel with restaurant and terrace just outside town.
Central 43270 Renaison
Tel (0)477 64 25 39
Good simple hotel with a restaurant in the Côte Roannaise.
Le Chêne Vert 35 boulevard Ledru-Rollin, 03500 **St-Pourçain-sur-Sioule**
Tel (0)470 45 40 65
Busy hotel with a good, comfortable restaurant.
Hôtel du Rhône 8 rue de Paris
03200 **Vichy** Tel (0)470 98 28 01
Hotel in central Vichy, which is not far from both St-Pourçain-sur-Sioule and the Côtes d'Auvergne vineyards.

RESTAURANTS

As elsewhere along the Loire, restaurants in Sancerre and Pouilly-sur-Loire feature fish dishes which match the local wines well. Further south in the more remote vineyards, meats, stews and other robust mountain cuisine become more common.

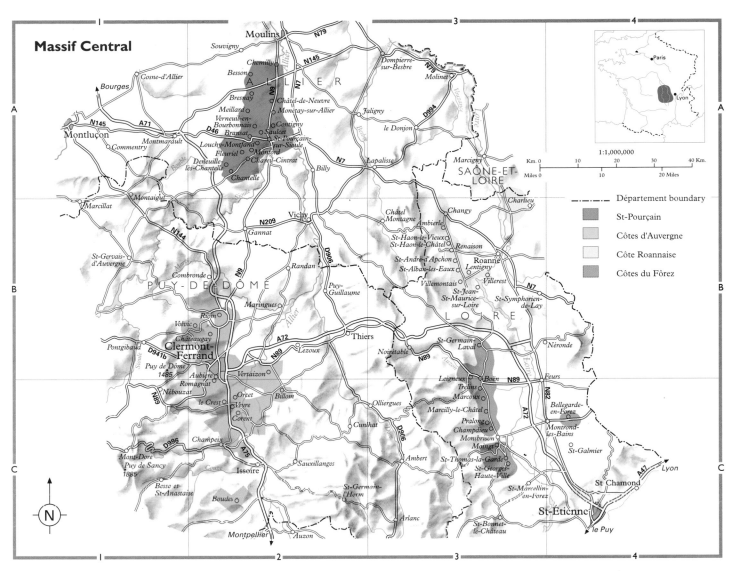

Massif Central

Souvigny • Moulins
Chemilly
Besson
Cosne-d'Allier
Bourges
Bresnay • Châtel-de-Neuve
Meillard • Monétay-sur-Allier
Montluçon • Verneuil-en-Bourbonnais • Contigny
Montmarault • Bransat • Saulcet • St-Pourçain-sur-Sioule
Commentry • Louchy-Montfand • Montord
Fleuriel • Chareil-Cintrat
Deneuille-les-Chantelle • Chantelle
Marcillat • Montaigut
Billy • Lapalisse
Vichy
Marcigny • SAÔNE-ET-LOIRE
Charlieu
ALLIER
Dompierre-sur-Besbre • Molinet
Jaligny • le Donjon

Km. 0   10   20   30   40 Km.
Miles 0   10   20 Miles
1:1,000,000

Paris • Lyon

Département boundary
St-Pourçain
Côtes d'Auvergne
Côte Roannaise
Côtes du Fôrez

St-Gervais-d'Auvergne
Combronde
PUY-DE-DÔME
Riom
Volvic
Châteaugay
Clermont-Ferrand
Puy de Dôme 1485
Aubière
Romagnat
Nébouzat
le Crest • Orcet
Veyre • Corent
Champeix
Mont-Dore • Puy de Sancy 1885
Besse et St-Anastaise
Boudes
Issoire
Sauxillanges
Maringues
Vertaizon
Billom
Lezoux
Thiers
Noirétable
Olliergues
Cunlhat
Ambert
St-Germain-l'Herm
Arlanc
Auzon
Montpellier

Randan
Gannat
Puy-Guillaume
Châtel-Montagne • Ambierle
St-Haon-le-Vieux
St-Haon-le-Châtel
St-André-d'Apchon
St-Alban-les-Eaux • Renaison
Roanne • Lentigny
Villemontais • Villerest
St-Jean-St-Maurice-sur-Loire
St-Symphorien-de-Lay
LOIRE
St-Germain-Laval • Néronde
Leigneux • Boën • Feurs
Trelins
Marcoux
Marcilly-le-Châtel
Pralong • Bellegarde-en-Forez
Champdieu • Montrond-les-Bains
Montbrison • Moingt
St-Galmier
St-Thomas-la-Garde
St-Georges-Haute-Ville
St-Marcellin-en-Forez
St-Chamond • Lyon
St-Étienne
St-Bonnet-le-Château
le Puy
Changy

SANCERRE AND POUILLY

Le Caveau de Bué 18300 Bué
Tel (0)248 54 22 08
Restaurant in the heart of the Sancerre village of Bué.

Auberge La Treille
18300 **Chavignol**
Tel (0)248 54 12 17
Good country cooking.

Le Laurier 29 rue de Commerce
18300 **St-Satur** Tel (0)248 54 17 20
Solid, sensible restaurant just below the hill of Sancerre.

Restaurant de la Tour 31 place de la Halle, 18300 **Sancerre**
Tel (0)248 54 00 81
The best restaurant in Sancerre with panoramic views of the vineyards.

OTHER REGIONS

Le Vigosche 2 rue du Château
63119 **Châteaugay**
Tel (0)473 07 21 12
In a small town in the Côtes d'Auvergne giving views across to Clermont-Ferrand.

Au Piet à Terre
place de la Gendarmerie

18370 **Châteaumeillant**
Tel (0)248 61 41 74
Comfortable and well run restaurant.

Troisgros place de la Gare
42300 **Roanne**
Tel (0)477 71 66 97
The incomparable Troisgros has a worldwide reputation. Hotel rooms are available.

PLACES OF INTEREST

SANCERRE AND POUILLY

Bourges Richly endowed capital of the Cher with the Gothic cathedral of St-Étienne and the Palais Jacques Coeur.

Chavignol Charming valley village, noted for its cheese and an elm planted by Henri IV (who reckoned the wine was the best he had tasted).

Menetou-Râtel Not far to the west of this Sancerre village is Château Boucard, a moated 15th–16th-century castle.

Sancerre Attractive hill-top town with narrow, steeply sloping streets and a market square. The Tour de

Fiefs is what remains of a castle that once dominated the town.

Sury-en-Vaux Beautiful 13th-century church tower.

Verdigny The Sancerre regional wine museum is located here.

OTHER REGIONS

Ambierle This Roannais community amid the vineyards has a beautiful 15th-century monastery with paintings attributed to the Flemish master Rogier van der Weyden.

Châteaugay Côtes d'Auvergne village situated on a hill around a 14th–16th-century castle. The castle has a wine-tasting hall.

Issoire The large 12th-century church of St-Austremoine is a perfect example of the Romanesque Auvergnat style.

Menetou-Salon Imposing 15th-century château built by Jacques Coeur, finance minister to Charles VII.

Morogues The Château de Maupas has a large collection of plates. The village's 14th-century church has an unusual wooden canopy.

Parc Naturel Régional des Volcans d'Auvergne
Taking in much of the Auvergne, this is the largest nature park in France.

St-Pourçain-sur-Sioule Parts of the church date from the 12th century and there is a Musée de la Vigne et du Vin.

Saulcet Wine village near St-Pourçain with a 13th-century church.

An annual fête is held in honour of the local speciality Crottin de Chavignol, an unctuous ewes'-milk cheese.

Champagne

Of all the great wines of France, champagne is the most paradoxical. For many people it is bottled laughter, euphoria at the pop of a cork; a frivolous draught more like a ceremonial libation than a serious drink, especially in the worst-case scenario where grand prix drivers shower each other with precious fizz. Yet behind the bubbles is a complex wine made by hard-working perfectionists in a very special place.

The heart of the Champagne region is about 145 kilometres north-east of Paris, centred on the cathedral city of Reims and the wine town of Épernay. The three principal wine-growing districts are Montagne de Reims, Vallée de la Marne and Côte des Blancs. Around 112 kilometres away to the south-east, the Aube too is Champagne, even if it is geographically closer to Burgundy. Champagne grapes are also grown across the Aisne, Seine-et-Marne and Haute-Marne. The region covers 34,000 hectares, of which 31,000 are currently planted.

These are among the most northerly vineyards in the world, so spring frosts, summer rain and variable sunshine pose potential problems to the quality and quantity of the grapes produced. Fortunately the chalky sub-soils of the Champagne heartland provide a refuge where classic grape varieties can produce exceptionally delicate and pure-flavoured juice – the ideal base for a sparkling wine.

Three grapes dominate the vineyards of Champagne. Pinot Noir, accounting for 37.5 per cent of production, is planted mainly on the chalky/sandy hillsides of Montagne de Reims; it is also the predominant grape of the Aube. The vigorous Pinot Meunier is better suited to the colder soils of Vallée de la Marne where it is popular for its high yields of soft fruity wine, an important component in an attractive non-vintage champagne. Pinot Meunier covers well over a third of the vineyards, so claims by some champagne producers (rarely the best) that they never use it should be taken with a pinch of salt!

The aristocratic Chardonnay thrives in the deep chalk of the Côte des Blancs. Ripening earlier and more reliably than Pinot Noir, Chardonnay is a vital component in the finer champagne

Left: The vineyards of Ville-Dommange, just south-west of Reims, provide Pinot Noir for the historic grande marque *house of Veuve Clicquot.*

Champagne

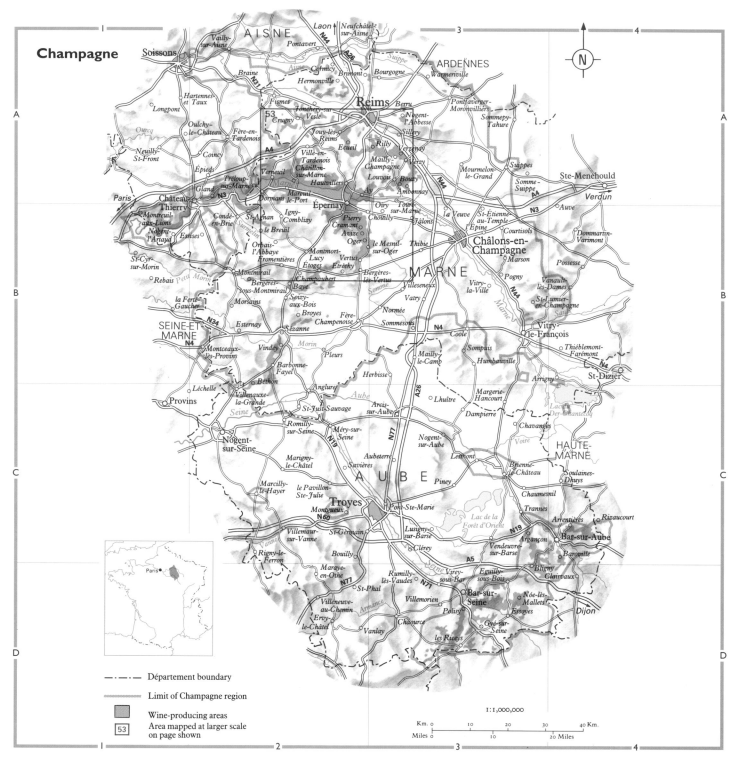

Département boundary

Limit of Champagne region

Wine-producing areas

53 Area mapped at larger scale on page shown

1:1,000,000

Km. 0   10   20   30   40 Km.

Miles 0   10   20 Miles

blends, providing delicacy, freshness and elegance to balance Pinot's greater weight and richness. Pure Chardonnay champagne, known as Blanc de Blancs, is very fashionable just now, though the repertoire of Chardonnay flavours ranges widely from youthful, incisive, apéritif styles through to mature, opulent, near-Burgundian expressions of the grape.

Champagne Making

At vintage time harvesting machines are banned: all picking is by hand. This is because most champagne is the product of white wine made predominantly from black grapes – the two Pinots – and it is essential that the neutral-coloured juice should not be put in contact with the surfaces of the skins which would taint it. The pressing itself must be conducted without delay; by the time of the '96 harvest, more than 2,000 pressing centres had been registered across the region to accelerate the transport of grapes.

The grapes are pressed gently in large, low traditional presses or in modern pneumatic ones, 4,000 kilos at a time. This gives 2,550 litres of juice obtained by two pressings. The first, the *cuvée*, produces 2,050 litres; the second, the *taille*, 500 litres. There used to be a third pressing, but this was effectively abolished in 1992. And a good thing too, for with each successive press the quality of the juice diminishes. In practice, the best firms tend to use only the *cuvée*. The clear juice then goes through its first fermentation, which usually takes place in stainless-steel tanks. A few great houses such as Krug and Jacquesson still ferment in wood, as do adventurous growers like Selosse and Tarlant.

Méthode champenoise is the name for the process of making a still wine sparkle by allowing it to ferment for a second time in the bottle. It is now used to make impressive sparkling wine around the world, but the blender's skill puts champagne into a separate class. Each January, the *chef de caves* (cellarmaster) starts to compose his non-vintage *cuvée*. He and his team will taste hundreds of new still wines, eventually arriving at a selection of those that marry well, consistent with the established style of the house. The *chef de caves* will also call on reserve wines from older vintages to make up for any deficiencies: thus, in the best hands, a technical function is elevated into an art form.

Once the blend is assembled, the *liqueur de tirage* (yeasts, old wine and sugar) is added and the wine bottled. The slow process known as the *prise de mousse* will produce a persistent stream of tiny bubbles. The second fermentation takes place with the bottles binned on their sides. Deposits are formed, mostly of dead yeasts, which add complexity to the wine's flavour.

After a lengthy ageing period (usually three years) the bottles are placed in holed racks called *pupitres* and are turned and tilted every day, eventually coming to an almost vertical position, neck downward. This induces the deposit to slide down and settle on the cork. The bottles are then easily disgorged of their deposit. To compensate for a certain loss of wine during disgorging, an equal amount of *liqueur de dosage* (cane sugar and still champagne) is added: the sugar content of the liqueur will determine the wine's degree of sweetness.

MERCHANTS, GROWERS AND COOPERATIVES

In the English-speaking world the champagne market is dominated by the *grandes marques*, the great merchants. In fact, the *grandes marques* own only about 14 per cent of the vineyards and rely on 15,500 growers to provide them with grapes.

Some of these growers, the *récoltants-manipulants*, make small amounts of champagne of their own, whose quality varies from the abysmal to the sublime. The best of these champagne growers are described on pages 54–55.

The cooperatives are a powerful force in Champagne and greatly feared by the merchants (often needlessly so). Two or three of the giant cooperative-unions each produce 10 million bottles of still wines and champagnes a year, many of which can be good value for money.

THE HEART OF CHAMPAGNE

Just south of Reims looms the Montagne, the first and most impressive of a series of chalky hills which provide enough protection from the elements to grow champagne grapes successfully. Montagne de Reims (not a mountain as such) comprises the Grande Montagne to the east of the N51 and the Petite Montagne to its west. The landscape is dominated by a vast forest rich in deer, wild boar and rare species of trees. About 7,000 hectares of vines are grown on the north-, east- and south-facing slopes, the *crus* ranking among the best in Champagne.

This is Pinot Noir country. The great vineyards on the northern slopes, especially those in Verzenay, reputedly produce the blackest grapes and the strongest wines. The vines extend east and south-east through Verzy and Beaumont-sur-Vesle, finally ending in the *premier cru* villages of Villers-Marmery, Trépail and Vaudemanges. These last three produce fruity, early-maturing Pinot. A little Chardonnay of a very particular type is also grown on the lower slopes of the eastern Montagne above Puisieulx and Sillery. More fleshy and rounded than the Chardonnay of the Côte des Blancs, the Montagne Chardonnay is much used in the *cuvées* of Ruinart, Reims' oldest champagne house. On the south side of the Montagne, the *grands crus* of Bouzy and Ambonnay are famous for sumptuous Pinots rich in alcohol and extract, tempered by a fine clarity of flavour.

From east to west, Vallée de la Marne is divided viticulturally into the Grande Vallée between Tours-sur-Marne and Dormans, and the Petite Vallée which extends as far as Château-Thierry, a mere 96 kilometres from Paris. The best vineyards – Mareuil-sur-Aÿ, Aÿ and Dizy – are all situated on the north bank of the river near Épernay. Smooth, harmonious Pinot Noirs are sourced from these sunny sites and, in exceptional years, the Côte aux Enfants vineyard on the south-west slopes of Aÿ yields an aromatic, still red wine which tastes like a light Burgundy. Good red wines are also made in the village of Cumières above Épernay. Higher still in the neighbouring commune of Hautvillers, the abbey where Dom Pérignon was cellarer from 1668 until his death in 1715 commands magnificent views over the Marne.

From Cumières to Dormans, mainly Pinot Meunier vines cover both banks of the river. Contrary to what one might expect, the quality of the grapes scarcely varies whether the vineyards face north or south. Pinot Meunier ripens easily but is a challenging grape to vinify. The cooperative at Leuvrigny west of Oeuilly

Before vines can be planted or re-planted, Champagne's Chartre de Qualité *dictates that soil and the subsoil be analysed and any deficiencies corrected.*

*The Pommery cellars, on the site of Gallo-Roman chalk-pits (*crayères*), are the finest in Reims. They maintain an even temperature of 10°C all year round.*

consistently makes the best Meunier wine, most of which is sold under contract to four of the greatest champagne houses – Krug, Roederer, Pol Roger and Billecart-Salmon – for judicious use in their non-vintage *cuvées*.

Pinot Meunier vines are also tended sporadically on the tributaries of the Marne, particularly in a south-east direction along the Surmelin for a distance of 40 kilometres to Orbais L'Abbaye. West of Dormans toward Château-Thierry, the soils become heavier and the wines increasingly coarse.

Épernay, close to the three principal wine-growing districts, is the wine capital of Champagne. To the south of the town in the valley of the Cubry, there is also a succession of lesser-known vineyards. The best of these is the *premier cru* Pierry. Its name (meaning 'stony') derives from the flinty soil which reputedly gives the wines their minerally taste. Pinot Meunier is the dominant grape but both Pinot Noir and Chardonnay can and do produce excellent results.

Nearby, the historic Château de la Marquetterie, once the haunt of Voltaire and Beaumarchais, is worth a visit by arrangement with the owners, Champagne Taittinger. Further down the D10 are the fine vineyards of Grauves and Cuis where the soils are chalkier, making them ideal for Chardonnay. The wines of Cuis in particular are firm, with high acidity – "you grip the table when you taste them", according to leading grower Didier Gimmonet. A lovely Romanesque church is set on a terrace above the village.

The Côte des Blancs starts just east of Épernay in the *grands crus* of Chouilly and Oiry. The Côte is a barrier of east-facing hills which runs south for 19 kilometres to the Mont Aimé. Chardonnay is grown almost exclusively, giving wines of rare finesse which sparkle vigorously. The vineyards are more homogeneous than those of Montagne, so the differences in taste from one wine village to another are subtle.

Travelling south, the four stars of the Côte are Cramant, Avize, Oger and Le Mesnil-sur-Oger. The wines of Cramant often have a spectacular perfume, those of Avize a superb purity of flavour. The flavours of Oger are all delicacy, those of Le Mesnil powerful and acidic when young but they have the potential to live to a magnificent old age: the opportunity to taste a 20-year-old Mesnil from a great producer such as Salon or Alain Robert is worth a long journey. At the southern end of the Côte, the small town of Vertus is known for fruity, charming Chardonnay and useful Pinot Noir.

The Côte de Sézanne is an extension of the Côte des Blancs, separated from the latter by the Marais de St-Gond. The soils are still chalky, the slopes of favourable aspect. Well made Chardonnay champagne can be found in this up-and-coming area, especially at Le Brun de Neuville, the admirable local cooperative. In blind tastings its Blanc de Blancs often shows the competition the door.

THE GRADING OF CHAMPAGNE GRAPES

All the champagne region's wine-growing villages are classified on a percentage scale known as *l'échelle des crus* (the 'ladder' of growths.) It is geographically based but is essentially an index of price, graded on the reputed quality of grapes from particular communes. *Grands crus* rate 100 per cent; *premiers crus* 90–99 per cent; *deuxièmes crus* 80–89 per cent.

Like most vineyard classifications, the *échelle* is less than perfect. Its main weakness is that it makes no qualitative distinction between individual vineyard sites within the same commune. And it obviously cannot take account of the all-important human factor. Clearly, a careful grower producing ripe, 80-per-cent-rated grapes is a much better source of supply than an incompetent grower producing sour, 100-per-cent-rated fruit.

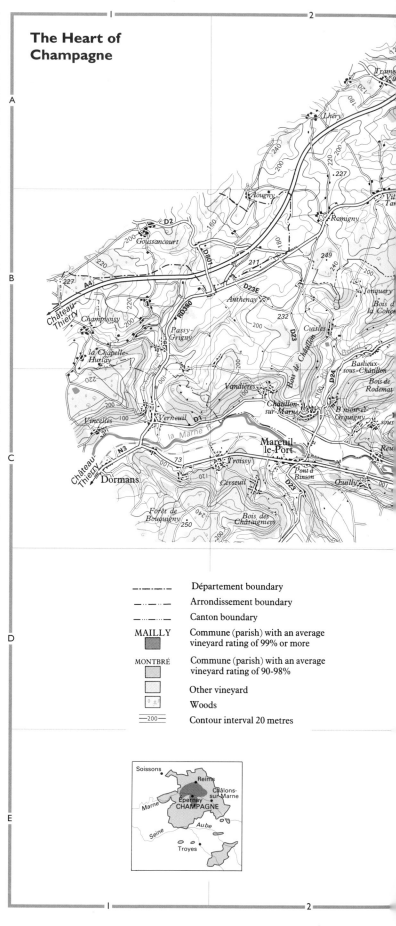

The Heart of Champagne

	Département boundary
	Arrondissement boundary
	Canton boundary
MAILLY	Commune (parish) with an average vineyard rating of 99% or more
MONTBRÉ	Commune (parish) with an average vineyard rating of 90-98%
	Other vineyard
	Woods
200	Contour interval 20 metres

Reims

Tinqueux

Janvry
Gueux
Vrigny
Ormes
Cité
Charbonneaux
Méry-
Prémecy
la-Montagne
St-Euphraise-
et-Clairizet
PARGNY-
LES-REIMS
JOUY-
LES-REIMS
LES MESNEUX
BEZANNES
CORMONTREUIL
Bouilly
VILLE-
DOMMANGE
TROIS-
PUITS
TAISSY
Bligny
SACY
VILLERS-
AUX-NOEUDS
Champfleury
SILLERY
Mont de
la Cuche
Courmas
le Bois de
la Fosse
ECUEIL
MONTBRE
PUISIEULX
Chaumuzy
CHAMERY
Mont
Trouilly
BEAUMONT-
SUR-VESLE
Marfaux
RILLY-LA-
MONTAGNE
Chemin de la Barbarie
VERZENAY
Pourey
Sermiers
CHIGNY-
LES-ROSES
VERZY
Courtagnon
VILLERS-
ALLERAND
LUDES
MAILLY
VILLERS-
MARMERY
Nanteuil-
la-Forêt
Bois de
St-Quentin
FORÊT DE LA MONTAGNE DE REIMS
Ville-
en-Selve
Belval-
sous-Châtillon
Bois de
Nanteuil
Germaine
TRÉPAIL
Mont Tournant
BILLY-LE-
GRAND
Bois de Fleury
Etang de
Nanteuil
St-Imoges
Bois du
Gouffre
Bois du Mont
St-Hubin
LOUVOIS
Bois des Dames
VAUDEMANGES
Fleury-
la-Rivière
Romery
Etangs des
Sentelles
Mont Hurlet
TAUXIÈRES-
MUTRY
BOUZY
Cormoyeux
CHAMPILLON
Fontaine-
sur-Ay
Mt
Ecoué
AMBONNAY
HAUTVILLERS
Bois de
St-Mare
CUMIÈRES
Bois de
Charlefontaine
MUTIGNY
AVENAY-
VAL D'OR
Mt
des Plantes
Damery
la Marne R.
DIZY
MAGENTA
Mont Charlier
TOURS-
SUR-
MARNE
Condé-
sur-Marne
Mardeuil
AY
MAREUIL-SUR-AY
BISSEUIL
Vauciennes
la Marne R.
Epernay
CHOUILLY
OIRY
Etang
d'Orléans
Châlons-
sur-Marne
Forêt d'Epernay
PIERRY
RD3
Etang
Neuf
Moussy
D40a
Vinay
CHIS
Butte
de Saran
Ch. de Saran
Chavot-
Courcourt
Monthelon
Mancy
CRAMANT
Morangis
AVIZE
Moslins
GRAUVES
B. d'Avize
OGER
Forêt d'Oger
LE MESNIL
SUR-OGER
Forêt du Mesnil
Forêt de Vertus
VILLENEUVE-
RENNEVILLE-
CHEVIGNY
VOIPREUX
VERTUS

1:157,000

Km. 0   1   2   3   4   5   6 Km.
Miles 0   1   2   3   4 Miles

53

PRODUCERS OF SPECIAL INTEREST

REIMS

Henri Abelé 51100 Reims
Very old champagne house (1785) now owned by Freixenet, the Spanish Cava producer. Fine Chardonnay-style champagnes. Good Sourire de Reims non-vintage Brut.

Charles Heidsieck 51100 Reims
Financed by Rémy-Cointreau, *chef de caves* Daniel Thibault has hugely improved the quality of this *grande marque*. The non-vintage Brut Réserve is a blended *cuvée* of up to 200 wines, creamy, vanilla-rich, perfectly balanced. The Blanc des Millénaires is a wonderful Blanc de Blancs on a winning streak ('83, '85, '89).

Henriot 51066 Reims
Joseph Henriot took the firm out of the Moët group in 1994. The champagnes are as fine drawn as ever. Incisive Blanc de Blancs and magnificent prestige Cuvée des Enchanteleurs (the '85 had years of life ahead a decade later).

Jacquart 51100 Reims
Sixth-largest champagne firm, Jacquart is the brand name of the CRVC cooperative. Two non-vintages: Brut Tradition, soft and round; Brut Sélection, Chardonnay-driven, tighter. Good vintage champagnes (the '90 is fabulous).

Krug 51100 Reims
The grandest name in Champagne and ruinously priced. The wines are unique, all fermented in small oak barrels. The Grande Cuvée multi-vintage is ultra-complex; always rich, nutty and profound, it has had an extra dimension of elegance recently. The rosé is a masterpiece, intensely fruity yet firmly dry. Lovely vintage wines (the legendary '64 is a collectors' item) and the austere but great Clos du Mesnil, a single-vineyard

Notre-Dame cathedral: a stunning example of 13th-century Gothic architecture at its finest.

pure-Chardonnay champagne that should not be drunk until it is 12–15 years old.

Lanson 51056 Reims
A question mark hangs over this famous old house taken over by the Franco-British group in 1992. Black Label non-vintage can taste green but the rosé is fine and delicate. Up to '90, the vintage champagnes are excellent, the prestige Noble Cuvée of rapier-like elegance.

Mumm 51100 Reims
This *grande marque* has received a mixed press but there are signs of improvement. The Cordon Rouge non-vintage is a straightforward wine and the Mumm de Cramant a fresh single-village Blanc de Blancs though with a highish dosage.

Bruno Paillard 51100 Reims
A relative newcomer, this house founded in 1981 makes elegant champagnes of real interest. The first-rate *première cuvée* is part-fermented in wood.

Palmer 51100 Reims
A small cooperative making a balanced fruity Brut non-vintage and a powerful mature prestige *cuvée* Amazon.

Piper-Heidsieck 51100 Reims
The same Thibault touch but in a lighter, crisper style than at Charles Heidsieck. Excellent, racy, vintage-dated Piper-Heidsieck Rare.

Pommery 51083 Reims
Delicate, refined vintage champagnes are the strong card of this historic house. Immaculate prestige *cuvée* Louise Pommery (superb '89) and the newly launched Flacons d'Exception (which are mature vintage champagnes in magnums freshly disgorged to order).

Louis Roederer 51100 Reims
A great family-owned champagne house. The high standards are due to the firm's choice vineyards (which supply 70% of its needs) and the perfectionist winemaking which includes ageing the reserve wines in wood. Rich vanilla-like Brut Premier non-vintage is Pinot-dominant. Cristal is the most sought-after prestige *cuvée* of all (a fabulous '89). Rare gently sparkling Blanc de Blancs.

Ruinart 51100 Reims
The oldest champagne house (1729) now owned by Moët. The Montagne Chardonnays in the Dom Ruinart Blanc de Blancs make for a sumptuous *cuvée*; equally brilliant is the Dom Ruinart Rosé.

Taittinger 51100 Reims
An important force in the champagne world since 1945. The firm has large vineyards in the Côte des Blancs and the Aube. The champagnes are floral, buttery, Chardonnay-led. The once-inconsistent Brut Réserve non-vintage is much improved. The Comtes de

Champagne Blanc de Blancs is always exciting ('82, '85, '86, '88).

Alain Thiénot 51063 Reims
A former broker, the dynamic Thiénot is a merchant to watch. Natural champagnes full of character. Beautiful Pinotish Grande Cuvée (great '85) and a fine-grained rosé.

Veuve Clicquot Ponsardin 51100 Reims
The Widow goes from strength to strength. Splendid full-flavoured Yellow Label non-vintage Brut, luscious vintage wines and the superb La Grande Dame prestige *cuvée* ('85 and '88 are classics).

MONTAGNE DE REIMS

Michel Arnould 51500 Verzenay
Arnould still grows for Bollinger but sells more champagne under his own label. The *grand cru* Brut is a true Verzenay Blanc de Noirs: powerful, deep-flavoured but with a fine creamy finish. Excellent rosé too.

Paul Bara 51150 Bouzy
Bara is one of Bouzy's leading grower-winemakers. Both his Brut Réserve and Grand Rosé de Bouzy are ample champagnes with strawberryish fruit.

Henri & Serge Billiot 51150 Ambonnay
The Billiots are growers making tiny quantities of outstanding Pinot Noir champagne. Superb prestige *cuvée* Laetitia, a blend of many vintages.

Canard-Duchêne 51500 Ludes
After a weak period at the beginning of the 1990s, this *grande marque* is back on form. The Brut non-vintage is full-flavoured, ideal with food. Excellent nutty, rich prestige *cuvée* Charles VII.

Daniel Dumont 51500 Rilly-la-Montagne
A nurseryman working with his sons, Dumont raises 200,000 vines a year for sale to other producers. His own champagnes are pure in flavour. The Grand Réserve has lovely toasty fruit.

Mailly Grand Cru 51500 Mailly-Champagne
Every one of the 70 member-growers of this exclusive cooperative owns *grand cru* vines in Mailly. Full, powerful yet well balanced champagnes across the range with at least 70% Pinot Noir in each blend. Successful Extra Brut and excellent Coteaux Champenois Rouge.

AŸ AND VALLÉE DE LA MARNE

Beaumont des Crayères 51530 Mardeuil
This small cooperative just west of Épernay produces admirable champagne at kind prices. The Meunier-dominated Cuvée Reserve Brut would make a perfect party fizz.

Billecart-Salmon 51160 Mareuil-sur-Aÿ
Always a highly respected *grande marque*, the firm is scaling new heights under François Roland-Billecart, a straight-talking perfectionist. The Brut non-vintage is faultless, fresh and racy yet mature. Wonderful vintage wines such as the late-disgorged Grande Cuvée '85.

Bollinger 51160 Aÿ
A true 'great', the firm makes muscular Pinot-led champagnes. Barrel-fermented Grande Année vintages need long ageing, though the '89 is a charmer.

Deutz 51160 Aÿ
With Roederer's investment, the Cuvée Classique is complex and vinous. The prestige *cuvée* William Deutz is a great wine.

Gatinois 51160 Aÿ
A small *manipulant*, Gatinois makes a strong, deep-coloured *grand cru* Brut and excellent still red in great years.

René Geoffroy 51480 Cumières
Vignerons since the 16th century, the family use traditional methods such as part-fermentation in wood and late-disgorging of vintage champagnes. Brilliant Cuvée Prestige '90.

Gosset 51160 Aÿ
A range of traditional full-flavoured champagnes from an old *grande marque*. The multi-vintage Grande Réserve and the rosé are the best wines.

Jacquesson 51530 Dizy
Founded in 1798, this low-key house is altogether excellent. Part wood-fermented champagnes, creamy and long-flavoured, is the constant style. The exquisite Blanc de Blancs is a pure Avize.

Laurent-Perrier 51150 Tours-sur-Marne
The champagne success story of the post-1945 period, Laurent-Perrier produces the most varied and imaginative range of wines in the region. Stars of the offerings are the now consistent and poised Brut L-P, the bone-dry Ultra Brut and the ever-splendid prestige Grand Siècle, a blend of three vintages.

Joseph Perrier 51000 Châlons-en-Champagne
With new finance from Laurent-Perrier, the fruit-laden champagnes of this house are even better. First-rate Cuvée Royale non-vintage, rich yet balanced, and spectacular Cuvée de Luxe Josephine, Chardonnay to the fore.

Tarlant 51480 Oeuilly
Jean-Mary Tarlant is a gifted *récoltant-manipulant* who vinifies the wines from different parts of his vineyards separately so that they may best express the character of their respective soils. His Krug-like Cuvée Louis is a great bottle.

ÉPERNAY AND CÔTE DES BLANCS

Duval Leroy 51130 Vertus
An important house with 130ha mainly on the Côte des Blancs, the firm has specialised in supplying 'buyer's own brand' champagnes on the export market. Its own-label Fleur de Champagne (75% Chardonnay) is excellent.

Gimmonet 51530 Cuis
Important growers with choice holdings on the Côte des Blancs, the Gimmonets make champagnes of rare finesse. Pick of the range are the vital Maxi-Brut (without dosage) and the honeyed Brut Fleuron.

Alfred Gratien 51201 Épernay
Rigorously old-fashioned, all Gratien champagnes are fermented in wood, with no malolactic fermentation in order to ensure a long life. The Brut non-vintage is spicy and mouth-filling, the prestige *cuvée* Paradis a masterpiece of refinement.

Larmandier-Bernier 51130 Vertus
From his 12-ha estate, Pierre Larmandier makes impressively pure-flavoured Chardonnay champagnes. The Blanc de Blancs Premier Cru is incisive, a perfect apéritif, the '90 Cramant Grand Cru is subtle, complex and well-flavoured.

R & L Legras 51530 Chouilly
Growers-turned-merchants. The exemplary *grand cru* Blanc de Blancs is sold mainly to Michelin-starred restaurants in France.

Moët & Chandon 51333 Épernay
A bottle of Moët is uncorked somewhere in the world every two seconds. For such a vast champagne operation (20 million bottles a year) the quality is extremely high: reliable Brut Impérial non-vintage, excellent vintages and sumptuous prestige Dom Pérignon.

Perrier-Jouët 51200 Épernay
The firm's superb Chardonnay vineyards in Cramant and Avize shape some first-rate vintage champagnes. The Blason de France is a well structured non-vintage.

Pol Roger 51206 Épernay
The Pol Roger family still makes the blends of this outstanding smallish *grande marque*: subtle White Foil non-vintage, exquisite Blanc de Chardonnay, elegant Cuvée Prestige PR and the majestic Pinot-led Sir Winston Churchill.

Alain Robert
51190 Le Mesnil-sur-Oger
No one makes better Blanc de Blancs champagne than Alain Robert, a leading Mesnil grower and driven perfectionist. The Mesnil Sélection, never less than 12 years old, is a magnificent mouthful of evolved Chardonnay flavours.

Salon 51190 Le Mesnil-sur-Oger
Salon is the only house to produce just one type of champagne, always a Blanc de Blancs, always vintage-dated and only in exceptional years. The latest release, the '83, has bell-like clarity of fruit and walnut aromas so typical of this great firm. Older vintages such as '66 and '64 are still in their prime.

Jacques Selosse 51190 Avize
Anselme Selosse is an original. Trained in Beaune, he ferments his top Cuvée d'Origine in new-oak barrels as if it were a great white Burgundy. Wonderfully full yet balanced wines that extend the taste spectrum of champagne.

Union Champagne 51190 Avize
The outstanding cooperative of the region, the union's greatest assets are its members' vineyards in the finest sites of the Côte des Blancs. Delectable Orpale Blanc de Blancs.

HOTELS AND RESTAURANTS

THE MARNE

Côte 108 N44, 02190 **Berry-au-Bac**
Tel (0)323 79 95 04
This is where the Champenois go when they want to eat really well. The finest ingredients are blended to create an unerring harmony of flavours. Great wines at fair prices.

Hôtel de l'Angleterre 19 place Mgr Tissier, 5100 **Châlons-en-Champagne** Tel (0)328 68 21 51
Solid, comfortable hotel with Michelin-star restaurant. Jacky Michel's cooking delights at every turn. Reasonable prices for this quality.

La Garenne N13, 51370 **Champigny-sur-Vesle**
Tel (0)326 08 26 62
On the Soissons road close to Reims golf course, this elegant, unfussy restaurant has the winning combination of first-rate cooking and reasonable prices, especially at lunchtime. Charming service.

Royal Champagne N2051, 51160 **Champillon** Tel (0)326 52 87 11
This Relais et Châteaux hotel-restaurant commands magnificent views over the Marne. A welcoming atmosphere; precisely timed, imaginative, consistent cooking. Superb champagne list. Also 27 luxury bedrooms, most with a splendid view.

Chez Pierrot 16 rue de la Fauville 51200 **Épernay** Tel (0)326 55 16 93
A minuscule picture-filled restaurant in a quiet street. Pierre Trouillard's bourgeois cooking wins high marks for true flavours at low prices.

Hôtel de la Cloche 5 place Mendès France, 51200 **Épernay**
Tel (0)326 55 24 05
Right by Épernay's Notre-Dame church and close to the station, this simple clean hotel is a budget choice. Also a restaurant.

Le Mesnil 2 rue Pasteur 51190 **Le Mesnil-sur-Oger**
Tel (0)326 57 95 51
Traditional French cuisine – mostly fish and seasonal game – and an impressive list of Chardonnay champagnes.

Au Petit Comptoir 17 rue du Mars, 51100 **Reims**
Tel (0)326 40 58 58
A fashionable meeting place, this stylish fin-de-siècle bistro offers 'French Grandmother's cooking' adapted to modern tastes. From bouillabaisse of rascasse (scorpion fish) to navarin of lamb, Fabrice Maillot's food is delicious and matched by good, fairly priced wines. Book.

Les Crayères 64 boulevard Henri-Vasnier; 51100 **Reims**
Tel (0)326 82 80 80
Part of the Relais et Châteaux association, this grand 1900 town house is world famous for the Michelin three-star cooking of Gérard Boyer. Wonderful fish dishes. Luxurious bedrooms overlook a beautiful park. High prices.

Holiday Inn Garden Court 46 rue Buirette, 51100 **Reims**
Tel (0)326 47 56 00
In the heart of the city close to the brasseries of the place d'Erlon, this is the best of the hotels in the middle-price range. Modern, simply elegant design, very comfortable; spotless bedrooms; helpful staff.

Le Grand Cerf
N51, 51500 **Rilly-la-Montagne**
Tel (0)326 97 60 07
A handsome inn. Rich classical cuisine tempered by a light touch. Outstanding cellar, knowledgeable sommelier.

PLACES OF INTEREST

THE MARNE

Châlons-en-Champagne The administrative capital of the Marne *département*, this is an important military centre. Rather sober in atmosphere, the town does have some fine churches, notably the 12th- and 13th-century Église de Notre Dame en Vaux, a lovely mix of Romanesque and Gothic styles. Visit by appointment the cellars of Joseph Perrier, one of the hidden jewels of the champagne world. Châlons is a good place to stay overnight en route to the Aube and Burgundy.

Épernay This is a working wine town, by no means beautiful but with pleasant parks and gardens such as the Jardin de l'Hôtel de Ville. Of the various organised tours of champagne firms, Moët & Chandon's is the most complete, that of Mercier the most fun, for you can travel daily along 16km of wide subterranean galleries on the firm's miniature electric train.

Le Mesnil-sur-Oger This large wine village, home to one of the greatest *crus* of the Côte des Blancs, has a wine museum with a fine collection of 17th–19th-century presses.

Montagne de Reims The regional nature park created in 1976 covers 123,500 acres between Reims, Épernay and Châlons-en-Champagne. More than a third of the park is forest and includes the macabre Faux de Verzy, a copse of ancient stunted beeches which would make an ideal set for the witches' scene in Macbeth.

Reims Once the spiritual capital of medieval France, Reims is a prosperous town best known for its fine Gothic cathedral and exquisite Romanesque Basilica of St-Rémi. As over three quarters of the city was destroyed during World War I, Reims is a unified example of 1920s architecture traversed by elegant boulevards. The cafés and brasseries of the lively place Drouet de l'Erlon are its social heart. A visit to the cellars of one of the famous champagne firms is highly recommended, particularly the Roman chalk-pits (*crayères*) of Ruinart which are classified as a national monument.

The best and most common champagne press is the traditional vertical coquard.

The Aube

Wine grapes were probably first planted in the Aube by the Romans, but it was the monks at Clairvaux and neighbouring abbeys who developed the vineyards on a serious scale in the 11th and 12th centuries. The wine region benefited around this time from its proximity to the great city of Troyes, then the capital of Champagne.

Despite wars, suffering and deprivation, the vineyards continued to flourish and expand over the next 700 years. By 1852 they covered about 23,000 hectares, planted mainly with Pinot Noir and traditional varieties such as Savagnin and Arbanne.

The period 1850–1950 was hard for the Aubois. The improved transport associated with the arrival of the railway brought competition from the cheaper wines of the Midi and the Aubois saw their champagne markets in the north of France and Flanders contract drastically. The phylloxera aphid which devastated all the vineyards of Champagne in the late 1880s resulted in the reduction of the Aube area under vine to just 6,000 hectares by 1911. A bad situation was made worse by widespread replanting with the Gamay grape, which although prolific and resistant to spring frosts, produced inferior juice for the purposes of champagne making. The manipulative Marnois growers around Reims and Épernay also tried to exclude the Aube from the champagne-growing zone, but eventually the region became part of an enlarged champagne appellation in 1927.

Courageous growers like 'Papa Pinot' Drappier started to replant Pinot Noir at Urville in the 1930s but it was not until the 1960s that noble varieties such as Chardonnay as well as the predominant Pinot were replanted in a systematic way. More than a third of the growers cultivating this relatively new vineyard were born after 1960.

It is remarkable that the Aube should be quite so far from the classic heartland of the Marne (Reims to Bar-sur-Seine is a 145-kilometre journey) and yet be an integral part of the champagne production structure. The Aube produces the equivalent of 50 million bottles of champagne a year, of which probably 40 million are transported, either in the form of juice or still wine, to the cellars of the *grandes marques* for use in their non-vintage *cuvées*. Demand is high because the Aube does produce grapes of excellent quality in a fine environment.

Known generically as the Côte des Bar, the Aube vineyards divide naturally into two main regions: the Barséquenais, centred on Bar-sur-Seine, and the Barsuraubois, further to the east below the A26 Troyes–Chaumont autoroute.

The Barséquenais is the larger of the regions, encompassing 33 wine communes in five valleys – the Seine of course, but also the Sarce, the Laignes, the Ource and the Arce. With 4,460 hectares in production, its vineyards have expanded two and a half times since 1971, representing the greatest increase in the whole of Champagne. The countryside is very like neighbouring Burgundy. Wooded hills and valleys are dotted with picturesque market towns and villages. Vines cling to sunny hillsides; meadows and farmland border the rivers, growers have a ready smile and will draw a cork on the slightest pretext.

In the extreme south-east corner of Champagne the Barsuraubois (or Baralbin) is more open country, also colder and more vulnerable to spring frosts. The vines on steep escarpments alternate with large forests and arable land. Twenty-seven communes make up this wine region, if the two tiny villages of

A tranquil stretch of the River Laignes, which snakes its way south from Polisy and through the three villages which make up Les Riceys.

Argentolles and Rizaucourt (which are actually in the Haute-Marne) are included. The total surface area of the Barsuraubois vineyards is 1,800 hectares.

Isolated from the rest of the Aube vineyards, the chalk hill of Montgueux just west of Troyes has an importance out of all proportion to its size, for 90 per cent of the vineyard is planted with Chardonnay. Soft, golden and fruity, Montgueux Chardonnay can be a luxuriant component in a champagne blend, as the *chefs de caves* at Veuve Clicquot and Charles Heidsieck will tell you. But the Aube is overwhelmingly planted (84 per cent) with Pinot Noir which is well suited to the limestone soil also found at Chablis in northern Burgundy and at Sancerre in the Upper Loire. This soil (known as Kimmeridgian) allied to the more continental climate of the Aube, produces ripe early-maturing Pinot Noir of real quality.

Aube Champagnes from the Producer

About ten million bottles of Aubois champagnes, labelled with the name of the producer, are made every year for sale in France and other countries of the European Union. These are sourced from 12 *négociants* (merchant-houses), 363 *récoltants-manipulants* (grower/champagne makers) and 1,882 *récoltants* (grape growers), most of the last-named selling their crop to cooperatives. The Union Auboise is the most powerful cooperative, producing fine, consistent champagnes at fair prices. The usual grape mix for an Aubois non-vintage champagne is 75 per cent Pinot Noir and 25 per cent Chardonnay. But the real glories of the Aube in my opinion are those champagnes made almost entirely from Pinot Noir – their mouth-filling richness can be truly exciting. Aubois rosé champagnes are also particularly good.

Rosé des Riceys

The steep slopes of the Les Riceys at the southern end of the Barséquenais are home to one of the finest still rosé wines in the world. Made in tiny quantities on average one year in three, Rosé des Riceys is the product of mature low-yielding Pinot Noir vines. The seeping juice macerates on essentially uncrushed grapes in the fermenting vat for three to six days until just the right light-ruby tint and characteristic *goût des Riceys* are achieved. The scent has a haunting aroma of Pinot red wine with none of its tannic hardness; on the palate, the fruitiness is delicate but persistent. A great '64 with a taste of liquorice from Jacques Defrance was still in good shape in 1996.

PRODUCERS OF SPECIAL INTEREST

THE AUBE
Albert Beerens
10200 Bar-sur-Aube
A small grower, Beerens has a loyal following among restaurateurs in Britain. Both the Brut and the rosé are full, rich champagnes – ideal partners for dressed crab.
Alexandre Bonnet
103460 Les Riceys
The firm's vineyards around Les Riceys are beautifully tended, the grapes from these sites as well as those bought in from the best *crus* of the Marne producing vinous champagnes of real character. The Cuvée Madrigal is a lovely full champagne redolent of orchard fruits.
Jacques Defrance
103460 Les Riceys
Under young Christophe Defrance this domaine continues to make the best and most consistent Rosé des Riceys from this rare appellation. Delicate with a lingering vinosity, great vintages like '64 and '90 can easily live for 30 years.
Drappier 10200 Urville
This medium-size firm is one of the most dynamic and quality-conscious in the Aube. Dijon-trained oenologist Michel Drappier keeps standards up as the company expands. Impressive Brut Zéro (without dosage) and magnificent prestige Grande Sendrée in full Pinot-led style.
J P Fleury 10250 Courteron
Biodynamic viticulture and Fleury's own talent produce exciting pure-flavoured champagnes made entirely from Pinot Noir. His Fleur de l'Europe has fruit and complexity, the '88 a lovely toasty note.
Lassaigne-Berlot
10150 Montgueux
A leading grower, Christian Lassaigne makes excellent ripe Chardonnay champagnes under his own label. First-rate Cuvée Scintillante.
Raymond Laurent
10110 Celles-sur-Ource
A great character of the Aube, Laurent is an outstanding grower with a range of older champagne vintages. Superb Blanc de Noirs back to '76.
Serge Mathieu 10349 Avirey-Lingey
At this immaculate, long-established domaine M Mathieu makes hedonistic champagnes of great class. The Cuvée Sélect is richly mature but vitally fresh, the rosé Brut sumptuous yet super-fine. Older vintages of his Coteaux Champenoise rouge are little gems.
Cristian Senez 10360 Fontette
Starting in 1955 with half a hectare of vines Senez is now a sizeable Aube producer (32ha). A brilliant winemaker, he always achieves exemplary finesse in his champagnes.

This is a source of old champagne vintages at keen prices (marvellous '73). Excellent fruity Coteaux Champenois Rouge.
Veuve A Devaux
10110 Bar-sur-Seine
Devaux is the premium label of the powerful Union Auboise, the grapes sourced from the 1,300ha of the member growers' vineyards. Unusually for a champagne cooperative, the aim is to establish the Devaux brand on world markets. The exceptional Grande Réserve non-vintage – aromatic, spicy, evolved – is the work of Claude Thibaut, a former winemaker at both Iron Horse and Jordan wineries in California.
Marcel Vézien
10110 Celles-sur-Ource
Mayor of his village, Vézien is famous for his Cuvée Double Eagle II, a sensuous Pinot-dominated champagne named after American balloonists who celebrated their safe arrival on French soil with a bottle of this nectar.

HOTELS AND RESTAURANTS

Le Parc de Villeneuve route de Dijon (N71), 10110 **Bar-sur-Seine**
Tel (0)325 29 16 80
An oasis in the gastronomic dessert of the southern Aube, Le Parc won a Michelin star in 1996 for the cooking of Bruno Caironi. Several dishes have a Mediterranean influence: a chartreuse of langoustines with aubergine, courgette and tomato, served in a light champagne butter, is a winner.
Bistrot du Pont 5 place de Charles de Gaulle, 10151 **Pont Ste Marie**
Tel (0)325 80 90 99
A warm welcome and gently priced menus featuring excellent salads, fish, meat and cheese make this bistrot 5km from the city a must for those on a budget. With your coffee, order a glass of Prunelle de Troyes, a delicious fruit brandy made by an old distiller in the shadow of Troyes Cathedral.
Auberge de Ste-Maure 99 route de Méry, 10150 **Ste-Maure**
Tel (0)325 76 90 41
By the D78 8km north of Troyes, this congenial restaurant (with river terrace) sports the newly gained Michelin-star cooking of Thierry Grandclaude. The set menus are excellent value. Try the local speciality, andouillette de Troyes with Chaource butter, and the pain perdu de pain d'épices aux poires, a French version of bread-and-butter pudding.
Le Champ des Oiseaux 20 rue Linard Gonthier, 10000 **Troyes**
Tel (0)325 80 58 50
Right by the cathedral in a quiet cobbled street, this bijou hotel has been sensitively restored to its original

15th- and 16th-century style by the charming Boisseau family. The 12 bedrooms around a courtyard have immense character and every comfort. No restaurant, but super light breakfasts. Middle-range prices.
Hôtel de la Poste 35 rue Émile Zola, 10000 **Troyes**
Tel (0)325 73 05 05
This welcoming city-centre hotel has comfortable, modern and well insulated bedrooms. The revamped restaurant serves good fresh seafood.

PLACES OF INTEREST

Colombey-les-deux-Églises The Boisserie, Charles de Gaulle's country house, is partially open to the public. An hour's drive east of Troyes.
Troyes The capital of Champagne in the early Middle Ages, the city is rich in churches, museums and timbered houses. The magnificent Cathedral of St-Peter-et-St-Paul (13th–17th centuries) has fine stained-glass windows. The 12th-century Église Ste-Madelaine and the Renaissance Jubé are well worth a visit. The city is also a centre of hat manufacture.

Half-timbering, steep gables, projecting upper storeys and cob walls characterise the ancient houses in the centre of Troyes.

Resplendent stained glass and delicate tracery combine perfectly in a rose window at Troyes Cathedral.

Alsace

Lying on the border of France and Germany, tucked between the Vosges Mountains to the west and the River Rhine to the east, the pretty region of Alsace offers unique appeal, in both its wines and its culture.

Alsace belonged to Germany for several centuries but is French by adoption. Set in splendid countryside, many of the wine towns and villages have the romantic, almost fairy-tale charm characteristic of the Central Europe of old. Most lie between or on the slopes of outliers of the Vosges range, which runs parallel with the Rhine and shelters Alsace from rain-laden west winds.

The region expresses its own, separate identity in a number of ways. The language spoken, known as *Elsässich* – not quite German, certainly not French – is incomprehensible to outsiders. The costume is distinctive and the cuisine combines German amplitude with French finesse. Even though the grapes are usually the same as those grown just to the east in Germany, the resulting dry, firm and aromatic wines are very different. In the lee of the Vosges the dry and sunny vineyards yield grapes with good sugar levels from which winemakers can create intensely flavoured, fresh and fragrant wines.

Alsace wines are predominantly white (the only red variety cultivated is Pinot Noir) and they are mainly 'varietals', made from single varieties and labelled as such. Grapes are categorised as 'noble' or superior varieties – the four noble whites being Gewürztraminer, Muscat, Riesling and Tokay-Pinot Gris – and ordinary varieties such as Sylvaner, Chasselas and Pinot Blanc.

The finest variety is the widely planted Riesling. It gives distinctly dry wines that vary in style from fresh, open and elegant to supple, firm and aromatic, often depending on the soil type. Rieslings from light soils can be drunk young; those from limestone-based soils often benefit from ageing.

The second important grape is Gewürztraminer, of which there is almost as much planted as there is Riesling. As the name suggests (*Gewürz* is German for 'spice') the wine has a spicy aroma which is sometimes so sultry that its dryness comes almost as a surprise. Its natural strength allows good examples to mature well.

The Vosges Mountains form the eastern rim of the wide Paris Basin and France's natural frontier. The vast mock-medieval castle of Haut-Koenigsbourg (far left) overlooks the Alsace plain from its lofty rock among the treetops.

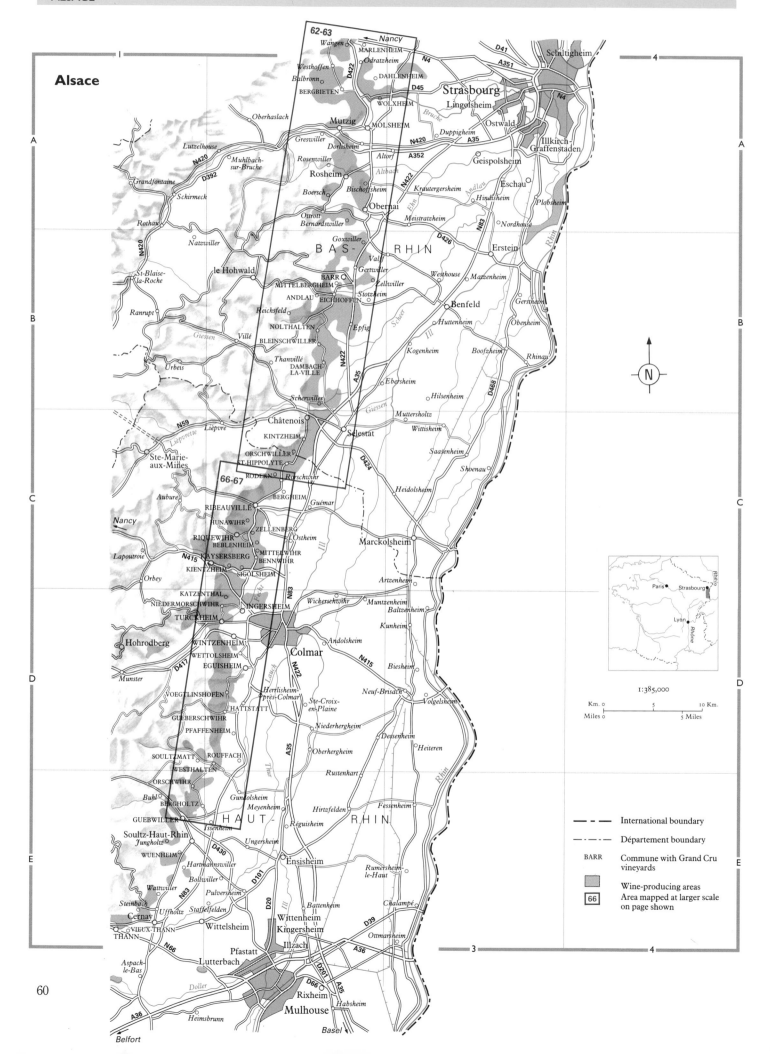

Alsace

62-63
Nancy

Wangen
MARLENHEIM
Odratzheim
DAHLENHEIM
N4
D41
A351
Schiltigheim

Westhoffen
Balbronn
BERGBIETEN
D422
WOLXHEIM
D45
Strasbourg
Lingolsheim
N4

Oberhaslach
Mutzig
MOLSHEIM
Duppigheim
A35
Ostwald
Illkirch-Graffenstaden

Lutzelhouse
N420
Greswiller
Dorlisheim
N420
A352
Geispolsheim

D392
Muhlbach-sur-Bruche
Rosenwiller
Altorf
Altbach

Grandfontaine
Rosheim
Boersch
Bischoffsheim
N422
Krautergersheim
Hindisheim
Eschau
Plobsheim

Schirmeck
Boersch
Bernardswiller
Obernai
Meistratzheim
N83
Nordhouse

Rothau
N420
Natzwiller
Goxwiller
BAS-RHIN
D426
Erstein

St-Blaise-la-Roche
le Hohwald
BARR
Valff
Gertwiller
Westhouse
Matzenheim

Ranrupt
MITTELBERGHEIM
Zellwiller
Stotzheim
N83
Benfeld
Gerstheim

Giessen
Villé
REICHSFELD
NOLTHALTEN
ANDLAU
EICHHOFFEN
Epfig
Huttenheim
Obenheim
Rhinau

Urbeis
Thanvillé
BLEINSCHWILLER
DAMBACH-LA-VILLE
Scheer
Kogenheim
Boofzheim
Ill

Scherwiller
Ebersheim
Hilsenheim
D468

Châtenois
KINTZHEIM
Sélestat
Wittisheim
Saasenheim

66-67
ORSCHWILLER
ST-HIPPOLYTE
RODERN
Rorschwihr
D424
Heidolsheim
Shoenau

Ste-Marie-aux-Mines
BERGHEIM
Guémar
RIBEAUVILLÉ
Marckolsheim

Nancy
HUNAWIHR
ZELLENBERG
Ostheim

RIQUEWIHR
BEBLENHEIM
MITTELWIHR
BENNWIHR
Ill

Lapoutroie
N415
KAYSERSBERG
KIENTZHEIM
SIGOLSHEIM
Artzenheim

Orbey
KATZENTHAL
NIEDERMORSCHWIHR
Wickerschwihr
Muntzenheim
Baltzenheim

TURCKHEIM
INGERSHEIM
N83
Kunheim

Hohrodberg
WINTZENHEIM
Andolsheim

WETTOLSHEIM
Colmar
N415
Biesheim

Munster
D417
EGUISHEIM
N422
Neuf-Brisach
Volgelsheim

VOEGTLINSHOFEN
Herrlisheim-près-Colmar
Ste-Croix-en-Plaine

GUEBERSCHWIHR
HATTSTATT
Niederhergheim

PFAFFENHEIM
Oberhergheim
Dessenheim
Heiteren

SOULTZMATT
ROUFFACH
Rustenhart

WESTHALTEN
Thur

ORSCHWIHR
Buhl
Gundolsheim
Meyenheim
Hirtzfelden
Fessenheim

BERGHOLTZ
HAUT-RHIN
Réguisheim

GUEBWILLER
Issenheim
Ungersheim
Rumersheim-le-Haut

Soultz-Haut-Rhin
Jungholtz
Ensisheim

WUENHEIM
D430
Hartmannswiller
Ill

Bollwiller
D101
Chalampé

Wattwiller
Pulversheim
D20

Steinbach
Staffelfelden
Battenheim

Cernay
Uffholtz
Ill
D39

VIEUX-THANN
Wittelsheim
Wittenheim
Kingersheim
Ottmarsheim

THANN
N66
Ilzach
A36

Aspach-le-Bas
Pfastatt
Rixheim
Habsheim

A36
Lutterbach
D201
A35
Mulhouse
D66

Belfort
Heimsbrunn
Doller
Basel

France inset map: Paris, Strasbourg, Lyon, Rhein, Rhône

1:385,000

Km. 0 — 5 — 10 Km.
Miles 0 — 5 Miles

— — — International boundary

— · — · Département boundary

BARR Commune with Grand Cru vineyards

Wine-producing areas

66 Area mapped at larger scale on page shown

Several times a day at the foot of the ruins of Château de Kintzheim, some 50 birds of prey take part in a free-flying display known as La Volerie des Aigles.

Another great Alsace grape is Pinot Gris (the wine is called Tokay-Pinot Gris). Locally the grape is often referred to Tokay d'Alsace despite an EEC ruling in 1980 prohibiting use of the name (in case it should be confused with Hungary's Tokay). Typically the wine has a firm structure and an intriguing aroma and taste. Sometimes a slight smokiness can be detected, sometimes a hint of nuts or honey. It was because of this exotic, mysterious character that the wine acquired the sobriquet 'Sultan'.

Last among the noble varieties is Muscat: Alsace is one of the rare wine regions where it makes dry wine. It has a wonderfully fruity aroma and is light enough to be served as an apéritif, but little is made. Because of their delicacy, Muscat grapes are planted on only about three per cent of the vineyard area.

Alsace has other versions of white Pinot: the tart Pinot Blanc and the softer Pinot Auxerrois. These are often blended, but single varietals are also made. Clevner is the Alsace name for Pinot in general, and blends of Pinots Blanc and Auxerrois are sold as Clevner or Klevner, but these should not be confused with the Savagnin Rosé/Klevener grape (see below). With its supple, fresh, aromatic character, Pinot Blanc makes a popular accompaniment to quiches, choucroute and many other dishes. It is also often used as the base for sparkling Crémant d'Alsace.

Sylvaner, along with Riesling, Gewürztraminer and Pinot Blanc, produces a large volume of wine, the four varieties accounting for about 80 per cent of Alsace vines. Light and sometimes pleasantly tart, Sylvaner generally yields an appealing, easy-drinking white but it has little depth or personality. When planted on limestone-rich soil, however, such as that of the Zotzenberg vineyards in Mittelbergheim, its wines can be delicious, light, spicy and fruity It is also blended with other grapes.

Chasselas is a traditional Haut-Rhin speciality, producing light, fruity wines, but the vineyard area planted with it represents only a tiny percentage of Alsace's total. The rarest Alsace wine is Klevener de Heiligenstein which originates in Heiligenstein and a few neighbouring communes and is made from the Savagnin Rosé grape. This variety has similarities with both Savagnin Blanc of the Jura and Gewürztraminer. Its wine has a distinctive, mild aroma and a fresh finish.

Last come the Pinot Noir reds. Until the late 1980s Pinot Noir was used only to make rosés but more recently producers have been making quality regional reds: ruby wines, often with soft strawberry fruit. Increasingly, they are aged in small oak vats.

CLASSIFICATION

Alsatian wines are named, quite simply, after their grape varieties. Even mention of the vineyard is the exception rather than the rule.

Top of the range are *grand cru* wines. This 'reserve' appellation was first introduced in 1983 and named 25 vineyards. A further 25 were added in 1993. Stringent rules govern the *grand cru* status; only wines made from the four noble white varieties planted on specified sites may be labelled *grand cru,* and yields are restricted to 70 hectolitres per hectare, (compared to the 100 hectolitres per hectare allowed for generic AC Alsace wines). Besides these *grands crus* a few other vineyards of great repute have their names on labels. These vineyards are referred to as a *lieux dits* ('named places'): the Kaefferkopf at Ammerschwihr and the Gaensbroennel at Barr are two examples. At the other end of the scale is Edelzwicker, an everyday wine almost always blended from Chasselas, Pinot Blanc and Sylvaner and often sold in litre bottles.

The rich, powerful Vendange Tardive wines and the even rarer Sélection des Grains Nobles, made from grapes individually picked for their super-ripeness, are worth seeking out. Like Sauternes these 'sweet' wines are intense, but by no means cloying or sugary-sweet.

Alsace has its own *méthode champenoise* sparkling wine AC Crémant d'Alsace, made mainly from Pinot Blanc. There are also crémants made solely from Riesling.

Bas-Rhin

Bas-Rhin is 'low' only in the sense of being lower down the Rhine. The region extends from Wissembourg, bordering Germany, to Orschwiller near Sélestat. Marlenheim, one of the oldest wine villages in Alsace, is the starting point proper of the Bas-Rhin. Its reputation is based on Pinot Noir which thrives on its calciferous soils. Once famous for light-red Vorlauf, the village is now better known for its fruity Rosé de Marlenheim. Among 75 hectares there is one *grand cru* vineyard, Steinklotlz, where fine Riesling grows. Further south in Traenheim, excellent Gewürztraminer and Riesling are produced from nearby *grand cru* Altenberg de Bergbieten. These grapes also perform well on the limestone soils around Molsheim, especially on *grand cru* Bruderthal.

Sylvaner appears next, in Rosheim, where soft, fresh examples are made. Pinot Noir reasserts itself in the small town of Ottrott. In neighbouring Obernai, sandy soils prevent vineyards from enjoying *grand cru* status, but Schenkenberg is one to look out for.

The first place of note in the southern half of Bas-Rhin is Heiligenstein, famous for its Klevener de Heiligenstein. The next is Barr, whose *grand cru* Kirchberg is known for its rich, spicy Gewürztraminer, and Clos Gaensbrunnel (part of Kirchberg) which yields distinctly smoky Gewürztraminer and Sylvaner. This last grape really shines at nearby Mittelbergheim, where the limestone soil yields light, elegant wines, but these are now difficult to find as Sylvaner is no longer permitted on *grand cru* sites.

The soil becomes rockier in the Vosges foothills and at Andlau this is reflected in some excellent Riesling with ageing potential from the *grands crus* Kastelberg, Moenchberg and Wiebelsberg. Delicious Tokay-Pinot Gris and Gewürztraminer are also grown, as are outstanding Vendange Tardive wines from Kreydenweiss. Continuing south, Itterswiller, Nothalten and Blienschwiller are packed with wine producers. Wonderful Rieslings are made from *grand cru* Muenchberg in Nothalten while in Blienschwiller a modern-style oak-aged Pinot Noir is produced by Cave de la Dîme.

With over 500 hectares Dambach-la-Ville (formerly Dambach-la-Vigne) is the largest Bas-Rhin commune. Several well known producers and the local cooperative are based here. The one *grand cru* – Frankstein – accounts for 11 per cent of the vineyard land. Riesling and Gewürztraminer are the main grapes, planted on the granitic slopes of the Vosges rather than in the foothills. The Riesling has renowned ageing potential and the Gewürztraminer has a distinct spiciness; the best come from the Breitstein vineyard. Award-winning Sylvaner, Pinot Blanc and Edelzwicker can also be found, and Pinot Noir is grown successfully nearby at Dieffenthal, where a sheltered location provides a warm microclimate.

Dambach is the last main wine point on the Bas-Rhin tour before you reach the Haut-Rhin *département*.

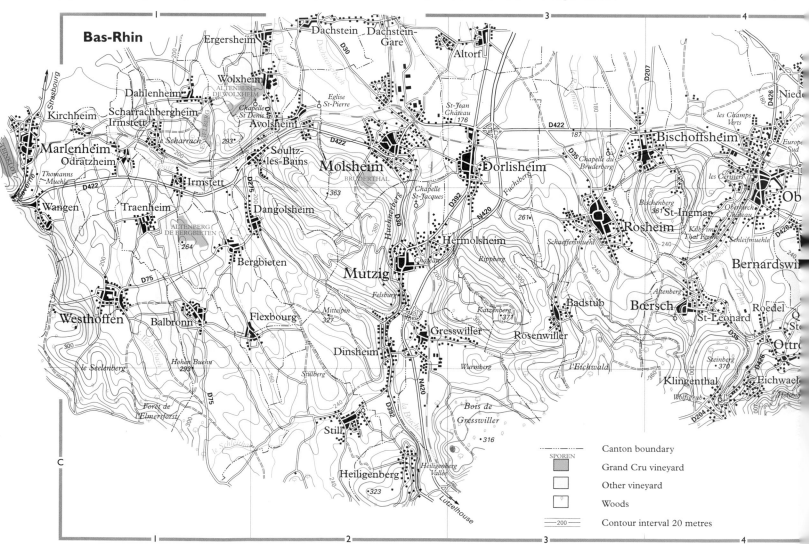

PRODUCERS OF SPECIAL INTEREST

Alsace Willm 67140 Barr
One of Barr's top producers.

Pierre Arnold
67650 Dambach-la-Ville
Excellent generic Riesling and Riesling Frankstein.

Eugène Blanck et Fils
67210 Obernai
Top wines include Tokay-Pinot Gris and Rouge d'Ottrott.

Claude Bléger 67600 Orschwiller
Award-winning wines from organically cultivated vineyards.

E Boeckel 67140 Mittelbergheim
Négociant/grower with 20ha in six villages. Traditionally made wines: spicy Riesling Brandluft and soft, smooth Riesling Wiebelsberg.

CV Obernai 67210 Obernai
Elegant Gewürztraminer and Tokay-Pinot Gris Clos Ste-Odile.

Laurent Dietrich & Fils
67650 Dambach-la-Ville
Consistently well made wines.

Jean-Louis Dirringer
67650 Dambach-la-Ville

Christian Dolder
67140 Mittelbergheim
Delicious Sylvaner Zotzenberg and Riesling Brandluft.

André Dussourt 67750 Scherwiller
Award-winning Riesling and Gewürztraminer Réserve Prestige. Good Sylvaner, Pinot Blanc and Tokay-Pinot Gris.

Raymond Engel 67600 Orschwiller
Large, reliable estate.

Romain Fritsch 67520 Marlenheim
Good Tokay-Pinot Gris Steinklotz, Pinot Noir and Rosé de Marlenheim.

Fritz 67530 Ottrott
Good Rouge d'Ottrott, Auxerrois and Gewürztraminer Affenberg.

Armand Gilg & Fils
67140 Mittelbergheim
20ha and a trend-setting approach to production methods. Fine Muscat.

Louis Gisselbrecht
67650 Dambach-la-Ville

Willy Gisselbrecht & Fils
67650 Dambach-la-Ville
Award-winning wines.

J Hauller & Fils
67650 Dambach-la-Ville
Former cooper, now a *négociant*.

Top Rieslings and Gewürztraminers from *grand cru* Frankstein. Exceptional Vendange Tardive wines.

Louis Hauller/Domaine du Tonnelier 67650 Dambach-la-Ville
Classy Klevner and Gewürztraminer Frankstein. Fine Riesling Fronholtz, Winzenberg and Pinot Noir.

Hering 67140 Barr
Gewürztraminer Kirchberg and Riesling Kirchberg are especially good.

Jean Heywang 67140 Heiligenstein
Excellent barrel-fermented wines.

Lucien Kirmann & Fils
67560 Rosheim

Antoine et Robert Klingenfus
67120 Molsheim
Good Gewürztraminer Bruderthal and Muscat Finkenberg. Special Bugatti Gewürztraminer 'Pur Sang'.

Domaine Klipfel 67140 Barr
Attractive, traditionally-styled wines.

Jean-Marie Koehly
67600 Kintzheim
Wonderful oak-aged Pinot Noir.

Laugel 67520 Marlenheim
Good Rosé de Marlenheim, crémants, Riesling and Tokay-Pinot Gris Steinklotz.

Philippe Lorentz 67310 Traenheim
Jacques Maetz 67560 Rosheim
Small grower with two specialities: soft, fresh Sylvaner Westerberg and a Pinot Blanc-Auxerrois blend.

Frédéric Mochel 67310 Traenheim
Some excellent wines: generics (Muscat and Pinot Noir), *grands crus* (fruity Gewürztraminer, elegant Riesling Altenberg de Bergbieten) and Crémant d'Alsace.

Mosbach 67520 Marlenheim
One of Marlenheim's best, with cellars and a *winstub* on the main street.

Gérard Neumeyer
67120 Molsheim
Large grower, with much land on the Bruderthal. Attractive Riesling, Tokay-Pinot Gris and Gewürztraminer.

Bernhard Reibel 67730 Châtenois
Intense Riesling Weingarten and Tokay-Pinot Gris Cuvée St-Hubert.

Ruhlmann-Dirringer
67650 Dambach-la-Ville
Alluring Muscat and Riesling Frankstein.

Schaeffer-Woerly
67650 Dambach-la-Ville

Schaetzel 67530 Boersch
Vineyards mainly in Ottrott. Reception

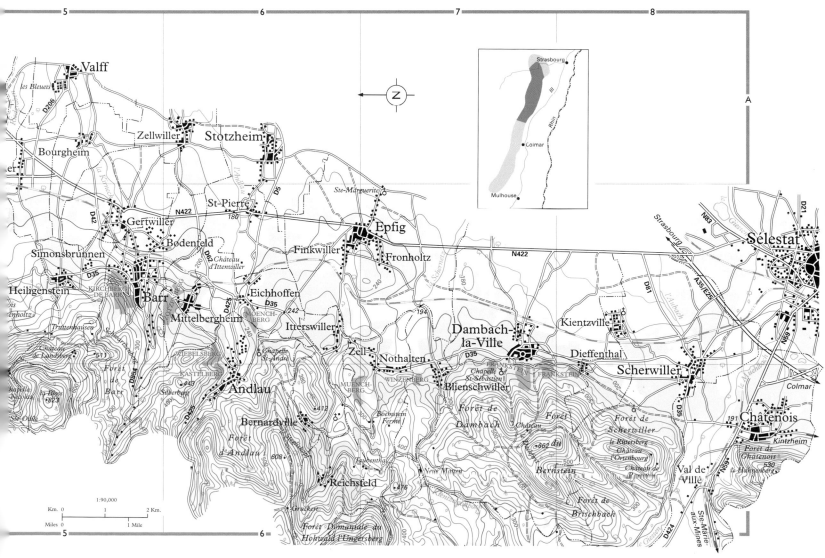

for group visits at Le Châtelain. Try the Rouge d'Ottrott Cuvée Châtelain.
Roland Schmitt 67310 Traenheim
Fresh Gewürztraminer and wonderful Riesling Altenberg de Bergbieten.
Seilly 67210 Obernai
A Seltz & Fils 67140 Mittelbergheim *Négociant* producing stunning Sylvaner from *grand cru* Zotzenberg. Good Réserve and Réserve Particulière Klevener, Gewürztraminer Zotzenberg and Muscat.
Louis Siffert & Fils 67600 Orschwiller
Excellent Riesling Praelatenberg, Gewürztraminer and Pinot Noir.
Charles Wantz 67140 Barr *Négociant* making juicy-fruity Rouge d'Ottrott.
Bernard Weber 67120 Molsheim
Serious producer offering terrific crémant, elegant Riesling Bruderthal and Tokay-Pinot Gris Finkenberg.

FÊTES

Dambach-la-Ville 'Open cellars' on the first Saturday in July; Fête des Vins de France August 14 and 15.
Scherwiller Art, Artisanat et Riesling celebrated on the penultimate weekend in August.

WINE INFORMATION

Maison du Vin d'Alsace 12 avenue de la Foire aux Vins, 68000 Colmar
Tel (0)389 20 16 20

HOTELS

Château de l'Andlau 67140 Barr
Tel (0)388 08 96 78
In the peaceful wooded Kirneck Valley.
Maison Rouge 67140 Barr
Tel (0)388 08 90 40
Large, half-timbered hotel with brasserie and restaurant. Fair prices.
Au Raisin d'Or 67650 Dambach-la-Ville
Tel (0)388 92 40 08
Pleasant, small, rural hotel owned by a wine producer. Also has a restaurant which serves regional dishes.
Le Vignoble 67650 Dambach-la-Ville Tel (0)388 92 43 75
Intimate hotel set in a delightful old building.
Les Châteaux 67850 Dieffenthal
Tel (0)388 92 49 13
Large hotel just outside town amid vineyards. Over 30 bright rooms, all with good views. Restaurant, bar, *winstub* and cellar.

Relais du Klevener 67140 Heiligenstein
Tel (0)388 08 05 98
Family-run, renovated in 1988. Ask for rooms overlooking the Rhine Valley.
Hostellerie Reeb 67520 Marlenheim Tel (0)388 87 52 70
Over 30 modernised rooms. Comfortable, stylish restaurant with a good choice of wines by the glass.
Winstub Gilg 67140 Mittelbergheim Tel (0)388 08 91 37
Hotel-restaurant: simple rooms round an inner courtyard. Good wines.
Hôtel Diana 67120 Molsheim
Tel (0)388 38 51 59
Modern hotel, close to old centre. 'Gastronomic' restaurant and *winstub*.
À la Cour d'Alsace 67210 Obernai
Tel (0)388 95 07 00
Obernai's most luxurious hotel; large rooms around a courtyard.
Le Parc 67210 Obernai
Tel (0)388 95 50 08
Truly Alsatian setting and good value. Delicious food; good choice of *eaux-de-vie*. An outdoor and indoor swimming pool and a sauna.
Le Clos des Délices 67530 Ottrott
Tel (0)388 95 81 00
Lovely rural setting, 25 rooms, a swimming pool and good restaurant.

Hostellerie du Rosenmeer 67560 Rosheim Tel (0)388 50 43 29
Modern hotel next to a *winstub*.
Monopole-Métropole 16 rue Kuhn 67000 Strasbourg
Tel (0)388 32 11 94
Congenial Alsatian atmosphere.
Hôtel des Rohan 17 rue Maroquine, 67000 Strasbourg
Tel (0)388 32 85 11
Comfortable hotel near the cathedral.

RESTAURANTS

Le Châtelain 67530 Boersch
Tel (0)388 95 83 33
Small and central. Owned by wine producer Schaetzel. Creative cooking.
À l'Arbre Vert 67650 Dambach-la-Ville
Tel (0)388 92 42 75
Unfussy establishment serving good choucroute, baeckoeffe, tarte flambée.
Au Raisin d'Or 67140 Heiligenstein
Tel (0)388 08 95 23
Cosy, rural; good three-course menu.
Auberge St-Martin 67600 Kintzheim Tel (0)388 82 04 78
Central. The speciality is tarte flambée.
Le Cerf 67520 Marlenheim
Tel (0)388 87 73 73
One of the best places to eat in Alsace, with prices to match. Traditional and modern cuisine, with fish specialities. Good rooms.
Relais de la Route du Vin 67520 Marlenheim Tel (0)388 87 50 05
Simple, cosy dining room serving regional dishes. Friendly service.
Au Cheval Blanc 67120 Molsheim
Tel (0)388 38 16 87
Attractive prices. Rooms available.
L'Agneau d'Or 67210 Obernai
Tel (0)388 95 28 22
Great little *winstub* serving excellent regional dishes quite cheaply.
Beau Site 67530 Ottrott
Tel (0)388 95 80 61
Reliable. Regional fare and game in season (perfect with Rouge d'Ottrott). Large wine-list. Comfortable rooms.
Winstub à l'Ortenbourg 67750 Scherwiller Tel (0)388 92 06 37
Unpretentious restaurant owned by grower Dussourt.
Chez Yvonne (S'Burgerstuewel) 10 rue Sanglier, 67000 Strasbourg
Tel (0)388 32 84 15
Famous *winstub*. Regional dishes served in generous portions.
Le Crocodile 10 rue de l'Outre 67000 Strasbourg
Tel (0)388 32 13 02
The city's best restaurant; culinary masterpieces served under large 19th-century works of art.
Maison Kammerzell 16 place Cathédral, 67000 Strasbourg
Tel (0)388 32 42 14
Set in a historic monument. Traditional cooking downstairs, contemporary on the two upper floors. Also a *winstub*.

Exquisite details in the well preserved cité *attest to the prosperity Riquewihr enjoyed during the 16th and 17th centuries.*

PLACES OF INTEREST

Dambach-la-Ville Within its walls is a charming historic centre. Amid vineyards above the village is the 14th-century St-Sebastien chapel with a carved wooden baroque altar.

Haut-Koenigsbourg The much visited fortress (see pages 58–9) was commissioned by Kaiser Wilhelm II.

Kintzheim La Volerie des Aigles (see page 61). Higher up is La Montagne des Singes, where 300 monkeys wander through woodland.

Molsheim A museum is set in the 1525 *Metzig* (Butchers' Guildhouse), there is a 17th-century church and the legendary Bugatti cars were made here.

Mont Ste-Odile Many pilgrims and tourists visit the convent founded by St Odile in the 7th century, especially its chapel, cloisters and terrace.

Obernai The 16th-century town hall and Halle aux Blés (also the museum) and 13th–15th-century Tour de la Chapelle are well worth a visit.

Rosheim The 12th-century Heidenhüss, the oldest house in Alsace is well worth a detour, as are the three gates and the Romanesque church of St-Pierre-et-St-Paul. Between mid-July and mid-August a steam train runs to Ottrott.

Strasbourg A university and music city, a Rhine port and the seat of the Council of Europe, Strasbourg also has more than its share of important museums. The old centre clusters around the magnificent 12th–15th-century cathedral of Notre-Dame. Beside the cathedral stands the early-18th-century Château des Rohan. La Petite France is the city's most charming quarter. The beautiful Orangerie park was designed by André Le Nôtre in 1692. Gutenberg invented printing in Strasbourg between 1434 and 1444.

Wissembourg After Strasbourg Cathedral, the town's church of St-Pierre-et-St-Paul is the region's most important Gothic structure.

Many attractive old buildings add to the charm of Wissembourg. Lying on the German border, this is the northernmost town of Alsace.

Haut-Rhin

In Haut-Rhin the Vosges Mountains offer protection from the wet, west winds. Hot, dry summer days encourage rich, ripe, healthy grapes – indeed the climate here is one of the best in France for grape-growing. Most of Alsace's finest classic varietals, especially Gewürztraminers and Rieslings, come from Haut-Rhin. Colmar lies at the centre of this region, whose vineyards extend north and south in a long, narrow stretch.

St-Hippolyte is the most northerly point. With neighbouring Rodern, this was the first village in Alsace to gain a reputation for Pinot Noir. You can still find soft, cherry-fruit-flavoured Rouge de St-Hippolyte, but Gewürztraminer and Riesling are also well produced. Rodern also has an interest in the *grand cru* Cloeckelberg, source of a stylish Tokay-Pinot Gris.

Just down the road is Rorschwihr which boasts several good vineyards and world-renowned winemaker Rolly Gassmann. Two *grand cru* vineyards join Rorschwihr with neighbouring Bergheim: Altenberg de Bergheim and Kanzlerberg, whose limestone and clay soils produce elegant Riesling and Gewürztraminer. Both wines benefit from several years' ageing but some refreshing, early-drinking Sylvaner can also be found in Bergheim.

Ribeauvillé, formerly the wine capital of Alsace, is next on the wine trail south. This pretty town's three *grand cru* vineyards – Geisberg, Kirchberg and Osterberg – all produce mature, classic Riesling. Trimbach is the top producer owning land in Ribeauvillé and makes one of the region's finest Rieslings, but other noble varieties also perform well. Even the lowly Chasselas (famous in the 1800s for its Vin de Paille – sweet wine from sun-dried grapes) grows well here thanks to the sandstone and marl soil. An outstanding Chasselas is produced by the André Kientzler estate.

Near Ribeauvillé is the small village of Hunawihr with its *grand cru* Rosacker and, within it, the tiny Clos Ste-Hune which can yield marvellous Riesling. Neighbouring Zellenberg, whose wines were unfashionable for many years, is rebuilding its name for fine wines thanks largely to the innovative producer Jean Becker. His family

firm has introduced wines such as Sylvaner F, made from Sylvaner grown on the *grand cru* Froehn. Once again, the wine cannot be sold as a *grand cru* since Sylvaner is not a noble grape.

Riquewihr, one of France's most glorious wine villages, comes next. Full of 16th- and 17th-century architecture, it is also home to some of Alsace's leading wine merchants and producers including Dopff 'au Moulin', a top Alsatian sparkling-wine producer, and Hugel & Fils, established here in 1639. Blended *cuvées* are one of Riquewihr's specialities; many famous names produce them from *grand cru* Sporen and will continue to do so for as long as the regulations allow blended wine to be made from these sites. Schoenenbourg, the other famous *grand cru*, is planted almost exclusively to Riesling and the resulting wines are rich, classic examples that benefit from extended ageing.

On to Beblenheim, past the *grand cru* Sonnenglanz ('sun glow', ideal for Gewürztraminer) which was one of the first vineyards to be formally cited for its first-class wine in 1935. Further south are two villages which have grown almost into one: Mittelwihr and Bennwihr. The mild microclimate in the former is ideal for viticulture: on the limestone and gravel soil of *grand cru* Mandelberg, Gewürztraminer and Riesling yield intense, long-lived wines. In Bennwihr, the highly productive Chasselas was planted to replace vineyards lost in World War II but since the 1970s the vine has gradually been ousted by more interesting varieties. To finance this replanting the growers formed a cooperative, CV Bennwihr, which has developed into one of the largest and most successful in Alsace. Its cellars lie on the edge of *grand cru* Marckrain, a vineyard shared with neighbouring Sigolsheim.

En route to Sigolsheim you pass the *grand cru* Mambourg which, at about 65 hectares, is one of the biggest in Alsace. Records first mention vineyards here back in 785. Sigolsheim also has part of the *grand cru* Furstentum and from these two prime sites come fine examples of the four noble varieties.

The two *grands crus* of nearby Kientzheim are Schlossberg (which was the first Alsace vineyard to be granted the status in 1975) and Furstentum. Riesling and Gewürztraminer from both these sites have successfully established Kientzheim's place on the wine map, as has the *lieu-dit* vineyard Altenbourg. Kientzheim is

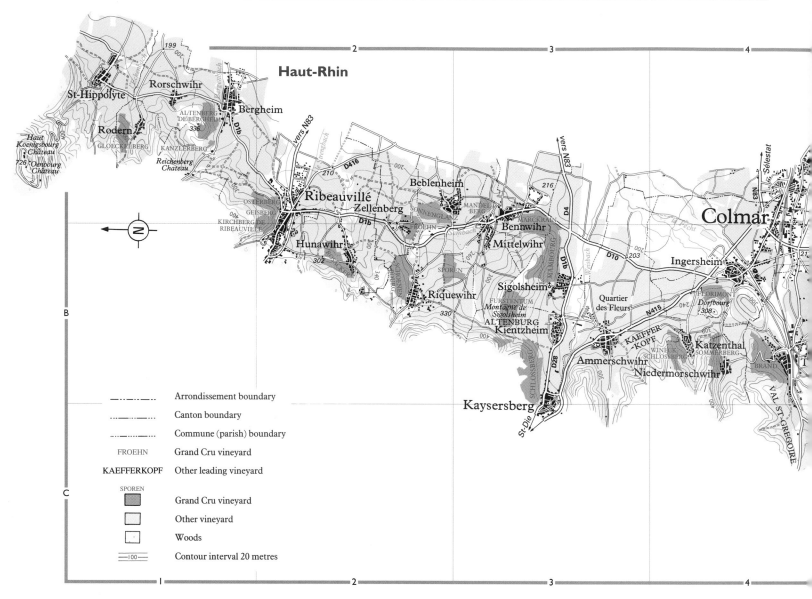

Haut-Rhin

Arrondissement boundary
Canton boundary
Commune (parish) boundary
FROEHN — Grand Cru vineyard
KAEFFERKOPF — Other leading vineyard
SPOREN
Grand Cru vineyard
Other vineyard
Woods
100 — Contour interval 20 metres

also home to the Alsace wine fraternity La Confrérie St-Étienne, whose headquarters are in the Château de Kientzheim. Just outside Kientzheim lies one of Alsace's most highly prized wine sites, the Clos des Capucins, at Domaine Weinbach. This fine estate produces intense Cuvée Théo Riesling, Cuvée Théo Gewürztraminer and floral Tokay-Pinot Gris Ste-Catherine.

A little further south at Kayserberg, the best sites are the Schlossberg and Bixkoepflé vineyards. The better Schlossberg land is in fact mostly in the commune of Kientzheim, and Bixkoepflé is not classified as *grand cru*, but its Gewürztraminers are some of Kayserberg's best. Concentrated Gewürztraminer is made from the tiny part of the *grand cru* Schlossberg that falls within the Kayserberg boundary.

The vineyards of Ammerschwihr, the largest wine commune in Haut-Rhin, stretch out next on the slopes behind the village. Their limestone base ensures subtle Gewürztraminers and Rieslings with youthful charm. The Riesling wines from the granite-based *grand cru* Kaefferkopf nearby are comparatively complex and intense and often need several years' ageing.

There are three more wine centres before Colmar: Katzenthal, whose best Rieslings come from the steep slopes of the *grand cru* Wineck-Schlossberg; the sheltered Niedermorschwihr and Ingersheim. Part of the *grand cru* Kaefferkopf also falls within Katzenthal's boundaries. *Grand cru* Sommerberg is well sheltered

and is renowned for its Riesling, Tokay-Pinot Gris and Muscat. Colmar itself has 350 or so hectares of vines and most of the area is divided among growers and cooperatives from neighbouring communes (although there are several good producers based in Colmar). The Harth vineyard, north of the town, is the most notable.

Turckheim, just five kilometres from Colmar, is home to the famous *grand cru* Brand. Its steep southerly slopes, perfect for ripening red grapes, yield some of Alsace's finest Pinot Noir. However Brand has grown to encompass more than 55 hectares and now supports a large variety of other grapes including Gewürztraminer, Riesling, Muscat and Pinot Gris.

Turckheim is famous for another name, that of Domaine Zind-Humbrecht, one of Alsace's top producers. The Domaine has sites on Brand as well as owning the famous *grand cru* Rangen in Thann. Zind-Humbrecht produces the finest *grand cru* wines from the Hengst vineyard in neighbouring Wintzenheim, where limestone soil favours Gewürztraminer and Riesling.

Wettolsheim, another dormitory village for Colmar, has over 200 hectares of vineyard and several notable producers. Tokay-Pinot Gris and Riesling are successful here. Gewürztraminer shines in the *grand cru* Steingrubler vineyard and in neighbouring Eguisheim on the *grand cru* Eichberg.

On to the highest wine village in Alsace, Husseren-les-Châteaux. For many years the village was not concerned with viticulture but

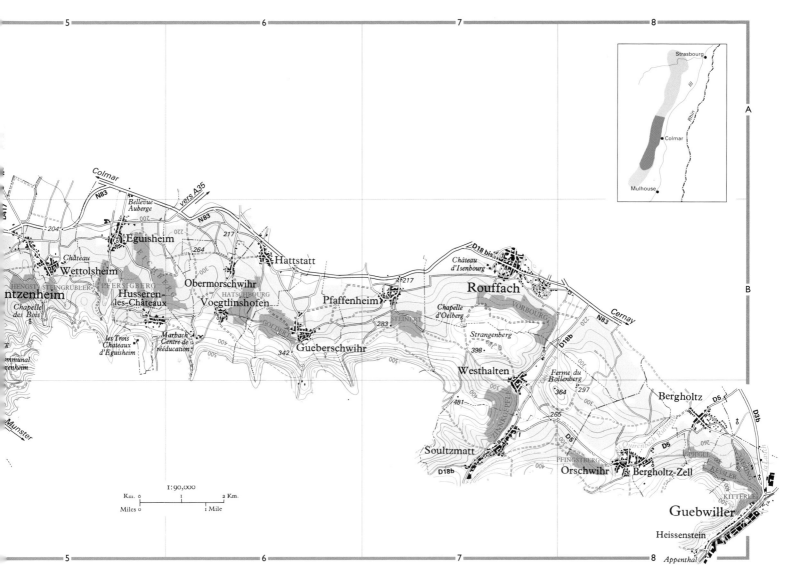

distilled the fruits of the surrounding forests into *eaux-de-vie*. Today Husseren's sandstone and granite vineyards yield lively wines with an attractive fresh taste.

From here, Muscat lovers should continue to Voegtlinshoffen. Wine-growing is a relatively recent business in this village, which was not granted vineyard land of its own until 1887. In spite of this late start it now produces rich yet fresh Muscat and wonderful examples of Gewürztraminer and Tokay-Pinot Gris. Much of the village's success is rooted in the limestone *grand cru* Hatschbourg, which is shared with the village of Hattstatt.

Just a few kilometres further is Gueberschwihr, a flourishing wine village with the *grand cru* Goldert, named after the rich golden Gewürztraminer and aromatic Muscat it yields. Ernst Burn is one of the names to look out for; he is the sole owner of Clos St-Imer on Goldert and produces extraordinary Muscat, Riesling and Gewürztraminer. Pinot Blanc comes into its own at Pfaffenheim, especially that grown in the Schneckenberg ('snail's hill') vineyard. Tokay-Pinot Gris from the *grand cru* Steinert is also making a name for itself, as are crémants.

Just a handful of wine villages remain at the lower end of the Haut-Rhin. Rouffach, with its 450 hectares set on slopes behind the village, is best known for its *grand cru* Vorbourg. Within this is Clos St-Landelin, owned by the best local producer, Muré. Westhalten, protected by the hills and based on sandstone and

granite soils, boasts just under half of the famous 60-plus hectares of *grand cru* Zinnkoepflé. Although Pinot Blanc and Tokay-Pinot Gris are considered to be Westhalten's best wines, the south-facing slopes of Zinnkoepflé also yield intense, full-bodied Gewürztraminer and great Rieslings. The lion's share of Zinnkoepflé, however, belongs to Soultzmatt.

The next village, Orschwihr, owns much of the sunniest part of Bollenberg's vineyards. Look out for *grand cru* Pfingstberg and named vineyard Lippelsberg, which is considered one of the village's best.

The route through the Haut-Rhin then leads to Bergholtz and, rising behind the village, *grand cru* Spiegel, whose southerly area belongs to the village while the rest falls within the district of Guebwiller. Guebwiller can also claim *grands cru*s Kessler, Saering and Kitterlé. The last, with its sandy limestone soil, is perhaps the finest.

From here the land flattens and vineyards temporarily disappear. At Thann some 20 kilometres away is the famous Rangen *grand cru* which was revived only in the 1970s by Léonard Humbrecht of Domaine Zind-Humbrecht. The steep slopes are owned by this estate and Schoffit. Dedication and investment are now paying off: exceptional Riesling, Pinot Gris and Gewürztraminer are being produced. The Clos St-Urbain plot on Rangen is now recognised for its supreme Riesling.

67

PRODUCERS OF SPECIAL INTEREST

Adam 68770 Ammerschwihr
Rich, traditional, long-lived wines.
Lucien Albrecht 68500 Orschwihr
High-quality wines. Renowned Riesling Pfingstberg and Tokay-Pinot Gris.
Domaine Barmès Buecher
68920 Wettolsheim
Good range of wines – from generics to grands crus from Herrenweg, Hengst and Steingrubler.
Jean-Jacques Baumann & Fils
68340 Riquewihr
High-quality wines.
François Baur Petit-Fils/ Maison Léon Baur & Fils 68420 Eguisheim
Top Riesling Cuvée Elisabeth Stumpf.
Jean Becker/Gaston Becker
68340 Zellenberg
Old, small, award-winning family firm.
Léon Beyer 68420 Eguisheim
High-class, firmly structured wines. Powerful Gewürztraminer and Tokay.
Luc Beyer 68420 Eguisheim
The top wine is Riesling Pfersigberg.
André Blanck & Fils
68240 Kientzheim
Excellent Riesling Cours des Chevaliers from grand cru Schlossberg.
Paul Blanck/Domaine des Comtes de Lupfen
68240 Kientzheim
Dynamic family firm producing reliable wines. Good-tasting room/cellars.
Bott Frères 68150 Ribeauvillé
Small firm producing elegant wines from its own vines.
Bott-Geyl 68980 Beblenheim
Small merchant with atmospheric wine cellar.
Albert Boxler & Fils
68230 Niedermorschwihr
Top producer, great wines.
Justin Boxler
68230 Niedermorschwihr
Attractive Riesling from Brand.
Ernst Burn
68420 Gueberschwihr
Owns the 5ha Clos St-Imer on grand cru Goldert. Sublime Muscat, Riesling, Tokay-Pinot Gris, Gewürztraminer.
Joseph Cattin & Fils
68420 Voegtlinshoffen
Specialities are the Muscat, Riesling, Tokay-Pinot Gris, Gewürztraminer Hatschbourg and crémant.
Theo Cattin & Fils
68420 Voegtlinshoffen
Supple, soft but well structured wines.
CV Bennwihr 68630 Bennwihr
Top wines include crémant, oak-aged Pinot Noir and Gewürztraminer Vendange Tardive.
CV Eguisheim 68420 Eguisheim
Alsace's largest cooperative.
CV Hunawihr 68150 Hunawihr
A good range with many highlights.
CV Kientzheim-Kayserberg
68240 Kientzheim
Heavy investment is reflected in

excellent and extensive range. Tasting rooms in Kientzheim and Kayserberg.
CV Pfaffenheim 68250 Pfaffenheim
A top cooperative. Excellent range.
CV Ribeauvillé 68150 Ribeauvillé
The oldest wine cooperative in France. Top wines include Rieslings Kirchberg and Osterberg, and wines from the Clos du Zahnacker.
CV Turckheim 68230 Turckheim
Exemplary Pinot Noir Cuvée à l'Ancienne. Many wines are sourced from grand cru Brand.
CV du Vieil-Armand
68500 Wuenheim
Part of the Eguisheim cooperative. Riesling and Gewürztraminer Ollwiller and crémant recommended.
CV Westhalten 68250 Westhalten
Lovely Pinot Blanc, Riesling, Muscat, Gewürztraminer Zinnkoepflé and crémants are all produced here.
Domaine Marcel Deiss
68750 Bergheim
Run by Jean-Michel Deiss. Good range includes quality Gewürztraminer Altenberg de Bergheim and Riesling.
Claude Dietrich
68770 Ammerschwihr
Robert Dietrich
68920 Wettolsheim
Diringer 68250 Westhalten
Excellent Zinnkoepflé wines.
Jean-Pierre Dirler 68500 Bergholtz
Small producer; stunning wines.
Dopff 'au Moulin' 68340 Riquewihr
One of Alsace's most important producers, especially for sparkling wines. Also excellent generic wines.
Dopff & Irion 68340 Riquewihr
A large export firm with well made wines. Tastings and cellar visits.
François Ehrhart
68920 Wettolsheim
Impressive Gewürztraminers.
Henri Ehrhart
68770 Ammerschwihr
Pure, fragrant Gewürztraminer.
Faller/Domaine Weinbach
68240 Kayserberg
Wines are not cheap, but offer quality.
Robert Faller 68150 Ribeauvillé
Specialities are Riesling Geisberg and Gewürztraminer Kirchberg.
Joseph Freudenreich & Fils
68420 Eguisheim
Pierre Frick 68250 Pfaffenheim
Biodynamic viticulture, charming wines, especially from lieu-dit Rot-Murlé.
Lucien Gantzer
68420 Gueberschwihr
Domaine Rolly Gassmann
68590 Rorschwihr
Internationally famous, exceptional quality. Full, aromatic, powerful wines.
Jérôme Geschickt & Fils
68770 Ammerschwihr
Good Riesling and Gewürztraminer.
Paul Ginglinger 68420 Eguisheim
Traditional winemaking. Top-quality Eichberg wines and good Riesling and Gewürztraminer.

Pierre-Henri Ginglinger
68420 Eguisheim
Delicious crémant and Gewürztraminer Eichberg.
Jean Greiner 68630 Mittelwihr
André Hartmann & Fils
68420 Voegtlinshoffen
'Armoirie' wines especially good.
Gérard et Serge Hartmann
68420 Voegtlinshoffen
Albert Hertz 68420 Eguisheim
Award-winning Pinot Noir and excellent generic and Eichberg wines.
Hugel & Fils 68340 Riquewihr
Top family firm with 25ha in Riquewihr (just 0.4ha in Zellenberg). Wines are full and rounded, especially the Vendange Tardive.
Marcel Humbrecht
68420 Gueberschwihr
Delicious Riesling and Goldert wines.
Bruno Hunold 68250 Rouffach
One of the few independent growers who live in Rouffach. Fine Riesling and Gewürztraminer Vorbourg.
Auguste Hurst & Fils 68230 Turckheim
Owns much of Brand. Quality Riesling, Gewürztraminer and Pinot Noir.
Jacques Iltis 68590 St-Hippolyte
High-quality Rouge de St-Hippolyte and Riesling Schlossreben.
Josmeyer 68920 Wintzenheim
Small firm; exemplary wines. Pinot Blanc is a speciality.
André Kientzler 68150 Ribeauvillé
Among the best in Alsace. Several extraordinary wines.
Roger Klein 68770 Ammerschwihr
Owns the tiny Clos Meywihr (situated on the Kaefferkopf).
Klur-Stoecklé 68230 Katzenthal
Expressive Riesling Wineck-Schlossberg; good Gewürztraminer.
Charles Koehly & Fils
68590 Rodern
Stylish, balanced wines.
Koerberlé-Klein 68590 Rodern
Kuehn 68770 Ammerschwihr
Elegant Riesling, Pinot Blanc, Gewürztraminer Cuvée St-Hubert.
Alphonse Kuentz
68420 Husseren-les-Châteaux
Notable Riesling and Gewürztraminer from grand cru Pfersigberg.
Kuentz-Bas
68420 Husseren-les-Châteaux
A top producer with splendid wines. All have class.
Seppi Landmann 68570 Soultzmatt
Characterful wines including Sylvaner and crémant and rich, dry wines from grand cru Zinnkoepflé.
Domaine Langehald
68230 Turckheim
Excellent Gewürztraminer Brand.
Philippe Leisbach
68340 Riquewihr
Aromatic Muscat, excellent Chasselas.
François Lichtlé
68420 Husseren-les-Châteaux
Small producer; renowned crémant.

Gustave Lorentz 68750 Bergheim
Fine Riesling and Gewürztraminer Altenberg de Bergheim, and Riesling and Gewürztraminer Kanzlerberg.
Jean-Luc Mader 68150 Hunawihr
Up-and-coming small producer.
Frédéric Mallo & Fils
68150 Hunawihr
Soft, classy wines.
Albert Mann 68920 Wettolsheim
Reliable, rich, balanced wines.
Materne Haegelin
68500 Orschwihr
Rich, long-lived Tokay-Pinot Gris Cuvée Élise.
Mittnacht-Klack 68340 Riquewihr
Good grand cru Rieslings and Gewürztraminers.
Marcel Mullenbach
68230 Niedermorschwihr
Wines of quality and personality.
Müller-Koenerlé 68590 St-Hippolyte
Attractive Rouge de St-Hippolyte and Tokay-Pinot Gris Vieilles Vignes.
Muré 68250 Rouffach
Owns the 16-ha Clos St-Landelin on the grand cru Vorbourg. Old, low-yielding vines produce outstanding quality wines. Good tasting rooms.
Preiss-Zimmer 68340 Riquewihr
Clean, dry, lively wines.
Edmond Rentz 68340 Zellenberg
Excellent Tokay-Pinot Gris.
Joseph Rieflé & Fils
68250 Pfaffenheim
Renowned Tokay-Pinot Gris, good Gewürztraminer.
Ringenbach-Moser
68240 Sigolsheim
Small producer specialising in Gewürztraminer and Tokay-Pinot Gris.
François Runner 68250 Pfaffenheim
Lovely Pinot Noir, Riesling and Gewürztraminer.
Salzmann Thomann
68240 Kayserberg
Attractive Riesling and Gewürztraminer Schlossberg.
Edgar Schaller & Fils
68630 Mittelwihr
Classic dry wines made for ageing. Excellent Rieslings and crémant.
Philippe Scheidecker
68630 Mittelwihr
Lovely Muscat; elegant Rieslings.
Louis Scherb & Fils
68420 Gueberschwihr
André Scherer
68420 Husseren-les-Châteaux
Family firm. Good Muscat Cuvée Jean Baptiste, Riesling and Gewürztraminer Eichberg.
Charles Schleret 68230 Turckheim
Small producer, consistently fine wines.
Domaine Schlumberger
68500 Guebwiller
A large and important estate. Rich, rounded, powerful wines.
Raymond Schmitt 67120 Soultz
Small grower with land on grand cru Ollwiller. Good Riesling and Gewürztraminer.

Maurice Schoech
68770 Ammerschwihr
Domaine Schoffit 68000 Colmar
Easy, elegant wines. Award-winning
Gewürztraminer and Chasselas.
Exceptional Tokay-Pinot Gris and
Riesling from *grand cru* Rangen.
Gérard Schueller
68420 Husseren-les-Châteaux
Lovely Riesling, fine Tokay-Pinot Gris.
Sick-Dreyer
68770 Ammerschwihr
Fine-quality wines.
Jean Sipp 68150 Ribeauvillé
Delicious wines for ageing.
Louis Sipp 68150 Ribeauvillé
31ha in Rodern, Bergheim and
Ribeauvillé. Long-lived and dry wines.
Bruno Sorg 68420 Eguisheim
Flawless, charming wines.
Pierre Sparr 68240 Sigolsheim
Established family firm; the quality of
the wines has risen since the 1980s.
Specht 68630 Mittelwihr
Good Muscat, Tokay-Pinot Gris and
Riesling Mandelberg.
Jean-Martin Spielmann
68750 Bergheim
Wines of finesse and elegance.
Bernard Staehlé
68920 Wintzenheim
Fabulous crémant and top Riesling
Cuvée Dame Blanche.
Aimé Stentz 68920 Wettolsheim
Fernand Stentz
68420 Husseren-les-Châteaux
Individualistic style.
Antoine Stoffel 68420 Eguisheim
Domaine Thomann
68040 Ingersheim
Trimbach 68150 Ribeauvillé
A reputation across the world for
aromatic, pure, refined wines. The
Riesling Clos-Ste-Hune is the epitome
of fine Riesling.
Vignobles Reinhart
68500 Orschwihr
Fine Riesling Bollenberg, rich Tokay-
Pinot Gris Cuvée Charlotte.
**Domaine Viticole de la Ville de
Colmar** 68000 Colmar
Sound, well-made wines.
Château Wagenbourg
68570 Soultzmatt
Pleasant, easy-drinking wines. There is
a tasting room in the castle annexe.
A Wischlen 68250 Westhalten
Wunsch et Mann
68920 Wettolsheim
Big and powerful wines including the
Riesling and Tokay Pinot-Gris Cuvée
Joseph Mann.
Jean-Jacques Ziegler-Mauler
68630 Mittelwihr
Domaine Zind-Humbrecht
68230 Turckheim
Superb range of wines with distinctive
style and quality. The firm owns 30ha
of the top sites in the Haut-Rhin.
Valentin Zusslin 68500 Orschwihr
Aromatic Muscat Cuvée Maxie, classy
Tokay-Pinot Gris Cuvée Jean-Paul.

Vineyards covering the hillsides around Riquewihr come right up to the double ring of walls which encircles the town.

FÊTES

Colmar The great Foire Régionale
des Vins d'Alsace in the first two
weeks in August.
Eguisheim Presentation of the new
wines on the last Sunday in March;
Fête des Vignerons on the last Sunday
in August.
Gueberschwihr 'Open cellars' on
the penultimate weekend in August.
Guebwiller Foire aux Vins on
Ascension Day.
Orschwihr Fête du Crémant on the
first weekend in July; 'open cellars' on
August 15.
Ribeauvillé Fête des Ménétriers
(minstrels) on the first Sunday in
September.
Riquewihr Fête du Riesling on the
penultimate weekend in July.

WINE INFORMATION

Maison du Vin d'Alsace 12 avenue
de la Foire aux Vins, 68000 Colmar
Tel (0)389 20 16 20

HOTELS

À l'Arbre Vert
68770 Ammerschwihr
Tel (0)389 47 12 23
Neat, simple rooms; good regional
cooking in the restaurant.
Hôtel de la Fecht 1 rue de la Fecht
68000 Colmar Tel (0)389 41 34 08
Convenient hotel with some 40 stylish
rooms. Also a restaurant.
Terminus-Bristol 7 place de la
Gare, 68000 Colmar
Tel (0)389 41 10 10
Traditional city hotel; 70 comfortable
rooms. Also a luxurious restaurant.

Hostellerie du Pape 68420
Eguisheim Tel (0)389 41 41 21
Comfortable rooms. Also a restaurant.
Le Relais du Vignoble
68420 Gueberschwihr
Tel (0)389 49 22 22
Over 30 smart rooms. The restaurant's
regional specialities are often served
with Sélection des Grains Nobles
from the hotel's Domaine Scherb.
Husseren-les-Châteaux 68420
Husseren-les-Châteaux
Tel (0)389 49 22 93
Modern, peacefully situated hotel with
38 masionettes. Indoor swimming
pool, children's playroom, tennis court.
Excellent cooking, many local wines.
À l'Arbre Vert 68240 Kaysersberg
Tel (0)389 47 11 51
Comfortable 20-room hotel on the
main square. A good restaurant. La
Belle Promenade is a more modern
and luxurious annexe with 30 rooms.
Hôtel des Remparts 68240
Kaysersberg Tel (0)389 47 12 12
Peaceful hotel near the vineyards and
woods. Around 30 rooms.
L'Abbaye d'Alspach 68240
Kientzheim Tel (0)389 47 16 00
Typical Alsace decor. No restaurant.
L'Ange
68230 Niedermorschwihr
Tel (0)389 27 05 73
Old building around a beautiful
courtyard. Has a restaurant.
Le Ménestrel 68150 Ribeauvillé
Tel (0)389 73 80 52
Colourful, cheerful rooms. Offers
sauna and Turkish bath.
Les Seigneurs de Ribeaupierre
68150 Ribeauvillé
Tel (0)389 73 70 31
Handsomely furnished 17th-century
building filled with atmosphere.

Auberge du Schoenenbourg
68340 Riquewihr Tel (0)389 47 92 28
One of the region's best hotels. Light
and stylish interior. Fresh ingredients
are prepared in an inventive way.
Le Riquewihr 68340 Riquewihr
Tel (0)389 47 83 13
Amid vineyards just outside the village.
Rustically decorated rooms. Sauna.
À la Ville de Lyon 68250 Rouffach
Tel (0)389 49 65 51
Over 40 neat rooms. Brasserie and
stylish restaurant; pleasant service.
Château d'Isenbourg 68250
Rouffach Tel (0)389 49 63 53
Luxury Relais & Châteaux hotel in an
elegant 19th-century château. First-
class restaurant in the vaulted cellars.
Aux Ducs de Lorraine 68590
St-Hippolyte Tel (0)389 73 00 09
Traditional, welcoming hotel.
Substantial regional cuisine and wines
from the family estate in St-Hippolyte.
À la Vallée Noble 68570
Soultzmatt Tel (0)389 47 65 65
Chalet-style hotel. Restaurant,
swimming pool, sauna and gym.
Berceau du Vigneron place
Turenne, 68230 Turckheim
Tel (0)389 27 23 55
Ideally situated; over 15 stylish rooms.
Domaine du Bollenberg 68920
Westhalten Tel (0)389 49 62 47
Peaceful hotel. Serves good regional
dishes and its own wines and spirits.
Au Riesling 68340 Zellenberg
Tel (0)389 47 85 85
Fairly modern hotel with 36 rooms,
some with good views. Restaurant.
Le Schlossberg 68340 Zellenberg
Tel (0)389 47 93 85
A friendly hotel in the old centre.
Cosy dining room and bar serve good,
local food. There is a large wine-list.

RESTAURANTS

Aux Armes de France 68770
Ammerschwihr Tel (0)389 47 10 12
The most famous restaurant in Alsace.
Gigantic wine-list; delicious food.
Excellent, reasonably priced Riesling by
the carafe. Ten hotel rooms.

Le Bouc Bleu 68980 Beblenheim
Tel (0)389 47 88 21
Rustic yet inventive cuisine.

Winstub du Sommelier 68750
Bergheim Tel (0)389 73 69 99
Quality regional dishes; large, expertly
chosen wine-list (some by the glass).

Au Fer Rouge 52 Grand' Rue
68000 Colmar Tel (0)389 41 37 24
Creative modern cuisine in a fine
half-timbered house. High prices.

Chez Hansi 23 rue des Marchands
68000 Colmar Tel (0)389 41 37 84
Unpretentious *winstub*.

Schillinger 16 rue Stanislas, 68000
Colmar Tel (0)389 41 43 17
Classically furnished restaurant and
high-quality cooking. Impressive cellar.

La Grangelière 68420 Eguisheim
Tel (0)389 23 00 30
Quality cooking, chic interior.

S'Wenzer Stewa 68420 Eguisheim
Tel (0)389 24 01 90
Good-value regional dishes and wines
from the Zinck-Fuermann estate.

La Taverne du Vigneron 68500
Guebwiller Tel (0)389 76 81 89
Good food at good prices.

Auberge de l'Ill 68970 Illhaeusern
Tel (0)389 71 89 00
One of France's finest restaurants, the
three-star Auberge is a 15-minute
drive from town. France's best wine-
waiter takes care of the wines. Menu:
expensive. Rooms are available.

Taverne Alsacienne 68040
Ingersheim Tel (0)389 27 08 41
A wide choice of dishes; Alsace wines.

Au Lion d'Or Grand' Rue, 68240
Kayserberg Tel (0)389 47 11 16
Popular restaurant; local cuisine.

*The great rose window of Strasbourg
Cathedral with its 16 radiating petals.*

Chambard 68240 Kayserberg
Tel (0)389 47 10 17
Spacious and stylish. Refined, original
and tasty dishes. Attentive service.
Large wine-list. Also 20 rooms.

Château du Reichenstein 68240
Kientzheim Tel (0)389 47 15 88
Restored 15th-century castle. Regional
and international classics are served in
the vaulted hunting hall.

Caveau Morakopf
68230 Niedermorschwihr
Tel (0)389 27 05 10
Alsace cuisine and good carafe wines
at reasonable prices. Must book.

Clos St-Vincent 68150 Ribeauvillé
Tel (0)389 73 67 65
Glorious situation high above town
amid vineyards. Good cooking; the
week-day lunch menu is good value.
Also a luxurious hotel.

Zum Pfifferhüss 68150 Ribeauvillé
Tel (0)389 73 62 28
An almost legendary *winstub* with its
half-timbered façade and beautiful
woodwork. Regional dishes only.

Le Sarment d'Or 68340 Riquewihr
Tel (0)389 47 92 85
Vaulted dining room. Regional
specialities prepared with care; good
wines. Value-for-money three-course
meals. Rooms available.

La Table du Gourmet 68340
Riquewihr Tel (0)389 47 98 77
Traditional Alsace decor. Well-known
regional specialities as well as more
international fare.

Au Bon Coin 68240 Sigolsheim
Tel (0)389 78 22 33
Simple restaurant on the church
square. Good fish dishes.

Klein 68570 Soultzmatt
Tel (0)389 47 00 10
Cosy village restaurant. Extensive
wine-list; good variety on a classic
menu. Seven rooms also available.

Hôtel Moschenross 68800 Thann
Tel (0)389 37 00 86
Large restaurant serving tasty local
dishes such as truite au Pinot Noir.
With 25 rooms.

À l'Homme Sauvage 68230
Turckheim Tel (0)389 27 56 15
Good restaurant with talented chef.

Au Cheval Blanc 68920
Westhalten Tel (0)389 47 01 16
Comfortable dining room. Fresh local
food; the wine-list includes own wines.

Auberge du Père Floranc 68920
Wettolsheim Tel (0)389 80 79 14
Specialities include foie gras and quail
pie (torte de cailles). Extensive wine-
list. About 30 rooms and a garden.

Au Bon Coin 68920 Wintzenheim
Tel (0)389 27 48 04
Simply furnished establishment serving
delicious regional dishes. Fish in
Riesling sauce and game in season.

Maximilien 68340 Zellenberg
Tel (0)389 47 99 69
Michelin-starred restaurant. Modern
cuisine in a modern setting.

PLACES OF INTEREST

Ammerschwihr In the church is a
wooden figure of Christ dating from
1606. A winding road takes you up to
Les Trois-Épis (viewing point with a
number of hotels and restaurants).

Andlau The abbey of Ste-Richarde
was founded in 880 and rebuilt in
1049. The abbey church has a 30-m
frieze full of curious animal figures.

Avolsheim In a field to the south-
east of this village stands the 11th-
century Dompeter church, the oldest
in Alsace, with its fortified churchyard.

Barr Small wine town with a maze of
winding streets. The St-Martin church
tower is Romanesque below and
Gothic above. 17th-century town hall.
The Musée de la Folie Marco displays
furniture, pewter and pottery.

Bergheim Atmospheric old centre
partly surrounded by walls with three
towers. The sandstone church has
frescoes. A footpath (*sentier viticole*) is
marked through the vineyards.

Boersch *Hôtel de ville* dating from
1578, fine well from 1617, picturesque
houses and three medieval gates.

Châtenois The Romanesque church
has four turrets. Inside are 16th-
century bas-reliefs. The *hôtel de ville* is
late 15th century.

Colmar The centre has many
notable places of interest. Among
them are the Maison Pfister (1537);
the Maison des Têtes (1608); the
Ancienne Douane (1480); and the
cathedral of St-Martin (13th–14th
century). In the cathedral is the
beautiful Schongauer painting of
Madonna in the Rose Garden. The
famous Musée Unterlinden (1 rue
Unterlinden), is in a 13th-century
former Dominican monastery and has
a magnificent collection of medieval
and Renaissance art and an interesting
section devoted to wine. The Musée
Bartholdi (30 rue des Marchands) is
Colmar's historical museum.

Eguisheim Photogenic wine village.
The walk through the rue des
Remparts is one of the prettiest in
Alsace. The central Château
d'Eguisheim (birthplace of Pope Leon
IX) has an 8th-century outer wall.

Guebwiller Still functioning as
churches are St-Léger (12th century,
with two bell-towers and ladders left
by 15th-century besiegers) and
Notre-Dame (18th century). The
town hall dates from 1514.

Hunawihr The 14th–16th-century
fortified church is surrounded by a
thick, hexagonal wall. Outside the
village there is a centre for breeding
and reintroducing much-loved storks.

Kaysersberg Many half-timbered
and Renaissance houses. Highlights
include the town hall, the church
(a 1518 altarpiece), the two-storey
St-Michel chapel, the Oberhof chapel
(with a 15th-century figure of Christ
with a bunch of grapes) and the
fortified bridge over the Weiss. Steep
paths lead up to the castle ruins which
overlook the town. Albert Schweitzer
was born in Kaysersberg in 1875.

Kientzheim The local château
belongs to La Confrérie St-Étienne
and houses the Musée du Vignoble et
des Vins d'Alsace (open from July to
the end of September).

Lapoutroie A distillery museum with
displays of apparatus and a collection
of French liqueurs from the 1920s.

Mulhouse Many fine museums.
Europe's largest car collection is in the
Musée National de l'Automobile (192
avenue de Colmar). Also the finest
railway museum of continental
Europe. The town's zoo is laid out in a
park with rare trees.

Obermorschwihr A gilded statue
of the Virgin watches over the village
fountain. The church has a unique
half-timbered tower.

Ribeauvillé Very pretty small town
with many old buildings and three
ruined castles. The 18th-century town
hall contains a museum of goblets and
gold- and silversmith's work.

Riquewihr Masses of visitors flock to
this village, which has been declared a
historic monument. Riquewihr ('rich
village') is one big museum: 90% of
the marvellous houses date from
before 1640. Shops, tasting rooms,
wine firms and restaurants all
contribute to the atmosphere. There
is a museum of history in the
Dolder, (a half-timbered tower built in
1291) and a further museum set in
the Tour des Voleurs (prison and
torture chamber).

Rouffach Around the large place de
la République stand the cathedral-like
church of Notre-Dame-de-
L'Assomption (Romanesque and early
Gothic); a corn exchange with
stepped gables (15th–16th century), a
former town hall (16th and 17th
century) and the 13th–15th-century
Tour des Sorcières (Witches' Tower).

Sigolsheim War graves are laid out
on a wide hill above the vineyards.
The village church has an attractive
Romanesque porch.

Thann The church of St-Thiébaut is
built in Flamboyant Gothic style and is
a masterpiece of its kind. Thann also
has a museum of history and a
13th–15th-century Witches' Tower.

Turckheim Half-timbered houses,
three 14th-century town gates and a
wine museum. Every summer evening at
10pm a nightwatchman, complete
with halberd and lantern, tours the
little town.

Ungersheim An Ecomusée has
been created in this village east of
Guebwiller. A reconstruction of a
traditional Haut-Rhin village, it has 20
half-timbered farmhouses.

Lorraine

The four *départements* of Lorraine lie between Alsace and Champagne. Until late in the last century thousands of hectares of vineyard were cultivated, but these fell into decline and only a few dozen remain. They are divided between two small VDQS districts: Côtes de Toul and Vins de Moselle. Most of the production is concentrated in Côtes de Toul, whose 40 or so hectares lie to the north and south-west of the fortified town of Toul, west of Nancy.

The Côtes de Toul speciality is Vin Gris, a light, fresh rosé usually made from Gamay which makes an excellent accompaniment to the region's own dish, quiche Lorraine. The reds can also be pleasant, particularly if they have been made from ripe Pinot Noir. The whites, especially those from Auxerrois, can be fresh, aromatic and attractive.

The extensive Vins de Moselle area is divided into three zones. The most northerly lies near the West German-Luxembourg border, the southern zone near Vic-sur-Seille, to the cast of Nancy. The district's tiny production (from about 20 hectares) is concentrated to the south of Metz; the emphasis is on refreshing, light white wines, although some rosés and reds are also made.

PRODUCERS OF SPECIAL INTEREST

CÔTES DE TOUL
Michael et Marcel Laroppe
54200 Bruley
Dedicated producer of some of the region's very best wines, including a Vin Gris, a red Pinot Noir and a white Auxerrois.
Lelièvre Frères
54200 Lucey
This family estate that dates from 1915. The Vin Gris can be especially delicious.
Les Vignerons du Toulois 54113 Mont-le-Vignoble
Small cooperative offering two versions of Vin Gris, one made from 100% Gamay.

VINS DE MOSELLE
Claude Gauthier
57590 Manhoué
One of the region's most successful growers making commendable reds as well as whites.
Centre de Laquenexy
57530 Laquenexy
Viticultural centre that also produces some attractive wines.
J Mansion-Welferinger
57480 Contz-lès-Bains
Pinot Blanc is the speciality.
Michael Maurice
57130 Ancy-sur-Moselle
A quality white wine.

WINE ACTIVITIES

Côtes de Toul has its own wine fraternity, **Les Compagnons de la Capucine**.

HOTEL

Hôtel de l'Europe 35 avenue Victor-Hugo, 54200 **Toul**
Tel (0)383 43 00 10
Simple, adequate provincial hotel with just over 20 rooms.

RESTAURANTS

La Belle Époque
31 avenue Victor-Hugo
54200 **Toul**
Tel (0)383 43 23 71
Stylish small restaurant specialising in fish dishes.
Le Dauphin
route de Villey-St-Étienne
54200 **Toul**
Tel (0)383 43 13 46
Rather unattractive location (5km from the town centre on an industrial estate), but the cooking at this modern restaurant is highly inventive.

PLACES OF INTEREST

Blénod-lès-Tours The local church is set in the courtyard of a former castle. Just south of the village is the 16th–18th-century Château de Tumejus.
Metz This industrial town was badly damaged in World War II, but well worth seeing are the Gothic cathedral of St-Étienne with its beautiful windows, the 13th–16th-century fortified Porte des Allemands and the Musée d'Art et d'Histoire (2 rue du Haut-Poireu).
Nancy A large, industrial town but with a beautiful baroque centre. The former ducal palace, the church and

Fabulous wrought-iron tracery by master iron-worker Lamour encloses the place Stanislas. A gilded portico, embellished with stylised leaf and shell motifs, frames the fountains of Neptune and Amphitrite by the sculptor Guibal.

monastery of the Cordeliers (Franciscans) and the Porte de la Graffe are now museums. The place Stanislas, formerly the Palace Royal dedicated to Louis XV, is the focal point of the Stanislas Buildings which constitute a masterpiece of baroque town planning.
Toul Seventeenth-century walls with four gateways surround the centre of this once-important town on the Moselle. The former cathedral of St-Étienne was badly damaged during World War II but has been restored. Its façade in Flamboyant Gothic was completed in 1496 and is flanked by two 65-m octagonal towers. There

are Renaissance chapels on either side of its splendid nave and the cloisters have 13th–14th-century galleries on three sides. The cloisters of the church at St-Gengould are even more beautiful.
Verdun The seat of bishops since the 4th century, Verdun has a predominance of ecclesiastical buildings including the composite cathedral of Notre Dame, begun in the 11th century. The nearby Bishop's Palace illustrates 18th-century architecture at its best. Some 800,000 soldiers died in the Battle of Verdun, (*L'Enfer de Verdun*), which was fought here over ten months in 1916.

Burgundy

Burgundy lies in the very heart of France. When rain falls on the little hamlet of Maconges near Pouilly-en-Auxois, some drops may find themselves en route to the English Channel by way of the rivers Armançon and Seine, others will end up in the Atlantic via the Arroux and the Loire while the remainder will trickle into the Ouche and thence the Saône, Rhône and Mediterranean.

Yet Burgundy was once almost a kingdom in its own right when the Valois dukes ruled from Dijon in the 14th and 15th centuries. Now it is a French province made up of four *départements*: the Yonne, Nièvre, Côte d'Or and Saône-et-Loire. For wine purposes however the Nièvre is excluded (its few vineyards make Pouilly-Fumé, which is considered to be Loire wine) while the Beaujolais (which lies mostly in the Rhône *département* and whose wines are made with a different grape variety on a different soil) is included.

In prehistoric times Burgundy lay beneath the sea. That sea dried up, the marine life fossilised and became what is now known as oolitic limestone. This is the bedrock of Burgundy as it is of Champagne: in both areas Chardonnay and Pinot Noir flourish. The former is now at home in almost every wine-producing country in the world, though Burgundy remains the originator. There is a small village in the Mâconnais called Chardonnay – although whether the grape owes its name to the village or vice versa is unclear. Mixed in with the Chardonnay *encépagement* there may still be plantings of Pinot Blanc and Pinot Gris (known here as Pinot Beurot) while lesser, though refreshing, wine is made from the Aligoté grape which is bottled separately under its own name.

The red wines, being made from Pinot Noir, are more problematic. This thin-skinned grape is prone to over-sensitivity – to disease in the vineyard and to any clumsiness in the winemaking. But patience with sensitive things can pay off – do not look for deep colour and massive body but savour instead the subtlety, elegance, fragrance and lingering intensity.

The wine districts of Burgundy are easy to visit, being linked by the autoroute A6 from Paris to Lyon. An hour and a half south of Paris, take the exit for Auxerre Sud and Chablis is just ten minutes' drive down the road. In this area of rolling limestone hills surrounding the Serein Valley, keen local interest is resurrecting

Flemish splendour in the heart of Burgundy. The Hospices, built in the 15th century by Nicolas Rollin, continued to receive the sick until the late 1940s.

Layers of dust from the Comblanchien quarry cover the surrounding countryside.

pockets of vineyards such as the Côte St-Jacques at Joigny, Épineuil near Tonnerre and, further to the south, Vézelay.

Rejoin the A6 and continue south, taking the A38 spur to Dijon, former capital of the Duchy of Burgundy. There is much to visit here including the old ducal palace which houses the Musée des Beaux Arts, and some notable hotels and restaurants.

Abandon the autoroute temporarily and drive south of Dijon on the RN74: every village name – Gevrey-Chambertin, Morey-St-Denis, Chambolle-Musigny – conjures up the magic of Burgundy. This is the Côte de Nuits, which begins in the outskirts of Dijon at Marsannay-la-Côte and stretches beyond Nuits-St-Georges, and this is where the most glorious red wines of Burgundy are made. The end of the Côte de Nuits gives way to the first vineyards of the Côte de Beaune, notably those on the landmark hill of Corton overlooking the villages of Aloxe and Pernand, both of which are distinguished by the brightly-tiled roofs of their church and château.

The main road soon leads into Beaune itself. Parking is becoming difficult inside the town, but a visit inside is worthwhile, whether for the excellent food and wine shopping or for the wealth of historical interest – above all in the captivating Hôtel Dieu.

The road divides on the southern edge of town and the RN74 traverses the foot of the slope past Pommard, Meursault and Puligny-Montrachet. An alternative route is to take the right fork (RN73) which goes through Pommard, past Volnay, between Meursault and Monthelie on to Auxey-Duresses and below St-Romain. Both routes offer marvellous views of the vineyards that provide the glorious red and white wines of the Côte de Beaune.

Hereafter vineyards become more scattered as the escarpment which provides the focus for the great wines of the Côte d'Or turns westward and dwindles. First the hamlet of Bouzeron, noted for its Aligoté, then the larger villages (or small towns) of Rully, Mercurey and Givry make up the Côte Chalonnaise, along with the appellation of Montagny around the town of Buxy. Decent red and white wines are made in this area as well as a certain amount of sparkling Crémant de Bourgogne.

The countryside soon becomes more gently pastoral and the first evidence of the south appears – more chirping crickets, southern-style roof-tiles and Romanesque churches in every village. This is the Mâconnais, which can be explored either by taking the back roads off the Route du Vin which descends from the villages of the Chalonnais towards Cluny, or by making forays off the autoroute. Viticulture seems almost incidental, except in pockets round villages such as Lugny and Viré, until you reach the last outcrop of the limestone soil, the crags of Solutré and Vergisson, towering over the vineyards of Pouilly-Fuissé.

Here the white soil of Burgundy proper gives way to the reddish granitic schist and sand of the Beaujolais. Neither Chardonnay nor Pinot Noir feels at home here but Gamay thrives, making succulent red wines which are mostly drunk young – a fair proportion within a few months of the harvest as 'Beaujolais Nouveau'.

So far, so good and apparently simple – clearly defined regions with wines made from single grape varieties. Yet the reality of Burgundy is enormously more complex. Where Bordeaux is content with a handful of appellations in which each producer makes only one or two wines, Burgundy has more than 100 distinct appellations, a dozen or more of which might be on offer from any given producer. This wealth of appellations makes buying more difficult, especially as the individual holdings of land are so fragmented. The French laws of inheritance provide for property to be divided equally among all children. In an agricultural region like Burgundy this has meant that vineyard land has become parcelled out into ever-smaller strips, estates being divided at the demise of one generation to be reformed in a different pattern with the marriages of the next. Now there is a tendency to put the family property into the form of a company (as has tended to happen in Bordeaux) so that shares in the whole can be distributed to the heirs.

Producers come in three main shapes: domaines, cooperatives and *négociants* (merchants). Growers who do everything at their own property (grow and pick the grapes, vinify and mature the wine, bottle it and sell it) can be distinguished on the label by the words 'Propriétaire-Récoltant' and the legend 'Mise en bouteilles au domaine'. Many of the greatest bottles of Burgundy come from these individual producers who can attain the peaks of glory, albeit in very small quantities. Conversely, there are plenty of growers who lack the technical skills to master vinification, maturation or bottling even if they can produce near-perfect raw material.

Outside the Côte d'Or, where lower prices make domaine bottling less tempting, many villages have cooperatives to which most of the growers belong. These are usually sources of competently made wine in large quantities at a lower price, while some (Buxy, Chablis, Lugny and Viré, for example) can produce better *cuvées* with some flair.

Still the largest sector of Burgundian commerce is that of the merchants, or *négociants*, who buy in grapes or grape juice or fermented wine and blend it in their own cellars to produce homogeneous lots in more commercial quantities than individual growers can manage. Many of the merchants have developed a recognisable house style: a bonus in terms of security and recognition, though perhaps also a loss for individuality.

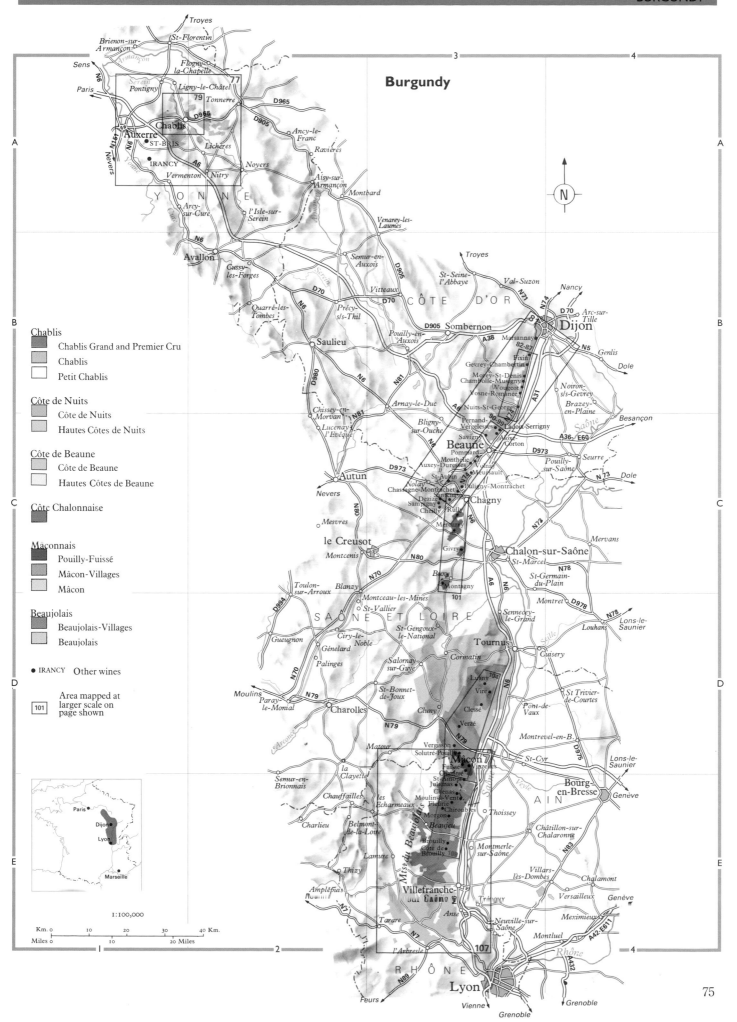

Chablis

Why is Chablis such an evocative name? Small though the region is it has been the most imitated of all – by other French wines masquerading under its popular name and by having that name used as a generic term for otherwise anonymous white wine in the US. The real thing is sublime, having all the character and concentration of the Chardonnay grape as well as an additional steeliness, a mineral austerity of its own.

Wines have been made here at least since the 11th century when the Abbey of Pontigny was founded. Some of Chablis' old streets such as the rue des Moulins are still flanked by wine-growers' houses, a number of of which have cellars dating from the 13th century. The relative proximity of Paris, by river from Auxerre, stimulated trade to the extent that 15th-century Chablis was more prosperous and more heavily populated than it is today.

Before phylloxera and warfare destroyed large areas of the vineyards in the late 19th and early 20th centuries, there were some 40,000 hectares under vine in the *département* of the Yonne. This diminished to under 1,000 hectares during the difficult times of the 1950s, though planting has boomed since. There are now four classifications of Chablis which comprise (in ascending order) 260 hectares of Petit Chablis; 2,630 hectares of Chablis including 670 hectares designated as *premier cru*, and 97 hectares of *grand cru* Chablis.

The vineyards are planted on rolling limestone hills, not unlike the English South Downs, with a top-soil known as Kimmeridgian clay. There was some controversy when the Chablis appellation was extended to cover land with a similar soil, Portlandian clay. This is not the real thing, according to local sticklers, although you or I might have difficulty in distinguishing between the two.

Delicious though successful results may be, it is not easy to make wine in and around Chablis. This far north, frost is a real problem: crops sustained significant damage in years such as 1981, 1985, 1991 and 1994. Distortions in yield tend in turn to affect the pricing of Chablis which, disconcertingly, vacillates more than that of most other appellations. Measures can be taken to protect the vines from frost but they are not universally successful nor indeed financially sustainable in the lesser vineyards. The main options are to burn stoves in between the rows of vines or to spray the vines at the critical moment hoping that the water will freeze in a protective layer around the plant, preventing a further drop in temperature. The latter is known as the water aspersion method.

Petit Chablis covers lesser vineyards on the fringes, especially around the villages of Lignorelles, Maligny and Beines. Some thought has been given to changing the name of the appellation since 'petit' is considered derogatory, but actually the wine sells extremely well, to the extent that there is now scarcely any difference in price between the lesser version and Chablis itself. This is partly due to the wine's scarcity, since many former Petit Chablis vineyards have been upgraded. However new land is being planted as rapidly as permission is granted.

Wines sold as Chablis, unless of *premier cru* status, may not bear any other vineyard designation. As a result the consumer is faced with a sea of Chablis – good, bad and indifferent – without any distinguishing characteristic save the all-important name of the producer. The name itself has such cachet that it used to be said that far more Chablis was sold in a year than was ever produced. Happily, pretenders are much rarer now although consumers in the US still need to note the difference between the French appellation and the inexpensive jug wine produced in the US under the generic title of 'Chablis'. Many producers of genuine Chablis are consciously trying to make softish, accessible, international Chardonnay-style wine. Some however remain faithful to the more austere, flinty, racy original, which is a classical accompaniment to oysters.

The situation regarding the *premier cru* vineyards is typically complicated. There are 17 different principal names: Mont de Milieu, Montée de Tonnerre, Fourchaume, Vaillons, Montmains, Côte de Léchet, Beauroy, Vau Ligneau, Vau de Vey, Vaucoupin, Vosgros, Les Fourneaux, Côte de Vaubarousse, Berdiot, Chaume de Talvat, Côte de Jouan and Les Beauregards. The first five of these are the most commonly seen and in general the best, the last five are the least well known. In addition, a further 23 vineyards (which

Vines sprayed with water at the critical moment develop a thin coating of ice which is designed to insulate them against any further drop in temperature.

Slow-burning chaufferettes *or stoves are placed between rows in this Chablis vineyard in an effort to minimise the damage caused by freezing conditions.*

Chablis

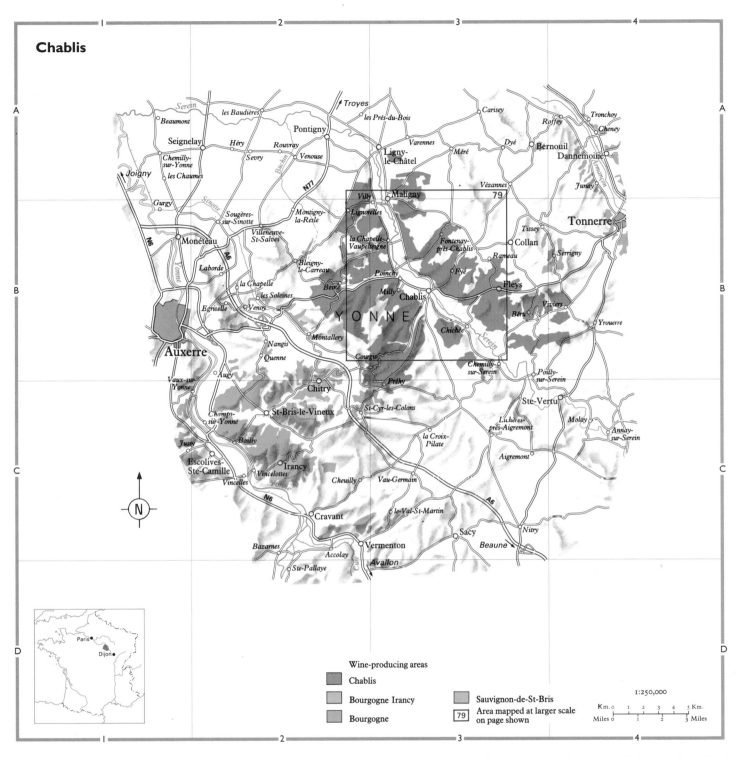

are effectively enclaves within one or other of the 17 principal names) may be specified. Of these you will sometimes see Chapelot (within Montée de Tonnerre), l'Homme Mort and Vaulorent (Fourchaume) and Forêt and Butteaux (both in Montmains).

Chablis *premier cru* should have an extra dimension, additional subtleties of flavour and a layer of concentration that takes time to develop fully.

The seven *grand cru* vineyards are concentrated on a steep slope overlooking the River Serein, just north of the town of Chablis. The vineyards of Blanchots, Les Clos, Valmur, Grenouilles, Vaudésir, Les Preuses and Bougros produce the most powerful Chablis of all, which needs a good seven to ten years in bottle and is capable of

ageing much longer. Some growers like to give their top wines the oak treatment, fermenting and maturing them in barrel. A few go for the intrusive flavour of new oak though many prefer the gentler effect of older barrels, which may be of the standard size or take the form of the traditional 132-litre Chablis *feuillette*.

Elsewhere in the Yonne *département* wine is made at Coulanges-la-Vineuse (noted for good Bourgogne Blanc and Rouge); Chitry (noted for its Aligoté); St-Bris-le-Vineux, which has a private VDQS appellation for its Sauvignon, and Épineuil and Irancy, the source of the region's best reds. Not all the red need be Pinot Noir however – a peculiarity of the Yonne is that the indigenous and somewhat rustic César and Tressot grapes may be included.

PRODUCERS OF SPECIAL INTEREST

CHABLIS

Michel Barat 89800 Milly
Jean-Claude Bessin
89800 La Chapelle-Vaupeltigne
Domaine Billaud Simon
89800 Chablis
Pascal Bouchard 89800 Chablis
Adhémar Boudin
89800 La Chapelle-Vaupeltigne
Jean Marc Brocard 89800 Préhy
Cave Coopérative La Chablisienne 89800 Chablis
Responsible for a third of the region's production. Reliable quality, prices dependent on the variations of the bulk-wine market.
Domaine des Courtis 89800 Milly
René & Vincent Dauvissat
89800 Chablis
Top domaine now run by Vincent for old-fashioned, barrel-fermented Chablis of the highest pedigree that ages extremely well.
Domaine Jean Defaix 89800 Milly
Jean-Paul Droin 89800 Chablis
Domaine de l'Églantière (Jean Durup) 89800 Maligny
A large and ever-expanding company embracing various 'domaine' names such as Domaine de l'Églantière and Château de Maligny. Wines competently made without use of barrels.
GAEC de Chantemerle
89800 La Chapelle-Vaupeltigne
GAEC du Colombier
89800 Fontenay-près-Chablis
Alain Geoffroy 89800 Beines
Jean-Pierre Grossot 89800 Fleys
Thierry Hamelin 89800 Lignorelles
Domaine Laroche 89800 Chablis
An ambitious and able business, partly domaine, partly *négociant*, whose headquarters are in the lovely 15th-century Obédiencerie in the town centre.
Roland Lavantureux
89800 Lignorelles
Domaine Long Depaquit
89800 Chablis

Domaine de la Maladière (William Fèvre) 89800 Chablis
Very good wines from across the spectrum, including vines in all but one of the *grands crus*. Noted for his use of barrels and for his fight to uphold traditional Chablis production.
Domaine des Malandes 89800 Chablis
Domaine des Maronniers (Bernard Legland) 89800 Préhy
Louis Michel & Fils 89800 Chablis
J Moreau & Fils 89800 Chablis
Sylvain Mosnier 89800 Beines
André Philippon 89800 Fleys
Gilbert Picq & Ses Fils
89800 Chichée
Domaine Pinson 89800 Chablis
Denis & Laurence Race
89800 Chablis
François & Jean-Marie Raveneau
89800 Chablis
At this legendary estate Jean-Marie is responsible for producing intense and long-lived Chablis *premier* and *grand cru*. Sometimes ungainly when young, these wines are worth the wait.
A Regnard et Fils 89800 Chablis
Domaine Ste-Claire
89800 Préhy
Olivier Savary 89800 Maligny
Roger Seguinot 89800 Maligny
Simonnet-Febvre 89800 Chablis
Gérard Tremblay 89800 Poinchy
Domaine de Vauroux
89800 Chablis
Domaine Robert Vocoret & Fils
89800 Chablis

THE AUXERROIS

COULANGES-LA-VINEUSE
Christophe Auguste 89580 Coulanges-la-Vineuse
Raymond Dupuis 89580 Coulanges-la-Vineuse
GAEC du Clos du Roi 89580 Coulanges-la-Vineuse

ÉPINEUIL
François Collin 89700 Épineuil
Émmanuel Dampt
89700 Épineuil

IRANCY
Léon Bienvenue 89290 Irancy
Bernard Cantin 89290 Irancy
Anita & Jean-Pierre Colinot
89290 Irancy
Roger Delalogue 89290 Irancy
Jean Podor 89290 Irancy

ST-BRIS-LE-VINEUX
Domaine Bersan & Fils
89530 St-Bris-le-Vineux
Caves de Bailly (in Bailly)
89530 St-Bris-le-Vineux
Robert & Philippe Defrance
89530 St-Bris-le-Vineux
Hervé Felix 89530 St-Bris-le-Vineux
Anne & Arnaud Goisot
89530 St-Bris-le-Vineux
Ghislaine & Jean-Hugues Goisot
89530 St-Bris-le-Vineux
Domaine Verret
89530 St-Bris-le-Vineux

WINE FÊTES

Chablis The Fête du Chablis is held on the fourth Sunday in November.
St-Bris-le-Vineux The Fête du Sauvignon takes place during the weekend preceding November 11.

WINE INFORMATION

The **Maison du Vin** is located near the Hostellerie des Clos and supplies wine and tourist information.

HOTELS

Hostellerie des Clos 89800 Chablis
Tel (0)386 42 10 63
This hotel and restaurant was opened in 1986. Comfortable and modern rooms. À la carte dishes are expensive and variable in quality, so keep to the menus.
Le Relais St-Vincent 89144 Ligny-le-Châtel Tel (0)386 47 53 38
About 10km from Chablis. Small, quiet hotel (a good choice for breakfast).
L'Abbaye St-Michel
89700 Tonnerre Tel (0)386 55 05 99
About 15km from Chablis. Luxurious hotel and restaurant with a medieval interior, a view over a river valley and meticulously executed cuisine.
Hôtel du Centre 89700 Tonnerre
Tel (0)386 55 10 56
Almost opposite the Ancien Hôpital. Mid-range.

RESTAURANTS

Au Vrai Chablis 89800 Chablis
Tel (0)386 42 11 43
Recently changed hands. Simple and dependable central restaurant.
Auberge du Bief
89144 Ligny-le-Châtel
Tel (0)386 47 43 42
Good cooking and an agreeable atmosphere. Very popular with locals.

Le St-Bris 89350 St-Bris-le-Vineux
Tel (0)386 53 84 56
You can enjoy a good-value menu and local wines either inside the old building or out on the terrace.
La Petite Auberge 89290 Vaux
Tel (0)386 53 80 08
The inn, beside the Yonne, is furnished in rustic style. Refined dishes.

PLACES OF INTEREST

Auxerre A town of churches. The 13th–16th century cathedral was built on the site of its Romanesque predecessor, the 11th-century crypt of which still remains. The single 68-m tower can be climbed. In the old centre of the town is the splendid Tour d'Horloge, a gateway with a large clock that shows the movements of the sun and moon.
Irancy A charming village nestling in a valley with vineyards and cherry trees.
Chablis Unfortunately the centre was largely destroyed by shelling in 1940, but several old streets, such as the rue des Moulins, remain. Some houses have cellars dating from the 13th century. In the centre stands the church of St-Martin which contains a diversity of religious art treasures. Just outside the village is the 12th-century church of St-Pierre, which is classified as a historic monument.
La Chapelle-Vaupelteigne A classic wine village. The church dates from the 12th and 13th centuries.
Maligny The château was once a feudal castle, unusually built not on a hill but in a valley. The 12th-century structure, rebuilt in the 18th, was patiently restored by wine-grower Jean Durup. The kitchen is vast, the salons contain interesting collections and ancient trees grow in the park.
Milly In the medieval chapel is a fine sculpture of a kneeling monk. The château dates from the same period. Climb *premier cru* Côte de Léchet for a splendid view over Chablis.
Noyers A small, beautifully preserved medieval walled town. Many wine cellars open onto its narrow streets.
Pontigny The magnificent 12th- and 13th-century monastery church is a remarkable example of Cistercian architecture. The monks of Pontigny were making wine in the Middle Ages.
St-Bris-le-Vineux Stone from here was used for the Panthéon in Paris. St-Bris also has an interesting partly-13th-century church.
Tanlay The château dates mainly from the 17th century and is one of the most sumptuous of the Burgundian Renaissance.
Tonnerre The old hospital, built in the 13th century, has an imposing roof and an oak-panelled hall 80m long.
Villy The village church has a pretty Romanesque porch.

Among St-Bris' many caves, one 'wine cathedral' can accommodate a million bottles.

The Heart of Chablis

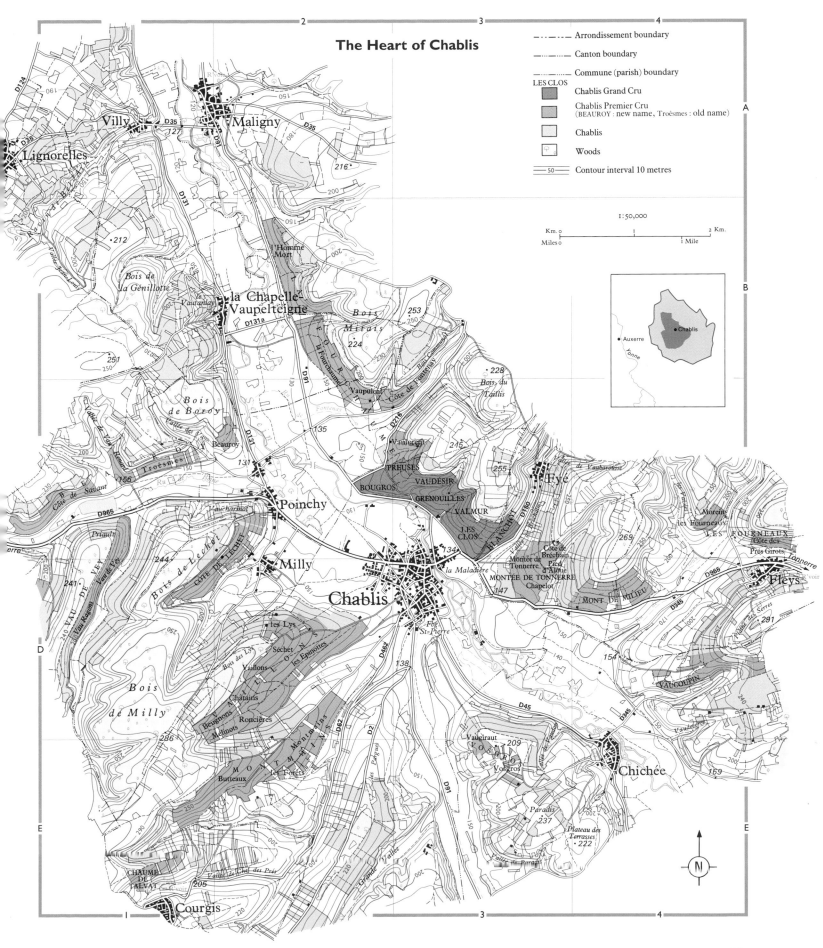

Legend:
- — ·· — ·· — Arrondissement boundary
- — · — · — Canton boundary
- — — — — Commune (parish) boundary

LES CLOS
- Chablis Grand Cru
- Chablis Premier Cru (BEAUROY : new name, Troësmes : old name)
- Chablis
- Woods

—50— Contour interval 10 metres

1 : 50,000

Km. 0 ... 1 ... 2 Km.
Miles 0 ... 1 Mile

Place names and features on map:

D124, 061, 190, Villy, D35, 127, Maligny, D35, D91, 216, 200, 150, 180, 150, Lignorelles, D36, D131, 212, 200, l'Homme Mort, Bois de la Génillotte, le Vaudanlay, la Chapelle-Vaupelteigne, D131a, 253, 250, Bois Mirais, 224, 251, 250, F O U R C H A U M E, la Fourchaume, Vaupulent, 228, Côte de Fontenay, Bois du Taillis, Bois de Boroy, Fontenay, 135, Vallée de Vau Renard, Vallée des Laus, Beauroy, D131, Vaulorent, 245, 255, Vallée de Vaubarousse, Troësmes, 131, PREUSES, VAUDÉSIR, Fyé, Côte de Savant, 156, Ru de Bréchain, BOUGROS, GRENOUILLES, VALMUR, D160, Morein, les Fourneaux, B. de Savant, 229, 200, Priault, Vaucharmot, Poinchy, VALMUR, LES CLOS, BLANCHOT, Vallée de Vauhupin, 269, LES FOURNEAUX, Côte des Prés Girots, Tonnerre, D965, Vau de Vey, Vard Vey, Bois de Léchet, CÔTE DE LÉCHET, Milly, Chablis, la Maladière, 134, Côte de Bréchain, Pied d'Aloue, Montée de Tonnerre, MONTÉE DE TONNERRE, Chapelot, 147, Mont de Milieu, Fleys, D345, 241, 244, VAU DE VEY, Vau Ragens, les Lys, Séchet, les Epinottes, Fbg St-Pierre, 138, 291, Bois de Milly, Vaillons, Châtains, Beugnons, Roncières, Mélinots, MONT MAINS, 286, V A I L L O N S, D62, D2, 154, VAUCOUPIN, D45, D345, Vaudevey, Vaugiraut, 209, VOSGROS, Vosgros, Chichée, 169, Butteaux, les Forêts, M O N T M A I N S, D91, Paradis, 237, Plateau des Terrasses, 222, Vallée de Paradis, CHAUME DE TALVAT, 205, Vallée de Chef des Prés, Grande Vallée, 220, Courgis

Auxerre, Chablis, Yonne

N

The Côte d'Or

The heart of Burgundy is the Côte d'Or, a long, irregular escarpment starting just south of Dijon and running south-south-west past Nuits-St-Georges and Beaune to Santenay, more than 50 kilometres away. The wine villages and their vineyards are linked by the RN74 in a chain punctuated by the marble quarries of Comblanchien and Corgoloin. The escarpment marks the edge of the hilly plateau which stretches back across the Morvan towards the Massif Central. From the top of the slope the view extends across the valley of the Saône towards the foothills of the Alps.

The vineyards are divided into four classifications. The most lowly are the generic vineyards, most of which lie on the fertile valley floor either side of the main RN74. They stretch towards the railway which runs parallel to the east. The wines are called Bourgogne Rouge and Bourgogne Blanc if made from Pinot Noir and Chardonnay; Bourgogne Aligoté if from the grape of that name, or Bourgogne Passe-Tout-Grains if from a blend of Pinot Noir (minimum one third) and Gamay. Bourgogne Rouge or Blanc made by a grower in one of the leading villages from vineyards just outside the well known appellation are excellent sources of inexpensive, decent-quality Burgundy. So too are the vineyards which lie in the hills behind the escarpment. They have their own subdivision of the generic appellation and are known as Bourgogne Hautes-Côtes de Nuits and Bourgogne Hautes-Côtes de Beaune.

The main Côte d'Or classification is by village appellation: Gevrey-Chambertin, Morey-St-Denis, Chambolle-Musigny, Vosne-Romanée and Nuits-St-Georges (the best known in the Côte de Nuits) and Aloxe-Corton, Beaune, Pommard, Volnay, Meursault, Puligny-Montrachet and Chassagne-Montrachet in the Côte de Beaune. The vineyards usually lie on the lower part of the slope, above the main road and around the villages. Certain lesser known Côte de Beaune villages may sell their wine under the collective title of Côte de Beaune-Villages while Brochon, Comblanchien, Corgoloin and one or two other locations may sell theirs only as Côte de Nuits-Villages.

The better vineyards within each village are designated as *premier cru* and show the village followed by the vineyard name on the label (Meursault Perrières and Pommard Rugiens, for example). If the wine is a blend of several different vineyards from the same village, or if the producer does not care to pinpoint the site's precise location, the wine can be labelled simply as (for example) Pommard Premier Cru. Vineyards in this classification tend to lie further up the slope where drainage and exposure are better and the soil is less fertile. Each of these named vineyards should have earned its rank by being able produce wine of a defined individual character.

This is certainly true of the 30 vineyards designated as *grand cru*. These titles stand proudly without mention of their village provenance – although their respective villages have chosen to append such names as Chambertin, Musigny, Corton and Montrachet to their own. Although there is a blurring of the edges between the best *premiers crus* and the lesser *grands crus*, by and large these giants of the Burgundian scene live up to their reputations.

As well as a number of fine vineyards and a beautiful church, the village of Fixin boasts François Rude's monumental statue Reveil de Napoléon, *set in the Parc Noiset.*

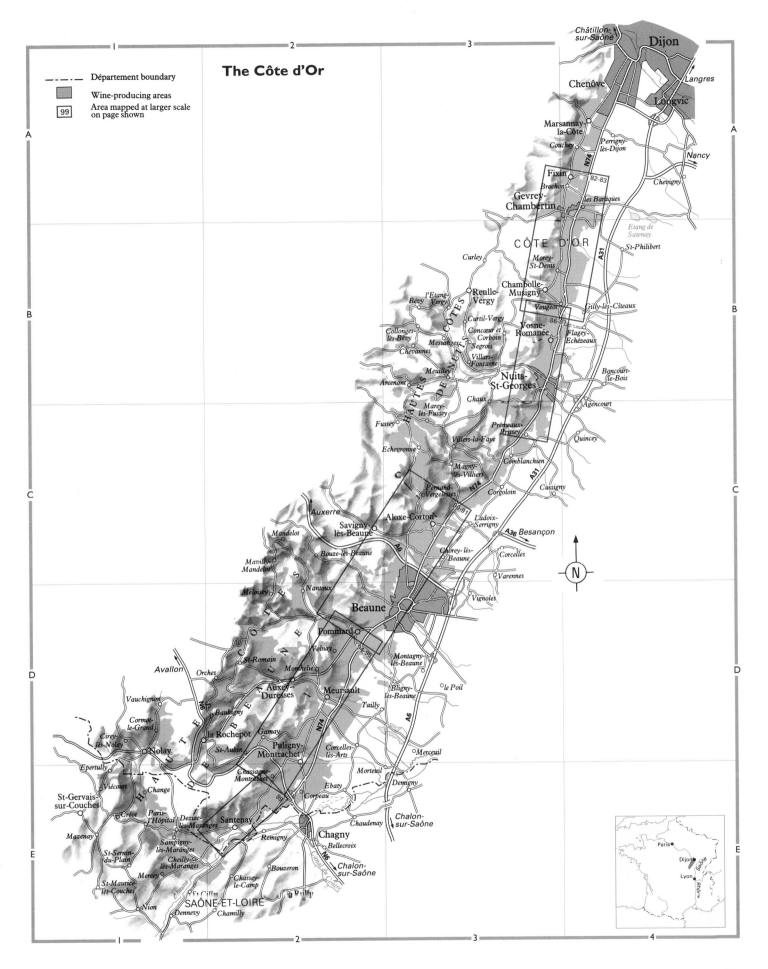

The Côte d'Or

- – – – Département boundary
- Wine-producing areas
- 99 Area mapped at larger scale on page shown

Châtillon-sur-Saône

Dijon

Chenôve

Longvic

Langres

Marsannay-la-Côte

Couchey

Perrigny-lès-Dijon

Nancy

Fixin

Brochon

Chevigny

Gevrey-Chambertin

les Baraques

CÔTE D'OR

Étang de Satenay

St-Philibert

Curley

Morey-St-Denis

l'Etang-Bévy

Reulle-Vergy

Chambolle-Musigny

Vougeot

Gilly-lès-Cîteaux

Curtil-Vergy

Collonges-lès-Bévy

Concœur et Corboin

Vosne-Romanée

Flagey-Echézeaux

Messanges

Segrois

Chevannes

Villars-Fontaine

Boncourt-le-Bois

Meuilley

Nuits-St-Georges

Arcenant

Marey-lès-Fussey

Chaux

Agencourt

Fussey

Préméaux-Prissey

Quincey

Echevronne

Villers-la-Faye

Magny-lès-Villiers

Comblanchien

Auxerre

Pernand-Vergelesses

Corgoloin

Cussigny

Mandelot

Savigny-lès-Beaune

Aloxe-Corton

Ladoix-Serrigny

Bouze-lès-Beaune

Besançon

Mavilly-Mandelot

Chorey-lès-Beaune

Corcelles

Meloisey

Nantoux

Varennes

Beaune

Vignoles

N

Pommard

Volnay

Montagny-lès-Beaune

Avallon

Orches

St-Romain

Monthelie

Bligny-lès-Beaune

le Poil

Vauchignon

Auxey-Duresses

Meursault

Cormot-le-Grand

Baubigny

Tailly

Cirey-lès-Nolay

la Rochepot

Gamay

Corcelles-lès-Arts

Nolay

St-Aubin

Merceuil

Epertully

Puligny-Montrachet

Morteuil

Denigny

Viécourt

Change

Chassagne-Montrachet

Ebaty

Corpeau

Chalon-sur-Saône

St-Gervais-sur-Couches

Créot

Paris-l'Hôpital

Dezize-lès-Maranges

Santenay

Chaudenay

Mazenay

Sampigny-lès-Maranges

Rémigny

Chagny

Bellecroix

St-Sernin-du-Plain

Cheilly-lès-Maranges

Bouzeron

Chalon-sur-Saône

Mercey

St-Maurice-lès-Couches

Chassey-le-Camp

Nion

Denevy

Chamilly

SAÔNE-ET-LOIRE

HAUTES CÔTES DE NUITS

HAUTES CÔTES DE BEAUNE

N74

A31

A36

A6

N6

Paris

Dijon

Lyon

Saône

Rhône

81

The Côte de Nuits

FROM DIJON TO CHAMBOLLE

For all the charm of its medieval centre, Dijon suffers inevitably from urban sprawl: American-style ribbon developments clutter the arterial roads such as the RN74 which runs south from Burgundy's capital city, and encroach on the vineyards. Those of Chenôve are all but lost, the remaining vestiges now being incorporated with the vineyards of Marsannay-la-Côte, the first village to hold its own against the suburban tide. Although Marsannay-la-Côte was once a lesser appellation confined to the production of rosé wine – fine, perfumed and more than just a local curiosity – since 1987 it has been made in all three colours. The whites are modest, the rosés still delicious and the reds (which constitute 75 per cent of the production) are interesting and charming in a light, easily approachable style. The appellation also covers neighbouring Couchey. Its best vineyards (Marsannay-la-Côte has no *premier cru* vineyards) include Champs Perdrix, Clos de Jeu, Monchenevoy and Clos du Roy in Chenôve.

Next in line is the village of Fixin. Many growers make wine both here and in Marsannay-la-Côte, but the two appellations are quite different in style. Fixin wines tend to be deeper in colour,

firmer in fruit and sturdier in structure. Amongst the best vineyards are *premiers crus* Clos de la Perrière, Clos du Chapitre and Clos Napoléon. Though Fixin wines are in most respects superior to those of Marsannay-la-Côte, they sometimes suffer from being regarded as lesser versions of Gevrey-Chambertin, whereas Marsannay-la-Côte stands as a style of its own.

Brochon does not merit an appellation of its own: most of the wines here must be sold as Côte de Nuits-Villages (as those of Fixin may be) though the vineyards bordering Gevrey-Chambertin benefit from their neighbour's grand name. Gevrey alternates between periods of fame and periods of infamy, depending on whether the vignerons are living up to the reputation of their vineyards or merely living off the popular name. Fortunately there are currently more producers worth their salt than ever before. A typical Gevrey-Chambertin should be relatively deep in colour, firm and well structured in style and capable of taking on rich, meaty flavours as it ages.

Normally, vineyards on the 'wrong side' of the main road are confined to the generic Bourgogne ACs though here the village vineyards of Gevrey-Chambertin lie on both sides of the RN74. Some that lie below are clearly not worthy although there are occasional good plots such as Clos de la Justice. Other 'village' Gevrey-Chambertins to look out for are Champs Chenys and Clos Prieur. Notable *premier cru* vineyards lie in a swathe above the

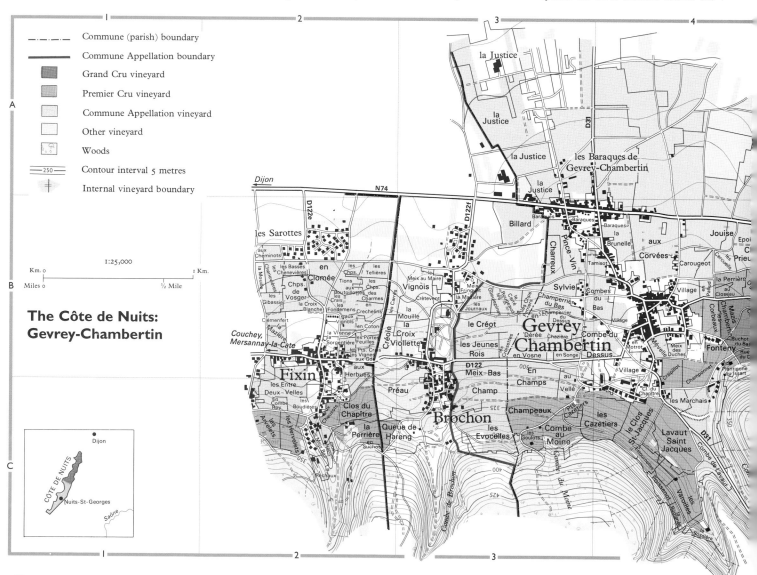

Key to map:
- Commune (parish) boundary
- Commune Appellation boundary
- Grand Cru vineyard
- Premier Cru vineyard
- Commune Appellation vineyard
- Other vineyard
- Woods
- Contour interval 5 metres
- Internal vineyard boundary

1:25,000

Km. 0 ————— 1 Km.
Miles 0 ————— ½ Mile

**The Côte de Nuits:
Gevrey-Chambertin**

village under the crown of the hill. Cazetiers, Lavaux St-Jacques and Verroilles are promising names but the stars are Clos St-Jacques which many would promote to *grand cru* – indeed it used to be regarded as the best vineyard in Gevrey after Chambertin – and Clos de Bèze. These last two lie with the other *grands crus* either side of the lesser road to Morey-St-Denis, proudly christened the Route des Grands Crus. On the right are Mazis-Chambertin and Ruchottes-Chambertin in a tiny enclave with thin stony soil which yields elegant wines, then the two giants, Chambertin and Chambertin Clos de Bèze (the latter may go under the former's name but not vice versa), followed by racy, lacy Latricières-Chambertin. On the left are Chapelle-Chambertin which frequently disappoints; small but distinguished Griotte-Chambertin, Mazoyères and Charmes-Chambertin (the former may go under the name of the latter but not vice versa) where some wines are excellent but many are not worth their *grand cru* status.

The Route des Grands Crus crosses the border into Morey-St-Denis and passes the vineyards of Clos de la Roche (potentially outstanding); Clos St-Denis (characteristically soft yet substantial); Clos des Lambrays, which was promoted to *grand cru* in 1981 yet despite determination and investment is still to show its true colours; and Clos de Tart, a monopoly of the house of Mommessin. Morey also contains the northern tip of Bonnes Mares, a vineyard which belongs to Chambolle-Musigny. Other leading vineyards in

Chambertin and its noble cousins lie among much more commonplace vineyards.

Morey-St-Denis are Clos de la Bussière and Les Monts Luisants where Domaine Ponsot makes an unusual white wine.

Fine though they are, the wines of Morey-St-Denis suffer from an identity crisis. In the days before *appellation contrôlée* they were sold either as Chambolle-Musigny or Gevrey-Chambertin. Even now it is difficult to define a Morey style: the wines range from delicate, elegant and Chambollesque to a firmer, tougher style akin to Gevrey-Chambertin. The *premier cru* Les Millandes and *grand cru* Clos St-Denis are probably the purest expressions of Morey although Clos de la Roche is ranked higher in many estimations.

Chambolle-Musigny boasts majesty – with discretion. It is the Margaux of Burgundy. There is less clay and more limestone in the soil, causing the vines to suffer more from chlorosis (slightly paler foliage can be noticed in high summer). This translates into the wines which are not as deep in colour as a Gevrey-Chambertin or Nuits-St-Georges but are magical in fragrance, purity of fruit and persistence. At the top level, the village's two *grands crus* Le Musigny and Bonnes Mares have been described as iron fists in velvet gloves. Bonnes Mares, which borders and indeed stretches into Morey-St-Denis, has a firm bone-structure overlaid with the ample seductive fruit of Chambolle.

Musigny at the other end of the village is one of Burgundy's greatest sites, whose wine was poetically described by Gaston Roupnel as being of "silk and lace", while its perfume put him in mind of "a damp garden, a rose and a violet covered in morning dew." Another vineyard of sublime potential is Les Amoureuses, adjacent to Le Musigny and scarcely inferior. By reputation and price it is of *grand cru* status although it is classified as *premier cru*. Les Charmes and Les Fuées are further Chambolle vineyards of note.

CLOS DE VOUGEOT TO NUITS-ST-GEORGES

The Clos de Vougeot is a microcosm of Burgundy: history, pageantry, pomp and circumstance, fascinating complexity and a frustrating lack of consistency. By the time the monks of Cîteaux had planted the vines and enclosed them within stone walls in 1336, they had a 50-hectare vineyard from which they made a harmonious wine by blending the component parts. Today the Clos de Vougeot is so fragmented (having about 80 different owners) that each wine can reflect only where it comes from within the Clos and of course the greater or lesser skills of the winemaker. The top of the Clos has fine, well drained soil suitable for making the classiest wines; down at the bottom by the main road the soil is heavy, the drainage poor and as a result the wines are clumsier.

Within the walls lies the austere 16th-century stone structure of Château du Clos de Vougeot, which is now the headquarters of the Confrérie des Chevaliers du Tastevin. It also houses a museum of vineyard and cellar implements. The colourful Chevaliers are dedicated to promoting Burgundy through patronage and pageantry. They raise funds – and raise the wine's profile – by holding glamorous dinners, banquets, enrolment ceremonies and tastings in the château itself and through the administration of the *tastevinage* awards. Growers submit wines

Clos de Vougeot's forbidding château, built by the monks of Cîteaux in the 16th century, has since 1944 been the property of the Chevaliers du Tastevin.

for blind tastings and those whose wines are accepted may pay a premium to sell their wines with a numbered *tasteviné* label.

Outside the Clos a tiny amount of village Vougeot is produced and a little more *premier cru*, including some interesting white wine. A local cheese-maker also produces a Vougeot and a Vieux Chambolle to go with the better known Amour de Nuits and Ami de Chambertin cheeses.

The village of Flagey Échézeaux lies on 'the wrong side of the tracks'. By convention the wines of this commune are labelled as Vosne-Romanée although the two best vineyards (both *grands crus*) go by their own names, Échézeaux and Les Grands Échézeaux. The former is too big to be consistent, the latter is rather finer. Domaine de la Romanée-Conti has land in both as it does also in the Vosne-Romanée *grands crus* Romanée-St-Vivant and Richebourg. It also owns La Tâche and Romanée-Conti itself. In these vineyards Burgundy can achieve its greatest expression.

Two other tiny *grands crus* are La Romanée and La Grande Rue. The latter, a monopoly of Domaine Lamarche, was promoted only in 1991 despite its location sandwiched between Romanée-Conti and La Tâche. Other excellent wines are made in the *premier cru* vineyards of Les Beauxmonts, Les Suchots and Aux Brulées.

Vosne-Romanée gives way to Nuits-St-Georges, capital of the Côte de Nuits and its commercial centre. The town is home to many of the region's *négociants* including Faiveley, Labouré-Roi and Jean-Claude Boisset, whose dynamic operation has steadily been taking over less successful *négociant* houses.

Nuits-St-Georges itself is somewhat spoilt by having the main road still running through the middle of the town, but there is some good shopping, including a first-class butcher, Gil Vié (7 rue Paul Cabet). On Palm Sunday Nuits-St-Georges holds its annual charity auction, the Hospices de Nuits: junior perhaps to the Hospices de Beaune although the wines are easier to make sense of in the spring than they are in November.

The vineyards of Nuits-St-Georges lie in three sectors. On stony and chalky soil between Vosne-Romanée and the town of Nuits the most elegant wines from *premiers crus* such as Boudots, Murgers and Vignes Rondes are grown. Just south of Nuits, where the soil is mostly clay mixed with gravel, is the heartland of the appellation providing the richest and longest lived wines including Les Pruliers, Les Porrets, Les St-Georges and Vaucrains. No vineyard is ranked as *grand cru,* although Les St-Georges would be the prime candidate. The fact that no sites attained that status is sometimes attributed to the modesty at the time of the classification of the town's mayor, Henri Gouges.

The third sector lies in the village of Prémeaux-Prissey where the soil is mostly of a reddish clay. The best vineyards here are the Clos des Argillières, Clos de l'Arlot and Clos de la Maréchale. A few growers also produce some white Nuits-St-Georges, usually made with a version of Pinot Blanc rather than with Chardonnay.

The Côte de Nuits ends with Comblanchien and Corgoloin, dusty villages spattered with the detritus of the important marble quarries. The vineyards here make wines that can be sold only as Côte de Nuits-Villages. The final vineyard, marking the historical limit of the diocese of Langres and the end of the Côte de Nuits, is the Clos des Langres.

In the hills behind the Côte de Nuits lie a group of small scattered villages, many of which produce agreeable and relatively inexpensive red and white wine under the appellation of Hautes-Côtes de Nuits. Plenty of Crème de Cassis and other fruit liqueurs are produced in villages such as Arcenant. In Marey-lès-Fussey the Maison des Hautes-Côtes has a wine-tasting room and restaurant promoting the products of this part of the region.

Light, lime-bearing soil gives Chambolle-Musigny exceptionally fine structure.

PRODUCERS OF SPECIAL INTEREST

MARSANNAY-LA-CÔTE
Domaine Bart
21160 Marsannay-la-Côte
Bruno Clair
21160 Marsannay-la-Côte
Bernard Coillot
21160 Marsannay-la-Côte
Domaine Collotte
21160 Marsannay-la-Côte
Domaine Fougeray de Beauclair
21160 Marsannay-la-Côte
Château de Marsannay
21160 Marsannay-la-Côte

FIXIN
Vincent & Denis Berthaut
21220 Fixin
Pierre Gelin 21220 Fixin
Philippe Joliet 21220 Fixin
Jean-Michel Molin 21220 Fixin

GEVREY-CHAMBERTIN
Denis Bachelet
21220 Gevrey-Chambertin
Lucien Boillot
21220 Gevrey-Chambertin
Pierre Bourée
21220 Gevrey-Chambertin

Alain Burguet
21220 Gevrey-Chambertin
Camus Père et Fils
21220 Gevrey-Chambertin
Philippe Charlopin
21220 Gevrey-Chambertin
Pierre Damoy
21220 Gevrey-Chambertin
Domaine Drouhin Laroze
21220 Gevrey-Chambertin
Claude & Maurice Dugat
21220 Gevrey-Chambertin
Bernard Dugat-Py
21220 Gevrey-Chambertin
Michel Esmonin et Fille
21220 Gevrey-Chambertin
Dominique Gallois
21220 Gevrey-Chambertin
Geantet-Pansiot
21220 Gevrey-Chambertin
Philippe Leclerc
21220 Gevrey-Chambertin
René Leclerc
21220 Gevrey-Chambertin
Henri Magnien
21220 Gevrey-Chambertin
Domaine Maume
21220 Gevrey-Chambertin
Domaine Denis Mortet
21220 Gevrey-Chambertin
A rising star as evidenced by

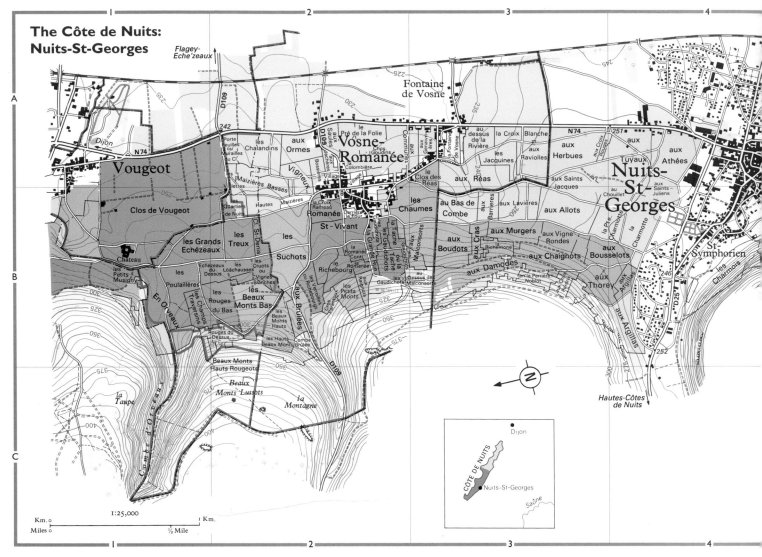

The Côte de Nuits: Nuits-St-Georges

1:25,000

Km. 0   1 Km.

Miles 0   ½ Mile

CÔTE DE NUITS

Hautes-Côtes de Nuits

---

superlative '93s with a clutch of single-vineyard Gevrey-Chambertins and a tiny holding of *grand cru*. Fine, deep-coloured wines with definition.

Thierry Mortet
21220 Gevrey-Chambertin

Henri Rebourseau
21220 Gevrey-Chambertin

Philippe Rossignol
21220 Gevrey-Chambertin

Joseph Roty
21220 Gevrey-Chambertin
Maverick winemaker of skill and passion who employs new oak to good use. Wines of power and purity which age well, especially the Charmes-Chambertin from exceptionally old vines.

Domaine Armand Rousseau
21220 Gevrey-Chambertin
The grand old domaine of Gevrey-Chambertin. Grandson Eric is making wines as fabulous as ever – majestic Chambertin, Chambertin Clos de Bèze and Gevrey-Chambertin Clos St-Jacques lead the field.

Serafin Père et Fils
21220 Gevrey-Chambertin

Domaine Tortochot
21220 Gevrey-Chambertin

Louis Trapet
21220 Gevrey-Chambertin

Vachet Rousseau
21220 Gevrey-Chambertin

Domaine des Varoilles
21220 Gevrey-Chambertin

MOREY-ST-DENIS

Domaine Pierre Amiot et Fils
21220 Morey-St-Denis

Domaine Arlaud
21220 Morey-St-Denis

Guy Castagnier
21220 Morey-St-Denis

Clos de Tart 21220 Morey-St-Denis

Domaine Dujac
21220 Morey-St-Denis
A domaine created over the last 30 years by owner Jacques Seysses. He specialises in fabulously elegant, perfumed wines which are deceptively long lived even if light in colour.

Robert Groffier
21220 Morey-St-Denis

Domaine des Lambrays
21220 Morey-St-Denis

Georges Lignier
21220 Morey-St-Denis

Hubert Lignier
21220 Morey-St-Denis

Henri Perrot Minot
21220 Morey-St-Denis

Domaine Ponsot
21220 Morey-St-Denis
Produces of a range of *grand cru* wines in Morey-St-Denis and Gevrey-Chambertin. The grapes are picked late, the wine is aged for nearly two years in cask and is bottled without being fined, filtered or sulphured. In great vintages the wines are outstanding.

Bernard Raphet
21220 Morey-St-Denis

Domaine Jean Raphet
21220 Morey-St-Denis

Domaine Louis Rémy
21220 Morey-St-Denis

Domaine B Serveau et Fils
21220 Morey-St-Denis

Domaine Taupenot-Merme
21220 Morey-St-Denis

J Truchot Martin
21220 Morey-St-Denis

CHAMBOLLE-MUSIGNY

Barthod-Noëllat
21220 Chambolle-Musigny

Domaine Bertheau
21220 Chambolle-Musigny

Château de Chambolle-Musigny
21220 Chambolle-Musigny
Proprietor Frédéric Mugnier has been making increasingly fine wines since 1985: perfumed Chambolle, luxurious Amoureuses, firmer Bonnes Mares and a sumptuous Musigny – all of which are precisely defined.

Domaine Comte Georges de Vogüé 21220 Chambolle-Musigny
Georges de Vogüé has the largest holdings of Bonnes Mares and Musigny and, especially since 1990, has made breathtaking wines. Also makes a rare white Musigny, though the old vines have just been replanted.

Domaine Henri Felletig
21220 Chambolle-Musigny

Daniel Moine Hudelot
21220 Chambolle-Musigny

Domaine Georges Roumier
21220 Chambolle-Musigny
Now in the able hands of grandson

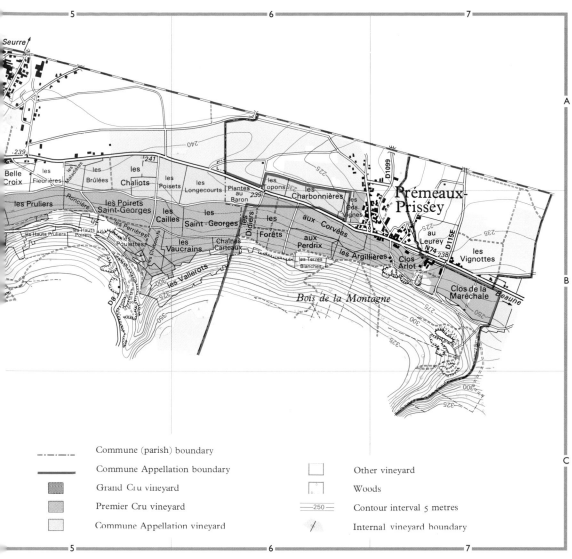

Commune (parish) boundary

Commune Appellation boundary

Grand Cru vineyard

Premier Cru vineyard

Commune Appellation vineyard

Other vineyard

Woods

—250— Contour interval 5 metres

Internal vineyard boundary

vineyards as Vosne-Romanée, Cros Parentoux and Échézeaux.

Jacqueline Jayer
21700 Vosne-Romanée

Domaine Lamarche
21700 Vosne-Romanée

Domaine Leroy
21700 Vosne-Romanée
Built up since 1988 by Lalou Bize-Leroy from the former Domaine Charles Noëllat along with additional purchases. Sublime wines made from almost ridiculously low yields from bio-dynamically cultivated old vines. Some mistrust the cult status and prices while admiring the wines. Leroy also exists as a *négociant* house in Auxey-Duresses.

Domaine Méo-Camuzet 21700 Vosne-Romanée
First made famous when Henri Jayer was responsible for the wines (until 1988). Exemplary intense and oaky wines, wonderfully expressed in the major vintages. A fine range throughout Vosne-Romanée and Nuits-St-Georges plus Corton and Clos de Vougeot.

Domaine Mongeard-Mugneret
21700 Vosne-Romanée
Jean Mongeard retired after his 50th vintage ('95) having created a loyal following for his charming, softly oaked and ripely fruity wines.

Domaine Mugneret Gibourg
21700 Vosne-Romanée

Domaine Pernin-Rossin 21700 Vosne-Romanée

Domaine de la Romanée-Conti
21700 Vosne-Romanée
Produces only *grand cru* wines: Échézeaux, Les Grands Échézeaux, Romanée-St-Vivant, Richebourg, La Tâche and Romanée-Conti. The last two are monopolies, all are fabulous in price and (usually) in quality. Also produces a little white, Le Montrachet.

Émmanuel Rouget
21700 Vosne-Romanée

Robert Sirugue
21700 Vosne-Romanée

Jean Tardy 21700 Vosne-Romanée

NUITS-ST-GEORGES

Marcel Bocquenet
21700 Nuits-St-Georges

Domaine Jean Chauvenet 21700 Nuits-St-Georges

Robert Chevillon
21700 Nuits-St-Georges
Makes an attractive and reasonably priced range of Nuits-St-Georges *premiers crus* from this long-standing domaine – notably Les St-Georges, Vaucrains, Chaignots and Pruliers.

Domaine Guy Dufouleur 21700 Nuits-St-Georges

Domaine Henri Gouges 21700 Nuits-St-Georges
One of the original domaine bottlers in the 1930s, Gouges came back on

Christophe, Roumier has a fine range of wines from Chambolle-Musigny, Morey-St-Denis and Gevrey-Chambertin plus a touch of Corton Charlemagne. The best of old-fashioned methods have been updated with modern competence.

Hervé Roumier
21220 Chambolle-Musigny

VOUGEOT

Domaine Bertagna 21640 Vougeot

Georges Clerget 21640 Vougeot

Domaine Engel
21700 Vosne-Romanée

Domaine Jean Grivot
21700 Vosne-Romanée

Domaine Anne et François Gros
21700 Vosne-Romanée

Domaine Alain Hudelot-Noëllat
21640 Vougeot

Domaine Méo-Camuzet
21700 Vosne-Romanée (see also Vosne-Romanée)

Domaine Denis Mortet
21220 Gevrey-Chambertin

Domaine Jacques Prieur
21190 Meursault

Domaine Jean Raphet
21220 Morey-St-Denis

Château de la Tour
21640 Vougeot

VOSNÉ-ROMANÉE

Robert Arnoux
21700 Vosne-Romanée

Jacques Cacheux
21700 Vosne-Romanée

Domaine Sylvain Cathiard 21700 Vosne-Romanée

Jacky Confuron Cotidot 21700 Vosne-Romanée

Domaine René Engel 21700 Vosne-Romanée
Grandson Philippe makes his small range of wines including *grands crus* Les Grands Échézeaux and Clos de Vougeot to a standard that would have delighted his legendary grandfather René.

Domaine François Gerbet 21700 Vosne-Romanée

Domaine Jean Grivot 21700 Vosne-Romanée
Expect great things now that Étienne Grivot has matured as a winemaker

after an uncertain learning curve. A clutch of Nuits-St-Georges and Vosne-Romanée *premiers crus* leads up to Clos de Vougeot and a sublime Richebourg.

Domaine Anne et François Gros
21700 Vosne-Romanée

Domaine Anne-Françoise Gros
21700 Vosne-Romanée

Domaine Gros Frère et Soeur
21700 Vosne-Romanée

Jean Gros 21700 Vosne-Romanée
Patriarch of a distinguished family which includes sons Michel (responsible for Domaines Jean Gros and Michel Gros), Bernard (Domaine Gros Frère et Soeur), daughter Anne-Françoise (Domaine Anne-Françoise Gros) plus niece Anne (Domaine Anne et François Gros). Excellent wines overall, especially from Anne-Françoise Gros.

Michel Gros 21700 Vosne-Romanée

Henri Jayer 21700 Vosne-Romanée
Now retired, Henri is still everybody's hero for the magnificently harmonious perfumed wines of great depth and complexity that he made from such

87

form in the late 1980s with high-class Nuits-St-Georges from such *premiers crus* as Les St-Georges, Vaucrains, Chaignots and Pruliers plus a monopoly of Clos des Porrets St-Georges.

Hospices de Nuits
21700 Nuits-St-Georges
Dominique Laurent
21700 Nuits-St-Georges
Domaine Lecheneaut
21700 Nuits-St-Georges
Maison Jean Claude Boisset
21700 Nuits-St-Georges
Maison F Chauvenet
21700 Nuits-St-Georges
Maison Dufouleur Père et Fils
21700 Nuits-St-Georges
Maison Joseph Faiveley
21700 Nuits-St-Georges
One of Burgundy's most uncompromising and reliable *négociants* making mostly red wines which are built to last. A good

number of vineyards, mainly in Nuits-St-Georges and Mercurey.
Maison Geisweiler & Fils
21700 Nuits-St-Georges
Maison Labouré-Roi
21700 Nuits-St-Georges
Maison Moillard
21700 Nuits-St-Georges
Domaine Alain Michelot
21700 Nuits-St-Georges
Domaine Remoriquet
21700 Nuits-St-Georges

PRÉMEAUX-PRISSEY
Domaine Ambroise
21700 Prémeaux-Prissey
Domaine de l'Arlot
21700 Prémeaux-Prissey
Owned by AXA-Millésimes, the estate is run by Jean Pierre de Smets who makes expressive, deliciously fruity Nuits-St-Georges from several vineyards and a good white Clos de l'Arlot.

Robert Dubois
21700 Prémeaux-Prissey
Domaine Machard de Gramont
21700 Prémeaux-Prissey
Domaine Daniel Rion et Fils
21700 Prémeaux-Prissey
Produces deeply coloured, tightly constructed Nuits-St-Georges, Vosne-Romanée, Chambolle-Musigny and Clos de Vougeot in a style which impresses when young but needs time to open out.
Domaine Patrice & Michèle Rion 21700 Prémeaux-Prissey

HAUTES-CÔTES DE NUITS
Domaine Marcel & Bernard Fribourg 21700 Villers-La Faye
Yves Chaley 21220 Curtil-Vergy
Claude Cornu 21700 Magny-lès-Villers
Bernard Hudelot-Verdel
21700 Villars-Fontaine
Robert Jayer-Gilles
21700 Magny-lès-Villers
Henri Naudin-Ferrand
21700 Magny-lès-Villers
Simon Fils 21700 Marey-lès-Fussey
Thévenot-le-Brun & Fils
21700 Marey-lès-Fussey
Alain Verdet 21700 Arcenant
Thierry Vigot 21220 Messanges

WINE ACTIVITIES

France's best-known wine fraternity is undoubtedly **La Confrérie des Chevaliers du Tastevin**, which promotes the wines of the Côte d'Or in an intelligent and exuberant fashion. The 'Knights' are owners of the Château de Vougeot, where several times a year banquets and enthronements are organised. In addition there are wine-tastings twice a year: wines that pass the panel's tasting are distinguished by the epithet 'tasteviné' and are given a special numbered label. Savigny-lès-Beaune has its own fraternity, **La Cousinerie de Bourgogne**.

WINE AUCTION

Nuits-St-Georges An auction at the Hospices de Nuits is held on the Sunday before Palm Sunday. On this day and on the Saturday before, hundreds of Côte d'Or wines can be tasted in the local salle des fêtes.

WINE FÊTE

On the Saturday after January 22 every year the villages take it in turns to celebrate the St-Vincent Tournant in which this patron saint of wine-growers is honoured by delegations from the whole district. Despite the winter cold this is usually a warming occasion, not least because the wine flows so liberally.

Morey-St-Denis On the Friday before Palm Sunday the village puts its wines on show in the salle des fêtes and visitors are welcome in the cellars. The occasion is called the Carrefour de Dionysos.

HOTELS

Hôtel Les Grands Crus
21220 **Gevrey-Chambertin**
Tel (0)380 34 34 15
Comfortable hotel built in 1976 in a quiet position near the local château. Stylish rooms and a garden.
Château de Gilly 21640 **Gilly-lès-Cîteaux** Tel (0)380 62 29 98
Grand hotel (Relais et Châteaux) originally belonging to the monks of Cîteaux who used to age their wines made in Clos de Vougeot here. Formal restaurant with extensive wine-list and learned sommelier.
Castel de Très Grand 21220 **Morey-St-Denis** Tel (0)380 34 33 09
Good sized rooms. Also a restaurant.
Hostellerie La Gentilhommière
21700 **Nuits-St-Georges**
Tel (0)380 61 12 06
A spacious old building in a peaceful setting west of Nuits, on the road to Meuilley. Good traditional food.

RESTAURANTS

Auberge du Moulin aux Canards
21170 **Aubigny-en-Plaine**
Tel (0)380 29 98 40
Secluded restaurant in a small village in the country. Specialises in duck, as you would imagine.
Le Chambolle 21220 **Chambolle-Musigny** Tel (0)380 62 86 26
Simple menu which does not change much (try compôte de lapereau à la confiture d'oignons followed by gâteau d'agneau au basilic). Good range of bottles from growers in the village, including some older vintages.
Thibert 21000 **Dijon**
Tel (0)380 67 74 64
Probably the most inventive cook in the Côte d'Or with a real flair for matching flavours. Also passionate about wine. Hôtel Wilson is attached.
Chez Jeannette 21200 **Fixin**
Tel (0)380 52 45 49
Rustic decor and traditional cuisine, plus a simple hotel.
Losset 21640 **Flagey Échézeaux**
Tel (0)380 62 88 10
Very popular with local wine-growers because of its well prepared regional dishes.
Les Millésimes
21200 **Gevrey-Chambertin**
Tel (0)380 51 84 24
A family concern with a friendly welcome. The dining room is a vaulted cellar which contained 48,000 bottles at the last count. Classic, fairly rich dishes.

The history of Clos de Vougeot's walled vineyard spans some 700 years.

Nuits-St-Georges, the geographical and busy commercial centre of the Côte de Nuits, bears one of the most evocative names in Burgundy.

Rôtisserie du Chambertin
21200 **Gevrey-Chambertin**
Tel (0)380 34 33 20
In a luxuriously converted 18th-century cellar. Escargots and coq au vin cooked with finesse. There is now also a bistro version.

Maison des Hautes-Côtes
21700 **Marey-lès-Fussey**
Tel (0)380 62 91 29
South-west of Nuits on the D115. Wines from the Hautes-Côtes are served with honest regional dishes.

Les Gourmets
21160 **Marsannay-la-Côte**
Tel (0)380 52 16 32
Full of atmosphere, and reliable food. Interesting paintings on the walls. Good-value set menus are served during the week.

La Côte d'Or 1 rue Thurot
21700 **Nuits-St-Georges**
Tel (0)380 61 06 10
Lies on a corner of the main street and offers fine cooking, an extensive wine-list and a pleasant ambience. The weekday menu is good value. Also has hotel rooms.

La Ferme de Rolle
Hameau de Rolle 21200 **Ternant**
Tel (0)380 61 40 10
Off the D35 beyond Ternant. A convivial place to eat, enthusiastically run in an old farmhouse. Regional cuisine with, for example, agneau en meurette, lapin à la moutarde, grills, and an interesting cheese board.

PLACES OF INTEREST

Arcenant (West of Nuits-St-Georges.) Fortified 13th-century monastery. An excellent source of Crème de Cassis and Framboise.

Bévy Artistic and cultural centre of the Hautes-Côtes.

Brochon Neo-Renaissance château that now serves as a school.

Chambolle-Musigny A 16th-century church with a separate tower and an ancient hollow lime tree in the churchyard. Also a triumphal arch erected for Henri IV.

Chenôve Two mighty, centuries-old wine presses stand in a cellar off the steep village street.

Cîteaux A short drive from Nuits-St-Georges are the remains of the Abbey of Cîteaux whose monks were responsible for developing viticulture in the Côte d'Or during the Middle Ages. Worth a visit for the Gregorian chants, cheese and honey sweets.

Collonges-lès-Bévy A Roman encampment, a Romanesque church and a 7th-century château.

Corgoloin The 18th-century Château de Cussigny forms a well preserved whole.

Curtil-Vergy (Hautes-Côtes.) Ruins of 9th-century St-Vivant abbey.

l'Étang-Vergy (North-west of Nuits.) Walls of a fortress dismantled in 1609.

Fixin In the Parc Noiset there is a museum dedicated to Napoleon and the monumental statue *Reveil de Napoléon* which the Dijon-born sculptor François Rude carved in 1846. Here too is the grave of Noiset himself, a former captain of the Imperial Guard.

Gevrey-Chambertin The 10th-century castle, restored by monks from Cluny in the 13th century, has vaulted wine cellars. The church dates from the 13th–15th centuries. In its interior are beautiful wood carvings and decorated tombstones.

Marey-lès-Fussey (South-west of Nuits-St-Georges.) An 11th-century church, remains of the abbey of Lieu-Dieu des Champs and the Maison des Hautes-Côtes, which offers a wine-tasting room and restaurant.

Nuits-St-Georges Finds from the Gallo-Roman excavations at Les Bolards are on show in the 17th-century bell tower. The church of St-Symphorien is late-Romanesque.

Ternant (North-west of Nuits-St-Georges.) Château dating from 1670. To the west towards Rolle there are two fine dolmens dating from 2000BC.

Villers-la-Faye (West of Comblanchien.) Church dating from the 11th century and a 13th-century château.

Vougeot The Château de Vougeot has a monumental kitchen and 14th-century presses (see also page 84).

The Côte de Beaune

FROM ALOXE-CORTON TO BEAUNE

The Côte de Beaune starts as the Côte de Nuits finishes, with a series of minor villages. Ladoix and Chorey-lès-Beaune are infrequently-seen labels though good wine can come from both. Ladoix' most valuable asset is its small share in the *grand cru* ACs of Corton and Corton-Charlemagne. Whereas most of the Côte d'Or escarpment faces east, the hill of Corton, an impressive landmark with its wood-capped summit, faces mostly south with wings exposed to east and west. The white wine, Corton-Charlemagne, is grown partly on the west-facing slope in the commune of Pernand-Vergelesses, partly on the south-facing slope in Aloxe-Corton and partly on a strip above the 300-metre contour under the crown of the hill which extends to the east as far as Ladoix-Serrigny. There is a greater concentration of limestone here, which makes it more suitable for the production of Chardonnay than of Pinot Noir. When Corton-Charlemagne is made to the highest standards it is majestic: all the power and intensity of great Chardonnay infused with a flinty, mineral quality that makes the palate sparkle.

The *grand cru* for red wines is Corton, though this name in fact covers 21 different vineyard sites including Le Corton. Wines from

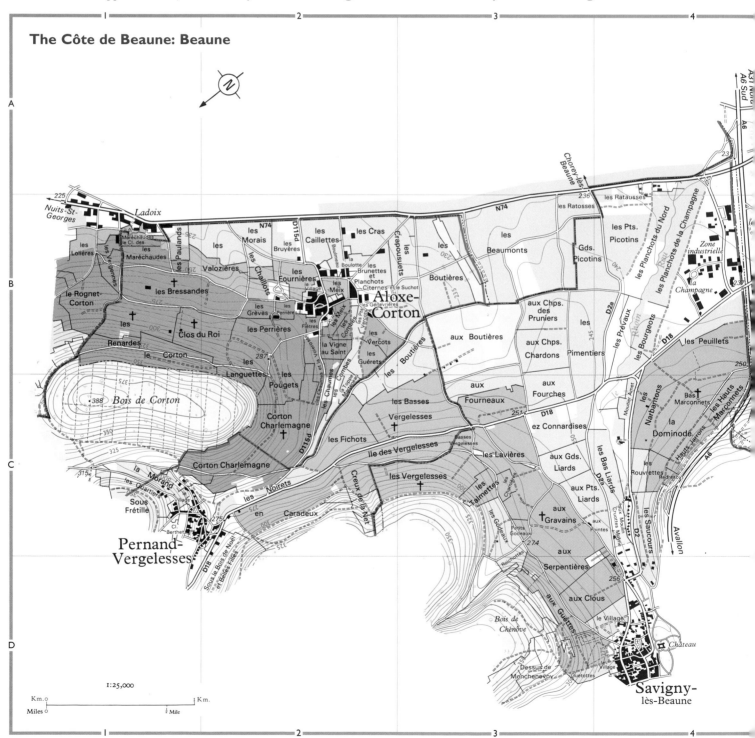

The Côte de Beaune: Beaune

any other part of the *grand cru*, the vineyards situated mid-slope on fine brown soil, may call themselves either Corton or Corton- followed by the name of the vineyard – Bressandes, Clos du Roi, Renardes and Pougets, to name the best of them.

A small quantity of white Corton (without the Charlemagne) is also made including the Corton Cuvée Paul Chanson, and this is sold at the Hospices de Beaune. Aloxe-Corton also produces good village and *premier cru* wine, although prices reflect the supposed added value of the Corton hyphenation.

Better value may well be found in Pernand-Vergelesses and Savigny-lès-Beaune. Pernand-Vergelesses is tucked away at the entrance to a valley leading down from the Hautes-Côtes de

Beaune. On one side are the west-facing vineyards of Corton- Charlemagne, after which Pernand's other best vineyards are Les Vergelesses and Île de Vergelesses which are well exposed on the opposite slope and capable of producing excellent red wines. The remaining reds of Pernand-Vergelesses tend to lack generosity, though there are some remarkable whites which have an interesting flinty, sub-Charlemagne character.

Savigny-lès-Beaune is similarly set back from the main thoroughfare which tends to mean that prices are more attractive. One swathe of vineyards continues from Les Vergelesses towards the village. The soil here is a mix of clay and limestone and the wines are full and long-lasting, if sometimes a little rustic. The

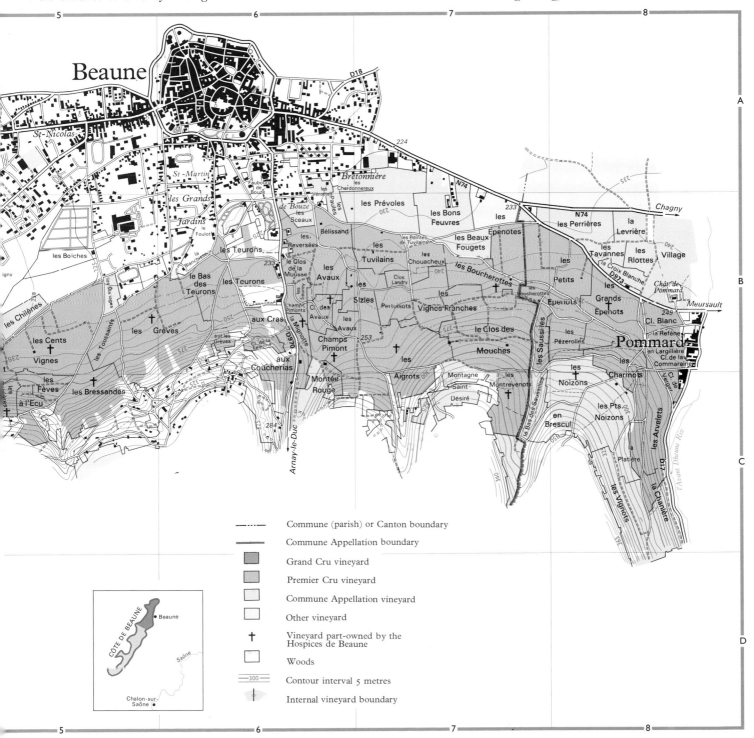

Commune (parish) or Canton boundary

Commune Appellation boundary

Grand Cru vineyard

Premier Cru vineyard

Commune Appellation vineyard

Other vineyard

✝ Vineyard part-owned by the Hospices de Beaune

Woods

══300══ Contour interval 5 metres

Internal vineyard boundary

Hospices de Beaune wines come under the hammer each November at the much fêted auction, launching the commercial campaign for the new vintage.

other major collection, on the far side of the little River Rhoin, is on sandier soil providing slightly lighter though elegant wines from vineyards such as Narbantons and Peuillets. Red Savigny, intriguingly described in a motto engraved above the Château door as "theological, nourishing and disease-defying", is often a sound bet for a decent, sensibly priced bottle of Burgundy. A tiny quantity of white wine is also produced.

The vineyards of Savigny are divided from those of Beaune itself by the A6 autoroute which sweeps down from the hills loaded with traffic from Paris. The Beaune vineyards at the northern end of the appellation continue on the same sandy soil as those at Savigny. The best known vineyards here are Marconnets, Bressandes and Cent Vignes. On the slopes above the town itself are Grèves and Teurons, followed by Vignes Franches and Clos des Mouches near the border with Pommard, where the wines take on a richer, more tannic character. Clos des Mouches is also noted for its highly sought-after, full-bodied and ageworthy white wine, especially that of Joseph Drouhin. Over 70 per cent of the Beaune appellation is ranked as *premier cru* and the great majority is in the hands of the *négociants*. There is a further mini-appellation confusingly known as Côte de Beaune which has a handful of vineyards on top of the Montagne de Beaune.

The town of Beaune is Burgundy's medieval capital and current vinous headquarters. Within the ramparts, much of which remain intact, reside the leading *négociants* or shippers who have dominated the wine scene for generations: Joseph Drouhin, Bouchard Père et Fils, Louis Latour, Louis Jadot and Chanson. Their presence is discreet but their wines may be bought at Denis Perret's wine shop on the place Carnot. Other shops in the vicinity offer a good range of growers' wines.

Not to be missed in Beaune is the Hôtel Dieu, the magnificent former charity hospital founded by Chancellor Nicolas Rolin in 1443. This was the traditional beneficiary of the world's greatest charity wine auction, held annually in Beaune on the third Sunday in November. Over the centuries the hospital has been donated plots in fine Côte d'Or vineyards. With the world's press looking on, burgundies from these sites, still young and in the cask, are sold at extremely high prices. The proceeds go towards the running of the large modern hospital behind the medieval building.

PRODUCERS OF SPECIAL INTEREST

CÔTE DE BEAUNE-VILLAGES
Capitain Gagnerot
21550 Ladoix-Serrigny
Domaine Chevalier Père et Fils
21550 Ladoix-Serrigny
Domaine Edmond Cornu
21550 Ladoix-Serrigny
Domaine Michel Mallard
21550 Ladoix-Serrigny
Domaine André Nudant & Fils
21550 Ladoix-Serrigny
Prince de Mérode
21550 Ladoix-Serrigny
Domaine Gaston & Pierre Ravaut 21550 Ladoix-Serrigny

CHOREY-LÈS-BEAUNE
Domaine Arnoux
21200 Chorey-lès-Beaune
Domaine Jacques Germain
21200 Chorey-lès-Beaune
Domaine Maillard
21200 Chorey-lès-Beaune
Domaine Maldant
21200 Chorey-lès-Beaune
Tollot-Beaut & Fils
21200 Chorey-lès-Beaune
Wide-ranging domaine making supple, attractive wines in Beaune, Aloxe-Corton and Savigny as well as in Chorey-lès-Beaune.

ALOXE-CORTON
Maurice Chapuis
21420 Aloxe-Corton
Château de Corton-André
21420 Aloxe-Corton
La Reine Pédauque
21420 Aloxe-Corton
Domaine Daniel Senard
21420 Aloxe-Corton
Produces a clutch of *grand cru* Corton wines of good quality despite or because of the controversial consultancy of Guy Accad.
Domaine Michel Voarick
21420 Aloxe-Corton

PERNAND-VERGELESSES
Domaine Bonneau du Martray
21420 Pernand-Vergelesses
The leading light in Corton-Charlemagne where the estate has a substantial block of perfectly placed vineyards. The wine is getting better and better under a new generation, as is the small holding of red Corton.
Domaine Marius Delarche
21420 Pernand-Vergelesses
Domaine Denis Père et Fils
21420 Pernand-Vergelesses
Domaine Dubreuil-Fontaine
21420 Pernand-Vergelesses
Domaine Laleure-Piot
21420 Pernand-Vergelesses
Domaine Rapet Père & Fils
21420 Pernand-Vergelesses
Domaine Rollin
21420 Pernand-Vergelesses

SAVIGNY-LÈS-BEAUNE
Domaine Simon Bize & Fils
21420 Savigny-lès-Beaune
A leading light in Savigny where Patrick Bize vinifies from half a dozen different vineyards and makes some intriguing Bourgogne Blanc which includes Pinot Blanc and Pinot Beurot.
Domaine Capron Charcousset
21420 Savigny-lès-Beaune
Domaine de Chandon de Briailles 21420 Savigny-lès-Beaune
Directed by mother and daughter who make often exciting reds from Savigny, Pernand-Vergelesses and Aloxe-Corton as well as a fine white Corton.
Maison Doudet-Naudin 21420 Savigny-lès-Beaune
Maurice Écard
21420 Savigny-lès-Beaune
Domaine Girard Vollot 21420 Savigny-lès-Beaune
Domaine Antonin Guyon 21420 Savigny-lès-Beaune
Jean-Marc Pavelot
21420 Savigny-lès-Beaune
Maison Henri de Villamont
21420 Savigny-lès-Beaune

BEAUNE
Domaine Besançenot
21200 Beaune
Domaine Cauvard Père & Fils
21200 Beaune
Hospices de Beaune
21200 Beaune
Various vignerons are contracted to look after extensive vineyards throughout the Côte de Beaune (and a couple in the Côte de Nuits). Grapes are vinified at the new Hospices *cuverie* by André Porcheret (since 1994) then matured by whichever *négociant* purchases them at the annual sale in November.
Maison Albert Bichot
21200 Beaune
Maison Bouchard Père et Fils
21200 Beaune
Maison Champy Père & Cie
21200 Beaune
Maison Chanson Père & Fils
21200 Beaune
Maison Joseph Drouhin
21200 Beaune
One of the great names for reds (for example Grands Échézeaux and Griotte-Chambertin) and whites (notably the Beaune Clos des Mouches). Excellent integration of oak and fruit.
Maison Camille Giroud
21200 Beaune
Maison Louis Jadot 21200 Beaune
One of the great houses of Beaune selling only Burgundy and Beaujolais. Long-lasting reds which benefit from extended maceration, and dynamic whites. Look out especially for the Corton-Charlemagne and Chevalier-Montrachet (*grand cru* whites) and

their range of reds from Beaune such as Clos des Ursules.

Maison Louis Latour
21200 Beaune
Makes some of the best white wines in the region from simple Montagny to luxurious Corton-Charlemagne, but the controversial reds rarely excite.

Albert Morot 21200 Beaune

Domaine Jean-Claude Rateau 21200 Beaune

WINE AUCTION

The auction (see page 92) is the climax of three days of festival, Les Trois Glorieuses. Wine-tasting and banquets are organised on the preceding Saturday and Beaune is decorated with flowers.

WINE INFORMATION

BIVB 12 boulevard Bretonnière, 21200 Beaune; Tel (0)380 24 70 20

HOTELS

Two busy routes to the south converge in the Côte d'Or, one from Paris and one from the North-East (Germany, the Benelux countries and Scandinavia). Travellers have used these routes for many centuries, thus Beaune has a tradition of hospitality.

Hôtel Clarion
21420 Aloxe-Corton
Tel (0)380 26 46 70
Small hotel with a good reputation. Rooms are furnished in styles from the 1930s and 1950s. Chassagne marble in the bathrooms and lounge.

Hôtel Bellevue 5 route de Seurre
21200 Beaune Tel (0)380 24 05 10
Simple but clean rooms. Restaurant.

Hostellerie de Bretonnière
43 Faubourg Bretonnière, 21200
Beaune Tel (0)380 22 15 77
A decent place to stay, built around an inner car park with a simple garden.

Le Cep 27 rue Maufoux, 21200
Beaune Tel (0)380 22 35 48
Stylish, luxurious rooms and an excellent restaurant under the name of Chef Bernard Morillon.

La Closerie 61 route de Pommard
21200 Beaune Tel (0)380 22 15 07
Functional comfort. Much used by wine merchants and their business customers.

Hôtel Grillon 21 route de Seurre
21200 Beaune Tel (0)380 22 44 25
Peaceful position just outside the centre. During the tourist season room bookings are sometimes conditional on eating in the mediocre restaurant.

Hôtel Henry II 12–14 Faubourg
Nicolas, 21200 Beaune
Tel (0)380 22 83 84
Comparatively new but in a historic

building. Attractive rooms.

Hôtel de la Poste Boulevard Clemenceau, 21200 Beaune
Tel (0)380 22 08 11
On the bypass road, near traffic lights, so for preference choose a room at the rear. Breakfast is excellent and you can eat very well in the elegant restaurant. Among the specialities are crayfish, tartare de saumon and civet de lotte aux pâtes fraîches. Large wine-list.

Samotel route de Pommard
21200 Beaune Tel (0)380 22 35 55
Perfectly adequate rooms overlooking the vineyards, but it may be better to avoid the restaurant.

Le Parc 21200 Levernois
Tel (0)380 22 22 51/(0)380 24 63 00
Quiet country hotel with rooms of rustic decoration and variable comfort.

l'Ouvrée
21420 Savigny-lès-Beaune
Tel (0)380 21 51 52
A pleasant place to sleep and eat. Demi-pension is obligatory during the summer season.

RESTAURANTS

Numerous hotels and restaurants serve regional dishes. These include escargots; jambon persillé (ham in a jelly made with white wine and parsley); eggs or fish en meurette (in a red wine sauce); pauchouse or pochouse (a casserole of freshwater fish); écrevisses (crayfish); coq au vin; boeuf bourguignon and fondue bourguignonne (meat fondue). Blackcurrants are often used in sauces and desserts. For hotels and restaurants see also Côte de Nuits and Chalonnais (pages 88–9 and 101).

La Crémaillière
21190 Auxey-Duresses
Tel (0)380 21 22 60
In some ways this above-average place was more pleasant when it was less formal (and the prices lower). However, the cooking is still good.

Au Bon Accueil La Montagne
21200 Beaune Tel (0)380 22 08 80
This is where the French eat, on the Montagne de Beaune. Strictly regional cuisine and low prices. Initiates call it 'Chez Nono'. Eat outside in summer. Take the D970 out of Beaune, turn right and continue up the hill.

Au P'tit Pressoir
15 place Fleury, 21200 Beaune
Tel (0)380 22 35 50
Simple, genial place to eat. Choose one of the set menus.

Auberge St-Vincent place de la Halle, 21200 Beaune
Tel (0)380 22 42 34
Rustic, but the food is good (magret de canard au baies de cassis, for example) and not too expensive.

Le Bistrot Bourguignon
8 rue Monge, 21200 Beaune
Tel (0)380 22 23 24
Wines by the glass and by the bottle with pâtés, salads, cheeses and other light dishes. Le Patron used to keep goal for Meursault.

La Ciboulette 69 rue Lorraine
21200 Beaune Tel (0)380 24 70 72
Small, pleasant place. Good food, reasonable prices. Friendly service.

Grand Café de Lyon 36 place
Carnot, 21200 Beaune
Tel (0)380 22 23 00
Beaune's favourite meeting place.

Hostellerie de l'Écusson
place Malmédy, 21200 Beaune
Tel (0)380 24 03 82
The cheapest set meal offers good value and the more expensive ones are also satisfactory. Lengthy wine-list.

Jacques Lainé 10–12 boulevard
Foch, 21200 Beaune
Tel (0)380 24 76 10
Old, dignified town house. Great care is taken with the cuisine. Marvellous lamb. Has own car park and terrace.

Rôtisserie de la Paix
47 Faubourg Madeleine, 21200
Beaune Tel (0)380 22 33 33
Tucked away in an alley. Dishes include raviolis de langoustines aux truffes and fricassée de pigeon au vinaigre. Good-value set menus.

Le Relais de Saulx 6 rue Louis-Véry, 21200 Beaune
Tel (0)380 22 01 35
Renowned locally. Small dining room with tiled floor and beams. Besides à la carte specialities such as feuilleté de bar en Crémant de Bourgogne and volaille de Bresse farcie there are attractive set menus. Booking essential.

Hostellerie du Vieux Moulin
21420 Bouilland Tel (0)380 21 51 16
Hotel with some charm. The lower-priced set menus are often more attractive than the dearer ones. Large, rather expensive wine-list.

La Bouzerotte
21200 Bouze-lès-Beaune
Tel (0)380 26 01 37
Simple local restaurant with hearty, nourishing food and a good choice of growers' wines at fair prices.

Le Bareuzai route de Dijon
21200 Chorey-lès-Beaune
Tel (0)380 22 02 90
Looks like a furniture shop from outside, but inside it has atmosphere. Acceptable quality and prices.

Érmitage-Corton route de Dijon
21200 Chorey-lès-Beaune
Tel (0)380 22 05 28
The interior has the grandeur of a small palace. The cuisine, including filet de St-Pierre au basilic, is excellent. Also a luxurious hotel.

Hostellerie de Levernois 21200
Levernois Tel (0)380 24 73 58
A great restaurant and a luxurious hotel surrounded by a spacious park.

PLACES OF INTEREST

Aloxe-Corton The 15th-century Château Corton-André belongs to a wine company. Tastings available.

Beaune A maze of wine cellars stretches under the beautifully preserved centre of Beaune, the capital of Burgundy, and above ground are dozens of wine firms and wine shops. A stroll through the narrow streets gives a glimpse of Beaune's rich architectural heritage. In place Monge, dominated by its 14th-century belfry, stands a tall tower with a remarkable wooden roof. No 10 rue Rousseau-Deslandes is one of the town's most remarkable buildings, the former Hôtel de Cîteaux, dating from the end of the 12th century. On the corner of rue de Lorraine stands the Hospice de la Charité, with its chapel and court. The hôtel de ville is housed in a 17th-century former Ursuline convent. The most beautiful of Beaune's town gates is the Porte St-Nicolas; nearby are the Chapelle de l'Oratoire, the much visited cellars of the firm of La Reine Pédauque and the basilica of Notre-Dame. Despite much alteration and rebuilding this church still has clear traces of Burgundian Romanesque architecture. From April to November marvellous wall tapestries depicting the 'Life of the Virgin' are displayed. The Musée du Vin de Bourgogne, which exhibits a rich collection of objects and works of art connected with wine, is housed in the former 15th–16th-century residence of the dukes of Burgundy.

The magnificent Hôtel-Dieu, completed in 1451, was built to the order of Nicolas Rolin, chancellor to Duke Philippe le Bon, and was in use as an old people's home until 1971. The main buildings, which are now a museum (a modern hospital has been built), have a colourful mosaic of enamelled roof tiles, a paved inner courtyard with old wells, a high-roofed hall for the sick with places for 28 beds, an enormous kitchen and a dispensary. In a second courtyard are statues of Nicolas Rolin and his wife Guigone de Salins together with an exhibition of tapestries, furniture and the sublime altarpiece by Rogier van der Weyden. The Last Judgement (1443), commissioned by the Hospice, is one of the transcendental masterpieces of Flemish art. It alone justifies a visit to Beaune.

Ladoix-Serrigny The 12th-century chapel of Notre-Dame-du-Chemin was for centuries a place of pilgrimage. Serrigny has an 18th-century château.

Savigny-lès-Beaune There is a motor museum in the local château. Note, too, the proverbs carved over various doorways in the village.

THE CÔTE DE BEAUNE:
FROM POMMARD TO PULIGNY-MONTRACHET

Historically, Pommard has a reputation for being the best red-wine village south of Beaune. Its wines should be dark in colour, relatively tough and tannic when young but have a core of fruit waiting to emerge at the end of a decade as the aggressive structure softens. This style is not altogether fashionable at the moment and several producers have run into difficulty by trying to achieve a commercial compromise. The resulting wines, though they may be more supple, are neither typical Pommard nor do they have sufficient charm to seduce the palate.

There is small wine shop just off the town's main road which offers products from a wide range of growers and vineyards.

As usual the favourite vineyards are located in mid-slope. On the Beaune side the best wines come from Les Pézérolles and Les Épenots (including, confusingly, Grand Clos des Épenots and Clos des Épeneaux). On the other side of the village the reddish, iron-rich soil of Les Rugiens yields some of Pommard's finest and longest-lasting wine.

Volnay is the perfect complement to Pommard. The wines are likely to be lighter in colour and overt structure but not in intensity of fruit. In the 18th century they were delicate and much sought-after rosés: today they are wines of grace and finesse comparable

with Chambolle-Musigny in the Côte de Nuits. If you follow the D973 southward, the best *premier cru* vineyards are Clos de la Bousse d'Or, Taillepieds and Clos des Chênes on your right; Champans, Les Caillerets and Santenots on the left. The last is in fact in Meursault, but goes under the courtesy title of Volnay.

Tucked in behind Volnay and Meursault is Monthelie, one of the Côte's most beautiful villages, characterised by narrow streets and gaily-coloured roof tiles. Most of the wines are red, similar to those of Volnay but in a lower key and a touch more rustic. Champs Fulliot, the best vineyards, abut Volnay and Les Duresses. The latter stretches into and gives its name to neighbouring Auxey-Duresses. Here the mix between red and white is more even. The wines of Auxey do not always ripen fully because they are exposed to the cool winds blowing down the valley from the direction of the Hautes-Côtes.

If you follow this valley on the RN73 you will come the village of St-Romain which is split into two halves above and below an impressive cliff face. St-Romain was promoted from being an 'Hautes-Côtes' village to full appellation only in 1967. The wines of both colours are less full bodied than most.

Back on the main face of the Côte d'Or escarpment, Auxey-Duresses' other neighbour is Meursault. Although it is one of the largest of the villages it is still relatively sleepy outside harvest time. Here some of the finest white Burgundy is made. Though

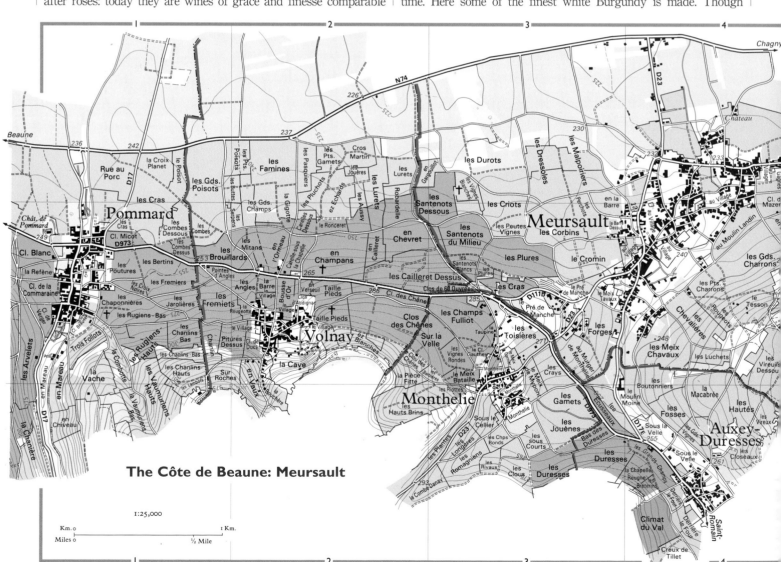

The Côte de Beaune: Meursault

1:25,000

Showplace Château de Meursault, bought by Beaune négociants Patriarche Père et Fils in 1973, has permanent wine-tasting facilities in its spectacular medieval cellars.

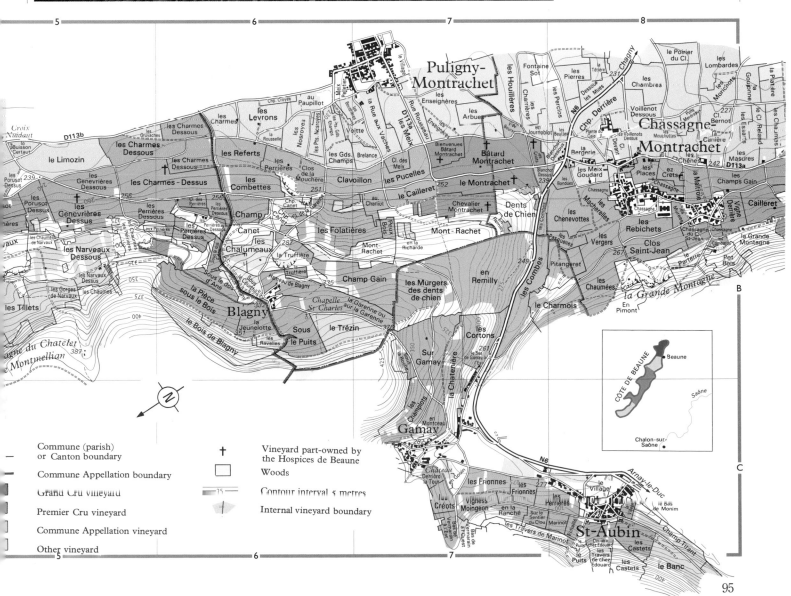

Commune (parish) or Canton boundary

Commune Appellation boundary

Grand Cru vineyard

Premier Cru vineyard

Commune Appellation vineyard

Other vineyard

Vineyard part-owned by the Hospices de Beaune

Woods

Contour interval 5 metres

Internal vineyard boundary

95

Meursault has no *grand cru* vineyard, it can boast three *premiers crus* of the highest class: Perrières, Genevrières and Charmes. Good Meursault is a rich, fat, buttery sort of wine which harmonises well with the oak in which it is fermented and matured.

The water table in Meursault lies considerably further down than in neighbouring Puligny, as a result of which the 'village' wines of Meursault are often superior as the vines' roots can go deeper into the soil. This feature also enables the vignerons to age their wines in cool, naturally insulated underground cellars in a way that is not possible in Puligny. There are many individual growers in Meursault, a number of whom advertise by means of large placards on their walls. It is sometimes wise to beware of those who advertise too forcefully.

The possession of part of the Montrachet vineyard has been a great boon to Puligny and Chassagne, both of which added Montrachet to their names late in the 19th century. In Puligny the top wines are magnificent: the *grands crus* Le Montrachet and Bâtard-Montrachet (both shared with Chassagne) as well as all of Chevalier-Montrachet and Bienvenues-Bâtard-Montrachet. The *premier cru* vineyards of Les Demoiselles, Les Caillerets, Pucelles and Combettes are not far behind in quality. Puligny-Montrachet should be the most refined of all white Burgundy, enticingly floral and nuanced in bouquet with a steely core on the palate, though 'village' level wines can be disappointing given their high price.

Those looking for value might do better to try St-Aubin, one of the villages set back up a side valley. About one third of the production is white in a style that has some affinity to Puligny. The remainder is red in a straightforward fruity vein, like red Chassagne-Montrachet only more supple. The best vineyards are Les Frionnes (for red), La Chatenière, En Remilly and the delightfully named Les Murgers Dents de Chien.

Mechanisation is a relatively new concept in the ancient vineyards of Volnay.

PRODUCERS OF SPECIAL INTEREST

POMMARD
Domaine Aleth LeRoyer Girardin 21630 Pommard
Domaine Billard Gonnet 21630 Pommard
Jean-Marc Boillot 21630 Pommard
Jean-Marc, grandson of the late Étienne Sauzet, has put together a sizeable domaine from his Boillot and Sauzet inheritances. He makes rich, oaky white wines mainly from Puligny-Montrachet and fine reds (Volnay, Pommard) of clearly defined vineyard character.
Domaine Comte Armand 21630 Pommard
Brilliant wines have been made by Pascal Marchand since '85: intense, deep-coloured Pommard Clos des Épeneaux of great ageing potential. The domaine was extended in 1994 and 1995 to include some Volnay, Meursault and Auxey-Duresses.
Domaine Coste Caumartin 21630 Pommard
Domaine de Courcel 21630 Pommard
The estate is best known for its rich if quite supple Pommard from leading vineyards such as Rugiens and Grand Clos des Épenots.
Domaine Michel Gaunoux 21630 Pommard
Domaine Jean-Luc Joillot 21630 Pommard
Domaine Raymond Launay 21630 Pommard
Domaine Lejeune 21630 Pommard
Domaine Mussy 21630 Pommard
Domaine Parent 21630 Pommard

VOLNAY
Domaine Bitouzet-Prieur 21190 Volnay
Jean-Marc Bouley 21190 Volnay
Domaine Yvon Clerget 21190 Volnay
Domaine Michel Lafarge 21190 Volnay
Sets the standard for red wines which are packed with fruit when young and open out very generously after a few years without ever losing their precise definition. A sumptuous Volnay Clos des Chênes.
Domaine du Marquis d'Angerville 21190 Volnay
The eminent Marquis owns a clutch of fine Volnay vineyards whose grapes are vinified with classical care and attention. Wines of great breeding, especially Clos des Ducs and Taillepieds.
Hubert de Montille 21190 Volnay
A distinguished range of Volnay and Pommard, austere when young but superlative when mature. He made the best '83 reds in Burgundy: his '85s were still not ready in 1996.

Domaine de la Pousse d'Or 21190 Volnay
Skillfully managed by Gérard Potel since 1984, now in conjunction with his son. Volnays of finesse, breeding and staying power (especially Clos de la Bousse d'Or and Clos des 60 Ouvrées) plus Pommard and Santenay.
Joseph Voillot 21190 Volnay

MEURSAULT
Robert Ampeau et Fils 21190 Meursault
A maverick in commercial policy but a main-liner for quality. The domaine's excellent range of Meursault, Puligny, Volnay and Savigny are sold only when approximately mature, at somewhere between five and 15 years old.
Domaine Ballot-Millot 21190 Meursault
Michel Bouzereau 21190 Meursault
Yves Boyer Martenot 21190 Meursault
Alain Coche-Debord 21190 Meursault
Jean-François Coche-Dury 21190 Meursault
This domaine, tiny in size but vast in stature, makes some of the most astonishingly fine white Burgundy of all including Meursault Perrières and Corton-Charlemagne.
Domaine des Comtes Lafon 21190 Meursault
Long known for its outstanding white wines of Meursault (Clos de la Barre, Charmes, Genevrières, Perrières) and Montrachet, the domaine now produces exceptional Volnay (Santenots, Clos des Chênes and Champans) as well.
Domaine Darnat 21190 Meursault
Jean-Philippe Fichet 21190 Meursault
Henri Germain & Fils 21190 Meursault
Domaine Albert Grivault 21190 Meursault
Patrick Javillier 21190 Meursault
Charles & Rémi Jobard 21190 Meursault
François Jobard 21190 Meursault
Joseph Matrot 21190 Meursault
Château de Meursault 21190 Meursault
Owned by the house of Patriarche which is justly proud of its flagship: intense, oaky Bourgogne Blanc Clos du Château (the front garden!) and a fine *cuvée* of Meursault made mostly from *premier cru* vineyards.
Domaine Michelot 21190 Meursault
Domaine Pierre Morey 21190 Meursault
Domaine Jacques Prieur 21190 Meursault
The domaine has been revived after

uncertain times by co-owner Antonin Rodet. It owns *grands crus* from one end of the Côte to the other, from Chambertin to Montrachet via Musigny and Clos de Vougeot.

Domaine Rougeot
21190 Meursault

Domaine Guy Roulot
21190 Meursault
A top name in Meursault, Roulot is now run with flair by Jean-Marc Roulot and his wife Alix (née de Montille). Look out for superb Meursault Tesson Le Clos de Mon Plaisir.

MONTHELIE
Domaine Darviot Perrin
21190 Monthelie

Paul Garaudet
21190 Monthelie

Château de Monthelie
21190 Monthelie

Domaine Monthelie Douhairet
21190 Monthelie

Domaine Potinet-Ampeau
21190 Monthelie

AUXEY-DURESSES
Jean-Pierre Diconne
21190 Auxey-Duresses

Maison Leroy 21190
Auxey-Duresses
A long-established *négociant* house, run by Lalou Bize-Leroy, with an awesome stock of some of Burgundy's grandest appellations going back over 50 years. Be prepared to pay handsome prices.

Michel Prunier
21190 Auxey-Duresses

Roger Prunier
21190 Auxey-Duresses

Roy Frères 21190 Auxey-Duresses

PULIGNY-MONTRACHET
Domaine Louis Carillon
21190 Puligny-Montrachet
An exemplary family estate which has upgraded itself in the 1980s and 1990s from a good performer to one of the very best.

Domaine Jean Chartron
21190 Puligny-Montrachet

Gérard Chavy et Fils
21190 Puligny-Montrachet

Philippe Chavy
21190 Puligny-Montrachet

Domaine Henri Clerc & Fils
21190 Puligny-Montrachet

Domaine Leflaive
21190 Puligny-Montrachet
The grandest name in Puligny in the heyday of Vincent Leflaive, now once again blazing a trail under the management of his daughter Anne-Claude who has been pioneering biodynamic techniques.

Olivier Leflaive Frères
21190 Puligny-Montrachet
A *négociant* business specialising in white wines that are beautifully made now by Franck Grux, and before

him by Jean-Marc Boillot.

Jean Pascal
21190 Puligny-Montrachet

Paul Pernot & Fils
21190 Puligny-Montrachet

Étienne Sauzet
21190 Puligny-Montrachet
Leflaive's long-term rival for the top spot with magnificent Puligny-Montrachet les Combettes and Bâtard-Montrachet. Now winemaker Gérard Boudot has also to buy in grapes to keep up with demand. Quality has not faltered.

WINE ACTIVITIES

Meursault On the Monday following Beaune's wine auction Meursault celebrates its Paulée in the Château de Meursault. This is a huge lunch party to which every grower takes bottles from his own cellar. Interest in the Paulée de Meursault is so great that every year many would-be participants have to be disappointed, so a second event of exactly the same kind has been created, the Banée de Meursault, held at the beginning of September. On the following day the Trinquée de Meursault, a tasting of local wines on a grand scale, takes place.

HOTELS

Les Charmes 21190 Meursault
Tel (0)380 21 23 23
Attractive hotel in the middle of the village. No restaurant.

Les Magnolias
21190 Meursault
Tel (0)380 21 23 23
Utterly delightful small hotel. without a restaurant. Beautifully appointed and well priced.

RESTAURANTS

Le Relais de la Diligence 21190 Meursault Tel (0)380 21 21 32
Not in the village itself but some distance east of the Route Nationale. Good traditional cooking.

Le Montrachet 21190 Puligny-Montrachet Tel (0)380 21 30 06
This restaurant is worth a detour. The cooking is excellent and the cellar has a choice selection of local and regional wines. Also a hotel.

Le Moulin d'Hauterive
71350 St-Gervais-en-Vallière
Tel (0)385 91 55 56
Outside the wine district, south-east of Beaune. A small hotel peacefully situated by a river. The cooking is recommended. Demi-pension obligatory in season.

L'Ouillette 21590 Santenay
Tel (0)380 20 62 34
Tasty country dishes such as perch in Aligoté sauce, coq au vin and entrecôte grillé.

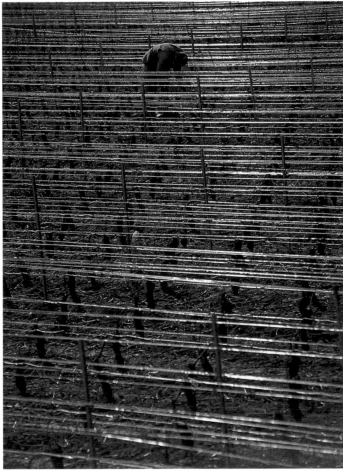

Wires are stretched between stakes to support the tender new growth.

Auberge des Vignes
N74, 21190 Volnay
Tel (0)380 22 24 48
The restaurant has a pleasant rustic interior and its expert chef produces good-value set menus. Dishes include a succulent roast quail - caille rôtie à la grume de raisin. Estate names appear on the wine-list – a practice which is less common than you might think in Burgundy.

PLACES OF INTEREST

Auxey-Duresses The 14th–15th century church shelters a 16th-century triptych.

Meursault The cellars of the Château de Meursault are impressive and well worth a visit. A wine-tasting is always laid out in the crypt-like vaults. The splendidly restored 15th- to 19th-century building now houses a wine farm. The Boisseaux family (of Patriarche Père & Fils) who own the château sometimes arrange exhibitions of paintings on a wine theme. The Paulée de Meursault (see Wine Activities above) takes place here every year in the *cuverie*. Meursault also has a fine town hall and the Gothic church of St-Nicolas.

Nolay Picturesque village with half-timbered houses and a 14th-century market hall.

La Rochepot Dominated by the 15th-century château and its polychrome roof which has a splendid dining hall and a terrace offering a fine view. In the village itself there is a 12th-century Benedictine church.

St-Romain A wine village in two parts, upper and lower. A signposted footpath takes you to the site of a medieval castle. Archaeological finds are displayed in the *mairie* from July to September.

Santenay One of the first Gothic churches of the region, St-Jean-de-Narosse was built here at the foot of the Mont de Sène at the beginning of the 13th century. The Mont, 521m high, has a viewing point. The Château Philippe-le-Hardi, in good condition and with a 14th-century keep and large cellars, belongs to a wine-grower. Santenay also has medicinal springs and a rather staid casino.

Volnay The 14th-century church has been carefully restored. A 16th-century chapel stands near the N73 and the village is dominated by the century-old statue of Notre-Dame-des-Vignes.

THE CÔTE DE BEAUNE:
SOUTH FROM CHASSAGNE

The main pre-autoroute Paris-Lyon road, the Route Nationale 6, separates most of Chassagne from Puligny. This might have an adverse commercial effect if Chassagne did not enjoy its share of Le Montrachet and Bâtard-Montrachet along with the tiny and rarely seen *grand cru* Criots-Bâtard-Montrachet.

Apart from these sites and a handful of excellent *premier cru* vineyards such as Les Caillerets, Ruchottes, Les Vergers and Chaumées, Chassagne-Montrachet becomes more of a red-wine village as the soil changes further south. Production of reds used to be significantly higher but the commercial success of the white wines, based partly on the vogue for Chardonnay and partly on the excellent quality of Chassagne's most suitable vineyards, has led to a great deal of 'red' soil being replanted with white. With occasional exceptions in vineyards such as Clos Jean or La Boudriotte, red Chassagne-Montrachet is too rustic and inelegant to be counted among the better wines of the Côte.

Visitors to Chassagne can taste an extensive range of wines at the *Caveau* attached to the local general store. Tasting is free if you subsequently buy, otherwise a small charge is made.

Beaune seems far away by the time you reach the next village, Santenay, which is divided into two: the main village below and an upper section complete with thermal baths and a modest casino above. Here the famous escarpment that allows the glories of the Côte d'Or to be realised starts to diverge from its north–south line towards the west. Santenay produces mostly red wines and these make up in body what they lack in elegance. The best vineyards such as La Comme, Gravières and Clos de Tavannes lie on the border with Chassagne.

Beyond Santenay, over the border in the Saône-et-Loire *département*, lie three villages, Dezize-lès-Maranges, Cheilly-lès-Maranges and Sampigny-lès-Maranges, each of which used each to have its own appellation although the wines were almost always sold as Côte de Beaune-Villages.

Since 1989, to the relief of all, the wines have gone under the appellation of Maranges, the principal vineyard being shared by the three villages. There is a clear determination to make something of this newcomer. The wines are mostly red, deep in colour with plenty of fruit, but there is a considerable tannic threshold to be overcome before they are ready to drink.

Above: Named after the first duke of Burgundy, Château Philippe le Hardi (Philip the Bold) in Santenay retains its massive 14th-century tower.

Far left and left: Wine drawn direct from the barrel is assessed by the maître de chais. *The silver tastevin maximises the reflection of light through the wine.*

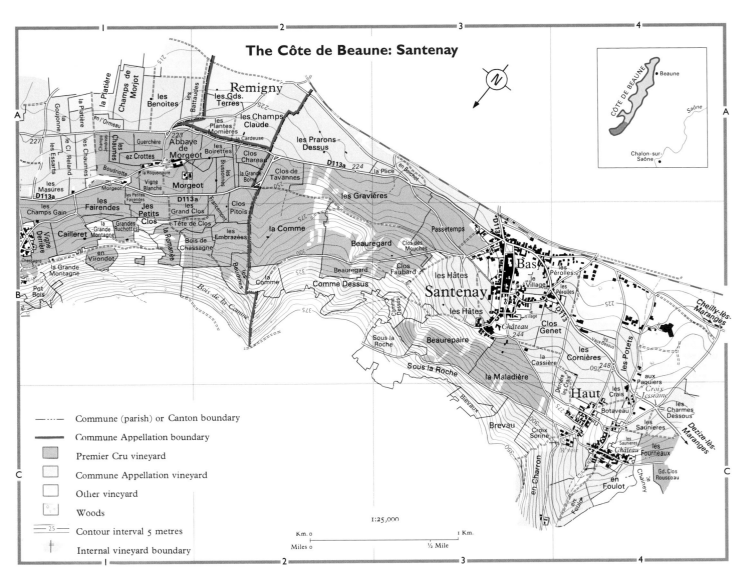

The Côte de Beaune: Santenay

Remigny

Santenay

Bas

Haut

Cheilly-les-Maranges

Dezize-les-Maranges

Commune (parish) or Canton boundary

Commune Appellation boundary

Premier Cru vineyard

Commune Appellation vineyard

Other vineyard

Woods

Contour interval 5 metres

Internal vineyard boundary

1:25,000

Km. 0   1 Km.

Miles 0   ½ Mile

PRODUCERS OF SPECIAL INTEREST

CHASSAGNE-MONTRACHET

Domaine Guy Amiot-Bonfils
21190 Chassagne-Montrachet
Among a good range the white
Chassagne Les Caillerets and Les
Vergers are recommended, as is the
memorable Montrachet.

Blain-Gagnard
21190 Chassagne-Montrachet
Small estate; distinguished range.

Michel Colin-Deleger
21190 Chassagne-Montrachet

Domaine du Duc de Magenta
21190 Chassagne-Montrachet

Fontaine-Gagnard
21190 Chassagne-Montrachet

Domaine Gagnard Delagrange
21190 Chassagne-Montrachet
Jacques Gagnard married the late
Edmond Delagrange Bachelet's
daughter. His sons-in-law continue the
story with Domaines Blain-Gagnard
and Fontaine-Gagnard. All produce
excellent white wines in and around
Chassagne-Montrachet.

Jean-Noël Gagnard 21190
Chassagne-Montrachet
Jean-Noël and his daughter make
clearly defined white wines in
Chassagne-Montrachet from village,
premier cru and *grand cru* (Bâtard-
Montrachet) vineyards.

Bernard Morey
21190 Chassagne-Montrachet

Jean Marc Morey
21190 Chassagne-Montrachet

Marc Morey
21190 Chassagne-Montrachet
Elegant, firm, white burgundies.

Michel Niellon
21190 Chassagne-Montrachet
Excellent Les Vergers.

Paul Pillot
21190 Chassagne-Montrachet
Attractive white *premiers crus*

Domaine Ramonet
21190 Chassagne-Montrachet
Brothers Noël and Jean-Claude make
superlative white wines, austere in
youth but magical with age, from half
a dozen vineyards in Chassagne-
Montrachet and three *grands crus*
including Le Montrachet itself.

ST-AUBIN

Gilles Bouton 21190 St-Aubin

Maison Raoul Clerget
21190 St-Aubin

Marc Colin 21190 St-Aubin
White *premiers crus* from St-Aubin
and Chassagne-Montrachet.

Dominique Derain
21190 St-Aubin

Hubert Lamy 21190 St-Aubin

Domaine Larue 21190 St-Aubin

Roux Père et Fils
21190 St-Aubin

Gérard Thomas
21190 St-Aubin

ST-ROMAIN

Alain Gras 21190 St-Romain

Taupenot Père et Fils
21190 St-Romain

**Domaine René Thevenin-
Monthelie et Fils**
21190 St-Romain

SANTENAY

Adrien Belland 21590 Santenay

Domaine Fleurot Larose
21590 Santenay

Domaine René Lequin
21590 Santenay

Domaine Prieur Brunet
21590 Santenay

Maison Prosper Maufoux
21590 Santenay

MARANGES

Bernard Bachelet & Fils
71150 Dézize

Paul Chevrot 71150 Cheilly

Y & C Contat-Grangé
71150 Cheilly

HAUTES-CÔTES DE BEAUNE

Denis Carré 21190 Meloisey

François Charles
21190 Nantoux

Jean-Yves Devevey
71150 Demigny

Lucien Jacob
21420 Échévronne

Jean Joliot 21190 Nantoux

Mazilly Père et Fils
21190 Meloisey

Claude Nouveau 21340
Marchezeuil-Change

The Côte Chalonnaise

After the escarpment of the Côte d'Or has faded beyond Santenay and Maranges, viticulture must compete with other crops for pride of place. However the most suitable slopes are still certain to be vine-clad in what is, for convenience, known as the Côte Chalonnaise after its principal town Chalon-sur-Saône. The Chalonnais 'Route du Vin' commences in Chagny, a dull town enriched by the three-star Lameloise restaurant of classical Burgundian cuisine. Unless you turn off to visit the hamlet of Bouzeron, which enjoys a consolation appellation for its delicious Aligoté known as Bourgogne Aligoté de Bouzeron, the D981 will take you first to Rully, which produces equal volumes of red and white wine and a certain amount of sparkling Crémant de Bourgogne. The wines are light, attractive and for early drinking, though more refined winemaking skills would be useful at a number of domaines. Among the white wines a fair amount of Pinot Blanc is planted alongside the expected Chardonnay.

South of Rully is Mercurey which produces the region's best red wines and charges a slight premium for them. They are firm and fruity enough to be able to age for a few years but most are just as attractive young as old. At least one reputable *négociant*, Antonin Rodet, is based in the region while others such as Joseph Faiveley control a significant amount of land in Mercurey. Rodet controls the making and marketing of the excellent Château de Chamirey and of Château de Rully.

The Mercurey appellation continues into neighbouring St-Martin-sous-Montaigu. Some bottles of Mercurey have a 'Chanteflûtage' label which is a local version of the 'Tastevinage' awarded in the Côte d'Or by the Chevaliers du Tastevin (see pages 84–5).

White Mercurey is rare but often interesting if drunk young. Though still very much a minority, Chardonnay is increasingly being planted in Givry, the next appellation to the south. Early results look promising from a handful of talented growers. The reds are not far behind Mercurey in quality and are usually less expensive. Labels on most bottles carry the legend that Givry was the preferred wine of King Henry IV of France (his mistress, Gabrielle d'Estrées, was a native of Givry). There is a sense of optimism in Givry and a fair amount of new planting. One promising site is Clos Jus, reclaimed from the wilderness in the early 1990s and a potential source of fine wines capable of ageing.

On the outskirts of the small town of Buxy is the appellation of Montagny which incorporates the communes of St-Vallerin and Jully-lès-Buxy and produces white wines only. These should be brisk, fresh wines with decent fruit and a fair amount of flesh. One reliable source is the cooperative at Buxy. A curiosity of the appellation is that most vineyards have the right to be labelled *premier cru* if they reach the desired degree of natural alcohol.

Throughout the region a fair amount of generic Burgundy is produced from vineyards that are not included in specific appellations. Since 1989 these wines have been labelled as Bourgogne Côte Chalonnaise. A little further west is another enclave of generic Bourgogne known as the Couchois, where some decent red wines are made.

Immaculately kept vines at Chagny, the largest town in northern Chalonnais.

PRODUCERS OF SPECIAL INTEREST

BOUZERON
Domaine de l'Hermitage Chanzy Frères 71150 Bouzeron
A & P de Villaine 71150 Bouzeron
Small private estate of Aubert de Villaine, co-owner of the Domaine de la Romanée-Conti, making impeccable reds and whites from the Côte Chalonnaise. Red Mercurey and white Rully are now included in the range.

RULLY
Domaine Belleville 71150 Rully
Domaine Chanzy 71150 Rully
Georges Duvernay 71150 Rully
Domaine de la Folie
71150 Chagny
Domaine de la Renarde
71150 Rully
Château de Rully 71150 Rully

MERCUREY
Château de Chamirey
71640 Mercurey
Michel Juillot 71640 Mercurey
Widely regarded as the top man in Mercurey for his various distinguished *cuvées*. Also makes a small quantity of sensational Corton-Charlemagne.
Maison Antonin Rodet
71640 Mercurey
A more-than-competent *négociant* house which co-owns Domaine Jacques Prieur (Meursault) and distributes the excellent Château de

Rully (Rully) and Château de Chamirey (Mercurey).
Domaine Protheau
71640 Mercurey
Domaine H & Y de Suremain
71640 Mercurey
Domaine Émile Voarick
71640 Mercurey

GIVRY
Domaine Chofflet Valdenaire
71640 Givry
Clos Salomon 71640 Givry
Michel Goubard 71640 Givry
François Lumpp 71640 Givry
Vincent Lumpp 71640 Givry
Domaine Gérard Mouton
71640 Givry
Domaine Ragot 71640 Givry
Michel Sarrazin 71640 Givry
Baron Thénard 71640 Givry

MONTAGNY
Domaine Bernard Michel
71390 Montagny
Cave des Vignerons de Buxy
71390 Buxy
Château de la Saule (Alain Roy)
71390 Montagny
Domaine Jean Vachet
71390 St-Vallerin

WINE FÊTES

Chagny The Foire des Vins takes place over several days around the middle of August. There is also a Paulée in November.

WINE INFORMATION

Maison des Vins de la Côte Chalonnaise promenade Ste-Marie 71100 Chalon-sur-Saône
Tel (0)385 41 64 00
La Confrérie des Vignerons de la Chanteflûté acts on behalf of Mercurey and the district's other wines.

HOTELS

See also the Côte d'Or and the Mâconnais listings, pages 88, 93, 97 and 110.
Hostellerie du Château de Bellecroix 71150 Chagny
Tel (0)385 87 13 86
Quietly situated just beside the N6. Comfortable rooms; good cooking.
Auberge du Camp Romain 71150 Chassey-le-Camp
Tel (0)385 87 09 91
In a tranquil setting with a fine view. Rooms simple but snug. Restaurant closed in winter.

RESTAURANTS

Lameloise place d'Armes, 71150 Chagny Tel (0)385 87 08 85
Excellent, famous and expensive restaurant where regional ingredients are prepared with great finesse. Splendid wine-list. Also a stylish hotel.
Auberge des Fontaines 71150 Fontaines Tel (0)385 91 48 00
Hotel and restaurant with local dishes and wines.
Auberge de la Billebaude 71640 Givry Tel (0)385 44 34 25
A bistro close to the church.
Hostellerie du Val d'Or 71640 Mercurey Tel (0)385 45 13 70
Well run village inn with finesse – and an excellent wine-list. Also a hotel.
Auberge du Moulin de la Chapelle 71940 Messey-sur-Grosne
Tel (0)385 44 00 58
Large riverside restaurant. Also a simple hotel.
Le Commerce 71150 Rully
Tel (0)385 87 20 09
Traditional dishes. Also a hotel.

PLACES OF INTEREST

Buxy Parts of the town walls and two fortified towers still stand. Attractive 15th-century houses and a Romanesque church.
Chalon-sur-Saône Once a great wine port: thousands of Roman amphorae have been found in the river. A good view from the Tour du Doyenné on an island in the Saône.
Givry Many 18th-century buildings. Mercurey Touches, just south of Mercurey, has a 12th-century church.
Rully Château de Rully, a 13th–16th-century castle with its own vineyard.

The Côte Chalonnaise

Canton boundary
Commune (parish) boundary
Vineyards
Woods
Contour interval 20 metres

1:100,000

The Mâconnais

The initial impetus for wine production in the Mâconnais came from the Romans established in the riverside town of Mâcon, and this was followed up by the monks of Cluny. These two influences combine in the scores of attractive Romanesque churches which dot the region. The feel of the South, scarcely apparent in the Chalonnais or Côte d'Or, becomes evident in the Mâconnais: curved rooftiles predominate, crickets chorus loudly on long, summer afternoons and the warm climate encourages earlier harvests.

Driving south on the D981 from Buxy towards Cluny, the first Mâconnais vineyards appear at St-Gengoux-le-National. (Alternatively, on the main RN6 the first Mâconnais vineyards appear at Sennecey-le-Grand, just north of Tournus.) On the former route vineyards are relatively sparse. Many of the best wine villages lie among the ridges and dales to the west of the Saône Valley and the main roads. The well signposted Route du Vin twists through the attractive polycultural countryside. Good wine can be had from cooperatives and growers in such villages as Chardonnay, Uchizy, Lugny and Viré (both have excellent cooperatives), Clessé, Igé, La Roche-Vineuse, Prissé and Chaintré. These are among the 43 communes that can sell their wines as either Mâcon-Villages or Mâcon followed by the specific village name. Such wines represent the bulk of the region's white, although straight Mâcon and Mâcon Supérieur also exist. Most white Mâcon is simple stuff, fermented in stainless steel and bottled early to keep the primary fruit. It is pleasant enough in its first year or two but is not for keeping. A handful of domaines are however making exciting barrel-fermented and matured wines which have greater character and stuffing than most Chalonnais wine.

White wine accounts for two thirds of the Mâcon appellations. Red (and rosé) Mâcon and Mâcon Supérieur are made from Gamay, thus they resemble Beaujolais although they are usually lighter: simple, quaffable and for drinking when young. Most red Mâcon comes from the villages in the south-west corner of the region where the soil is sandier, or at the extreme north. A fair amount of Pinot Noir is also grown although this has to be sold as Bourgogne Rouge.

The foundation – almost literally – of the whole of Burgundy is the limestone sub-soil. This shows to most advantage in the appellation of Pouilly-Fuissé where two great waves of limestone, resembling breakers about to topple (or else 1950s' haircuts), form the rocks of Solutré and Vergisson. On the slopes around these peaks in the four communes of Chaintré, Fuissé, Solutré-Pouilly and Vergisson lies the appellation of Pouilly-Fuissé. The wines are fat, broad-bottomed, rich in fruit, and usually quite high in alcohol – I have tasted examples verging on 16 per cent. They may miss the subtlety of great white burgundy from the Côte d'Or but otherwise they can be extremely satisfying, even if they are sometimes overpriced. Chaintré, in the south-east corner, seems to get the most sun – perhaps too much in the hot years, when the shadier Vergisson fares better.

Two lesser satellite appellations are Pouilly-Vinzelles and Pouilly-Loché. The latter may be and almost always is sold under the name of the former.

In 1971 a new appellation covering eight communes surrounding Pouilly-Fuissé was created: St-Véran. It is something of a hybrid since half the area is based on Mâconnais limestone while the vineyards in Chasselas, Leynes and St-Vérand (to confuse the issue) are on the much redder, sandier granitic soil of the Beaujolais which is less suited to white wine. Overall, a typical St-Véran has a little more body than a Mâcon-Villages, but does not achieve the weight or character of a Pouilly-Fuissé.

The village of Fuissé which, with neighbouring Pouilly in the extreme south of the region, makes the Mâconnais' most famous and most expensive wine.

PRODUCERS OF SPECIAL INTEREST

MÂCON AND MÂCON-VILLAGES

Domaine André Bonhomme
71260 Viré
The doyen of Mâconnais domaine bottlers, making impeccable wines from old vines.
Cave Coopérative 71570 Chaintré
Cave Coopérative 71960 Igé
Cave Coopérative 71620 Lugny
Cave Coopérative 71260 Viré
Roger Duboeuf & Fils
71570 Chaintré
Brother of the more famous George.
Henri Goyard Domaine de Roally 71260 Viré
Henri Lafarge 71250 Bray
Lycée Viticole et Agricle de Davayé 71960 Davayé
Maison Auvigue-Burrier-Revel
71850 Charnay-lès-Mâcon
Maison Mommessin
71850 Charnay-lès-Mâcon
Leading *négociant* for Mâconnais and Beaujolais wines as well as Burgundy from further north. Sole ownership of *grand cru* Clos de Tart in Morey-St-Denis. The firm took over Beaujolais specialist Thorin in 1994.
Domaine Mathias 71570 Chaintré
Domaine Mathias-Poncet
71850 Charnay-lès-Mâcon
Olivier Merlin, Domaine du Vieux St-Sorlin
71960 La Roche-Vineuse
A rising star noted for his barrel-fermented old-vine Mâcon La Roche-Vineuse and St-Véran from '96.
Domaine Talmard 71700 Uchizy
Jean Thévenet/Domaine de la Bon Gran 712600 Clessé
Maverick superstar specialising in ultra-rich late-picked wines, sometimes extending to a nobly rotten superstar *cuvée*. Very fine, expensive wines.
Trénel Fils
71850 Charnay-lès-Mâcon

ST-VÉRAN

Domaine Corsin 71960 Davayé
Domaine des Deux Roches
71960 Davayé
Ambitious and expanding business with an excellent price-to-quality ratio.
Corinne & Thierry Drouin
71960 Vergisson
Roger Luquet 71960 Fuissé
Jacques Saumaize 71960 Vergisson

POUILLY-FUISSÉ

Domaine Cordier 71960 Fuissé
Louis Curveux 71960 Fuissé
Jean-Jacques Denogent
71960 Fuissé
Domaine Ferret 71960 Fuissé
The legendary Mme Ferret died in her eighties, but her daughter continues to uphold this domaine's excellent reputation for long-lived wines.

Michel Forest Château de Fuissé, 71960 Fuissé
Jean-Jacques Vincent is responsible for the appellation's leading property which now makes a range of individual *cuvées* of Pouilly-Fuissé.
Dr Léger-Plumet 71960 Fuissé
Roger Luquet 71960 Fuissé
Jacques Saumaize 71960 Vergisson
Domaine Gérard Valette & Fils
71570 Chaintré

WINE ROUTE

In 1986 the **Route des Vins Mâconnais–Beaujolais** was opened. Some 450km long, it leads the traveller criss-cross through the two districts by means of a thousand or so signposts. Information about the route is supplied in the Cellier-Expo at Crèches-sur-Saône, a village just south of Mâcon on the N6.

WINE FÊTES

Lugny Foire des Vins du Haut-Mâconnais during the weekend of Palm Sunday.
Mâcon A wine fair of about ten days' duration takes place around May 20.

WINE INFORMATION

Maison Mâconnaise des Vins
avenue de Lattre-de-Tassigny
71000 Mâcon
Tel (0)385 38 36 70
Supplies information, sells wine and also has a simple restaurant.

HOTELS

Château de Fleurville 71260 Fleurville Tel (0)385 33 12 17
About 15km north of Mâcon. A pleasant place to stay – an old building surrounded by a park. With restaurant.
Château d'Igé 71960 Igé
Tel (0)385 33 33 99
Small 13th-century castle. Excellent rooms and a medieval ambience. The cuisine tends to be classical.
Hôtel du Centre 71620 Lugny
Tel (0)385 33 22 82
Small, charming village hotel, also a simple restaurant.
Altéa 26 rue de Coubertin, 71000 Mâcon Tel (0)385 38 28 06
Modern comfort. There are always fresh-from-the-market dishes on the restaurant menu.
Hôtel de Genève 1 rue Bigonnet 71000 Mâcon Tel (0)385 38 18 10
Not far from the station, a functional hotel with a restaurant.
Mapotel Bellevue 416 quai Lamartine, 71000 Mâcon
Tel (0)385 38 05 07
Comfortable hotel with a good restaurant.

Terminus 91 rue Victor-Hugo
71000 Mâcon
Tel (0)385 39 17 11
Fairly tastefully decorated rooms with sound-proofed windows. Also has a restaurant.

RESTAURANTS

In essence the gastronomy of the Mâconnais is still fully Burgundian – but with, if possible, an even greater supply of splendid ingredients including chickens from nearby Bresse and beef from the Charolais. For additional recommendations see the Chalonnais and Beaujolais listings pages 101 and 110–11.

Relais Lamartine 71960 Bussières
Tel (0)385 36 64 71
Regional dishes including andouillette au vin blanc and roast chicken.
Hôtel Le Moderne Le Pont de l'Étang, 71250 Cluny
Tel (0)385 59 05 65
Food of quality (charolais au jus de truffe, for example) and good value. Also a hotel. Demi-pension obligatory in summer.

Relais du Mâconnais 71960 La Croix-Blanche Tel (0)385 36 60 72
Near Sologny. The cooking is creative and light. Also a hotel.
Le Fleurville 71260 Fleurville
Tel (0)385 33 10 65
Traditional, straightforward cuisine. Also a cheap hotel.
Le Relais du Beaujolais-Mâconnais
71570 Leynes Tel (0)385 35 11 29
Simple, regional dishes. The restaurant faces the charming square at Leynes, one of the villages of St-Véran.
Restaurant St-Pierre 71620 Lugny
Tel (0)385 33 20 27
Wine-tasting room with a simple restaurant, open from March to the end of October. Panorama.
Au Rocher de Cancale
393 quai Jean-Jaurès, 71000 Mâcon
Tel (0)385 38 07 50
Good-value, carefully prepared set meals including at least one fish dish.
Auberge Bressanne 114 rue du 28-juin, 71000 Mâcon
Tel (0)385 38 07 42
A famous place. Specialities include feuilleté d'escargots à la crème d'ail, matelote d'anguille au Mâcon rouge.

Lamartine found solitude and inspiration in the grounds of Château de Montceau.

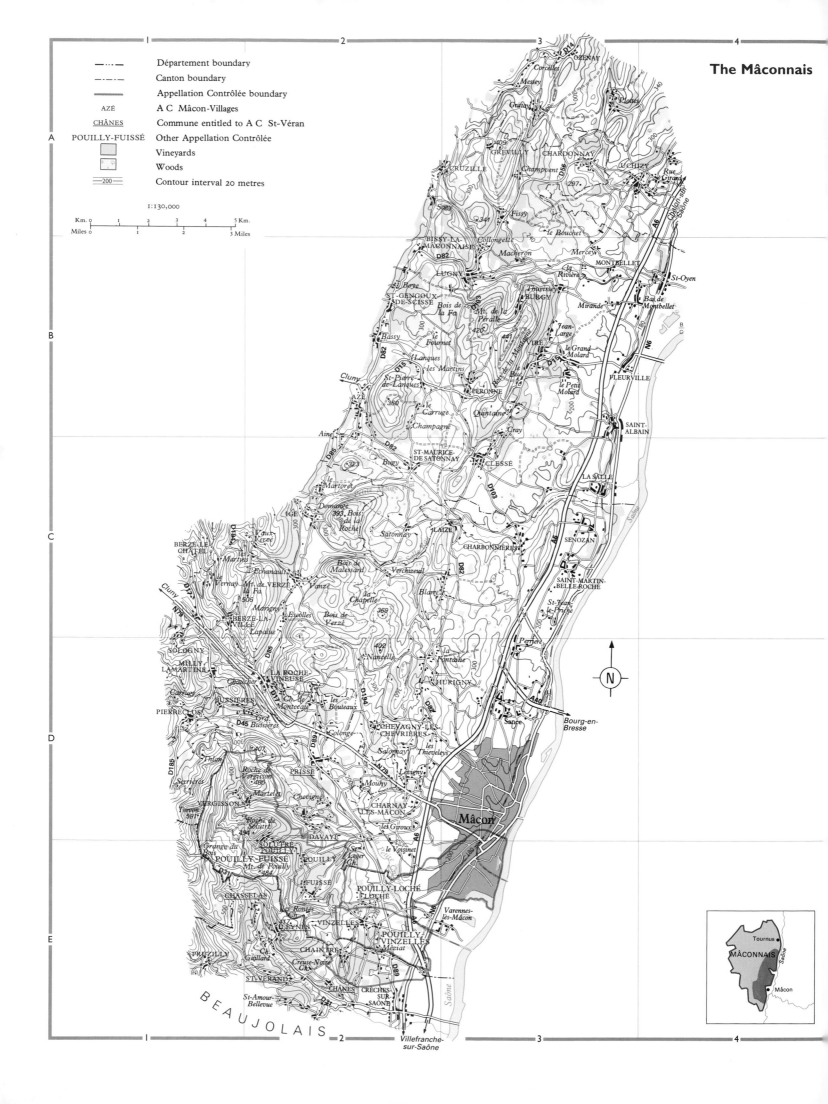

The Mâconnais

Corcelles
Messey
OZENAY
Grévilly
Plottes
GREVILLY
CHARDONNAY
CRUZILLE
Champvent
UCHIZY
Rue Grand
Sagy
Fissy
le Bouchet
Mercey
BISSY-LA-MÂCONNAISE
Macheron
MONTBELLET
LUGNY
la Rivière
St-Oyen
Boye
Thurissey
Bas de Montbellet
ST-GENGOUX-DE-SCISSE
BURGY
Mirande
Bois de la Fa
Mt. de la Péraille
Jean-Large
Bassy
Fournet
VIRÉ
le Grand Molard
FLEURVILLE
Cluny
Lanques les Martins
le Bue
St-Pierre-de-Lanques
PÉRONNE
le Petit Molard
AZÉ
le Carruge
Quintaine
Aine
Champagné
Gray
SAINT-ALBAIN
ST-MAURICE-DE-SATONNAY
Bugy
CLESSÉ
le Martoret
LA SALLE
Domange
Bois de la Roche
IGÉ
Satonnay
LAIZE
Vaux Verzé
Bois de Malessard
Verchizeul
CHARBONNIÈRES
BERZE-LE-CHÂTEL
Martins
SENOZAN
Echanault
la Chapelle
Blany
SAINT-MARTIN-BELLE-ROCHE
Mt. de VERZÉ la Fa
Vanzé
Marigny
St-Jean-le-Priché
BERZE-LA-VILLE
Escolles
Bois de Verzé
Lapalue
Perrière
SOLOGNY
Nancelle
la Fontaine
MILLY-LAMARTINE
Chauchet
HURIGNY
Carruge
les Bouteaux
BUSSIÈRES
Ch. de Monteau
PIERRECLOS
Colonge
Sance
CHEVAGNY-LES-CHEVRIÈRES
Grd Bussières
Bourg-en-Bresse
Thian
Salornay
les Theveleys
PRISSÉ
Lévigny
Serrières
Roche de Vergisson
Mouhy
Martelet
Chevigne
Tourron
CHARNAY-LES-MÂCON
VERGISSON
Mâcon
Roche de Solutré
DAVAYÉ
les Giroux
Grange du Bois
SOLUTRÉ-POUILLY
POUILLY
le Voisinet
POUILLY-FUISSÉ
Mt. de Pouilly
Loger Ch.
POUILLY-LOCHÉ
FUISSÉ
CHASSELAS
LOCHÉ
Ronze
Varennes-les-Mâcon
LEYNES
VINZELLES
POUILLY-VINZELLES
PRUZILLY
Ch. Gaillard
CHAINTRÉ
Méziat
Creuse-Noire Chs.
ST-VÉRAND
CHÂNES
CRÊCHES-SUR-SAÔNE
St-Amour-Bellevue

BEAUJOLAIS

Villefranche-sur-Saône

N

Tournus
MÂCONNAIS
Mâcon

Maison Mâconnaise des Vins
avenue de Latre-de-Tassigny
71000 **Mâcon**
Tel (0)385 38 36 70
A simple, spacious restaurant serving
tasty regional dishes. (See also Wine
Information page 103.)
Greuze 71700 Tournus
Tel (0)385 51 13 52
Jean Ducloux has been at the helm
for over 50 years. You need a big
appetite and a big wallet, but regulars
swear by this classical cooking.

PLACES OF INTEREST

Azé Prehistoric caves with an
associated museum (open only in
summer season).
Berzé-le-Châtel Large feudal
stronghold, once the seat of the first
barony in the Mâconnais.
Berzé-la-Ville The Romanesque
chapel of the Château des Moines has
wall-paintings from the 12th century,
rather Byzantine in style.
Bray Roman walls and an 11th-
century church.
Burgy Romanesque church (11th
century) on the hill above the village.
Bussières Beside the 12th-century
church lies the grave of Father
Dumont, the inspiration for the poet
Lamartine's *Jocelyn*.
Chaintré A 15th-century château.
Chardonnay Dolmen and a 16th-
century château.
Chasselas A 12th-century church
and a 15th-century château.
Clessé The 11th-century church
with its octagonal tower has
Lombardic elements.
Cluny In 910 an abbey was
founded here which, two centuries
later, was to have some 2,000
Benedictine daughter-houses
throughout Europe. Until the building
of St Peter's in Rome, the church at
Cluny was Europe's biggest. It had
seven towers, was 30m high and
187m long. Only the south wing
remains. There is a model of the
original building in the Musée Ochier.
Cluny town has many old houses and
monuments, the remains of its walls
and a second museum containing
early sculptures.
Cruzille-en-Mâconnais An
interesting museum here is devoted
to some 30 agricultural crafts and
occupations. It houses around
35,000 exhibits.
Farges-lès-Mâcon A small
Mediterranean Romanesque church
dating from the beginning of the
11th century.
Fuissé A 12th-century church.
Grévilly A Romanesque church
dating from the 12th century.
Igé Wine museum and tasting room
in a Romanesque chapel.
Leynes A 12th-century church.

At the foot of the Solutré rock lie the bones of some 100,000 wild horses driven over the cliff by prehistoric 'Solutréen' Man.

Loché A 12th-century church and, by
way of contrast, a station for the
high-speed TGV Paris-Lyon train,
which has brought the Beaujolais into
day-trip range from Paris.
Lugny Remains of a castle.
Mâcon The writer, poet and politician
Alphonse Prat de Lamartine was born
in 1790 in this commercial and
industrial town with its long riverside
quay. There is a museum dedicated to
him (21 rue Sigrogne), and a Circuit
Lamartine signposted around the
town. In the Musée des Ursulines (5
rue des Ursulines) prehistoric finds
and art of many periods are exhibited.
The Hôtel-Dieu (cours Moreau) has a
dispensary with, for example, earthen-
ware from the time of Louis XV.

Milly-Lamartine The house where
Lamartine lived as a child. The church
is 12th century.
Pierreclos A 15th-century castle.
Prissé Château de Montceau, which
was built in the 13th century.
La Roche-Vineuse Worth a visit if
only for the 12th-century bell tower,
but also has the remains of a feudal
stronghold and wonderful views over
the Charolais countryside.
St-Gengoux-de-Scissé Pretty
village with many old houses and an
11th-century church.
St-Vérand Ancient village with an
attractive Romanesque church. A
16th-century wine press stands in the
wine-tasting room.
Sologny An 11th-century church.

Solutré Situated near the foot of a
limestone cliff where fossilised bones
of thousands of horses lay – the horses
were apparently driven over the cliff
by prehistoric hunters. There is a small
museum of prehistory in the village.
Tournus A fine old abbey with the
twin-towered church of St-Philibert.
There is a museum dedicated to the
painter Greuze (1725–1805). See also
the restaurant of that name (above).
Uchizy Beautiful 12th-century church
with frescoes and a five-storey tower.
Vergisson Has a cliff similar to that
at Solutré and also a menhir.
Verzé A 12th-century chapel.
Vinzelles A feudal fort and a
Romanesque church.
Viré Has a small wine museum.

The Beaujolais

As limestone gives way to granite to the south of Pouilly-Fuissé, so Chardonnay makes way for Gamay, the grape that finds its most cheerful expression in Beaujolais. Logically this should not be part of Burgundy since soil, grape and culture are all different. Beaujolais is not even administratively in the province of Burgundy, but trading in both areas has historically been so closely connected over the years that the two remain lumped together for vinous purposes.

Beaujolais, the wine, bears little resemblance to Burgundy. A typical glass will be bright and purple in colour with a heady vinous bouquet, perhaps suggesting strawberries. Sometimes, especially with the 'nouveau' version, a whiff of bananas is detectable which has more to do with the methods of vinification than with the grape. Despite the wine's approachability and lack of intimidating structure, Beaujolais can be quite alcoholic stuff.

This is a beautiful part of the country. Densely wooded mountains rise behind the softer contours of gently rounded hills on which the grapes are grown. Its rural nature has been immortalised by Gabriel Chevallier's *Clochemerle*, a comic novel based on the village of Vaux-en-Beaujolais.

Roads are narrow and winding; an unwary traveller taking an unmarked road will frequently find that it peters out in the vineyards. Hamlets and villages, each dominated by its church, are scattered everywhere (according to the locals, the sharper the church spire, the more shrewish the women of the village) and enjoy a mild climate, being sheltered by the mountains from westerly winds.

The market for Beaujolais falls into two camps: one is concerned with the ten individual *crus*, the other with the mass-market Beaujolais, Beaujolais Supérieur and Beaujolais-Villages. About half of the second category's wine is sold as Beaujolais Primeur, which is available from the third Thursday in November each year. This is often referred to as Beaujolais Nouveau although officially that name signifies the wine of the new vintage whether sold in November or later. Whether the Primeur idea is a marketing triumph that celebrates the exuberant, fruity, quaff-me-quick nature of Beaujolais or an inoculation that cures one of the desire to drink Beaujolais for the rest of the year is open to question.

In total, Primeur or otherwise, about 45 per cent of the region's production is of Beaujolais and Beaujolais Supérieur, the remainder being split equally among Beaujolais-Villages and the ten *crus*. The *crus* are situated in the north of the region followed by the section afforded 'Village' status. Further south, towards Lyon, is flatter land where the simplest Beaujolais is made. Yet further into the hilly land west of Lyon, a new appellation has been created that makes similar light wines from the Gamay grape: the Coteaux du Lyonnais.

From north to south the *crus* are as follows: St-Amour, Juliénas, Chénas, Moulin-à-Vent, Fleurie, Chiroubles, Morgon, Régnié, Côte de Brouilly and Brouilly. St-Amour, with one foot in the limestone

Villages set among the quiet valleys and green hills of Beaujolais are characterised by the ochre-coloured pierres dorées *(gilded stones) from which they are built.*

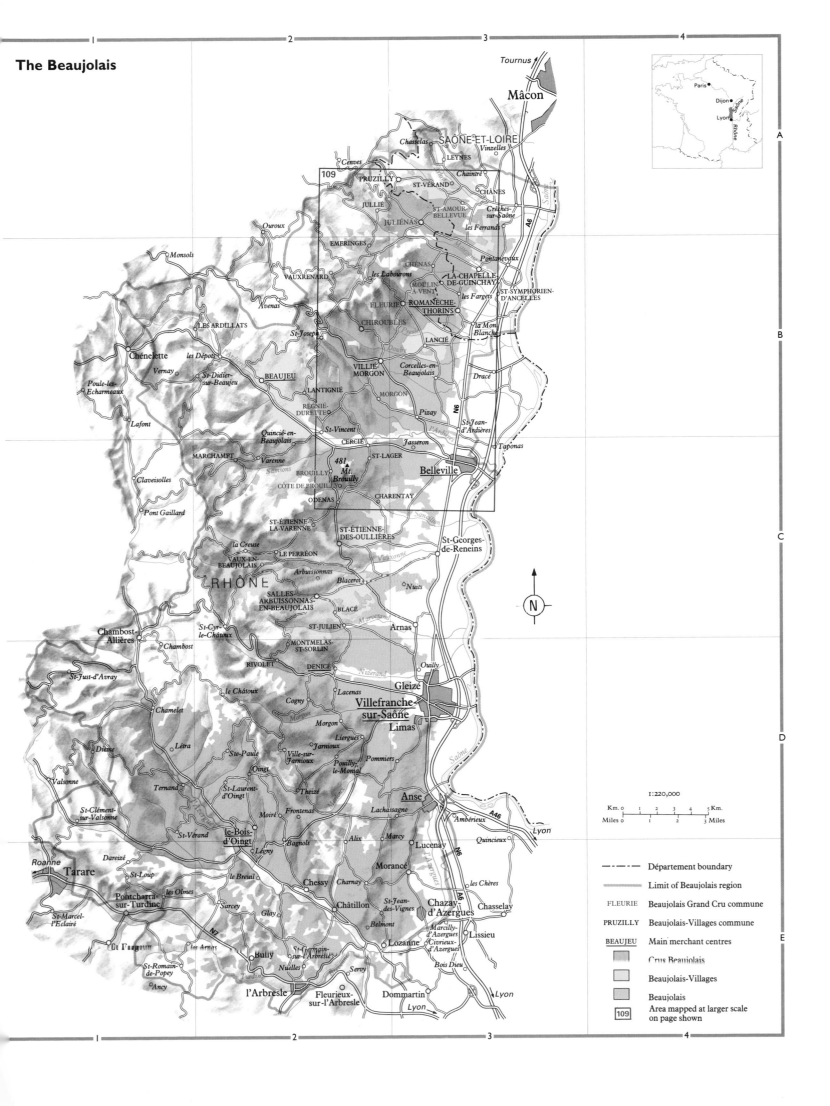

The Beaujolais

Mâcon

SAÔNE-ET-LOIRE

Tournus

Chasselas
Vinzelles
LEYNES
Cenves
Chaintré
109
PRUZILLY
ST-VÉRAND
CHÂNES
JULLIÉ
ST-AMOUR-
BELLEVUE
Crêches-
sur-Saône
Ouroux
JULIÉNAS
les Ferrands
EMERINGES
Pontanevaux
CHÉNAS
VAUXRENARD
les Labourons
LA-CHAPELLE-
DE-GUINCHAY
Avenas
MOULIN-
À-VENT
les Fargets
ST-SYMPHORIEN-
D'ANCELLES
LES ARDILLATS
FLEURIE
ROMANÈCHE-
THORINS
Monsols
CHIROUBLES
St-Joseph
la Mont
Blanche
Chénelette
les Dépôts
LANCIÉ
Vernay
St-Didier-
sur-Beaujeu
BEAUJEU
VILLIÉ-
MORGON
Corcelles-en-
Beaujolais
Poule-les-
Echarmeaux
LANTIGNIÉ
MORGON
Dracé
RÉGNIÉ-
DURETTE
Pizay
Lafont
Quincié-en-
Beaujolais
St-Vincent
St-Jean-
d'Ardières
St-Vincent
CERCIÉ
Jasseron
Taponas
MARCHAMPT
Varenne
ST-LAGER
481
Mt.
Brouilly
Belleville
Claveisolles
BROUILLY
CÔTE DE BROUILLY
Pont Gaillard
ODENAS
CHARENTAY
ST-ÉTIENNE-
LA-VARENNE
ST-ÉTIENNE-
DES-OULLIÈRES
St-Georges-
de-Reneins
la Creuse
VAUX-EN-
BEAUJOLAIS
LE PERRÉON
RHÔNE
Arbuissonnas
Blacéret
Nuits
SALLES-
ARBUISSONNAS-
EN-BEAUJOLAIS
BLACÉ
N
Chambost-
Allières
St-Cyr-
le-Châtoux
ST-JULIEN
Arnas
Chambost
MONTMELAS-
ST-SORLIN
St-Just-d'Avray
RIVOLET
DENICÉ
Ouilly
le Châtoux
Lacenas
Gleizé
Cogny
Villefranche-
sur-Saône
Chamelet
Morgon
Limas
Dième
Létra
Liergues
Ste-Paule
Jarnioux
Valsonne
Ville-sur-
Jarnioux
Pommiers
Ternand
Oingt
Pouilly-
le-Monal
St-Clément-
sur-Valsonne
St-Laurent-
d'Oingt
Theizé
Lachassagne
Anse
St-Vérand
Moiré
Frontenas
Ambérieux
Lyon
le-Bois-
d'Oingt
Légny
Bagnols
Alix
Marcy
Lucenay
Quincieux
Roanne
Dareizé
Tarare
St-Loup
le Breuil
Charnay
Morancé
les Chères
Pontcharra-
sur-Turdine
les Olmes
Sarcey
Chessy
St-Jean-
des-Vignes
Chazay-
d'Azergues
Chasselay
St-Marcel-
l'Eclairé
Glay
Châtillon
Belmont
Marcilly-
d'Azergues
Lissieu
Bully
Lozanne
Civrieux-
d'Azergues
St-Romain-
de-Popey
Nuelles
Servoy
Bois Dieu
Ancy
l'Arbresle
Fleurieux-
sur-l'Arbresle
Dommartin
Lyon
Lyon

1:220,000

Km. 0   1   2   3   4   5 Km.
Miles 0   1   2   3 Miles

---·--- Département boundary

〰〰〰 Limit of Beaujolais region

FLEURIE Beaujolais Grand Cru commune

PRUZILLY Beaujolais-Villages commune

BEAUJEU Main merchant centres

▨ Crus Beaujolais

▨ Beaujolais-Villages

▨ Beaujolais

109 Area mapped at larger scale
on page shown

soil of the Mâconnais, is the second-smallest of the ten. These seductive wines are much in demand on St Valentine's day and French commentators like to find raspberries, redcurrants, apricots and peonies in the bouquet. Juliénas produces about double the amount of wine produced by St-Amour and it is usually darker in colour, firmer in style and has greater depth of fruit so is more suitable for ageing. A man who drinks his Juliénas in one swallow, they say locally, is not to be trusted.

The road now leads down into a valley, back over a wooded hill and into Chénas, smallest of the *crus* and worthy of some attention for the extra complexity and spiciness which sits on top of the fruit. The appellation would be larger if two thirds of the commune's wines were not sold as Moulin-à-Vent. There is no village of this name, the wine comes from Romanèche-Thorins and Chénas, but it takes the name of the region's last surviving windmill. This is the Beaujolais with the most staying power. As it ages the flavours of Gamay seem to transmute into something akin to the decadent gaminess of venerable Pinot Noir. A top vintage of Moulin-à-Vent can keep for between 15 and 20 years.

Until recently Moulin-à-Vent was the most expensive Beaujolais, but modern taste has transferred its affections to neighbouring Fleurie, a totally different style of wine. Fleurie should be deliciously perfumed, supple, silky, and have plenty of fruit. It is designed to be drunk in its first two to three years. The village boasts a reliable cooperative and a distinguished restaurant.

A small detour into the hills behind is necessary to discover Chiroubles, the highest altitude *cru*. The wines are relatively light, attractive and certainly refreshing.

The next *cru*, Morgon, returns to the style of big, powerful Beaujolais – perhaps because the soil consists more of broken-down schist than the purer pinkish granite of Fleurie and Chiroubles. Morgon rivals Moulin-à-Vent for the title of the region's best keeping wine by virtue of its tannic structure. The Côte de Py to the south of the appellation is particularly favoured.

Régnié was promoted to AC status only in 1988, exchanging its position at the head of the Beaujolais-Villages for that of the lightest of the *crus*. The soil is sandier here, which limits the potential of Régnié to develop depth and complexity.

Rather more substance can be expected from Brouilly, the largest *cru* with vines in six communes. Given the size of the AC and the number of different producers, a typical Brouilly style is less easy to pin down. Stuck in the middle of it is an abrupt volcanic hill, Mont Brouilly, whose steep slopes bear vineyards designated as Côte de Brouilly. A good example is likely to be finer and longer lasting than the wines grown on flatter ground. However not much is produced and Côte de Brouilly lacks the identity that the wine deserves in the market place.

All the *crus* save Régnié may declassify their wine into Bourgogne Rouge, a ridiculous anomaly since one would reasonably expect to find Pinot Noir in a bottle so labelled. It is still possible to find a small amount of Beaujolais Blanc though this appellation has declined in volume since most of the best white-wine vineyards were renamed to help create St-Véran in 1971.

Good growers can be found throughout the Beaujolais and most villages boast a cooperative and a tasting *caveau*. Yet the fame of Beaujolais has been best promoted by its *négociants*: first by the long-established firms in the towns on the N6 and subsequently, in the last 30 years, by Georges Duboeuf.

'The prince of Beaujolais', Duboeuf can justly claim credit for a significant proportion of Beaujolais sales. His headquarters in Romanèche-Thorins seem constantly to expand and diversify: his huge business now includes a 'theme park' wine village.

Winter tranquillity in the pastures and vignobles *of rural Fleurie.*

PRODUCERS OF SPECIAL INTEREST

BEAUJOLAIS AND BEAUJOLAIS-VILLAGES
Château du Basty 69430 Lantignié
Château de Boisfranc 69640 Jarnioux
Cellier des Samsons 69430 Quincié
Chanut Frères 71570 Romanèche-Thorins
Jean Marc Charmet 69620 Le Breuil
Jacques Dépagneux 69400 Villefranche-sur-Saône
Georges Duboeuf 71570 Romanèche-Thorins
The living legend of the Beaujolais, now assisted by his son.
Éventail de Producteurs 69220 Corcelles-en-Beaujolais
Paul Gauthier 69460 Blacé
Domaines des Grandes Bruyères 69460 St-Étienne-des-Ouillières
Loron & Fils 71570 Pontanevaux
Maison Paul Beaudet 71570 Pontanevaux
Maison Pierre Ferraud 69220 Belleville
Maison Gobet 69460 Blaceret
Maison Paul Sapin 69220 Lancié
Maison Robert Sarrau 69220 Belleville
Maison Thorin 71570 Pontanevaux
René & Christian Miolane 69460 Salles-Arbuissonnas
Jean-Charles Pivot 69430 Quincié
Interesting grower making Beaujolais-Villages with minimal chaptalization.
Château de Pizay 69220 Pizay
Vins Dessalle 69220 St-Jean-d'Ardières
Vins Fessy 69220 St-Jean-d'Ardières
Les Vins Mathelin 69380 Châtillon-d'Azergues

ST-AMOUR
Domaine des Ducs 71570 St-Amour

Raymond Durand 71570 St-Amour
Francis Saillant 71570 St-Amour
Georges Trichard 71570 St-Amour

JULIÉNAS
Domaine de la Boittière 69840 Juliénas
Domaine Joubert 69840 Juliénas
Château de Juliénas 69840 Juliénas
Michel Tête 69840 Juliénas

CHÉNAS
Daniel Robin, Domaine des Brureaux 69840 Chénas
Domaine Louis Champagnon 69840 Chénas
Fine, rich, old-fashioned Chénas as well as Moulin-à-Vent and Fleurie.
Hubert Lapierre 69840 Chénas
A top name for concentrated Chénas and Moulin-à-Vent.
Pierre Perrachon, Château Bonnet 69840 Chénas
Domaine Bernard Santé 69840 Chénas

MOULIN-À-VENT
Domaine de la Bruyère 71570 Romanèche-Thorins
Domaine Louis Champagnon 69840 Chénas
Château des Jacques 71570 Romanèche-Thorins
Jacky Janodet 71570 Romanèche-Thorins
Hubert Lapierre 69840 Chénas
Château Moulin-à-Vent 71570 Romanèche-Thorins
Large estate owned by the Bloud family. Wine is aged in small casks.

FLEURIE
Domaine Bernard 69820 Fleurie
Domaine René Berrod 69820 Fleurie
Cave Coopérative 69820 Fleurie

The *Crus* of Beaujolais

Département boundary
Canton boundary
Commune (parish) boundary
Limits of Grands Crus
Vineyards
Woods
Contour interval 20 metres

1:75,000

Km. 0   1   2   3 Km.
Miles 0   1   2 Miles

Map labels

D469
Pruzilly
les Déburnays
la Combe Vineuse
Veaux
le Chapitre
Bessay
290
363
St-Vérand
D169
D31
St-Amour-Bellevue
Pirolette
304
205
Mont de Bessay
le Pavillon
375
les Poulets
Fouilouses
353
Vayollette
la Ville
St-AMOUR
les Champs Grillés
ST-AMOUR
les Thévenins
268
Ravinets
271
Julié
JULIÉNAS
les Chers
302
Château des Capitans
D486
Plâtre Durand
Château de Juliénas
379
Juliénas
la Bottière
330
les Chanoriers
les Janroux
D26
les Bucherats
D17
D68E
En Guinelay
227
les Paquelets
300
248
Bois Rétour
les Brureaux
CHÉNAS
les Daroux
D26
514
266
les Deschamps
Michelons
502
Château de Jean Loron
les Pinchons
Vieux Bourg
Chénas
510
la Tour du Bief
483
Pic de Rémont
les Verrillats
451
Rochegrés
D68
les Thorins
le Pic
la Rochelle
MOULIN-À-VENT
le Moulin-à-Vent
D186
484
Château de Poncier
les Moriers
Champ de Cour
le Carquelin
les Gimarets
D32
le Point du Jour
207
les Fargets
FLEURIE
les Garrants
la Roilette
D266
Château de Fleurie
Fleurie
les Guillattes
le Breynets
la Rivière
les Quatre Vents
la Biaune
Chafanjons
D32
le Vivier
Romanèche-Thorins
Chapelle des Bois
309
les Déduits
228
la Pierre
les Jacques
Mâcon
Tavernand
le Pont
le Moulin
D86
D119
CHIROUBLES
les Farges
SAÔNE ET LOIRE
Chatenay
Chiroubles
Château les Prés
RHÔNE
le Truges
St-Joseph
Bel Air
Côte Rôtie
254
Douby
Rau de Presle
les Vachats
Vermont
420
D18
les Chênes
Lancié
202
D86
les Fûts
Château de Bellevue
D86
256
le Plâtre
D119
D9
la Haute Ronze
Bellevue
360
Villié-Morgon
D119
Vieux Bourg
200
Corcelles-en-Beaujolais
Ruyère
les Gaudets
les Seve
D9
les Versauds
MORGON
les Bruyères
Vernus
352
les Marcelins
201
D78
les Chastys
Mont du Py
la Ronzière
D9
Haute Morgon
Javernière
la Plaigne
RÉGNIÉ
Morgon
les Forshets
320
D68
les Grands Cras
D69
Pizay
Régnié-Durette
Rayssie
Pónchon
Champ Lèvrier
les Bruyères
N6
St-Ennemond
195
St-Jean-d'Ardières
D68E
Beaujeu
D135
Ardières R.
D69
D18
St-Vincent
la Térrière
BROUILLY
240
199
St-Nizier
228
Gorge de Loup
D37
Jasseron
Belleville
Cercié
Château de Briante
les Ravaty
D43
St-Lager
400
Chavannes
CÔTE DE BROUILLY
le Pavé
les Nazins
les Pilliers
210
Mont Brouilly
368
les Gours
189
la Poyebade
Château Thivin
Bussières
Côte de Brouilly
197
D43
D68E
Ch. de Pierreux
Pierreux
214
D67
Odenas
les Combes
Charentay
Château de la Chaize
326
la Jardinière
D68
D62
210
Garanches
Château de Nervers
D43
Villefranche-sur-Saône

Inset map
Mâcon
Pontanevaux
Beaujeu
Saône
BEAUJOLAIS
Villefranche

1 · 2 · 3 · 4 · A · B · C · D · E

Michel Chignard 69820 Fleurie
Supplies many top French restaurants
from his domaine at 'Le Point du Jour'.
Guy Depardon 69820 Fleurie
Chignard's neighbour of equal
competence.
André Métrat 69820 Fleurie

CHIROUBLES

Georges Boulon 69115 Chiroubles
Domaine Cheysson-lès-Farges
69115 Chiroubles
Alain Passot 69115 Chiroubles
Georges Passot
69910 Villié-Morgon
Château de Raousset
69115 Chiroubles
Francis Tomatis & Fils
69115 Chiroubles

MORGON

**Gérard Brisson, Domaine des
Pillets** 69910 Villié-Morgon
Domaine de la Chanaise
69910 Villié-Morgon
Domaine Savoye
69910 Villié-Morgon

RÉGNIÉ

Domaine du Crêt des Bruyères
69430 Régnié-Durette
Joel Rochette
69430 Régnié-Durette
Château de la Tour Bourdon
69430 Régnié-Durette

CÔTE DE BROUILLY

Alain Bernillon 69220 St-Lager
Bernard Champier 69460 Odenas
Nicole Chanrion 69460 Odenas
Claudius Guérin 69460 Odenas
Château Thivin 69460 Odenas
Robert Verger 69220 St-Lager

BROUILLY

Alain Bernillon 69220 St-Lager
Château de la Chaize 69460
Odenas
Alain Michaud 69220 St-Lager
Château Thivin 69460 Odenas

WINE-TASTING

The Beaujolais has an exceptionally
large number of village *caveaux de
dégustation*, usually run by the wine-
growers of the commune.
Beaujeu Le Temple de Bacchus.
Variable opening times.
Châtillon-d'Azergues Le Pavillon
des Pierres Dorées. Open weekends.
Chénas Caveau du Cru Chénas, run
by the cooperative. Open daily mid-
July to mid-October, open weekends
only at other times.
Chiroubles The Terrasse de
Chiroubles. Open afternoons in
the season.
Cogny Le Caveau des Voûtes.
Variable opening times.
Fleurie Le Caveau de Dégustation
des Viticulteurs. Open daily.

Gleizé Le Caveau de Gleizé. In the
cooperative, open afternoons at
weekends and public holidays.
Juliénas Le Cellier de la Vieille Église.
Open daily. The cooperative has a
wine-tasting room in the 17th-century
Château du Bois de la Salle.
Jullié Caveau de Jullié. Open Sundays.
Leynes Le Relais du Beaujolais-
Mâconnais, mainly a simple restaurant
(see the Mâconnais listings, page 103).
Closed Wednesdays.
Pommiers La Terrasse de Beaujolais,
above the village at the Notre-Dame-
de-Buissante chapel. Also a restaurant.
Closed Wednesdays in winter.
Régnié-Durette Le Caveau des
Deux-Clochers. Open weekend
afternoons from Easter to
mid-September.
Romanèche-Thorins Le Caveau de
l'Union des Viticulteurs du Moulin-
à-Vent, by the N6. Also serves simple
dishes. A second tasting room, Le
Caveau du Moulin-à-Vent, is by the
famous windmill. Closed Tuesdays.
St-Amour Le Caveau du Cru
St-Amour. Variable opening times.
St-Jean-d'Ardières La Maison
des Beaujolais, on the N6, represents
the whole district. There is also a
restaurant. Closed Wednesday
evenings and Thursdays.
St-Jean-des-Vignes Le Refuge des
Pierres Dorées. Open Sundays and
public holidays.
St-Lager Le Cuvage des Brouilly.
Open daily except Tuesday mornings.
St-Vérand Le Caveau de l'Union des
Viticulteurs de St-Vérand. Variable
opening times.
Salles-Arbuissonnas La Tassée du
Chapitre. Open weekends and public
holidays, May to October.
Vaux-en-Beaujolais Le Caveau de
Clochemerle. Variable opening times.
Villié-Morgon Le Caveau des
Morgon. Variable opening times.

WINE ACTIVITIES

One of the greatest joys of the
Beaujolais is to visit a grower at
harvest-time when a fragrant must is
fermenting in the vats. The workers
permit themselves (with a degree of
caution) to try the heady, sweet,
perfumed half-made wine, 'paradis'.
More formal events, such as big
tastings, fairs and banquets, take place
almost every autumn weekend. The
declaration of the Primeur wines
(third Thursday in November) and the
Hospice de Beaujeu auction (second
Sunday in December) are highlights.
Three wine fraternities are active in
the Beaujolais: Les Compagnons du
Beaujolais (the whole district); La
Confrérie des Gosiers Secs (mainly
operating in Vaux-en-Beaujolais); and
La Confrérie des Grapilleurs des
Pierres Dorées (southern Beaujolais).

WINE INFORMATION

The unusually energetic **Union
Interprofessionelle des Vins du
Beaujolais**, 210 Boulevard Vermorel,
69400 Villefranche-sur-Saône, embraces
all the official bodies relating to
Beaujolais wine. In addition there is a
Maison des Beaujolais on the N6
between St-Jean-d'Ardières and
Belleville-sur-Saône, where information
can be obtained and which also has a
restaurant (see Restaurants below).

HOTELS

In the following listings, Beaujolais
is divided into a northern and a
southern half. The River Nizerand,
which flows into the Saône at
Villefranche, is the boundary.

NORTHERN BEAUJOLAIS

Anne de Beaujeu 69430 Beaujeu
Tel (0)474 04 87 58
Small, quiet hotel with regional food
served in the restaurant.
Hôtel des Grands Vins 69820
Fleurie Tel (0)474 69 81 43
Opened in 1985. Swimming pool.
Hôtel des Vignes 69840 Juliénas
Tel (0)474 04 43 70
Fairly modern. Tranquillity assured.
Le Rivage 01090 Montmerle-
sur-Saône Tel (0)474 69 33 92
Situated close to the east bank of
the Saône. Quite modern, with an
above-average restaurant.
Château de Pizay 69220 Pizay
Tel (0)474 66 51 41
Splendid château-hotel complex
between Pizay and Villié-Morgon.
It has apartments, a swimming pool,
a park and a good restaurant.
Les Maritonnes
71570 Romanèche-Thorins
Tel (0)385 35 51 70
Good hotel with a garden, swimming
pool and a renowned restaurant
among whose specialities are
andouillette au vin blanc, poulet de
Bresse au Beaujolais, Charolais beef
and soufflé glacé.

SOUTHERN BEAUJOLAIS

Hôtel-St-Romain 69480 Anse
Tel (0)474 60 24 46
A pleasant place to stay in a large old
building. Classic dishes and more
inventive ones such as salade tiède
d'escargots poêlés aux lardons.

RESTAURANTS

NORTHERN BEAUJOLAIS

Partly because of the proximity of
Lyon and other towns, many
restaurants at all levels thrive in this
district. They range from simple village
inns to veritable palaces with three
Michelin stars. Among the traditional
specialities are various kinds of

charcuterie (andouillette, cervelas,
Jésus de Lyon, rosette de Lyon,
saucisse), friture (freshwater fish fried
in butter), dishes with écrevisses
(freshwater crayfish) poultry from
Bresse and beef from the Charolais.
The dish that appears most frequently
is coq au vin, prepared in every
Beaujolais village with the local wine.

Le Beaujolais 40 rue Maréchal-Foch
69220 Belleville Tel (0)474 66 05 31
Fairly conservative, regionally
orientated and carefully prepared
cuisine. Also a hotel.
Le Beaujolais 69460 Blaceret
Tel (0)474 67 54 75
Restaurant with terrace. Strictly
regional cuisine and wine.
Le Relais Beaujolais
69220 Cercié
Tel (0)474 66 82 86
Traditional restaurant. Fine selection
of Brouilly wines.
Daniel Robin 69840 Chénas
Tel (0)385 36 72 67
Recommended for a quality meal
of regional fare. Shady terrace.
Auberge Le Cep 69820 Fleurie
Tel (0)474 04 10 77
Capable and inventive dishes: good
value but but not cheap.
Chez la Rose/Ma Petite Auberge
69840 Juliénas Tel (0)474 04 41 20
Regional cuisine. Also rooms.
Castel de Valrose
01090 Montmerle-sur-Saône
Tel (0)474 69 30 52
Classic cuisine is offered at this
hotel and restaurant on the east
bank of the Saône.
Christian Mabeau
69460 Odenas
Tel (0)474 03 41 79
Small, good-value restaurant.
La Vieille Auberge 69620 Oingt
Tel (0)474 71 21 14
Rustic decor, decent quality.
La Poularde
71570 Pontanevaux
Tel (0)385 36 72 41
Country cooking, reasonable prices.
Auberge du Paradis 71570
St-Amour Tel (0)385 37 10 26
Country cooking.
La Maison des Beaujolais
N6, 69220 St-Jean-d'Ardières
Tel (0)474 66 16 46
Good value regional set menus.
Also a wine information centre.
Hostellerie St-Vincent
69460 Salles-Arbuissonnas
Tel (0)474 67 55 50
Plenty of atmosphere, an owner who
knows his wine and full-flavoured,
often spicy dishes. Also a hotel with
park and swimming pool.
Au Chapon Fin
01140 Thoissey
Tel (0)474 04 04 74
Functional hotel and a fairly traditional
cuisine. Good wine-list.

Le Relais des Caveaux
69910 Villié-Morgon
Tel (0)474 02 21 77
Regional cuisine.
Georges Blanc 01540 Vonnas
Tel (0)474 50 00 10
In the centre of the village, south-east of Mâcon. One of the best restaurants in France. In warm, elegant surroundings you can enjoy crêpe parmentière au saumon, volaille de Bresse à la crème, agneau marine rôti à la fleur de sel and splendid wines. There is also a luxurious hotel.

SOUTHERN BEAUJOLAIS
Le Vieux Moulin 69380 Alix
Tel (0)478 43 91 66
Honest, carefully prepared dishes. Has a terrace for summer dining.
Auberge de la Brévenne 69690 Bessenay Tel (0)474 70 80 01
Simple establishment with a few rooms. Try the poulet aux morilles.
Les Marronniers 69830 Lozanne
Tel (0)478 43 70 15
At the southern tip of the Beaujolais. Good but rather expensive restaurant.
La Terrasse du Beaujolais
Buisante 69840 Pommiers
Tel (0)474 65 05 27
Specialités Beaujolaises.
Le Theizerot 69260 Theize
Tel (0)474 71 22 26
Sturdy cooking (entrecôte Charolais) and an attractive view.

LYONNAIS
Paul Bocuse
69660 Collonges-au-Mont d'Or
Tel (0)478 22 01 40
World-famous restaurant where you can enjoy classical and contemporary cuisine. Bocuse is a travelling ambassador for French gastronomy – and for himself.
Léon de Lyon 1 rue Pleney
69001 Lyon Tel (0)478 28 11 33
Very atmospheric interior. Serves perfectly prepared local specialities at very reasonable prices.
Les Acacias 69440 Taluyers
Tel (0)478 48 73 06
Pleasant place to eat in the southern Coteaux du Lyonnais, north-east of Mornant.

PLACES OF INTEREST

NORTHERN BEAUJOLAIS
Beaujeu Former capital of the Beaujolais. Displays in the Musée Audin include an 11th-century bas-relief, old interiors and dolls. Local objets d'art are on show in the Maison du Pays, near the St-Nicolas church (1130).
Corcelles-en-Beaujolais A 15th-century château that is also a wine estate. The artist Maurice Utrillo stayed here a number of times and also painted the castle.

The region's best wines are not identified on the label as Beaujolais but are known simply by the names of their crus.

Fleurie The view from the chapel above the village is worth the drive.
Juliénas The Château de Juliénas, which in parts is 14th century, has fine 18th-century cellars which are still used for storing wine.
Odenas Château de la Chaize is a historic monument. The *cuvier* and the immense cellar can be visited.
Quincié The Château de Varennes dates from the 15th century.
Romanèche-Thorins The windmill is at least 300 years old and gives its name to the Moulin-à-Vent *cru*. Next to it is a wine-tasting room.
St-Amour Beautiful Romanesque figure of Christ in the church.
St-Georges-de-Reneins The 12th-century church in this village is one of the most beautiful in the Beaujolais. There is a charming little port on the Saône (Porte-Rivière).
Salles-Arbuissonnas An attractive village and a glorious square with lime trees, an 11th- and 12th-century church, 12th-century cloisters and a monumental gate.
Vaux-en-Beaujolais Large wine commune. The picturesque village served as the model for *Clochemerle*, the comic novel by Gabriel Chevallier.

SOUTHERN BEAUJOLAIS
This district is known as the *pierres dorées* ('gilded stones') because many of its houses, churches and châteaux are built in an ochre-coloured stone.

There are two signposted 'Circuits des Pierres Dorées' tourist routes.

Anse Gallo-Roman mosaics are displayed in the 12th–13th-century Château de Tours (formerly the town hall). On the east bank of the Saône is Château de St-Bernard, where the artists André Utten, Suzanne Valadon and (Valadon's son) Maurice Utrillo lived between 1923 and 1935.
Bagnols Village near Le Bois-d'Oingt which has attractive old buildings and a 15th-century château.
Bully Handsomely restored 15th-century castle and old village centre.
Charney A feudal stronghold and Romanesque church.
Châtillon-d'Azergues A large, partly restored 12th-century castle rises above the village. There are wall paintings in the chapel.
Lacenas Village near Villefranche. The *cuvage* at Château Montauzon is in an enormous hall above a vaulted cellar where the Compagnons du Beaujolais hold their meetings.
Lachassagne Village near Anse with beautiful views of the countryside.
Oingt A medieval village with a fortified church.
Ternand On a hill near the Azergues. Formerly fortified and the summer residence of the archbishops of Lyon. There are 14th- and 15th-century houses and frescoes in the crypt of the 15th-century church.

Villefranche-sur-Saône Take time to look at the old buildings (numbers 476–834 and 375–793) in the rue National. The church of Notre-Dame-des-Marais has a late-Gothic front.

LYONNAIS
l'Arbresle Parts of the old fortifications (a gatehouse, two towers and a keep) remain and there are old houses, including one that belonged to Jacques Coeur (1395–1456).
Éveux The Couvent de la Tourette is by Le Corbusier.
Lyon It would be impossible to list here all the places of interest in Lyon, France's second city. It certainly merits a visit for its old centre and numerous museums at least. Detailed information can be obtained from the Syndicat d'Initiative, place Bellecourt (on the peninsula between the Rhône and the Saône).
Millery The most important wine village of the southern Lyonnais, situated high above the Rhône Valley.
Mornant Gothic church with beautiful wood carving. North of the village stands the only surviving arch of a Roman aqueduct.
Riverie Medieval village south-west of Mornant. An artists' colony.
Savigny West of Sain-Bel with an ancient abbey.
Soucien-en-Jarrest Remains of a Roman aqueduct over the Pilat east of the village (to the north of Mornant).

Savoie

The Savoie wine district consists of a number of small, isolated areas scattered like islands across four *départements*. Most of the vineyards are in Savoie and Haute-Savoie but Ain and Isère also produce a little wine. The distance between the most northerly areas by Lake Geneva (Lac Léman) and the most southerly below Chambéry (near Ste-Marie-d'Alloix) is more than 100 kilometres. The whole zone is affected by the proximity of the Alps, whose mountainous landscape is punctuated by some vast lakes including the biggest in France, Lac du Bourget.

Light, fresh and pure-tasting white wines are the speciality. Savoie whites are the perfect accompaniment to the many kinds of freshwater fish caught here and to various local cheeses – as well as being an attractive antidote to mountain thirst.

For a district that has only 1,500 hectares of vineyard, the number of different wines produced is disproportionally large. There are two main appellations: Vin de Savoie and Roussette de Savoie. Some 15 villages are allowed to append their names to the Vin de Savoie appellation and four to Roussette de Savoie, thus distinguishing the special *crus*. The best *crus* for white Vin de Savoie are, from north to south, Ripaille, Marignan (both grown in the Crépy neighbourhood), aromatic and slightly pétillant Ayze (from the Bonneville area), Apremont, Abymes, Chignin and Montmélian. The last four lie to the south of Chambéry. Of the Roussette de Savoie appellations, those wines from the *crus* of Frangy (11 villages north of Seyssel) and Marestel (on the west bank of Lac du Bourget) enjoy the best reputation.

The wine laws also distinguish between different district wines. One of the best known is Crépy. This appellation once almost disappeared but was rescued through the efforts of Douvaine's Léon Mercier and his son Louis. The exclusively white wine is made from the Chasselas grape (often called Fendant in Switzerland) and the better examples, like top-quality Muscadets, are bottled *sur lie*, making them slightly sparkling from the trapped carbon dioxide.

Another district appellation is AC Seyssel. It takes its name from the town of Seyssel, which is divided by the River Rhône so that the western part is in Haute-Savoie and the eastern part in Ain. Still white wine, dry and firm, and delicate sparkling wines of a high standard are made here from Roussette (or Altesse), which is said to be identical to the Hungarian Furmint and is the only grape permitted in this appellation.

The white Jacquère grape is used for Vin de Savoie, the most important appellation. Jacquère does well on both lime and gravel soils, yielding refreshing, crisply dry wines. White Vin de Savoie can also come from other varieties such as Roussanne (sometimes called Bergeron in Savoie); Gringet (the Savagnin of the Jura); Chasselas and Chardonnay.

Although Savoie is largely devoted to white wine, the reds should not go untasted. Black Mondeuse especially, rich in tannin and colour, makes excellent country wines which are full of character, exceptionally lively – and perfect after skiing. Mondeuse does well in Frangy, Chignin and Arbin. Pleasant Gamay wines are also made; the best come from Chautagne, halfway between Seyssel and Aix-les-Bains.

The VDQS district of Vin du Bugey, west of Savoie, has only 250 hectares under vine. Among a varied range of wines the Chardonnay, lighter and fresher than in Burgundy, is much the best. The most noteworthy of Bugey's various *crus* is the sparkling rosé of Cerdon.

Château de Ripaille was once the hunting castle of the Savoy Court.

PRODUCERS OF SPECIAL INTEREST

Belluard Fils 74130 Ayse
Delicious sparkling Ayze.
René Bernard 73190 Apremont
Apremont is the speciality here.
Chritian Bolliet 01450 Merignat
Pierre Boniface/Domaine des Rocailles 73190 Les-Marches
Top-quality Apremont; the Mondeuse also merits attention.
Domaine G et G Bouvet
73250 Fréterine
Produces range of fine wines.
Cave Coopérative de Chautagne 73310 Ruffieux
Red and rosé wines are the speciality, made from Gamay with a little Pinot Noir and Mondeuse.
Cave Coopérative de Vins Fins de Cruet 73800 Cruet
Large operation producing a range of wines from diverse grapes. Red Arbin, Mondeuse and white Chignin and Cruet are especially good.
Le Caveau Buguste 01350 Vognes
Caves de la Tour de Marignan 74140 Sciez
Bernard Canelli-Suchet uses an organic approach to winemaking. His range includes whites from Chasselas and some dry and medium-dry sparkling wine.
Domaine Dupasquier
73170 Jongieux
The clay/limestone soils on the slopes of the *cru* Marestel are well suited to the Altesse (Roussette) grape. The Roussette de Savoie Marestel is a deep golden yellow; rich, dry and refined. M Dupasquier likes to age his wines well before releasing them.
Genoux et Fils 73800 Arbin
Makes a very fruity Mondeuse.
Edmond Jacquin et Fils
73170 Jongieux
Attractive the Roussette de Savoie.
Domaine Louis Magnin
73800 Arbin
Wines from a substantial acreage of

vieilles vignes (these are over 80 years old) need time to age but develop into well structured, powerful yet elegant examples. The Chignin-Bergeron is also recommended.
Domaine Claude Marandon
73000 Chambéry
Passionate winemaker Claude Marandon works his tiny, steep 40-acre vineyard by hand. Careful use of barrel fermentation gives dry whites with no residual sugar.
L Mercier et Fils (La Grand Cave de Crépy) 74140 Douvaine
Large estate and *négociant* producing well made wines. The Crépy Goutte d'Or is excellent.
Jacques Métral 74140 Loisin
Produces a complex, minerally and stimulating Crépy.
Domaine Mollex 01420 Corbonod
Seyssel's top producer of still and sparkling wines.
Domaine Monin et Fils
01350 Vognes
Greatly respected family estate with an extensive range. The fragrant Chardonnay is usually bottled *sur lie*. Also produces Savoie wines.
Michel et Jean-Paul Neyroud
74270 Designy
Excellent Roussette from the Frangy *cru* – also makes traditional red Vin de Savoie from Mondeuse.
J Perrier et Fils 73800 Les-Marches
One of the area's largest firms, producing a range of sound wines.
André et Michel Quénard
73800 Chignin
This enthusiastic father-and-son team is dedicated to seeking out the best expression of terroir in their wines which include Chignin Blanc (made from Jacquère), Chignin-Bergeron (Roussanne) and Vin de Savoie (Mondeuse).
Domaine Raymond Quénard
73800 Chignin
This small estate owns Bergeron vineyards (almost 100 years old) which produce limited quantities of

fine, well balanced wines. Somewhat controversially for Savoie, M Quénard uses malolactic fermentation to give dry wines with no residual sugar.

Château de Ripaille
74200 Thonon-les-Bains
This lake-side estate benefits from a microclimate influenced by Lake Geneva. Fresh, lively, floral wines from Chasselas; splendid red Mondeuse.

Gilbert Tardy 73190 Apremont
Commendable Apremont with depth and complexity.

Varichon et Clerc 01420 Seyssel
Sparkling wine is the speciality, some of which is made from local varieties including Royal Seyssel. Others are made from bought-in grapes.

Le Vigneron Savoyard
73190 Apremont
Modern equipment at this small cooperative ensures well made, if rather straightforward, wines.

Château de la Violette
73800 Les-Marches
Daniel Fustinoni produces excellent whites from Jacquère (Abymes and Apremont) and Altesse. Long fermentation ensures richness.

HOTELS

Lille Le Grand Port
73100 **Aix-les-Bains**
Tel (0)479 63 40 00
Quietly situated near the lake-side harbour. The popular restaurant serves good regional cuisine.

Hôtel Bellevue 74130 **Ayse**
Tel (0)450 97 20 83
Balconied rooms offer fine views, but there is a certain lack of atmosphere. Peaceful position; restaurant.

Hôtel Sapeur place de l'Hôtel-de-Ville, 74130 **Bonneville**
Tel (0)450 97 20 68
Enjoy good food with a regional touch in the restaurant l'Eau Sauvage.

Hostellerie des Comtes de Challes 73190 **Challes-les-Eaux**
Tel (0)79 72 86 71
This château hotel is peacefully situated in its own park and has a swimming pool and restaurant.

Les Princes 4 rue de Boigne
73000 **Chambéry**
Tel (0)479 33 45 36
Sound-proofed rooms with modern comfort. Good restaurant.

Relais de Chautagne 73310 **Chindrieux** Tel (0)479 54 20 27
Country hotel with over 30 rooms. Also a restaurant.

Hôtel de la Couronne 74140 **Douvaine** Tel (0)450 94 10 62
The cuisine enjoys a good reputation.

Hostellerie Château de Coudrée 74140 **Sciez**
Tel (0)450 72 62 33
Beautifully situated in a medieval castle by Lake Geneva. Stylish rooms, a park, heated swimming pool and restaurant.

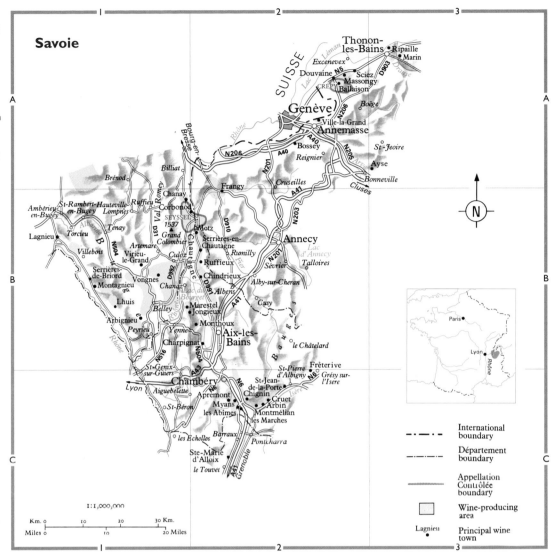

Savoie

RESTAURANTS

L'Essentiel 183 place de la Gare
73000 **Chambéry**
Tel (0)479 96 97 27
The town's best restaurant. Innovative Savoie cuisine; fine regional wines.

Auberge Gourmande 74140
Massongy Tel (0)450 94 16 97
Large, attractively decorated restaurant. Carefully executed country dishes; good set menus. Many regional wines.

Les Cinq Voûtes 73800
Montmélian Tel (0)479 84 05 78
Old vaulted dining rooms.

Rôtisserie du Fier 74190 **Seyssel**
Tel (0)450 59 21 64
Conservative, hearty cooking.

À la Vieille Port
74140 **Yvoire** Tel (0)450 72 80 14
Wonderful cellar hiding some rare Savoie wines. Terrace restaurant.

PLACES OF INTEREST

Aix-les-Bains The medicinal springs beside Lac du Bourget have been renowned since Roman times.

Gallo-Roman baths can still be seen beneath the present ones.

Belley Town in Bugey with the remains of Gallo-Roman fortifications, a medieval centre and the former bishop's palace. The cathedral of St-Jean has a 15th-century choir.

Bonneville Town in the Arve Valley with a museum of the Resistance. To the east the rare, slightly pétillant whites of the Ayze *cru* are grown.

Chambéry Many old buildings remain, among them the 13th–15th-century Château des Ducs de Savoie, (restored and extended in the 19th century). The interior of the Ste-Chapelle is painted with trompe-l'oeil. Until 1578 the *Saint Suaire* (Holy Shroud) was kept here (it is now in Italy). The Gothic cathedral of St-François-de-Sales (15th and 16th century) was once a chapel. The Fontaine des Éléphants is the town's most photographed monument. South-east of the town is Les Charmettes, where the writer and philosopher Jean-Jacques Rousseau lived with his mistress, Mme de

Warens, from 1735–41. He once wrote in praise of Savoie wines.

Culoz Bugey village where Henri Dunant, founder of the International Red Cross, was born. The Château de Montvéran is nearby.

Hantecombe This abbey projects into the Lac du Bourget on its west bank near Ontex. It was founded in this isolated spot in 1125 and contains the tombs of princes of Savoy.

Le-Bourget-du-Lac In this former seat of the House of Savoy there is a restored 13th-century monastery church with some beautiful carvings. Beside it are 15th-century cloisters and an Italian-style park.

Thonon-les-Bains Spa on Lake Geneva with some interesting churches and the local museum of the Chablais. Just to the north is Château de Ripaille, whose kitchen dates from the 15th century. The rare *cru* of Ripaille is produced nearby.

Yvoire Picturesque medieval village on Lake Geneva with old houses, a 14th-century castle, the remains of defensive walls and fortified gates.

Jura

The meticulously cultivated vineyards of the Jura are concentrated in a strip about ten kilometres wide that begins north of Arbois and ends south of Lons-le-Saunier. Large areas of the surrounding countryside remain untamed: about a third of the *département* (also called the Jura) is covered by forest interspersed with lakes and rugged rock formations. Roman amphorae found around Arbois, the Jura's wine centre and its largest appellation, testify to viticulture's long-standing association with the area.

The vineyard area of the Jura declined dramatically in the first half of this century. In the 19th century there were some 18,500 hectares, but this figure had shrunk to around 500 by just before World War II. Since then the area has gradually crept up to around 1,500 hectares, thanks largely to the work of grower and merchant Henri Maire who, in the 1950s and 1960s, stimulated expansion in the Jura and won recognition for its wines.

The Jura has a number of indigenous grape varieties found nowhere else in France. One is the black Poulsard, which gives a fairly delicate wine with little colour. It is often blended with Trousseau, which contributes more strength and colour. Among the white grapes, Savagnin, related to Gewürztraminer, is used for the rich Vin Jaune. Grapes from nearby Burgundy, including Pinot Noir, Chardonnay and Pinot Blanc, are also used.

About half the region's vineyards are on gently sloping hillsides around Arbois. Most of the producers make a wide range of wines – whites, rosés, reds, often a sparkling wine and a Vin Jaune – from the region's lime-, gravel- and clay-rich soil. The still wines are almost always light and may be produced either traditionally (wood-aged and fairly dour) or in a more contemporary fashion (without wood-ageing and with fruit and freshness in the taste). In general the white Arbois wines are better than the reds. The sparkling whites can also be attractive.

Vin Jaune is the great speciality of the Jura. By law this wine, made exclusively from Savagnin, must be matured for at least six years in oak casks. The casks are never completely filled and must not be topped up. A wrinkled film of yeast cells – resembling the *flor del vino* that gives sherry its distinctive nutty aroma – grows on the wine's surface. After six years, Vin Jaune is still fresh and lively: the layer of yeast cells absorbs oxygen and thus protects the wine from oxidation. Once bottled in its special 62-centilitre *clavelin*, a Vin Jaune can last for decades. The wine is similar to fino sherry, but in an unfortified form. Locally it is enjoyed with coq or poulet au Vin Jaune, as well as with the region's Comté cheese.

A superior Vin Jaune comes from the hill-village of Château-Chalon and a few adjoining communes. The small district of Château-Chalon is about 25 kilometres south of Arbois and forms an enclave in the Côtes du Jura appellation.

Côtes du Jura wines resemble those of Arbois but are a little lighter. Another small district within the Côtes du Jura is l'Étoile, where good-quality fresh, still and sparkling whites are made as well as Vin Jaune.

The rarest Jura wine, which was at one time virtually extinct, is Vin de Paille, made from bunches of grapes that have been laid out to dry. They used to be dried on straw (*paille*), but nowadays they are placed in small boxes in well-ventilated rooms. The grapes' sugar content increases as their moisture is lost, resulting in a wine with a mild yet fresh and lively taste, an aroma of nuts and figs, and at least 14.5 per cent alcohol. Production is limited and the wine is usually marketed in half-bottles.

PRODUCERS OF SPECIAL INTEREST

Château d'Arlay 39140 Arlay
Fine estate run by the Laguiche family. An excellent range of Jura wines made from traditional varieties. Look out for the unusual, deeply coloured red made from Poulsard, Trousseau and Pinot Noir, and the Vin Jaune, packed with nutty, spicy aromas.

Lucien Aviet
39600 Montigny-lès-Arsures
Excellent red Trousseau; good whites.

Jean Berthe-Bondet
39210 Château-Chalon
One of the area's star producers.

Domaine Désiré Petit
39600 Pupillin
Thanks to stainless-steel winemaking equipment, many of the whites, reds and rosés can now be drunk young.

Château de l'Étoile 39570 l'Étoile
Large producer specialising in sparkling wine made by the *méthode traditionnelle*. Also produces Vin Jaune and a red and rosé Côtes du Jura.

Fruitière Vinicole d'Arbois
39600 Arbois
This large cooperative, a regional institution, has done much for Jura wines by taking a more modern approach winemaking and producing fresher, less oxidised wines. Look out especially for the Cuvée Bethanie.

Fruitière Vinicole de Pupillin
39600 Pupillin
Small cooperative producing a range of wines, some of which are excellent. The whites are especially interesting. The cooperative also has some barrels of Vin Jaune with outstanding spicy aromas.

Domaine Michel Geneletti
39570 l'Étoile
Small family firm producing lovely buttery, hazelnutty whites. A little elegant Vin Jaune is also produced.

Domaine Grand Frères
39230 Passenans
Fairly large family estate, well known for its fruity, balanced red and white Côtes du Jura.

Domaine Frédéric Lornet
39600 Montigny-lès-Arsures
This energetic winemaker, based in an old abbey, is investigating the land of Arbois-aux-Salins with a view to reviving the vineyards in the north of the appellation. The reds (from Trousseau and Poulsard) are the most remarkable among his wines.

Domaine Jean Macle
39210 Château-Chalon
This estate owns some of the best vineyards of Château-Chalon including Les Dames, which yields well structured wines. Softer wines are made from the Sous Roche and Puits St-Pierre vineyards. Wines benefit from unusually long ageing.

Henri Maire (Château Montfort) 39600 Arbois
No-one has done more to revitalise and promote Jura wines than the energetic M Maire. All Jura AC wines and several brands are produced here, where the largest stocks of Vin Jaune are held.

Domaine Montbourgeau
39570 l'Étoile
High-quality Vin Jaune, barrel-aged Chardonnay, Vin de Paille and sparkling wine are produced at this extensive estate.

Pierre Overnoy
Pupillin, 39600 Arbois
M Overnoy takes a traditional approach in the vineyard and the winery. Wines are left on their lees for longer than usual giving rich, powerful aromas.

Domaine de la Pinte
Pupillin, 39600 Arbois
Large estate situated on the district's top sites. Classic Vin Jaune and Arbois Blanc are the highlights. The top *cuvées* of Savagnin and Trousseau peak at five to ten years.

Domaine Xavier Reverchon
39800 Poligny
In the heart of the Côtes du Jura this

The church of St-Just in Arbois is the focal point of the annual Fête de Biou.

young winemaker produces several outstanding wines including the rich, nutty Chardonnay/Savagnin blend from the Boutasses vineyard – and intense Vins Jaunes that demand patience!

Domaine Rolet 39600 Arbois
Family firm producing a large range of well made wine including Côtes du Jura (Chardonnay/Savagnin blend) and a fresh and fruity rosé from Poulsard.

André et Mireille Tissot
39600 Montigny-lès-Arsures
Family domaine where the whites are especially commendable. Rich yet fine Arbois Chardonnay and intense Vin Jaune. Reds are also produced.

Jacques Tissot 39600 Arbois
One of Arbois' leading producers with a range of well made wines. Those from Trousseau – supple, delicious and with red-berry aromas – are best but the rich, powerful Vin Jaune (which needs ageing) is also good.

WINE INFORMATION

Société de Viticulture
BP 396, avenue du 44 RI
39016 Lons-le-Saunier
Tel (0)384 24 21 07

WINE FÊTES

Arbois The Fête des Vins is celebrated around the middle of July. During the Fête du Biou on the first Sunday of September, wine-growers carry grapes through the streets to the church of St-Just.
Maynal The Foire des Vins du Sud-Revermont takes place at the end of July.

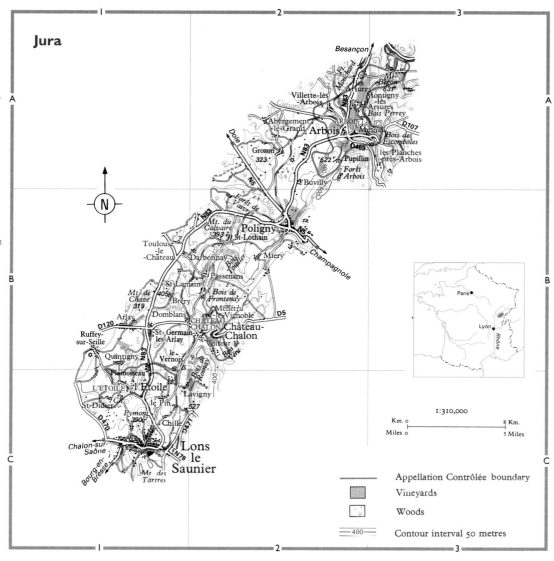

HOTELS

Hôtel Bourgeois 39110 Andelot-en-Montagne Tel (0)384 51 43 77
Simple yet welcoming and comfortable. The restaurant serves regional cuisine.
Hôtel de Paris 9 rue de l'Hôtel-de-Ville, 39600 Arbois
Tel (0)384 66 05 67
The main bedrooms have been refurbished but the annexe rooms, in an old presbytery, have better views. Good breakfasts. Also a fine restaurant (see Jean-Paul Jeunet, below).
Abbaye de Baume-les-Messieurs 39210 Baume Tel (0)384 44 64 47
Chambres d'hôtes are offered within the abbey walls.
Domaine de la Vallée Heureuse route de Genève, 39800 Poligny
Tel (0)384 37 12 13
Also a restaurant, the Moulin de la Vallée Heureuse (see below).
Hôtel des Deux Forts place du Vigneron, 39110 Salins-les-Bains
Tel (0)384 37 93 75
Modest hotel, well sited opposite the magnificent ancient buildings of Salins.

RESTAURANTS

Le Caveau 3 route de Besançon 39600 Arbois Tel (0)384 66 10 70
Overlooking the river. Well executed traditional dishes.
Jean-Paul Jeunet 9 rue de l'Hôtel-de-Ville, 39600 Arbois
Tel (0)384 66 05 67
Cuisine features wild plants and vegetables. Large wine-list, a third of which come from Jura. Modern decor. (See Hôtel de Paris, above.)
Les Templiers 35 Grande-Rue 39100 Dole Tel (0)384 82 78 78
Traditional cuisine plus more inventive dishes. Excellent wine-list, especially from the Jura.
La Grange Rouge 39570 Géruge
Tel (0)384 47 00 44
South of Lons, this is a great *ferme auberge* serving excellent meals.
Auberge de Rostaing
39230 Passenans
Tel (0)384 85 23 70
Situated between Poligny and Lons, offering good, honest, rustic cooking. Rooms are also available.

Moulin de la Vallée Heureuse route de Genève, 39800 Poligny
Tel (0)384 37 12 13
Simple but pleasant. Many well chosen Jura wines. (See Domaine de la Vallée Heureuse, above.)

PLACES OF INTEREST

Arbois This hard-working provincial town, plagued by heavy traffic, was the home of Louis Pasteur (1822–95). A small vineyard, now farmed by Henri Maire, once belonged to him. His parental home is now a museum. There is a Musée de la Vigne et du Vin in the basement of the town hall.
Arlay The château, built in classical style in the 17th century, rebuilt in 1774 and renovated in 1830, was originally a monastery. It is now a museum and one of the Jura's biggest and best wine estates.
Baume-les-Messieurs The village lies at the convergence of three valleys – one of them the imposing Cirque de Baume, a canyon with steep rock walls and caves. There is

an old abbey with a craft museum and a church with art treasures.
Château-Chalon The walls of a former castle are still standing. The church of St-Pierre dates from the 10th century. At the end of July and the beginning of August a *son et lumière* show depicts the conquest of the region by Louis XIV.
l'Étoile On the hill above the village (worth the climb for the panorama) stands the Château de l'Étoile, the most important local wine estate.
Lons-le-Saunier The crypt of the church of St-Désiré dates from the 11th century. The rue de Commerce has arcades full of atmosphere. The kitchen and dispensary of the 18th-century hospital are also worth visiting. The way into the old centre is via the Tour d'Horloge.
Le Pin A village just north of Lons-le-Saunier with a feudal castle. Its massive keep offers a panoramic view.
Poligny Old town full of treasures. The cooperative occupies a fine Gothic church, the vats fitting neatly in between the columns.

Bordeaux

If ever a place could symbolise wine, it would be Bordeaux. The Romans established viticulture in 'Burdigala' over 2,000 years ago, since when the corps, spirit and industry of the region has been inextricably linked to the vine. Far back in time the first commercial wines came from the hinterland along the Dordogne and from vineyards in Bordeaux' city limits, which are now demarcated by the urbanised appellation of Pessac-Léognan. The Médoc was developed in the 17th century when Dutch engineers made cultivation of the vine possible by draining this flat, marshland area.

Commerce is and always has been Bordeaux' raison d'être and consequently the region's evolution has been linked to its success as a centre for trade. Wine was already being exported across the Channel to England in the 12th century, after which commercial ties were established with northern Europe and the Hanseatic states. The 18th and early 19th centuries constituted a golden era for Bordeaux as trade with the West Indies generated untold wealth. Many of the great châteaux of the Médoc and much of the grand architecture within the city itself reflect the mercantile prosperity of this period.

The region has also had its periods of difficulty and depression. The onset of the fungal diseases oidium and mildew and the arrival of phylloxera in the late 19th century resulted in a devastation of the vineyards. The early 20th century was a period of economic gloom and the world oil crisis in 1973 had dire consequences in Bordeaux: stocks were off-loaded, merchants became bankrupt and properties changed hands with greater than usual rapidity.

Conditions of trade in the late 20th century are very different. Wine merchants long ago vacated their premises on the famous quai des Chartrons and moved to more modern, cost-effective constructions in the city's outer limits. Competition from overseas has become fiercer and has necessitated a more upbeat attitude towards marketing and promotion. Properties continue to change hands, but a greater percentage are now controlled by financial institutions and corporate enterprises.

Through all this Bordeaux can still justifiably claim to be the greatest fine-wine region in the world. There are presently 113,000 hectares of vineyard producing a yearly average of 700 million

The tidal Dordogne ebbs and flows alongside varied agricultural landscape, deciduous woodlands and mellow stone buildings in this welcoming region.

117

bottles of wine. This represents one quarter of all French AOC wine. On a human scale there are officially 13,951 wine-growers in the region, 4,000 of whom bottle their own produce.

No other region can match Bordeaux' output, but its reputation cannot be measured in production figures alone. Through the magic of its illustrious vineyard areas – Graves, Margaux, Pauillac, Pomerol, St-Émilion and Sauternes – and its prestigious estates such as Châteaux Latour, Pétrus and Yquem, Bordeaux remains the touchstone by which wine regions around the world measure their achievements.

Bordeaux is the collective image but this should not disguise the variety of wines produced. The evolutionary process of matching grape variety to *terroir* has led to a preselected list of varieties that are cultivated and blended according to the soil and climate in each sub-region. Hence the late-ripening Cabernet Sauvignon finds its full expression in the warm, free-draining gravel soils of the Médoc whereas Merlot is well suited to the cooler clay and limestone soils of St-Émilion and Pomerol. Add Cabernet Franc and you have the essential list of red varieties that are blended in different percentages to produce wines of varying nuance.

Eighty-three per cent of the region's wines are red, but its 17 per cent of white wines are of equal consequence. Sauvignon Blanc and Sémillon are the requisite white varieties and, depending on the conditions and winemaking techniques employed, can produce crisp, dry wines in Entre-Deux-Mers; rich, full, complex dry wines in Graves and voluptuously sweet wines in Sauternes.

The last area provides another example of nature's happy gifts to Bordeaux. The misty, humid conditions of Sauternes in early autumn allow for the onset of the prized noble rot or *pourriture noble*. This concentrates the sugar content of the grapes providing the rich base material for this heady style of wine.

Bordeaux' standing in the vinous world is closely tied to that of the great appellations and estates. But do not overlook the *petites appellations* where progress has been considerable over the last ten years. Improvements in viticultural and winemaking techniques, greater expertise and investment have led to overall improvements in quality that make these wines keen value for money.

The wines of The Côtes – Côtes de Bourg, Premières Côtes de Blaye, Premières Côtes de Bordeaux, Côtes de Castillon and Bordeaux-Côtes de Francs – and the lesser known Libournais: Lalande de Pomerol, Fronsac, Canon Fronsac and the St-Émilion satellites, are also important elements in the colourful mosaic that constitutes Bordeaux.

The pagoda and palace of Château Cos d'Estournel were built by a land-owner who chose to abandon wine-growing in favour of breeding Arab horses.

THE CITY OF BORDEAUX

France's fourth city, Bordeaux has many industries, an important university and a port, and many wine authorities and merchants have their headquarters here. The heart is the place de la Comédie with its splendid Grand Théâtre, designed by Victor Louis and completed in 1780. Europe's largest city square, the esplanade des Quinconces is only a few minutes' walk away, as is Le Vieux Bordeaux, the city's old quarter.

The city's vibrancy grows with acquaintance. It was Victor Hugo who said "Take Versailles, add to it Antwerp, and you have Bordeaux".

HOTELS

ALL ADDRESSES: 33000 **Bordeaux**
Burdigala Tel/Fax (0)556 90 16 16
Very comfortable; close to the centre.
Hôtel Etche Ona
Tel (0)556 44 36 49
Centrally located. Modest.
Normandie Tel (0)556 52 16 80
Fax (0)556 51 68 91
Large, traditional hotel.
Novotel-Bordeaux le Lac
Tel (0)556 50 99 70
One of the modern hotels in the exhibition area north of the city. Swimming pool and restaurant.
Royal Médoc Tel (0)556 81 72 42
Fax (0)556 51 74 98
Central, friendly and not too noisy. Popular with wine writers and buyers.

RESTAURANTS

ALL ADDRESSES: 33000 **Bordeaux**
Bistro des Quinconces
Tel (0)556 52 84 56

Market-fresh ingredients.
Bistro du Sommelier
Tel (0)556 96 71 78
Likable wines and inexpensive food.
La Chamade Tel (0)556 48 13 74
Pleasant atmosphere and food. A lower-priced lunch menu.
Le Chapon Fin
Tel (0)556 79 10 10
Top-class cooking in unique, grotto-like surroundings.
Chez Joël D Tel (0)556 52 68 31
For oyster-lovers.
Les Noailles Tel (0)556 81 94 45
Friendly brasserie open most hours. Simple fare.
Le Pavillon des Boulevards
Tel (0)556 81 51 02
Adventurous cooking with occasional oriental hints. A charming courtyard.
La Petite Brasserie
Tel (0)556 52 19 79
Bistro with good-value wine-list.
Jean Ramet
Tel (0)556 44 12 51
Distinctive atmosphere; fine cuisine.
La Tupina Tel (0)556 91 56 37
The cooking of the French south-west at its best.
Le Vieux Bordeaux
Tel (0)556 52 94 36
Classic cuisine in an atmospheric setting. Comprehensive wine-list.

WINE FÊTE

Every second year (1993, 1995, etc) VinExpo, the world's biggest wine fair for professionals, is held in June in the vast Parc des Expositions.

WINE INFORMATION

Maison du Vin 3 cours du 30-Juillet
33000 Bordeaux
Tel (0)556 00 22 88

Bordeaux

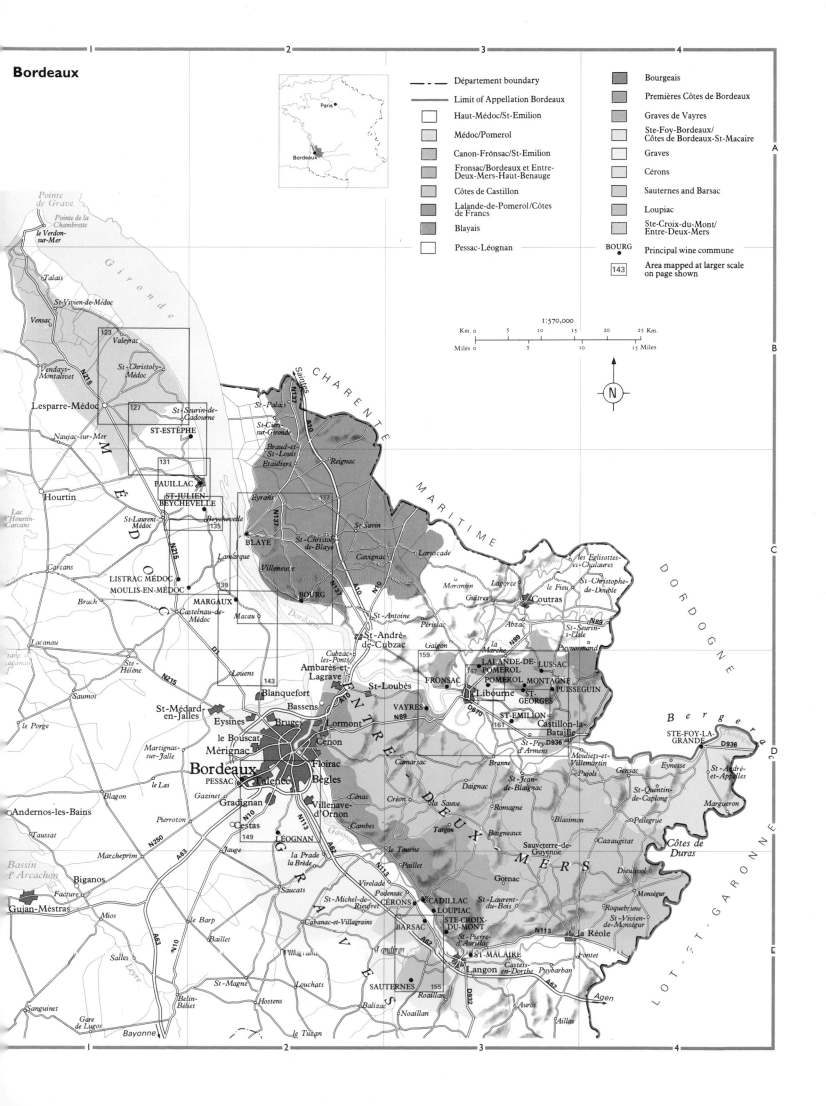

Département boundary
Limit of Appellation Bordeaux

Haut-Médoc/St-Emilion
Médoc/Pomerol
Canon-Fronsac/St-Emilion
Fronsac/Bordeaux et Entre-Deux-Mers-Haut-Benauge
Côtes de Castillon
Lalande-de-Pomerol/Côtes de Francs
Blayais
Pessac-Léognan

Bourgeais
Premières Côtes de Bordeaux
Graves de Vayres
Ste-Foy-Bordeaux/Côtes de Bordeaux-St-Macaire
Graves
Cérons
Sauternes and Barsac
Loupiac
Ste-Croix-du-Mont/Entre-Deux-Mers

BOURG   Principal wine commune

143   Area mapped at larger scale on page shown

Paris

Bordeaux

1:570,000
Km. 0   5   10   15   20   25 Km.
Miles 0   5   10   15 Miles

N

The 1855 Classification

Of the various wine classifications carried out in the Bordeaux region, that of the Médoc is not only the first and best known but also the most precise, consisting of 61 *grands crus classés* (including Haut-Brion in Graves) divided into five quality grades. The classification was drawn up in 1855 for the Paris World Exhibition by the courtiers (wine brokers) and was based on the price each wine had commanded over a long period (about 100 years), the wine's reputation and the current situation at the vineyard. There was nothing sensational about the classification, for comparable gradings had been in use among brokers and others for many years, but over 140 years later the classification is still valued and much used.

As well as the classified châteaux or *grands crus classés*, the Médoc has a large number of *crus bourgeois*, which now represent 49 per cent of the Médoc's total production. St-Émilion, Graves and Sauternes have their own classifications, which are discussed in the relevant sections.

Many of the châteaux welcome visitors, including the great names such as Haut-Brion, Haut-Bailly and de Chevalier. A telephone call or letter beforehand is advisable to check the opening hours and to find out whether an advance appointment is necessary. The most convenient times are usually from 10 to 12am and 3 to 5pm on week days, and some châteaux also welcome visitors on Saturday afternoons. Bear in mind, however, that the châteaux are particularly busy at harvest time, and that many properties close completely in August.

FIRST GROWTHS (PREMIERS CRUS)

Château Haut-Brion, Pessac, Graves
Château Lafite-Rothschild, Pauillac
Château Latour, Pauillac
Château Margaux, Margaux
Château Mouton-Rothschild, Pauillac
      (promoted in 1973 from second to first growth)

SECOND GROWTHS (DEUXIÈMES CRUS)

Château Brane-Cantenac, Cantenac-Margaux
Château Cos d'Estournel, St-Estèphe
Château Ducru-Beaucaillou, St-Julien
Château Durfort-Vivens, Margaux
Château Gruaud-Larose, St-Julien
Château Lascombes, Margaux
Château Léoville-Barton, St-Julien
Château Léoville-Las-Cases, St-Julien
Château Léoville-Poyferré, St-Julien
Château Montrose, St-Estèphe
Château Pichon-Longueville (Baron), Pauillac
Château Pichon-Longueville Comtesse de Lalande, Pauillac
Château Rauzan-Gassies, Margaux
Château Rauzan-Ségla, Margaux

Mouton-Rothschild was deservedly raised to parity with Lafite in 1973.

THIRD GROWTHS (TROISIÈMES CRUS)

Château Boyd-Cantenac, Cantenac-Margaux
Château Calon-Ségur, St-Estèphe
Château Cantenac-Brown, Cantenac-Margaux
Château Desmirail, Margaux
Château Ferrière, Margaux
Château Giscours, Labarde-Margaux
Château d'Issan, Cantenac-Margaux
Château Kirwan, Cantenac-Margaux
Château Lagrange, St-Julien
Château La Lagune, Ludon-Médoc
Château Langoa-Barton, St-Julien
Château Malescot St-Exupéry, Margaux
Château Marquis d'Alesme Becker, Margaux
Château Palmer, Cantenac-Margaux

Above: Local tradition has it that the gilded chais of Château Cos d'Estournel was inspired by the Sultan's palace at Zanzibar.

Left: The elegant moated 17th-century mansion of Château d'Issan lies in a charming spot where vineyard slope meets riverside meadow.

FOURTH GROWTHS (QUATRIÈMES CRUS)

Château Beychevelle, St-Julien
Château Branaire-Ducru, St-Julien
Château Duhart-Milon-Rothschild, Pauillac
Château Lafon-Rochet, St-Estèphe
Château Marquis-de-Terme, Margaux
Château Pouget, Cantenac-Margaux
Château Prieuré-Lichine, Cantenac-Margaux
Château St-Pierre, St-Julien
Château Talbot, St-Julien
Château La Tour-Carnet, St-Laurent

FIFTH GROWTHS (CINQUIÈMES CRUS)

Château d'Armailhac (formerly known as Château
  Mouton-Baronne-Philippe)
Château Batailley, Pauillac
Château Belgrave, St-Laurent
Château de Camensac, St-Laurent
Château Cantemerle, Macau
Château Clerc-Milon, Pauillac
Château Cos Labory, St-Estèphe
Château Croizet-Bages, Pauillac
Château Dauzac, Labarde-Margaux
Château Grand-Puy-Ducasse, Pauillac
Château Grand-Puy-Lacoste, Pauillac
Château Haut-Bages-Libéral, Pauillac
Château Haut-Batailley, Pauillac
Château Lynch-Bages, Pauillac
Château Lynch-Moussas, Pauillac
Château Pédesclaux, Pauillac
Château Pontet-Canet, Pauillac
Château du Tertre, Arsac-Margaux

The Médoc

The Médoc presents the gilded image of Bordeaux to the outside world. This is after all the region with a roll-call of prestigious châteaux and wines that, from the barrel to the auction room, are the source of dreams and giddy speculation. Geographically speaking, however, the Médoc is a rather flat and somewhat bleak peninsula to the north-west of the city of Bordeaux. The land is marshy but traversed by all-important undulating gravel ridges.

The region's early viticultural experiences were humble. Until the end of the 15th century the vine was planted in and around the villages of the southern Médoc and the wine drunk locally and in the city. In the 16th century the vineyards gradually spread northward to Margaux and elsewhere. A century later the great breakthrough came when, under the direction of Dutch engineers, marshes were drained and filled, bays and inlets reclaimed and coastlines straightened. The Dutch also regulated the courses of the many small streams (*jalles*) that flow through the Médoc and play an important part in its drainage. For many years the district near Bégadan in the northern Médoc was known as 'La Petite Hollande'.

Once the Médoc had been drained, the vineyard area grew rapidly. The world began to discover the wines from this new region, and the 'new French clarets' won a market in a by now prosperous England. At the end of the 17th and the beginning of the 18th century the first estate wines appeared. The first name to be noted was that of Haut-Brion, from the Graves district south of Bordeaux, but around 1703 those of Margaux, Lafite and Latour in the Médoc were also being reported. Almost all the wine estates were in the hands of Bordeaux' rich aristocracy who, as profits rose, were not slow to devote more land to vines. Even cornfields, hitherto so important to the region, had to make way for vineyards.

Fortune changed in the first half of the 19th century when wars and various political upheavals introduced the Médoc to a long period of depression. Prosperity, once so evident, was proving to be relative. In Bordeaux society it was said, 'there are three ways of ruining yourself: a *danseuse*, a racehorse and an estate in the Médoc. And the last is the quickest and surest!'. Despite this and later economic crises, the Médoc has continued to set the world's standards for red wine.

The key word is finesse: the subtleties possessed by the best Médocs are without equal. That such stylish, complex wines should be made here is due to a remarkable interplay of natural factors.

The Médoc has a notably mild climate in which extreme temperatures are exceptional. Its situation between two water masses – the Atlantic and the Gironde – contributes considerably to this (the name Médoc itself derives from words meaning 'middle land'). It does not have a damp, obviously maritime climate, despite its being near the sea, and this is due to the extensive pine-woods that shelter the wine-growing area from winds and rains from the west.

The mild climate is complemented by soil which has deep layers of gravel in many places. From the Tertiary period onwards this gravel has been carried down from the Massif Central and the Pyrenees and its complex composition is ever changing. The soil is generally poor, forcing the vines to push their roots deep into the subsoil to find nourishment: this factor is reflected in the complex wine. The high gravel content has the advantage of making the soil very permeable, resulting in good drainage which is improved further by the fact that many Médoc vineyards are on low, gently sloping hills. There is a saying in Médoc that from the best vineyards, you can always see the Gironde.

Because of the differences in soil, terrain and situation, each Médoc vineyard produces its own individual wine. Wines from neighbouring properties can be surprisingly different, even though the grape varieties cultivated are the same. Every wine-grower works with his or her own proportions of the main varieties Cabernet Sauvignon, Cabernet Franc and Merlot. Petit Verdot and Malbec are also grown on a small scale.

Wine-growing is practised in only a small part of the Médoc peninsula: a relatively narrow strip some 70–80 kilometres long that follows the Gironde from the first vineyards on the outskirts of Bordeaux almost to the northern tip. In only one place do vineyards reach about 12 kilometres inland from the river; usually the distance from the Gironde is less than five.

There are eight appellations: Margaux (which includes the southern Médoc communities Arsac, Cantenac, Labarde and Soussans); Moulis and Listrac-Médoc (in the central Médoc); St-Julien, Pauillac, St-Estèphe, the Haut-Médoc (which covers wines not included in the previous six) and Médoc (the northern, or Bas-Médoc). The classification of 1855 that divided the châteaux of the Médoc into five classes, or *crus classés*, is detailed on pages 120–21.

The large village of Soulac-sur-Mer on the Aquitaine coast developed from the Roman port of Noviomagnus. The ocean encroaches on the coastline here as the wind whips a constantly advancing sea of sand.

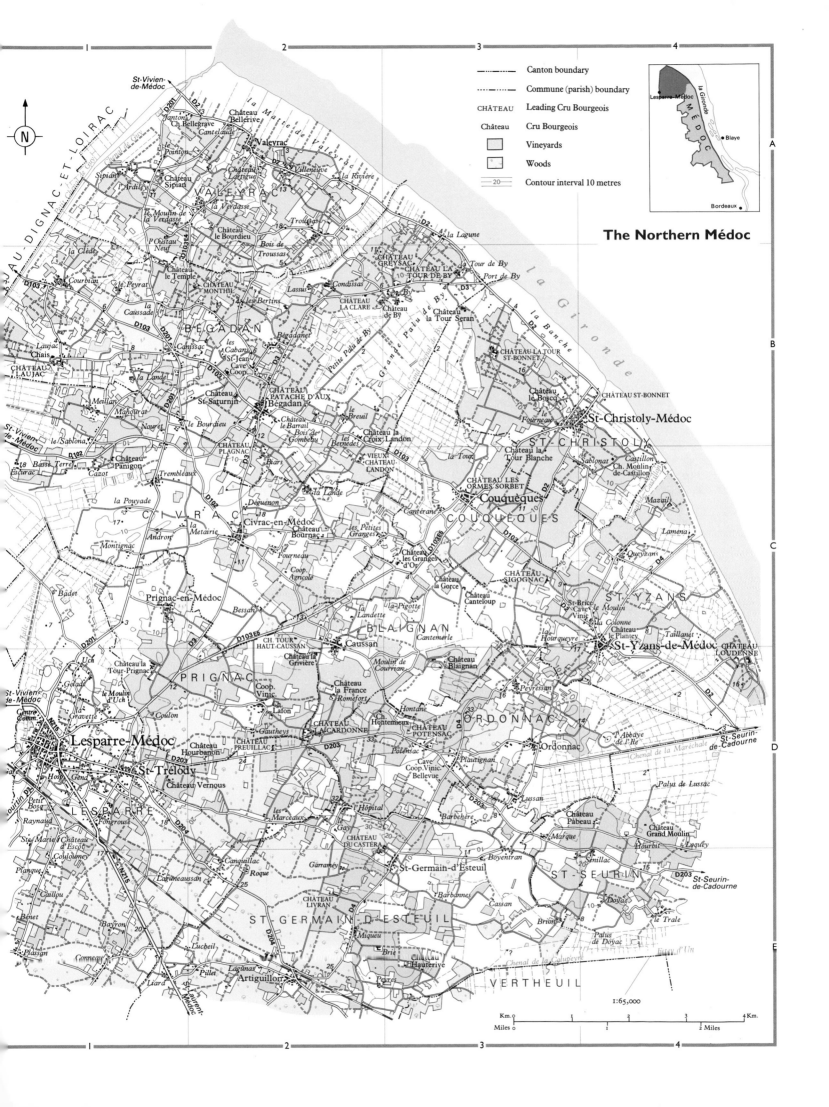

The Northern Médoc

Canton boundary
Commune (parish) boundary
CHÂTEAU Leading Cru Bourgeois
Château Cru Bourgeois
Vineyards
Woods
Contour interval 10 metres

1:65,000

Km.0 1 2 3 4 Km.
Miles 0 1 2 Miles

The Northern Médoc

The northern part of the peninsula is known as the Bas-Médoc or Lower Médoc. Wines from this region take the simple appellation Médoc in order to avoid the more derogatory title of Bas-Médoc. The surface area now covers some 4,700 hectares which represents 31.5 per cent of the vineyards in the Médoc peninsula.

Owing to the diversity of soils in this area, the wines vary in style. Some are robust verging on rustic, others have more delicacy with an attractive 'bright' fruit aspect, and a few have a more classic character but without the intensity of a *grand cru*. There is usually a high percentage of Merlot in the blend, making the wines more appealing at an earlier age.

The appellation Médoc starts just north of St-Seurin-de-Cadourne, the last commune of the Haut-Médoc, and is delimited to the north by the commune of St-Vivien-de-Médoc. There is a distinct change in the landscape, which becomes flatter, with more meadow land and fewer vine-clad slopes, and the villages seem smaller and quieter than those further south.

Until early in the 17th century this was mainly desolate and sparsely inhabited marshland. Then the first Dutch engineers, experienced in such matters, arrived to drain the marshes and build dikes. They left their mark: the name of the hamlet By, for example, near Bégadan, is probably of Dutch origin. Dutch influence extended even to the wine. In his *Traité sur les Vins du Médoc* of 1845, William Franck describes the wine from Château Livran in St-Germain-d'Esteuil as 'eminently Dutch' because of its soft characteristics, and the estate itself is called a *marque hollandaise*. There was also a period when a great deal of corn was grown in the northern Médoc and the district had numerous windmills. These have disappeared except for one: the splendidly restored mill, still in working order, near Château La Tour-Haut-Caussan at Blaignan.

Before the draining of the Médoc, the hills where the vines now grow formed islands of life and habitation. Roman foundations and mosaics have been discovered beneath the large *cuvier* at Château Laujac in Bégadan, and at St-Yzans-de-Médoc the remains of a Roman villa have been excavated. Wine-growing did not really make its breakthrough until the 19th century, but then the number of vineyards doubled between 1850 and 1895.

One reason for this spurt was the arrival at Château Loudenne of the Gilbey brothers, the London wine and spirits merchants. They bought this estate near the Gironde in 1875 to use as a depot from which they shipped vast quantities of Bordeaux wines to the British market. Walter and Alfred Gilbey (and their Grinling and Blyth cousins) built a cellar complex where 16,000 casks and 50,000 bottles could be stored, their own cooperage and a small railway to their dock on the busy river-front.

In the 19th century more land in the northern Médoc was planted with vines than is today, including large parcels of flat, low countryside. After the phylloxera disaster of the late 19th century and the subsequent crises in wine production, however, the growers concentrated their efforts on the better, higher land. As in the Haut-Médoc, there are hummocks of gravel outcrops that rise above the surrounding countryside, but they lie further apart and contain rather heavier clay soil, often combined with chalk. There are also sandy strips. As a result the wines are generally less fine and less complex than those from the southern Médoc. The influence of the sea is stronger in this part of the region, which makes it harder to grow Cabernet Sauvignon successfully. Many Médoc estates therefore plant high percentages of Merlot: 20–50 per cent is normal but as much as 60 per cent is sometimes encountered. The initial dour nature of many Médocs disappears with bottle-age. Like the wines of the Haut-Médoc they mellow, but this generally takes place over a shorter period.

Cooperatives play an important part, producing about 40 per cent of the Médoc's wine. Four out of the five cooperatives belong to the Uni-Médoc group which bottles an enormous quantity of wine – a third of all Médoc – at a vast centre at Gaillan. But increasingly it is the individual estates that are giving the appellation a good name and many of today's Médocs are of very high quality.

Château Loudenne, built on a hill of gravelly clay overlooking the river, has been in English hands for over 120 years.

PRODUCERS OF SPECIAL INTEREST

CRU BOURGEOIS CHÂTEAUX

Château Bellerive 33340 Valeyrac
Château Bellevue 33340 Valeyrac
Château Le Boscq
33340 St-Christoly-Médoc
Château La Cardonne
33340 Blaignan
The property was acquired by the (Lafite) Rothschild group in 1973 and considerable investments made. In 1990 it was sold to Guy Charloux. The wine is proficiently made in a modern, high-tech winery but can lack personality.
Château Castéra
33340 St-Germain-d'Esteuil
The château, a fine old castle with a drawbridge (the English laid siege to it in the 14th century), has been owned since 1986 by a German company.
Château La Clare
33340 Bégadan
This 20-ha domaine produces wines that are truly representative of the Médoc appellation. Grapes from the old vines are still hand picked, the rest are harvested by machine. A small percentage of the wine is aged in new-oak barrels and bottled with the mention 'Reserve du Château'.
Château Greysac
33340 Bégadan
The graceful grey white château is tastefully furnished. The wines are fresh and supple with good fruit expression. The better vintages have the potential to age ten years or so.
Château Lacombe-Noaillac
33590 Jau-Dignac-et-Loirac
One of the top properties in the far north of the Médoc appellation. The vineyard soils are of Garonne gravel, the installations modern and the winemaking highly proficient. The wines are well rounded with a subtle hint of oak.
Château Loudenne
33340 St-Yzans-de-Médoc
The English firm W & A Gilbey Ltd has its French headquarters here, which explains the large (now renovated) Victorian *chais*. The beautiful pale-pink château overlooking the river has its own gravelly vineyard producing a stylish, balanced Médoc that can mature over a long period. Loudenne also makes a delicious dry white Bordeaux from 50% Sauvignon, 50% Sémillon, which is unusual for the Médoc. Visitors are particularly welcome.
Château du Monthil
033340 Bégadan
Château Noaillac
33590 Jau-Dignac-et-Loirac
Located in one of the most northerly areas of the appellation, this property is owned by the Pagès family who are also associated with La Tour-de-By.

Fresh, vigorous wines with a marked fruit character for early drinking.
Château Les Ormes Sorbet
33340 Couquèques
An immaculate estate making polished, supple wines which last well.
Château Patâche d'Aux
33340 Bégadan
Substantial, mouth-filling wine, less reserved than other Médocs but with the ability to age well. The château is in the centre of Bégadan on the spot where stagecoaches used to stop.
Château Potensac
33340 Ordonnac
A most distinguished Médoc made by the Léoville-Las-Cases (St-Julien) Delon team: sinewy, with good colour and the odour of expensive barrels, a strong constitution, and fruit suggesting blackcurrants. The former church at Potensac (a hamlet near Ordonnac) functions as the cellar for the château.
Château Rollan de By
33340 Bégadan
One of the up-and-coming stars of the appellation situated on the gravel hillock of By, the best terrain in this zone of the Médoc. Wines are produced with the same attention to detail as is lavished on the *crus classés*.
Château St-Saturnin
33340 Bégadan
Château Sestignan
33590 Jau-Dignac-et-Loirac
Château Sigognac
33340 St-Yzans-de-Médoc
Château La Tour-de-By
33340 Bégadan
One of the larger properties with over 70ha under vine, but wines of a consistently high quality. The vineyard is situated on a gravel hill 400m from the Gironde and the vines now have an average age of 35–40 years. The wines are full bodied and firmly structured.
Château La Tour-Haut-Caussan
33340 Blaignan
A modest estate run by the friendly Philippe Courrian, who aims at no less than perfection. The wine is excellent, with elegance backed by wood and tannin. A superior version is called Réserve du Moulin after the restored windmill which graces the site.
Château La Tour-St-Bonnet
33340 St-Christoly-Médoc
The vineyard is set on a gravel ridge close to the estuary. The wines are made with a high percentage of Merlot and are concentrated and firmly structured. They have good ageing potential.
Château Tour Séran
33340 St-Christoly-Médoc
Château Vieux Robin
33340 Bégadan
Efficiently run 18-ha domaine situated on the road between Patâche d'Aux and La Clare. Well structured wines

Porte de Goulée, a charming little harbour just north of the village of Valeyrac.

with the ability to age. Bois de Lunier is the *cuvée speciale* aged in a percentage of new-oak barrels.

WINE FÊTES

Lesparre An annual wine fair at the beginning of August.
St-Yzans-de-Médoc Foire aux Sarments in mid-June.
Wine can be sampled at both events and food is available.

WINE INFORMATION

The **Maison du Médoc** in the place du Tribunalin, Lesparre, provides wine and tourist information and holds exhibitions of the work of local craftsman.

HOTELS

This part of the Médoc is thinly populated and off the main tourist route, so there are few hotels or restaurants of importance.

Château Layauga
33340 Gaillan-en-Médoc
Tel (0)556 41 26 83
A luxury hotel-restaurant with seven rooms, just north of Lesparre. The Michelin-starred restaurant provides fine classic dishes. Excellent wine-list.
Les Vieux Acacias 33340 Queyrac
Tel (0)556 59 80 63
On the D102E just north of Lesparre, in the peaceful setting of its own park.

RESTAURANTS

Lamb from Queyrac is a local speciality.

Auberges des Vignobles 33340 Blaignan Tel (0)556 09 04 81
Country-styled restaurant in the heart of the appellation. Hearty cuisine including foie gras, sweetbreads and grilled meats. Small but interesting

wine-list with the accent on the commune's wines.
La Maison du Douanier
33340 St-Christoly-Médoc
Tel (0)556 41 35 25
Situated near the harbour. Regional specialities such as lamproie, anguilles and duck at affordable prices.
Château Loudenne
33340 St-Yzans-de-Médoc
Tel (0)556 73 17 80
You can lunch in the Cuisine des Vendanges at the beautiful old Gilbey château overlooking the river, but make a reservation at least 48 hours in advance. The price includes a choice of two wines.
Hôtel-Restaurant des Pins
33780 Soulac-sur-Mer
Tel (0)556 09 80 01
Try the lamprey or the confit de canard here. There is also an interesting wine-list. Soulac is a typical seaside holiday resort at the northern extremity of the D101.
La Côte d'Argent
33123 Le Verdon-sur-Mer
Tel (0)556 09 60 45
Restaurant with a flower-filled terrace. Fruits de mer are the speciality. Near the tip of the Médoc peninsula.

PLACES OF INTEREST

Bégadan The church, which has an 11th-century apse, is classified as a historic monument.
By At Château La Tour-de-By, resplendent in the middle of the vineyard, there is an old beacon that was in service until 1860.
Lesparre A busy market town with good shops, Lesparre acts as a centre for the district. It also has a 14th-century square tower called the Honneur de Lesparre.
St-Yzans-de-Médoc A museum of winemaking equipment at Château Loudenne was destroyed by fire in 1986 but a new collection is being assembled.

St-Estèphe

Château Lafite stands on the northern boundary of Pauillac. To the north there is a meadow of tall poplars around a little stream (called a *jalle* in the Médoc) which marks the boundary of St-Estèphe. The road then bends and climbs to where a surprise awaits the traveller, for suddenly the outline of an oriental pagoda heaves into view. The pagoda, complete with bells, adorns a curious white building, the *grand cru classé* Château Cos d'Estournel. 'Cos' is a leader among the second growths of Bordeaux: wine of potent character with at least ten years of life.

After this bizarre prelude it hardly comes as a surprise to find that the landscape of St-Estèphe differs from that of the rest of the Médoc. After you turn right near Cos d'Estournel into a narrow minor road, the D2E3, a broad undulating plateau opens out, the green of its vineyards interrupted only by a few isolated châteaux.

St-Estèphe is the Médoc's biggest wine commune with 1,370 hectares under cultivation. A deep bed of gravel extends beneath the often sandy surface soil, especially in the south-east. The stones are sometimes so large, hard and translucent that they can be cut and polished into ornaments. (In the last century one grower had all the gravel removed from his land – and wondered why his wine declined in quality.) Chalk as well as gravel is found around St-Estèphe, particularly in the north-east, and clay is in the subsoil almost everywhere. There is generally a higher proportion of Merlot to Cabernet Sauvignon in the wines than there is farther south – up to 40 per cent on some estates.

This is *cru bourgeois* country where such estates represent 54 per cent of the production and a generally high quality level. There are only five classed growths, led by the two second growths Montrose and Cos d'Estournel. The wines are full of colour, vigorous, rather stronger and heartier than those of Pauillac, and as a rule generously provided with tannin. The better ones often demand years of patience: only after long maturing in bottle do their nuances of nose and taste develop while the tannin discreetly retreats in favour of smoothness and harmony.

The region's history goes back at least to Gallo-Roman times. Until the 18th century St-Estèphe was known as St-Estèphe-de-Calon, the calon probably derived from a Gaulish term meaning 'wood' or 'brushwood' (one of the district's best-known châteaux is Calon-Ségur). Wine-growing began to flourish in the 13th century thanks to the monks of the priory of Notre Dame des Couleys. The buildings of this former religious house still stand: rebuilt in 1662, they now serve as cellars for Château Meyney. When the monks

The long-lived St-Estèphe produced from Cos d'Estournel's vineyards develops finesse and breed in bottle and is regularly one of the Médoc's best wines.

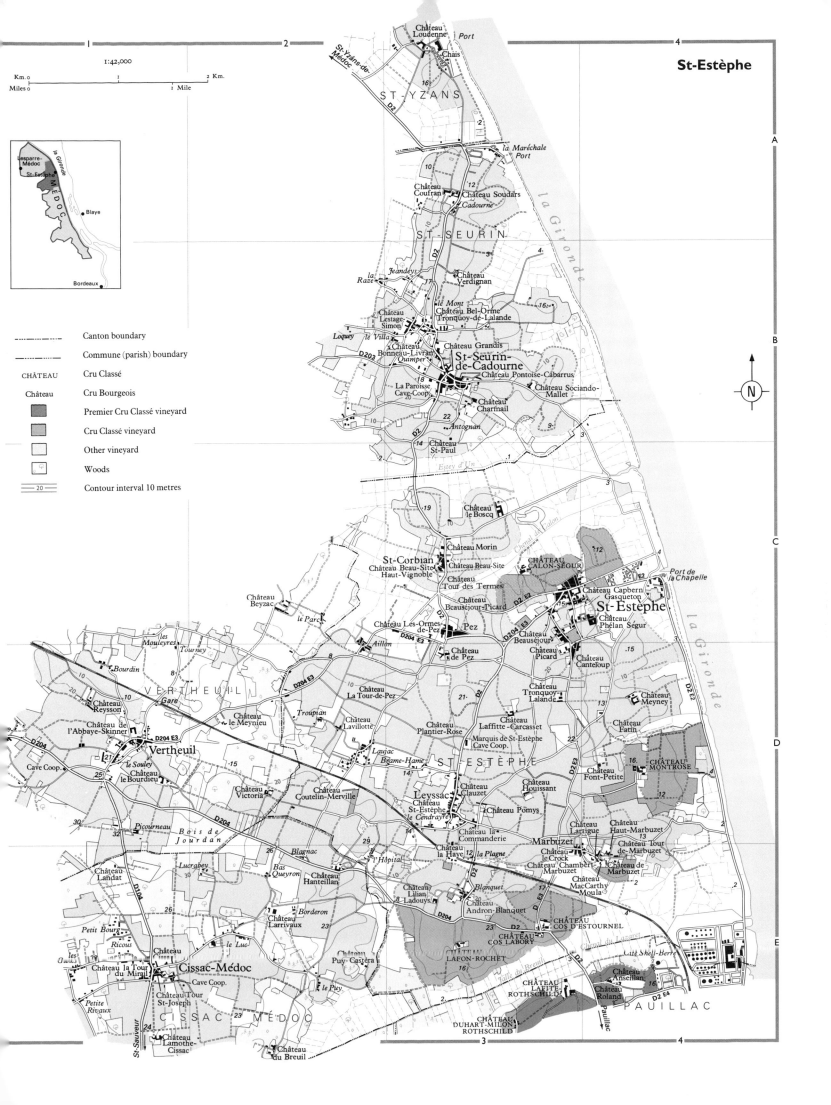

St-Estèphe

1:42,000

Km. 0   1   2 Km.
Miles 0   1 Mile

Lesparre-
Médoc
St-Estèphe
la Gironde
MÉDOC
Blaye
Bordeaux

- - - - -   Canton boundary

– – – –   Commune (parish) boundary

CHÂTEAU   Cru Classé

Château   Cru Bourgeois

Premier Cru Classé vineyard

Cru Classé vineyard

Other vineyard

Woods

═══ 20 ═══   Contour interval 10 metres

N

were establishing themselves, St-Estèphe itself was a busy port. A new, larger harbour had been created in the 12th century, which was used by merchant ships and also accommodated the steady traffic of pilgrims on their way to Santiago de Compostela. For many centuries, until 1704, the church of Notre Dame Entre Deux Arcs stood by the harbour and must have been a conspicuous landmark along the Gironde. Only a small chapel remains.

St-Estèphe's importance as a port was considerably enhanced in 1469 when Louis XI forbade English captains to sail up the Gironde beyond this point. The result was that for a while the harbour at St-Estèphe replaced that of Bordeaux. There is nothing now to be seen

of this proud past. The Port de la Chapelle is now just a small harbour frequented by fishing boats and yachts. A small modern residential quarter has been built close by.

St-Estèphe is surrounded by villages that belong to the Haut-Médoc appellation. To the north lies St-Seurin-de-Cadourne, which borders on the Médoc district; to the west are the partly wooded areas of Vertheuil and Cissac. Gravel is less prevalent here, though outcrops still occur, and the countryside is flatter. The wines from these neighbouring villages are rather less strong and less rich in tannin than those from St-Estèphe, but their quality can be surprising – a few of the *crus bourgeois* even reach *cru classé* level.

Above: A high proportion of Merlot in the blend gives St-Estèphe wines a unique succulence and persistence of flavour.

PRODUCERS OF SPECIAL INTEREST

ST-ESTÈPHE

Château Calon-Ségur
33250 St-Estèphe
3e grand cru classé
In the 17th century this estate was the favourite property of the rich and powerful Alexandre de Ségur, whose other possessions included Lafite, Latour, Mouton and de Pez. The château now belongs to the Capbern-Gasqueton (of Châteaux Capbern-Gasqueton, du Tertre, etc) and Peyrelongue families. The wine is intense and sinewy: a substantial St-Estèphe that lingers in the mouth.

Château Capbern-Gasqueton
33250 St-Estèphe
cru bourgeois
The château, just behind the church at St-Estèphe, is the home of the Capbern-Gasquetons, owners of Château Calon-Ségur. Sound, traditionally made wine for keeping.

Château Cos d'Estournel
33250 St-Estèphe
2e grand cru classé
The d'Estournel family had various properties in St-Estèphe in the 17th century, including a vineyard in the hamlet of Caux (the old spelling of Cos). After Gaspard d'Estournel took over the running of the wine properties in 1810 he decided to vinify the Cos wine separately. This 'Caux' proved in fact to be better than the other St-Estèphes that Gaspard produced, due largely to the very gravelly slopes on which the vines were planted. Today the Prats family owns Cos d'Estournel and, under the management of Bruno Prats, the château is perfectly maintained. The wine is excellent: distinguished, with a firm structure and beautiful balance. Normally it needs to age for at least a decade. Almost every vintage is matured in new-oak casks. During the summer months, visitors are welcomed by a multi-lingual guide.

Château Cos Labory
33250 St-Estèphe
5e grand cru classé
Although the vineyards of Cos Labory and Lafon-Rochet adjoin, they

Above: Behind the enclosing walls of Château Cos d'Estournel lie modern installations and a spacious cellar.

produce totally different wines. Cos Labory is a fairly soft St-Estèphe, accessible quite young, with more suppleness than finesse. There is a high percentage of Cabernet Franc planted at this domaine.

Château Le Crock
33250 St-Estèphe
cru bourgeois
The château, surrounded by a large park in the hamlet of Marbuzet, has the same owners as Léoville-Poyferré in St-Julien. Strong wine rich in tannin, excellent for laying down.

Château Haut-Marbuzet
33250 St-Estèphe
cru bourgeois
Wines from this estate are rich and voluptuous due to the production methods. Grapes are harvested at optimum maturity, vinified at a high temperature (up to 35°C) with a long period of maceration. The ageing takes place in 100% new-oak barrels. Unusually, 70% of Haut-Marbuzet is sold directly to private clients.

Château La Haye
33250 St-Estèphe
cru bourgeois

Château Houissant
33250 St-Estèphe
cru bourgeois

Château Lafon-Rochet
33250 St-Estèphe
4e grand cru classé
Lafon-Rochet, the only fourth growth in St-Estèphe, is the property of the Tesseron family which also owns Château Pontet-Canet in Pauillac. It was acquired in 1960 and over the years the vineyard, cellars and château have been steadily renovated. The wines, with around 55% Cabernet Sauvignon in the blend, are classically well-structured and long-lived.

Château Lilian-Ladouys
33250 St-Estèphe
cru bourgeois
The new star in St-Estèphe. A 50-ha property put together by Christian and Liliane Thiéblot in 1989, now making wine of *cru classé* quality.

Château Marbuzet
33250 St-Estèphe
cru bourgeois
A small vineyard with a fine Louis XVI château, owned by the Prats family of Cos d'Estournel. The wine used to be sold as the Cos second label but Marbuzet is now treated as a separate estate.

Château Meyney 33250 St-Estèphe
cru bourgeois
This perfectly preserved former abbey is now a flourishing wine estate making a highly reliable St-Estèphe.

Château Montrose
33250 St-Estèphe
2e grand cru classé
There are few estates that can match Montrose for the staying power of its wines. Vintages that date back to

More pleasantly rural than Pauillac, St-Estèphe comprises a scattering of hamlets, steepish slopes and wooded parks.

the early 1900s are seemingly years younger. Like Latour's, the wines are firm in their youth with a reserve of power and concentration. The property, which lies close to the Gironde estuary to the south of St-Estèphe, has been in the hands of the Charmolüe family since 1889. It is presently owned by Jean-Louis Charmolüe. The wines have around 65% Cabernet Sauvignon in the blend and the selection process allows for the production of an excellent second wine, La Dame de Montrose.

Château Les Ormes de Pez
33250 St-Estèphe
cru bourgeois
Owned by the Cazes family of Château Lynch-Bages. The *chais* was renovated in 1981 and the barrel cellar, which burned down in 1989, has been rebuilt. The wines are of a high standard.

Château de Pez 33250 St-Estèphe
cru bourgeois
Reliable estate now generally considered to be on a par with many classed growths. The wines are traditional in style with good concentration and firm structure.

Château Phélan-Segur
33250 St-Estèphe
cru bourgeois
One of the larger estates of the commune, next to Châteaux Montrose and Meyney. A magnificently refurbished house and cellars; now a wine to watch.

Château Pomys 33250 St-Estèphe
cru bourgeois

Tronquoy-Lalande
33250 St-Estèphe
cru bourgeois

HAUT-MÉDOC

Château Bel-Orme Tronquoy-de-Lalande
33250 St-Seurin-de-Cadourne
cru bourgeois
The small château was designed by the architect of the Grand Théâtre in Bordeaux.

Château Le Bourdieu
33250 Vertheuil
cru bourgeois
Makes a flawless wine.

Château du Breuil
Cissac 33250
cru bourgeois

Château Cissac Cissac 33250
cru bourgeois

Château Coufran
33250 St-Seurin-de-Cadourne
cru bourgeois
Attractive wines made from a high percentage of Merlot.

Château Hanteillan Cissac 33250
cru bourgeois
Well worth a visit: a great deal of money has been spent on the restoration of the splendid cellars.

Château Sociando-Mallet
33250 St-Seurin-de-Cadourne
cru bourgeois
The wines are consistently as good as many classed growths.

Château Verdignan
33250 St-Seurin-de-Cadourne
cru bourgeois

WINE INFORMATION

The little **Maison du Vin** of St-Estèphe [tel (0)556 59 30 59] is on the square facing the church. Information about the region is available here, but of even greater interest is the large range of wines on sale. Art exhibitions are held from time to time, mainly during the summer months.

HOTELS AND RESTAURANTS

There is a limited choice of hotels and restaurants in St-Estèphe and the surrounding area. *Cru bourgeois* **Château Pomys** in Leyssac [tel (0)556 59 73 44] offers bed and breakfast and has ten rooms available; otherwise it might be wiser to look for food and accommodation elsewhere in the Médoc.

Hôtel du Midi
33250 **St-Seurin-de-Cadourne**
Tel (0)556 59 30 49
For anyone who has been unable to find accommodation elsewhere. Totally without atmosphere. There is also a simple restaurant.

PLACES OF INTEREST

Cissac Ruins of an old castle close to the present Château du Breuil.
St-Estèphe The 19th-century church in the village square has a tower shaped somewhat like a bottle – a fact that the local wine-growers like to point out to their guests.
Vertheuil The Romanesque church was originally built in the 11th century but rebuilt in the 15th. In summer, exhibitions of work by artists and craftsmen of the region are held in what was the old monastery. The local château is private property and cannot be visited.

Pauillac

For many wine-lovers around the world, Pauillac embodies classic Médoc wine. With its dark intensity, sturdy frame that gives great ageing potential and distinctive bouquet of blackcurrants, mint, cedar and cigar box, it is the most imposing of wines. The region is also studded with a host of exceptional estates including three of the four Médoc first growths: Lafite-Rothschild, Latour and Mouton-Rothschild, as well as 15 other classed growths.

There is Pauillac the small provincial town with a tiny pleasure boat and fishing port, and there is Pauillac the appellation. The latter is bounded to the north by St-Estèphe and to the south by St-Julien. There are now around 1,200 hectares under vine with the *grands crus classés* representing 84 per cent of the appellation's production. The soils are composed of deep-bedded Garonne gravel. This provides excellent drainage as well as thermal heat, which helps to ripen the grapes. It is on these soils that the late-ripening Cabernet Sauvignon is at its best and, not surprisingly, this variety dominates in Pauillac.

The appellation is divided into two undulating plateaux lying north and south of the town and separated by the Chenal du Gaer. The two Rothschild properties, Châteaux Lafite and Mouton, are located on the northern plateau. Lafite, whose name originates from the old Médoc word for a mound or knoll, even has a small parcel of vines in St-Estèphe. Thanks to the life-long work of the Baron Philippe de Rothschild, Mouton was upgraded from second to first-growth in 1973. The motto on the legendary label was changed to read *Premier je suis, second je fus, Mouton ne change* (First I am, second I was, Mouton does not change).

A number of other classified growths in the northern part of Pauillac are also owned by the two Rothschild families. Château Duhart-Milon-Rothschild is owned by the Lafite-Rothschilds and the two fifth growths Clerc-Milon and d'Armailhac (known consecutively between 1933 and 1989 as Mouton d'Armailhacq, Mouton Baron Philippe and Mouton Baronne Philippe) are part of the dominion inherited by Philippine de Rothschild from her father the Baron Philippe. The other notable wine in this sector is Château Pontet-Canet.

In the very south of the appellation bordering St-Julien is Pauillac's other first growth, Château Latour. The saying in the Médoc is that the great estates can 'see' the Gironde: at some 200 metres from the estuary, Latour could not be much closer. The prestige of the wines can be traced back to the 16th century and, like Lafite and Calon-Ségur, Latour was once the property of one of the region's original great landowners Alexandre Marquis de Ségur, president of the Bordeaux Parlement.

In close proximity are the two second growths Pichon-Longueville Comtesse de Lalande and Pichon-Longueville (Baron). The former overshadowed Pichon-Baron, as it was known, for a number of years until the property was acquired by the Axa-Millésimes insurance group in 1987. Under the direction of Jean-Michel Cazes of Château Lynch-Bages the wines have since gone from strength to strength. Château Lynch-Bages, situated just to the north of these two estates, was classed as a fifth growth in 1855 but today the wines are more highly esteemed, selling at the same level as the second growths.

Another 'Bages' (the name refers to the plateau in the south) making fine wines is Château Haut-Bages-Libéral. Inland from these two properties, another fifth growth presently making eye-catching wines is Château Grand-Puy-Lacoste, owned by the Borie family of Château Ducru-Beaucaillou in St-Julien. The wines are long-lived and have the mineral or 'lead pencil' expression of a true Pauillac. Further west in the commune of St-Sauveur, the wines take on the appellation Haut-Médoc.

With the preponderance of classed growths in Pauillac there are few châteaux of *cru bourgeois* status. There are, however, several small growers attached to the local cooperative, which sells some of its production under the label La Rose Pauillac.

In days when Pauillac was an important port, the many islands studding the Gironde made navigation up-river to Bordeaux a hazardous business.

Pauillac

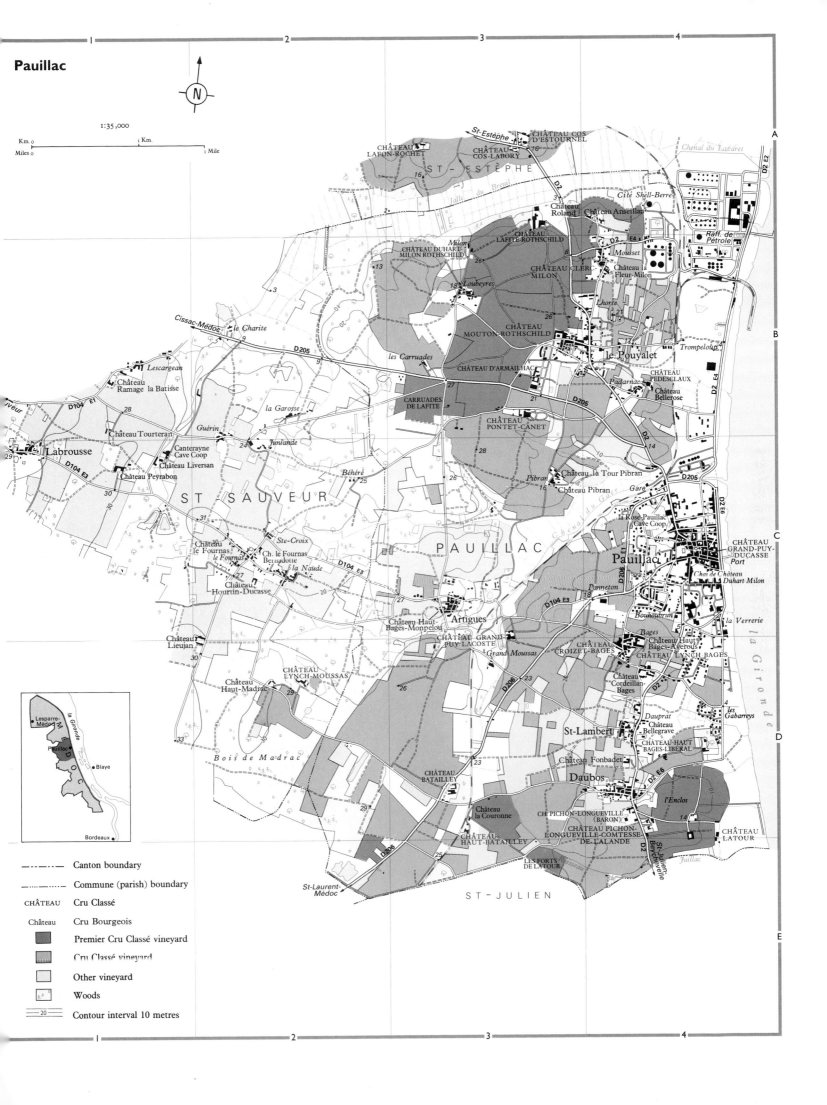

N

1:35,000

Km. 0 ___ 1 Km.

Miles 0 ___ 1 Mile

Legend

— ·· — ·· — Canton boundary

— · — · — Commune (parish) boundary

CHÂTEAU Cru Classé

Château Cru Bourgeois

Premier Cru Classé vineyard

Cru Classé vineyard

Other vineyard

Woods

—20— Contour interval 10 metres

Map labels

St-Estèphe
CHÂTEAU COS D'ESTOURNEL
CHÂTEAU LAFON-ROCHET
CHÂTEAU COS-LABORY
ST-ESTÈPHE
Cité Shell-Berre
Château Roland
Château Anseillan
CHÂTEAU LAFITE-ROTHSCHILD
Milon
CHÂTEAU DUHART-MILON ROTHSCHILD
CHÂTEAU CLERC MILON
Château la Fleur-Milon
Mousset
Raff. de Pétrole
Loubeyres
L'horte
Chenal du Lazaret
CHÂTEAU MOUTON-ROTHSCHILD
les Carruades
Cissac-Médoc
le Charite
le Pouyalet
Trompeloup
CHÂTEAU D'ARMAILHAC
CHÂTEAU PEDESCLAUX
Château Bellerose
Padarnac
Lescargean
Château Ramage la Batisse
CARRUADES DE LAFITE
CHÂTEAU PONTET-CANET
Château Tourteran
Guérin
la Garosse
Pibran
Château la Tour Pibran
Château Pibran
Canterayne Cave Coop
Château Liversan
Juniande
Gare
Béhéré
la Rose-Pauillac (Cave Coop)
Château Peyrabon
Labrousse
ST SAUVEUR
CHÂTEAU GRAND-PUY-DUCASSE Port
Ste-Croix
Château le Fournas
le Fournas
Ch. le Fournas Bernadotte
la Naüde
PAUILLAC
Pauillac
Chai de Château Duhart-Milon
Panneton
Château Hourtin-Ducasse
Bouboubrian
la Verrerie
Château Haut-Bages-Monpelou
Artigues
Bages
CHÂTEAU GRAND-PUY-LACOSTE
Château Haut-Bages-Averous
CHÂTEAU LYNCH-BAGES
Château Lieujan
Grand Moussas
CHÂTEAU CROIZET-BAGES
CHÂTEAU LYNCH-MOUSSAS
Château Haut-Madrac
Château Cordeillan-Bages
Dauprat Château Bellegrave
les Gabarreys
St-Lambert
CHÂTEAU HAUT-BAGES-LIBERAL
Château Fonbadet
Daubos
CHÂTEAU BATAILLEY
l'Enclos
Château la Couronne
Ch. PICHON-LONGUEVILLE (BARON)
CHÂTEAU HAUT-BATAILLEY
CHÂTEAU PICHON-LONGUEVILLE-COMTESSE-DE-L'ALANDE
CHÂTEAU LATOUR
St-Laurent-Médoc
LES FORTS DE LATOUR
St-Julien-Beychevelle
la Gironde
St-Laurent-Médoc
ST-JULIEN
Bois de Madrac

Inset map
MÉDOC
Lesparre-Médoc
la Gironde
Pauillac
Blaye
Bordeaux

PRODUCERS OF SPECIAL INTEREST

PAUILLAC

Château d'Armailhac
33250 Pauillac
5e grand cru classé
The former Mouton-d'Armailhacq was bought in 1933 by Baron Philippe de Rothschild of Mouton-Rothschild, the adjoining estate. The château, actually a half-completed villa, stands beside the Mouton-Rothschild drive. The wine is alluring and well balanced, lighter and quicker to develop than the Mouton-Rothschild. From 1956 until 1974 the estate was called Mouton Baron Philippe; 'Baron' was changed to 'Baronne' at the time of the 1975 vintage in honour of the Baron's late wife Pauline. Since the 1989 vintage, it has reverted to the original name: Château d'Armailhac.

Château Batailley
33250 Pauillac
5e grand cru classé
Trees from all parts of the world grow in the estate park and at harvest time the woodland floor is a carpet of pink cyclamen. Batailley is a respectable Pauillac that requires long ageing. Not renowned for complexity, it has good balance between fruit and tannin.

Château La Bécasse
33250 Pauillac

Château Clerc-Milon
33250 Pauillac
5e grand cru classé
Since Philippe de Rothschild bought the estate in 1970 the wine has merited attention. Recent vintages have been very good. A modest house serves as the château.

Château Colombier-Monpelou
33250 Pauillac
cru bourgeois

Château La Couronne
33250 Pauillac
cru bourgeois

Château Croizet-Bages
33250 Pauillac
5e grand cru classé
Earlier vintages have repeatedly given great pleasure but the estate seems to have been going through a difficult period. Even in such great years as '82, '85 and '88 the wines were below standard. In general the wines are early maturing.

Château Duhart-Milon-Rothschild
33250 Pauillac
4e grand cru classé
The vineyard borders on that of Lafite-Rothschild (which has the same owners) and produces a distinguished Pauillac. Produced and cellared in a *chais* in Pauillac, the wine is sturdy in style.

Château La Fleur Milon
33250 Pauillac
cru bourgeois
The vineyards of this small estate are located to the north of the town. The wines are firm, structured and long-lived.

Château Fonbadet
33250 Pauillac
cru bourgeois
The 19th-century château is surrounded by park land. The vines are old and the wines full flavoured and dense, in certain vintages on a par with a number of the Pauillac fifth growths.

Château Gaudin
33250 Pauillac

Château Grand-Puy-Ducasse
33250 Pauillac
5e grand cru classé
The château is on the quay at Pauillac, some distance from the three scattered plots that make up the 37-ha vineyard. Considerable investment since 1971 has meant that both production and quality have improved. The wine is sound, with fruit, plenty of colour and more than usual charm.

Château Grand-Puy-Lacoste
33250 Pauillac
5e grand cru classé

Fining or clarifying the wine with egg whites at Château Pontet-Canet.

This estate, in the hands of the Borie family of Ducru-Beaucaillou (St-Julien), produces a meaty Pauillac with plenty of depth and flavour and the class of a *troisième cru*. A little valley beside the château shelters a romantic private garden with hydrangeas, bordering a canal.

Château Haut-Bages-Libéral
33250 Pauillac
5e grand cru classé
This 25-ha estate has been under the same ownership as Château Chasse-Spleen in Moulis and Châteaux La Gurgue and Ferrière since 1983. The vineyard is well sited with a portion adjacent to the Latour vineyard. The wines are usually rich and aromatic and deserve their fifth-growth status.

Château Haut-Bages Monpelou
33250 Pauillac
cru bourgeois

Château Haut-Batailley
33250 Pauillac
5e grand cru classé
An unpretentious estate managed by François-Xavier Borie of Ducru-Beaucaillou: perhaps this is why the wine tends more to the amiability of St-Julien than the reserve of Pauillac.

Château Lafite-Rothschild
33250 Pauillac
1er grand cru classé
As you drive north from Pauillac, Lafite-Rothschild is the last château before St-Estèphe. A virile, hearty wine might be expected here on the very fringe of St-Estèphe – but not so. Lafite has a feminine grace, the subtlety and gentle finesse one would expect more from a St-Julien or a Margaux. Baron Eric de Rothschild took over the management in 1980. Visitors are not able to see inside the spacious 18th-century château but part of the magnificent new (1990) cellars may be visited by appointment. The wines are aged for up to 22 months in new-oak barrels produced by the estate's own cooperage.

Château Latour
33250 Pauillac
1er grand cru classé
The hamlet of St-Lambert used to be part of St-Julien, and a slightly different arrangement of the boundaries would have put Latour in the St-Julien appellation. Despite this, Latour is a thoroughbred Pauillac: concentrated and full of compact power. It can be described only in superlatives, as can its reliability. Latour produced successful wines even in such notoriously bad years as '63 and '65. The estate derives its name from a former fortress on the site: the solitary domed tower in the grounds today is not the remains of a medieval fortification but a *pigeonnier* (dove-cot). The actual château is a small, rather middle-class-looking Empire house surrounded by a little wooded garden. The roomy *chais* lies separately among the vines in a square around a small courtyard, perhaps where the long-destroyed fortress stood. Just as Latour wine contrasts strongly with Lafite, so do the installations: at Latour the wooden fermentation vats had been replaced by stainless-steel tanks by 1964. The very good second wine, Les Forts de Latour, is deemed as good as a second growth. Following a period of 30 years under English ownership, Latour was purchased in 1993 by French businessman François Pinault, chairman of The Printemps group.

Château Lynch-Bages
33250 Pauillac
5e grand cru classé
The working buildings dominate the pleasant house here. Both have been completely renovated by Jean-Michel Cazes. Lynch-Bages is a complete Pauillac: strong, often with a suggestion of mint in its perfume and an aroma of small red fruits. It is far better than its classification. Since 1990 a small amount of fine dry white wine, Blanc de Lynch-Bages, has been produced.

Château Lynch-Moussas
33250 Pauillac
5e grand cru classé
The property was purchased in 1969 by the Castéja family, owners of Château Batailley in Pauillac and the *négociant* house Borie-Manoux. The vineyards have since been replanted and cellars modernised. The wines are of average quality, lacking the depth and personality of true Pauillac.

Château Mouton-Rothschild
33250 Pauillac
1er grand cru classé
No other Bordeaux estate has had so much published about it, and no other *propriétaire* has been so much written about as the late Baron Philippe. When the management of Mouton passed to him in 1922 it was more a farm than a château. With great vision and tenacity, the Baron succeeded in making Mouton one of the most respected and most visited wine estates in the world; and this despite the fact that he was also a poet, playwright, film and theatre director and racing driver. With his American wife Pauline he created a unique wine museum and since 1946 commissioned a work by a famous artist each year for the Mouton label. Baron Philippe died in 1988 and the administration of the château was taken over by his daughter, Baronne Philippine. The Baron's greatest coup was the promotion of Mouton-Rothschild in 1973 from first of the second growths to its rightful place as a *premier cru* – the only change ever made to the 1855 classification. In character Mouton-Rothschild comes

closer to Latour than to Lafite: it has a luxurious, concentrated aroma of blackcurrant and cedarwood, plenty of tannin and an aftertaste that lasts in the mouth for minutes. A sumptuous Pauillac, prodigious in every respect.

Château Pédesclaux
33250 Pauillac
5e grand cru classé
This carefully made, concentrated and now somewhat soft Pauillac used to taste tougher. The vineyards are scattered around the commune.

Château Pibran 33250 Pauillac
cru bourgeois
Another Axa-Millésimes property whose wines were vinified at Château Pichon-Longueville (Baron) in 1996 while new cellars were being constructed. The wines are full-bodied, supple and flavoursome.

Château Pichon-Longueville (Baron) 33250 Pauillac
2e grand cru classé
A child asked to draw a château might come up with something resembling this affair of turrets and steep-pitched roofs. It was built in 1851 and lay empty until complete renovation in 1990 under the auspices of Jean-Michel Cazes and Axa-Millésimes, who bought the property from the Bouteiller family in 1987. The wine has also been restored to its former glory.

Château Pichon-Longueville-Comtesse de Lalande
33250 Pauillac
2e grand cru classé
'The Comtesse' is the larger portion of what was once a single estate. The balance is 'the Baron' (see previous entry). Since the second half of the 1970s enormous sums have been invested. The *chais* has been steadily renovated and since 1986 has boasted 33 temperature-controlled stainless-steel vats. Today the wines compete with the first growths in quality.

Château Pontet-Canet
33250 Pauillac
5e grand cru classé
The buildings where the wine is made are enormous. The loft over the *cuvier* can seat 600 (it is often used for receptions) and the high-ceilinged cellar where the casks are stored is almost cathedral-like. After a long period of mediocrity that lasted until well into the 1970s, Pontet-Canet is completely up to the mark again. The wine is dark, intense, with plenty of tannin and fruit that suggests currants: a very typical Pauillac and far superior to its fifth-growth status.

HAUT-MÉDOC
Château Peyrabon
33250 St-Sauveur
cru bourgeois
Queen Victoria once attended a concert here; the ceiling decorations are a reminder. Average wine.

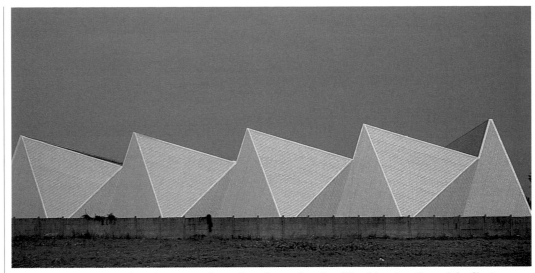
The futuristic lines of a maison de négoce: *a far cry from the merchants' traditional haunt on the quai des Chartrons.*

Château Ramage La Batisse
33250 St-Sauveur
cru bourgeois
Firm, balanced wine from this 55-ha estate.

WINE INFORMATION

Maison du Tourisme et du Vin de Médoc Tel (0)556 59 03 08
Reopened in 1986 after being burned down, the centre used to be based at Château Grand-Puy-Ducasse but is now in a modern-looking building south of the quay and is open throughout the year. You can ask here for information about visiting the châteaux.

HOTELS

The only first-class hotel-restaurant in Pauillac is Château Cordeillan-Bages (see below). Otherwise there are several simpler establishments situated alongside the quay.

Château Cordeillan-Bages
33250 **Pauillac**
Tel (0)556 59 24 24
A top-quality hotel-restaurant and a member of Relais et Châteaux group. The 17th-century château was renovated in 1989 and extensions built to provide a total of 25 luxuriously appointed rooms. Under the guidance of chef Thierry Marx the restaurant has become one of the best in the Bordeaux area and acquired a Michelin star in 1996. There is also a wine school, École de Bordeaux, which offers residents and students tutored tastings, wine courses and visits to châteaux.

Hôtel de France et d'Angleterre
33250 **Pauillac** Tel (0)556 59 01 20
An affordable hotel-restaurant, recently rebuilt down by the quay in

Roses mark the ends of rows and line a well used brick path at Pontet-Canet.

Pauillac. The hotel provides 29 rooms; the restaurant is good value and has a reasonable wine-list.

RESTAURANT

A speciality to look for here and elsewhere in Bordeaux is the now rare agneau de Pauillac. Made from lambs fed only on ewes' milk, it is very pale meat of incomparable flavour. The lamb you are likely to be served as agneau de Pauillac, which is certainly a delicacy to be enjoyed, comes from flocks that graze on the Médoc salt marshes (*prés-salés*).

La Salamandre, 33250 **Pauillac**
Tel (0)556 59 24 87
A simple restaurant opposite the port offering regional dishes. The wine-list is limited. Better known locally as Chez Johan.

PLACES OF INTEREST

Château Mouton-Rothschild
No visitor to the Médoc should leave without seeing the splendid wine museum opened at the château by Baron Philippe de Rothschild in 1962. A unique collection, beautifully displayed, shows how wine and art have been interwoven from early times. The main hall is a former wine cellar and six smaller rooms open off it. The collection includes Persian beakers from the 9th and 8th centuries BC, pre-Columbian sculptures, Alsace tapestries, Ming vases, Delft pottery, Venetian glasswork and much more. There are also works by modern artists. The museum can be visited only by appointment [tel (0)556 59 22 22] and is closed at weekends, on public holidays and during August.

133

St-Julien

St-Julien consistently produces some of the most exciting wines in the Médoc. Having only 910 hectares it is the smallest of the region's four famous communal appellations, but it boasts no fewer than 11 *crus classés*. These represent 80 per cent of the production, and there are also some outstanding châteaux at *cru bourgeois* level. There are no first growths, but the roll-call of estates includes the 'super-seconds' Châteaux Ducru-Beaucaillou, Gruaud-Larose and Léoville-Las-Cases as well as a number of other high-profile properties such as Châteaux Beychevelle, Lagrange, Léoville- and Langoa-Barton, Léoville-Poyferré, St-Pierre and Talbot. The winemaking at these estates is of the highest standard, making even the second labels a more-than-attractive proposition. Homogeneity across the board in St-Julien is provided by the compact nature of the appellation and the commitment of the producers.

Essentially, St-Juliens derive their qualities from the extremely gravelly soil of two large plateaux. The Beychevelle plateau is bounded on the south by the Jalle du Nord and on the north by a small valley, also with a stream. At the point where the D2 crosses this valley are the Langoa-Barton and Léoville-Barton estates. The second plateau, with the village of St-Julien-Beychevelle at its centre, runs north from the stream. The Ruisseau de Juillac forms the northern boundary and is also the line of demarcation between St-Julien and Pauillac.

The origin of St-Julien probably goes back to the 7th century but few traces of its early history remain. The 18th century, however, is splendidly represented by a number of châteaux including Beychevelle, Gruaud-Larose, Langoa-Barton, Branaire-Ducru and Lagrange. In the 16th century the Beychevelle estate with its riverside vineyards was called Château de Médoc, but this was changed after the Duke of Épernon, Admiral of France, received the property as a marriage portion. Ships on their way into Bordeaux were thereafter instructed to salute the château by lowering a sail as a sign of respect to the admiral, and the relevant order, *baisse voile* (or *bacha velo* in Gascon), became the name of the château ... or so the story goes. The Beychevelle label still shows a ship with lowered sail. The château of that time no longer exists; it was replaced in 1757 by a new building in Louis XV style. At the front it looks over a wide flight of steps and a beautiful garden to the distant Gironde; at the back, which can be seen from the road, there is a courtyard with virtuoso flowerbeds.

The regal 17th-century château of Beychevelle, flagged by its dazzling roadside flower beds, is one of the most beautiful in the Médoc.

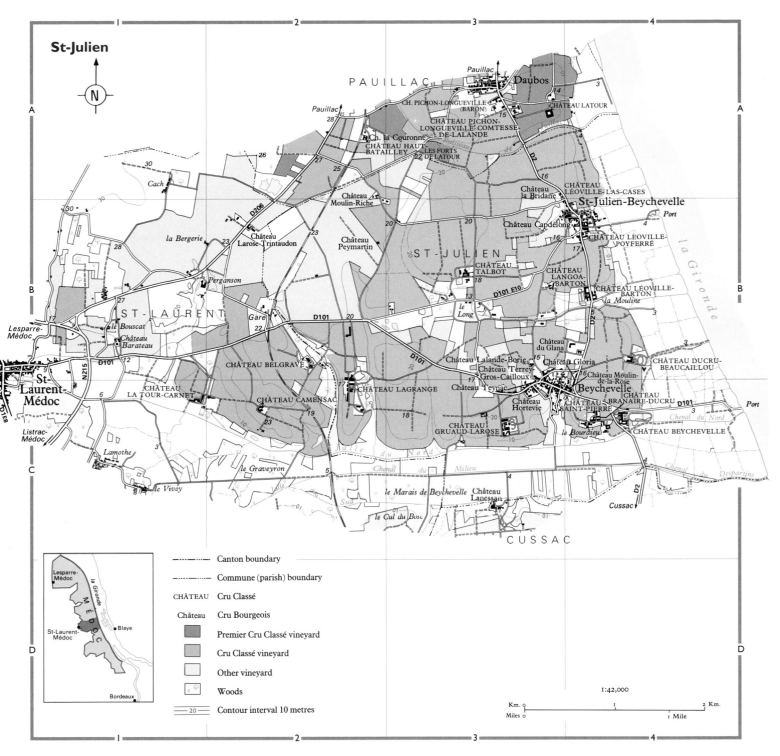

St-Julien

N

PAUILLAC
Pauillac
Daubos
Pauillac
CH. PICHON-LONGUEVILLE (BARON)
CHÂTEAU LATOUR
CHÂTEAU PICHON-LONGUEVILLE-COMTESSE-DE-LALANDE
Ch. la Couronne
CHÂTEAU HAUT-BATAILLEY
LES FORTS DE LATOUR
Cach
Château Moulin-Riche
Château la Bridane
CHÂTEAU LÉOVILLE-LAS-CASES
St-Julien-Beychevelle
la Bergerie
Château Larose-Trintaudon
Château Peymartin
Château Capdelong
Port
ST-JULIEN
CHÂTEAU LÉOVILLE-POYFERRÉ
Perganson
CHÂTEAU TALBOT
CHÂTEAU LANGOA-BARTON
CHÂTEAU LÉOVILLE-BARTON
la Mouline
ST-LAURENT
Gare
le Long
Lesparre-Médoc
le Bouscat
Château Barateau
St-Laurent-Médoc
CHÂTEAU BELGRAVE
Château Lalande-Borie
Château du Glana
Château Gloria
CHÂTEAU DUCRU-BEAUCAILLOU
Listrac-Médoc
CHÂTEAU LA TOUR-CARNET
Château Terrey Gros-Cailloux
Château Moulin-de-la-Rose
Beychevelle
CHÂTEAU CAMENSAC
CHÂTEAU LAGRANGE
Château Teynac
CHÂTEAU BRANAIRE-DUCRU
CHÂTEAU SAINT-PIERRE
Port
Lamothe
Château Hortevie
le Bourdieu
CHÂTEAU BEYCHEVELLE
CHÂTEAU GRUAUD-LAROSE
le Graveyron
le Marais de Beychevelle
Château Lanessan
Cussac
le Vivoy
le Cul du Bosc
CUSSAC

la Gironde
Chenal du Nord
Chenal du Milieu
Chenal du Despartins

Legend:

----·---- Canton boundary

------·------ Commune (parish) boundary

CHÂTEAU   Cru Classé

Château   Cru Bourgeois

Premier Cru Classé vineyard

Cru Classé vineyard

Other vineyard

Woods

══ 20 ══ Contour interval 10 metres

Lesparre-Médoc
MÉDOC
Blaye
St-Laurent-Médoc
Bordeaux

1:42,000

Km. 0   1   2 Km.
Miles 0   1 Mile

In this commune, which is dominated by elegant châteaux, some enchanting wines are made. They are rounded, have a deep colour, attractive bouquet, charm, grace and fruit: they are usually a little less powerful than those of Pauillac and often have the finesse of the most delicate Margaux *crus*.

The commune of St-Julien-Beychevelle has two hamlets of roughly equal size – the former Beychevelle and the original St-Julien. But apart from their wines and their châteaux, these little settlements do not have a great deal to offer the visitor.

Directly to the west of St-Julien-Beychevelle stretches the commune of St-Laurent-Médoc. The N215 Bordeaux–Soulac road used to run through St-Laurent but fortunately the traffic now bypasses the village. The wines of the commune often show a strong likeness to those of St-Julien and to allow them the same appellation would be justifiable (as has happened, for example, with the wines of Labarde and Arsac, which can now both be sold as Margaux). Fate however has decreed otherwise: St-Laurent is part of the Haut-Médoc appellation (although defined parcels of vines in this commune and that of Cussac are allowed in AOC St-Julien).

In St-Laurent also, wine-growing has been a way of life for hundreds of years. Wine from Château La Tour-Carnet – a genuine castle with a moat and a 13th-century bastion – was being sold at the beginning of the 15th century, and it commanded prices almost double those of the then much-sought-after red Graves.

PRODUCERS OF SPECIAL INTEREST

ST-JULIEN

Château Beychevelle
33250 St-Julien-Beychevelle
4e grand cru classé
In 1983 a French civil service pension fund (GMF) acquired a majority shareholding (later total control, after which 40% was sold to Suntory, owners of Château Lagrange) from the Achille-Fould family. Much-needed improvements have been made including the installation of stainless-steel fermentation tanks. Beychevelle wine has the stamina of a marathon runner and often shows its real class only after many years. The 17th-century château is one of the most beautiful in the Médoc.

Château Branaire-Ducru
33250 St-Julien-Beychevelle
4e grand cru classé
An alluring perfume of violets and a taste that is gentle yet firm are the most striking characteristics of the wine from this 50-ha property.

Operations in the winery are all handled by gravity. The immaculate château, set well back in its grounds, is opposite Beychevelle.

Château la Bridane
33250 St-Julien-Beychevelle
cru bourgeois

Château Ducru-Beaucaillou
33250 St-Julien-Beychevelle
2e grand cru classé
This château is set majestically against the east (riverside) slope of the more southerly of the St-Julien gravel plateaux. The façade, flanked by two stout Victorian towers, looks towards the Gironde and a magnificent park enhances the view. Thanks to the effort and expertise of the Borie family, Ducru-Beaucaillou, together with Léoville-Las-Cases, is among the top wines of St-Julien – and thus of the whole Médoc. It is a delicious, mouth-filling wine: mellow, stylish, and with sufficient strength for long maturing.

Château du Glana
33250 St-Julien-Beychevelle
cru bourgeois

Château Gloria
33250 St-Julien-Beychevelle
cru bourgeois

Château Gruaud-Larose
33250 St-Julien-Beychevelle
2e grand cru classé
This is one of the most consistent estates in the Médoc. The wines are rich, muscular and fruit laden, needing several years before they are at their best. The property was purchased in 1993 by French conglomerate Alcatel Alstom, but the previous owner, the *négociant* Cordier, still has the exclusive right to sales and oversees the winemaking. The second wine from this 84-ha estate, Sarget de Gruaud Larose, is also excellent value.

Château Hortevie
33250 St-Julien-Beychevelle

Château Lagrange
33250 St-Julien-Beychevelle
3e grand cru classé
Since it was taken over by the Japanese drinks' giant Suntory at the end of 1983, almost everything on this big estate has been altered or renovated, from the *cuvier* to the

lookout tower. This enormous effort has brought the wine right back up to standard after a long series of mediocre years. The first vintage – in the moderate year of '84 – produced an exquisite, satin-like wine of great finesse. The château's second wine, Les Fiefs de Lagrange, is regularly one of the most successful in the region. Lagrange is one of the most interesting Médoc châteaux to visit. It may be possible to make an appointment through merchants who import the wine.

Château Lalande-Borie
33250 St-Julien-Beychevelle
cru bourgeois

Château Langoa-Barton
33250 St-Julien-Beychevelle
3e grand cru classé
One of the gems of the Médoc: a country house built above its cellars has a lovely terraced garden behind. This is the only *cru classé* still owned and inhabited by the same family as in 1855 when the classification was made. The wine is made from the same proportions of grapes

Sailing ships passing Château Beychevelle on their way up the Gironde were once obliged to lower their sails in salute to the Admiral rank of the estate's founder.

(70% Cabernet Sauvignon, 7% Cabernet Franc, 15% Merlot, 8% Petit Verdot) as Léoville-Barton, and in the same conservative way with the same equipment. Not surprisingly there is a great family resemblance between the two wines, although Léoville is slightly ahead in finesse and complexity.

Château Léoville-Barton
33250 St-Julien-Beychevelle
2e grand cru classé
The smallest Léoville (50ha) has been in the Barton family since 1826. It is presently owned and managed by Anthony Barton and his daughter Lilian. The Bartons originate from County Kildare, Ireland. The wine, made at Langoa-Barton, is usually deep in colour, concentrated, structured, and takes longer to evolve than Langoa. It is one of the best buys in the Médoc, selling well under the price of the other second growths.

Château Léoville-Las-Cases
33250 St-Julien-Beychevelle
2e grand cru classé
After the French Revolution the estate of the Marquis de Léoville was split into three: the present château Léoville-Las-Cases (the largest), Léoville-Poyferré and Léoville-Barton. A large part of the vineyard is opposite Château Latour in Pauillac and the winery buildings are in St-Julien itself on either side of the street and next to the Poyferré cellars. Perfectionist management by Michel Delon produces memorable, flawless wine, intense and rich in colour,

fragrance and flavour. Even in lesser years its quality usually lives up to high expectations. Only 45% of the total production is used for Léoville-Las-Cases. The rest goes towards the excellent second label Clos du Marquis or is sold to *négociants*.

Château Léoville-Poyferré
33250 St-Julien-Beychevelle
2e grand cru classé
This part of the Léoville estate was bought by the Baron Poyferré in 1830, then by the present owners, the Cuvelier family, in 1920. The wines have shown a steady improvement since 1979 when Didier Cuvelier took over the management and the renovation of the cellars and installations began. Oenologist Michel Rolland has recently been called in to consult. Château Moulin-Riche is the second wine.

Château St-Pierre
33250 St-Julien-Beychevelle
4e grand cru classé
In its time St-Pierre has been divided, reunited and divided again, with different buildings functioning as the château. Since September 1982, however, a good deal of the original vineyard has been reunited with the original château. The man who brought this about was the late (1991) Henri Martin of Château Gloria, who had the château and surrounding park fully restored – although the château, originally a royal villa, is rather unfortunately faced by St-Julien's notorious giant bottle. The

Beychevelle gains silky, aristocratic elegance after a decade or so in bottle.

wine itself is generous and amiable with an aroma of soft fruits.

Château Talbot
33250 St-Julien-Beychevelle
4e grand cru classé
With more than 100ha of vines this is the largest property in St-Julien. The name comes from John Talbot, Earl of Shrewsbury, who lodged here in 1453 before departing to die in battle with the French at Castillon-la-Bataille. Château Talbot is rich in fruit extract, supple and aromatic. The second wine is called Connétable de Talbot. A fine dry white wine is made, sold under the name of Caillou Blanc.

Château Terrey-Gros-Cailloux
33250 St-Julien-Beychevelle
cru bourgeois

HAUT-MÉDOC
Château Belgrave
33112 St-Laurent-Médoc
5e grand cru classé
For a considerable time this estate did not deserve its place among the *grands crus* but the owners, *négociants* CVBG, have since 1979 invested a good deal in the vineyard and equipment. Recent vintages have confirmed the early promise of improvement in quality.

Château de Camensac
33112 St-Laurent-Médoc
5e grand cru classé
Meaty, lingering Haut-Médoc from an estate that has been painstakingly lifted out of its neglected state. The wine is comparable with many *4e grands crus classés*.

Château Caronne Ste-Gemme
33112 St-Laurent-Médoc
cru bourgeois
This isolated château (see the map of the Central Médoc on page 139) can be reached via the N215 just south of St-Laurent. The wine needs long maturing.

Château Larose-Trintaudon
33112 St-Laurent-Médoc
cru bourgeois
Despite the 172-ha vineyard, the

biggest in the Médoc, the wine is supple and reliable. The former proprietors (the Forner family, who own Château de Camensac) carried out many renovations before selling the estate in late 1986 to a French insurance company.

HOTELS

There is no hotel in St-Julien-Beychevelle, but it may be possible to stay at the Hôtel-Restaurant de la Renaissance in St-Laurent. See also Hotels in Bordeaux, Pauillac and Margaux (pages 118, 133 and 145).

RESTAURANTS

Although the wines of St-Julien and St-Laurent are served in the world's best restaurants, in the villages themselves you can enjoy them in simple eating houses – or in the châteaux, but this is a rare privilege.

Hôtel-Restaurant de la Renaissance 33112 St-Laurent-Médoc Tel (0)556 59 40 29
The patron supplies meals to the châteaux (and to pickers). Nourishing, regional fare.

PLACES OF INTEREST

St-Julien-Beychevelle and St-Laurent each have an interesting church. Apart from these, just admire the châteaux – and the wines.

THE CHÂTEAUX

Properties throughout the Médoc welcome visitors. Many require an appointment (the grander the château, usually the more necessary an appointment). Those open to casual visitors in St-Julien include Beychevelle, Branaire-Ducru and Lagrange. Typically, châteaux are open from 10 to 12am and from 3 to 5pm, Monday to Friday. Many close in August.

Grapes in douilles *are inspected before being tipped into the* fouloir-égrappoir.

The Central Médoc

Whereas the neighbouring communes of Margaux and St-Julien dazzle with their *grands crus*, the light in the Central Médoc is more subdued. There are no great aristocratic châteaux, just comfortably middle-class estates. This is *crus bourgeois* territory. The fact that there is not a single property with a higher classification is to be regretted, since several estates are producing wines that can match the *grands crus*: two convincing examples are Chasse-Spleen and Poujeaux in Moulis-en-Médoc.

The commune of Moulis has its own appellation (the other communes, apart from Listrac-Médoc, are simply Haut-Médoc) though the hamlet itself is little more than a single main street and a few houses. Grand Poujeaux, a few kilometres to the north-east, is more important, certainly as far as wine is concerned. Grouped in and around Grand Poujeaux are several good estates, many with 'Poujeaux' in their name. The name Moulis comes from *moulins* (windmills) as this used to be mainly corn-growing country, the landscape studded with windmills to grind the grain.

Vineyards were first planted in the 15th and 16th centuries and there are now some 600 hectares under production. Most of the fine wines come from the gravel plateau of Poujeaux and the south-east where the gravel is mixed with clay. In the south-west there is gravel and sand and around Moulis itself there is clay and chalk. These differences in the soil contribute to the various styles of wine in Moulis-en-Médoc. Some mature to the same kind of mellow refinement as St-Juliens; others are firmer and more reserved or striking for their suppleness, making few demands on the patience.

The other commune of the Central Médoc with its own appellation is Listrac-Médoc, west and north of Moulis. The appellation, which has a vineyard area of 670 hectares, used to be simply Listrac, but the name was changed in 1986 to Listrac-Médoc, allegedly to avoid possible confusion with Lirac in the Rhône. The N215 from Bordeaux (which in summer takes the Bordelais en masse to the beaches in the north) runs through the village and alongside the cooperative where about a third of the local wine is vinified. The village lies at the foot of the highest hill in the Médoc, which is 43 metres above sea level and topped by a fire tower (for looking out for forest fires). This plateau also acts as a watershed: the streams to its east flow into the Gironde, those to its west towards the sea. The subsoil varies, being partly gravel from the Pyrenees, partly clay and chalk and partly shingle brought down by the Garonne. Merlot used to be the main grape variety but on most estates today at least half the vines are Cabernet Sauvignon. This has increased the finesse of the wines, but Listrac-Médocs in general are fairly virile with plenty of body and a firm structure.

The other communes of the Central Médoc are entitled to the appellation Haut-Médoc. In Avensan and Arcins the wines can

Château Lamarque, the Médoc's finest medieval fortress and a former royal seat, retains its 11th- and 12th-century cellars and chapel.

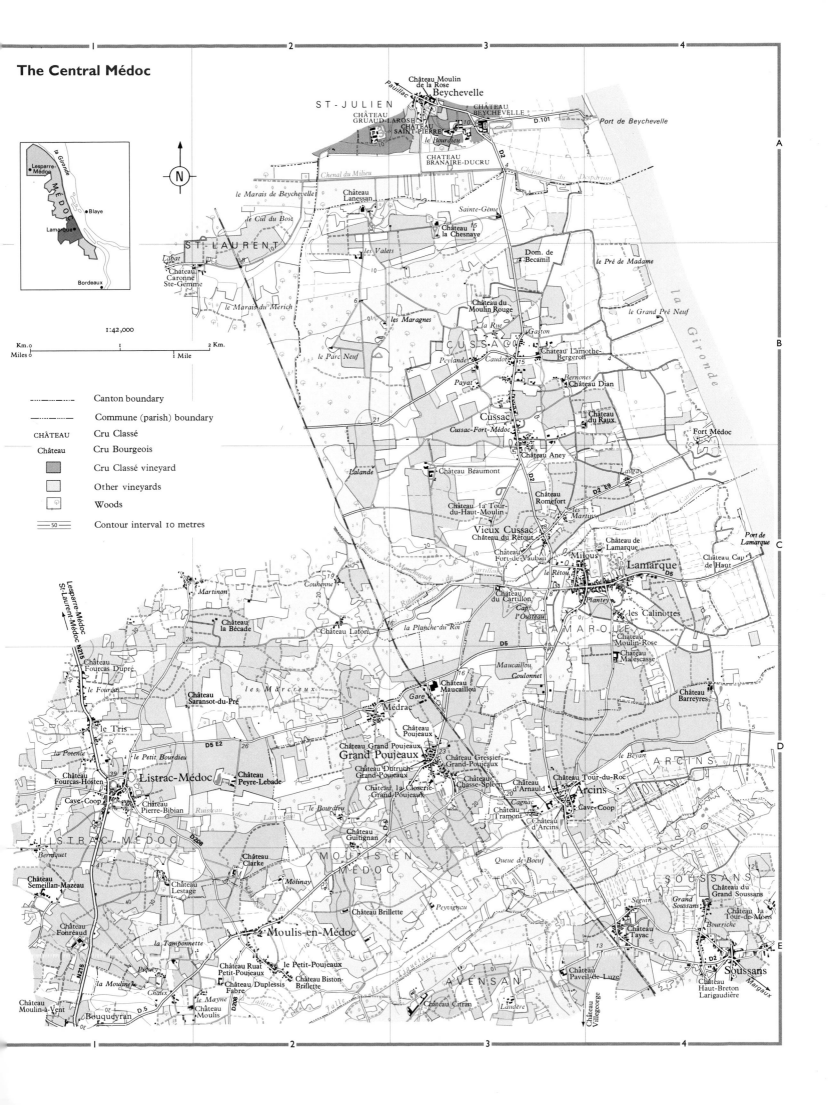

The Central Médoc

MÉDOC
Lesparre-Médoc
la Gironde
Blaye
Lamarque
Bordeaux

1:42,000

Km.0   1   2 Km.
Miles 0   1 Mile

Canton boundary
Commune (parish) boundary
CHÂTEAU   Cru Classé
Château   Cru Bourgeois
Cru Classé vineyard
Other vineyards
Woods
50   Contour interval 10 metres

N

Château Moulin de la Rose
Pauillac
Beychevelle
ST-JULIEN
CHÂTEAU GRUAUD-LAROSE
CHÂTEAU BEYCHEVELLE
CHÂTEAU SAINT-PIERRE
le Bourdieu
Port de Beychevelle
D.101
CHÂTEAU BRANAIRE-DUCRU
D.2
Chenal du Milieu
Chenal du Despartins
le Marais de Beychevelle
Château Lanessan
Sainte-Gême
le Cul du Bosc
ST-LAURENT
Labat
Château Caronne Ste-Gemme
les Valets
Château la Chesnaye
Dom. de Becamil
le Pré de Madame
le Marais du Merich
les Maragnes
le Grand Pré Neuf
le Parc Neuf
Château du Moulin Rouge
la Rue
Gaston
CUSSAC
Château Lamothe-Bergeron
Peylande
Caudot
Bernones
Château Dian
Payat
la Gironde
Cussac
Cussac-Fort-Médoc
Château du Raux
Fort Médoc
Château Aney
Château Beaumont
l'alande
Château la Tour-du-Haut-Moulin
Château Romefort
D.2
E9
les Martins
Vieux Cussac
Château du Rétout
Port de Lamarque
Château Fort-de-Vauban
Château de Lamarque
Château Cap de Haut
Milous
le Rétout
Lamarque
D.5
Martinon
Couhenne
Château du Cartillon
Plantey
les Calinottes
Château la Bécade
Château Lafon
la Planche du Roi
Cap l'Ousteau
LAMARQUE
Château Moulin-Rose
N215
Lesparre-Médoc
St-Laurent-Médoc
Château Fourcas Dupré
le Fourcas
Maucaillou
Coulonnet
Château Malescasse
Château Saransot-du-Pré
les Marceaux
Château Maucaillou
Château Barreyres
le Tris
Gare
Médrac
Château Poujeaux
ARCINS
la Potence
Château Grand Poujeaux
le Beyrat
Grand Poujeaux
Château Gressier Grand-Poujeaux
D5 E2
le Petit Bourdieu
Listrac-Médoc
Château Peyre-Lebade
Château Dutruch Grand-Poujeaux
Château la Closerie-Grand-Poujeaux
Château Chasse-Spleen
Château d'Arnauld
Château Tour-du-Roc
Arcins
Château Fourcas-Hosten
Château Pierre-Bibian
Cave-Coop
Château Tramont
Cagnac
Cave-Coop
Château d'Arcins
Ruisseau
Larravan
LISTRAC-MÉDOC
D208
le Bourdieu
Château Guitignan
Berraquet
Château Clarke
MOULIS EN MÉDOC
Queue de Boeuf
SOUSSANS
Château Semeillan-Mazeau
Château Lestage
Molinay
Château du Grand Soussans
Seguin
Grand Soussans
Château Fonréaud
Château Brillette
Peyvigneu
Château Tayac
Château la Tour-de-Mons
Bouriche
Moulin-à-Vent
Moulis-en-Médoc
le Petit-Poujeaux
Château Paveil-de-Luze
D.2
Soussans
N215
Château Ruat Petit-Poujeaux
Château Duplessis Fabre
Château Biston-Briffette
AVENSAN
Château Haut-Breton Larigaudière
la Mouline
Piquey
le Mayne
Château Citran
Château Moulis
Laudere
Château Villegeorge
Bouqueyran
D.208
Taillette
D.5

sometimes approach those of Margaux in style (the commune of Soussans, in the extreme south, is part of the Margaux appellation).

The village of Lamarque (from which there is a car ferry to Blaye) has rather low-lying land which is unsuitable for the production of quality wines. Farther inland however there are some flourishing estates including the splendid Château Lamarque, an ancient castle complete with towers, battlements and a courtyard with palms and white doves. The Cussac-Fort-Médoc commune consists of two small hamlets on the D2 (the 'route des Châteaux'). Wines produced by the vineyards on both sides of the road are generally classic in style and benefit from long maturing.

Top: Fishermen at work near Lamarque. The Gironde at this point was once heavily fortified; now a car ferry links the small village with Blaye on the opposite bank.

Above: With the citadel at Blaye, Fort Paté on the small Île Paté formed part of a line of fortifications designed to defend the Gironde against marauders.

PRODUCERS OF SPECIAL INTEREST

MOULIS

Château Biston-Brillette
33480 Moulis-en-Médoc
cru bourgeois

Château Branas Grand Poujeaux
33480 Moulis-en-Médoc

Château Brillette
33480 Moulis-en-Médoc
cru bourgeois

Château Chasse-Spleen
33480 Moulis-en-Médoc
cru bourgeois
Indeed an exceptional Moulis that has repeatedly shown itself to be the equal of a *grand cru*. The wine is matured in oak and usually half the casks are replaced each year. A small part of the vineyard is situated in Listrac-Médoc.

Château Dutruch Grand Poujeaux
33480 Moulis-en-Médoc
cru bourgeois
Wine with a good deal of reserve and tannin, demanding long maturing. The more modern-styled Château Anthonic is owned by the same family.

Château Gressier Grand-Poujeaux
33480 Moulis-en-Médoc
cru bourgeois

Château Maucaillou
33480 Moulis-en-Médoc
cru bourgeois
The name of the estate comes from an old description of the soil: *mauvais cailloux*, (bad pebbles), coined in the days when it was found too gravelly to grow corn (but proved later, of course, to be excellent for vines). At blind tastings the supple, nuanced wine is sometimes barely distinguishable from a *grand cru*. The château has an interesting wine museum.

Château Moulin à Vent
33480 Moulis-en-Médoc
cru bourgeois
The property is on the boundary of Moulis and Listrac-Médoc and, although a third of the vineyard is in Listrac-Médoc, all the wine is sold as Moulis. Dominique Hessel has invested considerable time and money in the estate since he bought it in 1977 – and this shows in the wine.

Château Poujeaux
33480 Moulis-en-Médoc
cru bourgeois
This is the largest estate in Moulis after Chasse-Spleen and, thanks to the efforts of the Theil family, the wine is well enough known to be sold directly from the château instead of via the Bordeaux trade. Dark and long-lived, it usually needs time to lose its reserve, but patience is richly rewarded. It can now rival some *grands crus*.

LISTRAC-MÉDOC

Château Cap Léon Veyrin
33480 Listrac-Médoc
cru bourgeois
The wines are Merlot dominated.
A few rooms above the *chais* are
rented to holidaymakers.

Château Clarke
33480 Listrac-Médoc
cru bourgeois
Since 1973 Baron Edmond de
Rothschild (of the Château Lafite-
Rothschild family) has spent millions
of francs in making this the most
spectacular and technically advanced
estate in Listrac-Médoc. The wines
are among the appellation's best.

Château Ducluzeau
33480 Listrac-Médoc
cru bourgeois
Belongs to the Boire family who
own Ducru-Beaucaillou in St-Julien
and other estates.

Château Fonréaud
33480 Listrac-Médoc
cru bourgeois

Château Fourcas-Dupré
33480 Listrac-Médoc
cru bourgeois
A concentrated Listrac-Médoc of
the highest standard. The vineyard lies
about 1km north of the village centre
on the D2 and has ample parking
space for visitors.

Château Fourcas-Hosten
33480 Listrac-Médoc
cru bourgeois
A fine wine with plenty of fruit and
tannin and the class of a *grand cru*.
The château is opposite Listrac-
Médoc's 13th-century church and
the splendid park at the back was
designed in 1830 by an Englishman.

Château Lestage
33480 Listrac-Médoc
cru bourgeois
An imposing château set in a park
of tall old trees. The owners also
own Château Fonréaud on the other
side of the hill at Listrac-Médoc.
The wine is an out-and-out Listrac-
Médoc which has improved since the
early 1980s.

Château Mayne Lalande
33480 Listrac-Médoc
cru bourgeois
Hand-crafted wines made from a
dominance of Cabernet Sauvignon
and aged in new-oak barrels.

Château Peyredon Lagravette
33480 Listrac-Médoc
cru bourgeois
A small family estate near the
hamlet of Médrac.

Château Saransot-Dupré
33480 Listrac-Médoc
cru bourgeois
A large estate making rich, supple
reds and a rare Sémillon-based white,
both of which have shown vast
improvement under Yves Raymond,
the third-generation owner.

Soutirage (drawing off) in the Lamarque cellars. Just after fermentation, the wine's colour is at its deepest.

HAUT-MÉDOC

Château d'Arcins 33460 Arcins
cru bourgeois
Conspicuous on the D2, the whole
complex has been restored and
enlarged by the Castel family (of
Castelvin table wine fame). The
Castels have also restored Château
Barreyres near the river. Their efforts
should make the name of Arcins
better known.

Château Arnauld 33460 Arcins
cru bourgeois
An elegant, fruity Haut-Médoc.

Châteaux Beaumont
33460 Cussac-Fort-Médoc
cru bourgeois

Château Citran 33480 Avensan
cru bourgeois
A solid *cru bourgeois*, Citran was sold
in 1986 to the Japanese Fujimoto
Company, and has since undergone
a physical and vinous transformation.
It changed hands again in 1996. The
wine now rivals a lesser *cru classé*.

Château Lachesnaye
33460 Cussac-Fort-Médoc
cru bourgeois
Located en route to, and shares
the same owners as, Lanessan.

Château Lamarque
33460 Lamarque
cru bourgeois
A generous, firm wine, sometimes
almost velvety after ageing, is expertly
produced at this splendid old castle.

Château Lanessan 33460
Cussac-Fort-Médoc
cru bourgeois
Classic, traditionally made, intense
wine that approaches a *grand cru*
in quality. There is also a carriage
museum at the château.

Château Malescasse
33460 Lamarque
cru bourgeois
Owned by the French conglomerate
Alcatel Alsthom.

Château Tour Carelot
33480 Avensan

Château Tour-du-Haut-Moulin
33460 Cussac-Fort-Médoc
cru bourgeois
Excellent, full-bodied wines in true
Haut-Médoc style.

Château de Villegorge
33480 Avensan
cru bourgeois
A Lucien Lurton estate, now managed
by daughter Marie-Laure. Gravelly soil.
The well rounded wine has plenty of
colour, a long finish and outstanding
ageing potential.

WINE INFORMATION

There is no Maison du Vin in the
Central Médoc but enquiries in the
larger villages such as Lamarque and
Grand Poujeaux about visiting the
local châteaux should prove helpful.
Visitors are particularly welcome at
Château Clarke in the commune of
Listrac-Médoc and Château
Maucaillou in Moulis, where there
is also a wine museum.

L'École du Vin A wine school
[tel (0)556 58 01 23] is run in Moulis-
en-Médoc by Château Maucaillou
(closed June through August).

HOTEL

Relais du Médoc 33460 Lamarque
Tel (0)556 58 92 27
Small, central hotel-restaurant.

RESTAURANTS

Le Lion d'Or 33460 Arcins
Tel (0)556 58 96 79
Plenty of atmosphere and tasty food.
Very popular locally (though most
tourists drive past). Owner Jean-Paul
Barbier allows customers to bring
their own wines.

Relais du Médoc 33460 Lamarque
Tel (0)556 58 92 27
Strictly regional cuisine (escargots
à la bordelaise are a speciality) and
excellent value.

PLACES OF INTEREST

Avensan The local church has
15th-century bas-reliefs.

Castelnau-de-Médoc A small
hamlet 6km south of Listrac-Médoc
with an interesting church.

Cussac-Fort-Médoc Fort Médoc,
by the Gironde, with it's ornamented
Louis XIV gateway, was built around
1690 by the military architect
Vauban. Also at Cussac is Château
Lanessan with its Musée du Cheval,
which houses a collection of carriages
dating from 1885 and an original
19th-century stables and saddle room.

Lamarque The great Château
Lamarque is a Médoc landmark. The
car ferry across the Gironde to Blaye
leaves from Lamarque's pier.

Listrac-Médoc The village has a
13th century Romanesque church
with Gothic elements.

Moulis-en-Médoc The Romanesque
church has a fortified tower and there
is an old water mill in the village, the
Moulin de Tiquetorte.

Margaux and the Southern Médoc

Initial impressions of the Médoc can leave the visitor bemused as to what the fuss is about. The route north from Bordeaux leads through the city's suburban sprawl, over the ring road or *rocade* and past a chequered pattern of industrial estates and expanding residential areas. Ribbon development has linked once independent communities, and only when you reach Ludon-Médoc does the importance of the vine appear to assert itself.

The most interesting route through the Médoc starts at Blanquefort, where you can take either the D2 north or the D210 that runs parallel to it to the east, closer to the Gironde. The D210 is quieter and passes through the peaceful wine villages of Parempuyre, Ludon-Médoc and Macau as well as by many of the châteaux, including the beautiful d'Agassac. The D2 has the advantage of running closer to such estates as Châteaux Cantemerle and Giscours, and it is easy to turn off for Le Pian-Médoc and Arsac, two wine communities deeper inland. At Labarde the two roads join, so a circular route could embrace both routes.

The wines of the most southerly villages – Macau, Ludon-Médoc, Le Pian-Médoc and, closer to Bordeaux, Le Taillon-Médoc, Parempuyre and Blanquefort – carry the Haut-Médoc appellation. On the flat lands near the river – the *palus* – the wines are simpler and have the appellation Bordeaux or Bordeaux Supérieur, as do the wines from the islands in the Gironde. The further north you go, the more the vineyards penetrate among the woods and meadows. Directly after the hamlet of Cantenac the landscape opens out, with impressive sweeps of vineyards stretching away on either side of the road. To the left, just past Château Prieuré-Lichine, is a classic example of the gravel plateaux so characteristic of the Médoc. The hill with its shallow vine-clad slope seems low, but in fact in this flat countryside it is high enough to block your view of Châteaux Brane-Cantenac entirely.

Here you are in the Margaux appellation, which covers some 1,341 hectares of vineyard out of the total for the Médoc of nearly 15,000. Margaux is the second largest (after St-Estèphe) of the Médoc's communal appellations, and with 21 *crus classés* has more than any of the others. As well as Margaux itself, the appellation includes Arsac, Cantenac, Labarde and Soussans, a quartet of adjoining communities. The long, low islands in the Gironde form a natural screen against cold winds from the north-east and the microclimate is a little milder than in the rest of the Médoc, which means that the grapes usually ripen eight to ten days earlier. The topsoil is the thinnest in the Médoc but rich in gravel, particularly in the eastern part of the appellation where a number of the delicate and delicious wines so characteristic of Margaux are made. To the west there is more clay and the wines are firmer.

Until late in the 17th century Margaux and the surrounding villages were sparsely populated, being the territory of a few wealthy seigneurs who lived in the châteaux of Margaux, d'Issan (in Cantenac) and La Tour-de-Mons (in Soussans). Châteaux Margaux and d'Issan still stand, but only parts of La Tour-de-Mons remain.

Today the township of Margaux has just under 1,400 inhabitants and is more village than town; the other villages of the appellation are little more than hamlets. Almost everyone in Margaux makes his or her living from wine and most of the châteaux lie in a neighbourly cluster around and in the centre of the town, their vineyards divided into small plots which are woven into the surrounding countryside.

Château Palmer's wines of finesse and voluptuous ripeness owe much to the vineyard's superb position on a gravel rise just above Château Margaux.

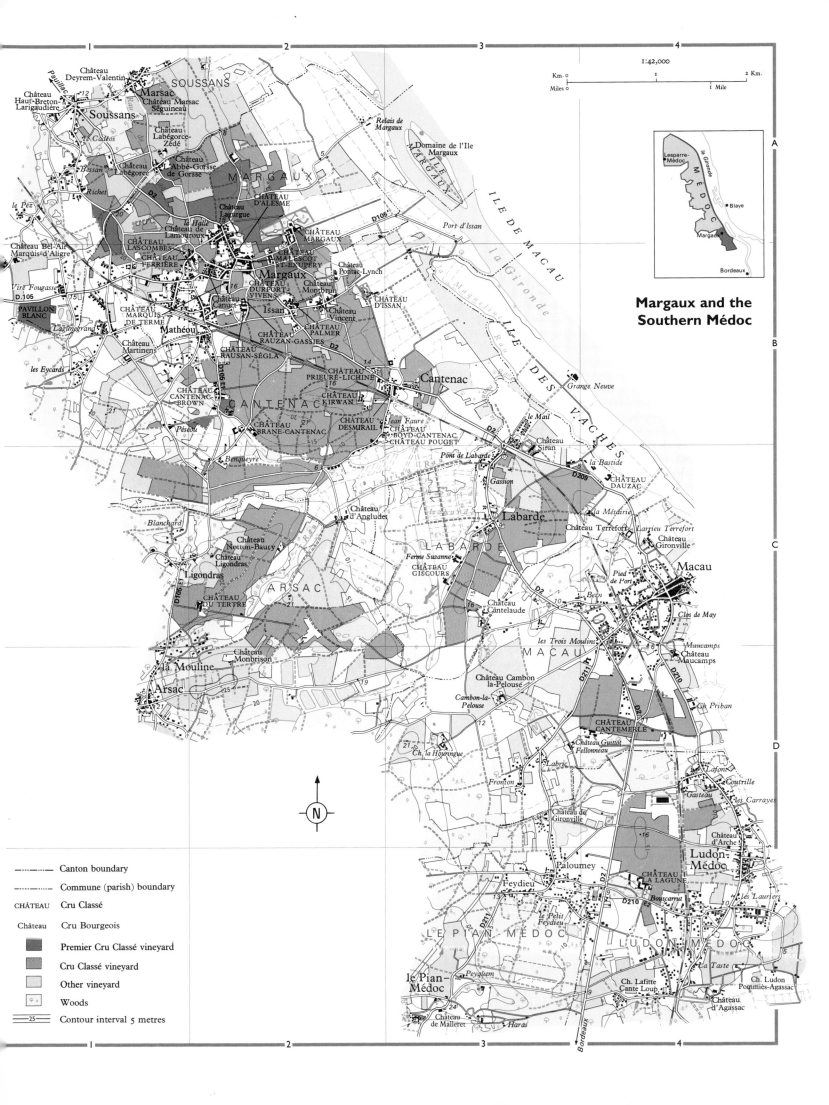

Margaux and the Southern Médoc

Scale 1:42,000

Km. 0   1   2 Km.
Miles 0   1 Mile

MÉDOC
Lesparre-Médoc
la Gironde
Blaye
Margaux
Bordeaux

SOUSSANS
Château Deyrem-Valentin
Marsac
Château Haut-Breton-Larigaudière
Château Marsac Séguineau
Soussans
Château Labégorce-Zédé
les Cailloux
Château Labégorce
Château l'Abbé-Gorsse de Gorsse
Bessan
Richet
le Pez
MARGAUX
Relais de Margaux
Domaine de l'Ile Margaux
ILE MARGAUX
Château D'ALESME
Château Lagurgue
la Halle
Château de Lamouroux
Port d'Issan
ILE DE MACAU
Château Bel-Air Marquis d'Aligre
CHÂTEAU LASCOMBES
Château FERRIÈRE
CHÂTEAU MARGAUX
CHÂTEAU MALESCOT ST-EXUPÉRY
Château Pontac-Lynch
Viré Fougasse
PAVILLON BLANC
Margaux
Château DURFORT-VIVENS
Château Canuet
Château Montbrun
CHÂTEAU D'ISSAN
Château Vincent
la Gironde
Château MARQUIS DE TERME
Mathéou
Issan
CHÂTEAU PALMER
ILE DES VACHES
Lagunegrand
Château Martinens
CHÂTEAU RAUZAN-GASSIES
CHÂTEAU RAUSAN-SÉGLA
les Eycards
CHÂTEAU PRIEURÉ-LICHINÉ
Cantenac
Grange Neuve
CHÂTEAU CANTENAC-BROWN
CANTENAC
CHÂTEAU KIRWAN
le Mail
Péséou
CHÂTEAU BRANE-CANTENAC
Château DESMIRAIL
Jean Faure
CHÂTEAU BOYD-CANTENAC
CHÂTEAU POUGET
Château Siran
la Bastide
Benqueyre
Pont de Labarde
Gassion
CHÂTEAU DAUZAC
la Métairie
Larrieu Terrefort
Château d'Angludet
Labarde
Château Terrefort
Château Gironville
Blanchard
Château Notton-Baury
LABARDE
Macau
Château Ligondras
Ferme Suzanne
Pied de Port
Clos de May
Ligondras
CHÂTEAU GISCOURS
ARSAC
CHÂTEAU DU TERTRE
Château Cantelaude
Bern
Maucamps
Château Maucamps
la Mouline
Château Monbrison
MACAU
les Trois Moulins
Arsac
Château Cambon la-Pelousé
Ch. Priban
Cambon-la-Pelouse
CHÂTEAU CANTEMERLE
Château Guittot Fellonneau
Ch. la Houringue
Lafont
Coutrille
Frontin
Labric
Château de Gironville
Gasteau
les Carrayes
Château d'Arche
Paloumey
Ludon-Médoc
Feydieu
CHÂTEAU LA LAGUNE
Bouscarrut
les Lauriers
LE PIAN-MÉDOC
le Petit Feydieu
LUDON-MÉDOC
Peyquem
la Taste
le Pian-Médoc
Ch. Lafitte Cante Loup
Ch. Ludon Pommiès-Agassac
Château de Malleret
Haras
Château d'Agassac

Legend

— · · · — Canton boundary

— · — · — Commune (parish) boundary

CHÂTEAU   Cru Classé

Château   Cru Bourgeois

▮ Premier Cru Classé vineyard

▮ Cru Classé vineyard

▯ Other vineyard

🌿 Woods

══25══ Contour interval 5 metres

PRODUCERS OF SPECIAL INTEREST

MARGAUX

Château d'Angludet
33460 Cantenac
cru bourgeois
The château, set in a peaceful park complete with grazing ponies, is the home of Peter Sichel, the English co-owner of Château Palmer. The wine is consistently of *grand cru* quality: complex and complete.

Château Boyd-Cantenac
33460 Cantenac
3e grand cru classé
The wine used to be identical to that of Pouget, the adjoining estate with the same owner, but is now vinified and bottled separately. Not a particularly subtle Margaux, it needs time to show its qualities.

Château Brane-Cantenac
33460 Cantenac
2e grand cru classé
This large estate on the Cantenac plateau is part of the Lurton stable of properties. It is managed by Lucien Lurton's son Henri. The wines in the past have been supple and forward, lacking the depth necessary for a *2e grand cru classé*. Perhaps the new generation will amend this character.

Château Cantenac-Brown
33460 Cantenac
3e grand cru classé
This imposing edifice looks more like an English country house than a château. The wine used to be rather old-fashioned but, since the estate joined the Axa-Millésimes group in 1989, it has become thoroughly concentrated and modern.

Château Dauzac 33460 Labarde
5e grand cru classé
Totally regenerated, the vineyard is now perfectly equipped after a long period of decline. The old château is no longer in use. The property is managed by André Lurton and the wines have been showing a marked improvement in quality.

Château Desmirail
33460 Cantenac
3e grand cru classé
A low grey building serves as the château; it lies on the left (from Bordeaux) before the crossroad in Cantenac. The Brane-Cantenac team makes the wine which is an elegant Margaux of unmistakable finesse.

Château Deyrem-Valentin
33460 Soussans
cru bourgeois

Château Durfort-Vivens
33460 Margaux
2e grand cru classé
Responsibility for this estate has now passed to Gonzague Lurton. The winery has recently been modernised and a new barrel cellar built. The actual château is no longer part of the wine estate. Recent vintages have shown a marked improvement in wines which, for some years, did not live up to their second-growth status.

Château Ferrière 33460 Margaux
3e grand cru classé
This tiny 5-ha property has undergone a recent renaissance. Purchased by the Merlaut family in 1992 it is now managed by Claire Villars (Chasse-Spleen and La Gurgue) and a team of able professionals. Before '93 the wines were of little interest.

Château Giscours 33460 Labarde
3e grand cru classé
A huge, rambling château and *chais* in a fine park with a lake sunk partly to influence the microclimate. Sinewy, concentrated wine with a solid reputation, even in lesser years. The estate was purchased in 1995 by Eric Albada Jelgersma.

Château La Gurgue
33460 Margaux
cru bourgeois
An avenue almost opposite the Maison du Vin leads to this restored château where, since 1978, remarkably good wines have been made. It is another of the properties owned and managed by the Merlaut-Villars family of Chasse-Spleen fame.

Château d'Issan 33460 Cantenac
3e grand cru classé
Beautifully restored by the Cruse family, this 17th-century moated castle is one of the most splendid sights in the Médoc. A musical programme is given in one of the cellars during the annual Bordeaux festival. The wine has consistency, elegance and finesse.

Château Kirwan 33460 Cantenac
3e grand cru classé
An 18th-century manor with a beautiful show of flowers in summer. The wines have improved since 1993. This could be linked to the recent modernisation of the *chais* and the fact that oenologist Michel Rolland is now consultant to the property.

Château Labégorce
33460 Margaux
cru bourgeois
A substantial château and close neighbour of Labégorce-Zédé (the two were once one part of the same estate). Supple, rounded, often almost fat wine. Very much improved under new ownership since the late 1980s.

Château Labégorce-Zédé
33460 Margaux
cru bourgeois
Luc Thienpont (of the Belgian family who own Vieux Château Certan in Pomerol and other estates) makes a very pure wine, full of character with a pleasing amount of fruit and good ageing potential.

Château Lascombes
33460 Margaux
2e grand cru classé
Excellently managed and maintained estate, one of the largest in the Médoc, with a rather ungainly Victorian château. The wines are elegant and mature outstandingly well in bottle. They are usually reliable in poor years too. The British brewery Bass Charrington took over in 1971 from Alexis Lichine.

Château Ligondras 33460 Arsac
A robust, old-fashioned wine for long cellaring.

Château Malescot St-Exupéry
33460 Margaux
3e grand cru classé
The château, dating from 1885, is in Margaux' main street; the vineyards are typically scattered and include plots in Soussans. The wine has plenty of colour and tannin, some fruit and a certain refinement; it usually demands years of patience.

Château Margaux 33460 Margaux
1er grand cru classé
An avenue lined with tall plane trees leads to a large country house with a palatial air. The late André Mentzelopoulos bought Margaux in 1977 and spared neither money nor effort to restore the château and the wine, which had declined in quality, to their former glory. His wife and daughters continue his work. Château Margaux can be the Médoc's best red: rich, stylish and very concentrated. Tasting it is a privilege. A second label is Pavillon Rouge. A white Bordeaux, Pavillon Blanc du Château Margaux, is also made from a separate vineyard of Sauvignon Blanc – the finest of the very rare white wines of the Médoc.

Château Marquis d'Alesme Becker 33460 Margaux
3e grand cru classé
In the same street as Château Margaux. The wine is usually reserved, but since 1979 when a modern *cuvier* and new *chais* were installed, it has become more supple and elegant, and more of a true Margaux.

Château Marquis-de-Terme
33460 Margaux
4e grand cru classé
During the 1980s a great deal has been invested in equipment, cellars and reception rooms. The wine has benefited: it is a pure, firm Margaux with colour, juice and tannin.

Château Martinens
33460 Margaux
cru bourgeois
Partly in Margaux and partly in Cantenac, the château was built, so the annals say, in 1767 by three English sisters called White. The pleasant wine seems to have improved in recent years.

Château Monbrison 33460 Arsac
cru bourgeois
Exceptional wines made from very low-yielding vines. Fine, subtle and complex, they are superior to many of the appellation's *crus classés*.

Château Palmer 33460 Cantenac
3e grand cru classé
The picture-book château with its four pointed towers produces splendid, balanced wine with great charm and finesse, obviously far better than its third-growth classification. The château flies British, Dutch and French flags, representing the nationalities of the owners and winemaker.

Château Paveil de Luze
33460 Soussans
cru bourgeois
A more-than-respectable Médoc *bourgeois* from Baron Geoffroy de Luze. The château is in the *chartreuse* (hunting lodge) style typical of the Médoc – long and low, with two wings and two square towers.

Château Pontac-Lynch
33460 Cantenac
cru bourgeois
A comparatively modest family estate combining two celebrated Bordeaux names. A correct wine.

Château Pouget 33460 Cantenac
4e grand cru classé
The château where the wine of Boyd-Cantenac was made until early 1983. Now a new *cuvier* and *chais* across the road from the old cellars (where Boyd-Cantenac is still made) produce sturdy, often rather steely wine with considerable tannin and colour. For long maturing.

Château Prieuré-Lichine
33460 Cantenac
4e grand cru classé
Probably the most hospitable *grand cru* in the Médoc. Visitors are always welcome. Prieuré-Lichine is a former monastery where Benedictine monks made wine centuries ago; the property was bought in 1951 by Alexis Lichine who painstakingly extended the vineyard area. The wine is well made with good balance and enough backbone for ageing. It is also good value for money.

Château Rauzan-Gassies
33460 Margaux
2e grand cru classé
The balance of the old Rauzan estate (see below). The wine is an atypical Margaux, rather hard and dour, but worth watching.

Château Rauzan-Ségla
33460 Margaux
2e grand cru classé
Older than most well-known Médoc estates, the Rauzan vineyards date back to 1661. The property was divided at the time of the French Revolution, a third of it becoming Rauzan Gassies. The château remained with the Ségla portion. For years the wine was not worthy of its second-growth status but since the early 1980s its quality has been remarkably restored. Bought in 1994 by Chanel Inc: from this vintage labels indicate Château Rauzan-Ségla with a 'z'.

Château Siran 33460 Labarde
cru bourgeois
A charming property famous for its vintage-time cyclamen as well as its extremely elegant wine. The owner, Alain Miailhe, aims to acquire the status *cru classé* for his wine, which it certainly deserves. His anti-nuclear shelter is thoughtfully stocked with his best vintages.

Château Tayac 33460 Soussans
cru bourgeois
Large, modern estate producing pleasant, mellow wine. The actual château is no longer occupied.

Château du Tertre 33460 Arsac
5e grand cru classé
The once-dilapidated building has been carefully restored; the wine had already improved. This relatively unknown Margaux is now one of the commune's most reliably satisfying.

Château la Tour-de-Mons
33460 Soussans
cru bourgeois
Tiny Soussans is the most northerly of the five villages entitled to the Margaux appellation. The property is rich in history and bears the remains of a castle whose construction was begun in the 13th century. In good years the wine is almost opaque; the perfume and taste develop only after long cellaring.

HAUT-MÉDOC
Château d'Agassac
33290 Ludon-Médoc
cru bourgeois
Ludon-Médoc vineyards spread out before the splendidly romantic 13th-century moated castle, behind which the woods of the Landes begin. The estate produces sound, sturdy wine that benefits from bottle-age.

Château d'Arche
33290 Ludon-Médoc
cru bourgeois
The modest château in the centre of the village, hidden behind a high wall, houses a pleasant little museum of antique winemaking equipment. The wines are conservative, reliable and still give pleasure after many years.

Château Cambon La Pelouse
33460 Macau
cru bourgeois
Mild, pleasant wine for early drinking.

Château Cantemerle
33460 Macau
5e grand cru classé
This fairy-tale château, hidden in romantic woodlands that flank the road, is marvellous to visit. Its wine went through a weak period in the 1970s but in 1980 the estate was taken over by a group who, with the help of the *négociants* Cordier, totally renovated the vineyard and cellars. The quality of the wine is now exemplary, with concentration, depth and length.

Château Clément-Pichon
33290 Parempuyre
cru bourgeois
Clément Fayat, owner of Château La Dominique in St-Émilion, acquired this property in 1976. The vineyards have been totally replanted and the château renovated. The wines have been improving steadily.

Château Dillon 33290 Blanquefort
cru bourgeois
Pleasant wine vinified by pupils of the local Lycée Agricole.

Château La Lagune
33290 Ludon-Médoc
3e grand cru classé
The 1730 château, a low-built villa characteristic of the Bordeaux region, was originally a Carthusian monastery. It produces a particularly reliable wine with fruit, mellow firmness, a slight spiciness and the characteristic hint of vanilla from new-oak casks. The estate is owned and meticulously managed by the champagne house Ayala.

Château Magnol
33290 Blanquefort
cru bourgeois
A mellow, fairly firm Haut-Médoc, ready for drinking within a few years. Since 1979 it has been made and sold by the *négociants* Barton & Guestier, whose buildings adjoin the vineyard.

Château de Malleret
33290 Le-Pian-Médoc
cru bourgeois
A pleasant family château with splendid stables. Owner Count Bertrand du Vivier is an enthusiastic horseman as well as a *négociant* and winemaker. Good, reasonably firm, balanced Haut-Médoc.

Château Maucamps 33460 Macau
cru bourgeois
Sound, pure Haut-Médoc with the elegance of a Margaux. Worth following, particularly from '81 on.

Château Sénéjac
33290 Le-Pian-Médoc
cru bourgeois
Owned by Charles de Guigné. The wines have improved under the guidance of New Zealand winemaker Jenny Dobson, now returned to her native land. The red is firm and concentrated and there is also a small production of very good white, Blanc de Sénéjac.

Château du Taillan
33320 Le Taillan
cru bourgeois
This is the first important estate to appear as you approach the Médoc from Bordeaux (the boundary between the Médoc and Graves actually crosses it). The monumental 18th-century château is beautifully preserved and its 300-year-old cellar has been declared a historic monument. The wine is comparatively mellow and supple. A pleasant white Bordeaux is also made.

Margaux' sumptuous wines mature in the estate's lofty, pillared chais.

WINE ACTIVITIES
The Commanderie du Bontemps de Médoc et des Graves represents the whole of the Médoc and also the Graves district. This Wine Order can be contacted through the **Maison du Tourisme et du Vin de Médoc** in Pauillac, but most of its events are attended by invitation only. In April there is a 'portes ouvertes' weekend in the Médoc when listed châteaux open their doors to visitors without appointment.

WINE INFORMATION
Maison du Vin 33460 Margaux
Tel (0)557 88 70 82
Information about visiting the châteaux is available; wine is on sale.

HOTELS
Relais de Margaux
33460 Margaux
Tel (0)557 88 38 30
Fax (0)557 88 31 73
This hotel and restaurant was opened in 1985. It is set in a large park close to Château Margaux and overlooks the river. The rooms are fairly small but modern and comfortable (though the walls are thin). In the restaurant, regional specialities in season include fish in red wine, scallops in Sauternes and Pauillac lamb.

Le Domaine des Ardillières
33160 Salaunes
Tel (0)556 58 58 08
Fax (0)556 58 51 01
This hotel and restaurant is set amid pinewoods and offers a heated swimming pool as well as a tennis court. Salaunes is about 20km west of Margaux on the D105 and N215 via Castelnau-de-Médoc, or you can take the N215 Bordeaux–Lacanau from Bordeaux via St-Médard-en-Jalles.

RESTAURANTS
Auberge des Criquets 33290 Blanquefort Tel (0)556 35 09 24
Specialises in game but other dishes are also generally of good standard. Friendly service. Eight rooms offer adequate accommodation.

Chez Quinquin 33460 Macau
Tel (0)557 88 45 89
A *guinguette* or small tavern located on the water's edge in the port of Macau. Fresh fish and shellfish are the specialities.

Auberge le Savoie 33460 Margaux
Tel (0)557 88 31 76
Congenial village restaurant with friendly service, a good wine-list and traditional and contemporary dishes.

PLACES OF INTEREST
Blanquefort South of the village centre, to the right of the D2 as you come from Bordeaux are the ruins of Château de Duras, a stronghold built in the 13th and 14th centuries and now a historic monument. In Blanquefort itself there is an agricultural and viticultural school with its own vineyard, Château Dillon. The American wine firm Barton & Guestier has its headquarters in the village.

Coast and Woodlands Excursions can be made by car, bike or canoe, or on foot or horseback, in and around the pinewoods west of the wine-producing area. A folder showing the various routes is available from the Information Touristique in Bordeaux. To enjoy sun and sand, go to the splendid beaches on the Atlantic coast, or to the two large inland waterways, Étang d'Hourtin and Étang de Lacanau.

Macau There is a charming harbour here. In summer you can enjoy fresh fruits de mer and a glass of white wine on the banks of the Gironde. Shad (*alose*) is the local speciality.

Graves

The disparate region of Graves, to the south of Bordeaux along the left bank of the River Garonne, is a difficult one to get to grips with. Geographically it is a continuation of the Médoc, but in the north many vineyards have disappeared beneath the urban sprawl of Bordeaux. This was once a region of many mediocre whites and a few aristocratic reds, but over recent decades the picture has changed almost beyond recognition.

The first vines in Bordeaux were cultivated within the city limits as far back as the Middle Ages and probably beyond, the port providing a ready market for wine. These vineyards, which gradually extended outward from Bordeaux, came to be known as the 'Graves de Bordeaux' (as did the wines, later) due to the gravelly nature of the soil. The vineyard of Château Pape-Clément, now in the city suburbs, was established in the 14th century.

The wines duly acquired an 'international' reputation, being exported first to England and then later to northern European countries and the Hanseatic states. The first Bordeaux wine to be referred to by the name of its estate was from the Graves: in 1663 the diarist Samuel Pepys noted that he had drunk "a sort of French wine called Ho Bryan that hath a good and most particular taste that I ever met with". Thomas Jefferson later approved the quality of Graves wines in the 18th century. The Graves remained highly regarded until the middle of the 19th century when it was overshadowed by the Médoc. At this point there were some 10,000 hectares of vineyard in the Graves.

Originally the Graves constituted all the vineyards from the Jalle de Blanquefort, the tiny stream just north of the city that marks the boundary with the Médoc, to the town of Langon 55 kilometres further south – excluding the sweet-wine appellations of Cérons, Sauternes and Barsac. To the east and west the region is bounded respectively by the Garonne and the pine forest of the Landes.

In 1987, however, a new appellation was created for the wines of the northern Graves: Pessac-Léognan. The southern Graves, which extends south from La Brède, and the tiny Saucats stream now constitute what is delimited as appellation Graves. There are approximately 3,100 hectares under production that take the appellation Graves and a further 400 hectares are reserved for sweet white Graves Supérieures.

The division into two appellations has caused some confusion not least because the *crus classés* of the Graves, a classification which dates from 1959, are all in Pessac-Léognan and because the inscription Vin de Graves or Grand Vin de Graves is permitted on the labels of wines from appellation Pessac-Léognan. The split also

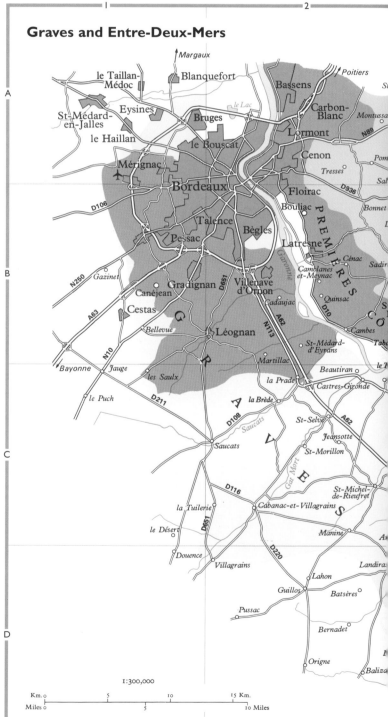

Graves and Entre-Deux-Mers

Château de Vayres, with its fine terrace and manicured gardens backing onto the Garonne, was once the property of Henry IV of France.

had the effect of notionally down-grading Graves, although some very good wines are produced there. The two wine-growers' associations (Pessac-Léognan and Graves) now work in tandem to promote the region's wines.

The southern Graves, now appellation Graves, used to produce mainly semi-sweet white wines. Now over half the wines are red and the white, around 35 per cent of the production, is mainly dry.

The grapes for red Graves are the same as those of the Médoc (Cabernet Sauvignon, Merlot and Cabernet Franc) but the wines are quite distinctive: being somewhat earthier than the Médocs, a little more supple and with an aroma that can be spicy, smoky or slightly resinous. They are also earlier-maturing. The English

wine writer Maurice Healey once compared the difference between a Médoc and a red Graves to that between a glossy and a matt print of the same photograph. The matt version is just as good as the glossy but less brilliant, its contrasts less marked.

Gravel terraces exist in the Graves but there is more sand and clay than is found further north in Pessac-Léognan. The fairly high calcium content is good for the white-grape varieties. White Graves is made from Sémillon, Sauvignon and sometimes a small percentage of Muscadelle. There is usually a higher percentage of Sémillon than Sauvignon. The dry whites are produced in two styles: one crisp, dry and fruity, the other embracing richer, more complex wines that have been been barrel-fermented and oak-aged.

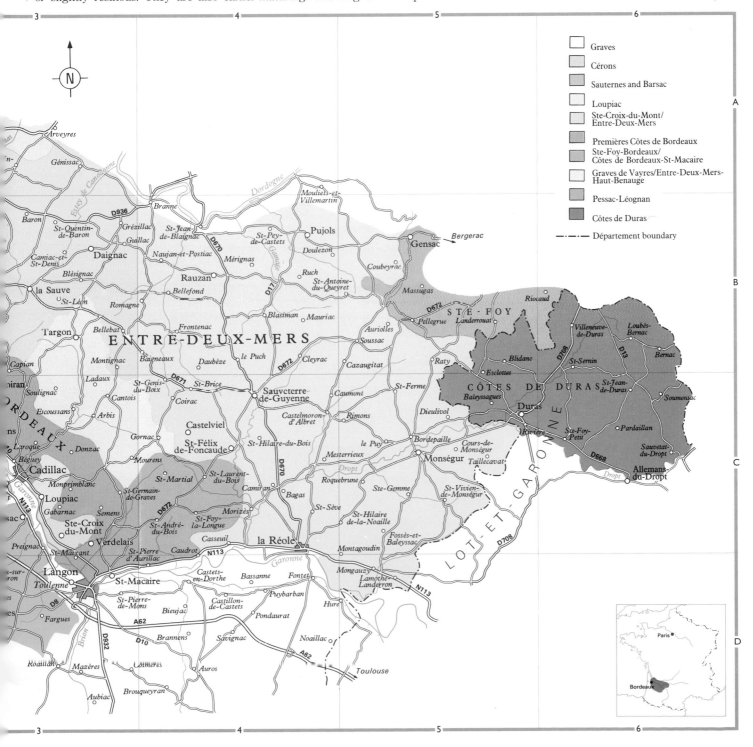

Entre-Deux-Mers

Entre-Deux-Mers is both a general description of the wedge-shaped region between the Dordogne and the Garonne rivers to the east of Bordeaux, and the designated appellation for the dry white wines produced in the greater part of this zone.

The area extends for some 80 kilometres south-east of Bordeaux and is about 30 kilometres across at its broadest point. This is one of the most beautiful regions around Bordeaux, where viticulture rubs shoulders with other forms of agricultural activity. Cereal crops, fruit trees and tobacco are cultivated alongside vines on an undulating terrain of hills and valleys. A plethora of monasteries, churches, castles and *bastides* or fortified towns attest to the region's rich and colourful history.

Both red and white wines are produced in Entre-Deux-Mers but as the red wines take either the appellation Bordeaux or that of Bordeaux Supérieur, precise figures for production and surface area are difficult to come by. The appellation Entre-Deux-Mers has approximately 2,300 hectares under production for dry white wines. The quality of its wines has improved tremendously from the days when they were either over sulphured or oxidised. Investment in modern equipment – mechanical harvesters, temperature-control systems, stainless-steel tanks and greater technical and viticultural expertise – has led to the production of cleaner, more aromatic wines. Large cooperatives dominate the scene but small estates that bottle their own wines do exist. Cabernet Sauvignon, Cabernet Franc and Merlot are used for the red wines, with the last dominating blends, while for white wines Sauvignon generally takes ascendancy over Sémillon and Muscadelle.

Haut-Bénauge is a small sub-district of Entre-Deux-Mers made up of nine villages between Targon and Cadillac. The wines made from Sémillon, Sauvignon and Muscadelle are seldom seen as they are unfashionably sweet. The region also produces dry white Entre-Deux-Mers, red Bordeaux and Bordeaux Supérieur.

The appellation Premières Côtes de Bordeaux runs parallel to the River Garonne for 60 kilometres, from just south of Bordeaux to St-Maixant, just north of Langon. At its widest point it is only five kilometres. The region was first cultivated by the Romans, became an important source of wine in the Middle Ages and is at present experiencing something of a renaissance. Foreign and national investors have been attracted to the region and provide a welcome injection of cash as well as a more open-minded attitude. Vineyards have been restructured, buildings and equipment improved and a greater percentage of new-oak barrels introduced. Producers offer both an oaked and an unoaked *cuvée*. The vineyards are situated on south-east-facing clay and gravel slopes on a limestone bluff that runs the length of the appellation. The red wines are aromatic, with an attractive purity of fruit. There are now 2,800 hectares producing red Premières Côtes de Bordeaux and 895 hectares in the southern half of the appellation destined for sweet white Premières Côtes de Bordeaux and Cadillac.

Just south of Cadillac the sweet-wine appellations of Loupiac and Ste-Croix-du-Mont face Sauternes across the Garonne. The wines do not have the same intensity as those of Sauternes but they are often better value for money than some of the dull yet expensive offerings from the superior appellation. The permitted grape varieties are the same – Sémillon, Sauvignon and Muscadelle – but permitted yields are higher at 40 hectolitres per hectare, although this is rarely attained. As in Sauternes the onset of *pourriture noble* (noble rot) is the critical factor determining the quality of the vintage. Being lighter in style these wines are generally drunk young as an apéritif, or occasionally as an accompaniment to white-meat dishes. Some of the better wines have the potential to age up to 20 years or more.

Further south around St-Macaire are the ten communes of Côtes de Bordeaux-St-Macaire. Most of the wine made here is sold as Bordeaux or Bordeaux Supérieur and about 90 hectares is set aside for the production of semi-sweet (*demi-sec*) or sweet appellation Côtes de Bordeaux-St-Macaire.

Another less well known appellation in the far north-eastern corner of the Entre-Deux-Mers region is Ste-Foy Bordeaux, named after the old town of Ste-Foy-la-Grande. The emphasis is on red and dry white here; some sweet wines are also permitted. Thanks to a charter of quality signed by all the better producers, the wines of Ste-Foy Bordeaux improved dramatically during the 1990s. Similarly on the left bank of the Dordogne, almost opposite Libourne, the appellation Graves de Vayres produces mainly red and dry white wines, and very occasionally a little *demi-sec,* from a total of 540 hectares. The local cooperative dominates the scene here but there are also a few individual producers.

The village of St-Macaire looks out over the Garonne through the fortified gates of its former defences. Narrow streets lined with medieval houses radiate from the magnificent 12th–14th-century church of St-Sauveur.

Pessac-Léognan

The appellation Pessac-Léognan was created only in 1987 but its history, like that of the Graves, dates back to beyond the Middle Ages. In fact Pessac-Léognan is in essence a Graves, having formerly been the northern part of that appellation with vineyards located in the western and southern reaches of Bordeaux' urban expanse. The appellation comprises ten communes with the two most important, Pessac and Léognan, providing its name and replacing two temporary designations, Graves de Pessac and Graves de Léognan. Its importance lies in the fact that all the châteaux nominated in 1959 as *cru classé* (a classification that designates both red and white wines) lie within its bounds.

One of the region's problems has been the continual urban expansion of Bordeaux. In 1850 Mérignac (now the location of Bordeaux airport) had 22 wine estates, compared with just one today. In the same period the number of estates in Pessac fell from 12 to four and in Talence from 19 to three. At the end of the 19th century there were approximately 5,000 hectares under production in this northern Graves zone. By 1975 this had been reduced to 550. The decline has since been reversed and the vineyard area has climbed to just over 1,300 hectares. It is still surprising to discover, however, that the vineyards of some of Pessac-Léognan's and Bordeaux' most famous estates, Châteaux Haut-Brion, La Mission-Haut-Brion and Pape-Clément, are surrounded by suburban sprawl.

The gravelly soils that have made this region so famous continue to exert their influence. They form gentle undulations providing excellent drainage, which is further reinforced by a network of tiny streams flowing into the Garonne. These gravel deposits can be found close to the city in the communes of Talence and Pessac but also appear further south in the more forested communes of Léognan and Martillac. The gravel also soaks up the sun's rays providing thermal heat for ripening the grapes. This, coupled with the temperate climate, results in most years in Pessac-Léognan harvesting earlier than the Médoc.

The northern Graves built a reputation for its red wines, 'the new French claret', from the end of the 17th century and Pessac-Léognan continues the tradition by producing mainly red. Cabernet Sauvignon, Cabernet Franc and Merlot are again the principal red varieties with greater emphasis on Cabernet Sauvignon here than in the Graves and Cabernet Franc playing a more significant role in hot, ripe years. The wines usually have a dark hue and are firmly structured with the classic aromas of blackcurrant and mint and a subdued mineral or smoky character. The quality of the wines in Pessac-Léognan has remained more consistent than it has in other Bordeaux appellations.

The white wines may represent a tiny percentage of the production but they are significant in terms of quality and value and usually command higher prices than their red counterparts. Sauvignon, Sémillon and Muscadelle are the varieties used but in a reversal of the trend in the Graves, Sauvignon is the dominant variety. At some top estates, Châteaux Couhins-Lurton, Malartic-Lagravière and Smith-Haut-Lafitte for instance, the white wines are made from 100 per cent Sauvignon. The white wines from Pessac-Léognan have considerable ageing potential and have great intensity, aroma and concentration. Fermentation and ageing in new-oak barrels with stirring of the lees is almost universally employed by the better estates.

The importance of the 16 classified growths in Pessac-Léognan cannot be understated. In particular, changes of ownership and new investment in these properties over the last few years have added momentum and given a new sense of dynamism to the entire appellation. The knock-on effect has been that those properties within the appellation which were not classified in 1959 have also found new ownership, and as a result are improving steadily.

Above: Administrator M Delmas believes in diversity and cultivates up to 400 different clones – excluding the roses – in the Château Haut-Brion vineyards.

Left: A museum of medieval imagery is conjured by the numerous statues that decorate the façade of Bazas' 13th-century cathedral.

PRODUCERS OF SPECIAL INTEREST

ENTRE-DEUX-MERS (WHITE), BORDEAUX AND BORDEAUX SUPÉRIEUR

Château de Beau Rivage
33880 Baurech
Château Beaulieu
33540 Sauveterre-de-Guyenne
Château Bonnet 33420 Grézillac
A pioneer estate for modern, fruity white wines. Also good reds. The property is owned by André Lurton.
Château de Bouchet
33420 Grézillac
Château Canet 33420 Guillac
Château de Castelneau
33670 St-Léon de Bordeaux
Full, fruity Entre-Deux-Mers and barrel-fermented Réserve du Château.
Château Cazeau
33540 Sauveterre-de-Guyenne
A reliable source of decent red AOC Bordeaux, produced by the mayor.
Domaine de Cazères
33550 Langoiran
Château Courson 33890 Gensac
Domaine de Courteillac
33350 Castillon-la-Bataille
Red wines produced with the same attention to detail as is given the *grands crus* – including barrel ageing.
Château Courtey 33490 St-Martial
Château La Croix du Moulin
33790 Soussac
Château Gamage
33350 St-Pey-de-Castets
Well made reds from this château with English partners.
Château les Gauthiers
33370 Bonnetan
Château Le Grand Verdus
33670 Sadirac
Consistently good red wines.
Château Lafite Monteil
33370 Salleboeuf
Château Launay 33790 Soussac
Another dependable address for crisp, fresh Entre-Deux-Mers whites.
Château Laurétan
33550 Langoiran
Château La Mongie 33240 Vérac
Château Moulin de Launay
33790 Soussac
Château Nardique la Gravière
33670 St-Genès-de-Lombaud
Château Pailhas 33790 Massugas
Château Pomirol du Pin
33490 Verdelais
Château Queyret-Pouillac
33790 St-Antoine-du-Queyret
Château Reynier 33420 Grézillac
Château Roquefort
33760 Lugasson
Very good white wines including an oaky barrel-fermented version.
Château La Rose St-Germain
33760 Romagne
Château de Sours
33750 St-Quentin-de-Baron
Owned by Scotsman Esme Johnson.

Firm, full reds and a refreshing rosé.
Château Thieuley 33670 La Sauve
Now a highly proficient, modern domaine. Various *cuvées* of red and white Bordeaux are available.
Château Toutigeac 33760 Targon
Château Turon La Croix
33760 Lugasson

PREMIÈRES CÔTES DE BORDEAUX, CADILLAC, BORDEAUX AND BORDEAUX SUPÉRIEUR

Château Anniche 33550 Haux
Château du Biac 33550 Langoiran
Château Brethous
33360 Camblanes et Meynac
Château Carsin 33410 Rions
A Finnish owner, a modern winery and an Australian winemaker. Very good Premières Côtes reds.
Domaine de Chastelet
33360 Quinsac
Château la Clyde 33550 Tabanac
Château Constantin
33880 Baurech
Château Fauchey
33550 Villenave-de-Rions
Château Fayau 33410 Cadillac
Château Génisson
33490 St-Germain-de-Grave
Château du Grand Mouëys
33550 Capian
Château Haux 33550 Haux
Château Jonchet 33880 Cambes
Château Labatut 33490 St Maixant
Château Lamothe de Haux
33550 Haux
Cellars in a quarried limestone cave. Well constituted red Premières Côtes.
Château Langoiran
33550 Langoiran
Cellars are beneath ruins of the 12th-century château. Fruity red Premières Côtes and a barrel-aged version.
Château Lézongars
33550 Langoiran
Château de Malagar
33490 St-Maixant
Château Marcelin Laffitte
33410 Gabarnac
Château Melin 33880 Baurech
Domaine de la Meulière
33360 Cénac
Château Montjouan 33270 Bouliac
Château de Paillet-Quancard
33550 Paillet
Château Péconnet 33360 Quinsac
Domaine du Pin Franc
33410 Donzac
Château Puy Bardens
33880 Cambes
Château Rauzé-Lafargue
33360 Cénac
Château Renon 33550 Tabanac
Château Reynon 33410 Béguey
Excellent reds and whites produced by owner Denis Dubourdieu, who is also a professor at Bordeaux University's Institute of Oenology.
Château de Rions 33410 Rions
Château Sauvage 33550 Haux

Château Le Sens
33880 St-Caprais-de-Bordeaux
Château Suau 33550 Capian
Monique Aldebert makes an attractive red Premières Côtes.
Château Tanesse 33550 Langoiran

CÔTES DE BORDEAUX-ST-MACAIRE, GRAVES DE VAYRES, LOUPIAC AND STE-CROIX-DU-MONT

Château Barre Gentillot
33870 Graves de Vayres
Clos Jean 33410 Loupiac
As good as some Sauternes in certain vintages.
Château Coullac
33410 Ste-Croix-du-Mont
Château de Cros 33410 Loupiac
Large and fairly consistent producer of sweet Loupiac and other appellations.
Château La Grave
33410 Ste-Croix-du-Mont
Château Lamarque
33410 Ste-Croix-du-Mont
Château Lesparre
33750 Bechau-et-Cailleau
The largest and best estate of Graves de Vayres.
Château Loubens
33410 Ste-Croix-du-Mont
Château de Loupiac-Gaudiet
33410 Loupiac
Château Lousteau-Vieil
33410 Ste-Croix-du-Mont
The vineyard is at the highest point in the commune. A larger-than-normal percentage of Muscadelle makes the wines aromatic and ready for early drinking.
Domaine de Majoureau
33490 Caudrot
Château Malromé
33490 St-André-du-Bois
Once the summer retreat and family home of French artist Henri Toulouse-Lautrec. Reliable red wines are produced on the estate.
Château Mazarin
33410 Loupiac
Château du Mont
33410 Ste-Croix-du-Mont
Château Pichon Bellevue
33870 Graves de Vayres
Château La Rame
33410 Ste-Croix-du-Mont
Top estate in this sweet-wine appellation.
Château de Ricaud
33410 Loupiac
Château la Serre
33490 St-André-du-Bois
Château du Vieux Moulin
33410 Loupiac

STE-FOY BORDEAUX

Château l'Enclos 33220 Pineuilh
Top-quality red wine dominated by Merlot.
Château Hostens-Picant
33220 Les Lèves-et-Thoumeyragues
Exceptional red and white wines.

WINE FÊTES

Créon In the first week in November.
La Réole At the beginning of June.
Ste-Croix-du-Mont At the end of July/beginning of August.
Sauveterre-de-Guyenne In the last week of July.

WINE INFORMATION

Maison du Vin Château des Ducs d'Épernon, Cadillac
Information and wine shop.
Maison de Qualité Opposite Beychac-et-Cailleau on the N9 Bordeaux-Libourne road. Also has a tasting room and information office.

HOTELS

Hôtel de France 33420 Branne
Tel (0)557 84 50 06
Country hotel on the banks of the Dordogne. Restaurant.
Château de la Tour 33410 Cadillac
Tel (0)556 76 92 00
Modern hotel with a view of the nearby Château des Ducs d'Épernon. Swimming pool, tennis court, terrace and restaurant serving classic dishes.
Hôtel St-Martin 33550 Langoiran
Tel (0)556 67 02 67
Simple hotel-restaurant by the river.
Château du Parc 33580 St-Ferme
Tel (0)556 61 69 18
Comfortable family-run *maison d'hôte*. Six rooms available in the 17–19th-century château. Reservations are needed for dinner.
Grand Hôtel
33220 Ste-Foy-la-Grande
Tel (0)557 46 00 08
Modernised town-centre hotel with character intact. Restaurant.

RESTAURANTS

Auberge du Marais 33270 Bouliac
Tel (0)556 20 52 17
Generous, seasonally based cuisine. Agreeably priced lunch menus.
Le St-James 33270 Bouliac
Tel (0)557 97 06 00
One of the best restaurants in the Gironde, overlooking the Garonne. Inventive cuisine; impressive, lengthy wine-list. Luxurious rooms also available. Next door is the bistrot Le Bistroy [tel (0)557 97 06 06].
La Fontine 33190 Fontet
Tel (0)556 61 11 81
A large farm offering friendly service and tasty food.
Le Coq Sauvage 33450 St-Loubès
Tel (0)556 20 41 04
Situated on the edge of the Dordogne. Classic regional dishes.
L'Abricotier 33490 St-Macaire
Tel (0)556 76 83 63
Pleasant restaurant with reasonably priced menus. Al fresco in summer.

PRODUCERS OF SPECIAL INTEREST

GRAVES

Château d'Archambeau
33720 Illats

Château d'Ardennes 33720 Illats

Château Le Bonnat
33650 St-Selve

Château de Chantegrive
33720 Podensac
A delicious red wine, aged in oak, and a very pure dry white. The Cuvée Caroline is the top white.

Clos Floridène
33210 Pujols-sur-Ciron
A top white Graves produced by Denis Dubourdieu, professor at Bordeaux University's Institute of Oenology. The vineyard is on the plateau of Barsac.

Pierre Coste 33210 Langon
This *négociant* has for a number of years produced crisp, fresh white Graves and supple, early-drinking reds.

Domaine La Grave 33640 Portets
Excellent red and white wines produced by Peter Vinding-Diers of Château de Landiras.

Château de Landiras
33720 Landiras
Another property belonging to Peter Vinding-Diers, making splendid 100%-Sémillon white Graves and some appealing red.

Château Magence
33210 St-Pierre-de-Mons

Château Magneau
33650 La Brède

Château Rahoul 33640 Portets
Solid red and aromatic white wines. Good but the white is not at the same level as it was in the 1980s.

Château Respide-Médeville
33210 Preignac

Château du Roquetaillade La Grange 33210 Mazères
Generous, meaty red Graves. The white tends towards gentleness.

Château Le Tuquet
33640 Beautiran

Vieux Château Gaubert
33640 Portets
The property includes an 18th-century château which is still to be renovated. Crisp, delicately aromatic white wines and supple reds.

PESSAC-LÉOGNAN

Château Bouscaut
33140 Cadaujac
cru classé (red and white)
The reputation of this property dates back to the 17th century when the vineyard was known as Haut-Truchon. It was totally restored in the 1970s with US dollars and acquired by Lucien Lurton in 1980. It is now owned and managed by his daughter Sophie. The white is made from a high percentage of Sémillon; the red is normally supple and medium weight.

Château Brown 33850 Léognan

Château Carbonnieux
33850 Léognan
cru classé (red and white)
A famous old estate taken over by Benedictine monks in 1741, now run by the Perrin family. With 82ha this is the largest of the *crus classés*. Considerable investment through the 1980s has been rewarded by an improvement in the quality of the wines. The white is now consistently one of the best in the appellation and the red is well crafted.

Château Les Carmes Haut-Brion 33600 Pessac
Quite elegant, respectable red-wine neighbour of Haut-Brion.

Domaine de Chevalier
33850 Léognan
cru classé (red and white)
This vineyard – remarkably situated in a clearing deep in the woods behind the village of Léognan – produces magnificent white wine that in complexity, length and stamina surpasses almost all the other dry white Bordeaux. It is made with meticulous attention to the smallest details. The red wine is also excellent, tending towards a great Médoc personality: only after 10–20 years does it start to reveal itself. The house itself is small and modest and the word 'château' is not used.

Château Couhins
33140 Villenave-d'Ornon
cru classé (white)
A large part of the vineyard is the property of INRA, a French agricultural research institute. The white is full and spicy; the red powerful. Various new grape varieties are being tried (see also Château Couhins-Lurton below).

Château Couhins-Lurton
33140 Villenave-d'Ornon
cru classé (white)
Reserved, long-lived white wine produced from 100% Sauvignon. The small vineyard was originally part of the Couhins estate but was bought from INRA by André Lurton in 1979.

Château de Cruzeau
33650 St-Médard-d'Eyrans
Estate on deep gravel, replanted when bought by André Lurton in the 1970s. Worth following for both its red and its white wines.

Château de Fieuzal 33850 Léognan
cru classé (red)
The red wine – now one of the best of the *crus classés* – is firm, packed with oaky fruit and typical of the district. Unfortunately not much of the *cru classé*-quality white wine is produced. De Fieuzal was purchased by a French bank in 1994.

Château de France
33850 Léognan
Lots of investment since the 1970s. Supple, well made red. The white dates from 1988 but has not yet reached its full potential.

Château Gazin 33850 Léognan

Château Haut-Bailly
33850 Léognan
cru classé (red)
An unspectacular-looking château making an almost satiny-soft, stylish and satisfying red Graves. Since 1979, after a short weaker period, the wine has remained consistent in quality. About a quarter of the vines are over 40 years old.

Château Haut-Bergey
33850 Léognan
Bought in 1991 by Sylvianne Garcin, sister of Daniel Cathiard (see Château Smith-Haut-Lafitte, page 153). The

winery has been completely rebuilt and the quality of the wines is on an upward curve.

Château Haut-Brion 33600 Pessac
cru classé (red) and
1er grand cru classé (1855)
Haut-Brion was the only Graves estate to be included in the classification of 1855 – and was classed in the top category. The substantial, 16th-century château used to be beyond the Bordeaux town boundary but is now surrounded by the suburb of Pessac. The vineyard is in two parts and slopes slightly on a deep layer of gravel. The red wine from this excellently managed estate is distinguished by a superb balance between fruity and earthy flavours, a noble, almost mild velvetiness, gentle strength and long aftertaste. The white wine, made only in very small quantities, is also outstanding. Stainless-steel fermentation tanks of the estate's own design were installed as early as 1961. Haut-Brion was bought in 1935 by the American banker Clarence Dillon; the current president is Dillon's granddaughter Joan, the Duchesse de Mouchy.

Château Haut-Gardère
33850 Léognan

Château Haut-Lagrange
33850 Léognan

Château Larrivet Haut-Brion
33850 Léognan
Plenty of investment at this estate. Wines improving but not yet up to the standard of the leaders.

Château Laville Haut-Brion
33600 Pessac
cru classé (white)
Together with that produced by the Domaine de Chevalier, this is the best dry white wine of Bordeaux. The aroma of the Sauvignon (40% of the *encépagement*) is strongly present in this Graves for four to five years. After this, however, the Sémillon (the other 60%) breaks through, giving rise to a concentrated, luxurious, wonderfully nuanced flavour. Since 1983 the modest estate has had the same owner as Haut-Brion.

Château La Louvière
33850 Léognan
Owned by André Lurton. Both the red and white wines of this property are at *cru classé* level. The beautiful château was designed by Victor Louis.

Château Malartic-Lagravière
33850 Léognan
cru classé (red and white)
Modern methods are used to make a traditional red wine with a distinct personality. It usually needs laying down for decades. The white (from 100% Sauvignon) is delightful when young and also after maturing. The property is owned by the champagne house Laurent-Perrier.

The 16th-century manor house at Haut-Brion is Bordeaux' oldest great château.

Château La Mission-Haut-Brion
33600 Pessac
cru classé (red)
For years this near-neighbour of Haut-Brion was its great rival, but today it is in the hands of the same owner, Domaine Clarence Dillon. La Mission is more sinewy and reserved, darker and earthier than Haut-Brion, and often just as fine. It can mature for decades, its original reserve giving way to warm, deep, mysterious and complex tones.

Château Olivier 33850 Léognan
cru classé (red and white)
The château is a splendidly medieval moated fortress. The gravelly vineyard produces a fresh, clean white and a red that has improved in recent years.

Château Pape-Clément
33600 Pessac
cru classé (red)
The estate was established in 1300 by Archbishop Bertrand de Goth of Bordeaux, later to become Pope Clement V (the label still carries the papal insignia). Today it is owned by Montagne & Cie. The wine is a broad, generous, almost creamy-tasting Graves with a strong constitution, due in part to the traces of iron in the soil. There is a small production of white – one of the best in Pessac-Léognan.

Château Picque-Caillou
33700 Mérignac
The only estate in Mérignac. Firm, lean, red wines and more recently a white of average quality.

Château Pontac-Monplaisir
33140 Villenave-d'Ornon
Mellow, nuanced white wine that can be among the best of all the Graves.

Château de Rochemorin
33650 Martillac
Exquisite red wine with body, wood and tannin. Sauvignon is the dominant variety in the white.

Château Le Sartre 33850 Léognan

Château Smith-Haut-Lafitte
33650 Martillac
cru classé (red)
One of the revelatory properties of the 1990s. Purchased in 1990 by French businessman and former ski-champion Daniel Cathiard, the estate has been completely renovated and the wines are now among the best in Pessac-Léognan. The white, made from 100% Sauvignon, is rich and aromatic; the red, produced from low-yielding vines, has since '94 been rich and concentrated.

Domaine de la Solitude
33650 Martillac
The property of a religious community. The wines are now made and the estate managed by the team at Domaine de Chevalier.

Château La Tour-Haut-Brion
33600 Pessac
cru classé (red)
For a long time the name of this château was used for La Mission-Haut-Brion's second wine. Today, however, this strong, tannic wine is once again solely the product of its own vineyard.

Château La Tour-Martillac
33650 Martillac
cru classé (red and white)
A modest little château with an old tower, the remnant of a 12th-century fort, in the inner courtyard. The *chais* has been renovated and the wines have improved enormously in the last few years. The white is an elegant barrel-fermented and oak-aged wine and the red a tight, medium-weight wine very much in the Graves style.

WINE FÊTE

Langon Foire aux Vins featuring wines from the Graves and Sauternes districts at the beginning of September.

WINE INFORMATION

The **Maison des Vins de Graves** at Podensac, just north of Cérons on the N113 [tel (0)556 27 09 25] provides information about visiting Graves and Pessac-Léognan and has a cellar where the district's wines are on sale. The **Maison du Vin** 1 cours du 30-Juillet, Bordeaux [tel (0)556 00 22 88] also provides information about the individual châteaux. **The Union des Crus Classés de Graves** has its headquarters at the same address.

HOTELS

La Réserve 33600 l'Alouette
Tel (0)556 07 13 28
Fax (0)556 36 31 02
A luxurious oasis surrounded by a park. Also a first-class restaurant.

Relais de Fompeyre
33430 Bazas
Tel (0)556 25 98 00
A spacious hotel with comfortable modern rooms, a swimming pool and restaurant.

La Grappe d'Or 33720 Cérons
Tel (0)556 27 11 61
On the D117E. Has charm without pretensions. Evening meals for residents only.

Le Chalet Lyrique 33170 Gradignan Tel (0)556 89 11 59
Hotel in a tranquil location with restaurant attached. Meat dishes are the speciality. Emphasis on the wines of Pessac-Léognan.

RESTAURANTS

La Maison des Graves
33650 La Brède
Tel (0)556 20 24 45
Restaurant in the centre of the village with modern cuisine. Original wine-list with plenty of unusual discoveries.

Bazas, famous for its cattle, has given its name to the powerful Bazadaise breed.

Pascal Le Bistrot 33610 Canéjan
Tel (0)556 89 18 57
Rustic style; traditional cuisine. Canéjan is about halfway between Pessac and Léognan, within easy reach of Bordeaux.

Claude Darroze 33210 Langon
Tel (0)556 63 00 48
The best restaurant of Graves/Sauternes. Stylish decor; such regional specialities as salade landaise, foie gras de canard, lamproie au blanc de poireaux and agneau de Médoc à l'estragon, and an extensive wine-list. Pleasant and comfortable rooms.

Le Grangousier 33210 Langon
Tel (0)556 63 30 59
On the D10 to Auros. An old manor house with a garden and a terrace. Regional cuisine.

La Maison de Cuisine 33650 Villenave-d'Ornon
Tel (0)556 87 07 59
Well executed regional and traditional cuisine. Reasonably priced menus.

PLACES OF INTEREST

The Graves district is easy to visit using Bordeaux as the departure point (see map page 119). A signposted wine road, the Circuit Touristique des Graves, takes in many of the world-famous châteaux. Further addresses, hotels and restaurants are listed in the Sauternes listings (page 157).

Bazas A good base from which to explore the Graves district, Bazas is about 15km south of Langon down the D932. A striking little town with a splendid square dominated by the Gothic cathedral of St-Jean-Baptiste. Nearby is the Jardin de l'Ancien Évêche on the former town walls. At the end of June/beginning of July a *son et lumière* display, with a cast of 400, bring the history of Bazas to life.

Budos This village a few kilometres west of Sauternes (take the D125) has the remains of a 14th-century feudal castle.

Cadaujac Romanesque church. (See also Château Bouscaut, page 150.)

Cérons and Illats Both have interesting churches.

Labrède Château de Labrède, a romantic moated castle, was the birthplace (in 1689) and home of the politician, writer and philosopher Charles de Segondat, Baron de La Brède and de Montesquieu. His library, containing some 7,000 works, is still intact. In Montesquieu's time the château was exporting wine to England; the estate still produces a modest amount of white.

Léognan Has a small, restored Romanesque church.

Mazères One of the most southerly communes in the Graves. Its pride is Château de Roquetaillade, a massive 14th-century fortress with six enormous round towers, a square keep and impressive vaulted chambers. It was built by a nephew of Pope Clement V and is well worth a visit (not least for the wine). Not far away are the ruins of a more primitive 12th- and 13th-century castle, and the beautiful St-Michel chapel with 14th-century paintings.

Podensac The Parc de Chavat has a display of curious statues sculpted between the two World Wars. The firm of Lillet in Podensac makes wine-based apéritifs.

St-Morillon A small village that still looks almost medieval.

Uzeste Has a splendid church built in 1312 to the orders of Pope Clement V (and rebuilt in the 16th century). The papal tomb lies here.

Villandraut Bertrand (Pope Clement V) was born in this small town which is ringed by woods. Bertrand built the local castle; of what remains, four large towers are particularly striking. There is also a small regional museum.

Villenave-d'Ornon Has a beautiful church, its nave flanked by two high aisles.

153

Sauternes

The Sauternes district is a small enclave in Graves devoted to the production of sweet white wine. It is located about 40 kilometres south-east of Bordeaux (see map on page 119). The autoroute des Deux Mers, the A62, crosses it and also partially delimits it, as does the River Ciron that flows into the Garonne here.

The 2,000-hectare appellation Sauternes extends over five communes: Barsac, Sauternes, Bommes, Fargues and Preignac. Each gives a different nuance to the character of the wines according to the local geological structure and climate. Bommes and Sauternes tend to produce rich, powerful wines. Barsac, on the opposite side of the tiny River Ciron, has its own appellation but can label its wines as either Barsac or Sauternes. They tend to be more delicate with a lively acidity due to the higher percentage of calcium in the soil and the proximity of the Ciron.

The secret of Sauternes lies not so much in the soil (gravel in many places, often mixed with clay) or in the grape varieties (mainly Sémillon, supplemented by Sauvignon and sometimes a little Muscadelle) but in the very specific mesoclimate. A warm temperate climate ripens the grapes through to July and August, then in the autumn the cold water from the Ciron flowing into the warmer water of the Garonne produces early-morning mists that envelop the vineyards until later in the day when the sun breaks through. The warm, moist conditions are ideal for provoking the onset of *Botrytis cinerea*, a fungus that attacks the grapes causing *pourriture noble*.

'Noble rot' precipitates a number of changes in the grapes. As they rot and shrivel on the vine, much of their moisture is lost, leaving the remaining juice concentrated, intensely sweet and rich in glycerine, capable of producing a wine of a minimum 13 per cent alcohol plus the residual sugar. Tannins are released and, critically, there is no loss of acidity. The aroma of the grapes is also altered, and this change is reflected in the wine.

Botrytis can occur only if the grapes are at optimum ripeness. This is why the harvest is much later in Sauternes than in the rest of Bordeaux – and prone to all the risks that a late harvest involves. The district enjoys a milder, somewhat drier climate than that of the surrounding areas but autumn rains can still spoil an entire vintage. Not all the grapes affected by noble rot – or not at the same time. In all but exceptional years the pickers must work through or *tri* the vineyard several times, picking the grapes from their bunches one by one as the rotting process becomes complete. In addition, the yield is low. The legal maximum is 25 hectolitres per hectare, but in practice this is rarely reached. At Yquem the average is only nine hectolitres, the equivalent of just one glass of wine per vine.

Such is the precarious nature of producing Sauternes that in some years very little is made. Sauternes was blessed with a string of great vintages in the 1980s: '83, '86, '88, '89 as well as '90. The early 1990s proved less fortuitous and due either to frost or to rain, certain estates did not declare a vintage in '91, '92 and '93 and made very little wine in '94.

A relatively new process, known as cryo-extraction, can help with water-bound years. The grapes are placed in the equivalent of a deep-freeze and those with the lowest sugar levels frozen and rejected. From an economic point of view, the production of great Sauternes is obviously a risky venture, and most of the best estates are now owned by solid family or business institutions.

Nature may provide the essential ingredients for these wines but their production still has to be handled with great delicacy. Stainless-steel tanks are used by some winemakers but many châteaux hold to traditional methods. The pressing of the grapes needs to be gentle and many leading estates, including Château d'Yquem, still prefer the old-fashioned vertical hydraulic presses. Fermentation then takes place in (new) oak barrels where the wine is matured for anything up to 36 months.

It is not exactly clear when the production of sweet wines in Sauternes became fully established but the process evidently existed in the late 18th century. Thomas Jefferson, American ambassador and later president, visited Sauternes and ordered cases of Yquem 1784 for his president, George Washington. The Russian court took to Sauternes in the early 19th century with the appearance of the much-acclaimed Yquem 1847. Sauternes was the only white wine to be included in the 1855 classification.

A good Sauternes is a feast for all the senses: its glowing colour of gold tinged with green; its luxurious perfume with overtones of ripe apricots, honey and nuts; its rich, intense, sweet yet vital taste. It can be delicious when young but it ages magnificently.

Château d'Yquem's Sémillon and Sauvignon grapes are perfectly placed for maximum exposure to – and subsequent concentration by – Botrytis cinerea.

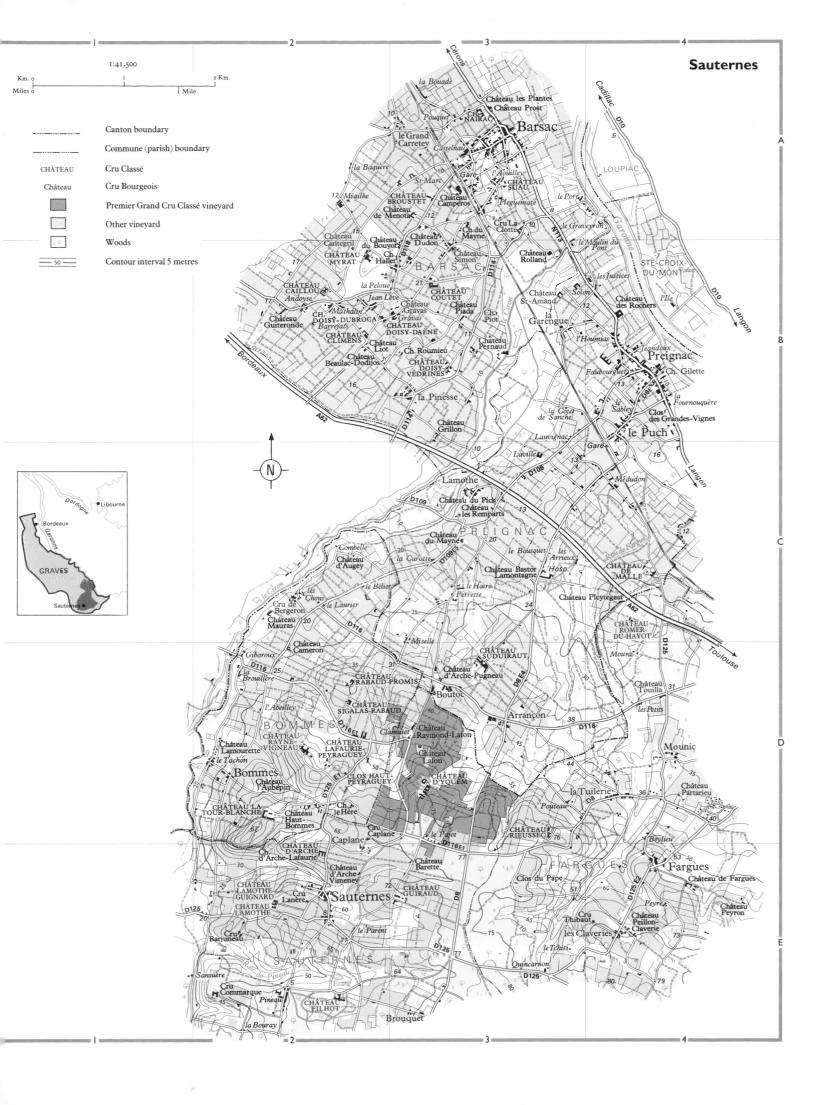

PRODUCERS OF SPECIAL INTEREST

SAUTERNES

(PROPERTIES IN BARSAC CAN LABEL WINES BARSAC OR SAUTERNES)

Château d'Arche
33210 Sauternes
2e cru classé

Château Bastor-Lamontagne
33210 Preignac
Owned by a French financial institution. One of the best-value Sauternes. Even the second wine, Les Remparts de Bastor, can be good value. There are 60ha under production.

Château Broustet 33720 Barsac
2e cru classé

Château Caillou 33720 Barsac
2e cru classé

Château Climens 33720 Barsac
1er cru classé
Climens is the quintessential Barsac: rich and concentrated but with great delicacy and finesse. The property was bought by Lucien Lurton in 1971 and is now owned by his daughters Brigitte and Bérénice. The vineyard has a prime site at the highest point of the Barsac plateau. Although some Sauvignon is planted the wine is made from practically 100% Sémillon.

Château Clos Haut-Peyraguey
33210 Bommes
1er cru classé
This 15-ha estate was separated from Lafaurie-Peyraguey when the original Peyraguey estate was split up in 1878. In the 1980s the wines were rather light but recent vintages have shown more concentration and expression of fruit.

Château Coutet 33720 Barsac
1er cru classé
One of Barsac's most influential estates. In the very best years a small amount of wine is selected for the Cuvée Madame, which approaches the class of Yquem. The present château is near a 13th-century tower, a reminder that the history of Coutet goes back to the Middle Ages.

Château Doisy-Daëne
33720 Barsac
2e cru classé
Technically a highly proficient domaine owned and managed by Pierre Dubourdieu. The wine is made principally from Sémillon grapes and vinified and matured in oak casks. There is also an excellent dry white Bordeaux, the Vin Sec de Doisy-Daëne. The trio of Doisy châteaux

were originally one estate that was divided and sold in the 19th century.

Château Doisy-Dubroca
33720 Barsac
2e cru classé
A tiny estate of just over 3ha owned by Louis Lurton. The wine is made from 100% Sémillon and vinified at Château Climens.

Château Doisy-Védrines
33720 Barsac
2e cru classé
The largest of the three Doisy estates, with the original 16th-century château and *chais*.

Château de Fargues
33210 Fargues
Estate with romantic old castle ruins owned by the de Lur Saluces of Yquem. A brilliant Sauternes, lighter than Yquem but certainly worth a place among the *crus classés*.

Château Filhot 33210 Sauternes
2e cru classé
Large estate on the southern boundary of Sauternes with a particularly fine château and park. Not a sumptuous Sauternes but a delicate and finely structured wine with plenty of fruit.

Château Gilette 33210 Preignac
The wine here is aged for at least 20

years in underground tanks before being bottled. This unique method produces sumptuous, warm-gold wines of tremendous vitality. A younger version is sold as Château Les Justices.

Château Gravas 33720 Barsac
One of the best of the Barsac *bourgeois*. The 16th-century château and its vineyards are in the heart of the Barsac appellation between the *premiers crus* Climens and Coutet.

Château Guiraud 33210 Sauternes
1er cru classé
Following the purchase of the property by Canadian Hamilton Narby in 1981, the wines improved dramatically. The estate is now managed for the Narby family by Xavier Planty. The grapes are selectively picked; the grape juice is fermented (since 1990) and aged in oak barrels, 50% of which are new. A dry white Bordeaux, G, is made, essentially from Sauvignon, as well as a red Bordeaux Supérieur.

Château Haut-Bergeron
33210 Preignac

Château Lafaurie-Peyraguey
33210 Bommes
1er cru classé
One of the oldest Sauternes châteaux,

Ste-Croix-du-Mont, wreathed here in the magical Botrytis-inducing mist, faces Sauternes and Barsac across the Garonne and produces comparable dessert wines.

part 13th-century fortress and almost as spectacular as Yquem. Starting with the '83 vintage this estate has produced some outstanding wines, putting it among the top half-dozen in the appellation. It is now owned by the Société Foncier des Domaines Cordier.

Château Lamothe
33210 Sauternes
2e cru classé

Château Lamothe Guignard
33210 Sauternes
2e cru classé

Château de Malle
33210 Preignac
2e cru classé
The showplace of Sauternes: the 17th-century chateau, its contents and gardens are enough to justify a visit to the region (see Places of Interest, Preignac, below). The wine has almost the delicacy of a Barsac. The estate also makes a dry white wine (M de Malle) and a red Graves.

Château de Myrat
33720 Barsac
2e cru classé

Château Nairac 33720 Barsac
2e cru classé
This is one of the best of the Barsacs. It is owned by Nicole Heeter-Tari and managed by her son Nicolas. Produced predominantly from Sémillon the wine has a fairly rich, concentrated, oaky style.

Château Rabaud-Promis
33210 Bommes
1er cru classé
The larger proportion of what was originally one estate, Château Rabaud (the balance is Château Sigalas-Rabaud). The château was built by Victor Louis, architect of the Grand Théâtre in Bordeaux. With more rigorous selection and an increase in the use of new-oak barrels the wines have improved through the 1980s.

Château Raymond-Lafon
33210 Sauternes
Although its 'château' is no castle, this is usually a splendid wine with the quality of a *premier cru*. It is made with exceptional care and expertise.

Château de Rayne-Vigneau
33210 Bommes
1er cru classé
Large estate celebrated in the late 1800s and early 1900s for the semi-precious stones found among the gravel in the vineyard; some are displayed in the *chais*. The wine has gone through a very weak period but since 1986 has been back up to standard.

Château Rieussec
33210 Fargues
1er cru classé
Generally the wine that comes closest to Yquem – and the two estates are neighbours, superbly situated on the highest hills in the district. Rieussec

is an impressive Sauternes, often reminiscent of ripe peaches or apricots. A dry white Rieussec is called R. In 1985 the French Rothschilds acquired a majority of the shares. There is no actual château but a rambling collection of various buildings, with a prominent ivy-clad lookout tower.

Château Romer du Hayot
33210 Preignac
2e cru classé

Château St-Amand
33210 Preignac

Château Sigalas-Rabaud
33210 Bommes
1er cru classé
Small domaine with a vineyard ideally situated on the hill slopes of Haut-Bommes. The quality of the wines improved through the 1980s. The style is usually more delicate and aromatic than the other wines from this sector.

Château Suau 33720 Barsac
2e cru classé

Château Suduiraut
33210 Preignac
1er cru classé
A splendid estate with a 17th-century château and a park designed by André Le Nôtre. For two decades the wine has been amongst the most opulent and impressive of the whole district. In 1991 the property was sold to Axa-Millésimes (See Château Pichon-Longueville-Baron, page 133).

Château La Tour-Blanche
33210 Bommes
1er cru classé
The estate where the German wine-grower Focke experimented with late harvesting from 1836. Today it is owned by the Ministry of Agriculture and is a school of viticulture. At one time the wines lacked great class but following a change in production methods they are now among Sauternes' best.

Château d'Yquem
33210 Sauternes
1er cru supérieur
The world's most famous sweet-wine estate – literally in a class of its own as the sole *premier cru supérieur* in the 1855 classification. For more than two centuries Yquem, with its superb château, belonged to the Lur Saluces family. In 1996 the luxury group LVMH acquired a controlling interest. Neither cost nor effort is spared to make the wine as perfect as possible. Harvesting might begin in mid-October (Yquem is always one of the last harvests in the district) and continue until the end of November or into December. The wine is fermented in new-oak casks and then matured for at least three years before being bottled. A dry white called Y (Ygrec) is produced in the same extravagantly expensive way.

Here at Yquem the wine is not bottled for three years, is unlikely to be sold for four and, in truly good vintages, it may not reach its peak for four decades.

WINE ROUTE

The **Circuit du Sauternais** is a signposted route that takes you, via pleasant country roads, through the vineyards and past many of the estates. Many of the châteaux or their cellars can be visited; ask at the Maison du Vin (see below) and look for *vente directe* (direct sales) on roadside signs.

WINE FÊTES

Barsac The **Commanderie du Bontemps de Sauternes-Barsac** organises a Fête du Vin Nouveau each September/October.
Langon Graves wine fair also featuring wine from Sauternes, in September.

WINE INFORMATION

The modest **Maison du Vin** is in the place de la Mairie, Sauternes [tel (0)556 76 69 83]. In Barsac, near the church, the **Office Viticole de Sauternes et Barsac** sells the region's wines as well as its own under the Terre Noble label.

HOTELS AND RESTAURANTS

Hotels and additional restaurants within easy reach of Sauternes are described in the Graves, Pessac-Léognan and Entre-deux-Mers listings (pages 151–53).
In local restaurants you can discover how excellent Sauternes can be as an apéritif and with the meal itself, as well as enjoying it as a superb dessert wine.

Restaurant du Cap
33210 **Preignac**
Tel (0)556 63 27 38
Mainly regional dishes and a delightful view over the Garonne.

Auberge Les Vignes
33210 **Sauternes**
Tel (0)556 76 60 06
Next door to the church. Regional dishes such as entrecôte bordelaise, without trimmings but with great care. Try the tarte aux poires, an excellent partner for a Sauternes. Wines are served by the glass as well as by the bottle and half-bottle.

Le Saprien 33210 **Sauternes**
Tel (0)556 76 60 87
The cooking is creative and the decor elegant.

PLACES OF INTEREST

Barsac The oldest wine village in the region. The Romans introduced wine-growing to Barsac and the remains of a Roman villa have been found alongside the church. The church itself has elements from the 16th, 17th and 18th centuries. Two marks high on the wall near the main door indicate the level reached by the water in the floods of 1770 and 1930 when the River Garonne burst its banks.

Preignac The château, flanked by pepper-pot towers, is the only historic monument in Sauternes; it dates from the 17th century and can be visited from Easter to mid-October. A splendid collection of furniture and objets d'art has been assembled in its rooms and the Italian-style garden is filled with statuary.

Sauternes A small but charming village; partly Romanesque church.

Libournais

The Libournais is the title given to the viticultural regions of St-Émilion, Pomerol (including the satellites) and Fronsac – in essence Bordeaux 'right bank'. It is home to a warm, aromatic, generous style of wine produced predominantly from the Merlot grape. The name comes from the most important town in the region, Libourne, but it has no legislative definition.

The walled town and port of Libourne was founded in 1270 under the aegis of Henry III of England in order to control the merchant trade along the River Dordogne. Although wine from the hinterland around Bergerac was exported through Libourne, much of the area (including St-Émilion) was devoted to grain growing.

Until the 18th century large areas of St-Émilion and Pomerol were controlled by the Church and religious institutions. Fronsac was the fife of the Ducs de Richelieu. This monopoly of ownership with its share-cropping economy and largely internal consumption meant that viticulture and commerce were slow to develop in the Libournais. The region was also distant from the mainstream commercial centre of Bordeaux, and physically separated by the Dordogne and Garonne rivers. Access, in the absence of bridges, was limited to river transport.

In the 17th century the vine was grown and exploited along the flat *palus* near Libourne, but it was not until the 1750s and 1760s that the vineyards of St-Émilion and Pomerol established, under separate ownership, and that trade outside the region developed more fully. Domaines such as Canon, Magdelaine and (Château) Belair in the St-Émilion Côtes made their first appearance as did Trotanoy, La Conseillante and Pétrus in Pomerol. Towards the end of the 18th century the wines of the Fronsac Côtes became as highly esteemed as those of St-Émilion. The Libournais missed out on the publicity coup of the 1855 Classification for the Exposition Universelle in Paris, and it was not until the end of the 19th century that the renown of its wines spread beyond traditional markets.

The pattern of commercial and viticultural development established in the Libournais in the latter half of the 18th century is still relevant today. Since their wines had been excluded from the Bordeaux Classification, Libourne merchants travelled north in search of new commerce and forged trading links in north-east France, Belgium, Luxembourg and the Netherlands, countries which still provide important markets for Libournais wines. In the aftermath of the French Revolution and the sale of lands owned by the Church and nobility, small, family-owned and managed domaines became the norm, contrasting in size with the large Médoc estates which were owned by often absentee Bordeaux proprietors.

In further contrast to the Médoc, the Libournais has generally hilly, undulating terrain with a wide variety of exposures. The soils too are different, composed essentially of a mix of limestone and clay with pockets of gravel and sand in areas of St-Émilion and Pomerol. These cooler limestone-clay soils have dictated that a higher percentage of the earlier-ripening Merlot is grown in the region, supported by Bouchet (as Cabernet Franc is known locally) with Cabernet Sauvignon this time taking the back seat.

The wines of the Libournais, dominated by the more supple Merlot, have a rich, sweet, generously fruity nature with power provided by a generally higher alcoholic degree than is found in the Médoc. The wines are well structured, allowing for good ageability, but the tannins appear softened by the Merlot fruit. When the Cabernet Franc ripens fully, it can add the extra touch of aromatic magic and complexity required of a great vintage.

Libournais

- – – – – Canton boundary
- – · – · – Commune boundary
- ───── Satellite commune permitted to add St-Emilion to its name
- Vineyards
- Woods
- 161 Area mapped at larger scale on page shown
- 100 Contour interval 20 metres

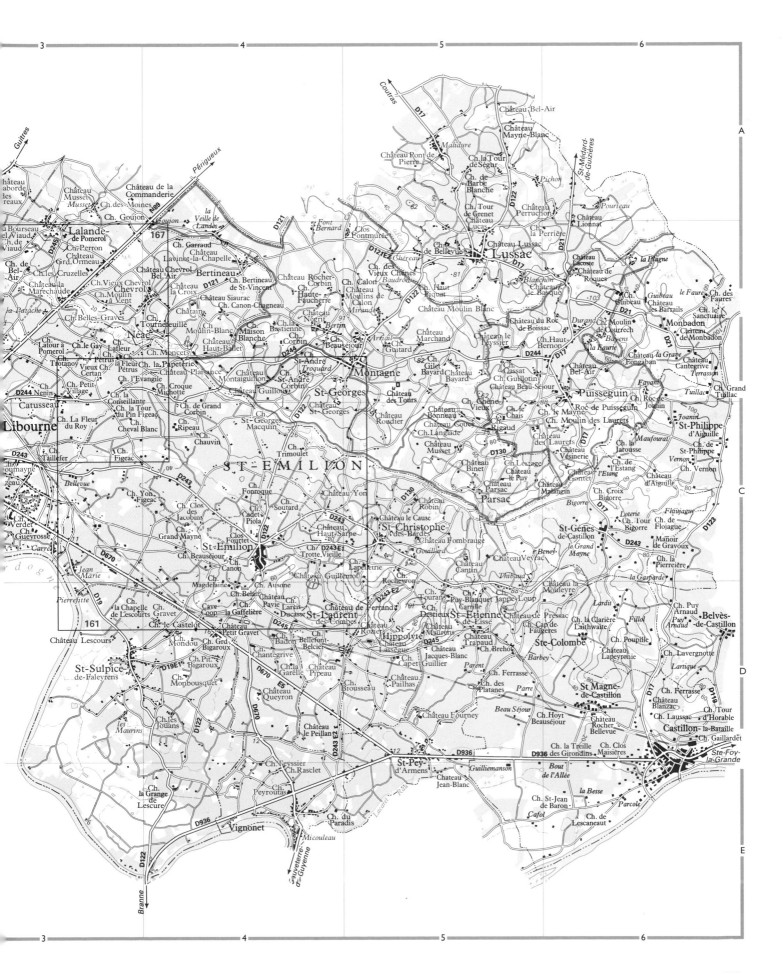

St-Émilion

The very name St-Émilion seems to melt on the tongue – warm, mellow and resonant, it suits the place and the wine. Both owe their character to thousands of years of development. Scratch the surface of the soil between the rows of vines and you may find a reindeer bone, a prehistoric stone axe, a Bronze-Age arrowhead or a fragment of Roman pottery. It was the Romans who laid the real foundations of the St-Émilion wine industry, bringing their own vines which they grafted onto the native ones, so founding a tradition that has continued unbroken to the present day. Growers still plant most of the vines, as the Romans did, in rows 1.33 metres apart, except where the width been increased to accommodate modern machinery.

The town is named after a holy man known as Aemilianus or Émilion who settled here in the 8th century with his group of followers. Later the Franciscans and Dominicans established monasteries here and the town came under a dual administration shared between a clerical chapter and a secular body known as the Jurade, instituted by King John of England and France in 1199.

The Jurade played a key role in the development of viticulture in the area and remains in existence today as probably the oldest body of its kind in France. It continues to regulate the local wine industry and promote its produce, and performs impressive ceremonies at which its members wear striking red robes.

The area of the St-Émilion appellation covers eight communes and part of Libourne (there are also four 'satellite' communes, see pages 170–71). It is one of the most intensively cultivated areas in the Bordeaux region, comprising 5,200 hectares of vineyards owned by just over 1,000 proprietors. Smallholdings are characteristically owned and managed by passionate individualists, rather than by absentee investors as tends more often to be the case in the Médoc. The average estate is therefore comparatively small and it is easy to lose your way among the lanes and the patchwork of vineyards.

The district is roughly divided into four geological zones. The Côtes is a limestone plateau and its slopes around the town of St-Émilion. The Plain, at the foot of the plateau to the south towards the river Dordogne, is sandy with gravel in some places. This flat countryside was the last to be planted with vines, mainly between the two World Wars. The Plateau des Sables to the west and north of St-Émilion is, not surprisingly, sandy and the Graves, just 60 hectares in the west adjoining Pomerol, has deep layers of gravel. The best – and usually the strongest – wines come from the limestone plateau and the gravelly areas.

In general the wines of St-Émilion are fuller, softer, fruitier, less astringent and easier to enjoy than those of the Médoc. They are also slightly more alcoholic, partly because of the richer soil and partly because a different balance of grape varieties is used. There is less of the rather austere Cabernet Sauvignon and more Merlot and Cabernet Franc. As a consequence many people find that St-Émilion wines are a good first step in learning to appreciate claret.

The ban des vendanges, *proclaimed in colourful ceremony by the Jurade de St-Émilion from the 13th-century Tour du Roi, signals that the harvest may begin.*

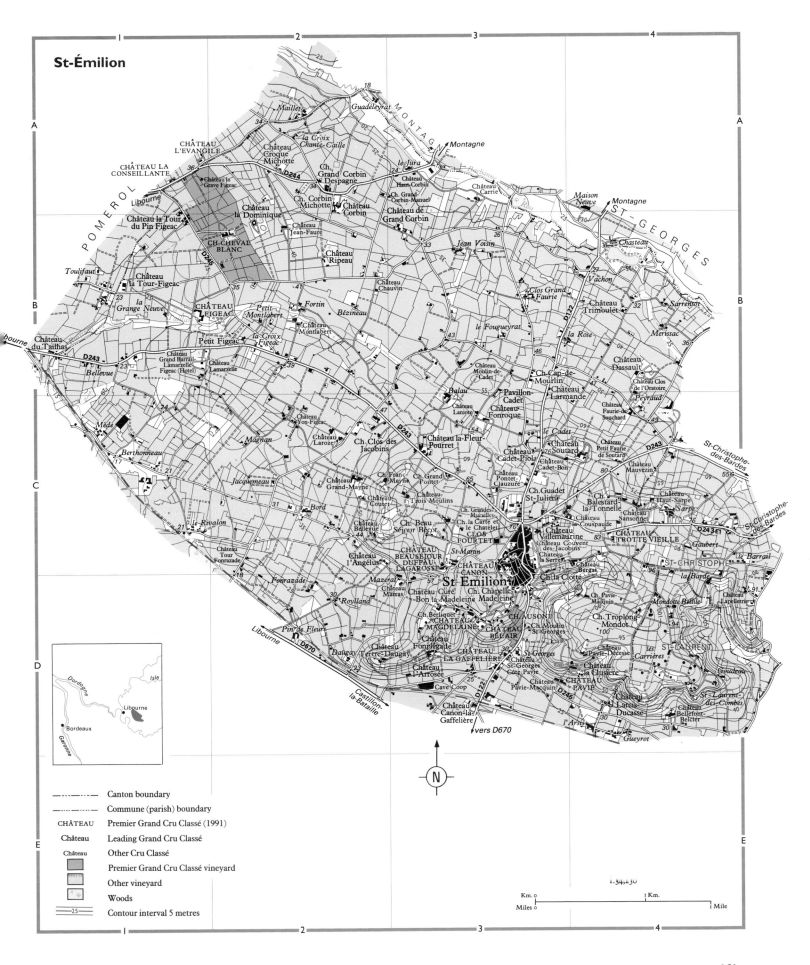

St-Émilion

MONTAGNE

Montagne

ST-GEORGES

POMEROL

Montagne

Libourne

CHÂTEAU L'EVANGILE

CHÂTEAU LA CONSEILLANTE

Maillet

la Croix Chante-Caille

le Jura

Château Croque Michotte

Ch. Grand Corbin Despagne

Barbanne

Ch. Corbin Michotte

Ch. Grand-Corbin-Manuel

Château Haut-Corbin

Château Carrie

Maison Neuve

Château la Grave Figeac

Château Corbin

Château de Grand Corbin

CH. CHEVAL BLANC

Château la Dominique

Château Jean-Faure

le Rau

Château la Tour du Pin Figeac

Château Ripeau

Jean Voisin

Château Trimoulet

Toulifaut

Château la Tour-Figeac

Château Chauvin

Vachon

Château

Sarrensot

la Grange Neuve

CHÂTEAU FIGEAC

Petit Montlabert

Fortin

Bézineau

Clos Grand Faurie

la Rose

Merissac

Château du Tailhas

Château Montlabert

le Fougueyrat

Château Dassault

bourne

Château Grand Barrail Lamarzelle Figeac (Hotel)

Petit Figeac

la Croix Figeac

Château Moulin-de-Cadet

Ch. Cap-de-Mourlin

Château Clos de l'Oratoire

Peyraud

Bellevue

Château Lamarzelle

Château Laniote

Château Larmande

Château Faurie-de-Souchard

Mède

Château Yon-Figeac

Balau

Pavillon-Cadet

Château Fonroque

D243

Magnan

Château Laroze

Ch. Clos des Jacobins

Château la-Fleur-Pourret

le Cadet

Château Soutard

Château Cadet-Piola

Petit Faurie de Soutard

Château Mauvezin

Berthonneau

Château Grand-Mayne

Ch. Franc-Mayne

Ch. Grand Pontet

Château Cadet-Bon

Château Pontet-Clauzure

Château Haut-Sarpe

Jacquemeau

Château Trois Moulins

Ch. Guadet St-Julien

Château Sarpe

Bord

Château Coutet

Ch. Grandes Murailles

Ch. Balestard la Tonnelle

Château Trotte Vieille

le Rivalon

Château Bellevue

Ch. Beau Séjour Bécot

Ch. la Carte et le Chatelet

CLOS FOURTET

la Couspaude

Château Villemaurine

St-Christophe des-Bardes

Château Tour Fonrazade

St-Martin

Château Couvent des Jacobins

Château Bergat

la Barde

le Barrail

CHÂTEAU BEAUSÉJOUR DUFFAU LAGAROSSE

Château la Serre

ST-CHRISTOPHE

Fonrazade

Château l'Angélus

Mazerat

CHÂTEAU CANON

Ch. la Clotte

Ch. Pavie-Macquin

Mondotte Bellisle

Royland

Château Mâtras

St-Émilion

Ch. Chapelle Madeleine

Château Lapelletrie

Château Curé-Bon la Madeleine

Ch. Troplong-Mondot

Pin de Fleur

Ch. Bérliquet

CHÂTEAU MAGDELAINE

CH. AUSONE

Ch. Moulin St-Georges

Libourne

Daugay

Château Tertre-Daugay

Château Fonplégade

CHÂTEAU BÉL AIR

Château Pavie-Décesse

Château la Clusière

St-LAURENT

Daugay

Château l'Arrosée

CHÂTEAU LA GAFFELIÈRE

St-Georges

Château Pavie-Macquin

CHÂTEAU PAVIE

Château Larcis Ducasse

Castillon-la-Bataille

Cave Coop

St-Georges Côte Pavie

Château la Clusière

Château Bellefont-Belcier

Château Canon-la-Gaffelière

St-Laurent-des-Combes

l'Arsé

Goudeau

vers D670

Gueyrot

Dordogne

Isle

Libourne

Bordeaux

Garonne

N

---|--- Canton boundary

--- Commune (parish) boundary

CHÂTEAU Premier Grand Cru Classé (1991)

Château Leading Grand Cru Classé

Château Other Cru Classé

Premier Grand Cru Classé vineyard

Other vineyard

Woods

25 Contour interval 5 metres

1:84,230

Km. 0   1 Km.

Miles 0   1 Mile

The classification of St-Émilion is a law unto itself. The Bordeaux classification of 1855 (which concentrated on the Médoc) ignored it altogether. Not until a century later did St-Émilion set up a system of four appellations, in ascending order: St-Émilion, St-Émilion *grand cru*, St-Émilion *grand cru classé* and St-Émilion *premier grand cru classé*. A revision in 1985 reduced these to two appellations: St-Émilion for the region's basic wines and St-Émilion *grand cru*. Since that time, if the St-Émilion *grands crus* meet certain requirements they can be considered for the status of *grand cru classé* or *premier grand cru classé*. The process of reviewal occurs theoretically every ten years with recommendations made by an independent commission. The regulations permit a maximum of 90 classified growths. *Premiers grands crus classés* are also rated *A* (that is Châteaux Ausone and Cheval Blanc) and *B* (the rest). The last revision of the classification occurred in 1996.

It is worth sampling a wide spectrum of St-Émilion wines: those lower down the scale can be agreeable surprises. The area itself is one of timeless beauty, where traditions are jealously guarded.

The Mur des Dominicans, the only remnant of a vanished 13th-century monastery, stands just to the north of St-Émilion's Porte Bourgeoise.

PRODUCERS OF SPECIAL INTEREST

PREMIER GRAND CRU CLASSÉ

Château L'Angélus
33330 St-Émilion
Significant investment and technical expertise have turned L'Angélus into one of St-Émilion's top estates. The vineyard has been restructured and new winemaking facilities constructed. The wines are rich, ripe and structured and are usually aged in 100% new-oak casks. L'Angélus was promoted to *premier grand cru classé* in 1996.

Château Ausone 33330 St-Émilion
The showplace of the Côtes and one of the two *premiers grands crus classés* A (the other is Cheval Blanc). The tiny 7-ha estate, named after the Roman consul and poet Ausonius, is on the edge of St-Émilion's limestone plateau commanding long views over other vineyards and the valley of the Dordogne. Its penetratingly perfumed wines can rival the great Médocs in style and finesse.

Château Beau-Séjour-Bécot
33330 St-Émilion
This estate was deprived of its *premier grand cru classé* status in 1985 but re-elected into that class in 1996. The wines have the quality and breed of a top-class St-Émilion and have improved under the direction of brothers Dominique and Gérard Bécot. The vineyards are located on the plateau and the Côtes.

Château Beauséjour
33330 St-Émilion
A pretty property on the west-facing Côtes. The traditionally made, concentrated wine has a lot of tannin and a refinement that demands patience: a wine for laying down.

Château Belair 33330 St-Émilion
Close to Château Ausone, the estate is owned by Madame Helyett Dubois-Challon, co-owner of Ausone. The wine is among the best of the Côtes, with a beautiful aroma of oak as a prelude to its silky substance.

Château Canon 33330 St-Émilion
A most distinguished, sturdy wine from a partly walled vineyard on St-Émilion's limestone plateau. It is made in the traditional way for long cellaring.

Château Cheval Blanc
33330 St-Émilion
The vineyard of this charming white château is close to the Pomerol boundary and has a lot of gravel in its soil. The wine (*premier grand cru classé* A) has luxury and refinement, strength and subtlety. Great vintages are legendary; unsurpassed even among the first growths of the Médoc.

Château Figeac 33330 St-Émilion
The dignified château has a long history; the estate once included what is now Cheval Blanc as well as other properties. The surrounding vineyard on low gravel hills is planted 70% to Cabernet (half Sauvignon, the highest proportion for St-Émilion) and the wine has a velvety softness and great allure. It can be drunk early but is also capable of long maturing.

Clos Fourtet 33330 St-Émilion
Owned by the Lurton family, this is one of the most interesting estates to visit. Its extensive cellars are hewn from the rock. The property sits just opposite the place de l'Église on the north-eastern perimeter of St-Émilion. The wines are typically full, structured and fruity but the quality could be more consistent.

Château La Gaffelière
33330 St-Émilion
The estate has been owned by the Malet-Roquefort family for the last 400 years. The vineyard is located on the Côtes and Pied de Côtes to the south of St-Émilion. The wines are delicately structured rather than powerful.

Château Magdelaine
33330 St-Émilion
This property, owned since 1952 by the Libourne-based *négociant* Jean-Pierre Moueix, has been extensively renovated and a new *chais* was opened in 1989. It lies to the south of the town near Belair and Canon. The wine, made from 90% Merlot, is rich and elegant in style.

Château Pavie 33330 St-Émilion
The château and its large vineyard lie on the south-west slope of St-Émilion's plateau; its cellars are hewn out of the limestone slope and the roots of vines growing 8m further up the hill penetrate the cellar ceiling. Stylish, supple, fragrant wine that matures excellently in bottle.

Château Trottevieille
33330 St-Émilion
The vineyard occupies an isolated site on the plateau to the east of St-Émilion, away from the other *premiers grands crus classés*. The wines are rich and powerful but over the years the quality has not matched that of Trottevieille's peers.

GRAND CRU CLASSÉ

Château l'Arrosée
33330 St-Émilion
A strong, generous wine of *premier cru* standard. The vineyard is on the south-west slope of the limestone plateau.

Château Balestard-la-Tonnelle
33330 St-Émilion
A very old estate – a verse from the 15th-century poet François Villon, reproduced on the label, refers to "the divine nectar...of Balestard". The wine today is full, vital and reliable. An old stone tower on the

estate has been restored and is used for receptions.

Château Bellevue 33330 St-Émilion
Château Bergat 33330 St-Émilion
Château Berliquet
33330 St-Émilion
A substantial house in a pleasant garden. The wine is well made under the direction of the local cooperative.
Château Cadet-Bon
33330 St-Émilion
Château Cadet-Piola
33330 St-Émilion
Generous wine: better than its status.
Château Canon-la-Gaffelière
33330 St-Émilion
Over the last ten years owner Stéphan de Neipperg has brought new life to this estate with its vineyards in the Pied de Côtes. The wines are now among the best in the appellation. Low yields, attention to detail, technical expertise and a high percentage of Cabernet Franc in the blend are responsible for the quality.
Château Cap de Mourlin
33330 St-Émilion
Under the same ownership as Balestard-la-Tonnelle, the estate makes rich, vibrant wines that age beautifully.
Château Chauvin
33330 St-Émilion
Clos des Jacobins 33330 St-Émilion
Under the wing of the Cordier establishment.

Clos de l'Oratoire
33330 St-Émilion
Clos St-Martin 33330 St-Émilion
Château La Clotte
33330 St-Émilion
Château La Clusière
33330 St-Émilion
Château Corbin 33330 St-Émilion
Château Corbin-Michotte
33330 St-Émilion
Château La Couspaude
33330 St-Émilion
Well situated property on the limestone plateau.
Couvent des Jacobins
33330 St-Émilion
Established in a former 13th-century monastery with splendid rock cellars. Excellent wine.
Château Curé Bon
33330 St-Émilion
Intense, formidable wine, usually from grapes at optimum ripeness.
Château Dassault
33330 St-Émilion
Château La Dominique
33330 St-Émilion
Next-door to Cheval Blanc. The wines are on the rich and generous side, but always stylish.
Château Faurie-de-Souchard
33330 St-Émilion
Château Fonplégade
33330 St-Émilion
A distinguished château producing a

firmly structured, stylish wine. Often undervalued.
Château Fonroque
33330 St-Émilion
Château Franc-Mayne
33330 St-Émilion
Château Grand-Mayne
33330 St-Émilion
Another St-Émilion estate that has improved dramatically over recent years. The wines are rich and powerful, aged in a high percentage of new oak.
Château Grand-Pontet
33330 St-Émilion
Château Grandes Murailles
33330 St-Émilion
Following demotion in 1985 this estate was re-selected for *grand cru classé* status in 1996.
Château Guadet St-Julien
33330 St-Émilion
Château Haut Corbin
33330 St-Émilion
Château Haut-Sarpe
33330 St-Christophe-des-Bardes
One of the most beautiful châteaux of St-Émilion, inspired by the Trianons at Versailles and set in a spacious park. The wine is well rounded and enjoys a good reputation in France.
Château Lamarzelle
33330 St-Émilion
Château Laniote
33330 St-Émilion

Château Larcis-Ducasse
33330 St-Laurent-des-Combes
Château Larmande
33330 St-Émilion
The wines from this well managed estate have improved steadily.
Château Laroque
33330 St-Christophe-des-Bardes
Known as the 'Petit Versailles de St-Émilion' due to its architecture, this estate was promoted to *grand cru classé* status in 1996.
Château Laroze 33330 St-Émilion
Château Matras 33330 St-Émilion
Château Moulin du Cadet
33330 St-Émilion
Château Pavie Décesse
33330 St-Émilion
Château Pavie Macquin
33330 St-Émilion
Managed by Nicolas Thienpont, the estate is run on biodynamic lines.
Château Petit-Faurie-de-Soutard
33330 St-Émilion
Château Le Prieuré
33330 St-Émilion
Château Ripeau 33330 St-Émilion
Château St-Georges Côte Pavie
33330 St-Émilion
Château La Serre
33330 St-Émilion
Château Soutard 33330 St-Émilion
Traditional, long-keeping wines from one of the larger (28ha) St-Émilion estates.

St-Émilion, built and in parts carved out of the pale local limestone, is named after a wandering Breton hermit, Atmilianus, who retired on the site in around 750.

163

Château Tertre Daugay
33330 St-Émilion
Château la Tour-Figeac
33330 St-Émilion
**Château La Tour-du-Pin-Figeac
(Giraud-Bélivier)** 33330 St-Émilion
**Château La Tour-du-Pin-Figeac
(Moueix)** 33330 St-Émilion
Firm, somewhat earthy St-Émilion
from the Moueix family.
Château Troplong-Mondot
33330 St-Émilion
Owned by the Valette family and
managed by Christine Valette,
Troplong-Mondot has been making
superbly concentrated wines in
recent years.
Château Villemaurine
33330 St-Émilion
The splendid cellars here are used for
banquets as well as wine. Since the
early 1980s the deep-coloured wine
has again been of impressive quality.
Château Yon-Figeac
33330 St-Émilion

GRAND CRU
Château Béard
33330 St-Laurent-des-Combes
Just outside the commune of
St-Émilion to the east, on the
limestone Côtes.
Château Bellefont-Belcier
33330 St-Laurent-des-Combes
Château Bigaroux
33330 St-Sulpice-de-Faleyrens
Château Bonnet
33330 St-Pey-d'Armens
A firmly constituted wine from a

family that has owned the estate for
six generations.
Château Carteau Côtes Daugay
33330 St-Émilion
Château La Chapelle-Lescours
33330 St-Sulpice-de-Faleyrens
Château Destieux
33330 St-Hippolyte
Château Faugères
33330 St-Étienne-de-Lisse
The estate has vines in St-Émilion and
the Côtes de Castillon and produces a
wine from each. High-tech winery.
Château de Ferrand
33330 St-Hippolyte
A little to the west of St-Étienne, also
at the foot of the limestone slope.
Château Fleur Cardinale
33330 St-Étienne-de-Lisse
Well placed at the foot of the
limestone scarp. Velvety wines.
Château Fombrauge
33330 St-Christophe-des-Bardes
Château Franc Pipeau
33330 St-Hippolyte
Château Gaillard
33330 St-Hippolyte
Often a very successful wine: it is
stylish as well as being generous and
concentrated.
**Château Grand-Corbin-
Despagne** 33330 St-Émilion
Château Grand-Pey-Lescours
33330 St-Sulpice-de-Faleyrens
Château Gravet 33330
St-Sulpice-de-Faleyrens
Repeatedly and deservedly an
award-winning wine with fruit, tannin
and vitality.

Château Gueyrosse
33330 Libourne
Château Haut-Segottes
33330 St-Émilion
Small family-run property on the
plateau not far from Figeac and
Cheval Blanc. Consistent wines of
good concentration.
Château Lapelletrie
33330 St-Christophe-des-Bardes
Château Lescours
33330 St-Sulpice-de-Faleyrens
Château Mauvezin
33330 St-Émilion
Château Monbousquet
33330 St-Sulpice-de-Faleyrens
Château Monlot-Capet
33330 St-Hippolyte
Château Moulin St-Georges
33330 St-Émilion
Owned and vinified by Alain Vauthier,
co-owner of Château Ausone.
Château Puy-Blanquet Carrille
33330 St-Christophe-des-Bardes
A lively, deep-coloured wine that
lingers beautifully in the mouth.
Château Le Tertre Roteboeuf
33330 St-Laurent-des-Combes
Of *grand cru classé* standard and
possibly above. Sells at the same price
as the *premiers*. Rich, unctuous wines
aged in 100%-new-oak barrels.
**Union des Producteurs de
St-Émilion** 33330 St-Émilion
The St-Émilion cooperative produces
a range of wines.
Château de Valandraud
33330 St-Émilion
Tiny 2.5-ha estate that has shot to

prominence. Rare and expensive but
deep, concentrated wines.
Domaine de la Vieille Église
33330 St-Hippolyte

WINE ACTIVITIES

La Jurade de St-Émilion was set
up in 1199 as a governing body for
the town and its wine. The body was
revived in 1948. At the end of
September it proclaims the *ban des
vendanges* from the top of the King's
Tower, after which the grape harvest
may begin. In mid-June a 'new wine'
festival is organised.

WINE INFORMATION

St-Émilion's **Maison du Vin** [tel
(0)557 55 50 55] is in the former
Maison de l'Abbé, one of the buildings
of the Cloître de la Collégiale. Wines
are offered for sale at château prices
and there is also a programme of
tutored wine tastings. For information
about wine and visits to the châteaux
you can also ask at the Office du
Tourisme around the corner. During
the summer, wine information is also
provided at the Pavillon d'Accueil at
St-Étienne-de-Lisse and the Pavillon
du Vin at St-Pey-d'Armens.

HOTELS

Auberge de la Commanderie
33330 St-Émilion Tel (0)557 24 70 19
Middle-range hotel with a simple,
brasserie-style restaurant.
Château Grand Barrail 33330
St-Émilion Tel (0)557 55 37 00
Luxury hotel with 28 rooms including
5 suites; 3km from the town centre
on the D243 to Libourne. The
restaurant is one of the region's best.
Hostellerie de Plaisance 33330
St-Émilion Tel (0)557 24 72 32
Situated on the square next to the
belfry tower and above the Église
Monolithe. Comfortable rooms are
named after wine estates. The mid-
priced restaurant is the best in town.
Logis des Remparts 33330
St-Émilion Tel (0)557 24 70 43
Well furnished rooms with every
comfort. Own car park.

RESTAURANTS

Bar de la Poste 33330 St-Émilion
Tel (0)557 24 70 76
Convivial spot in summer with meals
served on the terrace opposite the
Église Monolithe. Simple dishes with a
small list of wines offered by the glass.
Le Clos du Roy 33330 St-Émilion
Tel (0)557 74 41 55
Pleasing results from fresh ingredients.
L'Envers du Décor
33330 St-Émilion Tel (0)557 74 48 31
Wine bar serving simple fare and a

Château Belair wines, among the Côtes' best, acquire a delicious oaky aroma in the estate's own quarry caves.

selection of wines by the glass from St-Émilion and other French regions. Service in the garden in the summer.

Francis Goullée 33330 St-Émilion
Tel (0)557 24 70 49
Elegant decor and some very fine dishes such as soupe de foie gras.

Logis de la Cadène
33330 St-Émilion Tel (0)557 24 71 40
Excellent place for lunch: covered terrace and reasonable prices. Rich family cooking with regional dishes.

Le Tertre 33330 St-Émilion
Tel (0)557 74 46 33
Well executed traditional cuisine. Reasonable list of wines. Menus at varying prices as well as à la carte.

PLACES OF INTEREST

St-Christophe-des-Bardes One of the oldest castles of the district, Château Laroque was largely rebuilt in the 18th century but the keep is medieval. The local church with its rather worn carvings is a historic monument.

St-Émilion From any of its many vantage points, nothing breaks the delicate harmony of St-Émilion, clustered on its hillside, tier upon tier of old stone houses with red-tiled roofs. Sunlight forms age-old patterns of shadow on eaves and cloisters, archways and winding cobbled streets. It is reassuring to know that the whole town, shadows and all, is an ancient monument. These days such fragile beauty has to be protected by law.

It is hard to imagine the violent history of this tranquil little town. Founded in the 11th century, it came under English rule in the 12th, changed hands many times during the Hundred Years' War of 1337–1453, and was the scene of many battles during the 16th-century Wars of Religion and again during the French Revolution.

Between battles the town was an important resting place on the great medieval pilgrim route to Santiago de Compostela in north-west Spain. Today pilgrims of another kind flock to St-Émilion, drawn by the wine and the beauty of the place. When visiting it is best to leave your car in one of the six parks: in an afternoon's walk you can easily cover all the main sites.

The most memorable monument is the Église Monolithe (monolithic church), entered from the place du Marché. It was carved out of the limestone hill by Benedictine monks in the 11th and 12th centuries and is the largest chamber-cave of its kind in Europe. During the Revolution it was stripped of its adornments and turned into a saltpetre store, which ruined most of the frescos. It was re-consecrated in 1837 and is used now only on ceremonial occasions, such as

Château Cheval Blanc's legendary wines are grown near the Pomerol border on deep soils of gravel, sand and clay.

when members of the Jurade meet there in their scarlet robes. The subterranean church is an impressive but rather gloomy and forbidding place which, unfortunately, smells of dampness and mould.

Nearby is the small medieval Trinity Chapel, beneath which is the underground cavern that Émilion used as his hermitage. It contains the saint's stone bed, his altar and water supply from a spring. The less reverent of the local guides will tell you that young women complaining of infertility would go to the holy man for help and would invariably give birth nine months later. In the place du Clocher directly above the church, its belfry tower seems to thrust up from the cave below. From this square there is a fine view over the town and the surrounding vineyards.

Other religious buildings include the ruined Franciscan friary in the eastern part of the town, the Jacobin monastery, now the cellars of a château, and the splendid 12th-century Collegiate Church with its rich Romanesque façade. Of the 13th-century Dominican monastery nothing remains but a single high wall. Towering over the southern part of

the town is the King's Castle or Tower (Château du Roi) with its imposing quadrangular keep. It was probably built in the 13th century in the time of Henry III of England and is the only Romanesque donjon (fortress) in the Gironde. Also in the Romanesque style is the ruined Cardinal's Palace near the Porte Bourgeoise, former residence of the first dean of St-Émilion, Cardinal de St-Luce.

One of the town's most romantic touches is the stone archway called the Porte de la Cadène, a few steps away from La Commanderie; one of the city's oldest dwellings and former residence of the garrison's officers.

A vivid reminder of the French Revolution is given by the grotto where deputies of the Gironde hid for several months to escape the Terror.

The town is still encircled by stretches of the medieval ramparts but there remains only one of the old fortified gates, the eastern Porte Brunet. Just to the south of this gate is one of the watchtowers, the Tour du Guetteur.

The local museum in the Logis de Malet contains artefacts, documents and displays relating to St-Émilion's remarkably varied history.

A St-Émilion food speciality is a type of macaroon: a crunchy cake made from finely ground almonds, sugar and egg white which is remarkably good with the wines of the district. Michel Poupin in rue Guadet also sells chocolates with vinous themes, such as vine branches (sarments de vignes) – all thoroughly delicious, but not recommended with the wine.

St-Hippolyte Beneath the Château de Ferrand wine estate is a maze of underground passages, probably prehistoric, and a spring. The partly 14th-century village church stands on a hill that dominates the surrounding countryside.

St-Martin This little hamlet lies just west of St-Émilion and consists mainly of wine-producing châteaux (Château Canon, for example). The church is Romanesque.

St-Sulpice-de-Faleyrens North of St-Sulpice, near the little river harbour of Pierrefitte, is a well preserved prehistoric menhir. More than 5,000 years old, the hand-shaped stone is 5m high and 3m wide. The church of St-Sulpice dates from the 11th century. French monarchs, including Henry of Navarre, have stayed at nearby Château Lescours.

Pomerol

Pomerol is the smallest of Bordeaux' major wine regions, having only 780 hectares under production. Such is the acclaim for this unctuous, almost exotic wine however that merchants' order books could be filled several times over. But production of Pomerol, whose unique combination of flavour and texture is provided by the Merlot grape grown on clay soils, is limited by the size of the individual estates.

There is no village called Pomerol: the commune is made up of a number of small hamlets – Catusseau, Cloquet, Grand- and Petit-Moulinet, Maillet, Pignon and René – each of which is prefixed with 'Pomerol'. Administratively and socially the commune is based on Pomerol-Centre, which can be pinpointed on the rural landscape by the church steeple. The church, built in 1898, replaced one built in the 12th century by the Knights of St John (the Hospitaliers), later known as the Knights of Malta, who gave help and shelter to travellers at the time of the crusades. Pomerol was on one of the pilgrim routes to Santiago de Compostela in north-west Spain: there are still stone signposts marked with the Maltese cross near Châteaux Beauregard, Moulinet and La Commanderie, for example, and at a crossroads near the hamlet of Pignon a weathered column marks the old route. It is also probable that the knights stimulated vine-growing in Pomerol, if only to produce wine for Mass and medicinal purposes. This is why the local wine fraternity was given the name La Confrérie des Hospitaliers, and its members have a Maltese cross on their robes.

Pomerol's vineyards, introduced by the Romans, were destroyed during the Hundred Years' War. They were gradually restored during the 15th and 16th centuries but for several hundred years the district was regarded in wine terms – if considered at all – as part of St-Émilion. It did not acquire an identity of its own until 1923, and was confirmed by an *appellation contrôlée* in 1936. Today

the demand for Pomerol exceeds supply to the extent that the prices paid for the better wines can equal or surpass even those of renowned Médoc *crus classés*.

Pomerol itself has no classification system, mainly because the more important growers do not particularly want one. The leading estates, after Pétrus, are generally considered to be Châteaux Certan (De May de Certan), La Conseillante, l'Église-Clinet, l'Évangile, La Fleur de Gay (see La Croix de Gay), La Fleur-Pétrus, Gazin, Lafleur, Latour à Pomerol, Petit Village, Le Pin, Trotanoy and Vieux Château Certan. Other estates of special interest include châteaux Le Bon Pasteur, Gombaude-Guillot, La Grave (Trigant de Boisset), Lafleur-Gazin and Vray Croix de Gay.

The centre of Pomerol is a plateau some 35 metres high with an abundance of clay from which strong, generous, richly coloured wines are produced. Château Pétrus reigns supreme. Around the plateau there is a fairly narrow belt consisting of gravel, clay and sand: the wines grown here are robust and intense but often less rounded and luxurious than those from the plateau. To the west the land is flatter and the soil sandier, resulting in relatively light, supple wines. In many places there is a hard, compact layer of iron-bearing sandstone in the subsoil: this *crasse de fer* is said to give Pomerols their sometimes truffle-like aroma. A good Pomerol, however, will have other elements: of cocoa, blackberry and violets, roasted almonds, liquorice and oak.

Most Pomerols are more accessible, warmer, more charming and less reserved than wines from the other Bordeaux districts (although they can also mature well). Merlot, the grape that thrives on clay and loamy soils, contributes greatly to this and accounts for three-quarters of the vines.

The typical Pomerol château is comfortable rather than grand, and sits tranquil among its vines. There are some 180 growers, so in this small district most of the estates are small, averaging around ten hectares. Many have a mere hectare or two. Château Pétrus has only 11.4 hectares and by far the largest property is Château de Sales with 47.5 hectares.

Lambs en route to market temporarily evade their shepherd to investigate a Pomerol vineyard.

Pomerol

Canton boundary
Commune (parish) boundary
CHÂTEAU   Top-quality château
Château   Other good château
First-growth vineyard
Other vineyard
Woods
25   Contour interval 5 metres

St-Denis-
de-Pile
Château des
Annereaux
les Annereaux

Lalande-
de-Pomerol
Château
Castel Viaud
les Sablés
le Perron
Château Perron
Château
Bourseau
Viaud
le Sablot
Château
de Viaud
D245 E1

St-Médard-
de-Guizières
Château
Grand Ormeau

le Moulin
de Salles
Château de
Bel-Air
Canton
des-Chats
Bel-Air
18
15
Château
les Cruzelles
la Pignère

Château de Sales
Château la
Maréchaude
LALANDE-DE-LIBOURNE
Château
Vieux Chevrol

le Petit
Moulinet
Château
Moulinet
Domaine
de la Combe
D245
N89
D121 E3
Château
Moulin à Vent
Chevrol
le Moulin

15
Château
Patache
Marchesseau
le Moulin
de Lavaud
le Moulin
N É A C
la Forêt

Clos de
la Combe
15
Lavaud
Château
Belles
Graves
le Moulin
de Gazelis
Barbanne
13

le Grand
Garrouil
21
la
Patache
CHÂTEAU
LA GRAVE TRIGANT
DE BOISSET
CHÂTEAU
ROUGET
Château
Tournefeuille
Néac

Château
Grand-
Moulinet
Vieux
Château
Cloquet
D245
CHÂTEAU
LATOUR À
POMEROL
CLOS
L'EGLISE
Pignon
Château
Lafleur
Gazin
la Chichonne

CHÂTEAU
L'ENCLOS
Château
Rêve d'Or
le Grand
Moulinet
Pont de
Cloquet
21
Château
Feytit-Clinet
CHÂTEAU
CLINET
CH.
L'EGLISE-
CLINET
Domaine
de l'Eglise
CHÂTEAU
LE GAY
CHÂTEAU
LAFLEUR
CHÂTEAU
GAZIN

René
CLOS
RENÉ
Château
Bellevue
Château
Bel-Air
Château de
Bourgueneuf
Château
la Cabanne
Château la
Croix-de-Gay
CHÂTEAU
LA FLEUR-
PÉTRUS
Château
Franc-Maillet
Maillet

Château
Mazeyres
les
Barrières
les Ormeaux
Château
Lagrange
Château
Vray-Croix-
de-Gay
CHÂTEAU
PÉTRUS

Château
Cantereau
20
Château de
Grange-Neuve
COMMUNE
Trochau
CHÂTEAU
CERTAN GIRAUD
CHÂTEAU
GAZIN

Château
Clos Mazeyres
Béquille
Château
Bourgneuf-
Vayron
23
CHÂTEAU
TROTANOY
Clos du
Clochet
CHÂTEAU
CERTAN DE MAY
DE
P O M E R O L
CHÂTEAU
HAUT-MAILLET

Beauséjour
Château
Gombaude-
Guillot
D121 E4
Château
la Violette
VIEUX
CHÂTEAU
CERTAN
CHÂTEAU
LE BON PASTEUR

Château
Bonalgue
Bonalgue
N89
Château
la Pointe
35
38
CHÂTEAU
L'EVANGILE
CHÂTEAU
CROQUE
MICHOTTE

Château
Nénin
Château
Grate-Cap
D121
la Gravette
CHÂTEAU
PETIT
VILLAGE
D244
Montagne

D244
CHÂTEAU
LE PIN
Catusseau
Ch. la Croix
St-Georges
Ch.
la Croix
St-Georges
CHÂTEAU LA
CONSEILLANTE
36

Château
la Fleur
du Roy
Château
le Caillou
Château
la Croix
Château
Beauregard
36
Château la
Tour du Pin
Figeac
Château
la Dominique

Château
Plince
la Brandaude
30
33
CHÂTEAU
CHEVAL BLANC

Château la
Croix-du-Casse
Château
Ferrand
les Grands
Sillons
Toulifaut
St-Emilion
25

la Bordette
Château
la Commanderie
Ch. la Croix
Taillefer
Rouilledinat
23
Château
la Tour-Figeac

Libourne
la Lamberte
21
Château
Taillefer
la Grange Neuve

N
Taillas

Château
du Tailhas
D243
St-Emilion

1:25,000
Km. 0 _____ 1 Km.
Miles 0 _____ ½ Mile

PRODUCERS OF SPECIAL INTEREST

Given advance warning, many of the châteaux including Beauregard, La Conseillante, La Croix de Gay, Nenin, La Pointe, de Sales and Vieux Château Certan welcome visitors.

Château Beauregard
33500 Pomerol
Owned by a French financial institution, the estate includes a 17th-century château and a vineyard that is practically in one single plot. The wines have improved considerably since the estate's purchase by new owners in 1991.

Château Le Bon Pasteur
33500 Pomerol
A characteristic, generous Pomerol of high quality. The modest estate in the north-east corner of the district is owned by the well known oenologist Michel Rolland.

Château Bonalgue 33500 Pomerol
Situated to the north-east of Libourne on the sandy gravel soils. The wines are generally full and rich but have not the intensity of the top Pomerols.

Château La Cabanne
33500 Pomerol
Pleasant, supple wine with a distinct oak aroma. It often has a good colour and matures well.

Château Certan (De May de Certan) 33500 Pomerol
A small estate with modern equipment opposite Vieux Château Certan (they were once one estate). The wine has style and strength.

Château Certan-Guiraud
33500 Pomerol
Well sited property on Pomerol's central plateau. Ripe, full style of wine.

Château Clinet 33500 Pomerol
Clinet has become one of the stars of recent years, producing deeply coloured, opulent wines. The grapes are harvested late and the malolactic fermentation is completed in barrel.

Clos de l'Église 33500 Pomerol
Exquisite, not particularly broad wine that often demands years of patience.

Clos René 33500 Pomerol
Sound, serious Pomerol.

Château La Conseillante
33500 Pomerol
Estate on the St-Émilion/Pomerol boundary that has belonged to the family for more than a century. The wine is one of the finest of the district and has a delicate perfume and a firm yet silky taste of great distinction.

Château La Croix 33500 Pomerol
A fairly sturdy Pomerol that can age well but lacks real class. A small museum at the château houses items connected with the old pilgrim route to Santiago de Compostela.

Château La Croix de Gay
33500 Pomerol
A noble Pomerol with subtle nuances. A *supérieur* selection from a small plot is sold as Château La Fleur de Gay and can match the best in the district.

Château l'Église-Clinet
33500 Pomerol
Vital, stylish wine with a creamy roundness, tannin and a beautiful balance. The vineyards are of a good age and the wines expertly vinified by Denis Durantou.

Château l'Enclos 33500 Pomerol
Sound, reasonably generous wine with an unmistakable charm. It needs to age. L'Enclos proves what can be achieved on the flat, sandy land in the west of Pomerol – the secluded estate is in the hamlet of Grand-Moulinet, on the west side of the Libourne–Périgueux road.

Château l'Évangile 33500 Pomerol
Purchased by the Rothschild Group (Lafite) in 1990, the vineyard borders on Château Pétrus and produces a splendid, stylish Pomerol, characterised by a distinct impression of violets in the bouquet.

Château Feytit-Clinet
33500 Pomerol
The estate is managed by *négociant* Jean-Pierre Moueix. The wines are reliable rather than stunning.

Château La Fleur-Pétrus
33500 Pomerol
The château is striking for its egg-yellow shutters; the wine is a distinguished Pomerol with more subtlety than most but it tastes softer and less fat. It should be allowed to mature.

Château Le Gay 33500 Pomerol
Under the same ownership as Lafleur. Low yields produce concentrated, structured wines.

Château Gazin 33500 Pomerol
With 23ha this is one of the largest estates in Pomerol. The vineyard is adjacent to that of Pétrus. The wines improved greatly in the latter part of the 1980s and are now among the best in the appellation.

Château Gombaude-Guillot
33500 Pomerol
The vineyard is situated on sand, gravel and clay soils, the wines are powerful and concentrated. In exceptional years a *cuvée speciale* is produced from the best wines.

Château la Grave (Trigant de Boisset) 33500 Pomerol
Balance, refinement and a good deal of tannin mark this consistent wine, made from 90% Merlot.

Château Lafleur 33500 Pomerol
Initially very reserved, with colour and strength, Lafleur develops beautifully in bottle.

Château Lafleur-Gazin
33500 Pomerol
A carefully made, generous wine with fruit and wood.

Château Lafleur du Roy
33500 Pomerol
A fairly fresh, slender, classically made example.

Château Lagrange 33500 Pomerol
In terms of class and complexity Lagrange just misses the top group of Pomerols but is better than average.

Château Latour à Pomerol
33500 Pomerol
An almost corpulent, generous Pomerol with a lot of soft tannin and ripe fruit.

Château Mazeyres 33500 Pomerol
Sound but not very exciting wine.

Château Moulinet 33500 Pomerol
A rounded wine; reasonable tannin and sometimes an earthy aroma.

Château Nenin 33500 Pomerol
One of the bigger Pomerol estates, its handsome château is set in a large park. The compact, deep-coloured wine has less meat, depth or charm than its reputation might suggest, but it usually develops well in bottle.

Château Petit Village
33500 Pomerol
Excellent wine that is anything but *petit*. Owned since 1989 by Axa-Millésimes which purchased it from the Prats (Cos d'Estournel) family.

Château Pétrus 33500 Pomerol
For all its fame, Pétrus will disappoint anyone looking for a grand château – until they taste the wine. Pétrus is the Pomerol of Pomerols: a dark, exceptionally intense wine that overwhelms the senses with its authoritative power. Its unique class puts its price beyond the reach of ordinary mortals: it is three times the price of the Médoc first growths. The estate (the vines are 95% Merlot) belongs to Mme Lacoste and Jean-Pierre Moueix (of the Libourne firm of the same name). A Moueix team looks after the vineyard and makes the wine. Other Moueix properties in Pomerol include Feytit-Clinet, La Fleur-Pétrus, La Grave Trigant de Boisset, Lagrange, Latour à Pomerol and Trotanoy.

Château Le Pin 33500 Pomerol
This tiny 2-ha property has shot to stardom in recent years. It is owned by the Thienpont family of Vieux Château Certan. Some vintages now

Pomerol's eight small hamlets are administered from Pomerol-Centre.

sell at higher prices than Pétrus. The wines are aged in new-oak casks and are dense and aromatic.

Château Plince 33500 Pomerol
A relatively unknown Pomerol that deserves to be followed. Its has made great strides in quality in recent years.

Château La Pointe 33500 Pomerol
An extensive estate just outside Libourne, where two roads from Pomerol join at the Libourne boundary – hence the name La Pointe. The château itself looks out over a magnificent park with stately old trees. If conditions are favourable, La Pointe produces colourful wines with plenty of extract.

Château Rouget 33500 Pomerol
The ivy-covered country house, built in 1750, is one of the oldest châteaux in Pomerol. The wines, with a firm tannic structure that demands several years' bottle-age, are made for cellaring.

Château de Sales 33500 Pomerol
Pomerol's biggest estate with an impressive château set in an extensive park. The wine is always reliable with style, structure, a certain elegance and a fine aroma.

Château du Tailhas
33500 Pomerol
Broad, rounded wine made with modern equipment: reliable even in lesser years.

Château Taillefer 33500 Pomerol
A somewhat rustic wine that benefits from ageing. The wines are solid if somewhat unexciting.

Château Trotanoy
33500 Pomerol
A Moueix estate on Pomerol's central plateau: the wine is decidedly more grand than the pleasant country house which serves as a château. Trotanoy is an extraordinarily distinguished wine with plenty of colour, concentration and strength. If Pétrus is the Emperor of Pomerol, Trotanoy is the King.

Vieux Château Certan
33500 Pomerol
The Belgian owners (the Thienpont family) produce a flawless, charming wine with style and strength that gains in fragrance and complexity with the years. The bottle is easily recognised by its pink cap. A high percentage of Cabernet Franc and Cabernet Sauvignon is used in the blend.

Château La Violette
33500 Pomerol
A Pomerol with grace, a perfume of violets and a nice finish.

Château Vray Croix de Gay
33500 Pomerol
The age of many of the vines make this a good Pomerol with depth.

WINE ACTIVITIES

La Confrérie des Hospitaliers de Pomerol was founded in 1968 and

Osier stacked at Vieux Château Certan. These pliable water willow shoots are used to tie canes to wires after pruning.

named after the Order that built a hospital in Pomerol in 1298.

WINE INFORMATION

There is no Maison du Vin in Pomerol, but details about the wines and the châteaux should be available from the tourist information offices in Libourne and Bordeaux and the Maison du Vin in Bordeaux (see page 118). It is also worth making enquiries at the larger hotels or restaurants in Libourne.

HOTELS

Pomerol has no hotels or restaurants, so Libourne is the place to go. (See also listings for St-Émilion page 164.)

Hôtel Climat de France
33500 **Arveyres** Tel (0)557 51 41 41
Modern hotel with restaurant, opened at the beginning of the 1980s. Across the river from Libourne, opposite the quai du Priourat.

Hôtel de Gare 33500 **Libourne**
Tel (0)557 25 27 76
A simple, decent place to sleep. Also has a restaurant.

Hôtel Loubat 33500 **Libourne**
Tel (0)557 51 17 58
The best-known hotel in Libourne.

Near the station. The rooms have been modernised and the restaurant, Les Trois Toques, serves carefully prepared local dishes (entrecôte Libournaise, lampreys, etc) and a range of Pomerol wines.

RESTAURANTS

Auberge les Treilles
33500 **Libourne** Tel (0)557 25 02 52
Reasonably priced restaurant close to the river. Meals are served outdoors in summer. Also has rooms.

Le Bistrot Chanzy
33500 **Libourne** Tel (0)557 51 84 26
Small bistro near the railway station. The prices are affordable and the wine-list is good.

L'Étrier 33500 **Libourne**
Tel (0)557 51 26 99
A rather elegant establishment with prices to match, but the cooking is good and the wine-list tempting. For something cheaper, you could go to the grill next door.

PLACES OF INTEREST

Apart from its wine and a few reminders of the Order of St John, Pomerol has few attractions to offer visitors. Libourne, however, has plenty.

Libourne The town has around 25,000 inhabitants. It was founded in the 13th century by the Englishman Roger de Leyburn who built a fortified settlement where an earlier stronghold had probably stood. In 1270 Libourne was given its municipal charter. The old town walls have been replaced by quays and embankments lined with plane trees; most of the town's wine merchants are concentrated on the quai du Priourat, and behind their offices there are often extensive cellar complexes. Coming from Bordeaux, you can enter Libourne via a long 19th-century bridge (heavy through-traffic is diverted around the old centre). In the heart of town is the place Abel Surchamp, a large square surrounded by old houses, arcades and the 15th-century town hall which has a museum of archaeology and art, including paintings by René Princeteau who taught Toulouse-Lautrec. Three days a week the square comes to life when the market is held. Where the little River Isle flows past the quays and into the Dordogne is the Tour du Grand-Port, one of the two fortified towers remaining from the original town walls. This one used to command the harbour entrance.

169

Satellites of St-Émilion and Pomerol

The so-called satellites lie beyond the River Barbanne, the northern boundary of St-Émilion and Pomerol. The villages of Lussac, Montagne, Puisseguin and St-Georges each constitute an appellation whose wines can be sold under the name of the commune coupled with that of St-Émilion. The wines of Parsac were absorbed into the Montagne-St-Émilion appellation in 1992. To the west are the satellites of Pomerol: the communes of Lalande and Néac, most of whose wines carry the appellation Lalande-de-Pomerol.

On this north side of the river, small hills and charming valleys replace the well-ordered rows of vines found on St-Émilion's central plateau. There are woods and meadows as well as vineyards, small villages, winding roads and modest châteaux. The visitors who throng St-Émilion at weekends do not disturb the stillness here.

By far the most important appellation is Montagne-St-Émilion. The wines are often earthier and more robust than St-Émilions but can be of surprisingly high quality – and are often reasonably priced. As well as the wines from Montagne, most of those from St-Georges are also sold under the Montagne-St-Émilion appellation. The most important exception is Château St-Georges, the splendid estate that dominates the surrounding countryside and produces wine with at least the distinction of a St-Émilion *grand cru classé*. It proudly carries the St-Georges-St-Émilion appellation.

The wines of Lussac often seem a little fuller and more rounded than those of Montagne. Almost half the harvest is processed by the cooperative in Puisseguin, a commune which itself makes many agreeable, rounded and charming wines.

Château de Coucy in Montagne, the most productive of the satellite districts.

Like Pomerol, the commune of Lalande has many small properties: of some 210 growers, about 50 cultivate less than a hectare. The wines, too, show a family likeness with those of Pomerol although they have just a little less generosity, strength and appeal. The communes of Lalande-de-Pomerol and Néac are separated by the N89, but both comprise the appellation Lalande-de-Pomerol. As in Pomerol the soils vary with clay, gravel and sand evident. The producers of Néac are entitled to sell their wine either as Néac or as Lalande-de-Pomerol, and usually opt for the latter.

Certain growers in Montagne contend that the formation of the Barbanne Valley gives their vineyards a situation superior to some sites in St-Émilion proper.

PRODUCERS OF SPECIAL INTEREST

LUSSAC-ST-ÉMILION

Château de Barbe Blanche
33570 Lussac

Chateau Bel-Air 33570 Lussac
Consistent producer with a range of older vintages for sale.

Château Bellevue 33570 Lussac

Château de Bordes 33570 Lussac

Château La Claymore
33570 Lussac

Château du Courlat 33570 Lussac

Château Croix de Rambeau
33570 Lussac

Château La Grènière
33570 Lussac
Well made wines. The Cuvée de la Chartreuse is of particular note.

Château La Haute Claymore
33570 Lussac

Château du Lyonnat 33570 Lussac
Large estate producing attractive wines.

Château Mayne-Blanc
33570 Lussac
Satisfyingly mouth-filling St-Vincent Cuvée, with good firm tannins on the finish.

Château du Moulin Noir
33570 Lussac

Producteurs Réunis Puisseguin-Lussac 33570 Puisseguin
Located in Puisseguin but responsible for 50% of the production of Lussac. Cuvée Renaissance is the top wine.

Château Vieux-Fournay
33570 Lussac

MONTAGNE-ST-ÉMILION

Chateau Bonneau
33570 Montagne
Astute investment and good winemaking have improved the wines at this immaculately kept estate.

Château Calon 33570 Montagne
Merlot constitutes 70% of the blend. The owner also produces a Calon under the St-Georges label.

Château Corbin 33570 Montagne

Château Coucy 33570 Montagne

Château Croix-Beauséjour
33570 Montagne

Château Faizeau 33570 Montagne
Extremely polished wine produced by the owners of Château La Croix de Gay in Pomerol.

Château Grand Barrail
33570 Montagne

Château Haut Musset
33570 Montagne

Château Maison Blanche
33570 Montagne

Château de Maison-Neuve
33570 Montagne

Château des Moines
33570 Montagne

Château Montaiguillon
33570 Montagne
Structured wines with good fruit concentration even in lighter vintages.

Château Négrit 33570 Montagne

Château Roc de Calon
33570 Montagne
Attractive wines. The Cuvée Prestige is aged in new-oak barrels.

Château Rocher-Corbin
33570 Montagne

Château Roudier
33570 Montagne

PUISSEGUIN-ST-ÉMILION

Château de l'Anglais
33570 Puisseguin

Château Bel-Air
33570 Puisseguin

Château Durand-Laplagne
33570 Puisseguin
Structured, tannic wines produced at this estate by Bertrand Bessou. The Cuvée Sélection is the top wine.

Château Fongaban
33570 Puisseguin

Château Guibot La Fourvieille
33570 Puisseguin
The satellites' most modern winery. Wines are also bottled under the label Vieux Château Guibeau for some markets. The Sélection Henri Bourlon is aged in new-oak barrels.

Château Haut-Bernat
33570 Puisseguin

Château Lafaurie
33570 Puisseguin

Château des Laurets
33570 Puisseguin
At 81ha this is the largest property in the Libournais. It has been owned since 1993 by a banking group. The wines, some of which are bottled under the appellation Montagne-St-Émilion label, have good fruit extract.

Producteurs Réunis Puisseguin-Lussac 33570 Puisseguin

Château Soleil 33570 Puisseguin
Fruity, aromatic wines with tannic structure. The Cuvée Prestige et Tradition is heavily oaked.

ST-GEORGES-ST-ÉMILION

Château Bellevue
33570 St-Georges

Château Calon
33570 St-Georges

Château Le Roc de Troquard
33570 St-Georges

Château St-André Corbin
33570 St-Georges

Château St-Georges
33570 St-Georges
The flag-bearer for this appellation and in truth better than many *grands crus classés* in St-Émilion. Managed with élan for many years by Pétrus' Desbois and now by his son Georges.

Château Tour du Pas St-Georges 33570 St-Georges

Château Vieux Montaiguillon
33570 St-Georges
Plenty of depth and persistence in the wines from this estate. The quality of the terroir is evident.

LALANDE-DE-POMEROL

Château des Annereaux
33500 Lalande-de-Pomerol

Château Bel-Air
33500 Lalande-de-Pomerol

Château Bourseau
33500 Lalande-de-Pomerol

Clos de L'Église
33500 Lalande-de-Pomerol
A significant percentage of Cabernet Franc and Cabernet Sauvignon and even a little Malbec is used in these wines. There is no wood-ageing.

Clos des Templiers
33500 Lalande-de-Pomerol

Château La Croix Chenevelle
33500 Lalande-de-Pomerol
Produced essentially from Merlot. The percentage of new oak used for ageing has risen to around 35 in recent vintages.

Château Fougeailles
33500 Lalande-de-Pomerol

Château Grand Ormeau
33500 Lalande-de-Pomerol
In recent years this has been the estate of reference in Lalande-de-Pomerol. Rich, luxurious wines in the true Pomerol style.

Château Perron
33500 Lalande-de-Pomerol

Château Sergant
33500 Lalande-de-Pomerol

Château de Viaud
33500 Lalande-de-Pomerol

Domaine de Viaud
33500 Lalande-de-Pomerol

LALANDE-DE-POMEROL (OR NÉAC)

Château Belles-Graves
33500 Néac

Château Bertineau St-Vincent
33500 Néac

Château La Croix St-André
33500 Néac
Concentrated wines that have long ageing potential.

Château La Fleur St-Georges
33500 Néac

Château Garraud 33500 Néac
This is the largest domaine in the appellation and is rapidly becoming one of the leaders. Since 1990 new cellars have been built and work in the vineyard has become more selective. The wines are deeply coloured, concentrated and aromatic.

Château Haut-Chaigneau
33500 Néac

Château Les Hauts-Conseillants
33500 Néac

Château Haut-Surget 33500 Néac

Château Siaurac 33500 Néac

Château Tournefeuille
33500 Néac

WINE ACTIVITIES

The wine fraternity **Les Baillis de Lalande-de-Pomerol** has been active since 1984. The Montagne fraternity, **Les Vignerons de Montagne de St-Émilion**, is three years older. The **Échevins de Lussac-St-Émilion** was created in 1986.

WINE INFORMATION

Maisons du Vin
33570 Lussac
Tel (0)557 74 50 35
33570 Montagne
Tel (0)557 74 60 13
33570 Puisseguin
Tel (0)557 74 50 62

HOTELS

These rural villages have little to offer in the way of hotels and restaurants; see instead places to eat and stay in St-Émilion (pages 164–65) and Fronsac (page 175).

RESTAURANT

Restaurant de l'Aérodrome
33500 Les Artigues-de-Lussac
Tel (0)557 24 31 95
By the local airfield, close to the N89. A speciality is rôti de lotte au basilic. The wine-list has a generous selection including St-Émilions.

PLACES OF INTEREST

Cornemps Hamlet north-east of Lussac with a monastery where Henry of Navarre once stayed.

Lalande-de-Pomerol Well preserved 12th-century church with an open belfry.

Lussac The church has a bas-relief with harvest scenes. Just west of the village is the Picampeau menhir, sometimes called the Pierre des Martyrs because it was used as a sacrificial stone.

Montagne A 12th-century Romanesque church with a ribbed dome. The Éco-Musée de Montagne, next to the Maison du Vin, exhibits displays concerning rural life in times past. On a hill-top near the village are the five mills of Calong, a reminder that corn used to be grown here. Also close to Montagne is the Château des Tours, with 72ha of vineyards and an imposing 14th-century château.

Petit-Palais Attractive 12th-century church with two 16th-century belfries. The village is north-west of Lussac along the D21.

St-Georges High on the hill overlooking its sweep of vines is Château St-Georges, built in 1770 on medieval foundations by Victor Louis (architect of the Grand Théâtre in Bordeaux). Neither the château nor its wine should be missed. The cellar entrance bears the motto *vini templum* (temple of wines).

171

Côtes de Castillon and Bordeaux-Côtes de Francs

Immediately to the east of St-Émilion and its satellite communes of Montagne, Puisseguin and Lussac are nine villages entitled to the appellation Côtes de Castillon, upgraded from Bordeaux Supérieur Côtes de Castillon in 1989. The wines produced are all red. Near the Dordogne the landscape is fairly flat, but farther north it becomes hilly and very pretty.

The soils are clay-limestone with gravel and sand on the river plain. The better vineyards on the slopes behind Castillon have a higher percentage of limestone and a south-south-easterly exposure, which is an important consideration given the cooler soils. Merlot is the dominant grape variety, contributing as much as 70 per cent to most blends; it is complemented by Cabernet Franc and sometimes a little Cabernet Sauvignon.

There are now approximately 2,900 hectares under vine. Most of the holdings are under 10 hectares and only four domaines have more than 40. Of the 400 winegrowers, 240 vinify and bottle their own wines, the rest send their grapes to the local cooperative.

Until the latter half of the 1980s the Côtes de Castillon had excited little attention on the international scene; a recent injection of capital from outside investors however and a real focus on quality now makes this one of the most interesting appellations to watch. Improved disease control in the vineyard and a later harvesting date has led to fresher, fruitier wines. Their tannic structure is honed by their being aged in newer wood, which permits a certain amount of bottle-age. They are essentially St-Émilion in character and in a number of instances can be just as good as their more august neighbour.

The district derives its name from Castillon-la-Bataille, a market town on the Dordogne. It was here on 17 June, 1453 that a decisive battle was fought between the English and the French: the battle that parted Aquitaine from England after 300 years. The English commander Talbot, an old fighter in his 80s, lost the battle and his life. A single memorial to him stands to the east of the village.

To the north of Côtes de Castillon lies the small district of Bordeaux-Côtes de Francs: three communes and part of the Salles-de-Castillon commune (the other part of this village comes within the Côtes de Castillon). There was a Frankish settlement here in early times, which is commemorated by the hamlet of Francs.

The appellation comprises only 390 hectares. Principally red wines are produced and again Merlot dominates. There is also a small production of dry white wines made from the Bordeaux varieties of Sémillon and Sauvignon. In the 19th century the Côtes de Francs had a reputation for its sweet white wines.

Bordeaux-Côtes de Francs is a green and peaceful district with hills everywhere, including the highest in the entire Gironde *département*. The clay and limestone soil lends itself well to wine-growing and the microclimate is perhaps the warmest and driest in all Bordeaux. Some of the growers still have the 'St-Émilion' stamps for their casks: Côtes de Francs used to belong to that district but the adjustment of the appellations in the 1920s put an end to this arrangement and heralded the beginning of a rather wretched period. Many vineyards were dug up or planted with inferior grape varieties. Since the early 1980s, however, great interest has been shown in the Côtes, thanks to the achievements of the Belgian Thienpont family who own two leading estates, Puyguéraud and La Claverie. In 1985 two St-Émilion families (joint owners of Cheval Blanc and L'Angélus) bought the run-down Château de Francs with the aim of creating a first-class vineyard there.

Castillon-la-Bataille, where English rule in Aquitaine was ended in 1453.

Château Puyguéraud in remote and tranquil Bordeaux-Côtes de Francs.

The Église de St-Cibard in the Côtes de Francs, built in the 13th century in the region's characteristic gold-coloured stone, stands resplendent in the evening sun.

PRODUCERS OF SPECIAL INTEREST

CÔTES DE CASTILLON

Château d'Aiguille
33350 St-Philippe-d'Aiguille
Spanish Cava producer Raventos i
Blanc owns this property.

Château de Belcier
33350 Les Salles de Castillon

Château Blanzac
33350 St-Magne-de-Castillon

Château Cantegrive
33570 Puisseguin
This estate is owned by the
champagne producer Doyard. The
Cuvée l'An 1453 is the top wine.

Château Cap de Faugères
33330 St-Étienne-de-Lisse

Château La Clarière Laithwaite
33350 Ste-Colombe
British wine merchant Tony Laithwaite
is the driving force behind this
excellent 4-ha estate.

Château de Clotte
33350 Les Salles de Castillon

Château Côte Montpezat
33350 Belvès-de-Castillon

Château Lapeyronie
33350 Ste-Colombe

Château Peyrou
33350 St-Magne-de-Castillon

Château Pitray
33350 Gardegan et Tourtirac
A Côtes de Castillon producer of
note. The château is also of interest.

Château Poupille
33350 Ste-Colombe.
The estate's special *cuvée* Poupille is

made from 100% Merlot and aged in
new-oak barrels.

Château Robin
33350 Belvès-de-Castillon

Vieux Château Champs de Mars
33350 St-Philippe-d'Aiguille

BORDEAUX-CÔTES DE FRANCS

Cellier des Côtes de Francs
33570 Francs
This is the local cooperative. Duc de
Seignade is one of the labels
produced here.

Château Les Charmes-Godard
33570 St-Cibard
Another estate owned by the
Thienpont family. The best white wine
in the appellation is produced here
from mainly Sémillon grapes.

Château de Francs
33570 Francs

Château Laclaverie
33570 St-Cibard

Château Moulin de la Pitié
33570 St-Cibard

Château La Prade
33570 St-Cibard

Château Puyanché
33570 Francs

Château Puyguéraud
33570 St-Cibard
This flagship estate of the Thienpont
family puts as much as 45%
Cabernet Franc and Cabernet
Sauvignon in the wine blend, which
needs a certain amount of bottle-age.
The wine is made by Nicolas
Thienpont.

WINE FÊTE

Castillon-la-Bataille The annual
Foire aux Vins is usually held in the
second half of July.

WINE INFORMATION

Maison du Vin 33350 Castillon-la-
Bataille; Tel (0)557 40 00 88
Information about the wines and the
châteaux. Wines are also on sale.

HOTELS

The Côtes are not richly endowed
with hotels or restaurants; see
instead the listings for Entre-Deux-
Mers, St-Émilion and Bergerac (pages
153, 164–65 and 189).

RESTAURANT

Chez Régis 33350 Ste-Terre
Tel (0)557 47 16 21
You can lunch or dine here quite
inexpensively. Friture d'anguilles
(fried eel) is a speciality. Simple
accommodation is also available.

PLACES OF INTEREST

Belvès-de-Castillon In July and
August the battle between the English
and the French is re-enacted on open
ground next to the 15th-century
Château de Castegens. The spectacle
starts at 10.30pm and some 600
people in costume take part.

Castillon-la-Bataille Little river
town where in 1453 the historic
battle was fought that finally returned
Aquitaine to the French. In 1953
Castillon commemorated the 500th
anniversary of the event by adding 'la
Bataille' to its name. The local church
dates from the 18th century. The
mairie is in a former hospital.

Champ de la Hire In the Côtes de
Francs district between St-Cibard and
Salles-de-Castillon. A hill here was
fortified by the French during the
Hundred Years' War.

Francs The Château de Francs could
be partly 12th century, but most of
the buildings date from the 14th and
17th centuries. A fine gateway gives
access to the wine estate.

Gardegan Has an interesting 12th-
century church.

Monbadon A 14th-century feudal
castle crowns one of the hills.

Ste-Colombe Provides a panoramic
view of the surrounding countryside.
The church dates from the 11th and
12th centuries.

St-Genès-de-Castillon Has a
beautiful 15th-century house.

St-Magne-de-Castillon The church
is 11th or 12th century.

Salles-de-Castillon There is a
menhir (ancient stone) and a
Romanesque church.

Tayac The remains of a Gallic
settlement were found near this
hamlet in the Côtes de Francs in
the 19th century. The church is
Romanesque.

Fronsac

The River Isle meandering in its broad valley forms the boundary between Pomerol and Fronsac, two very different districts. Pomerol is a gently undulating plateau; Fronsac a tangle of small hills and valleys. The most important of the hills is the Tertre de Fronsac, which commands the surrounding countryside and provides a superb view of the Dordogne. The Gauls and then the Romans fortified it, and in 769 Charlemagne chose the site for a stronghold which for centuries was a residence for often tyrannical lords.

The castle's most notorious inhabitant was d'Argilemont, a seigneur who took delight in sinking any passing ship that did not immediately heave to when he fired a shot across its bows. In 1620 d'Argilemont was arrested on the orders of Louis XIII and died on the scaffold. Three years later the castle was dismantled and nothing now remains of it, nor of the later Italianate palace built on the hill by the Duc de Richelieu (great-nephew of the famous cardinal and military commander). The name of the local wine fraternity which was established in the late 1960s, Les Gentilshommes du Duché de Fronsac, is a reminder of this period. Today the Tertre de Fronsac is crowned by a pavilion, or lodge, built in the last century by a wealthy Libourne family. It is private property.

Grapes have been grown in Fronsac since very early times. Until the 18th century the wines were more highly valued than those of St-Émilion. It was only during the first half of the 19th century that St-Émilion began to outstrip Fronsac in reputation, although the first edition of *Bordeaux et ses Vins*, which appeared in 1850, described Fronsac as one of the communes "where the best wines of the Libourne *arrondissement* are harvested". But recovery from disasters such as phylloxera and economic depression has been less complete in Fronsac than in St-Émilion and Pomerol, and the name remained virtually forgotten until the 1960s.

The renewal of interest since then has been justified by the much improved wines. They are characterised are a strong, deep colour, plenty of power, a hearty finesse, a slightly bitter undertone and a long life. It is the soil that provides the potential for producing wines of this nature: a bedrock of limestone-clay-sand known geologically as *molasse du Fronsadais* is the key element.

The tiny appellation of Canon-Fronsac is located almost entirely on south-facing slopes, giving a greater homogeneity to its wines. Well sited vineyards can also be found in Fronsac. As in Pomerol and St-Émilion, Merlot is the dominant grape variety with Cabernet Franc and to a lesser extent Cabernet Sauvignon adding an extra dimension in the riper vintages.

The average holding in Fronsac is only about ten hectares, so the estates tend to be small family-run domaines. Some are still not sufficiently motivated by the idea of quality but there is now a solid core of young producers adding a new dynamism to the appellation. They have understood the importance of lower yields, riper fruit, control of the vinification and ageing in a certain percentage of new oak to soften the tannins, and appreciate that such measures are fundamental to improving the standard of the wine and of the appellation. Experts agree that of all the lesser-known appellations in Bordeaux, those of Fronsac and Canon-Fronsac are strong candidates for building a reputation at world level. A stimulus in this direction has already been given by the distinguished firm of Jean-Pierre Moueix of Libourne, which took over four leading châteaux in the 1970s and 1980s: Canon, Canon de Brem, Canon Moueix and La Dauphine and, in 1995, Château Charlemagne.

The Fronsac district, with some 1,100 hectares of vines (300 classified as Canon-Fronsac, 800 as Fronsac) is larger than Pomerol and is worth visiting for its landscape and architecture as well as for its wines. The châteaux display a great variety of styles. Some, such as Château La Rivière, are genuine castles. Others, such as Canon in St-Michel-de-Fronsac, are comfortable mid-19th-century country villas built by prosperous merchants from Libourne.

The ancient village of Fronsac on the Dordogne. The district's wines, drunk at court in the 18th century, once took precedence over those of neighbouring Pomerol.

Many of Fronsac's châteaux were originally built as country villas.

PRODUCERS OF SPECIAL INTEREST

CANON-FRONSAC

Château Barrabaque
33126 Fronsac
There are two *cuvées* produced at this estate: Tradition and Prestige.

Château Canon
33126 Fronsac
This tiny 1-ha estate has been owned by Christian Moueix since 1971.

Château Canon de Brem
33126 Fronsac

Château Canon Moueix
33126 Fronsac

Château Cassagne Haut-Canon
33126 St-Michel-de-Fronsac
A greater percentage of Cabernets Franc and Sauvignon is grown on this estate than on others in the district. La Truffière is the top *cuvée*.

Château Charlemagne
33126 Fronsac
The latest Moueix acquisition was formerly known as Château Bodet. It is a relatively large estate with 14ha under vine.

Château Coustolle
33126 Fronsac

Château La Fleur Cailleau
33126 Fronsac
Firm, balanced wines from this estate which is run on biodynamic principles. Fronsac's Château La Grave is under the same ownership.

Château Grand Renouil
33126 Fronsac

Château Mazeris
33126 St-Michel-de-Fronsac

Château Mazeris-Bellevue
33126 St-Michel-de-Fronsac

Château Moulin Pey-Labrie
33126 Fronsac
Rich, concentrated wines produced principally from Merlot.

Château du Pavillon
33126 Fronsac

Château Vray Canon Boyer
33126 St-Michel-de-Fronsac

FRONSAC

Château de Carles 33141 Saillans
Château Dalem 33141 Saillans
Concentrated, powerful wines with the potential for long ageing.

Château La Dauphine
33126 Fronsac
The least complex of the Moueix wines. The vineyard and château are situated close to the Dordogne.

Château Fontenil 33141 Saillans
This estate is owned by oenologists Dany and Michel Rolland.

Château La Grave 33126 Fronsac

Château Haut-Lariveau
33126 St-Michael-de-Fronsac
Grégoire Hubau of Château Moulin Pey-Labrie owns this estate which is planted with 100% Merlot.

Château Mayne-Vieil
33133 Galgon

Château Moulin Haut-Laroque
33141 Saillans
One of the stars of the appellation. Firm, balanced wines include a high percentage of old-vine Cabernet Franc.

Château Puy Guilhem
33141 Saillans

Château de La Rivière
33126 La Rivière
The district's showpiece property: a 13th-century castle flanked by two square towers and built against a wooded slope looking out over the Dordogne Valley. Extensive cellars.

Château Romagnac la Maréchale 33126 La Rivière

Château Rousselle
33126 La Rivière

Clos du Roy 33141 Saillans

Château La Vieille Cure
33141 Saillans

Château Villars 33141 Saillans
One of the pioneer estates of the appellation when it comes to improved quality. Consistently good wines.

WINE INFORMATION

Maison du Vin 33126 Fronsac
Tel (0)557 51 80 51

Les Gentilshommes du Duché de Fronsac fraternity has functioned since 1969.

HOTELS

The district is not yet equipped for tourism. See St-Émilion hotel and restaurant listings (pages 164–65).

RESTAURANT

Bord d'Eau 33126 Libourne
Tel (0)557 51 99 91
Modern, spacious restaurant located on the banks of the Dordogne. Classic dishes with a contemporary approach. The wine-list highlights the wines of Fronsac.

PLACES OF INTEREST

Asques This picturesque river village has an attractive view across the Dordogne Valley.

Cadillac-en-Fronsadais Village with a 19th-century chapel and the Ste-Ruffine fountain. The commune is actually outside the Fronsac appellation: Château de Cadillac, an impressive 12th-century fortress, produces red and white wines under the Bordeaux Supérieur and Bordeaux appellations.

Fronsac The ancient centre of the district, eclipsed in the 13th century by Libourne. The Romanesque church is a historic monument. There are also many lovely old houses, some dating from the 17th century.

St-Aignan The remains of a Gallo-Roman villa have been found here; the church is Romanesque.

St-Genès-de-Fronsac An 11th-century church, restored in the 16th century.

Vérac The church is 12th century, and a tower near the village was a corn mill until 1776. Lovers of cheese should make a point of visiting the dairy next to the 18th-century Château de Pommiers.

The smaller adjoining area of Canon-Fronsac occupies higher ground.

Côtes de Bourg and Côtes de Blaye

The wines of Bourg and Blaye may not rival those of the 'classic' regions but much progress has been made in recent years. The quality of Côtes de Bourg wines in particular has improved dramatically. Greater investment, better vineyard husbandry and carefully applied production techniques are evident in the character of the wines. Prices also remain competitive, placing Bourg and Blaye firmly in the value-for-money bracket among Bordeaux wines.

To reach Bourg from Bordeaux you can take either the D911 or the autoroute north-east to St-André-de-Cubzac. The D911 is slower as it passes through a number of villages but it has the advantage of taking you over Eiffel's remarkable bridge across the Dordogne, and in St-André-de-Cubzac the junction with the scenic D669 to Bourg is easy to find. The Cubzageais wine district around St-André makes a number of good wines under the Bordeaux and Bordeaux Supérieur appellations.

Bourg-sur-Gironde lies opposite the Bec d'Ambès, the spit of land that forms the northern tip of the Entre-Deux-Mers district and the site of a large industrial complex. The Bec has been built up by deposits of silt in the last 300 years: in the 17th century Bourg was called Bourg-sur-Mer and faced not the Dordogne but the Gironde. Bourg's strategic importance was recognised by the Romans and by the English, and a citadel was built in 1153. Later, the Château de la Citadelle served as a summer residence for the archbishops of Bordeaux; houses were built around the citadel and by the river and long flights of steps linked the two quarters. Today Bourg is little more than a picturesque and sleepy small town.

Essentially a red-wine region, Bourg has 3,700 hectares of vineyard devoted almost entirely to the production of Côtes de Bourg rouge. Viticulturally this appellation has a number of favourable features. The local climate is mild and is mediated by the proximity of the Dordogne and Gironde. Thus, in the 1991 and 1994 spring frosts, less damage was caused in the Côtes de Bourg than elsewhere in Bordeaux. In addition the vineyards are planted mainly on three hill slopes that run parallel to the Gironde, which give them decent drainage. Soils are varied but there is a good percentage of limestone, with gravel and marl further inland.

The wines are produced from a blend of Merlot, Cabernet Sauvignon, Cabernet Franc and often a little Malbec. Merlot however predominates, accounting for as much as 80 per cent at some estates. Grapes in the Côtes de Bourg in general ripen a week or two later than those in the Médoc, putting the earlier-ripening Merlot at an advantage. In recent years better vineyard management has allowed harvests to begin later, so providing riper fruit. As a result the normally full-bodied wines have a cleaner fruit expression with a little less 'earthiness' than they had in the past. Investment in oak barrels for ageing has also given the wines more definition and polished some of the harder rustic edges.

There are 536 wine-growers in the Côtes de Bourg and of these half are attached to one or other of the local cooperatives. These too have improved considerably, having updated methods and machinery. The largest at Tauriac and Pugnac are now turning out some more-than-respectable wines, and that of Lansac is improving. But the best come from individual producers: in the vanguard are a dozen or so *crus* led by François Mitjavile's Château Roc de Cambes.

From Bourg to Blaye is just under 15 kilometres and the most pleasant way to make the trip is via the D669E1, a narrow road that follows the river until it joins the D669. In summer the small gardens that line the river are bright with flowers. The little River Brouillon marks the boundary between the two districts.

Côtes de Bourg, on the right bank of the River Gironde, was a thriving vineyard long before the Médoc across the water was planted.

Côtes de Bourg and Côtes de Blaye

1:88,000

Km. 0   1   2 Km.
Miles 0   1 Mile

Arrondissment boundary
Canton boundary
Commune (parish) boundary
Vineyards
Woods
——100——   Contour interval 10 metres

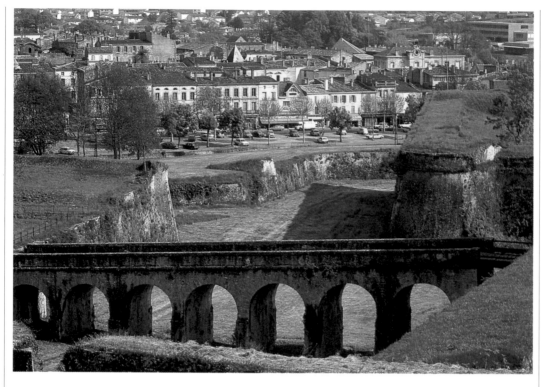

Blaye, like Bourg, has Roman origins. In the Middle Ages it was on one of the pilgrim routes to Santiago de Compostela and was a departure point for crusaders. Like Bourg it has a citadel, built in the late 1600s as part of a defensive line across the Gironde. Perfectly preserved, it stands high above Blaye's harbour, with a superb view of the river. Blaye itself is a pleasant little provincial town with some 5,000 inhabitants, a long street full of shops and cafés and a bustling market on Wednesdays and Saturdays. A car ferry that might have been designed expressly for wine-lovers on holiday links Blaye with Lamarque and the Médoc.

The wine-growing region of Blaye is much more dispersed than that of Bourg to the south. There are three principal viticultural zones: around the port of Blaye where many of the better reds are produced; in the north centred on St-Ciers where the soils suit the production of white wines, and in the south around St-Savin. The climate is fresher and well exposed slopes are essential. Owing to the variety of soils the wines are less uniform in style than those of the Côtes de Bourg. In all there are 3,950 hectares of vineyard producing red and white Premières Côtes de Blaye and white Côtes de Blaye and Blaye. Over three-quarters of the production is red, although there is also an undisclosed amount of white wine declared as AOC Bordeaux.

The Premières Côtes de Blaye are the most interesting wines. The better whites are usually produced from blends with a large proportion of Sauvignon and the reds, like Bourg, have a high percentage of Merlot. They are robust but lighter in weight than those from the Côtes de Bourg. The six cooperatives play an important economic role in the region, having over half the wine-growers attached to them.

Individually there has been less progress in Blaye than in Bourg. Lack of investment, often due to economic constraints, has been a barrier to general improvement. The quality of wines consequently varies considerably. One example of individual achievement in the region has been at Château Bertinerie where the vineyard has been refitted to the divided-canopy Lyre system of trellising to obtain greater ripeness of fruit.

PRODUCERS OF SPECIAL INTEREST

BORDEAUX AND BORDEAUX SUPÉRIEUR

Château du Bouilh
33240 St-André-de-Cubzac
The oldest vineyard in Bourg (see Places of Interest, page 179).

Château de Terrefort-Quancard
33240 Cubzac-lès-Ponts
This large property of the Quancard family (wine producer and merchant) demonstrates that pleasant wine can be made in this corner of Bordeaux.

CÔTES DE BOURG AND BOURG

Château de Barbe
33710 Villeneuve
An extensive estate with a spacious château producing a supple wine.

Château Beaulieu du Castenet
33710 Samonac

Château Bégot 33710 Lansac

Château Bruléscaille
33710 Tauriac
One of the top estates in the Côtes de Bourg. Grapes harvested at optimum maturity and wines aged in one-third new-oak barrels. Concentrated, structured wine.

Château Bujan
33710 Gauriac

Château Caruel
133710 Bourg-sur-Gironde

Château Castel La Rose
33710 Villeneuve

Château Le Clos de Notaire
33710 Bourg-sur-Gironde

Château Croûte Courpon
33710 Bourg-sur-Gironde

Château Falfas 33710 Bayon
The vineyards surround the beautiful 17th-century château. Aromatic, structured wines from this biodynamically run estate.

Château Fougas 33710 Lansac

Château Grand Launay
33710 Teuillac

Château Gravettes-Samonac
33710 Samonac

Château Gros Moulin
33710 Bourg-sur-Gironde

Château Guerry 33710 Tauriac
One of the best wines of the district; a quarter of the vines are Malbec.

Château Haut-Guiraud
33710 St-Ciers-de-Canesse

Château Haut-Macô 33710 Tauriac
This domaine has been totally restructured over the last 20 years. Merlot and Cabernet Sauvignon (50% of each) provide firm, fruity wines.

Château Macay 33710 Samonac
The 34-ha vineyard has a south-south-easterly exposure. The wines, vinified in a modern winery with modern equipment, are attractively fruity.

Château Mercier 33710 St-Trojan
Property of the same family for 12 generations. The 22-ha domaine has a mix of gravel and clay soils. The Cuvée Prestige is aged in one-third oak barrels and there is a small production of white wine.

Château Nodoz 33710 Tauriac

Château Le Piat 33710 Tauriac
The showpiece of the excellent cooperative at Tauriac.

Château Roc de Cambes
33710 Bourg-sur-Gironde
Bourg's leading estate. The vineyard has been restructured since its purchase in 1988 by François Mitjavile. Late harvesting and limited yields provide concentrated, balanced wines.

Château Rousset 33710 Samonac
Consistently well made wines. The Grande Réserve is a selection from old vines aged in new-oak barrels.

Château Tayac
33710 Bourg-sur-Gironde
The river-front vineyard of this fine châteaux gets the maximum possible sun, and from the château there is a splendid view across the Gironde. The wine is rich in colour and strong in constitution, especially the Cuvée de Prestige.

PREMIÈRES CÔTES DE BLAYE, BLAYE AND CÔTES DE BLAYE

Château Bertinerie
33620 Cubnezais
The most innovative estate in Blaye.

Excellent red and white Premières Côtes de Blaye. The top of the range for both red (75% Cabernet Sauvignon) and white (100% Sauvignon) are labelled Château Haut Bertinerie.

Château Charron
33390 St-Martin la Caussade

Duchesse de Tutiac
33860 Marcillac
Good Sauvignon-based white wine produced by the cooperative at Marcillac, the Cave des Hauts de Gironde. The Excellence de Tutiac has more oak influence.

Château Les Graves
33920 St-Vivien-de-Blaye

Château Haut-Grelot
33820 St-Ciers-sur-Gironde
One of several estates in the north of the appellation making consistently good red wine. There is also a small production of white.

Château Les Jonqueyres
33390 St-Paul-de-Blaye
A small but very individual domaine run by Pascal Montaut. Solid, concentrated red Premières Côtes de Blaye made from a Merlot-dominated blend. Also a good Côtes de Bourg, Clos Alphonse Dubreuil.

Château Loumède
33390 Blaye
Balanced, fruity wines with just a hint of oak are made on this 18-ha estate close to Blaye.

Château Roland-La-Garde
33390 St-Seurin-de-Cursac

Château Sociondo 33390 Blaye

WINE ACTIVITIES

The **Connétable de Guyenne** wine fraternity, established in 1952, is active in Bourg and Blaye as well as in Entre-Deux-Mers and the Premières Côtes de Bordeaux.

WINE INFORMATION

Maisons du Vin
33710 Bourg-sur-Gironde
Tel (0)557 68 46 47
33390 Blaye (across from Vauban's citadel); Tel (0)557 42 91 19
Information available from both for châteaux visits; also tastings and wine for purchase at cellar-door prices.

HOTELS

Tourism here is relatively undeveloped and it is not a prosperous region, so the number of good hotels and restaurants is rather limited.

Hôtel Bellevue 33390 Blaye
Tel (0)557 42 00 36
Country-style hotel in the town. Has a simple restaurant.

Hôtel La Citadelle 33390 Blaye
Tel (0)557 42 17 10

The Gironde estuary is guarded by the citadel of Blaye, which was completed in the late 17th century by Vauban.

Modern hotel in Blaye's citadel, with a swimming pool and a panoramic view over the Gironde. Also a restaurant.

La Closerie des Vignes
33710 St-Ciers-de-Canesse
Tel (0)557 64 81 90
Ten quiet, spacious rooms offer modern comfort. Also a restaurant and swimming pool.

RESTAURANTS

La Filadière 33710 Gauriac
Tel (0)557 64 94 05
Owned by a Swiss couple and situated on the banks of the Gironde. Pleasant spot for lunch. Menu includes salads, cold dishes and fish. Small list of regional wines.

Au Sarment 33240 St-Gervais
Tel (0)557 43 44 73
Located in a former primary school near St-André-de-Cubzac. Classic dishes with a modern touch. Average price and good quality.

PLACES OF INTEREST

CUBZAGEAIS
St-André-de-Cubzac (Where the D669 meets the routes from Bordeaux.) Has a fortified church with a Romanesque apse. Not far to the north of St-André-de-Cubzac is Château du Bouilh, one of the district's landmarks and a historic monument. The château was never

completed: building began in 1787 under the direction of Victor Louis (who designed the Grand Théâtre in Bordeaux) but was stopped at the outbreak of the French Revolution. The château, where wine is still made, can be visited, mainly at weekends.

BOURG
Bayon Has a 12th-century Romanesque church.
Bourg-sur-Gironde From the shaded terrace by the town hall there is a splendid view over the Gironde and the Bec d'Ambès. The Château de la Citadelle has a museum and there is a maze of underground passages.
La Libarde Just north of Bourg; an 11th-century Romanesque crypt.
Margrigne Near Tauriac, has a Templar chapel.
Marmisson Along the D669E towards Blaye; a prehistoric site.
Prignac-et-Marcamps Close to the D669 en route from St-André-de-Cubzac to Bourg are the Pair-non-Pair caves, discovered in 1881, with some 60 prehistoric wall paintings of animals. The paintings depict bison, mammoth and wild-horse hunting.
Tauriac Splendid, weathered Romanesque church, possibly the most beautiful in the district.
Teuillac 9th-century sarcophagi in the church.

BLAYE
Blaye The great citadel of Blaye, almost 1km long, was built between 1685 and 1689 on the ruins of the St-Romain church, where Charlemagne is said to have buried his nephew Roland in 778. Within the citadel there is virtually a small village with streets and gardens, the remains of the triangular Château des Rudel and a 17th-century monastery. There is also a hotel (see Hotels), a camping site, a museum of local art and history, and the Tour de l'Aiguillette, a lookout post.
Marcillac Just east of St-Aubin, off the A10 Autoroute l'Aquitaine is a 12th-century church and a distillery producing 'fine' bordeaux (this is after all on the fringe of cognac country).
Montuzet For a panoramic view over the surrounding countryside, go up the hill from Plassac to Château Bellevue. From here it is a short walk to the Butte de Montuzet and its statue.
Plassac During the summer months the small museum displays finds from the Gallo-Roman period.
St-Ciers-sur-Gironde On flat land unsuitable for vines near the Gironde there is an enormous nuclear reactor that supplies about 8% of France's electricity. Visitors are welcome. In St-Ciers itself by contrast there is a museum of prehistory (open in July and August).

Cognac

The only area in the world where cognac may legally be made lies directly north of the Bordeaux region. It takes in the whole of the Charente-Maritime *département*, a large part of the Charente and two small enclaves in Dordogne (to the south-east) and Deux-Sèvres (to the north). Cognac may also be produced on two off-shore islands.

The landscape is a harmonious one of gently sloping hills with fields and small woods, peaceful villages and isolated, often walled farms. Hazy sunlight makes colours more mellow, contours less sharp, and across the region flows the languid browny-green Charente. Haste is an unfamiliar concept: not for nothing are the inhabitants nicknamed *cagouillards* after the small cagouille snails of the region.

Various remains show that the Romans were here in considerable numbers: the arena at Saintes, for example, could hold 20,000 people. They probably introduced viticulture, but for many centuries wine was made only for local consumption. The first and most important export was salt, from which Cognac derived its prosperity from the 11th century onward. It was not until the second half of the 17th century that a brisk trade in wine became established.

During the Middle Ages the region exported a great deal of wine to Britain and the Low Countries. In the 17th century the Dutch started to import wine for distilling. Their *brandewijn* (burnt wine) gave us our word 'brandy'. Later the wines were increasingly left to be distilled in their region of origin. At first this *eau-de-vie* was drunk with water, but the qualities of pure, wood-aged cognac became increasingly appreciated until in the 17th and 18th centuries it began to enjoy a worldwide reputation. The 19th century saw the rise of many of the great cognac houses and of the sale of cognac in bottle.

The name and origin of cognac were given legal protection in 1905 when the boundaries of its production area were laid down. Official recognition of the zones that make up the district followed almost 30 years later.

The zones lie in concentric circles around Cognac itself. The heart is the chalky area of Grande Champagne, which is surrounded in succession by Petite Champagne, Borderies, Fins Bois, Bons Bois and Bois Ordinaires. The proportion of chalk in the soil decreases successively through these zones – which directly affects the quality of the cognacs produced. To achieve a balanced and consistent quality, most houses use cognacs from different zones and of various ages. Fine Champagne, a special quality, is a blend of Grande Champagne (at least 50 per cent) and Petite Champagne.

The age of a cognac is also indicated by a range of legally protected terms. For three-star cognac (or VS) the minimum age of the youngest brandy used is 30 months. For VSOP (Very Superior Old Pale), VO and Réserve this minimum is raised to four and a half years, and to six years for XO, Vieille Réserve, Napoléon, VVSOP,

Mellow brickwork harmonises with the landscape at Bouteville. The reputation of cognac rests on the chalky constituents of the region's gently rolling hills.

Royal and so on. In practice, conscientious cognac firms maintain much stricter norms. At the extreme, the youngest brandy from the house of Delamain, its Pale and Dry, is on average 20 years old.

The basis for cognac is a thin, acidic white wine from Ugni Blanc (known here as St-Émilion), the grape that accounts for 95 per cent of the vineyard area. This is distilled twice in a special pot-still, or alembic. At this stage the colourless liquid – very alcoholic at around 70 per cent – is not yet cognac. Only a quarter of the eventual quality is present; the rest comes from the oak of the maturing casks (made from Limousin or Tronçais oak), the quality of the cellar in which it is aged and the length of time it is kept there. During its time in cask the alcohol content gradually

decreases, while every year three to four per cent of the volume is lost by evaporation. This 'angel's share' amounts to an annual loss for the whole district of 22 million bottles.

The normal drinking strength of around 40 per cent alcohol is achieved by diluting the distillate, usually with distilled water, but some firms mix the distilled water with a little very old cognac.

Not all the wine of the Cognac region passes through the stills. Partly in order to soak up the surplus of grapes, the wines of the Charente have been given vin de pays status. One more interesting drink is Pineau des Charentes, a mixture of unfermented grape juice and brandy, which must spend a year in wood and reach between 16 and 22 per cent alcohol. It is pleasant chilled as an apéritif.

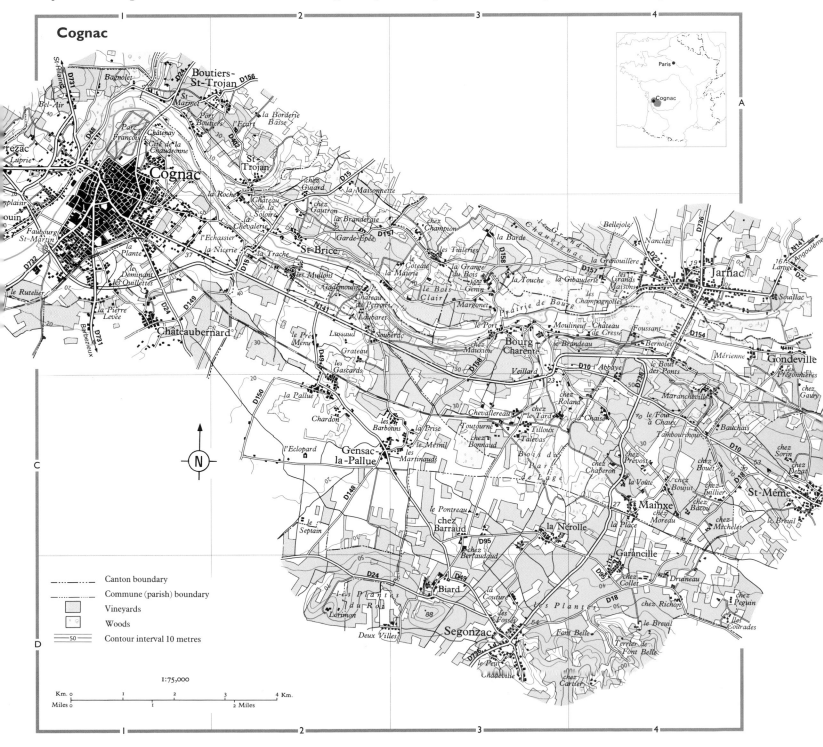

Cognac

Canton boundary
Commune (parish) boundary
Vineyards
Woods
Contour interval 10 metres

1:75,000

PRODUCERS OF SPECIAL INTEREST

COGNAC

Camus 16101 Cognac
Still in family hands, the firm was founded in 1862 as La Grande Marque – a name it still uses – a consortium of growers headed by Jean-Baptiste Camus. Its present status is due to the former chairman, Michel Camus, who rescued the firm in the 1960s by concentrating on duty-free sales in the Far East. Its best cognac is the Château de Plessis, made at the family's property in the Borderies.

Courvoisier 16200 Jarnac
An important firm now owned by the British group Allied-Domecq, which used to rely heavily on the image of Napoleon. Courvoisier's brandies have always been full and rich. It has recently reblended its XO. The new bottle is elegant and the contents round and well balanced.

Croizet BP3 16720 St-Même-lès-Carrières
Old-fashioned family firm with a good reputation for the brandies from the family vineyards. Its stock controls were so good that it was one of the first firms to be allowed to sell cognacs of individual vintages, many of which are old and delicious.

Delamain 16200 Jarnac
Both the firm and its cognacs are unique. Its brandies, notably the Pale & Dry, the firm's standard-bearer, are classically elegant, almost ethereal, exclusively from the Grande Champagne and designed to appeal to the taste of British aristocratic connoisseurs.

AE Dor 16200 Jarnac
A small family firm which specialises in selling some of the fine, very ancient cognacs acquired by the family in the past – some in the 19th century.

Frapin 16130 Segonzac
The biggest of the few firms based in Segonzac, the 'capital' of the Grande Champagne. The Frapins have been growing grapes in the region for 700 years and their direct descendants, the Cointreau family, now sell a range of fine cognacs from their estates including the elegant Château de Fontpinot.

De Fussigny 16200 Jarnac
An enterprising new firm created by Alain Royer whose family owned Louis Royer (see below). He specialises in selling a series of old cognacs bought from growers in the best sub-regions. These are now firm favourites with major restaurants the world over.

Leopold Gourmel 16016 Cognac
A firm created recently by M Voisin to promote the fine, floral brandies made in the Fins Bois d'Archiac. The brandies are carefully distilled, blended and sold under names that indicate their age. The youngest is Age des Fruits, then comes the Age des Fleurs, Age des Épices and last the intense Quintessence.

Jas Hennessy 16101 Cognac
Founded by Irish émigré Richard Hennessy in 1765, this is now the biggest of all the cognac firms with the largest stock of old brandies. It is well known for the rich, round style of all its cognacs. Hennessy invented the XO quality and its present offering is a fine example of the type. The firm has recently opened the region's most elegant and ambitious museum.

Hine 16200 Jarnac
Hine, founded in 1791, has always been a traditional firm supplying fine elegant brandies largely to the British market. Though now a subsidiary of Hennessy, the brandy is still blended by Bernard Hine and it retains its own style, elegant but rather rounder than that of Delamain with which it is often compared. Its basic Signature is probably the best of all, and its better qualities, notably in its Fine Champagne Antique, live up to the firm's reputation. Also noted for the Early Landed single-vintage cognacs shipped to Britain to be matured in damp dock-side warehouses.

Martell 16101 Cognac
The oldest of the major cognac houses. It was founded in 1715 by Jean Martell, a smuggler from the Channel Islands who married twice, both times to members of old cognac dynasties. The firm's cognacs, especially its up-market Cordon Bleu, have always been noted for their nuttiness which is due to a high proportion of brandies from the Borderies. Now a subsidiary of the giant Canadian drinks firm, Seagram.

Ragnaud-Sabourin, Domaine de la Voûte Ambleville 16300 Barbezieux
For over half a century the family has been selling direct some of the finest cognacs, produced in the heart of Grande Champagne. The range is quite extensive, with the 35-year-old Fontvieille among the finest: rich and balanced, fruity with a touch of rancio. Connoisseurs wanting a taste of what cognacs were like before the onset of the phylloxera epidemic can find it in the family's Le Paradis.

Rémy-Martin 16100 Cognac
The most striking success story in the modern history of Cognac. The firm was founded in 1724 but was a virtual shell when it was taken over by André Renaud in 1924. Since then he and his son-in-law André Heriard-Dubreuil have built up an important firm based on a fine, elegant VSOP, the best of is type and a Fine Champagne (made purely from brandies from Grande and Petite Champagne).

Renault-Bisquit, Domaine de Lignières 16170 Rouillac
Two historic names now both owned by the apéritif firm of Pernod-Ricard and based at a high-tech new distillery in the Fins Bois, 32km north-east of Cognac. Renault sells only one cognac, the nicely rounded, rich, up-market Carte Noire Extra. Bisquit, founded in 1819, also has a tradition of rich and fruity brandies. Its VS is particularly successful.

Louis Royer 16200 Jarnac
Founded in the 19th century, Royer used to specialise in bulk cognacs. In the early 1980s Alain Royer produced some fine blends before leaving the family business to found de Fussigny. Royer has now been taken over by the Japanese giant Suntory which has introduced a full range of well balanced brandies.

WINE FÊTE

Cognac The Fête des Vendanges is held every year around harvest time.

WINE INFORMATION

The Confrérie du Franc Pineau was established in 1982 (Pineau des Charentes is an apéritif made from the juice of white or black grapes and cognac).
Several of the cognac houses are happy to show visitors around. Information concerning such visits can be obtained from the **Office de Tourisme** place J-Monnet 16101 Cognac.

HOTELS

The coast of the Charente-Maritime and the islands just off-shore attract many tourists in summer and are liberally provided with hotels and restaurants. There are also many inland places where it is pleasant to stay.

Les Relais Bleus 16100 Châteaubernard Tel (0)545 35 42 00 Modern comfort.
L'Auberge 13 rue Plumejeau 16100 **Cognac** Tel (0)545 32 08 70 Central yet calm. Fish specialities

Rural charm at Château de Bourg, home of the firm of Marnier Lapostelle.

include mouclade, soupe de poisson and the fabulous eel dish, lotte au poivre vert flambée au cognac.

Hôtel François Ier
3 place François Ier, 16100 **Cognac**
Tel (0)545 32 07 18
Centrally located.

Mapotel Le Valois
34 rue du 14-juillet, 16100 **Cognac**
Tel (0)545 82 76 00
Business-like comfort.

Les Bosquets route de Rochefort
17100 **Saintes** Tel (0)546 74 04 47
Set in the middle of woods. There is also a restaurant.

RESTAURANTS

Gastronomic specialities include oysters, especially those of Marennes and Oléron; mussels (try the mouclade); snails (called *cagouilles* here); asparagus, and the region's delicious butter.

La Ribaudière
16200 **Bourg-Charente**
Tel (0)545 81 30 54
By the river, with a terrace. Excellent regional cuisine and a good wine-list.

Le Relais 17120 **Boutenac-Touvent**
Tel (0)546 94 13 06
Traditional decor and cuisine.

Le Coq d'Or 33 place François Ier
16100 **Cognac** Tel (0)545 82 02 56
Excellent for oysters.

La Halle aux Vins
7 place François Ier, 16100 **Cognac**
Tel (0)545 32 07 51
Honest country dishes such as mouclade and choucroute, and regional wines.

Les Pigeons Blancs 10 rue Jules-Brisson, 16100 **Cognac**
Tel (0)545 82 16 36
Good cooking based on produce fresh from the market. Try the foie gras de canard au Pineau and sole aux essences de Cognac. Also a hotel.

Restaurant du Château
16200 **Jarnac** Tel (0)545 81 07 17
Serves regional dishes including snails (*cagouilles*).

Grottes de Matata
17120 **Meschers-sur-Gironde**
Tel (0)546 02 70 02
In one of the local caves (see Places of Interest), with a large terrace. Try the oyster or fresh fish dishes.

Auberge Pontoise 17800 **Pons**
Tel (0)546 94 00 99
Plenty of atmosphere. Oysters (huîtres chaudes au beurre rouge) and duck (magret de canard) are among the specialities. Also a hotel.

l'Auberge 17350 **St-Savinien**
Tel (0)546 90 20 33
Mainly regionally based cooking.

Mancini rue des Messagiers
17100 **Saintes** Tel (0)546 93 06 61
Famous establishment with good cuisine (including canard aux pêches

fraîches). The hotel is more rural than its central situation implies.

Le Relais du Bois St-Georges
rue de Royan, Cours Genêt
17100 **Saintes**
Tel (0)546 93 50 99
Inventive menu and a country atmosphere. Also a luxury hotel, 1km from the autoroute with an indoor pool, a large park and a lake.

Le Soubise 17780 **Soubise**
Tel (0)546 84 93 36
Excellent restaurant with hotel.

PLACES OF INTEREST

Aulnay Superb 12th-century church with a wealth of sculpture.

Bourg-Charente Romanesque church and the Château de Bourg.

Brouage A former harbour built by the military architect Vauban, with 17th-century walls and seven bastions.

Châteauneuf-sur-Charente
The bell tower of Bassac abbey is a regional landmark. The abbey itself was founded in 1002 but rebuilt in later centuries.

Cognac Many of the well known cognac houses have their warehouses here. The black fungus on the roofs and walls arises from the evaporation of cognac, stored here in casks by the thousand: the fungus lives on the fumes. The most famous building of the locality is the Château des Valois, also known as Château de Cognac, where King Francis I was born in 1492. The château belongs to the cognac firm of Otard. Visitors can see a vaulted prison chamber (with inscriptions made by British prisoners of war at the end of the 18th century) and there is also a *son et lumière* display. Near the château stands the Porte St-Jacques with its two thick round towers, where pilgrims to Santiago de Compostela used to lodge. The part 12th-century church of St-Léger has a painting from 1629 by Jacques Blanchard, and the Musée de Cognac has a wine press that dates back to 1760. Rest and shade can be found in the large François Ier park by the river on the northern outskirts of the town.

Crazannes The present Château de Crazannes dates from the 15th century but it stands on the site of an 11th-century structure whose chapel remains.

Le Douhet The bishops of Saintes built the rather austere château here. Beneath it is an 11th-century hall.

Fenioux Next to the partly Romanesque church is the imposing Lanterne des Morts, a funerary tower that can be climbed from inside by a spiral stairway.

Jonzac A 12th- and 13th-century castle (three French kings stayed there at various times).

Top-quality oak casks are imperative in the production of good cognac. Several large firms have private cooperages – Hennessy even has its own oak forest.

Marennes Famous for its oysters (there is a diorama of oyster culture).

Meschers-sur-Gironde Prehistoric caves; there is a pleasant restaurant in one of them (see Restaurants).

Pons Medieval town built for defensive purposes on a hill. Exhibitions are held in the enormous castle keep which was built in 1187.

Port d'Envaux The Château de Pauloy is an excellent example of Louis XV architecture; it also includes parts of an older castle. It has a fine dining hall and a dovecote that dates from 1620.

Rochefort-sur-Mer A former naval town, now a resort. The house of the writer Pierre Loti is its most remarkable sight; among other things it has a Turkish salon. The old rope-yard beside the harbour is now a museum. Rochefort also has a maritime museum with beautiful models of ships, and a Musée des Beaux-Arts.

Royan Devastated in World War II; now a harbour and holiday resort with the remarkable 20th-century church of Notre-Dame.

St-Cybardeau 'Les Bouchauds' is a Gallo-Roman theatre from the 1st century AD which can seat nearly 10,000 people.

St-Fort-le-Né Beside the D44 is one of the region's stone dolmens.

St-Jean-d'Angély A former halt for pilgrims, with half-timbered houses of the 15th and 16th centuries.

St-Porchaire Just north of this village is Château de la Roche Courbon, which the writer Pierre Loti (see Rochefort-sur-Mer above) called 'Sleeping Beauty's castle'. The 15th-century château contains furniture and paintings and is surrounded by a charming garden. Prehistoric caves nearby can be visited.

Saintes Contains good examples of Roman and Romanesque art. The Germanicus arch (by the Charente) was built by the Romans, and the Roman arena could hold 20,000 people. The Romanesque church of Ste-Eutrope has a large crypt; the Abbaye aux Dames with its church of Ste-Marie is partly 12th, partly 16th century. Saintes also has museums of archaeology, art and regional history.

The South-West

Inland from Bordeaux stretches the great river basin, Aquitaine as it was once called, 'the land of waters'. It was down these rivers and not by the sea that the Romans came to Bordeaux. Wine was being made in Gaillac while the savages of Bordeaux were still brewing home-made beer.

The vineyards of the South-West are some of the oldest and most varied in France. Leaving Bordeaux, the traveller comes to the satellites – Bergerac, Duras, Marmande – so-called because they use the same grapes as, and their vineyards adjoin those of, Bordeaux. The further inland you go, the hillier the countryside becomes, and each wine area uses grapes specific to itself to give the wines their individual character. In Cahors it is Malbec, in the far South-West Tannat, in Marcillac Fer-Servadou and in Fronton Négrette none of which features elsewhere in significant quantities. Jurançon and Gaillac are made from grapes unheard of in Graves or Sauternes.

The vineyard landscape varies as much as the grapes. Cahors is made mostly in the Lot Valley, which is wide enough to sustain a varied agriculture, but also on the higher stony ground through which the river has eroded its sinuous course. Marcillac is made in a precipitous gorge where soil and wine are as purple as the sunset; Gaillac on rolling down-land, Jurançon and Irouléguy on almost vertical terraces against a backdrop of the high Pyrenees and picture-postcard skies of cobalt blue.

The winemakers are as individual as their wines, but travellers are greeted warmly everywhere. Production often polarises between the giant – usually excellent – cooperatives and the small independent growers. Large private estates are the exceptions rather than the rule. Some of the best wines are produced by families for whom winemaking has been a way of life rather than a business for centuries. The younger generation will almost certainly have trained as oenologists but for them, sometimes even more than for their parents, passion is still the key word. The proof of it is in the glass. 'Le Grand Sud-Oest' offers the wine explorer a different experience; one which will leave him or her wondering why these wines are not more readily available at home.

Part of the charm of the Dordogne countryside lies in its great variety: gently undulating landscape of orchards and fields is punctuated by dramatic swathes of dark forests, steep ravines and swift-flowing rivers.

The South-West

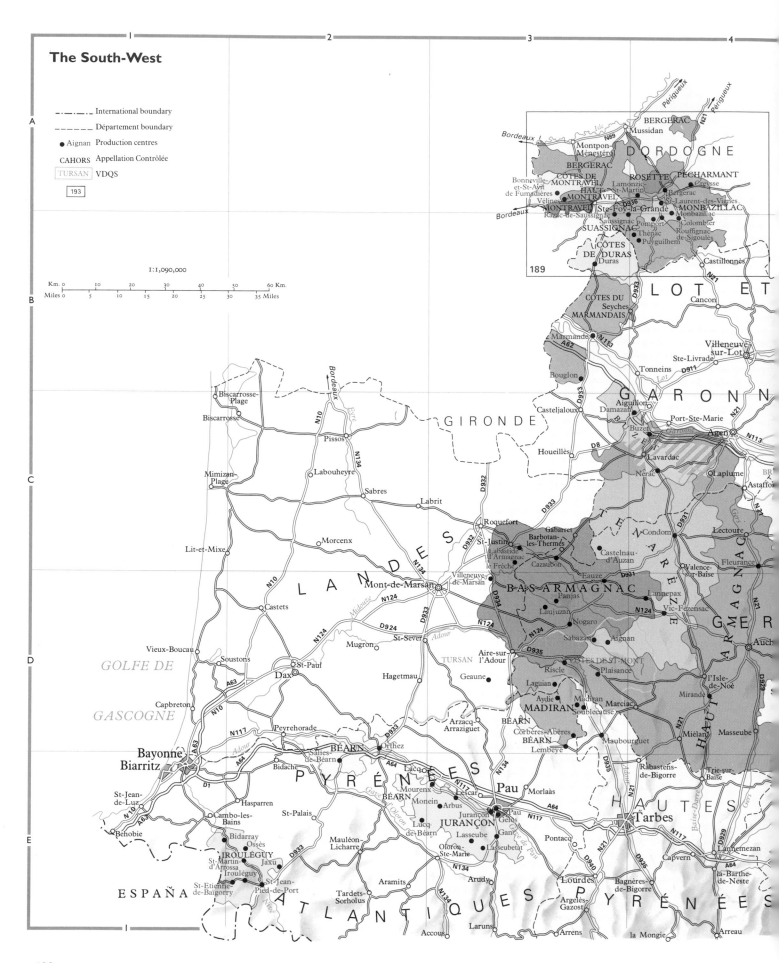

International boundary

Département boundary

● Aignan   Production centres

CAHORS   Appellation Contrôlée

TURSAN   VDQS

193

1:1,090,000

Km. 0   10   20   30   40   50   60 Km.

Miles 0   5   10   15   20   25   30   35 Miles

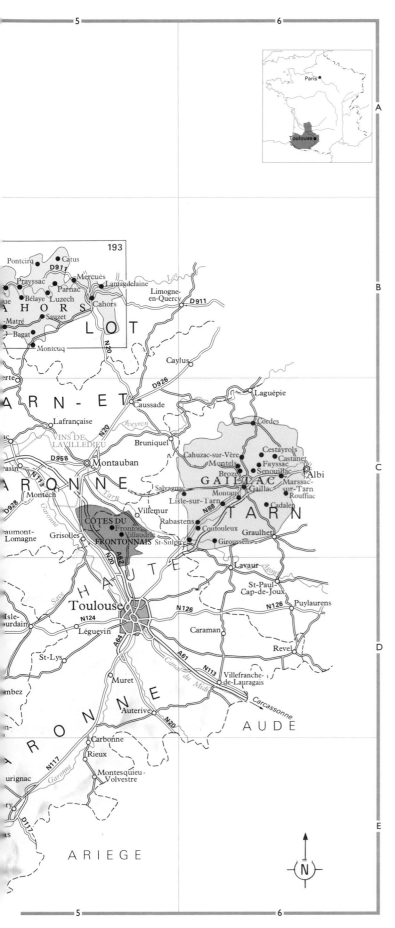

Bergerac

The Dordogne might have been expressly designed to attract visitors. It is rich in prehistory and well endowed with impressive châteaux, old fortified villages and medieval strongholds as well as having a dramatic variety of attractive landscape. Little wonder that the area – often called Périgord after the former provincial name – draws crowds of tourists every year.

Wine-growing is concentrated around the town of Bergerac in the south of the *département*. There has always been fierce competition with Bordeaux: for centuries Bordeaux' merchants tried to exclude the wines of the 'hinterland', but the wines of Bergerac were still exported in large quantities. In the 17th and 18th centuries Holland was the biggest market, taking about half of every vintage. The wines were then mainly white and sweet, a style that declined markedly in popularity after World War II. Many growers turned increasingly to red wine, which now represents nearly two thirds of production. The grapes used are those of Bordeaux: the two Cabernets, Merlot and sometimes Malbec. Most of the wines are lighter than the average claret but some better growers make more full-bodied examples which can also have depth and finesse and an affinity with those of St-Émilion. The best reds come from the small district of Pécharmant just north-east of Bergerac, but there are many other good examples. Those called Côtes de Bergerac are usually better than Bergerac *tout simple*.

Among the dry white wines, those made solely from Sauvignon grapes are fashionable, cheap Bordeaux look-alikes. White Bergerac is made mainly from Sémillon, Sauvignon and Muscadelle. Production of semi sweet white wines, once in sharp decline, shows signs of revival. There are six appellations: Bergerac Sec, Côtes de Bergerac, Saussignac, Côtes de Montravel, Haut-Montravel and Rosette (which once almost disappeared).

Dominating the sweet white wines is Monbazillac, the district due south of Bergerac. There is also a village of that name, which apparently derived from Mont Bazailhac, 'Mountain of Fire' or 'Mountain of Gold'. Vineyards had already been planted here in the 11th century and by the 16th the wine's fame reached as far as Rome. Later, French ambassadors served Monbazillac as a 'wine of peace', and Talleyrand introduced it at the Congress of Vienna.

Despite its almost legendary reputation, the demand for Monbazillac declined so dramatically after World War II that the appellation was almost lost. Only through measures taken in the 1970s, including the limitation of production per hectare, was the quality rescued. The local cooperative, which is now responsible for the wine of Château de Monbazillac, played a key role in this revival. There are now 130 or so independent producers and the wine is enjoying something of a vogue.

A good Monbazillac is akin to Sauternes. The grape varieties are the same: mainly Sémillon with a little Sauvignon and Muscadelle, and harvesting is left as late as possible to take advantage of overripeness and noble rot. In luxury, sweetness and concentration Monbazillac can rival all but the best Sauternes; though the *rôti* aroma so characteristic of the latter is less distinct. There is a more refined and elegant style in some, which are therefore not rich enough to accompany sweet desserts. On the other hand all Monbazillacs taste delicious with foie gras, with fish or poultry served with a sweet sauce, with nuts, with not-too-sweet cake or simply chilled as an apéritif. They also often have a formidable capacity to mature in bottle. A wine from the fabulous 1811 vintage was served over a century later to an admiring French president.

PRODUCERS OF SPECIAL INTEREST

RED WINES: PÉCHARMANT

Domaine de Bertranoux
24100 Creysse
Château de Biran
24100 St-Sauveur de Bergerac
Château Champarel Pécharmant
24100 Bergerac
Domaine du Haut-Pécharmant
24100 Bergerac
At 23ha, the second-largest Pécharmant vineyard. Owner Michel Roches is keen to experiment and engages high-flying winemaker Daniel Hecquet as consultant. Try his Cuvée Veuve Roches, (70% Cabernet Franc).
La Métairie 24100 Bergerac
Vinification of up to four weeks is followed by ageing in one-year-old oak. By common consent one of the best Pécharmants.
Château de Tiregand
24100 Creysse
La Comtesse de St-Exupéry is the owner of this, the biggest and most handsome property in Pécharmant. Wine from new vines (called Clos de la Montalbanie) is much lighter.

BASIC RED BERGERAC

Château Court-lès-Mûts
Razac-de-Saussignac, 24240 Sigoulès
A specialist in sweet white Saussignac, Pierre-Jean Sadoux also produces one of the best of all Bergerac reds. Unwooded, straightforward and a worthy multi-medal-winner.
Domaine de Gouyat
24610 St-Méard-de-Gurçon
In the north-west corner of the Bergerac area the Dubard family produces a first-class red as well as dry and *moelleux* Montravel and an oaked red called Château Laulerie.
Château Grinou 24240 Monestier
Guy Cuisset is another all-rounder

making good red Bergerac as well as both dry and medium-sweet white.
Château de la Mallavieille
24120 Montfaucon
Château Le Raz
24610 St-Méard-de-Gurçon

WHITE WINES: MONBAZILLAC

Domaine de l'Ancienne Cure
24560 Colombier
Château de Bélingard-Chayne
24240 Pomport
Beautiful vineyard; wines to match.
Château la Borderie Monbazillac
24240 Sigoulès
Also owner of nearby Château Treil-de-Nailhac. Both are Monbazillacs of the highest quality, aged for as long as four years in huge old vats. Treil-de-Nailhac has a distinct Muscat taste due to the high proportion of Muscadelle.
Clos Fontindoule
24240 Monbazillac
Gilles Cros, the archetypical old-style vigneron, is making some of the most astonishing wines of the area, matured in huge old barrels and not bottled for at least six years – often longer.
Château le Fagé Pomport
24240 Sigoulès
François Gérardin is an all-rounder but his Monbazillac, from a high 90% Sémillon, attracts the plaudits.
Château Haut-Bernasse
24240 Monbazillac
Cello-playing vigneron of highest quality.
Château le Mayne 24240 Sigoulès
Château Poulvère Monbazillac
24240 Sigoulès
Most of the wines are marketed as Domaine des Barses, the name Poulvère being reserved for the flagship Monbazillac. The family also owns Château de la Haute-Brie-et-du-Caillou, the two properties together covering over 80ha. The house style is elegance rather than lusciousness.

Château de Theulet
24240 Monbazillac
Pierre Alard's Monbazillac is old-fashioned and very rich but its sweetness is redeemed by a lovely twist of acidity.
Domaine la Truffière-Tirecul
24240 Monbazillac

SAUSSIGNAC

Château Court-Les-Mûts
Razac-de-Saussignac, 24240 Sigoulès
Château les Miaudoux
24240 Saussignac
Gérard Cuisset is one of the pioneers of the new-style ultra-sweet Saussignac whites. Pressed direct into new wood, the wines are every bit as good as the best Monbazillacs.
Domaine de Richard
La Croix-Blanche, 24240 Monestier
Englishman Richard Doughty, like Cuisset, is experimenting with a similar style of Saussignac. He also relies on his dry white Bergerac for a living but his heart is in making the sweet wine.

MONTRAVEL

Château Calabre and **Château Puy-Servain** 33320 Port Ste-Foy-et-Ponchapt
Daniel Hecquet's own vineyards. Calabre wines are made without the benefit of wood while Puy-Servain is oaked. The Haut-Montravel sweet wines reflect the current styles in Monbazillac and Saussignac. Expertly made and long-lived.
Domaine de Krével
33320 Port, Ste-Foy-et-Ponchapt
This new vineyard, which has Pécharmant-owner Kreusch as part-proprietor, is making fashionable oaked wines from 90% Sauvignon and 10% Muscadelle.
Domaine de Libarde
24230 Nastringues
A fascinating example of the sweet Haut-Montravel style from one of its leading exponents. Jean-Claude Banizette was president of the Montravel Syndicat of growers for four years.
Château de Montaigne
24230 St-Michel-de-Montaigne
White *moelleux* is the speciality here in what was once the home of the famous French essayist.
Château Pique Sègue
33220 Ponchapt
Château la Raye 24230 Vélines
Château la Ressaudie
33220 Port, Ste-Foy-et-Ponchapt

ROSETTE

Clos Romain
Les Côtes, 24100 Bergerac
One of only six growers declaring under this appellation, Mme Bourgès makes a distinctive half-sweet wine with fruit and body. It is splendid as an apéritif or with mushroom dishes.

Domaine de Puypézat Rosette
24100 Bergerac

BASIC DRY WHITE BERGERAC

Château du Bloy Bonneville
24230 Vélines
A Montravel property which sometimes markets its wine under that name, sometimes as plain Bergerac. The pure Sauvignon wine is the one to go for here, bottled and marketed young.
Domaine de Constant
24680 Lamonzie-St-Martin
Domaine de la Jaubertie
Colombier, 24560 Issigeac
Flying winemaker Hugh Ryman has taken over this important property, best known for its dry white Bergerac, from his father Henry. Techniques learned in Australia enable him to produce a crisp 100%-Sauvignon wine.
Château de Panisseau
24240 Thénac
La Tour des Gendres
24240 Ribagnac
Owned by Luc de Conti. Stylish and unusual dry wine from 100% Sémillon which is bottled on its lees to give it extra character and has a distinct flavour of citrus fruits.

WINE INFORMATION

Bergerac's **Maison du Vin** [tel (0)553 63 57 57], facing the small harbour, merits a visit for the information you can obtain and the wines you can sample, but also for its location in the Cloître des Récollets, a 17th- and 18th-century monastery in the heart of the old town. The cloisters enclose a magnificent flowering paulownia tree.
In the wine districts there is a signposted **Route des Vins.**

HOTELS

Hôtel de Bordeaux 24100 **Bergerac** Tel (0)553 57 12 83
Family-run provincial hotel. In fine weather you can eat in the garden or on the terrace.
Hôtel La Flambée 24100 **Bergerac** Tel (0)553 57 52 33
Comfortable country hotel with a large park, a swimming pool and restaurant.
Hôtel du Château 24150 **Lalinde** Tel (0)553 61 01 82
A small château by the river, with a terrace. Regional cuisine. Demi-pension is obligatory in season. The Beatles once stayed here.
Relais de Saussignac 24240 **Saussignac** Tel (0)553 27 92 40
Friendly village hotel surrounded by vineyards. Adequate, if sometimes slightly noisy, rooms and strictly regional cuisine. Simple restaurant.

Showpiece Château de Monbazillac is now owned by the local cooperative.

RESTAURANTS

The Dordogne's two supreme specialities, foie gras and truffles, feature on many menus; goose and duck are widely used. The district is also famous for its walnuts which are used for making superb oil and liqueurs, and – more recently – for its strawberries.

Le Cyrano 24100 Bergerac
Tel (0)553 57 02 76
Bergerac's best restaurant with distinctive regional cuisine. There is usually a choice of three menus and a good selection of local wines.
Château de Monbazillac 24240 Monbazillac Tel (0)553 58 38 93
Visitors to the château can eat in the restaurant here, which serves sustaining regional dishes.

PLACES OF INTEREST

Bergerac Bustling provincial town with an atmospheric old centre where there is a museum of wine and inland waterways, an interesting tobacco museum (with a local history department) and a museum of religious art. The town hall is a former convent dating from the 18th century.
Les Eyzies-de-Tayac A visit to this village makes a most interesting day-trip: there are world-famous prehistoric caves and also the French national museum of prehistory. If you follow the little River Vézère northward for 25km you reach Montignac where there is a replica of the Lascaux cave with its renowned animal paintings (Lascaux itself is closed for reasons of conservation).
Malfourat South of Bergerac and the highest point of the locality with a superb view of the surrounding countryside. A restored windmill allows you to climb still higher.
Monbazillac The château is the region's showpiece, a handsome 16th-century fortress that now functions as a museum. Château de Monbazillac wine is on sale at the entrance: it is a good idea to buy it here for it is sold almost nowhere else.
St-Michel-de-Montaigne The essayist Montaigne was born at Château Michel-de-Montaigne in 1533. The Tour de la Librairie where he wrote is still intact but the rest of the château was destroyed by fire in 1885 and subsequently rebuilt. It is owned by the Mähler-Besse *négociant* family of Bordeaux, co-owners of Château Palmer. Wine is still made at the château.
Saussignac This wine village's château, a vast building surrounded by 200-year-old cedars, is best viewed from the west side. It is in the process of being restored.

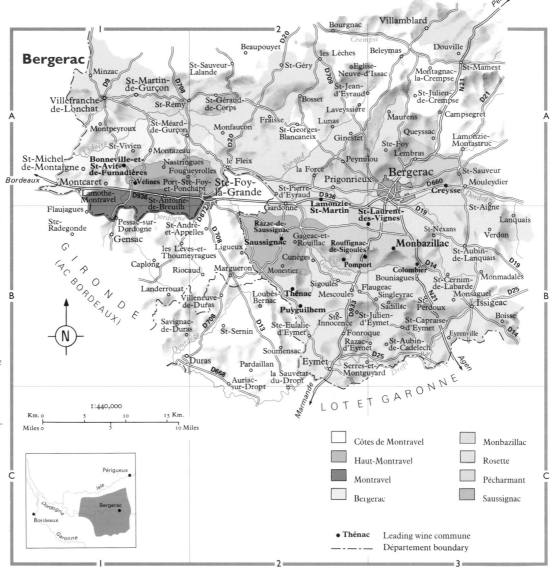

1:440,000

Km. 0   5   10   15 Km.
Miles 0   5   10 Miles

	Côtes de Montravel		Monbazillac
	Haut-Montravel		Rosette
	Montravel		Pécharmant
	Bergerac		Saussignac

● **Thénac**   Leading wine commune
– ⋅ – ⋅ –   Département boundary

The reindeer and other animals depicted on the walls of the Lascaux cave were painted around 20,000 years ago.

189

Lot-et-Garonne

The green landscape, mild climate and soft light of Lot-et-Garonne once put Stendhal in mind of Tuscany. There are indeed landscapes in the *département*, which largely corresponds with ancient Agenais, that are reminiscent of Italy. The scenery is varied: in the east it is hilly, a large part of the west is woodland and in between is the broad flat valley of the Garonne, fed by its many tributaries including the Lot. These streams, flowing down from the Massif Central, have brought a good deal of fertile soil to Lot-et-Garonne, rendering it ideal for the cultivation of fruit and vegetables.

Because the Garonne Valley forms the most convenient corridor, the region has always been an important link between the Atlantic and the Mediterranean. It has a rich history and boasts many old towns and villages, castles and churches. The recent history of its wine, however, is brief. Only since the 1970s have four districts acquired a modest renown. From north to south they are the Côtes de Duras, Côtes du Marmandais, Buzet and the Côtes du Brulhois.

The Côtes de Duras takes its name from the little hill town of Duras which is just short of the Gironde *département* boundary – and the Bordeaux appellation. Its wines show a strong resemblance to those of Bordeaux, the more so since the same grape varieties are used. The most interesting Côtes de Duras is the white wine made from Sauvignon. This can be fresh and fragrant and have sound balance. Today there are two cooperatives and about 50 private growers. The cooperatives also make a fruity, supple style of red for drinking earlier than the average Bordeaux.

The town of Marmande is about 20 kilometres south of Duras on the Garonne, where wine grapes are grown on both sides of the broad valley. More than 95 per cent of production comes from the two cooperatives. The better, at Cocumont, uses modern equipment and experiments continuously with new grape varieties. Almost all Côtes du Marmandais wine is red and until recently it has mostly been a fairly light, reasonably supple wine. Now that the rules of its production require the use of more local grapes, however, it is developing rather more personality.

At Buzet (formerly the Côtes de Buzet) a single cooperative processes some 95 per cent of the harvest from the scattered vineyards and uses modern winemaking methods before maturing the red wine in oak in the traditional way. The casks – more than 5,000 – are made by the cooperative's own cooper. Buzet's red wine is closely related to that of Bordeaux but is rather more accessible and has a little less finesse. Thanks to the sound quality and very reasonable prices of its wine, the area of vineyard in this extensive district of 27 communes has been able to increase steadily, and continued growth is forecast. The vineyards intermingle with those of Armagnac; much of the appellation is also in the Haut-Armagnac zone and a portion overlaps with one of the other Armagnac districts, Ténarèze.

The standard of the wine has also been improving, particularly since the cooperative has been vinifying wines from some of the member châteaux separately, according to grape variety. Château de Gueyze is usually very successful. The top wine is Baron d'Ardeuil (formerly Cuvée Napoléon) made with selected grapes from the best vineyards in the district. There are about eight good private growers, worth searching out because their wines have a distinct local character rather than being imitations of Bordeaux.

As at Buzet, the Côtes du Brulhois lie on the south bank of the Garonne, this time around the valley of Gers and not far from Agen. Part of the district is in the adjoining *département* of Tarn et Garonne. There is a cooperative for each *département*, and they share virtually the whole production. The mainly red wines of the Côtes du Brulhois, where there are no private producers, are more rustic in character than the others of the *département*.

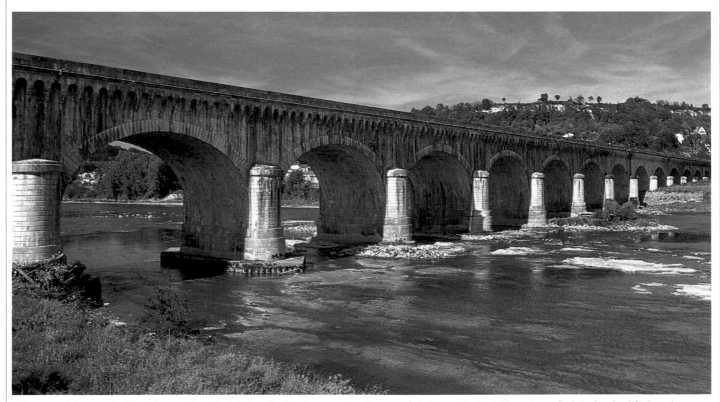

The town of Agen on the River Coronne flourished during the Renaissance, attracting many scholars to the 11–12th-century collegiate church of St-Caprais.

PRODUCERS OF SPECIAL INTEREST

Few tourists go to see the smaller wine-growers of Lot-et-Garonne, so visitors are usually very welcome. The cooperatives are also pleased to have you taste their wines and you can also buy bottles directly from them.

CÔTES DE DURAS

Domaine Amblard
47120 St-Sernin
Guy Pauvert's 65-ha vineyard is the largest in Duras. His dry white, based on Sauvignon, is sometimes found under the name of Domaine la Croix-Haute.

Château Bellevue-Haut-Roc
47120 Esclottes

Domaine de Durand
47120 St-Jean de Duras
There are still some 100-year-old Sémillon vines in Michel Fonvielhe's centuries-old vineyard. His are serious wines made for keeping.

Domaine de Ferrant
47120 Esclottes

Château la Grave-Béchade
47120 Baleyssagues
Daniel Amar's comfortable *gentilhommière* is the only wine-making property in the region aspiring to the status of a real château. Using ultra-modern technology, his winemaker Daniel Bensoussan produces wines worthy of *bourgeois château* status in Bordeaux terms.

Château Lafon
47120 Loubès-Bernac
The hobby-vineyard of Sancerre-grower Pascal Gitton.

Domaine de Laulan 47120 Duras
Gilbert Geoffroy is a native of Chablis: appropriately his white wines are outstanding. Made entirely from Sauvignon, they come with and without oak and are among the region's best.

Château la Moulière
47120 Duras
The brothers Blancheton take particular pride in their vin doux which is wonderful with foie gras – and nearly as expensive. Their shop in Duras stocks their full range.

Domaine du Vieux Bourg
47120 Pardaillan

CÔTES DU MARMANDAIS

Château de Beaulieu
47250 Cocumont

Cave Coopérative de Cocumont
47250 Cocumont
The latest state-of-the-art technology means that vinification is achieved electronically and by remote control. The mainstream red wine called Tradition is excellent in its class.

Les Vignerons de Beaupuy
47200 Beaupuy
Right-bank wines are said to age more slowly than left-bank wines, so this cooperative ages some of its lines in new wood. About 40% of the production is of Vins de Pays d'Agenais or vins de table.

Vignobles Boissonneau (Domaine des Géais)
33190 St-Michel-de-Lapujade
The owners take as much trouble over their Marmande wines as they do over their Bordeaux from vineyards just over the border in Entre-Deux-Mers.

BUZET

Château du Frandat 47600 Nérac
Domaine du Pech
47310 Ste-Colombe-en-Brulhois
Château Sauvagnères
47310 Ste-Colombe-en-Brulhois
Domaine de Tourné
47600 Calignac
Domaine de Versailles
47600 Montagnac-sur-Auvignon
Les Vignerons Réunis Buzet-sur-Baise, 47160 Damazan
A model cooperative with its own cooper. The red wines are aged in the home-made barrels. New wood is used for the top range called Baron d'Ardeuil and then passed on to the second-in-line Carte d'Or, finally to the least expensive range called Tradition. The cooperative also makes wines for individual properties, the best being Château de Gueyze. The Cave makes no secret of its aim to establish a monopoly, which is a pity because the private growers listed above are just a selection of those making wines that have more local character.

CÔTES DU BRULHOIS

Château la Bastide
47270 Clermont-Soubiran
Mme Orliac supplies many restaurants in the region.

Cave Coopérative de Donzac
82340 Auvillar

Cave Coopérative de Goulens-en-Brulhois 47390 Donzac

Domaine de Coujétou-Peyret
82340 Donzac
The Hébrard family make an excellent vin de pays as well as their more pedigree VDQS wines, which have surprising body and rustic character.

WINE ACTIVITIES

Buzet Centre for the energetic Confrérie du Vin de Buzet.
Duras There is usually a Foire aux Vins in the second half of July.

HOTELS

Résidence des Jacobins
47000 Agen Tel (0)553 47 03 31
Despite its central position, a quiet hotel with atmosphere.

Château de Gueyze is isolated and barely inhabited, but the estate's 80 hectares in rolling countryside in the Côtes produce Buzet's best single-domaine wine.

Hostellerie des Ducs
47120 Duras
Tel (0)553 83 74 58
Comfortable, with a good restaurant.

Auberge de Guyenne
47200 Marmande
Tel (0)553 64 01 77
Peaceful hotel with restaurant.

Le Capricorne
47200 Marmande
Tel (0)553 64 16 14
Modern-style hotel and restaurant with garden and pool.

Moulin de la Belle Gascogne
47170 Poudenas
Tel (0)553 65 71 58
Delightful converted mill with only six rooms. Ideal for recovering from Mme Gracia's Gascon generosity. Luxury hotel; good restaurant.

L'Aubergade 47270 Puymirol
Tel (0)553 95 31 46
One of the best tables in France with accommodation to match, in a medieval village just outside Agen.

RESTAURANTS

Marmande is renowned for its tomatoes but asparagus, peaches, plums, melons and other fruit and vegetables are also grown. Agen is famed for its prunes which, like its fresh plums, appear in many dishes.

Les Cygnes 47190 Aiguillon
Tel (0)553 79 60 02
Attractive place to stay and to dine, with a garden and terrace.

La Corne d'Or
47450 Colayrac St-Cirq
Tel (0)553 47 02 76
A few km west of Agen, by the Garonne. Classical and contemporary cuisine. Also a hotel.

Auberge du Château
47120 Duras
Tel (0)553 83 70 58
Simple, honest regional dishes. This establisment is also a hotel.

Auberge des Quatre Vents
47190 Lagarrigue (east of Aiguillon)
Tel (0)553 79 62 18
Situated high above the hamlet, with a fine view. Large terrace. Try the salads; also agreeable local wines.

La Chaumière d'Albert
47230 Lavardac
Tel (0)553 65 51 75
Generous helpings of regional dishes at reasonable prices. Large garden and a terrace.

Auberge du Moulin d'Ané
47200 Virazeil Tel (0)553 20 18 25
In an old mill; serves grills as well as more sophisticated dishes. The village is just east of Marmande.

PLACES OF INTEREST

Agen The Quartier des Cornières, the old district by the cathedral of St-Capras, is picturesque and full of atmosphere. The Musée Municipale des Beaux Arts has paintings by Goya and a Greek marble Venus.
Duras The local château dates from the 14th century and is now a museum housing many wine exhibits.
Le Mas d'Agenais Village of Roman origin. In the 12th-century church (ask the priest for the key) there is an early Rembrandt, *The Crucifixion*. In front of the church are 16th century wooden market halls.
Nérac Well known small town south of Buzet whose Renaissance château, partly destroyed in 1793, now houses a museum. Beside the Garonne is the old quarter of Petit Nérac.

Cahors

The ancient town of Cahors, founded by the Gauls, occupies a spectacular site in a loop of the River Lot. Cahors used to be not only an important trading place but also one of Europe's banking centres, making loans in the 13th century to kings and even to the Pope. It also had a university for some 400 years, founded in 1332 by Pope John XII who was born in the town and had Cahors wine delivered to his palace at Avignon. By this time the district's winemaking tradition was already old: documents suggest that Cahors wine has been made since at least the 7th century.

For hundreds of years the wine enjoyed such an excellent reputation that King Francis I tried to imitate it at Fontainebleau using vines imported from the region. In the mid-19th century the Lot *département* – of which Cahors is the capital – had nearly 60,000 hectares of vineyards. After this a decline set in: plant diseases and economic problems caused an enormous reduction in both the quantity and quality of the wine, and all but a few growers gave up. Cahors wine nearly disappeared, although the vineyards continued to produce a good deal of ordinary wine.

Recovery did not begin until after World War II and was due largely to the energetic cooperative at Parnac. At first the cooperative, set up in 1947, could only check further decline, but the great frost of 1956 forced a change of direction. At the urging of the cooperative the devastated vineyards were largely replanted with the traditional Cahors grape Auxerrois (the local name for Malbec, also known, confusingly, as Cot). This variety thrives on the rugged limestone plateaux, the *causses*, found on either side of the Lot. The sand and gravel terraces of the Lot Valley are also excellent sites for the grape.

Investment in the new plantings brought a good return – there was a marked improvement in the quality of the wines and in 1971 Cahors was given its *appellation contrôlée*. The Parnac cooperative has ceded a deal of ground to the independent growers, who now number 200 compared with the score or so that existed here in 1971.

These growers, particularly those whose roots in Cahors are well established, make the best wines. A number of newcomers and wine traders have also cashed in on the renaissance, but they tend to produce wines of a more generalised character, less typical of Cahors and sometimes, short-sightedly, wines for early drinking. Classic Cahors is deep in colour, often almost opaque, and rich in flavour and tannin. It needs considerable ageing because the Auxerrois grape gives a basically austere, reserved wine. For this reason some growers add a proportion of Merlot to give roundness to their wines. The so-called 'Black Wine' is now a thing of the past, having disappeared after World War I.

PRODUCERS OF SPECIAL INTEREST

In Cahors, which is not overrun by tourists, the wine-growers are generally happy to welcome visitors.

Château la Caminade
46140 Parnac
Architecturally striking, this old Quercynois presbytery is now the home of high-class viticulture. The Resses family make an oaked premium wine called La Commendery and a lighter-style called Château Peyrouse, but their mainstream wine remains the most typical of Cahors.

Château du Cèdre 46700 Viré
Pascal and Jean-Marc Verhaeghe saw nearly all their 1995 crop destroyed by hail. They are among the most respected winemakers in the appellation. Long *cuvaisons* of up to four weeks.

Clos la Coutale 46700 Viré
The Bernède family have been making wine here since before the Revolution. Today it is noted for its round charm and is often successful in difficult years like '87 and '92. A small quantity of white vin de table called Clos Valmy is also made.

Clos Triguedina
46700 Puy-l'Evêque
This 40-ha estate dating back to 1830 makes wines that need some ageing. There is a special generously oaked *cuvée* called Prince Probus and a lighter wine for earlier drinking sold as Domaine Labrande.

Château La Coustarelle
46220 Prayssac
Domaine de Decas
46090 Trespoux-Rassiels
Château Eugénie 46140 Albas
Jean and Claude Couture make their premium wine (Réserve de l'Aïeul) exclusively from Auxerrois while their other two wines, Etiquette Noire and Cuvée des Tsars, have only a little Merlot and Tannat respectively. Traditional and high class.

and **Château de Cayrou**
46700 Puy-l'Evêque
The colourful Jean Jouffreau who died in 1996 will be hard to follow at these two properties, but his son-in-law, Yves Hermann-Jouffreau has the necessary talent. The 10-ha Gamot vineyard has been in the family since 1610 and is planted exclusively with Auxerrois. The Cayrou vineyard was bought in 1971 and is planted with a more modern mix of grapes including some Merlot and Tannat. Gamot can last as long as great claret; Cayrou is a little lighter in style, with considerable elegance.

Clos de Gamot 46220 Prayssac
Château de Gaudou
46700 Viré
Château de Haute-Serre
46230 Cieurac
Château les Ifs
46220 Pescadoires
The quality of the grapes harvested from the Buris' ground close to the river enable first-class wine to be made. Full and generous, with the typical flavour of almonds and damsons, the wines are good keepers.
Château Lacapelle-Cabanac
46700 Lacapelle-Cabanac

The central tower and lookout post of Pont Valentré, built over the Lot in 1308, is known as the Tour du Diable.

Château Lamartine
46700 Soturac

Château Latuc 46700 Mauroux
An English couple, Colin and Penelope Duns, have made an exciting start to their new careers as vignerons. Their '95 has enormous promise.

Le Manoir du Rouergou
46150 St-Médard-Catus

Château de Mercuès
46090 Mercuès

Château de Nozières 46700 Viré

Domaine de Paillas
46700 Floressas
M Descombes makes a *causses* wine that can be drunk younger than many others. His crop suffered badly in the 1995 hail but the wines, stylish and attractive rather than big and rustic, are sure to recover their former standing.

Domaine du Pech de Jammes
46090 Flaujac-Poujols
Owned by Americans Stephen and Sherry Schechter, this 10-ha vineyard produces the best of all the wines made by the *négociant* Georges Vigouroux. Marketed in anglophone countries by the owners, elsewhere by Vigouroux.

Domaine du Pic 46140 Douelle

Domaine Pineraie
46700 Puy-l'Evêque
Robert Burc is another lover of Auxerrois, which occupies 90% of his vineyard. The best wine comes from the ground which rises towards the *causses*. The wine from the lower ground is called Pierre Sèche.

Prieuré de Cénac 46140 Albas

Château la Reyne
46700 Puy-l'Evêque
This old established estate, whose private cellars like those of the Jouffreaus have bottles going back to the 19th century, is planted mostly to Auxerrois. Some of the vines are 80 years old. A section of the 20-ha vineyard is called Clos des Batuts.

Château St-Didier-Parnac
46140 Parnac

Domaine des Savarines
46090 Trespoux-Rassiels
Danielle Biesbrouck planted these 8ha in 1970 in the middle of nowhere up on the *causses* above Cahors town. She is able to reduce the *cuvaison* to 12 days, but in spite of this the wine has good tannins, is attractively perfumed and soft in texture.

Domaine du Souleillou
46140 Douelle

WINE FÊTE

Viré-sur-Lot The Fête des Vins de Cahors takes place at the end of July.

WINE INFORMATION

The region's fraternity is **La Confrérie du Vin de Cahors**.

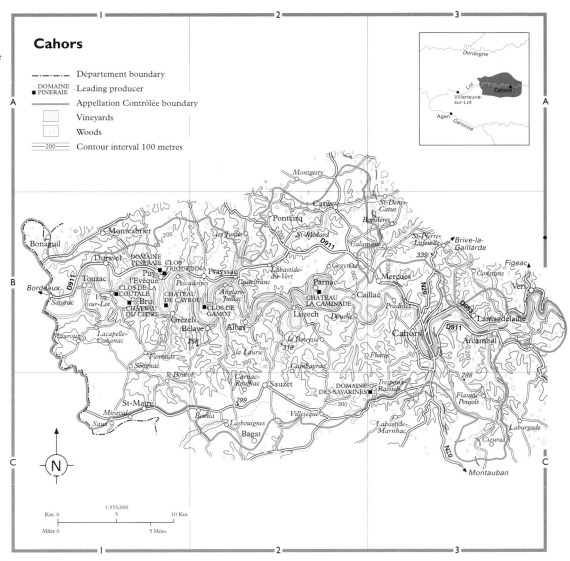

Cahors

- —·—·— Département boundary
- DOMAINE ■ PINERAIE · Leading producer
- ——— Appellation Contrôlée boundary
- ☐ Vineyards
- ☐ Woods
- ══200══ Contour interval 100 metres

1:333,000

HOTELS

La France 46000 Cahors
Tel (0)565 35 16 76
Somewhat colourless but comfortable modern hotel, not far from the station.

Terminus 46000 Cahors
Tel (0)565 35 24 50
Provincial hotel; the excellent restaurant is separate (see Le Balandre below).

Le Vert 46700 Mauroux
Tel (0)565 36 51 36
Rustic but comfortable, on the *causses* south of Puy-l'Evêque. Good food.

Château de Mercuès 46090
Mercuès Tel (0)565 20 00 01
A luxury château hotel high on a rock, with a park and swimming pool. An expensive establishment.

Hôtel Bellevue 46700 Puy-l'Evêque
Tel (0)565 21 30 70
A good view – as the name suggests – and dependable country cooking.

Moulin de la Source Bleue
46700 Touzac Tel (0)565 36 52 01
Attractively set in a 14th-century water-mill. Also a restaurant.

RESTAURANTS

Le Balandre 46000 Cahors
Tel (0)565 30 01 97
Connected to the Terminus hotel. The style is fin de siècle; that of the talented chef's cooking, contemporary.

La Taverne 46000 Cahors
Tel (0)565 35 28 66
Strictly regional: the truffe en croustade here is famous.

Marco 46090 Lamagdelaine
Tel (0)565 35 30 64
One of the region's best restaurants, in a remarkable vaulted dining hall. An excellent selection of wines.

Le Gindreau 46150 St-Médard
Tel (0)565 36 22 27
A serious restaurant 15km from Cahors. A speciality is foie gras de canard chaud aux cèpes. The sommelier is expertly informed about the outstanding list of Cahors wines.

PLACES OF INTEREST

Cabrerets This village (about 30km east of Cahors) lies outside the actual wine district, but it has the prehistoric Pech-Merle cave in which human hand-prints as well as wall paintings of animals can be seen.

Cahors The town is full of history and splendid old buildings – ask at the Office de Tourisme (12 boulevard Clemenceau) for a plan of the town showing the main points of interest. There is also a pleasant walk up to the viewpoint on Mont St-Cyr, the hill directly to the south of Cahors. A market for the region's famous truffles and foie gras is held here on Saturdays from the beginning of November to the end of March.

Château de Bonaguil A stronghold of enormous dimensions – one of the largest in France. The partly ruined structure dates from the 13th century.

Lalbenque The weekly truffle market, held here at 2.30pm every Tuesday in season, is world famous.

Puy-l'Evêque An important wine community, formerly a fortified town: the central tower gives a view over the surrounding district and the old houses in the centre.

Gaillac

To the west of the lovely cathedral town of Albi, the capital of the Tarn *département*, lies Gaillac, one of the largest and most productive wine districts of south-west France. It embraces at least 73 communes, and vines have probably been grown here for almost 20 centuries.

The district takes its name from the little town on the right bank of the River Tarn where Benedictine monks became established in the 10th century. As elsewhere in France, viticulture flourished under their care. Gaillac wines were already being exported in the 12th century, and from the 14th their authenticity was guaranteed by the cock (from the town's coat of arms) branded on the barrels. This was why Gaillac wines were long known as Vins de Coq.

For a variety of reasons Gaillac winemaking experienced a serious decline from the mid-19th to the mid-20th century. One cause was the dwindling demand for sweet wine, in which Gaillac had specialised. During the 1960s, however, some energetic producers (including cooperatives) took the initiative and began to plant black grapes, mostly of strictly local varieties, for the production of red and rosé wines.

At its best, the red is a fairly rustic wine with a pleasant perfume, a full-flavoured taste, hints of fruit and a good deal of tannin, but there are also lighter wines including some Vins de Primeur. Gaillac red comes in many styles and this is true to an even greater extent of the white wines. There are four main categories: dry; semi sweet; sweet and *perlé* (slightly sparkling). In addition the district produces two types of (fully) sparkling wine – a dry wine made by the *méthode champenoise* and a semi-sweet *méthode gaillaçoise* (in which fermentation is interrupted and then continues in bottle). As every producer makes his own version of the various kinds, the resulting picture is too complex for convenient survey. This may be why exports have been slow. Locally, however, the wines are drunk with great enthusiasm. The better restaurants in particular often carry an exciting selection.

As a general rule the best white wines come from the area between Gaillac and Cordes. The red wines are more difficult to localise: they represent two thirds of the local production. There are three cooperatives, whose whites are on the whole better than their reds, and there are now over 100 private producers – a ten-fold increase since 1971. Most growers make a rosé wine, usually from Gamay and sometimes including some Syrah. Another range of wines called Vin de Pays des Côtes du Tarn is made in the Gaillac area and in the country south of the Tarn as far as the River Agoût.

Gaillac red, produced as it is in at least four different styles from various combinations and proportions of grape varieties, is a difficult wine to define.

194

PRODUCERS OF SPECIAL INTEREST

GAILLAC

Cave Coopérative de Técou
81600 Técou
The best all-rounder of the three cooperatives. Marketing is aimed largely at the restaurant trade.

Domaine de Labarthe
81150 Castanet
Especially good white perlé and sweet white from Mauzac, basic red and Rouge Primeur from Gamay.

Mas d'Aurel 81170 Donnazac
M Ribot has 14ha seemingly on top of the world just south of Cordes. His red wines are always reliable while his dry sparkler regularly wins prizes.

Mas Pignou 81600 Gaillac
Dry Gaillac from this 20-ha property ages well, unlike most. The sweet wine is a stunner from Mauzac. The prestige red is Cuvée Mélanie but the basic red is also excellent.

Vignobles Robert Plageoles et Fils 81140 Cahuzac
Robert Plageoles produces an astonishing range of varietal wines from 15ha planted with the traditional Gaillac varieties. A 100% Duras, a Gamay, dry and sweet whites exclusively from Mauzac, a dry sparkler made according to the old Gaillac method, sweet wines from 100% Ondenc and another from Muscadelle. The range is rounded off with the old sherry-type maderized white wine, also from Mauzac.

RECOMMENDED FOR PARTICULAR STYLES: WHITE PERLÉ

Cave Coopérative de Labastide-de-Lévis 81150 Labastide-de-Lévis
Cave Coopérative de Rabastens 81800 Rabastens-sur-Tarn
Domaine de Salmes 81150 Bernac
Exceptionally full and fruity, a '95 prize-winner at the Gaillac Fair.

DRY WHITE

Domaine de Long Pech
81310 Lisle-sur-Tarn
Stylish wine based on Sauvignon.
Domaine de la Ramaye Ste-Cécile d'Avès, 81600 Gaillac
Long-lived wines of some complexity. Only 4ha of vines.

SWEET WHITE

Mas de Bicary 81600 Broze
Moelleux rather than sweet, lovely mid-morning or as 'le five o'clock'.
Château de Mayragues
81140 Castelnau-Montmirail
Scotsman Alan Geddes and his French wife Laurence have produced prize-winners in two years out of three. *Coup de coeur* with the French media.
Domaine de Vayssette Laborie 81600 Gaillac

RED

Domaine d'Escausses
81150 Ste-Croix
Rustic and traditional but somehow strikingly original at the same time.
Domaine du Moulin 81600 Brens
M Hirissou makes red wines which are consistently admired.
Domaine de la Ramaye
Ste-Cécile d'Avès, 81600 Gaillac

ROSÉ

Château de Candastre
81600 Boissel
One of the largest estates. The rosé is its best wine.
Domaine de Gayssou 81600 Broze
Domaine de Moussens
81150 Cestayrols

SPARKLING DRY

Domaine de Canto Perlic
81600 Gaillac
Ex-patriates Alex and Claire Taylor make a delicious sparkler from Mauzac and *méthode champenoise* Len de l'El.
Domaine René Rieux
81600 Boissel
Run by a charitable foundation for the mentally handicapped, all the patients have some winemaking function. The wines are as good as they were in old M Rieux' day which, according to the locals, says a great deal.

SPARKLING SWEET

Domaine d'Escausses
81150 Ste-Croix
Domaine de Moussens
81150 Cestayrols
Domaine René Rieux 81600 Boissel
Domaine de la Tronque
81140 Castelnau-Montmirail
Biodynamic methods are used in the vineyard. Stylish wine.
Domaine de Vayssette Laborie
81600 Gaillac

WINE FÊTE

Gaillac The Cocagne des Vins takes place on the first weekend in August, during which the wines of the region can be sampled in abundance.

WINE INFORMATION

Maison de la Vigne et du Vin
Abbaye St-Michel, 81600 Gaillac
Tel (0)563 57 15 40
The local fraternities are **l'Ordre de la Dive Bouteille de Gaillac** and **La Commanderie des Maîtres Vignerons du Frontonnais**.

HOTELS

Le Grand Écuyer 81170 Cordes
Tel (0)563 56 01 03
Sumptuously furnished Relais et Château hotel. Famous cuisine, especially desserts.

Burning les sarments *at the highly original estate of Les Très Cantous.*

Le Vieux Cordes
81170 Cordes
Tel (0)563 56 00 12
This hotel in a centuries-old building has the same owner as the restaurant Le Grand Écuyer in the same street.
La Réserve 81000 Fonvialane
Tel (0)563 47 60 22
Prestige hotel beautifully situated a few km outside Albi. Swimming pool. The restaurant is recommended.
L'Occitan 81600 Gaillac
Tel (0)563 57 11 52
Adequate but not very large hotel. Warm welcome but no restaurant.

RESTAURANTS

Hostellerie St-Antoine/Mapotel
81000 Albi Tel (0)563 54 04 04
Stylish, with an indoor garden. Also a comfortable hotel. Restaurant good, hotel excellent.
Hostellerie du Parc
81170 Cordes
Tel (0)563 56 02 59
Excellently prepared dishes with a local accent such as lapin aux choux. Also a hotel, surrounded by a park.
L'Échauguette
81500 Giroussens
Tel (0)563 41 63 65
Beautiful terrace overlooking the Agoût. Excellent country cooking: the patron is a wine buff.

Hostellerie du Pré Vert
81800 Rabastens-sur-Tarn
Tel (0)563 33 70 51
Also a hotel, in an 18th-century building with a garden and terrace. Restaurant simple; hotel mid-range.

PLACES OF INTEREST

Albi Just outside the wine area but well worth a visit. Near the imposing cathedral is the house where the painter Henri de Toulouse Lautrec was born: a collection of his work is exhibited in the Palais de la Berbie.
Cordes A medieval hill village, dating in part from 1222, which has been splendidly restored. Narrow, steeply sloping cobbled streets lead to the church, from whose tower there is a fine view.
Gaillac Has the church of St-Michel (11th–13th century), the Parc de Foucaud laid out by André Le Nôtre and a wine museum in the Tour Pierre de Brens.
Lisle-sur-Tarn Once fortified, as can be seen from the central square. There are fine old half-timbered houses and a museum with local archeological finds and art.
Rabastens-sur-Tarn The castle of St-Céry has a monumental 14th-century entrance and the kitchen also dates from this time.

195

Aveyron

Of great importance locally but unknown elsewhere are the wines from the Aveyron *département*, which has three tiny districts among its mountains, valleys and ravines. The Marcillac district lies north-west of the old town of Rodez; Estaing, Entraygues and Le Fel, further north, can be reached only by way of extraordinarily narrow twisting roads over hills or through river valleys. With some 99 hectares, Marcillac is the biggest of the districts; Estaing, Entraygues and Le Fel together make up only one sixth of this area.

Marcillac is all red or rosé and made from the Fer-Servadou grape, locally called Mansois. In this setting it makes a grassy, light-red wine, slightly reminiscent of a Loire red but more rustic. It has an unmistakable aroma and taste of soft red fruits. Production is dominated by the cooperative at Valady but there are in addition six or so excellent private growers. Marcillac has enjoyed AOC status since 1990.

Entraygues comes in all three colours but the white wine from Chenin Blanc is usually the best, though on the slopes overlooking the River Lot some good red wines are also made. The wines of Estaing are similar and the cooperative is again the main producer, as it is in the village of Aguessac at the mouth of the Tarn Gorges near Millau. A full range of country wines is made here. Entraygues, Estaing and Millau all enjoy VDQS status.

PRODUCERS OF SPECIAL INTEREST

MARCILLAC

Cave des Vignerons du Vallon
12230 Valady
Produces red and rosé wines fully characteristic of the Mansois grape and excellent value for money.

Domaine du Cros
12390 Goutrens
Philippe Teulier makes two categories of red: neither is oaked. The basic version is more characteristic of the appellation but the prestige wine is more sophisticated.

Le Vieux Roche (Jean-Luc Matha)
12330 Bruéjols
Matha's wines generally show less finesse than Teulier's, but they have an appealing gutsiness instead.

ENTRAYGUES ET LE FEL

François Avallon
12140 Entraygues

Laurent Mousset
12140 Entraygues
A young grower with an almost vertical vineyard. Light wines (red only) for summer drinking.

Jean-Marc Viguier
12140 Entraygues
Avallon and Viguier have white Entraygues fairly buttoned up between them. Avallon's wines are drier but Viguier's have more body and will age.

ESTAING

Michel Alaux
La Frayssinette, 12190 Estaing
Two very small growers, but the (red) wines are distinctive and full of character.

Le Caveau de Viala
12190 Estaing

Monique Fages
La Ponsarderie, 12190 Estaing
Good for white wine.

MILLAU

Domaine de la Cardabelle
12640 Rivière-sur-Tarn
Jean Meljac is a rare independent producer of country-style red wines of character.

Cave des Vignerons des Gorges du Tarn 12520 Aguessac
The Cave has a virtual monopoly of the wines of Millau – except, that is, for Domaine de la Cardabelle.

HOTELS

Le Vieux Pont 12390 Belcastel
Tel (0)565 64 52 29
A few rooms across the River Aveyron complement the fabulous cooking of the Fagegaltier sisters. Inventive, rustic and sophisticated all at once. Good hotel, top restaurant.

La Truyère 12140 Entraygues
Tel (0)565 44 51 10
Modernised riverside coaching house with traditional rooms and food.

La Terrasse 15120 Vieillevie
Tel (0)471 49 94 00
Quiet, comfortable but simple hotel with tennis courts and swimming pool. Plain, well prepared food. The strawberries are wonderful in season.

RESTAURANT

Goûts et Couleurs 12000 Rodez
Tel (0)565 42 75 10
The patron Monsieur Fau is a self-taught painter as well as chef, and highly talented in both fields. Good place to taste the regional wines.

PLACES OF INTEREST

The wine towns are all medieval at their centre. Visit also the beautiful Lot Valley between Espalion and Decazeville and the splendid Romanesque abbey and pilgrimage church of Ste-Foy in Conques with its 14th-century bell tower and 'treasure' – the finest of all great French medieval collections.

The 11th–12th-century church of Ste-Foy in Conques houses a fabulous collection of stones, enamels and precious metals.

Côtes du Frontonnais

Directly west of Gaillac between Montauban and Toulouse is a relatively young appellation, the Côtes du Frontonnais. The district was given its *appellation contrôlée* in 1975 – although as early as 1119 a papal document was full of praise for wine from the 'Négret' grape, known today as the Négrette. This local variety needs plenty of sun and is vulnerable to rain, so it thrives in the sunny, dry climate that is typical the Côtes. A cooperative is active in the district as are 50 or so independent growers. The bulk of the red wine can be drunk early and is characterised by soft fruitiness but there are also wines with more colour, strength and tannin for laying down. If the wine comes from specified communes, 'Fronton' or 'Villaudric' can be added to the label. The district takes its name from the old village of Fronton which is recognisable from a distance by the square red-brick church tower.

North-west of the Côtes du Frontonnais is the small wine district of Lavilledieu. Négrette is planted here, too, with other mainly local varieties. The cooperative at La Ville Dieu du Temple controls production. Red Lavilledieu wine comes somewhere between a simple Bordeaux and a Côtes du Rhône and production is restricted to the area around nearby Montauban. The cooperative also makes a range of vins de pays from Montauban, the Côteaux de Quercy and the region around Toulouse.

Fronton is either red or rosé: there is no such thing as white Fronton. The appellation area is a combination of the two former districts of Fronton and Villaudric, which were fierce rivals for many years. Producers in the appellation can still add either name (as appropriate) to their wines, and many Villaudric growers still use Burgundy-shaped bottles to distinguish themselves from their Fronton rivals. Villaudric used also to have its own cooperative, but it has now been merged with the Gaillac cooperative at Rabastens.

As the wines gain popularity, producers are reinvesting in modern equipment.

The reputation of Fronton wine is founded on the small, perfectly rounded Négrette, rich in the taste of ripe-red fruits and ideal for quick-maturing wine.

PRODUCERS OF SPECIAL INTEREST

Château Baudare
82370 Labastide-St-Pierre
Château Bel Air 31620 Fronton
Château Bellevue-la-Forêt
31620 Fronton
With 113ha under vine, Patrick Germain is the largest producer in the South-West. Deservedly popular rosé.
Château la Bruyère
82370 Campsas
M Duplan has just started to make and market his own excellent Fronton.
Château Cahuzac 82170 Fabas
Firmer-style wines than many; good fruit and dark colour.
Domaine de Callory
82370 Labastide-St-Pierre
Mme Montels works in the local pharmacy as well as in the vineyards. Her vin de pays is almost as good as her AOC.
La Cave de Fronton
31620 Fronton
A worthy cooperative combining the vineyards of Fronton and Villaudric.
Domaine Caze 31620 Villaudric
Martine Rougevin-Bazille makes full-bodied wines in a *chais* that resembles the prow of a galleon.
Château la Colombière
31620 Villaudric
M Le Baron de Driesen is the only Fronton grower to make wines by *macération carbonique*. Unusually, the method here yields wines that keep well and develop character in bottle.
Château Devès
31620 Castelnau-d'Estrefonds
Château Flotis
31620 Castelnau d'Estrefonds
M Kuntz' good commercial wines sell well in Toulouse bars and brasseries.
Domaine de Joliet 31620 Fronton
François and Marie-Claire Daubert specialise in an all-Négrette red, perhaps the best of its style in the region. A delicious sweet vin de pays from Mauzac is also made.

Château la Palme
31340 Villemur-sur-Tarn
Château Peyreaux
31340 Villematier
Mme Vovette Linant de Bellefonds is one of the characters of the appellation, making wines of old-fashioned splendour.
Château Plaisance
31340 Vacqueris
Marc Pénévayre and his father make three styles of Fronton in addition to a good rosé: a so-called Vin de Printemps, whose style speaks for itself, an excellent mainstream red and an oaked prestige wine called Thibault de Plaisance.
Château le Roc 31620 Fronton
The Ribes family wines are more structured than most and need cellarage. A fascinating contrast with Daubert's (see Domaine de Joliet above).

HOTELS

Hôtel Ingres 81000 Montauban
Tel (0)563 63 36 01
Modern and comfortable, 350m from the station but quiet. No restaurant. Swimming pool and garage.
Villa Les Pins 31340 Vacqueris
Tel (0)561 84 96 04
Peaceful hotel in the midst of woods. Comfortable rooms, good restaurant.

RESTAURANTS

La Cuisine d'Alain 82000 Montauban Tel (0)563 66 06 66
Opposite the station. A sensibly up-dated version of local cooking. Strong on local wines.
Le St-Porquier 82700 St-Porquier Tel (0)563 68 73 14
Simple restaurant with a terrace – and marvellous cassoulet.
La Ferme de Bernadou
31340 Villemur-sur-Tarn
Tel (0)561 09 02 38 A country inn with pleasant local wines.

Armagnac

After cognac, armagnac is France's greatest spirit. It is also probably France's oldest distillate of wine: a document of 1411 in the Musée de l'Armagnac at Condom shows that wine was already being distilled in Gascony at that time, centuries earlier than it was in Cognac, although the *eau-de-vie* may have been used only for medicinal purposes.

Armagnac comes from a part of the former province of Gascony: a few hundred hectares are in the *départements* of Landes and Lot-et-Garonne, but some 90 per cent of the vineyard area is in Gers. This is a beautiful rural region, as yet undiscovered by mass tourism. Its friendly landscape is threaded by small rivers and streams and has an abundance of ancient towns, villages and hamlets as well as the sweet-smelling forests known as the Landes. It is also a region of cellars and kitchens. Gascon cuisine is one of the richest in France: foie gras, goose and duck are served in all kinds of ways and in exuberant quantities. The hearty local cooking has given rise, with admirable logic, to the *trou gascon*, the glass of young white armagnac traditionally taken halfway through a meal to clear the way for the courses still to come.

The area entitled to the appellation armagnac was defined in 1905 and divided into three zones, each of which has its own distinctive characteristics. The most westerly is Bas-Armagnac, also known as Armagnac Noir because of its dark oak forests. The landscape here is relatively flat and the soil mainly of clay and sand. Sixteen communes are included in the (unofficial) zone of Grand Bas-Armagnac, whose fine and subtle product represents, for connoisseurs, the zenith of armagnacs.

The central district is Ténarèze, which from early times has functioned as a corridor between the Pyrenees and Bordeaux. Its capital, the market town of Condom, is one of the main centres of the armagnac trade (the others are Eauze in Bas-Armagnac and Auch, on the River Gers in Haut-Armaganc). In the gently rolling countryside of Ténarèze there are orchards as well as vineyards, wooded hills and fields of maize and sunflowers. The chalk and clay soil produces full-flavoured armagnac with plenty of character.

Armagnacs from the eastern district, Haut-Armagnac (also called Armagnac Blanc), lack the character and quality of those from the other districts. The soil is mainly chalk which is well suited to vines, but the wines are soft and better for drinking than distilling. Much of the relatively small quantity of spirit is used in liqueurs. This is the largest district in Armagnac, most of it in the *département* of Gers, whose steep hills in the south border the Hautes-Pyrénées.

The main grapes of Armagnac are the Folle Blanche (known here, appropriately, as Picpoule, or 'lip stinger'), Ugni Blanc, Colombard and the hybrid Baco Blanc – all varieties that produce wines low in alcohol, high in acidity and ideal for distilling. Production of armagnac is, in fact, steadily decreasing. Only around 20,000 hectolitres per hectare of pure alcohol is now produced, less than half the amount made in the late 1980s and enough for rather less than seven million bottles.

An important difference between cognac and armagnac lies in the method of distillation. For cognac the thin, light white wine is distilled twice. Armagnac has its own alembic, or distilling vessel, in which the wine is heated twice but distilled only once. As a result, pure armagnac has less alcohol than cognac (between 53 and 63 per cent, as against cognac's 70), but possesses more of the elements of perfume and flavour. It is also drier, since sugar is not normally added.

Under the influence of cognac houses that have acquired interests in armagnac, more and more armagnac is being double-distilled in pot-stills, as in Cognac. In addition, the local dark, hard oak in which armagnac is traditionally matured has become scarce, and increasingly wood from other areas is being used. Some armagnacs are thus growing closer to cognac in style. Whereas production of cognac is dominated by large firms, the armagnac houses are on a smaller scale and many producers market their spirit directly. As a result the diversity of styles between producers, and from vintage to vintage (the year of vintage may be indicated on armagnac labels) is enormous. It is also fascinating to explore.

The pine forests of the Landes have replaced what was once a sandy wilderness. In clearings among the trees lie small rural communities surrounded by fields of maize and tobacco, and gaggles of geese.

PRODUCERS OF SPECIAL INTEREST

Castarè de Pont-de-Bordès
47230 Lavardac
The oldest family business in Armagnac, founded in 1832. Concentrates its efforts on selling a wide variety of vintage brandies at their natural strength to up-market establishments throughout Europe.

Chabot Compagnie Viticole des Grands Armagnacs 16101 Cognac
Formerly a cooperative, now owned by the Cognac firm of Camus. Buoyant sales of armagnacs in France, thanks partly to the excellent brandies produced by the firm's own vineyards.

André Daguin 32000 Auch
M Daguin is the high priest of local gastronomy (see Restaurants, Hotel de France, below), so it is natural for him to buy small, carefully selected lots of brandies from individual growers throughout the region. These include, unusually, brandies from the increasingly unfashionable Haut-Armagnac.

Francis Darroze 40120 Roquefort
M Darroze, the self-styled 'antiquary of Armagnac', is the son of a famous local restaurateur. He sells dozens of brandies from individual estates which have been distilled without additives; brandies which he stores in special cellars, sometimes for several decades.

Gélas 32190 Vic-Fézensac
An old-fashioned, traditional family business which also owns the well known Château de Martet. Brandies are distilled to a very low strength and kept in new wood, thus ensuring that they all have a – traditional – warmth.

Janneau 32100 Condom
The biggest firm in Armagnac, founded in 1851. After an unhappy period as an associate and then a subsidiary of Seagram, it is now owned by an Italian whisky importer. Recently it has revamped its range of armagnacs, recognising that the brandy needs more age than cognac, and also taking into account the modern taste for lighter brandies.

Gérard Laberdolive, Domaine d'Escoubes
40240 Labastide d'Armagnac
For half a century now the family have been selling single-vintage, single-vineyard armagnacs, distilled 'at home' and matured in oak from the estate. Customers include many of France's best restaurants.

Larressingle 32100 Condom
A family firm still owned by descendants of the remarkably-named Hippolyte Papelorey who founded it in 1837. The family owns the magnificent Château de Larressingle, a walled village built back in 1250. The cellars in a former Carmelite convent are equally remarkable.

Samalens 32110 Laujuzan
Until 1970 the family sold only brandies distilled and matured in their native village – and as a result they have one of the region's finest stocks of old armagnacs. They now sell other brandies but the best remain typical of its base in the Bas-Armagnac.

Sempé 32290 Aignan
A recent success story, Henri-Abel Sempé founded the firm in 1934 and combined his business with a political career which included a long spell as senator for the local *département*. In his early days Sempé's brandies were unremarkable, but the firm now offers some fine older armagnacs.

FÊTES

Armagnac
The Foire aux Eaux-de-Vie is held at the end of May/beginning of June.

Mauvezin
A garlic festival on the third Monday in August.

Samatan
The national foie gras fair takes place here during the fourth weekend in August.

WINE INFORMATION

At the end of 1986 the **Maison du Floc de Gascogne** was opened in Eauze to provide information about this Armagnac speciality: white or red grape must mixed with armagnac, comparable to Pineau des Charentes.

HOTEL

Many Armagnac hotels are combined with restaurants (see below).

Le Relais de Gascogne
5 avenue de la Marne
32000 Auch
Tel (0)562 05 26 81
Comfortable and fairly modern hotel which also has a restaurant.

RESTAURANTS

The numerous restaurants keep mainly to regional cuisine, with foie gras, goose and duck in abundance.

Hôtel de France
place de la Libération, 32000 Auch
Tel (0)562 61 71 71
Central, comfortable hotel with a restaurant where Gascon cuisine is splendidly represented. The foie gras is excellent and so is the lou magret (breast of duck). Owner and chef is André Daguin. Also a first-class hotel. Regional products are on sale at a shop here and there are separate restaurants for simpler meals.

Claude Laffitte
38 rue Dessoles, 32000 Auch
Tel (0)562 05 04 18
Good cooking without fuss.

At Sempé in Ténarèze, brandies are stored for almost two years in new oak.

Le Florida 32410 Castéra-Verduzan
Tel (0)562 68 13 22
Congenial inn and hotel situated in a small spa town.

La Table des Cordeliers rue des Cordeliers, 32100 Condom
Tel (0)562 68 28 36
Housed in a 14th-century chapel. Contemporary cuisine. Also a modern hotel.

Restaurant de l'Armagnac 32800 Eauze Tel (0)562 09 88 11
Pleasant and convivial.

Le Moulin du Pouy 32800 Eauze
Tel (0)562 09 82 58
A good place to eat out of doors. Regional cooking.

Le Fleurance 32300 Fleurance
Tel (0)562 06 14 85
Regional wines and cooking. Generous helpings. Pleasant hotel.

Château Larroque 32200 Gimont
Tel (0)562 67 77 44
Luxurious château hotel; demi-pension obligatory in season. Try the soufflé au foie gras and visit the colourful local market on Sunday. Also a good restaurant.

Le Relais d'Armagnac 32110 Luppé-Violles Tel (0)562 08 95 22
Regional cooking. Also a hotel.

La Rapière 32120 Mauvezin
Tel (0)562 06 80 08
Charming, busy address; menu includes confit de canard.

Hôtel des Pyrénées 32300 Mirande Tel (0)562 66 51 16
Hotel and restaurant. Local dishes and fish are prepared with great care.

La Gare 32250 Montréal-du-Gers
Tel (0)562 29 43 37
A former railway station. One of the platforms has been converted into an attractive terrace. Fish specialities and regional dishes.

Le Relais de Cardneau 32450 Ste-Christie Tel (0)562 64 33 90
Traditional cooking and local wines.

La Ferme de Flaran 32310 Valence-sur-Baïse Tel (0)562 28 58 22
Ideal for lunch after visiting the abbey. The hotel has a swimming pool.

Le Relais des Postes 32190 Vic-Fézensac Tel (0)562 06 44 22
Provincial hotel with regionally based cuisine. Book very early if you want to attend the local (bloodless) bullfights at Whitsun.

PLACES OF INTEREST

Auch The region's biggest town. The old centre is perched on a hill overlooking the river. The cathedral of Ste-Marie has superb choir stalls and 16th-century stained-glass windows. Some 232 steps link the quai de Gers with the place Salinis and its tall Tour d'Armagnac. A statue of d'Artagnan commemorates the famous Gascon musketeer whose adventures were immortalised by Alexandre Dumas. A market for armagnac is held on most Thursdays in the town centre.

Castelnau-Barbarens Village encircling its church. There is a fine viewpoint at the D349 and D626 intersection.

Condom Gothic cathedral and a museum with armagnac as its theme.

Fources Fortified village or *bastide*, a rare circular example. The central square is surrounded by houses and a wooden gallery. Also a Gothic bridge and a 15th-century castle.

Gimont A bustling market town with a 13th-century fortified church.

Labastide d'Armagnac Viticultural museum at Château Garreau.

Mauvezin An octagonal tower, winding streets and a covered market.

Montréal-du-Gers One of the first and finest *bastides* in Gascony.

St-Puy Château Monluc makes Pousse Rapière, a potent liqueur, and sparkling white wine.

Seviac A luxurious Gallo-Roman villa with colourful mosaics.

Termes d'Armagnac Exhibitions are held in the historic castle keep. One hall is devoted to wine.

Valence-sur-Baïse The 12th-century Cistercian abbey functions as a cultural centre for Gers.

The Pyrenees

Some of France's least well known wine districts lie in and around the foothills of the western Pyrenees. Their wines are also among the most exciting and dramatically improved in the whole of the South-West.

Not far out of the western suburbs of Toulouse is the boundary with the *département* of Gers, the beginning of Gascony. Here a number of vins de pays have become popular and widely available on account of their fresh, fruity character as well as their exceptional value for money. Whether called Gers, Côtes de Gascogne, Côtes du Condomois, Montestruc or Landes, they have a remarkable similarity. Mostly dry and white, they are based on Colombard and Ugni Blanc – grapes which used to go into the making of wine for distillation into Armagnac until the demand for that brandy started to decline in the early 1970s. Local growers were, fortunately, able to make drinkable wines from raw materials that had previously been consumed only domestically. Commercial realisation of this fact was almost entirely due to the enterprise of those who recognised the Colombard's potential, having followed its spectacular success in the US.

The Gers is the watershed between the river basins of the Garonne and the Adour. In the hills through which the Adour flows, some of the best of these wines are made. Pierre Dubosc, the

At Clos Urolat, pliable water willow shoots are still used to tie the vines.

man behind the Colombard revolution, almost single-handedly created the trio of cooperatives based on Plaisance, St-Aignan and St-Mont, grouped together as Plaimont, and the area now enjoying VDQS status (soon almost certainly to be raised to AOC) called Côtes de St-Mont. St-Mont wines are closely modelled on the wines of Madiran and Pacherenc further south. The reds are based on the Tannat grape but given shorter vinification so that they mature earlier. The whites are based on the two Manseng varieties (Gros and Petit) and a local grape called Arrufiac. Plaimont also makes and sells Côtes de Gascogne as well as Madiran proper for members qualifying for the latter appellation.

The vineyards of Madiran adjoin St-Mont immediately to the south. The area used to be called Vic-Bilh – its white wine is still called Pacherenc du Vic-Bilh. As early as the 16th century Madiran wines were being exported via Bayonne as far as Finland and Russia. One reason for a decline in production this century was the virtual disappearance of the essential Tannat grape, which was almost totally wiped out by phylloxera. Most of those growers who replanted their vineyards chose to do so with inferior hybrid varieties which produced much higher yields. As at Cahors, a few growers were responsible for keeping true Madiran going – but only just: in the 1950s there were only six hectares of vines planted with the appropriate grapes. Again, as in Cahors, it was the local cooperative, this one at Crouseilles, that launched the rebirth of Madiran and today there are 60 or so independent producers as well as the cooperative at St-Mont, and another smaller one within the Madiran appellation.

Classic Madiran is a deep but lively red with a firm taste full of tannin. It needs a good five years of bottle-age but the reward is wine of singular silky fluidity; no country boy this but a courtier of character. Fruit can also be present, particularly cherries and currants. The white Pacherenc comprises only ten per cent of the wine made in the area. It comes in at least two styles, both of which have an exotic fragrance: dry or fairly sweet, the latter sometimes being matured in oak. The better examples are sometimes akin to the richer Jurançons, but on the whole the style is a little lighter. The reds accompany the hearty stews and game of the region to perfection while the whites are good with the local foie gras and the hard ewes' cheeses from the mountains.

To the west of Madiran lies Tursan, a district that produces red, white and rosé wines of VDQS level, almost all processed by the cooperative at Geaune. There are only two private producers, but one of them is master-chef Michel Guérard who now makes his own wine at his country home, Château de Bachen. Tursan, whose reds are also based on the Tannat grape, is taking the opposite road from Madiran. Using increasingly large proportions of Cabernet Franc, the aim is to produce soft, supple wines for early drinking but with some fruit and a good colour. A fair amount of rosé is also made here, mostly from Cabernet Franc, to meet the demand of the Atlantic tourist trade in the summer. The white wine is all dry in style and made from a mysterious local variety called Barroque, with just a little Sauvignon to give it some zing. Again the style is much lighter than that of the dry Pacherencs, and in flavour quite different from the Côtes de Gascogne because there is no Colombard in the vineyards. Guérard's wines are not typical of the appellation; they are substantial and rather New World in style and as original as his cooking.

There are two other vins de pays to the west of Tursan: that of the Chalosse, based on a cooperative at Mugron, and the Landes, used largely for a small production of local wines grown just behind the sand-dunes of the Atlantic Ocean. Sometimes called vins de sable, they are rarely seen outside local restaurants.

The Béarn appellation, spread over three *départements*, is also dominated by a cooperative at Bellocq, a village north-east of Orthez. The wines of all three colours enjoy AOC status but the best-known is the rosé, which came to prominence after World War II and made the name of Béarn before Madiran and Jurançon had staged their come-backs. The appellation is also used by the Madiran cooperative for its pink wine and by growers in Jurançon for their red wine, neither of which can be sold under their local appellation. The rosé, made mostly from Cabernet Franc, can be a particularly delicious thirst-quencher.

Just south of the spa town of Pau is Jurançon, one of the most beautiful wine districts in all France. Vines on steep hillsides that are the first convulsions of the Pyrenean chain alternate with a luxuriant covering of trees, whose intense green foliage gives way in autumn to gold-brown tints, often lit by radiant sunshine and warmed by the balmy south wind from over the mountains.

Apart from those few made as red or pink Béarn, wines from this little paradise are almost entirely white; the name Jurançon cannot be applied to any other colour. Classic Jurançon is made from overripe grapes but differs from Sauternes in that conditions here do not allow the development of botrytis, or noble rot. The wines are still concentrated, sweet and memorable; acids that give them hints of grapefruits, mangoes and other exotic fruits are noticeably present and balance the sweetness beautifully.

Recent years have seen the development of a drier style of wine, for which there is a separate appellation, Jurançon Sec. At its best this too has a substantial character and ages well. There are three grape varieties: Gros Manseng which can go into wines of both styles; Petit Manseng which has smaller and sweeter fruit and goes

Away from the battle grounds in the north and east, the medieval town of Salies-de-Béarn was able to develop a lively commerce in relative peace.

into the dessert wines, many of which contain no other variety; and Petit Courbu, a drier grape which is rather difficult to cultivate but which some growers use to introduce an element of freshness and youth to Jurançon Sec. There is but one cooperative, whose top-of-the-range wines at least are as good as most produced by the 50 or so independent producers. The latter include several very serious growers who are set on re-establishing their wines as some of the best in the South-West.

Irouléguy, whose bizarre name betrays its position as the only AOC-producing area of the French Basque country, is an isolated district near St-Jean-Pied-de-Port not far from the Spanish frontier and in the lee of the mountains. It is a very small district, covering a total of about 170 hectares. The wines are mostly red and these are the most interesting; some rosé is also made and there is a small production of white, largely from the Petit Courbu grape. There are five private growers, including the famous distillery family of Brana, but the bulk of the production is still in the hands of the excellent cooperative at St-Étienne-de-Baïgorry.

Irouléguy red is not unlike Madiran in style, more rustic and without some of the silkiness. It suits admirably the rather rugged landscape, the beautiful mountain scenery and the gutsy Basque cuisine. It also suits the temperament of a people devoted to bullfights, pelota and rugby football. The rosé is perfect for a picnic in the mountains, while the white is an interesting rarity not unlike a dry Jurançon and delicious with the trout from the mountain streams or the exotic variety of fish from the nearby ocean.

PRODUCERS OF SPECIAL INTEREST

CÔTES DE GASCOGNE

Domaine de Bergerayre
32110 St-Martin d'Armagnac
Jean-Marc Sarran has 20ha of vines around his aunt's delightful auberge at St-Martin d'Armagnac. By using more of the two Manseng varieties he hopes to make a better style of Côtes de Gascogne.

Domaine de Laballe
40310 Parleboscq
Noël Laudet used to be the *régisseur* at Château Beychevelle and now works from his home in Bas-Armagnac. His dry white wine has proved enormously successful.

Domaine de Lahitte
Ramouzens 32800 Eauze
A wine for those who like the pear-drops character of the Colombard.

Domaine Mesté-Duran
32100 Condom
The red wines here are made by Patrick Aurin with the Bordeaux grapes rather than the more traditional Gascon varieties.

Domaine le Puts (also called **Bordès**) 32100 Gondrin
'Flying winemaker' Hugh Ryman has helped with the making and marketing of this agreeably typical wine.

Château de Tariquet, Domaine de Rieux, Domaine de Plantérieu, La Jalousie (the Grassa family) 32800 Eauze
With four adjoining estates near Eauze, the Grassa family has been partly responsible for putting the Côtes de Gascogne wines on the map.

TURSAN

Château de Bachen Duhort-Bachen, 40800 Aire-sur-l'Adour
The home and vineyard of world-famous chef Michel Guérard. A fifth of the production goes to his restaurant complex at Eugénie-lès-Bains. No ordinary Tursan this but New World in style and generously oaked.

Domaine de Perchade-Pourrouchet 40320 Geaune
Les Vignerons de Tursan (Cave Coopérative) 40320 Geaune
The cooperative has a monopoly of Tursan except for the two growers listed above. The product, especially the rosé, is aimed at the summer tourist trade.

ST-MONT

Château de la Bergalasse
32400 Aurensan
Domaine de Maouries
32400 Labarthète
Plaimont Producteurs (Cave Coopérative) St-Mont, 32400 Riscle
A truly dynamic cooperative producing a complete range of wines from Côtes de Gascogne, St-Mont and Madiran – all of which are widely available in the UK.

MADIRAN AND PACHERENC

Château d'Aydie (Domaines Laplace) 64330 Garlin
The Laplace family are Madiran veterans. The château gives its name to their prestige wine. The principal red is named after grandfather Frédéric. They think highly of white Pacherenc and its future: their own Pacherenc is superb.

Château Barréjat
32400 Maumusson
Domaine Berthoumieu
32400 Viella
Didier Barré's Madirans are more approachable and mature sooner than many. Barré goes through the vineyard selecting his white grapes no less than five times, (each trawl, whose purpose is to select only those grapes which have reached optimum ripeness) is known as a *triage*) and his sweet Pacherenc is made from grapes harvested in the last three.

Domaine Capmartin
32400 Maumusson
Guy Capmartin is one of the promising young stars of the appellation, though his vineyard is tiny.

Domaine de Crampilh
64350 Aurions-Idernes
The dry Pacherenc is consistently one of the best.

Cru du Paradis 65700 St-Lanne
Domaine Damiens 64330 Aydie
Château de Fitère 32400 Cannet
Particularly good-value wines of consistently high quality. Unusually approachable when young.

Domaine Labranche-Laffont
32400 Maumusson
Yvonne Dupuy and her daughter Martine are rapidly making a name for themselves in this male-dominated appellation. Their *vieilles vignes* took first prize at the important local show in '95 and their Pacherenc is also among the best.

Château Laffitte-Teston
32400 Maumusson
Jean-Marc Laffitte's Madirans are good but his Pacherencs are consistently magnificent. Good-value wines.

Domaine de Maouries
32400 Labarthète
Château Montus and Domaine Bouscassé 32400 Maumusson
Alain Brumont is the high priest of the Tannat grape. The premium wines from his two properties, which cover 61ha, are both 100% Tannat and they are vinified for five weeks. A third wine called Domaine Meinjarre is priced at bargain level. There is also a range of Pacherenc, good vins de pays and more recently a range of varietals.

Domaine Mouréou
32400 Maumusson
Patrick Ducournau is the think-tank of Madiran, much admired as one of the bright young hopes of the South-West. Although a devotee of 100%-Tannat wines he is also keen to shorten the period of maturation and has invented a system of oxygen-injection to reduce the need for frequent *remontage* and disturbance of the wine in *cuve*.

Château Pichard
65700 Soublecause
Domaine Sergent
32400 Maumusson
Les Vignerons du Vic-Bilh-Madiran 64350 Crouseilles
A first-class cooperative whose top wine Château de Crouseilles (a property owned by the cooperative) is among the best. The mainstream Madirans and Pacherencs are also good and there is a large production of rosé and red Béarn as well as vin de pays.

Vignobles du Domaine de Diusse 64330 Aydie

BÉARN

Cave Coopérative Bellocq, 64270 Salies-de-Béarn
Produce a wide range of Béarn AOC and vin de pays of which the rosé is the best.

Clos Mirabel La Chapelle-de-Rousse, 64110 Jurançon
Red Béarn based on Cabernet Franc from a Jurançon grower.

Domaine de Guilhémas (Domaine Lapeyre)
64270 Salies-de-Béarn
Béarn's one independent producer outside the other areas of Madiran and Jurançon. Prize-winning wines.

JURANÇON

Domaine Bellegarde
64360 Monein
Pascal Labasse is the prototype new-wave Jurançon-grower. His bone-dry sec ages well. The *moelleux* is called Cuvée Thibault and the ultra-sweet *cuvée* is called Sélection Petit Manseng.

Domaine Bru-Baché
64360 Monein
Claude Loustalot has taken over from his uncle Georges Bru-Baché. Both dry and *moelleux* wines are top-notch and sold under the name of Cuvée des Casterasses.

Domaine Capdevielle
64360 Monein
Traditional grower who keeps up well with the youngsters.

Domaine de Castéra
64360 Monein
Christian Lihour scorns the use of new wood but manages to make superb wines of all three styles.

Domaine Cauhapé 64360 Monein
Henri Ramonteu is the best known private grower, with the second-largest vineyard of 25ha. The benchmark for modern Jurançon. An impressive range includes two ultra-luscious and expensive oaked wines from Petit Manseng grapes that have been allowed to shrivel on the vine.

Cave des Producteurs de Jurançon 64290 Gan
The 300 members of this cooperative have only 546ha between them. Most of the production is of dry wine, of which there are three grades. The highest, Peyre d'Or, is one of the appellation's best.

Clos Guirouilh 64290 Lasseube
Wines of tremendous style and elegance, the taste of apples and pears giving way with age to citrus fruits. Guirouilh is a master of the discreet management of new wood.

Clos Lamouroux La Chapelle-de-Rousse, 64110 Jurançon
Richard Ziemeck-Chigé abhors new oak and does not believe in Jurançon Sec. He makes wines in varying degrees of sweetness as they always used to be in Jurançon.

Clos Lapeyre La Chapelle-de-Rousse, 64110 Jurançon
Jean-Bernard Larrieu is another exciting young producer in this predominantly young appellation. Top of the range is a superb 100% Petit Manseng Vendange Tardive.

Rounds of ewes' milk cheese mature in temperature-controlled cellars at Gabas.

Clos Uroulat 64360 Monein
Charles Hours is president of the
Syndicat of local growers and makes
elegant and stylish rather than fat and
luscious wines.
**Clos de la Vierge (Domaine
Concaillaü)** 64150 Mourenx
A property of long-established
excellence. The Barrère family kept
the flame of Jurançon alive almost
single-handed for some years.
Domaine Gaillot 64360 Monein
Château Jolys
La Chapelle-de-Rousse
64100 Jurançon
With 36ha Robert Latrille is the
largest grower in Jurançon. Good,
middle-of-the-road wines.
Domaine Larrédya La Chapelle-
de-Rousse, 64110 Jurançon
Domaine Mondinat 64290 Gan
With rustic simplicity and
excellence such as this – who needs
modern technology?
Domaine de Nays La Chapelle-
de-Rousse, 64110 Jurançon
Château de Rousse La Chapelle-
de-Rousse, 64110 Jurançon
Monsieur Labat still uses the Petit
Courbu grape to give extra vitality to
his wines.

IROULÉGUY
Domaine Abotia 64220 Ispoure
Domaine Arretxea
64220 Irouléguy
Domaine Brana 64220
St-Jean-Pied-de-Port
With fabulous views of the Pyrenees,
the splendid winery is hewn out of
the mountainside. There is but 30%
Tannat and the *cuvaisons* are shorter
than at Ilarria (see below) so the
wines mature earlier.
Domaine Etchegaraya
64430 St-Étienne-de-Baïgorry
Domaine Ilarria
64220 Irouléguy
Peio (Pierre) Espil has only 6ha of
vines, but he makes two ultra-typical
reds from 80 and 100% Tannat
respectively. The latter is called Cuvée
Bixintzo (the Basque name for St
Vincent). *Cuvaisons* are long and the
wines are aged for 18 months in a
mixture of new and old wood.
**Les Maîtres Vignerons
d'Irouléguy**
64430 St-Étienne-de-Baïgorry
Many holdings are tiny since 49
members share 350 acres. Nearly half
the production is of rosé. There are
special *cuvées* and a small production
of white in addition to the basic range:
Domaine de Mignaberry, Domaine
Iturritze (quicker maturing) and
Domaine Mendisokoa.

WINE FÊTE

Madiran A Fête des Vins is held on
August 14 and 15.

Pau, Henry IV's town or 'Nouste Henric' as the Béarnais say, is the principal town of the Pyrénées-Atlantiques département.

WINE INFORMATION

Maison du Vin Gan
Tel (0)559 06 53 25)
One local fraternity is the **Viguerie
Royale de Madiran**, based in
Jurançon. The headquarters of the
Commanderie des Chevaliers
is in Tursan. The *syndicat* of Madiran
growers in Madiran is also a good
source of local information.

HOTELS

GASCONY, ST-MONT
AND MADIRAN
Michel Guérard
Les Pres et les Sources d'Eugénie
40320 Eugénie-lès-Bains
Tel (0)558 05 06 07
A place of pilgrimage for gastronomes
but also for weight-watchers.
Impressive wine-list including Guérard's
own Tursans. Luxurious and expensive.
The same proprietor's Relais des
Champs [tel (0)558 51 18 00] and the
pub-inspired Maison Rose are nearby.
Hôtel de France 40320 Geaune
Tel (0)558 44 51 18
This simple country hotel, set in the
heart of the Tursan region, offers
comfort and good value.
Hôtel Ripa-Alta
32160 Plaisance
Tel (0)562 69 30 43
Inventive but distinctly regional
cooking. Rooms less ambitious.
Auberge de Bergerayre
32110 St-Martin d'Armagnac
Tel (0)562 09 08 72
Just a few km from St-Mont, set in
quiet countryside. With swimming
pool. Traditional Gascon cooking.

JURANÇON
Mapôtel Continental
2 rue Maréchal-Foch, 640000 Pau
Tel (0)559 27 69 31
Long regarded as Pau's best hotel.
Rooms well sound-proofed, good
service. Smart restaurant.

Renaissance boulevard Cami-Salié
64000 Pau Tel (0)559 80 20 51
Near the motorway exit but in quiet
grounds. Modern, spacious rooms.
Locally-inspired cooking.
Roncevaux 25 rue Louis-Barthou
64000 Pau Tel (0)559 27 08 44
An old mansion in the centre. Good-
sized rooms and a family feel.
Courtyard parking. No restaurant.

IROULÉGUY
Hôtel Arcé 64430 St-Étienne-
de-Baïgorry Tel (0)559 37 40 14
The quintessential auberge. Terrace
and rooms overlook the river.
Les Pyrénées 64220 St-Jean-
Pied-de-Port Tel (0)559 37 01 01
Undoubtedly the classiest hotel and
restaurant of the district. Monsieur
Arrambide specialises in transcendental
rustic cuisine of the highest order. Ask
for rooms at the back.
Eskualduna 64780 St-Martin
d'Arrossa Tel (0)559 37 71 72
Many rooms are in a separate building,
200 yards away but totally quiet and
with views over the valley. Simple but
excellent, like the Basque cooking.

RESTAURANTS

GASCONY, ST-MONT
AND MADIRAN
Chez l'Ahumat 40800 Aire-
sur-l'Adour Tel (0)558 71 82 61
Traditional regional food. Crowded,
cheap and cheerful. Excellent value
but the town is noisy.
Pain, Adour et Fantaisie
40270 Grenade sur-l'Adour
Tel (0)558 45 18 80
Fashionable newcomer, innovative
cuisine. Much praised locally.
Expensive. There are a few rooms
overlooking the river.

JURANÇON
Le Tucq route de Laruns
64290 Gan Tel (0)559 21 61 26
Convenient when visiting the Cave

Coopérative. Good-value set menus, à
la carte more expensive. Local
specialities and wines.
Le Berry 4 rue Gachet
64000 Pau Tel (0)559 27 42 95
Excellent value. Inexpensive brasserie
with South-West specialities.
Pierre 16 rue Louis-Barthou
64000 Pau Tel (0)559 27 76 86
The best as well as the most
expensive of Pau's restaurants. Wine-
list strong on claret.

IROULÉGUY
(see also Hotels above)
Auberge Etche Goyen
Esterençuby 64220 St-Jean-
Pied-de-Port Tel (0)559 37 09 77
Simple, with well prepared food and
good choice of local wines.

PLACES OF INTEREST

Irouléguy There is little to rival the
local scenery. St-Jean-Pied-de-Port
itself, dominated by a 15th-century
citadel, is attractive but noisy in
season. The scallop shell, which is
the symbol of Santiago de
Compostela (St Jacques), is still
much in evidence.
Orthez Pleasant town with a
13th-century fortified bridge.
Pau Here (so the story goes) the
infant lips of King Henry IV were
rubbed at birth with garlic and
Jurançon wine. He was born in the
château, a gracious palace that now
contains two museums. Nearby are
the ancient Parc National and the
boulevard des Pyrénées which, when
the weather is clear, gives breathtaking views of the nearby and often
snow-capped mountains. The
boulevard leads to the Parc
Beaumont, the most beautiful in Pau.
Salies-de-Béarn A spa with many
17th-century houses. Salt from Salies
is essential to authentic Bayonne
Ham, most of which is cured at
Orthez and Sauveterre.

203

The Rhône

The Rhône is France's largest quality-wine region after Bordeaux. The river valley from south of Lyon almost to its mouth at Marseilles is a natural home for the vine. Intense viticulture starts south of Vienne and continues, with a break somewhere roughly in the middle, as far as Avignon.

That break seems almost to mark a divide between the wines of central France and those of the South. The vineyards of Côte Rôtie and Hermitage, home to the Syrah grape, may produce wines of great power but they seem more closely related to the vineyards of Burgundy than to those of the Côtes du Rhône further south. In their narrow valley they rely – as do the vines of Burgundy – on the exposure provided by slopes to bring the grapes to maximum ripeness. They need the intense heat which steep hillsides and proximity to water (where the heat reflects from its surface) can offer. Further south, the vines can afford to stretch luxuriously across the valley, only occasionally creeping up slopes to claim a little extra heat.

Wines and vines have been the common currency of the Rhône since before the time of Christ. Greeks – even Phoenicians, perhaps – brought vines to Marseilles and thence up the natural waterway of the Rhône. The Syrah, with its almost mythical origins in Persia, is one of the most ancient of French vines. One of the great attractions of this part of France is the wealth of Roman remains – some of which, as at Orange, are of immense scale and grandeur.

Travelling from the north of France you meet the Rhône Valley vineyards at Vienne. If you turn off the A7 autoroute and follow the river as it enters a narrow defile you pass hillsides planted with terraced vineyards: the Côte Rôtie, St-Joseph, Cornas, Crozes-Hermitage and Hermitage. After the Hermitage hill the valley widens to leave broad expanses between the receding hills. The landscape reflects its more southerly postion, with cypress trees acting as windbreaks against the feared *Mistral* and olive trees complementing vines to create a truly Mediterranean landscape.

Red wines are the speciality of the Rhône. Many young Côtes du Rhône are cheap and easy to drink but the area also offers some of the finest of French reds – those from Châteauneuf-du-Pape and

Left: September harvest on the Côte Rôtie above the village of Ampuis. The best red wines from these slopes are deep-coloured, tannic, rich and concentrated and reward long cellaring; whites can be powerful and aromatic.

Northern Rhône

Hermitage. The small quantities of white wine produced here also deserve attention since they include those from the original Viognier appellations. This grape was once confined to Condrieu and Château Grillet but its worldwide renown is now growing. Rosé wines are also made, especially in the village of Tavel, whose cooperative proclaims that it makes the 'Premier Rosé de France'.

The Rhône is perfect wine-touring country, combining as it does the pleasures of the vine with fine landscape and charming, picturesque towns and villages as yet unspoilt by tourism. The many small cellars in the wine villages are just as welcoming as the larger establishments.

A small stone chapel crowns the steep hill of Hermitage just behind the town. It is maintained by the Jaboulet family of Tain l'Hermitage who bought it for just 500Ffr in 1929, and it lends its name to their flagship wine, Hermitage La Chapelle, which has introduced wine-lovers around the world to the magnificence of Rhône Syrah.

In northern Rhône vineyards, Syrah is king and Viognier is queen. These two grapes, currently among the most fashionable in the international wine world, come from vineyards that cling often precariously to the hillsides of the river's narrow gorge between Vienne and Tain-l'Hermitage. The slopes may be difficult to work but their near-perfect exposure to the heat of the sun was recognised as long ago as the Roman era, if not before. The very name of the south-east facing Côte Rôtie – the 'roasted slope' – suggests that this is the place to ripen grapes for full-bodied wines.

The wines of this section of the river, from Côte Rôtie in the north to Cornas and St-Péray in the south, were famous well before those of Bordeaux or even Burgundy. In the last century the wines from Hermitage hill commanded prices as high as those of the best Bordeaux. They were also – somewhat less alluringly – used as

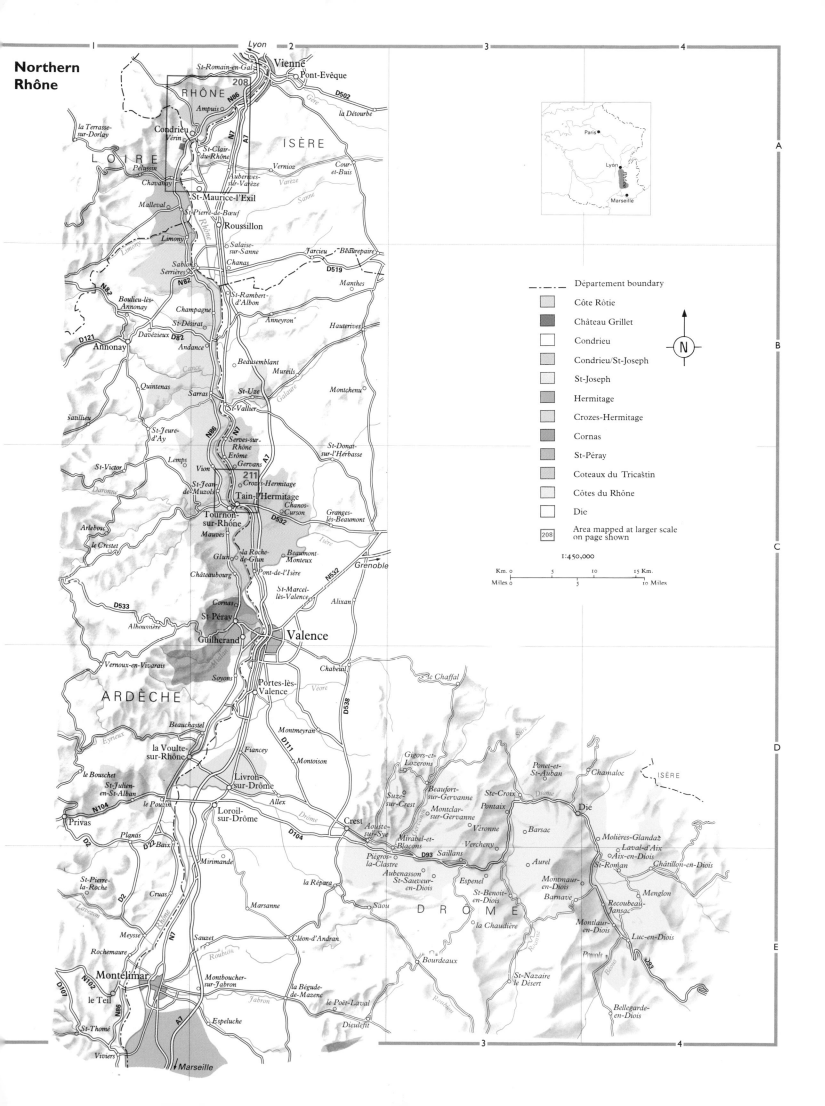

Northern
Rhône

Lyon

St-Romain-en-Gal
Vienne
Pont-Evêque
208
RHÔNE
D502
N86
Ampuis
la Détourbe
N7
A7
Condrieu
Vérin
ISÈRE
la Terrasse-
sur-Dorlay
St-Clair-
du-Rhône
Vernioz
Cour-
et-Buis
LOIRE
Pélussin
Auberives-
sur-Varèze
Varèze
Chavanay
St-Maurice-l'Exil
Sanne
Malleval
St-Pierre-de-Bœuf
Roussillon
Limony
Salaise-
sur-Sanne
Tarcieu
Beaurepaire
N82
Sablons
Serrières
Chanas
D519
Manthes
Boulieu-lès-
Annonay
St-Rambert-
d'Albon
N82
Champagne
Anneyron
Hauterives
St-Désirat
D121
Davézieux
D82
Andance
Beausemblant
Annonay
Mureils
Quintenas
Sarras
St-Uze
Montchenu
Satillieu
t-Vallier
St-Jeure-
d'Ay
N86
N7
Serves-sur-
Rhône
St-Donat-
sur-l'Herbasse
Lemps
Erôme
A7
Gervans
St-Victor
Vion
211
Daronne
St-Jean-
de-Muzols
Crozes-Hermitage
Tain-l'Hermitage
Chanos-
Curson
Granges-
lès-Beaumont
Tournon-
sur-Rhône
D532
Mauves
Isère
Arlebosc
la Roche-
de-Glun
le Crestet
Glun
Beaumont-
Monteux
Châteaubourg
Pont-de-l'Isère
N532
St-Marcel-
lès-Valence
Grenoble
D533
Cornas
Alixan
Alboussière
St-Péray
Guilherand
Valence
Vernoux-en-Vivarais
Chabeuil
le Chaffal
Soyons
Portes-lès-
Valence
ARDÈCHE
Véore
D538
Beauchastel
Montmeyran
Eyrieux
Gigors-et-
Lozerons
Sire
la Voulte-
sur-Rhône
Fiancey
D111
Montoison
Ponet-et-
St-Auban
Chamaloc
ISÈRE
le Bouschet
Livron-
sur-Drôme
Beaufort-
sur-Gervanne
Ste-Croix
Drôme
St-Julien-
en-St-Alban
Allex
Montclar-
sur-Gervanne
Pontaix
Die
N104
le Pouzin
Loriol-
sur-Drôme
Suze-
sur-Crest
Véronne
Barsac
Privas
Drôme
Crest
D104
Aouste-
sur-Sye
Molières-Glandaz
Planas
Mirabel-et-
Blacons
D93
Saillans
Vercheny
Laval-d'Aix
D2
D22
Baix
Piégros-
la-Clastre
Aurel
St-Roman
Châtillon-en-Diois
Mirimande
Aubenasson
St-Sauveur-
en-Diois
Espenel
Montmaur-
en-Diois
Menglon
St-Pierre-
la-Roche
la Répara
St-Benoit-
en-Diois
Barnave
Recoubeau-
Jansac
D2
Cruas
Marsanne
Saou
la Chaudière
DRÔME
Montlaur-
en-Diois
Luc-en-Diois
Meysse
Sauzet
Cléon-d'Andran
Rochemaure
Roubion
Bourdeaux
Montélimar
N102
Montboucher-
sur-Jabron
la Bégude-
de-Mazenc
St-Nazaire-
le Désert
Bellegarde-
en-Diois
le Teil
N86
A7
Espeluche
le Poët-Laval
D101
St-Thomé
Espeluche
Dieulefit
Viviers
Marseille

Paris

Lyon

Marseille

Département boundary
Côte Rôtie
Château Grillet
Condrieu
Condrieu/St-Joseph
St-Joseph
Hermitage
Crozes-Hermitage
Cornas
St-Péray
Coteaux du Tricastin
Côtes du Rhône
Die
208 Area mapped at larger scale
on page shown

1:450,000

Km. 0   5   10   15 Km.
Miles 0   5   10 Miles

N

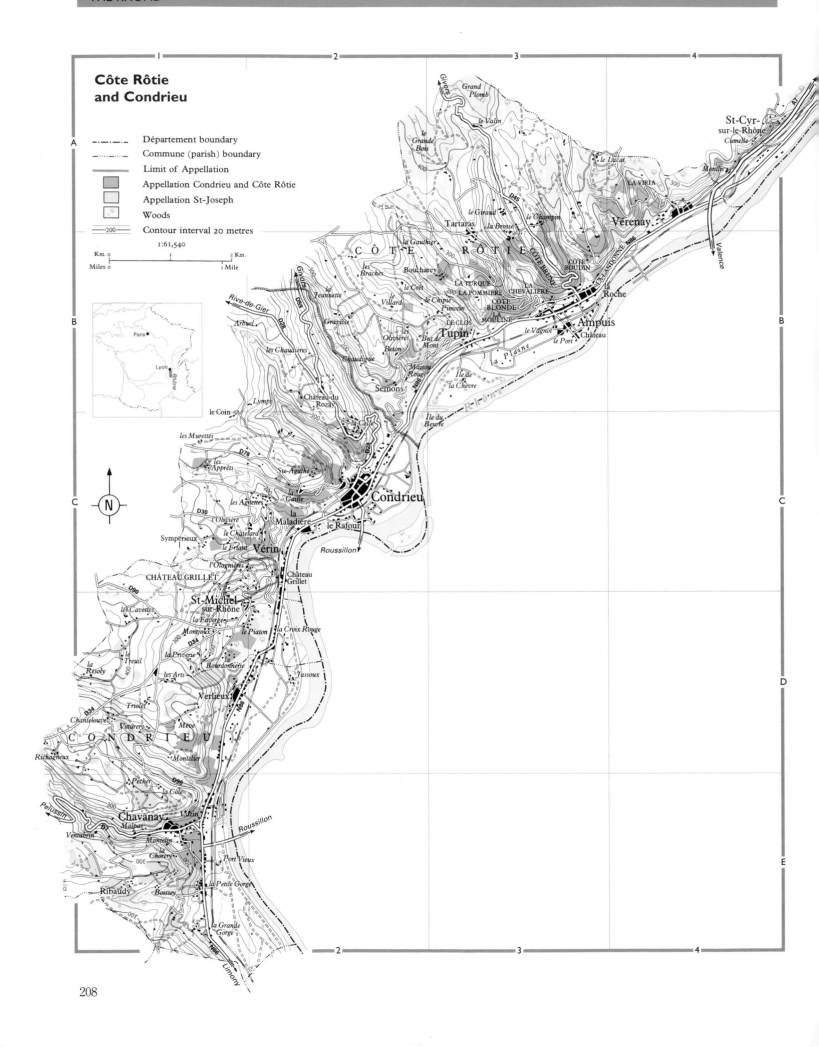

Côte Rôtie
and Condrieu

make-weight and to add strength when Burgundy producers needed some assistance. Today their reputation is higher than ever thanks to a coterie of fine producers, many of whom craft the smallest quantities of wine in cellars which look as though they have hardly changed in the last 100 years.

Travellers from Vienne should leave the autoroute and take the N86 which plunges immediately into the Rhône Gorge. The river cuts through the last outcrops of the Massif Central. Schistose soil has had to be blasted out for vines to be planted but – as in the Douro Valley in Portugal – it retains moisture as well as heat during the long, often dry summers. The first vineyard is the Côte Rôtie, a steeply sloping series of terraces which tower over the village of Ampuis. Legend has it that the two most famous slopes, the Côte Brune and Côte Blonde, are named after the hair colour of the two sisters who once owned them. More prosaically, their names are likely to have been prompted by the different colour of the soils: one is dark brown with iron, the other lighter with chalk.

The Côte Rôtie marks the most northerly appearance of the Syrah grape in France. And yet such is the power of its wines that it has traditionally been blended with small proportions of the white Viognier to soften tannins and reduce weight. Viognier comes into its own in the next two appellations, Condrieu and Château Grillet. Condrieu, with its apricot and peach flavours, powerful but with charmingly delicate aromas, is one of the most enticing white wines of southern France. It is strange to think that until the last decade this appellation was in decline: in 1965 there were only eight hectares in production. Today that figure has augmented to 80 and there are a further 20 hectares coming on stream, representing a huge increase – even if the size of the appellation is still tiny compared with the worldwide demand for Viognier wine. As with Côte Rôtie, the best slopes are the hardest to work: tiny terraces that demand back-breaking cultivation by hand since no machines can operate on such steep inclines.

Next door to Condrieu is the even smaller appellation of Château Grillet – all 3.8 hectares of it. This is one of the curiosities of the French system: an appellation that consists of just one estate. It is planted entirely with Viognier and, because of the vineyard's size and the minute quantities produced, the wine is always expensive. On the basis of the wines made in the 1980s many would argue that it does not merit its high price, but they have improved since then. Nevertheless this sunbaked bowl of vines, etched with apparently random terraces, is certainly an uplifting sight.

After this white-wine interlude the Syrah grape returns. The appellation of St-Joseph is not perhaps the best known of the northern Rhône vineyards, as a result of which its softer, less pronouncedly tannic wines are generally good value. Plantings were traditionally on the slopes rising from the river but new vineyards on the plateau above have changed the character of some of the wines – not, say the experts, for the better.

As the Rhône reaches the small twin towns of Tournon-sur-Rhône on the west bank and Tain-l'Hermitage on the east, the river turns east. The hills on the left bank terminate abruptly in a sharply conical hill which faces almost due south. This is the hill of Hermitage, an 180-degree circle of vines, terraced and heavily cultivated, topped by a small hermit's chapel. The wines of Hermitage – the reds made from Syrah and the whites from Marsanne and Roussanne – are the most famous of the northern Rhône wines and are now greatly in demand around the world. The reds in particular are the most long-lived of Syrahs: hugely powerful, dense, concentrated and deeply coloured, they need many decades to open out. The whites, produced in smaller quantities, are full-bodied with surprising depth and flavour.

Crozes-Hermitage, the vineyards that stretch to the north and the south of the Hermitage hill, have long been unfairly compared to their more elevated cousin. The wines do not achieve the power, intensity or long life of Hermitage wines but, with the advent of a new generation of producers and the example of some of the better local *négociants,* the wines are now attaining a considerable following for their immediate attractiveness and their relatively accessible prices.

There is one further powerful expression of Syrah in this northern part of the Rhône Valley. Below the east-facing slopes south of Tournon-sur-Rhône and still on the main N86 road south is the straggling village of Cornas. Above it are its vineyards: 80 hectares planted all to Syrah and extending around a steep-sided bowl. The wines produced by the granitic soil are more full-bodied than Côte Rôtie; they are possibly more powerful and certainly more brooding than Hermitage. Yet, for various reasons which have more to do with local politics than with wine quality, they are still relatively undervalued.

After this dramatic statement the northern Rhône ends with a curious whimper in the vineyards of St-Péray, where still and *méthode champenoise* sparkling white wines are made. They have a fair local reputation but few of them travel beyond the confines of the village. Pleasant enough to drink, they are not in the same class as their northern neighbours.

The main Rhône vineyards peter out at Valence just south of St-Péray and do not resume until south of the nougat capital of Montélimar. Eastwards along the valley of the Drôme and in the foothills of the Alps, however, lie the superbly beautiful vineyards of Die. The most famous product here is sparkling wine. There are two versions: Crémant de Die, a dry style made mainly from Clairette grapes using the *méthode champenoise*; and Clairette de Die Tradition, a semi-sweet style made from Muscat grapes using the *méthode diose.* The local cooperative is the centre of a revived tradition for these wines.

At St-Péray, Syrah grapes (above) give way to Marsanne, Roussanne and Roussette, to produce wines ranging from light to rich and broad.

PRODUCERS OF SPECIAL INTEREST

Domaine Gilles Barge
69420 Ampuis
Gilles Barge has taken over from his father Pierre the running of this small domaine. The estate concentrates mainly on Côte Rôtie.

Guy de Barjac 07130 Cornas
Traditional, powerful wines.

Buffardel Frères 26150 Die
Sweet and dry Clairette de Die Tradition are the only wines produced by this firm of *négociants*.

Domaine Bernard Burgaud
69420 Ampuis
A relatively young vineyard situated mainly at the top of the Côte Rôtie with a portion on the plateau above.

Cave des Clairmonts
26600 Beaumont-Monteux
Red and a small amount of white Crozes-Hermitage are made in this modern grouping of four growers headed by Jean-Michel Borja.

Cave Coopérative de Tain-l'Hermitage 26600 Tain-l'Hermitage
Besides having members with vineyards in Crozes-Hermitage, St-Péray, St-Joseph and Cornas, this cooperative controls two-thirds of the Hermitage AC.

Cave de St-Désirat
07340 St-Désirat
Good standards of St-Joseph.

Jean-François Chaboud
07130 St-Péray
The best-quality St-Péray.

Émile Champet 69420 Ampuis
The main part of M Champet's vineyard is on the Côte Brune and he owns a portion of the La Viaillère vineyard.

M Chapoutier
26600 Tain-l'Hermitage
A leading producer of Hermitage. Quality at this firm has risen dramatically in recent years.

Jean-Louis Chave
07300 Tournon-sur-Rhône
One of the great producers of Hermitage.

Domaine du Chêne
42410 Chavanay
Marc Rouvière makes both Condrieu and St-Joseph from his vineyards.

Auguste Clape 07130 Cornas
Superb wines are made by M Clape in his small cellar on the main road of Cornas. He is now joined by his son.

Domaine Clusel Roch
69420 Ampuis
Old vines give fruit for the Grandes Places *cuvée*.

Jean-Luc Colombo 07130 Cornas
A modernist producing good wines in a traditional appellation.

Domaine Pierre Coursodon
07300 Mauves
Le Paradis, St-Pierre and l'Olivaie are some names used by M Coursodon

for his red and white wines produced from vineyards in the southern part of the St-Joseph AC.

Delas Frères
07300 Tournon-sur-Rhône
An old established firm of *négociants* which owns vineyards in the main northern Rhône appellations.

Desmeure Père et Fils
26600 Mercurol
Soft but well made Crozes-Hermitage.

Pierre Dumazet 07340 Serrières
Produces tiny quantities of Condrieu plus some St-Joseph.

Domaine des Entrefaux
26600 Chanos-Curson
High-quality wines made with some new oak.

Philippe Faury 42410 Chavanay
Condrieu and St-Joseph.

Jules Fayolle et ses Fils
26600 Gervans
Crops are vinified separately from each parcel of land: Le Dionnières for Hermitage, Le Pontaix and Les Voussères for red Crozes-Hermitage, Les Blancs for white.

Domaine Florentin 07300 Mauves
Low-yielding vines produce concentrated wines.

Marius Gentaz-Dervieux
69420 Ampuis
Wines from the Côte Brune vineyard.

Alain Graillot
26600 Tain-l'Hermitage
One of the rising stars of Crozes-Hermitage.

Château Grillet 42410 Vérin
The only producer of this appellation. Now making fine wines from the Viognier grape.

Bernard Gripa
26600 Tain-l'Hermitage
One of the finest St-Joseph producers.

Jean-Louis Grippat
07300 Tournon-sur-Rhône
A small yield from the terraces of St-Joseph gives an intense wine.

Étienne Guigal 69420 Ampuis
The stunning wines owe much to the use of new wood.

Paul Jaboulet Aîné
07300 Tournon-sur-Rhône
Successful producer of wines from most parts of the northern Rhône. Hermitage La Chapelle is the star.

Robert Jasmin 69420 Ampuis
A traditionalist with fine wines.

Marcel Juge 07130 Cornas
Classic wine style.

Robert Michel 07130 Cornas
M Michel makes three styles of Cornas. The wine is bottled unfined, giving a very rich, earthy taste. Old-fashioned style.

André Perret
42410 Chavanay
Concentrated Condrieu.

Domaine Pochon
26600 Chanos-Curson
Good use of wood ageing is at the heart of the top wines.

Domaine Pradelle
26600 Chanos-Curson
Traditional well made red Crozes Hermitage produced.

René Rostaing 69420 Ampuis

Domaine Raymond Roure
26600 Gervans

Château du Rozay
69420 Condrieu
Two styles of Condrieu, one made from old vines for ageing.

Marc Sorrel 26600 Tain-l'Hermitage
Old vines are behind the quality achieved from this small vineyard where traditional methods reign.

Union Producteurs du Diois
26150 Die
The largest producer making good-quality wines of the Die appellations.

Georges Vernay 69420 Condrieu
The key figure in Condrieu, this producer has done much to achieve recognition for the appellation.

Noel Verset 07130 Cornas
Truly long-lived wines.

Vidal-Fleury 69420 Ampuis
Founded in 1781, the firm is the oldest in the Côte Rôtie area. Its reputation has remained high for much of that time.

Alain Voge 07130 Cornas
M Voge must be one of the few producers of Cornas who uses cement tanks in his cellar.

WINE ACTIVITIES

Chavanay, Condrieu A wine market is usually organised at the end of November.

Cornas A local wine market is usually arranged in December.

St-Péray A market for Rhône wines is held at the beginning of September.

HOTELS

Domaine de Clairefontaine
38121 Chonas l'Amballan
Tel (0)474 58 81 52
A converted 18th-century mansion on the edge of a Rhône Valley village. The rooms are clean and functional, the restaurant now quite superior.

Hôtellerie Beau Rivage 69420 Condrieu Tel (0)474 59 52 24
A riverside hotel dominated by the water and by the vineyards above the village. Terrace dining and river-facing bedrooms.

Hôtel St-Domingue 26150 Die
Tel (0)475 22 03 08
Simple holiday hotel with regional cooking in the restaurant.

L'Abricotine 26600 Mercurol
Tel (0)475 07 44 60
Small, quiet villa-hotel in a village in the Crozes-Hermitage.

Auberge des Cimes
43290 St-Bonnet-le-Froid
Tel (0)471 59 93 72
About 30km west of the Rhône in the

Massif Central, an attractive auberge with 16 bedrooms in a new annexe. Starred Michelin cooking.

Hôtel les Bains 07130 St-Péray
Tel (0)475 40 30 13
Quiet provincial hotel with its own grounds. Rooms were renovated for 1997 season.

Hôtel du Commerce 69 avenue Jean-Jaurès, 26600 Tain-l'Hermitage
Tel (0)475 08 65 00
Comfortable hotel with garden and restaurant.

Le Manoir 07300 Tournon-sur-Rhône Tel (0)475 08 20 31
Small hotel on the road to Lamastre. Swimming pool.

RESTAURANTS

La Vieille Auberge 07800 Charmes-sur-Rhône
Tel (0)474 60 80 10
High in a village on the west bank of the river. Sound, traditional cooking.

Le Caveau 26410 Châtillon-en-Diois Tel (0)475 21 18 77
Simple home cooking in a delightful rural setting.

Alain Charles 42410 Chavanay
Tel (0)477 87 23 02
Restaurant in the appellation of Condrieu. Regional cuisine

Beau Rivage 62420 Condrieu
Tel (0)474 59 52 24
High-standard, classic cuisine and a good wine-list. The restaurant overlooks the river.

Restaurant Ollier 01730 Cornas
Tel (0)475 40 32 17
Auberge-style cooking with good hearty local dishes.

La Porte de Montségur 26400 Crest Tel (0)475 25 41 48
On the north bank of the Drôme. Fine cooking is based on colourful, fresh ingredients.

Les Cèdres 26600 Granges-lès-Beaumont Tel (0)475 71 50 67
An attractive restaurant on the road from Tain-l'Hermitage to Romans. Terrace dining in the summer.

Michel Chabran 26600 Pont de l'Isère Tel (0)475 84 60 09
Just outside Valence, this Michelin-starred restaurant aims high and generally hits the mark.

Terminus 26240 St-Vallier
Tel (0)475 23 01 12
Attractive set menus and many local wines. Also a hotel.

Restaurant Reynaud 82 avenue Président-Roosevelt, 26600 Tain-l'Hermitage Tel (0)475 07 22 10
Contemporary cuisine and an extensive wine-list.

Pic 285 avenue Victor Hugo, 26000 Valence Tel (0)475 44 15 32
One of the most welcoming of France's great restaurants. Excellent cuisine and range of wines. High standards throughout.

Hermitage

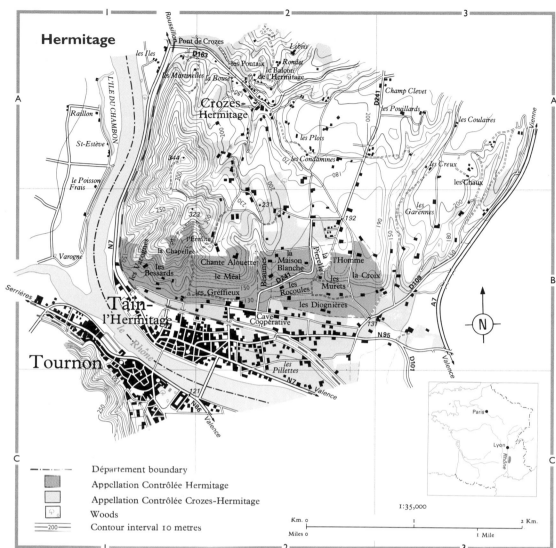

The sweeping terraces of the Courbis vineyard trace elegant curves along south-facing slopes at Châteaubourg Les Royes.

Département boundary

Appellation Contrôlée Hermitage

Appellation Contrôlée Crozes-Hermitage

Woods

—200— Contour interval 10 metres

1:35,000

PLACES OF INTEREST

The main roads through the region are always crowded, carrying traffic to and from the Mediterranean. But it is possible to turn both east and west and quickly leave the beaten track. The journey along the Drôme Valley to Die and beyond to Crest is particularly rewarding.

Ampuis Drive up one of the narrow, winding streets to the Côte Brune or the Côte Blonde for a fine impression of the vineyard terracing as well as a view across Ampuis and the Rhône.

Condrieu In the old town centre is the striking 16th-century Maison de la Gabelle where salt tax used to be collected. Its grey-stone façade is covered with medallions. An annual river tournament is held in August.

Crest One of France's tallest castles dominates Crest and guards the Drôme Valley as it emerges from the Alps.

Malleval Close to Condrieu, this village has 16th-century houses as well as castle remains.

St-Vallier-sur-Rhône Fine views from here over the Défile de St-Villier, a beautiful part of the Rhône Valley. The nearby château once belonged to Diane de Poitiers.

Tain-l'Hermitage From the town you can drive up to the top of the hill of Hermitage to the hermit's chapel and look down on the wonderfully positioned vineyards.

Tournon-sur-Rhône From the terrace of the 15th–16th-century castle there is a fine view of Tain-l'Hermitage and the hill of Hermitage. During the tourist season a steam train departs for Lamstre every morning to take a four-hour journey up the Doux Valley.

Vienne The town is just outside the vineyard zone, but a visit is well worth the detour if only to see its Roman remains, museums and medieval buildings. One of the largest surviving Roman amphitheatres is found here, as is the temple of Augustus and Livia and the 23m-high Pyramid, which lends its name to the nearby Pyramide restaurant.

*A strict pruning policy helps to reduce yields and so to concentrate the flavour of the grapes that subsequently develop. The cuttings (*les sarments*) are often burned in the vineyard in makeshift portable 'incinerators'.*

Côtes du Rhône

As the Rhône flows southward past Valence and Montélimar its valley opens into a wide plain bounded on the west by the Ardèche and on the east by the foothills of the Alps. Occasional ridges and mountains stand sentinel on the approaches to the city of Avignon and around these outcrops the main vineyards of the Côtes du Rhône are found.

Almost into Provence, this is true southern-French countryside. Olives make their first appearance alongside the vine, bringing a distinctly Mediterranean flavour to the pretty hillside villages. Larger towns, many with Roman origins, are strategically placed on the main routes. They once presented hideous bottlenecks as travellers from the north headed to the southern beaches: today that same traffic charges past on the main autoroute leaving the townspeople in peace to sit outside cafés, or play boules in dusty squares beneath flaking plane trees.

It is easy to grow vines here: the weather is kind and the wines have a southern, perfumed feel. Long, hot summers are tempered by the *Mistral* wind which, while it may drive men and dogs mad, does at least keep the vineyards free from humidity and the grapes free from rot. What little rain there is falls in the winter and spring.

Red wines are the principal product. North of Avignon, broad washes of vines fill the valley that shelters beneath the strange rock formation of Dentelles de Montmirail (the name rather fancifully suggests a lace-like shape). From here come some of the finest wines of the Côtes du Rhône. The names of villages such as Sablet, Séguret, Beaumes-de-Venise, Rasteau and Cairanne can be attached to the general appellation of Côtes du Rhône as an indication of extra quality. The Muscat wines of Beaumes-de-Venise and the sweet red vin doux naturel of Rasteau also come from here.

Two villages in this stretch have become sufficiently distinguished to gain their own separate appellations. Gigondas can produce hugely powerful wines from bowl-shaped land in the mountains which allows the vines a small but significant amount of extra heat. The wines of neighbouring Vacqueyras are slightly less classy, but they too have considerable finesse and quality.

These villages are the heart of any wine tour of the Côtes du Rhône vineyards. The wine road runs between the agricultural and truffle centre of Carpentras and the ancient Roman town of Vaison-la-Romaine. To the right as you travel north are the rocks of Montmirail; to the left, vines stretch away towards the distant Rhône in a panorama of uninterrupted grape-growing rare even in France. Enticements to stop, taste and buy are everywhere – not just from the cooperatives attached to each village but increasingly from the many private estates which have found it worthwhile to build small tasting rooms alongside their cellars.

On the far eastern side of the Dentelles de Montmirail another, tighter valley is the home of the Côtes du Ventoux. These vineyards, stretching southward towards the Lubéron and producing wines of good value and increasingly good quality, are dominated in their turn by the massive hump of Mont Ventoux.

On facing banks of the Rhône just north of Avignon are two enclaves of wines of superior fame and quality. On the left bank is Châteauneuf-du-Pape (see pages 216–21), while on the right are the almost twin appellations of Lirac and Tavel – twins because most producers in the area make both styles of wine. Lirac wines are superior those of Côtes du Rhône. Tavel produces what is reputed to be the best rosé in France – although until recently that claim rested more on its former quality than on reality.

Southern countryside typified by the village of Brantes, a scattering of pale stone buildings reflecting the glare and intense heat of the afternoon sun.

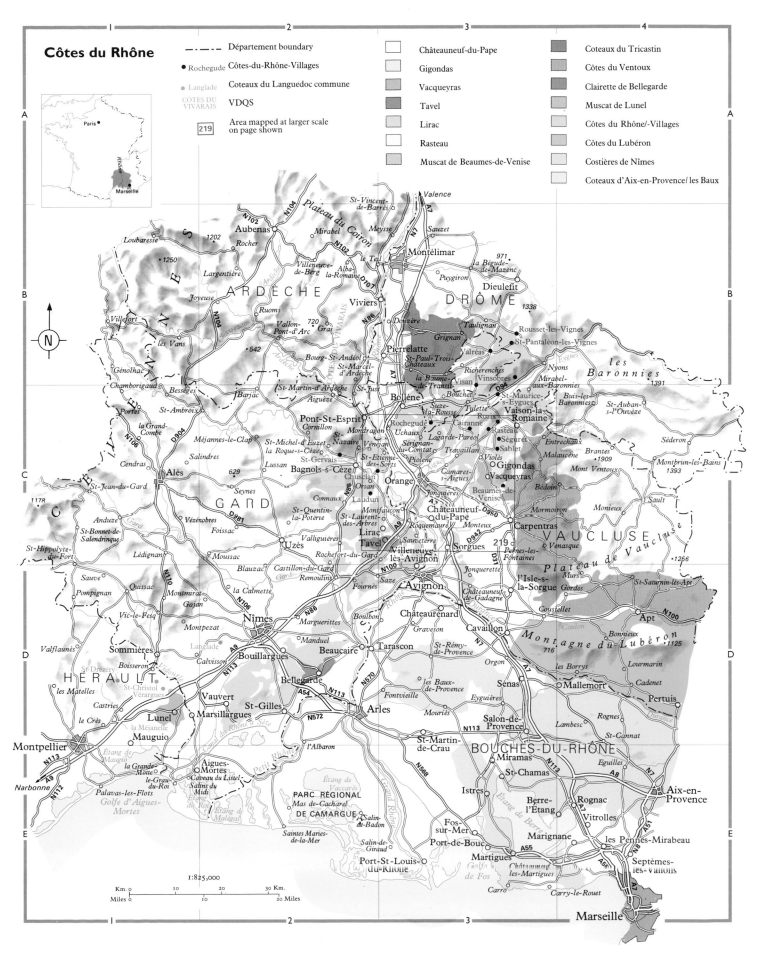

The medieval village of Séguret, nestling in the wooded hills of the jagged Montmirail escarpment among orchards, olives and vines, has been declared a historic monument in its entirety. Its Côtes du Rhône-Village red is peppery and full, its white rounded and clean.

Grape varieties are many and varied in these vineyards. Grenache dominates in reds and rosés. Carignan and Cinsault were once the normal blending partners with Grenache but increasingly they have been superseded by superior vines such as Syrah and Mourvèdre. Intriguingly, there are also producers who makes convincing special *cuvées* from old Cinsault vines.

Recent changes that have been made (especially by the dominant cooperatives) both in the blends and in the winemaking practices themselves, have meant a general improvement in the style of Côtes du Rhône wines and a very pleasant increase in their drinkability. Many are made to be drunk young but there are producers, especially among the increasing number of private estates that make and bottle their own wine, who also make *cuvées* fine enough to put away for a few years. Gigondas and Vacqueyras in particular are regarded as having considerable ageing potential.

PRODUCERS OF SPECIAL INTEREST

CÔTES DU RHÔNE AND CÔTES DU RHÔNE-VILLAGES

Domaine des Amoureuses
07700 Bourg-St-Andeol

Domaine Michel Bernard
84100 Orange

Domaine des Bernardins
84190 Beaumes-de-Venise

Domaine de Boissan 84110 Sablet
Makes a deeply coloured Côtes du Rhône-Villages Sablet that has 10% Syrah and 2% Mourvèdre in its blend.

Domaine du Cabanon
30650 Rochefort-du-Gard
M Payan uses some carbonic maceration for his red Côtes du Rhône, the only wine he makes.

Domaine de Cabasse
84110 Séguret
A hotel and restaurant are also run on the estate.

Cave Coopérative
84190 Beaumes-de-Venise
Known equally for its Muscat-based Beaumes de Venise and its red Côtes du Rhône-Villages.

Cave Coopérative 30200 Chusclan

Cave Coopérative 84110 Puyméras

Cave Coopérative 84110 Rasteau
A top Rhône Valley cooperative with a speciality in the local sweet Rasteau vin doux naturel.

Cave Coopérative
26130 Rochegude

Cave Coopérative
26230 St-Pantaléon-lès-Vignes

Cave Coopérative
26130 Suze-la-Rousse

Domaine de Cayron
84190 Gigondas
High-quality wines produced in an ancient cellar.

Cellier des Dauphins
26130 Tulette
Huge cellars produce a mixed range.

Cellier des Princes
84350 Courthézon
Large cooperative with good wines.

Chambovet Père et Fils
84100 Orange
Côtes du Rhône wines from three estates: Château d'Estagnol, La Serre du Prieur and Domaine Ste-Marie.

Domaine du Charavin
84110 Rasteau

Domaine le Clos des Cazeaux
84190 Vacqueyras
Produces Vacqueyras and Gigondas.

Domaine de Coyeux
84190 Beaumes-de-Venise
Spectacular vineyard under the heights of the Dentelles de Montmirail making Muscat de Beaumes-de-Venise as well as red wines.

Cru du Coudoulet
84350 Courthézon
A Côtes du Rhône estate owned by the same family as Château de Beaucastel in Châteauneuf-du-Pape.

Château de Deurre
26490 Vinsobres
Domaine de Durban
84190 Beaumes-de-Venise
Fine Muscat as well as Côtes du
Rhône-Villages.
Domaine de la Fourmone
84190 Vacqueyras
Makes Vacqueyras and Gigondas to a
high standard.
Domaine les Goubert
84190 Gigondas
Modern cellars and elegant wines.
Domaine du Grand Montmirail
84190 Gigondas
Château du Grand Moulas
84420 Mornas
Good-value, very drinkable Côtes
du Rhône.
Domaine de la Grand'Ribe
84290 Ste-Cécile-lès-Vignes
Domaine des Grands Devers
84600 Valréas
A sturdy Valréas Côtes du Rhône
made from 90% Grenache.
Domaine de la Grapillon d'Or
84190 Gigondas
Good solid Gigondas with plenty of
weighty fruit.
Domaine de la Janasse
84350 Courthézon
Both Châteauneuf-du-Pâpe and
Côtes du Rhône are made here from
50 different parcels of widely
scattered vineyard.
Claude et Nicole Jaume
26490 Vinsobres
Domaine des Lambertins
84190 Vacqueyras
A traditional family firm producing
Vacqueyras and Côtes du Rhône
wines, both in red only.
Gabriel Meffre 84190 Gigondas
The largest producer of Gigondas,
Meffre has done much to help the
reputation of the AC area.
Domaine de l'Olivet
07700 Bourg-St-Andeol
Domaine de l'Oratoire
St-Martin 84290 Cairanne
A top-notch domaine making big,
quite tannic wines, still with a majority
of Grenache but with increasing
amounts of Syrah and Mourvèdre.
Domaine Pélaquié 30290 Laudun
Domaine de la Présidente
84290 Ste-Cécile-lès-Vignes
Domaine Rabasse-Charavin
84290 Cairanne
Energetic owners make an
overwhelming array of fine wines.
Domaine Raspail-Äy
84190 Gigondas.
Some of the area's best wines.
Domaine de la Réméjeanne
30200 Cadignac
Domaine de la Renjarde
30200 Cadignac
Deep, peppery Côtes du Rhône
Cuvée Henri Fabre (60% Syrah). The
domaine also produces a Côtes du
Rhône-Villages.

Domaine Marcel Richaud
84290 Cairanne
Domaine de Ste-Anne
30200 St-Gervais
Attractive, spicy reds and good whites
including one of 100% Viognier.
Domaine St-Appolinaire
84110 Puyméras
Château St-Estève 84100 Uchaux
Impressive property with a wide
range of wines.
Domaine le Sang des Cailloux
84190 Vacqueyras
Vacqueyras with herby, spicy fruit and
touches of wood tannin.
Domaine de la Soumade
84110 Rasteau
Innovative wines as well as more
classic products.
**Union des Vignerons de
l'Enclave des Papes** 84600 Valréas
Domaine de Verquière
84110 Sablet
Traditional reds and a Rasteau vin
doux naturel.
La Vieille Ferme 84100 Orange
Merchant firm established by the
Perrins of Beaucastel.
Vignerons Ardechois
07120 Ruoms
This huge cooperative is the largest
producer in the Rhône Valley.
**Les Vignerons des Quatre
Chemins** 30290 Laudun

LIRAC AND TAVEL
Château d'Aquéria 30126 Tavel
Classic Tavel: a raspberry flavour and a
good balance of acidity and fruit.
Domaine de Castel-Oualou
30150 Roquemaure
Domaine Jean-Pierre Lafond
30126 Tavel
Deliciously fruity, fresh Tavel. Also red
Lirac and Côtes du Rhône.
Domaine Maby 30126 Tavel
Fresh Tavel and Lirac for ageing.
Château de Trinquevedel
30126 Tavel
Domaines Verda
30150 Roquemaure
There are two Lirac estates owned by
the Verda family: Château St-Roch and
Domaine Cantegril-Verda.

CÔTES DU VENTOUX
Domaine des Anges
84750 Montmoiron
Grenache, Syrah, Cinsaut and
Carignan make a full, fresh, easy-
drinking Côtes du Ventoux.
Cave Coopérative
84750 Montmoiron

FÊTES
Bédoin Fête des Vignerons de Mont
Ventoux around August 10.
Gordes Fête des Côtes du Ventoux
around July 14.
Ruoms Fête des Vignerons
d'Ardèchois around August 10.

Ste-Cécile-lès-Vignes A festival
of wine and music takes place around
November 20.
St-Maurice-sur-Eygues Wine
festival around August 10.
St-Victor-la-Coste Festival of Côtes
du Rhône around June 15.
Vacqueyras Fête des Côtes du
Rhône-Villages around July 14.
Vinsobres Côtes du Rhône
festival and competition at the
beginning of March.

WINE INFORMATION
Maison des Vins 6 rue des Trois
Faucons, 84024 Avignon
Tel (0)490 27 24 00

HOTELS
Château de Coulorgues route
d'Avignon, 30200 Bagnols-sur-Cèze
Tel (0)466 89 52 78
Small château surrounded by a park.
Restaurant and swimming pool.
Domaine de St-Luc
26790 La Baume-de-Transit
Tel (0)475 98 11 51
East of Bollène, this rustic Provençal
farmhouse provides simple rooms in a
beautiful remote setting.
Fiacre 153 rue Vigne, 84200
Carpentras Tel (0)490 63 03 15
Set in an 18th-century building in the
centre of town.
La Genestière 84170 Monteux
Tel (0)490 62 27 04
Comfortable rooms; attractive
location; swimming pool.
Les Frênes 84140 Montfavet
Tel (0)490 31 17 93
Luxurious hotel set in a park in the
suburbs of Avignon. Good restaurant.
Hôtel Arène place de Langes
84100 Orange Tel (0)490 34 10 95
A quiet hotel in a central location not
far from the Roman arena.
La Bellerive 84110 Rasteau
Tel (0)490 46 10 20
This modern hotel, part of the Relais
du Silence group, is set in some fine
gardens in the heart of the Côtes du
Rhône vineyards.
Château de Rochegude 26790
Rochegude Tel (0)475 04 81 88
Comfortable castle hotel with
swimming pool and impressive
underground cellars.
Domaine de Cabasse 84110
Séguret Tel (0)490 46 91 12
The hotel is part of a wine estate.
Good restaurant and swimming pool.
Le Relais-du-Château 26130
Suze-la-Rousse Tel (0)475 04 87 07
Modern hotel with swimming pool
and relaxed restaurant.
Hostellerie le Beffroi
84110 Vaison-la-Romaine
Tel (0)490 36 04 71
A good place to stay and to eat in the
old part of this ancient town.

l'Atelier 5 rue de la Foire
30400 Villeneuve-lès-Avignon
Tel (0)490 25 01 84
Comfortable central hotel.
Le Prieuré 30400 Villeneuve-
lès-Avignon Tel (0)490 25 18 20
Elegant and luxurious, this ancient
hotel faces Avignon across the
Rhône. Dining in the coutryard
during summer. There is some
noise from passing trains.

RESTAURANTS
Le Bistrot d'Avignon
1 place Jean-Vilar, 84000 Avignon
Tel (0)490 88 06 45
Popular with tourists. A good
selection of wines by the glass.
Brunel 46 rue de la Balance
84000 Avignon Tel (0)490 85 24 83
Inventive, light cuisine served here,
as well as splendid desserts.
La Fourchette 17 rue Racine
84000 Avignon Tel (0)490 82 56 01
A local favourite. Regional cooking
and pleasant atmosphere.
Le Vernet 58 rue Joseph-Vernet
84000 Avignon Tel (0)490 86 64 53
A large garden outside, paintings
inside, fresh ingredients on the plate.
l'Oustau d'Anaïs 84410 Bédoin
Tel (0)490 65 67 43
At the foot of Mount Ventoux in
the midst of lovely country. Good
country food.
l'Orangerie 26 rue Duplessis, 84200
Carpentras Tel (0)490 67 27 23
Inconspicuous from the outside but
attractive inside. A garden, good
food and an expertly chosen wine-list.
St Hubert 84340 Entrechaux
Tel (0)490 36 07 05
Convenient for visiting nearby
Vaison-la-Romaine. Shady terrace
and inexpensive food.
Le Val des Fées 84220 Roussillon
Tel (0)490 75 64 99
A small restaurant serving generous
helpings of colourful, but not
sophisticated, cooking.
Le Relais 84290 Ste-Cécile-
lès-Vignes Tel (0)490 30 84 39
A congenial restaurant. High
standards are set by the cuisine.

*Botrytis-affected Muscat yields the
high-flavoured, subtle and lingering
dessert wine Beaumes-de-Venise.*

Once a supplier of wine to Burgundy for blending, Gigondas won appellation contrôlée *status in 1971. Now ninety per cent of the local population depend on wine for their livelihood.*

La Table du Comtat 84110 **Séguret** Tel (0)490 46 91 49 Excellent cooking and good local wine-list in a picturesque village with good views.

Auberge de Tavel 30126 **Tavel** Tel (0)466 50 03 41 Top-class wine-list and food. Also a hotel.

La Ferme du Champ-Rond 84600 **Valréas** Tel (0)490 37 31 68 Charming old farmstead. The cuisine offers modern interpretations of classic dishes.

Le Prieuré 26110 **Vinsobres** Tel (0)475 27 63 32 Country inn with local-style cooking.

Le Mas de Bouvan 84150 **Violès** Tel (0)490 70 84 08 Carefully prepared regional dishes.

PLACES OF INTEREST

Avignon Full of tourists during the season. The papal palace, huge and forbidding, is better from outside than inside but is still worth a visit. The gardens of the Rocher des Doms beside the cathedral have fine views of the Rhône and the Pont St-Bénézet (the 'Pont d'Avignon' of the song) is intriguing, although it now has only four arches instead of the original 22 and a busy dual carriageway passes underneath it. Good shopping but, as in most cities, beware of pickpockets.

Beaumes-de-Venise Village with a medieval bastion, caves, and remains of a prehistoric burial chamber.

Carpentras A busy market town, also the centre of the truffle trade. The Arc de Triomphe dates from Roman times and the Musée de Poésie is unique in France. There is also a good regional museum.

Fontaine-de-Vaucluse A tourist spot with a spring at the edge of a cliff. A museum is devoted to the poet Petrarch, who climbed nearby Mont Ventoux.

Gigondas Attractive wine village at the foot of the Dentelles de Montmirail. Remains of old fortifications and a castle. There is a tasting room in the village.

Gordes Straggling hill village rescued by local artists.

Grignan The imposing castle was made famous through the letters of the Marquise de Sévigné, whose daughter and son-in-law lived here. Summer organ recitals in the church.

Nyons Town noted for wine, olives, jam and truffles. A pleasant old quarter.

Orange A sizeable town in Roman times where many remains can be seen. The theatre, the finest to survive from that era, is still used and a large triumphal arch depicts Caesar's victories over the Gauls.

Roussillon Hill-top village in the Côtes du Ventoux district.

Sablet Built in step formation up a hill alongside the remains of old fortifications.

Séguret An almost perfect medieval village straggling down a hillside.

Suze-la-Rousse A wine university was set up in the château in 1977. Activities cover the whole gamut but concentrate on the Rhône region.

Vaison-la-Romaine Extensive Roman remains, a museum to house the finest finds and the 7th-century church of Notre-Dame-de-Nazareth make this one of the region's most interesting towns.

Visan A fortified village with castle ruins. A pilgrimage is made every year to the church of Notre-Dame-des-Vignes.

Viviers-sur-Rhône Small medieval town with a 12th-century cathedral.

Châteauneuf-du-Pape

From Avignon the approach to Châteauneuf-du-Pape is gradual. Industrial activities give way to vines; the ground begins to slope and eventually a strange ruin looms on the horizon: apparently a solid wall leading from nowhere to nowhere and pierced by a huge arch. Houses cluster down the hillside below. The ruins are of the summer palace built by the 14th-century popes when the papacy had installed itself in Avignon. The village, now better known for its wines than its papal connections, recalls that time of fame and glory in its name.

In this and in many other sections of the Châteauneuf vineyards, short stumpy vines grow apparently out of stone. The soil, such as it is, lies buried under thick layers of huge pebbles. By both reflecting the sun onto the grapes and storing heat during the day to release after sunset, the stones contribute to the power and intensity of so many of the village's wines.

The special qualities of Châteauneuf's wines have long been recognised. They were certainly prized by the papal court during the 14th century, at which time as many as three million vines were under cultivation. But the wines' fame did not die with the return of the papacy to Rome. By the early-18th century, only grapes from within the commune boundaries of Châteauneuf were allowed to be be processed there. Two centuries later in 1923, the rules for the production of Châteauneuf drawn up by Baron Pierre le Roy de Boiseaumarie of Château Fortia became the forerunners of the *appellation contrôlée* rules established in the mid-1930s.

Modern Châteauneuf wines are the southern Rhône Valley's best. While a good proportion of them (some good, some less so) are still handled by négociants and cooperatives, the influence and reputation of the top estates is increasing worldwide. Some, such as Château La Nerthe, are very grand while others are headquartered in small houses or in twisting cellars dug into the earth.

One of the appellation's claims to fame is that 13 grape varieties are permitted in the wines. The list includes a number of white grapes that can be put into the red wine or be used to make Châteauneuf whites. Few estates use more than the three or four leading varieties – Grenache, Syrah, Mourvèdre plus probably Cinsault – but two of the top producers, Château de Mont Redon and Château de Beaucastel, make use of all 13 in different *cuvées*.

Blending, both of grape varieties and of wines from different parcels of soil, is part of the producers' stock-in-trade here. Grapes from the red earth under those pebbles, or from gravel soils or the clay soils nearer the Rhône, are blended to give Châteauneuf wines their complexity and subtle nuances.

The village is entirely dedicated to the vine. A good number of producers have tasting cellars and the many restaurants serve the local wines. The surrounding countryside has gentle slopes and wide plateaux across which the vines spread. In the height of the summer the reflected heat combined with the intense southern sun brings these open spaces to furnace-like temperatures, with the result that many of the wines have a huge alcoholic content. Once it seemed that strength was all that they had to commend them, but today as producers experiment with some barrique ageing (as

Right: The apparent tranquillity of the papal ruins – whose vast cellars are still used by the local confrérie for tastings and banquets– belies the enormity of the Châteauneuf-du-Pape winemaking operation. In excess of a million cases are produced each year.

distinct from ageing in traditional large wooden barrels) there are more and more subtleties appearing in the wines.

One of the distinguishing characteristics of many bottles of Châteauneuf is the insignia of the papal crossed-keys embossed on the glass. Its presence indicates that the wine has been bottled in the appellation, rather than having been transported considerable distances before being bottled, as still happens with many *négociant* wines. Although the symbol may not guarantee quality, it does guarantee authenticity of provenance and recalls the medieval origins of this distinguished papal wine.

Above: Thirteen different grape varieties are permitted in the dark, strong, long-lived wines of Châteauneaf-du-Pape, so the final product relies heavily on the artistry of the blender as well as on the quality of the grapes.

Châteauneuf-du-Pape

—·—·—·— Département boundary

—·—·—·— Arrondissement boundary

—·—·—·— Canton boundary

—·——·— Commune (parish) boundary

CH. DE SÉGRIERS Leading producer

Bédarrides Châteauneuf-du-Pape commune

SABLET Côtes du Rhône-Villages commune

—————— Appellation communale boundary

[shaded] Vineyards

[symbol] Woods

Contour intervals:
below 120 metres every 20 metres
above 120 metres every 40 metres

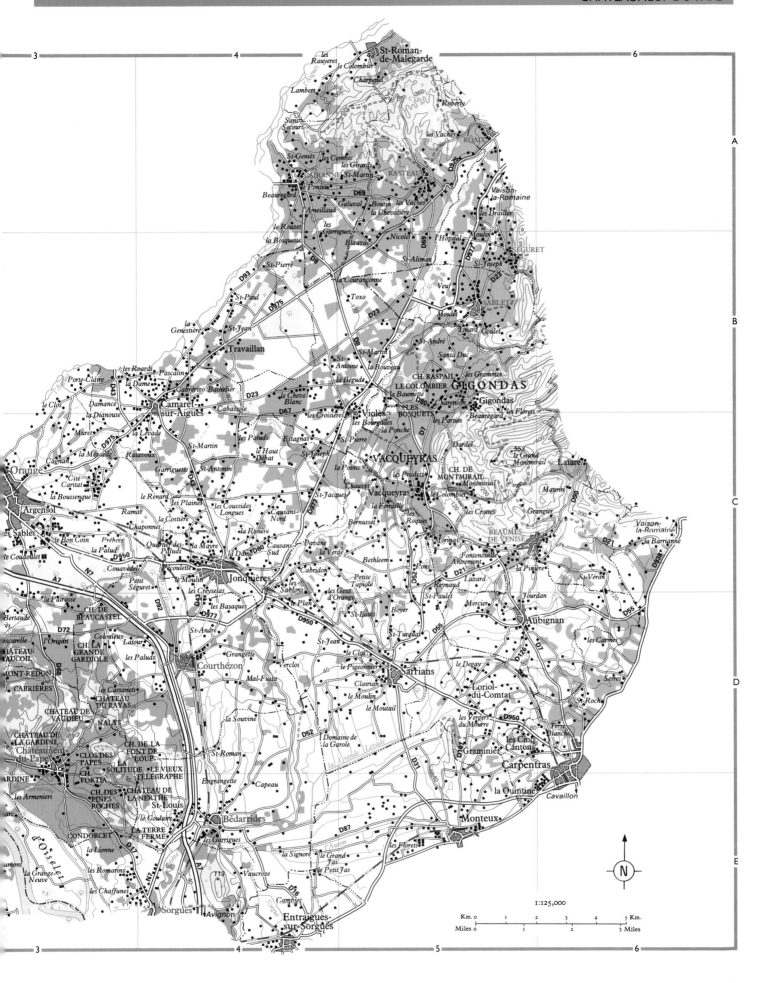

Above: Châteauneuf-du-Pape's famous vineyard stones, the Alpine quartzite drift-boulders, are known as galets roulés. *The vines are deliberately pruned low and bush-like which protects them to some extent from the merciless sweep of the* Mistral *winds.*

PRODUCERS OF SPECIAL INTEREST

Château de Beaucastel
84350 Courthézon
The Perrin family use all 13 permitted grape varieties in their justly famed wines and practise strictly organic methods in vineyard and cellar.

Domaine de Beaurenard
84230 Châteauneuf-du-Pape
Founded in 1695, this is one of the area's oldest estates.

Domaine Berthet-Rayne
84230 Châteauneuf-du-Pape
This small estate produces Châteauneuf and Côtes du Rhône using thermo-vinification at controlled temperatures.

La Bosquet des Papes
84230 Châteauneuf-du-Pape
Close to the papal palace ruins.

Domaine de Cabrière-lès-Silex
84230 Châteauneuf-du-Pape
High up in the appellation with the classic pebbly soil in its vineyards.

Les Cailloux
84230 Châteauneuf-du-Pape
Owned by André Brunel who also makes a Côtes du Rhône.

Domaine Chante Cigale
84230 Châteauneuf-du-Pape
Traditional estate; long-lived wines.

Domaine Chante Perdrix
84230 Châteauneuf-du-Pape
Big, old-style wines are made on this estate on the western edge of the Châteauneuf AC area.

Domaine les Clefs d'Or
84230 Châteauneuf-du-Pape
Traditional, powerful, rich wines.

Clos des Papes
84230 Châteauneuf-du-Pape
Well structured, long-lived wines.

Domaine Durieu
84230 Châteauneuf-du-Pape
The wines are not too heavy, they have an elegant style and mature well for up to ten years.

Château des Fines Roches
84230 Châteauneuf-du-Pape
The vineyard surrounds the hotel and is owned by the Musset family, important local *négociants*.

Château de la Font du Loup
84350 Courthézon
The red is elegant and less tannic than some Châteauneuf. The white is produced in small quantities.

Château Fortia
84230 Châteauneuf-du-Pape
One of the finest examples of the old-style wines.

Château de la Gardine
84230 Châteauneuf-du-Pape
The Brunels produce a Cuvée Génération which is entirely aged in new wood – as are portions of the white wine.

Domaine du Grand Tinel
84230 Châteauneuf-du-Pape
Powerful wines are made here by Elie Jeune.

Domaine de Montpertuis
84230 Châteauneuf-du-Pape
Superb Cuvée Tradition made entirely from old-vine Grenache.

Château de Mont Redon
84230 Châteauneuf-du-Pape
One of the largest and best estates.

Domaine de Nalys
84230 Châteauneuf-du-Pape
On the eastern side of the AC area. All 13 Châteauneuf varieties are planted at this large estate, which has been in existence since 1778.

Château La Nerthe
84230 Châteauneuf-du-Pape
The estate's reputation for elegant wines is soaring.

Château Rayas
84230 Châteauneuf-du-Pape
Small estate but highly regarded wines.

Domaine de la Solitude
84230 Châteauneuf-du-Pape
The wine has a high proportion (20%) of Mourvèdre which gives some power as well as an attractive perfume.

Domaine de La Vieille Julienne
84100 Orange
Côtes du Rhône as well as Châteauneuf is produced at this estate which is situated at the northern edge of the appellation.

Domaine du Vieux Télégraphe
84230 Châteauneuf-du-Pape
An estate whose traditional style is now evolving with greater elegance.

FÊTES

Châteauneuf The Fête de St-Marc takes place around April 25; the Fête de la Véraison is on the first weekend of August; the Ban de Vendanges celebrates the beginning of the harvest around the second half of September.

HOTELS

For hotels in the area surrounding Châteauneuf-du-Pape, see Côtes du Rhône listings, page 215.

Hostellerie du Château des Fines Roches
84230 Châteauneuf-du-Pape
Tel (0)490 83 70 23
Seven luxurious rooms in a castle flanked by crenellated towers. The restaurant food is equally impressive. The wine estate here is run by different owners.

La Sommellerie
route de Roquemaure
84230 Châteauneuf-du-Pape
Tel (0)490 83 50 00
Good value for money and one of the region's most pleasant places to stay. It has a dozen comfortable rooms (plus two suites), a fine restaurant (with terrace) and a swimming pool.

RESTAURANTS

For restaurants in the area surrounding Châteauneuf-du-Pape see Côtes du Rhône listings, page 215–16.

La Garbure
84230 **Châteauneuf-du-Pape**
Tel (0)490 83 75 05
Good-value country cooking in an attractive setting. A few simple rooms are also available.

La Mule du Pape
84230 **Châteauneuf-du-Pape**
Tel (0)490 83 79 22
On the first floor of a building in the village centre. Great care is taken with Provençal cooking.

Le Pistou 84230 **Châteauneuf-du-Pape** Tel (0)490 83 71 75
Traditional cooking.

La Porte des Princes avenue de la République, 84350 **Courthézon**
Tel (0)490 70 70 26.
Good country cooking.

PLACES OF INTEREST

Châteauneuf-du-Pape The remains of the Popes' summer palace still dominate the village skyline. The vast cellar hall is still intact and used for local festivities. The village's main concern is wine, and everywhere there are cellars and other signs of viticultural activity. Various producers have their cellars and tasting rooms in the centre while on the route into town from Avignon, producer Père Anselme has established a small wine museum. One of the better known exhibits is a 4,000-litre cask.

Top: Restoration of Château La Nerthe, its vineyards and cellars, began in 1985. Châteauneuf's most substantial and elegant property, it is unusual in having its 90-ha vineyard in a single block around the château.

Above: The chais at Château de la Gardine where Patrick and Maxime Brunel produce consistently fine Châteauneuf-du-Pape. Some cuvées are treated to 70% cask ageing in new wood for two years or more.

221

Provence

Forget the mass tourism and the millionaires' yachts; forget the image of local wine being a rather heavy rosé made to be drunk on the spot. There is much more to Provence, both as a holiday destination and as a wine region, than these stereotypes suggest.

The part of Provence most usually associated with tourists is confined to a narrow coastal strip. There are vineyards in some of the most popular destinations, especially around St-Tropez, but there are many more of them inland. This is where the real Provence is found, a land wild and untamed where silver-grey barren mountains rise above the scattered pines and bushes of the *garrigue* – the moor or wasteland. It is as remote and as beautiful as anywhere in France. Under the lee of these mountains, in land often torn from the scrub, lie the Provence vineyards.

There was a time when Provence was concerned only with rosé. With a few important exceptions, standards were low because growers could sell all they made to summer visitors. This is still the case at some estates, but at many others producers are investing in serious winemaking. Much of the excitement started with red wines. The use of modern production techniques has increased, as has the practice of ageing in new wood rather than in ancient barrels, and varieties such as Cabernet Sauvignon and Syrah have been introduced. Provence's local grapes – Grenache and Cinsaut, along with the much more exciting Mourvèdre of Bandol – are capable of producing some enticingly herbal wines full of southern character, but for real class the Grenache and Cinsaut at least need to be blended with the new arrivals. Some producers, particularly in Les Baux-de-Provence and Aix-en-Provence, have produced startling results with a richness of fruit reminiscent of New World examples by using almost entirely Cabernet Sauvignon. Others have combined southern warmth with northern structure to produce reds worthy of serious consideration.

Much has been done to bring rosés up to standard: vinification in stainless steel, which preserves the wines' freshness, has limited the appeal of the familiar orange-coloured, high-alcohol, siesta-inducing examples. In the Côtes de Provence, the region's largest appellation, rosés are still the main product and are worth seeking out to enjoy with Provençal cuisine.

Left: Les Baux, a 200 x 800m promontory of the Alpilles scored on either side with vertical ravines, rises majestically from a bare rock spur.

Provence

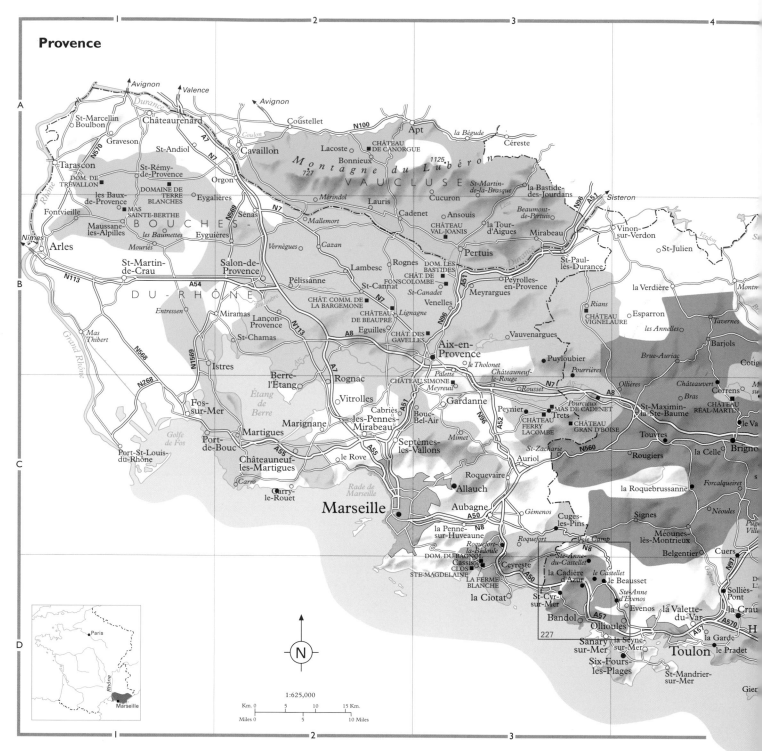

There are two pockets of traditional white-wine interest in Provence, one at each extremity of the region. Close to Nice is the small appellation of Bellet whose light, fresh wines, based on local grapes such as the Rolle combined with Roussanne and even Chardonnay, are quickly consumed along the Promenade des Anglais. In the west, the fishing port of Cassis produces a dry, tangy white, the perfect accompaniment to the local fish dishes.

Provence wine country stretches right across the region. In the west are the high-quality appellations of Les Baux-de-Provence and Aix-en-Provence: some of the best estates are found around the Alpilles Mountains of the former, where production of organic wines is concentrated. To the south are Cassis with its white wines

and Bandol, set in hilly country around a huge bowl of a valley, with its Mourvèdre-based reds. Dynamic young winemakers have helped some of these long-lived monsters to enjoy a recent revival.

The Coteaux Varois, further inland and to the east, is a lightweight prelude to the Côtes de Provence proper. There are various concentrations of the Côtes de Provence: around Mont Ste-Victoire in the west, Les Arcs-sur-Argens in the centre and in the peninsula of St-Tropez in the south. Ste-Victoire has some excellent individual estates while Les Arcs-sur-Argens is home to the local Maison des Vins which has a helpful tasting centre as well as a restaurant. St-Tropez is, well, fashionable ... but its wines should not be ignored for that reason alone.

Organic techniques are used at Domaine Richeaume to farm the firm's 54 acres on the sun-baked slopes of Mont Ste-Victoire.

PRODUCERS OF SPECIAL INTEREST

BANDOL

La Bastide Blanche
83330 Ste-Anne-du-Castellet
The white is the star, although the reds can have good weight and tannin.

Domaine Bunan
83740 La Cadière d'Azur
Bandol's most dynamic producer.

Domaine du Cagueloup
83270 St-Cyr-sur-Mer
Reds with fruit and a typical herbiness.

Domaine de Frégate
83270 St-Cyr-sur-Mer
The reds are at their best after five to six years.

Domaine le Galantin
83330 Le Plan-du-Castellet
A fragrant red from 60% Mourvèdre, 20% Grenache and 20% Cinsaut.

Domaine Lafran-Veyrolles
83740 La Cadière d'Azur

Domaine la Laidière
83330 Ste-Anne d'Évenos
Careful destalking and long, slow fermentation processes help to produce fine wines.

Domaine de la Noblesse
83740 La Cadière d'Azur

Château de Pibarnon
83740 La Cadière d'Azur
The highest-altitude estate in Bandol, making wines of great interest.

Château Pradeaux
83270 St-Cyr-sur-Mer
Traditional wines from old vines.

Domaine Ray-Jane
83330 Le Plan-du-Castellet
Traditional wines full of tannin and powerful fruit.

Château Ste-Anne
83330 Ste-Anne d'Évenos
The reds are wood-aged for up to 22 months.

Domaine Tempier
83330 Le Plan-du-Castellet
Big, powerful reds.

Château Vannières
83740 La Cadière d'Azur
Vineyard dates from the 16th century.

BELLET

Château de Bellet
St-Roman-de-Bellet 06200 Nice
A serious producer.

Château de Crémat
St-Roman-de-Bellet, 06200 Nice
Prestigious estate, leading this small appellation. Produces light, long-lived reds; good rosés and top-class whites.

CASSIS

Domaine du Bagnol 13260 Cassis
High quality from a tiny domaine.

Clos Ste-Magdelaine 13260 Cassis
Delicious straw-coloured white with a nutty bouquet and tinges of green from the Sauvignon in the blend.

La Ferme Blanche 13260 Cassis
The largest estate in the appellation.

Map legend

— · — · — Département boundary

• Wine commune

■ CHÂTEAU Cru Classé and other top producers

Côtes du Lubéron

Coteaux d'Aix-en-Provence/les Baux

Palette

Cassis

Bandol

Coteaux Varois

Côtes de Provence

Bellet

227 Area mapped at larger scale on page shown

Verdon's spectacular 21-km river gorge, known as the Grand Canyon du Verdon divides the limestone plateau of Upper Provence.

COTEAUX D'AIX-EN-PROVENCE

Domaine les Bastides
13610 Le Puy-Ste-Réparade
Organically cultivated vineyards.
Château de Beaupré
13760 St-Cannat
An 18th-century house and estate on the edge of the town.
Château Commanderie de la Bargemone 13760 St-Cannat
Château la Coste
13610 Le Puy-Ste-Réparade
A large estate. Especially good reds.
Château de Fonscolombe
13610 Le Puy-Ste-Réparade
Some of the region's best-value wines.
Château des Gavelles
13540 Puyricard
Ancient house making modern wines.
Château Vignelaure 83560 Rians
Now making fine wines after something of a lean period.

LES BAUX-DE-PROVENCE

Mas de la Dame
13520 Les Baux-de-Provence
Mas de Ste-Berthe
13520 Les Baux-de-Provence
Domaine des Terres Blanches
13210 St-Rémy-de-Provence
Noël Michelin's classically southern wines are organically produced.
Domaine de Trévallon
13150 St-Étienne-du-Grès
Subtle reds: some of the district's best.

CÔTES DU LUBÉRON

Château de Canorgue
84480 Bonnieux
Biodynamic methods produce easy-to-drink wines.
Cellier de Marrenon
84240 La Tour d'Aigues
The region's largest cooperative.
Château Val-Joanis 84120 Pertuis
This model estate has set new standards for the Lubéron.

CÔTES DE PROVENCE

Domaine de l'Aumérade
83390 Pierrefeu-du-Var
The huge vineyard is owned by the Fabre family.
Château Barbeyrolles
83580 Gassin
Domaine de la Bernarde
83340 Le Luc
The vineyard lies north of Les Maures at an altitude of 300m.
Château de Berne 83510 Lorgues
Well-equipped estate.
Domaine de Bertaud-Belieu
83990 Gassin
The exotic winery and cellar are built like a Roman temple.
Domaine des Campaux
83230 Bormes-les-Mimosas
Castel Roubine 83510 Lorgues
Commanderie de Peyrassol
83340 Flassans-sur-Issole
Special *cuvées* are the stars.
Domaine des Féraud
83550 Vidauban
High-quality winemaking using Cabernet Sauvignon.
Château Ferry Lacombe
13530 Trets
Château des Garcinières
83310 Cogolin
Domaines Gavoty
Cabasse 83340 Le Luc
Fresh and attractive wines.
Château Grand'Boise
13530 Trets
Domaine du Jas d'Ésclans
83920 La Motte
The red, with Mourvèdre and Syrah in the blend, is smooth and has firm fruit.
Château de Jasson
83250 La Londe-lès-Maures
All three styles – red, white and rosé – have won awards.
Les Maîtres Vignerons de la Presqu'île de St-Tropez
83990 Gassin
Good cooperative.

Mas de Cadenet 13530 Trets
The red is the best wine: spicy and rich, it has ageing ability and also comes through well when young.
Château Minuty 83580 Gassin
Large estate. The Cuvée de l'Oratoire is the top wine.
Domaines Ott 06600 Antibes
One of the leading producers in Provence, owning several properties including Château de Selle, Clos Mirielle and Château de Romassan.
Domaine des Planes
83520 Roquebrune-sur-Argens
Exemplary wines.
Château Réal-Martin 83143 Le Val
Domaine Richeaume
13114 Puyloubier
An admirable estate for both its architecture and its wines.
Domaine de Rimauresq
83790 Pignans
Domaine St-André de Figuière
83250 La Londe-lès-Maures
Organic vineyard.
Château Ste-Roseline
83460 Les Arcs-sur-Argens
Domaine de la Source Ste-Marguerite
83250 La Londe-lès-Maures
The rosé and whites have benefited from modern winemaking techniques.
Vignobles Crocé-Spinelli
83460 Les Arcs-sur-Argens
Owners of three estates based at Château des Clarettes.

PALETTE

Château Simone 13590 Meyreuil
Fascinatingly herbal, rich reds.

WINE FÊTES

Brignoles Wine fair in April.
Cogolin Wine festival in September.
Fréjus Fête du Raisin on the first Sunday after August 6.
La Motte Wine festival in September.
St-Tropez Wine festival in August.

WINE INFORMATION

Maison des Vins des Côtes de Provence 83460 Les Arcs-sur-Argens
Tel (0)494 73 33 38

HOTELS

The following listings include only those hotels located in the wine districts.
Le Ventoux 67 avenue Victor Hugo
84400 Apt Tel (0)490 74 07 58
Well-run middle-range hotel.
Mas de l'Oulivié
13520 Les Baux-de-Provence
Tel (0)490 54 35 78
Attractively situated hotel near Les Alpilles Mountains and not far from Avignon. No restaurant, but eat at the famous Oustau de Baumanière, (see Restaurants below), and sleep here.

Relais Ste-Victoire
13100 Beaurecueil
Tel (0)442 66 94 98
Pleasant restaurant with comfortable rooms beneath the peaks of Mont Ste-Victoire.
L'Aiguebrun
84480 Bonnieux
Tel (0)490 74 04 14
On the edge of Peter Mayle country (but most attractive in spite of that) with a delightful country setting.
Hostellerie Bérard
83740 La Cadière d'Azur
Tel (0)494 90 11 43
One of the best and smartest hotels in the Bandol region. A fine view of the vineyards from the restaurant.
Hostellerie Lou Calen
83570 Cotignac Tel (0)494 04 60 40
Friendly and simply furnished; a delightful terrace. Swimming pool.
Les Moulins de Paillas
83420 La Croix-Valmer
Tel (0)494 79 71 11
Modern hotel not far from St-Tropez but with unspoilt coastline. Comfortable rooms, mostly with balconies, and a good fish restaurant.
La Grillade au Feu de Bois
03340 Flassans-sur-Issole
Tel (0)494 69 71 20
Stylish and attractive rooms behind a pleasant grill restaurant.
Villa de Belieu 83580 Gassin
Tel (0)494 56 40 56
This old farmhouse (now a luxury hotel with swimming pool) and nearby winery Domaine de Bertaud-Belieu are just outside St-Tropez.

RESTAURANTS

Traditional Provençal cuisine, the basis of the Mediterranean diet, emphasises olive oil, fish, simple vegetables such as tomatoes, peppers and garlic and plenty of herbs. Perhaps the best-known Provençal dish is bouillabaisse, fish soup which, at its most typical in Marseilles, is filled with succulent portions of fish and shellfish. Eating out in Provence can range from the pretentious and expensive – especially on the coast – to the fascinating and delicious, inland and nearer the main wine districts. The selection given below concentrates on the latter.

Arbaud 19 cours Mirabeau
13100 Aix-en-Provence
Tel (0)442 26 66 88
Restaurant with a tea-room which *le tout monde* of Aix used to frequent – it has the antique decor to go with it.
Le Logis de Guetteur 834460
Les Arcs-sur-Argens
Tel (0)494 73 30 82
Hotel with restaurant in an attractive and quiet location in the Côtes de Provence vineyards.

La Maison des Vins
83460 Les Arcs-sur-Argens
Tel (0)494 47 47 70
Newly established within the centre
of the Côtes de Provence wine trade.
Naturally enough it has a fine list of
local wines and a tasting room.

L'Oustau de Baumanière
13520 Les Baux-de-Provence
Tel (0)490 54 33 07
Probably the best restaurant in
western Provence, with prices to
match. Attractive terrace, good
service and fine views of Les Baux.

La Tonnelle des Délices
83230 Bormes-les-Mimosas
Tel (0)494 71 34 84
Contemporary regional dishes and
good regional wines. Popular.

Le Flibustier 13260 Cassis
Tel (0)442 01 02 73
A colourful location at the harbour
entrance. Good fish terrine, grilled
rougets and filet de morue.

Auberge Provençale 13810
Éygalières Tel (0)490 95 91 00
Simple dishes well prepared and
served on a terrace. Also a few
beautiful rooms.

Bruno 03510 Lorgues
Tel (0)494 73 92 19
Jet-set guests enjoy generous dishes
often loaded with truffles.

Les Sarments 13114 Puyloubier
Tel (0)442 29 32 07
Provençal cuisine with flair and
imagination.

L'Oustau du Vin 13530 Trets
Tel (0)442 61 51 51
Attractive menu with seasonal dishes.
Expertly chosen wine-list.

Au Bien-Être 83690 Villecroze
Tel (0)494 70 67 47
Hidden from the road, a restaurant
with a few rooms and a talented
owner/chef.

PLACES OF INTEREST

With its delightful climate, its
Roman remains, ancient towns and
villages and often unspoilt
countryside, Provence has strong
connections with many artists: Picasso
in Antibes, Renoir in Cagnes-sur-Mer,
Chagall in Nice and Cézanne in St-
Rémy-de-Provence.

Aix-en-Provence The Cours
Mirabeau, a long avenue shaded by
plane trees, is the centre of this
elegant university town.
Apt Busy town in the Lubéron. The
old cathedral of Ste-Anne has two
crypts, one above the other.
Les Arcs-sur-Argens This medieval
village on the Argens is now the centre
of the Côtes de Provence wine region.
Les Baux-de-Provence Mountain-
top village with castle ruins.
Spectacular views. A visit is best made
outside the busy summer season.

Bonnieux Lovely Lubéron village
built on a hillside. Famous for the fact
that author Peter Mayle lived nearby.
Bormes-les-Mimosas Picturesque
old town with steep streets and
flowers everywhere.
Cassis Harbour town with good
restaurants, pretty vineyards and
famous associations with painters.
Gassin Hilltop village close to
St-Tropez. Very attractive for an
evening stroll.
Grand Canyon du Verdon
Away from the wine regions but

nevertheless one of the area's great
sights. Depths range between
200–1,500m along this 21-km stretch
of river gorge.
Marseilles The largest conurbation
in Provence and, despite its rather
raffish associations, well worth a visit.
Pertuis Known as 'the gate to the
Lubéron', this village has a historic
centre with old houses and a castle.
St-Maximin-la-Ste-Baume
Formerly a place of pilgrimage.
The local basilica dates back to the
13th century.

St-Tropez Much publicised,
overblown and over-crowded, but
there is still something extremely
appealing about this harbour village
with its lovely waterfront buildings and
narrow streets.
Taradeau A comfortable, attractive
little town away from the tourist
routes but close to the vineyards.
La Tour d'Aigues Exhibitions are
held in the 16th-century castle ruins.
Also a Romanesque church.
Tourtour 'Village in the sky' built, for
defence purposes, on a hill-top.

Languedoc-Roussillon

It does not seem long ago in the history of wine that the twin regions of Languedoc and Roussillon – especially Languedoc – were dismissed from textbooks as the sources of only the basest wines. If they attracted any attention it was with their rich, fortified vins doux naturels made from either Muscat or Grenache. These, so it was deemed, were the only product of distinction from a region which otherwise produced a great deal of very ordinary wine.

Much has changed, even in the last decade since the first edition of this Atlas was published. Although vins de pays existed then, their influence was not widespread. Today Vin de Pays d'Oc is a familiar name to every wine-drinker whether in Europe or the US: it is the wine of the future from the vineyard of the future, which uses modern winemaking techniques, varietal labelling and a New-World approach to marketing.

In parallel with this transformation, the more traditional regions have also been improving. Many have gained *appellation contrôlée* status which has boosted the winemakers' confidence as well as giving them the opportunity to charge higher prices and so invest revenue in new equipment.

In every area of winemaking the producers of Languedoc and Roussillon have been striving to achieve quality over quantity. Vineyards have been uprooted all across the fertile plains and attention switched to sites on slopes and in other areas where grape-growing conditions are favourable.

Growers appreciate that they have to grow good-quality grapes if they are to realise a decent price from the producer – whether it be a cooperative or a large private firm. Producers in their turn know that in order to survive they must make wines of a quality comparable with that of estate wines from other regions of France – and indeed from outside France.

This is an exciting region to visit. There are huge, stainless steel wineries which would not look out of place in Australia or in California's Central Valley and an increasing number of small estates are making the region's top wines. In between are the cooperatives which still dominate both Languedoc and Roussillon in terms of the volume of grapes they handle. But these are now

Left: The sunny, fertile plains of Languedoc have been given over to the region's other agricultural crops as growers concentrate on cultivating quality vineyards on more suitable land.

Languedoc-Roussillon

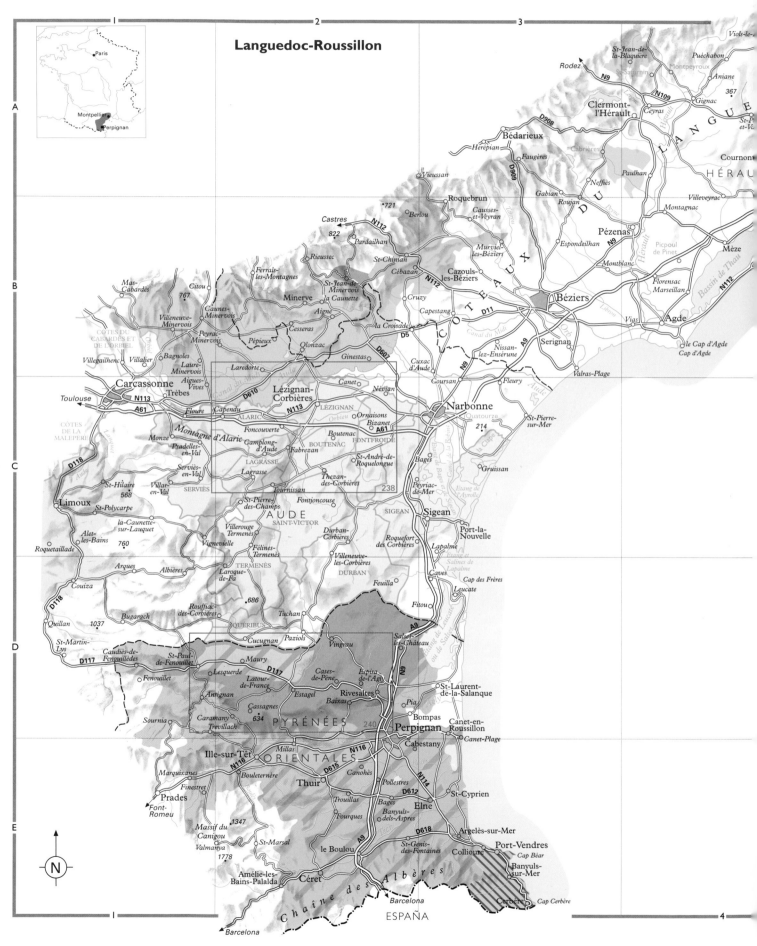

International boundary

Département boundary

Appellations Contrôlées

Clairette du Languedoc

Faugères

St-Chinian

Minervois

Corbières (= sub-divisions)

Fitou (included in Corbières)

Blanquette de Limoux

Côtes du Roussillon

Côtes du Roussillon-Villages
(includes AC villages Caramany and
Latour-de-France)

Collioure

la Clape   Coteaux du Languedoc commune

Vins Doux Naturels

Muscat de Lunel

Muscat de Mireval

Muscat de Frontignan

Muscat de St-Jean de Minervois

Maury

Banyuls

Rivesaltes

VDQS

238   Area mapped at larger scale
on page shown

1:1,000,000

Km. 0   5   10   15   20 Km.

Miles 0   5   10 Miles

divided into two distinct categories: those that have banded together into large marketing and production organisations, such as the Vignerons Catalans in Roussillon and the Vignerons du Val d'Orbieu in Languedoc; and those that have been left behind.

This large region, from Montpellier in the east to Perpignan in the south, embraces the flat plains by the sea and the rugged, remote mountains of the interior; hideous urban developments and remote villages ... and a cuisine full of simple pleasures. There is delicious shellfish from the coast; hot, spicy sausages from inland, bouillabaisse from the sea and cassoulet from the mountains. For any wine-lover, it beckons as a voyage of discovery.

Languedoc

As the French Mediterranean coast curves gradually round from the mouth of the Rhône towards the Spanish border, the coastal plain widens and the mountains recede into the distance. Flat, alluvial land with sandy soil stretches ahead, interspersed with rocky barren outcrops. In the inhospitable, wild and beautiful mountains that fringe the flat land, the summer heat is intense. Ancient cities – many dating from Roman times – are strung out along the main route that leads from France into Spain, tracing the path once travelled by Roman legions and merchants.

Almost a third of all France's vineyards are concentrated in the region on the plains between Montpellier and Narbonne. This land, facing out toward the Mediterranean, has for a century or more been the provenance of *gros rouge*, the workman's vin de table, the vin very *ordinaire* of France. Fertile soil and an easy climate meant that the effort involved in viticulture was small compared to that

The elegant Pont du Gard was constructed as an aqueduct and bridge by the Romans in 18 BC, to bring water to the town of Nîmes.

231

South of Pézenas lies Picpoul de Pinet, an appellation exclusively devoted to the old white-wine variety Picpoul. Beyond lies the colourful port of Sète, its centre divided by canals and basins.

needed to coax wine from lands further north. Since the level of wine consumption in Paris had reached five million hectolitres a year by 1900, vast plantations of highly productive grape varieties were necessary to meet a virtually insatiable demand. Quantity was everything, and in striving for it at the cost of quality, the better vineyard land in the mountains was neglected.

Slowly, however, the tide has turned. The demand for cheap 'plonk' has dramatically diminished. Some of those flatland vineyards are being uprooted while enterprising vignerons, many from outside the region, are replanting on land that last saw vines perhaps 100 years ago. Experimentation is in the air in this region more than anywhere else in France: producers feel the same freedom, the same determination to try anything at least once, that inspires the producers of Australia or California. Not for nothing is this called Europe's New World of wine.

In this rapidly changing environment, one piece of wine legislation has proved of inestimable value. This is the creation in the late 1970s of the category of vin de pays. It was an attempt – created very much with this region in mind – to bring some quality back into vineyards which could hardly aspire to *appellation contrôlée* but which nevertheless produced better than simple vin de table. The creation of a vin de pays designation for the wines of a particular zone allowed wines with some regional or local character to be recognised and perhaps developed.

Hundreds of vins de pays were created; some have proved highly successful in reviving viticulture or improving its quality. The most successful of the vins de pays however have not been those which aimed to revive a local character but those which created almost instant 'traditions'. These were the departmental vins de pays – wines which could be grown anywhere in a French *département*; and the regional vins de pays – those which could come from anywhere in a grouping of *départements*.

The reason why these two categories were so successful was that they allowed the production of *vins de cépage* – wines made from one variety only and labelled as such. It was this which led to the huge success of the Vin de Pays d'Oc which covers wines from the *départements* of Gard, Hérault and Aude and which has led to

the creation of a new generation of wines, many inspired by New World models or even made by New World producers. Often the wines are made using techniques such as new-wood ageing: such enterprise suggests a desire to make and market wines whose quality is well above simple vin de pays.

In a similar spirit of discovery other producers, particularly in the mountainous hinterland of the Hérault, have set about producing fine wines made with varieties such as Cabernet Sauvignon and Chardonnay which are not native to the region but thrive in the harsh, hot conditions.

While vins de pays have been reviving the viticultural fortunes of Languedoc, the traditional quality areas have been enjoying their own successes. First among these, certainly, are the twin appellations of Corbières and Minervois (see pages 237–39). The scattered vineyards of the Coteaux du Languedoc are also producing wines of a quality which simply would not have been expected even a few years ago, particularly in the sub-areas of La Clape, Quatourze and Montpeyroux.

Smaller appellations dot the landscape: St-Chinian is known for its full-bodied reds, as is neighbouring Faugères, while Clairette du Languedoc makes what can be a fruity white from the Clairette grape. A handful of estates in Costières de Nîmes (the renamed Costières du Gard) have achieved more than local renown.

There are also two wine traditions that have a special place in the history of Languedoc. In the hills of Limoux, a sparkling wine (once called Blanquette de Limoux, now Crémant de Limoux) is produced which, it is claimed by its adherents, predates champagne. Made from the Blanquette grape – the local name for the Mauzac – this can be a delightful light-hearted wine with with fragrance, finesse and just a hint of pepper.

On the shores of the Mediterranean another tradition continues, even though under threat from changing fashions. Sweet, fortified wines made from the Muscat grape are produced in a number of communes, of which Frontignan is perhaps the most important in Languedoc. This is an ancient tradition – it is recorded by Pliny the Younger in the Roman era – and it would be a great shame if the current trend against somewhat more alcoholic, sweeter wines should become the pretext for its disappearance.

Languedoc is enjoying a renaissance: it is becoming increasingly pleasant to visit its estates, wineries and cooperatives. The Comité Interprofessionel has set up tasting rooms at Montpellier and Narbonne, both of which are worth visiting before setting out on any exploration. The sheer variety of the wines made suggests that the region's potential is only just beginning to be realised.

Above: Massive 13th-century fortifications reflected in the waters of the Chenal Maritime. The wide sunny beaches and lagoons of the Languedoc coast are now favoured sites for holiday and leisure complexes.

Left: The futuristic stainless-steel winery of the Limoux cooperative, the region's dominant producer, invites comparison with its New World counterparts.

Left: The old port of Sète, whose colourful history includes notoriety for trafficking in bogus wines.

Right: The chapel of St-Jul de Salinelles stands amid the vineyards of Costières de Nîmes (formerly Costières du Gard), which were awarded AC status in 1986.

PRODUCERS OF SPECIAL INTEREST

CRÉMANT DE LIMOUX
Cave Cooperative
11300 Limoux
The region's dominant producer, making quality Crémant de Limoux as well as still wines.

COSTIÈRES DE NÎMES AND CLAIRETTE DE BELLEGARDE
Domaine de l'Amarine
30127 Bellegarde
Both Costières de Nîmes and Clairette de Bellegarde are produced on this large estate.
Château de Belle-Coste
30132 Caissargues
Bertrand du Tremblay's family has run this estate for more than a century. Red, rosé and white Costières de Nîmes are made.
Château Roubaud
30600 Vauvert
Some of the wine is sold in bulk but bottled red, white and rosé Costières de Nîmes are also made using modern techniques.
Château de la Tuilerie
30000 Nîmes
Go-ahead estate making a wide range of quality wines.

FAUGÈRES
Cave Coopérative
34480 Faugères
Domaine du Fraisse
34480 Magalas
Jacques Pons uses carbonic maceration for his red Faugères which is made from Carignan, Grenache, Syrah and Cinsaut grapes.

Domaine de la Grange des Aires
34480 Magalas
The classic regional grape varieties make long-lived reds.
Bernard et Claude Vidal
34480 Magalas
Carbonic maceration techniques are used here to gain maximum fruit.

COTEAUX DU LANGUEDOC AND CLAIRETTE DU LANGUEDOC
Abbaye de Villemagne
34140 Mèze
Ancient abbey, now in private hands. Good reds.
Château la Condamine Bertrand 34230 Paulhan
Coteaux du Languedoc and Clairette du Languedoc both made here.
Château de l'Engarran
34880 Laverune
Fine wood-aged reds and vin de pays.
Château Notre Dame du Quatourze 11100 Narbonne
Aromatic wines with plenty of Mourvèdre and Syrah in the blend.
Château Pech-Céleyran
11110 Coursan
Viognier and Merlot are planted for vin de pays. Wood-aged La Clape.
Château Pech-Redon
11100 Narbonne
Domaine du Poujol
34570 Vailhauques
A newly-acquired British-owned property which produces Coteaux du Languedoc in red and rosé and vin de pays.
Château de Ricardelle
11100 Narbonne
Organic vineyard; attractive La Clape.

Château Roquette-sur-Mer
11100 Narbonne
Wood-aged wine from La Clape.
Les Vins de St-Saturnin
34725 St-Saturnin
Coteaux du Languedoc-St-Saturnin's main cooperative. Specialises in the rosé Vin d'Une Nuit brand.

CABARDÈS
Domaine de Rayssac
11600 Conques-sur-Orbiel
Château Rivals
11600 Conques-sur-Orbiel
Cabardès and some Bordeaux-style vin de pays.
Château Youclary
11600 Conques-sur-Orbiel

CÔTES DE LA MALEPÈRE
Château de Malvies-Guilhem
11300 Malvies

MUSCAT
Domaine de Belle Côte
34400 Lunel
Cave Coopérative
34100 Frontignan
This is by far the biggest producer of sweet Muscat de Frontignan, the only wine it makes.
Cave Coopérative
34360 St-Jean-de-Minervois
Responsible for 90% of local production.
Cave Coopérative de Rabelais
34840 Mireval
Domaine du Grès St-Paul
34400 Vérargues
Also makes Coteaux du Languedoc.
Château de la Peyrelade
34100 Frontignan
One of the area's best producers.

VIN DE PAYS
Domaine de la Baume
34290 Severin
Australian-owned winery making a range of varietal Vin de Pays d'Oc.
Les Caves du Sieur d'Arques
11300 Limoux
Brand name of the dynamic Limoux cooperative.
Listel/Salins du Midi
30220 Aigues-Mortes
The largest vineyard expanse under single ownership in France. Inexpensive vin de pays.
Mas de Daumas Gassac
34150 Aniane
Famous estate producing wines of sensational quality from Cabernet Sauvignon in a style that owes much to the classed growths of Bordeaux. Also produces Rosé Frisant and a sumptuous white.
Seigneurie de Peyrat
34120 Pézenas
A huge range of good-value Vin de Pays d'Oc.
Skalli Fortant de France
34204 Sète
Important producer of varietal vin de pays. Consistently well made wines from a spectacular winery site.
Vignerons du Val d'Orbieu
11100 Narbonne
The region's largest producer with a huge range and good standards.
Vignobles James Herrick
11100 Narbonne
Australian-inspired estate which produces Vin de Pays d'Oc Chardonnays.
Domaines Virginie
34500 Béziers
Fine range of clean, balanced wines.

The ramparts of Aigues Mortes, a 13th-century town built in the midst of salt marshes and completely surrounded by towers and walls.

Maison de la Blanquette
11300 **Limoux**
Tel (0)468 31 01 63
Wine growers' wives serve the food and there is a choice of cooperative-produced wine.
Hostellerie du Palais 34400 **Lunel**
Tel (0)467 71 11 39
Traditional food in a rural setting.
Manpotel Impérator/l'Enclos de la Fontaine quai de la Fontaine
30000 **Nîmes** Tel (0)466 21 90 30
Pleasant restored house with a charming garden.
La Tour Sarraisne 34310
Pilhes-la-Romain Tel (0)467 93 41 31
A former smithy with modern paintings and stylish cooking.
Lou Flambadou 34360 **St-Chinian**
Tel (0)467 38 13 12
Regional dishes and wines.
La Palangrotte 1 rampe Paul-Valéry
34200 **Sète** Tel (0)467 74 80 35
Probably the region's best fish restaurant.

PLACES OF INTEREST

Aigues-Mortes The town of 'dead water' (see picture, left). Visit the vast cellars of the salt and wine company, Salins du Midi, just outside the town.
Béziers Prosperous town and centre for the Hérault wine trade. Many museums, some dedicated to wine, and the fine cathedral of Ste-Nazaire.
Carcassonne Showplace of inland Languedoc, a complete medieval-style fortified town. Largely the work of the 19th-century architect Viollet-le-Duc, it nevertheless looks very convincing. The lower town beneath the walls is perhaps more genuine.
Clermont-l'Hérault Old fortified township with medieval walls, a 12th-century castle and many churches.
Frontignan This seaside town is home to Muscat de Frontignan and the cellars of vermouth producer Noilly-Prat.
Montpellier Busy, ever-expanding city which has retained its old quarter and elegant views from Le Peyrou, a promenade along the highest points. The university has France's biggest viticulture and winemaking faculty.
Nîmes Rich in Roman architecture such as the Maison Carrée, a perfectly preserved temple, and the amphitheatre. Opposite the Maison Carrée is the beautiful modern building of the Carrée d'Art.
Remoulins Near this small village stands the greatest of monuments to Roman engineering, the Pont du Gard.

FÊTES

Béziers The Fête du Vin Nouveau takes place in October.
Carcassonne Harvest festival in September/October.
Nîmes Wine fair in the first weekend in November.
St-Chinian Wine festival in the second half of August.

WINE INFORMATION

There are two main centres of wine information for Languedoc: 9 cours Mirabeau, 11100 Narbonne [tel (0)468 90 38 30] and Mas de Saporta, 34970 Montpellier, just off the A9 [tel (0)467 06 04 28] where there is also a restaurant.

HOTELS

For hotels in Narbonne see Corbières and Minervois listings, pages 238–39.
Hôtel Lou Tamarou
route de Pézenas, 34500 **Béziers**
Tel (0)467 30 12 76
Very comfortable modern hotel conveniently situated near the entrance to the town.

Côte Bleue 34140 Bouzigues
Tel (0)467 78 31 42
Modern hotel on the Bassin de Thau near Sète. Also a fish restaurant.
Domaine d'Auriac 11000
Carcassonne Tel (0)468 25 72 22
Luxury hotel surrounded by a park and vineyards. Good restaurant.
Hôtel le Guilhem 18 rue Jean-Jacques Rousseau, 34000 **Montpellier**
Tel (0)467 52 90 90
Attractively restored hotel in the centre of the city's old quarter.
Les Hauts de Mourèze
34800 **Mourèze** Tel (0)467 96 04 84
Simple, friendly hotel set in wild countryside west of Montpellier.
Hôtel du Cheval Blanc
30000 **Nîmes** Tel (0)466 67 20 03
Near the Roman arena.
Le Mas de Clergues
34800 **Octon** Tel (0)467 96 02 65
A simple but comfortable small hotel in a converted farmhouse.
Hôtel Genieys 34120 **Pézenas**
Tel (0)467 98 13 99
Small town hotel with simple rooms.
Auberge de la Tour
34290 **Valros** Tel (0)467 98 52 01
The rooms at the back look out over an attractive courtyard. Average food.

RESTAURANTS

Fish, shellfish and eels come from the Mediterranean and from the *étangs*, the enclosed salt-water lakes which line the coast. The food of the mountains comes in the form of confits and cassoulets, hearty meat and sausage stews, and in rough terrines. Olive oil is also produced locally. Honey from the wild flowers and herbs of the *garrigue* is some of the best in France.

For restaurants in Narbonne see Corbières and Minervois listings, pages 238–39.
L'Oliver 12 rue Boildieu
34500 **Béziers** Tel (0)467 28 86 64
Small bistro-style restaurant offering creative cooking.
La Madrague 34140 **Bouzigues**
Tel (0)467 78 32 34
Attractive menu based on fish and shellfish.
Le Languedoc 32 allée d'Iéna, 11000
Carcassonne Tel (0)468 25 22 17
Good regional menu.
Capion 34150 **Gignac**
Tel (0)467 57 50 83
Regional dishes; set menus; local wines.

Corbières and Minervois

Away from the plains of Languedoc, the hilly landscape rapidly turns into dramatic mountain country, bristling with sharp peaks and fierce rocks and slashed with narrow valleys. Ancient stones are gouged by rivers flowing headlong through gorges that have been channelled over centuries. High up where the air is cooler, secret valleys open out to reveal lush pastures where sheep and goats graze and cheese and milk are still made on small farms. The villages of these regions are often dominated by brooding castles, once the strongholds of medieval heretics or local robber barons but now imposing ruins which demand a strenuous climb to reach.

The wine regions of both Corbières and Minervois have always been set apart from those of the flat lands nearer the sea. Their vineyards have benefited from the hillside sites and harsh soils in which vines thrive. They have always made better wines than the average Languedoc patch so it is hardly surprising that, having made great improvements themselves, they are still the region's *cru* vineyards. Closely related to both regions is the smaller wine region of Fitou, carved out of part of Corbières.

The regions share certain characteristics including the mix of grapes cultivated. Carignan and Cinsault were the traditional varieties; Grenache arrived some time ago but newer arrivals Syrah and Mourvèdre are the aristocrats here. These are being blended to make some sophisticated wines, some of which have a degree of barrique ageing. The wine styles also have similarities, from the extremely rustic to the stylish, elegant *cuvées*. While Corbières tends to chunkiness, Minervois is leaner and more taut. The wine of Fitou, the smallest region of the trio, is often drunk young.

Soils vary throughout both regions to the extent that in Corbières there has been a move to divide the appellation into separate terroirs. Whether or not a sub-division into 12 different areas will mean anything to the average consumer is debatable; whether or not it is possible to taste differences between wines produced in the high country of Durban and the softer Orbieu Valley of the Lagrasse area is also difficult to say. But this division does draw attention to the huge expanse of Corbières: there are up to 30,000 hectares now under vine in many different valleys and hillsides, and an annual production of about 900,000 hectolitres.

Minervois by contrast is more compact, and many of the vineyards are on the softer slopes facing south across the Aude Valley. However, even Minervois has contrasting areas – the pebbly coastal soil of the eastern district of Ginestas, for example, and the harsh, mountain conditions of the Haut-Minervois around the village of Minerve.

All three appellations provide some of the most spectacular touring country in southern France. It is certainly exhilarating to round the end of the Tuchan Gorge and see the valley of Cucugnan spread before you; the village perched on its hill, dominated on the southern side by the Château of Quéribus. And in the Minervois there is something equally wonderful about driving along the tortuous road to Minerve and watching the village appear and disappear behind the jutting mountain.

This too is unspoilt countryside, far enough from the main tourist routes to attract only the curious or wine-lovers. Summer heat can be intense but spring or autumn, when mountain flowers are blooming and the wild heath-lands of the *garrigue* are alive with colour or when the vines change colour and the harvest is gathered, are both marvellous times to visit this spectacular and apparently changeless part of France.

The fortified town of Minerve was once a stronghold of heresy: in 1210 over 150 of its inhabitants were burned at the stake for their beliefs.

PRODUCERS OF SPECIAL INTEREST

CORBIÈRES

Château La Baronne
11700 Fontcouverte
Hand-picked Carignan and Grenache plus Syrah and Mourvèdre undergo *maceration carbonique* at this estate.

Château de Cabriac
11600 Douzens
Château Chasse-Spleen in Bordeaux holds shares in this estate, which produces Corbières red and white.

Château de Caraguilhes
11220 St-Laurent-de-la-Cabrerisse
A soft red is made here using *maceration carbonique*.

Cave Coopérative Embres et Castelmaure 11360 Durban
One of the best of Corbières' many cooperatives. The white wines are especially good.

Château de Gasparets
11200 Luc-sur-Orbieu
Mourvèdre and Grenache are blended at this estate to make a particularly fine wine.

Château du Grand Caumont
11200 Lézignan
Cuvée Tradition is Corbières' best. Vin de pays is made from Merlot, Cinsaut, Cabernet Sauvignon and Carignan.

Château de Lastours
11490 Portel des Corbières
Top-class Corbières including Cuvée Simone Descamps.

Château les Ollieux 11200 Lézignan
Modern wines from an old monastery.

Domaine des Pensées Sauvages
11360 Albas
Wood-aged Corbières.

Domaine du Révérend
11350 Cucugnan
Owned by Bordeaux merchant Peter Sichel, as is nearby Domaine du Trillol.

Château St-Auriol
11220 Lagrasse
Wood-aged reds and whites.

Château Villemagne
11220 Lagrasse

Domaine de Villemajou
11200 St-André-de-Roquelongue
Top-class Corbières.

Château de la Voulte-Gasparets
11200 Lézignan

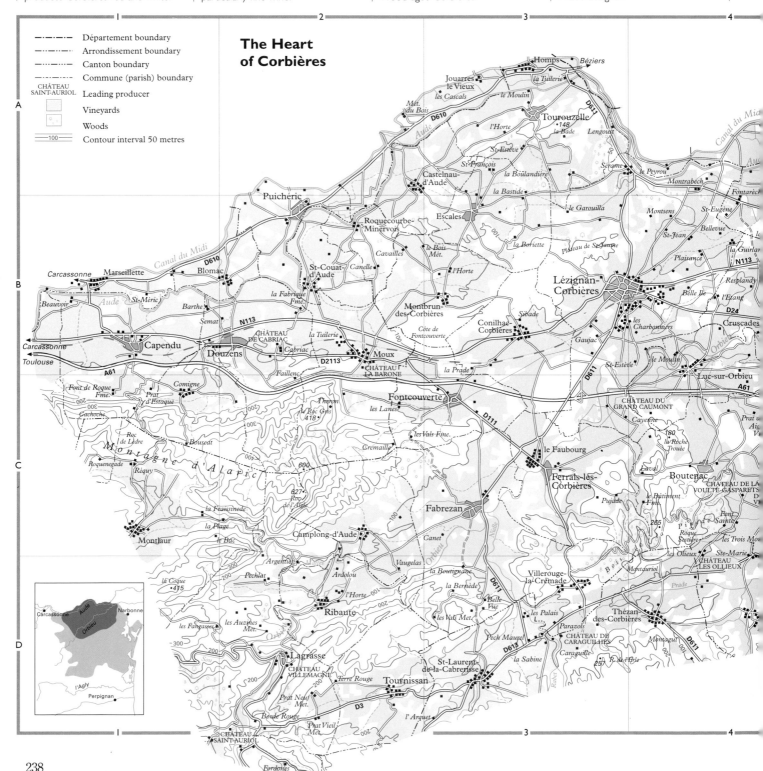

The Heart of Corbières

Département boundary
Arrondissement boundary
Canton boundary
Commune (parish) boundary
CHÂTEAU SAINT-AURIOL Leading producer
Vineyards
Woods
Contour interval 50 metres

FITOU
Cave Coopérative
11510 Fitou
Château de Nouvelles
11350 Tuchan
Les Producteurs de Mont Tauch 11350 Tuchan
A leading cooperative. The top brand is Cuvée Madame Claude Parmentier.

MINERVOIS
Château de Blomac
11700 Capendu
Produces an impressive selection of vins de pays including one interesting example made from Tempranillo.
Château Canet 11800 Rustiques
Red made from Carignan, Syrah, Grenache and Cinsaut is aged for six months in wood; white from Roussanne, Bourboulenc and Terret for three months.
Cave Coopérative
34210 La Livinière
Domaine Daniel Domergue
11160 Caunes
Fascinating Syrah-dominated wines.
Château de Fabas 11800 Trèbes
There is quite a high percentage of Syrah and Mourvèdre in this vineyard and more is being planted.
Château de Gourgazaud
34210 Olonzac
The region's showpiece estate with interesting *cuvées* from Cabernet Sauvignon and Merlot.
Domaine de l'Herbe Sainte
11120 Ginestas
Many interesting varietal wines as well as more classic Minervois.
Domaine Jacques Maris
34210 Olonzac
Red, rosé and white Minervois are the main products at this large estate in the heart of the Minervois AC, northwest of Olonzac.
Château de Paraza
11200 Lézignan
An important estate which uses traditional methods.
Château de Paulignan
11160 Caunes
Domaine du Pech-d'André
34210 Olonzac
Excellent examples of Minervois quality.
Château de Pouzols
11120 Ginestas
Also produces vin de pays.
Domaine Ste-Eulalie
34210 La Livinière
Delicious Minervois, rich in fruit.
Les Vignerons de Haut-Minervois 34210 Azillanet
Château Villerambert-Julien
11160 Caunes
The top wine is the Cuvée Trianon.
Château de Villerambert Moreau 11160 Caunes
Owned by the same group as Château Villegly, also in Caunes.

FÊTES

Lézignan-Corbières Wine festival in mid-July.
Minerve Minerve 1210: a festival of song, dance, food and drink at the end of July.

HOTELS

Le Tassigny 11200 Lézignan-Corbières Tel (0)468 27 11 51
Classically furnished rooms. The restaurant, Le Tournedos, is much favoured by locals.

La Résidence 6 rue de 1er mars 11100 Narbonne
Tel (0)468 32 19 41
Pleasant hotel in the town centre.
Le Relais Val d'Orbieu 11200 Ornaisons Tel (0)468 27 10 27
Quiet, high-class hotel with good cuisine and a swimming pool.
Château de Violet 11160 Peyrac-Minervois Tel (0)468 78 10 42
Beautifully furnished château hotel with park and swimming pool.

RESTAURANTS

Many kinds of traditional farming are being revived in Corbières and Minervois. Real farmhouse cheeses, made from the milk of ewes or goats fed on high mountain pastures, are one speciality. Honey, made from the wild flowers and herbs which grow profusely in the valleys and on the hillsides, is another.

Local cuisine is typified by sturdy terrines and cassoulets which are often accompanied by spicy sausages – a reminder of a more southern influence of Spain. Other tempting dishes include excellent bouillabaisse and grilled langoustine

Auberge de Cucugnan
11350 Cucugnan
Tel (0)468 45 40 84
Coq au vin is a speciality.
Le Moulin 11360 Durban-Corbières
Tel (0)468 45 81 03
High-class restaurant (try the lamb!) set in an old mill on a hill.
Chez Odette 11560 Fitou-Village
Tel (0)468 45 72 89
Regional dishes.
Auberge de l'Arbousier
route de Carcassonne, 11200 Homps
Tel (0)468 91 11 24
Elegant restaurant, picturesquely sited by the Canal du Midi.
La Horte Restaurant à la Ferme
11220 Lagrasse
Tel (0)468 24 06 01
Simple cooking with friendly service.

The unique terroir of the Grau de Maury vineyard is much in evidence in its wines.

Relais Chantovent 34120 Minerve
Tel (0)468 91 22 96
Atmospheric surroundings.
L'Alsace 2 avenue Pierre-Semard 11100 Narbonne
Tel (0)468 65 10 24
Le Petit Comptoir
11100 Narbonne Tel (0)468 42 30 45
Good-value bistro in a busy city.
Le Réverbère 4 place des Jacobins 11100 Narbonne
Tel (0)468 32 39 18
Highly respected restaurant in the style of the belle époque.

PLACES OF INTEREST

Abbaye de Fontfroide 12th- and 13th-century Cistercian abbey built in light-pink stone.
Caunes-Minervois Fortified village at the mouth of the Gorges de l'Argent Double with houses dating from the 16th and 17th centuries.
Cucugnan Wine village built on a hilltop and surrounded by mountains. Nearby is the Château de Quéribus, the last stronghold of the Albigensians.
Duilhac-sous-Peyrepertuse
The château, which overlooks the village, is a splendid example of local military architecture.
Lagrasse This fortified village, the 'prettiest in France', has the River Orbieu running through its centre.
Lézignan-Corbières Interesting Musée de la Vigne.
Minerve Village perched on a narrow redrock ledge above a gorge where two rivers meet.
Narbonne A bustling commercial centre which has preserved some of its southern charm. The 13th-century cathedral of St-Just is worth a visit.
Tuchan One of the centres for Fitou wines. Nearby are the ruins of the 12th-century Château d'Aiguilar.

Map labels
le Pech Dalcy
St-Martin
Marcorignan
Canet
le Cnon. de la Plaine
Raissac-d'Aude
Villedaigne
Névian
Laparre
Villenouvette
St-James
Roc d'Agel Fme,
Col de la Muette
Narbonne
la Cendrillou
les Auberges
St-Antoine
aisons
D224
Labastide
Bizanet
Narbonne
Dom. de Quillanet
les Cayrels
les adels
rbousier
St-Maurice
Jardin de St-Julien de Septime
St-Martin de Toques
Beauregard
les Pres Vieux
ndré de uelongue
Bois de
Coudé

N

1:125,000
Km. 0   1   2   3   4   5 Km.
Miles 0   1   2   3 Miles

Roussillon

Roussillon may technically and politically be part of France, but there will always be something in the heart of a true Roussillonais that looks over the Pyrenees towards Catalonia. Four centuries of rule by the kings of Mallorca from their castle in Perpignan have left their mark: in the local dialect, which is close to Catalan; in the local cuisine, and viticulturally in the grapes and the tradition for sweet red fortified wines.

This is the warmest, driest part of France and the land has a tired, wind-swept air about it, refreshed only by the proximity of the snow-covered mountains and sea breezes. In summer, roads need the shade of the plane trees, dogs lie panting in the coolest spots and villages simmer in remorseless heat. In winter, cold, crisp days follow one another, blue skies often seeming endless. Ancient hilltop towns and fortified castles speak of a past when this was disputed frontier country.

There are two traditions of wine in this land. One is for sturdy reds made from ancient Carignan vines which still grow in short stumps, trailing their tendrils along the ground. In recent years growers of these hugely powerful, alcoholic wines have begun to strive for quality. With such excellent potential in the raw material

their job was half done, but they have added to their success by bringing in other grape varieties: Grenache, Syrah and Mourvèdre, all of which thrive in this climate, along with Cabernet Sauvignon and Merlot in more recent years.

Roussillon reds come in a number of different appellations. The most basic and widespread is Côtes du Roussillon, which covers much of the plain land and is centred on Perpignan. It produces reds and whites, the latter from the Catalan Macabeo and Malvoisie. Certain villages in the valley of the Aigly River northwest of Perpignan are allowed a superior appellation of Côtes du Roussillon-Villages while two – Caramany and Latour-de-France – can in addition append their names to the label.

A small red appellation, Collioure, clings to the hillsides of Mount Albères near Banyuls-sur-Mer. Sadly, local demand for seaside housing has reduced the production area of this big, strong red wine to a mere 50 hectares.

The other tradition in Roussillon is for fortified wines. Fortified Muscats made in the village of Rivesaltes are in a style similar to that of the Muscats made further north in Languedoc. Demand for these wines has fallen to such an extent that in 1996 the producers decided to turn the whole crop into delicious Muscat jellies.

A fine sweet red vin doux naturel is also still made in Rivesaltes, in neighbouring Maury and, more importantly, in the seaside resort of Banyuls-sur-Mer which is close to the Spanish border.

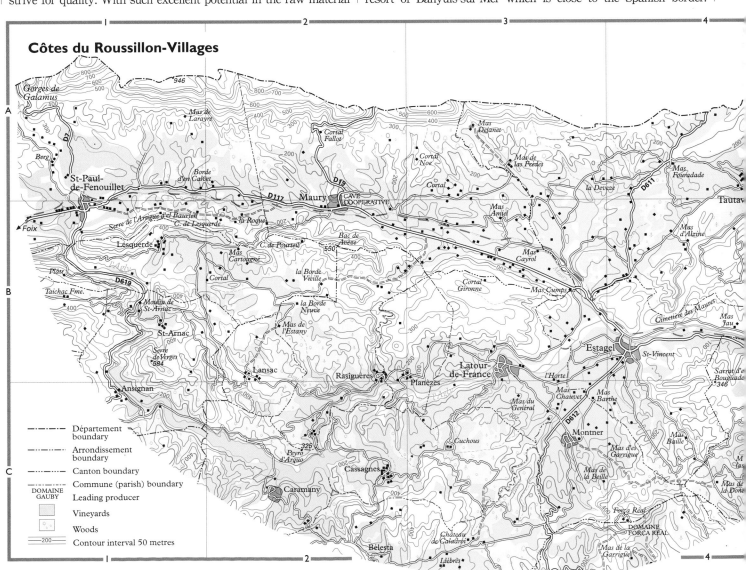

Côtes du Roussillon-Villages

Département boundary

Arrondissement boundary

Canton boundary

Commune (parish) boundary

DOMAINE GAUBY Leading producer

Vineyards

Woods

200 Contour interval 50 metres

Banyuls, technically a distant relation of port, is produced chiefly from Grenache grapes grown on steep terraces of dark-brown schist just north of the Spanish frontier.

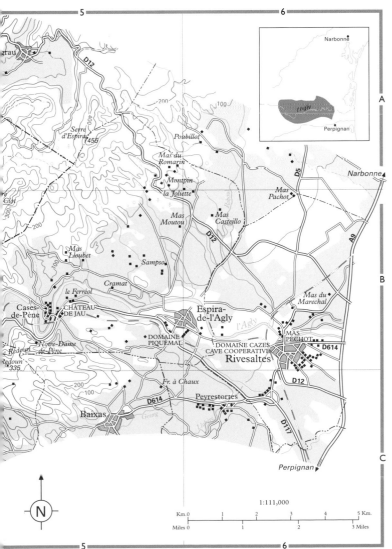

Made from Grenache and reminiscent of port, it comes in both red and tawny styles depending on how much time it has spent in oak. Certain special Banyuls are aged in wood in the open air and these develop a concentrated character; almost (but not quite) oxidised. The wines are known as Banyuls Rancio.

Built in 1276 for the ruler of the newly-found kingdom, the Palais des Rois de Majorque was once surrounded by extensive fig and olive groves.

PRODUCERS OF SPECIAL INTEREST

Domaines de Canterrane
66300 Trouillas
The estates of the Conte family include Château de Canterrane and its associated La Tour de Canterrane.

Cave Coopérative 66460 Maury
The vin doux naturel of Maury in all its forms is what matters at this cooperative.

Cave Coopérative
66370 Pézilla de la Rivière
The best cooperative in the region.

Cave Coopérative 66602 Rivesaltes
The largest cooperative in the region and the largest producer of Côtes du Roussillon as well as Rivesaltes.

Domaine Cazes 66602 Rivesaltes
Enterprising firm with successful experiments in top-class wines from Cabernet Sauvignon and Merlot.

Château de Corneilla
66200 Corneilla del Vercol
15th-century castle producing excellent Côtes du Roussillon.

Domaine Força-Réal 66170 Millas
Produces wood-aged Côtes du Roussillon and fine Rivesaltes.

Domaine Gauby 66600 Calce
Small domaine inclined to experiment – with excellent results.

Château de Jau
66600 Cases de Pène
Top-quality and good-value Côtes du Roussillon along with Collioure from an estate at Banyuls-sur-Mer. Art exhibitions and a restaurant in the summer.

Domaine du Mas Blanc
66650 Banyuls-sur-Mer
Excellent Banyuls and Collioure.

Mas Péchot 66600 Rivesaltes
The Muscat de Rivesaltes produced at this estate has a deservedly high reputation.

Domaine Piquemal
66600 Espira d'Agly
A wide range of quality wines including a Merlot-dominated red.

Château Planères
66300 St-Jean-Lasselle
Good-quality Côtes du Roussillon.

Domaine de la Retorie
66650 Banyuls-sur-Mer

Domaine Sarda-Malet
66000 Perpignan
New-wood-aged wines have expanded this quality-oriented range.

Vignerons Catalans
66000 Perpignan
Huge operation producing wines of a good standard.

Aged in wood in the open air, Banyuls Rancio develops an intense, highly fragrant character. Dark amber in colour, its taste is fresh and clean yet lingers in the mouth.

The colourful Procession de la Sanch weaves its way through Perpignan.

The elegant 12th-century cloister at Elne contains various funerary monuments.

WINE FÊTES

Perpignan Fête de la St-Bacchus and the Salon des Vins in June; Fête du Vin Nouveau in mid-October.
Rivesaltes Fête de Rivesaltes in July.

HOTELS

Le Catalan 66650 **Banyuls-sur-Mer**
Tel (0)466 88 02 80
A modern hotel built on the rocks.
La Terrasse au Soleil 66400 **Céret**
Tel (0)468 87 01 94
Modern hotel built in traditional Catalan style in a small village in the foothills of the Pyrenees.
Les Caranques 66190 **Collioure**
Tel (0)468 82 06 68
Modern, family-run seaside hotel.
La Casa Pairal 66190 **Collioure**
Tel (0)468 82 05 81
Luxuriously appointed in a flower-filled park. Swimming pool.
Park Hotel 18 boulevard Jean-Bourrat, 66000 **Perpignan**
Tel (0)468 35 14 14
Old-fashioned comfort in central Perpignan. Michelin-starred restaurant.

L'Île de la Lagune
66750 **St-Cyprien-Sud**
Tel (0)468 21 01 02
Modern hotel in a futuristic resort. Bungalows are set around a lagoon.

RESTAURANTS

Catalan flavours and the use of garlic come together in dishes such as cargolade, snails barbecued over vine cuttings with lashings of all y oli, a paste of garlic, lemon and olive oil. Game birds from the mountains are traditionally cooked à la Catalane with peppers and bitter Seville oranges, while lamb is braised en pistache, in a gloriously pungent white sauce with garlic and pistachio nuts. Aubergines and red and green peppers are the basis of the salads; savoury tarts use tomatoes, anchovies and olives.

Restaurant l'Hostal
66300 **Castellnou**
Tel (0)468 53 45 42
Set in a spectacular hillside village. Traditional local dishes.

Restaurant Les Feuillants
66400 **Céret**
Tel (0)468 87 37 88
Elegant restaurant with a mix of French and Catalan dishes and an extensive wine-list.
La Bodega 66190 **Collioure**
Tel (0)468 82 05 60
Regional cooking of a good standard in a former wine cellar.
Les Templiers
66190 **Collioure**
Tel (0)468 82 05 58
Come for the art as much as the cooking: artists such as Picasso and Dufy paid their bills in pictures and the results hang on the walls.
Casa Sansa 3 rue Fabrique Couverte, 66000 **Perpignan**
Tel (0)468 34 21 84
Traditional Catalan restaurant with live music in the evenings.
Relais St-Jean 1 cité Bartissol
66000 **Perpignan**
Tel (0)468 35 16 16
Contemporary cuisine in the old quarter. Good wine-list and many wines by the glass.

PLACES OF INTEREST

Baixas Village on the plain. Remains of defensive walls and a Gothic church.
Banyuls-sur-Mer Seaside resort and centre of the sweet vin doux naturel producers.
Céret This attractive village, full of winding narrow streets, is dominated by the Pyrenees.
Elne Lovely old city with a beautifully preserved 11th-century cathedral.
Perpignan Capital of the region, supposedly the hottest and driest city in France. The palace of the kings of Mallorca still stands in the centre surrounded by the old quarter within the inevitable modern outskirts.
Tautavel The 450,000-year-old skull of Homo Tautavelensis was discovered here in 1971. There is a museum devoted to it, but the village setting is perhaps finer than the museum.
Thuir Famous for the cellar belonging to apéritif producer Byrrh with its million-litre-capacity barrel. There is also a chocolate factory and the remains of ancient town walls.

243

Corsica

Compared to the wine regions of the French mainland, Corsica is like another world. Guy de Maupassant called the extraordinarily mountainous island "a mountain in the sea". Over 90 per cent of Corsica is 100 or more metres above sea level and the island boasts 20 peaks over 2,000 metres high. Only along the east coast is there a large area of flatter land. The country's mountainous landscape has naturally played an important part in the development of its wine culture.

The Corsicans are mountain people, proud and reserved – their island has been invaded so many times that they have developed an innate suspicion of foreign influences. Most villages were built in defensive positions high on slopes or hill-tops.

When the Phoenicians discovered this island in the 6th century BC they called it Korsaï, meaning 'covered with forests'. The description is still partly true today, for more than a quarter of Corsica's surface is covered with woodland, some of it of superlative pines, and the brushwood and low trees of the *maquis* are everywhere. Other peoples, both before and since the Phoenicians, have inhabited the island, among them the Etruscans, the Syracusans, the Carthaginians and the Romans. Evidence of their presence is displayed in the local museums.

In 1347 the Genoese took possession of the island's coastal areas – Genoese watch towers still stand at various points around the coast – but they did not venture into the interior. With one short interruption, Italian domination lasted for almost four centuries, which explains why in many respects Corsica, the Île de Beauté, is more Italian than French. The dialect (taught as part of the school curriculum) is closely related to Italian; the architecture looks Italian; the place-names are Italian; the food features pasta and other Italian specialities and even the grape varieties are Italian.
A Genoese order of 1572 gave Corsican wine-growing an initial impetus by directing every family to plant four vines, but it was only under French rule, especially after the French Revolution, that viticulture became really important. By about 1870 Corsica had some 15,000 hectares of vineyard and three quarters of its income came from wine – though the arrival of phylloxera put an end to this period of prosperity.

The proud independence of Corsica, an island of dramatic mountain peaks and fragrant scrubland, has been shaped by its rich and warlike history.

It was not until the 1960s that restoration really began. This was due largely to repatriates from Algeria who, with government help, soon reclaimed the malarial Eastern Plains and planted them with vines. Once again wine became Corsica's most important agricultural product. Unfortunately, however, quantity prevailed over quality at that time and most of the island's production consisted of cheap vins de table which were used to strengthen the lighter wines of the Languedoc region. Vins de pays were also produced, including some AC wines, but for many years these represented only three per cent of the total production. The proportion gradually increased to around 20 per cent, but even that was not enough to avert a crisis in the 1980s – as a result of which three quarters of the vineyards were uprooted.

At this point many wine-growers switched to the financially more rewarding cultivation of kiwi fruit. However, when kiwi production started to increase throughout the world, prices fell and Corsican farmers were facing a new dilemma. Only a return to the production of high-quality wines – and the attendant direct financial returns – could save the situation.

Mainly on the initiative of the island's cooperatives, large areas were planted with international grape varieties. Chardonnay, Cabernet Sauvignon, Merlot and Pinot Noir vines among others began to be cultivated on the gentle rolling hills of the Eastern Plain. The area devoted to wine-growing has now increased to 32,000 hectares.

The varietal wines are marketed as Vin de Pays de l'Île de Beauté and are meeting with great success in all export markets. These 'imported' varieties, together with native varieties,

Bonifacio, on an extraordinary site atop a sheer cliff, is linked to the citadel.

are thriving on the Eastern Plain partly because of the soil (which contains clay and shale among other things, with tuff in the subsoil) and partly because of the microclimate. Even during the summer, humidity is between 90 and 95 per cent, so by early morning the grapes are bathed in dew which somewhat tempers the effect of the burning sun later in the day.

The high mountain ranges also play an important role by providing excellent protection against the weather fronts from the west. Every evening around nine o'clock a cooling wind blows from the mountains over the vineyards. The resulting drop in temperature helps to retain the fruit flavour in the grapes, which in turn yield aromatic wines – wines of a mountainous rather than a Mediterranean nature.

Besides producing almost all the vins de pays, the Eastern Plain also produces three quarters of all Corsica's AC wines. This proportion is bound to rise further, as there are plans to increase the wine-growing area by several thousand hectares in years to come.

The basic varieties for Corsica's red and rosé AC wines are Sciacarello and Nielluccio, which complement each other perfectly. Sciacarello produces rather elegant, lively wines with red fruit, a slightly peppery, spicy aroma, and a bright colour. Nielluccio (which is related to Sangiovese) produces a more colourful wine, relatively robust and with fair amounts of tannin. When submitted to a special vinification process – as is practised by the Uval group in Borgo on the Eastern Plain – the grape can also produce pleasantly fruity, not-too-heavy wines with traces of blackberries and black cherries. Most dry white AC wines should contain at least 75 per cent Vermentino, a variety identical to Rolle which occurs in Provence among other places. Vermentino yields pleasant wines, full of character and fruit, which often have a fragrance of jasmine and aniseed. Corsica also produces some excellent sweet Muscat wines. Most bear the appellation Muscat du Cap Corse. They have a golden colour and a sumptuous taste.

In addition to the Eastern Plain – whose wines are marketed under the name of Vin de Corse – there are other wine regions along the coast. The most northern wines come from the Coteaux du Cap Corse and are grown on the narrow, calcareous cape of the same name. The dry white wines, such as those of Clos Nicrosi, are among the best in the island. The fact that there is also an apéritif named Cap Corse is rather confusing: apart from its name this bitter-sweet drink has no connections with the wine region. On the south-west side of the Cape is the Patrimonio wine region which consists of seven communes. The vineyards are laid out in the shape of a gigantic amphitheatre situated between a mountain ridge and a bay. Some 30 wine-growers produce a range of attractive rosé, red and white wines which tend to be of high quality. Further down the rugged, dry west coast lies the wine district of La Balagne, famous for good, robust reds that are marketed under the name Vin de Corse-Calvi. This region also produces refreshing, fruity whites. Ajaccio is one of the most active districts. The black Sciacarello grape predominates for red wines; again Vermentino is the basis of a number of pleasant whites.

The old fortified town of Sartène on its hillside is the centre of a district whose wines are mainly firmly structured reds. The southernmost wine area, Figari, is suffering a decline although the local cooperative is going to great lengths to earn recognition for its supple wines, particularly the reds. Not far from Figari is the busy holiday resort of Porto-Vecchio which, thanks to the grower Christian Imbert, is still numbered among the wine districts.

Deep in Corsica's interior (in Ponte-Leccia, a village situated between Ajaccio and Bastia) there is one important domaine producing wines from Corsica's mountain region, Domaine Vico.

PRODUCERS OF SPECIAL INTEREST

AJACCIO

Clos d'Alzeto 20151 Sari d'Orcino
Produces a selection of fruity reds, the best and most robust among them being the Cuvée Prestige. Rosé and whites are also produced. The owner is Napoléon Albertini.

Clos Capitoro 20166 Pisciatella
Jacques Bianchetti welcomes visitors to his cellars where they can taste a range of excellent wines including his red Cuvée Réservée (100% Sciacarello), an attractive rosé, a sweet dessert wine produced from Malvoisie plus Grenache and a lively mousseux from Vermentino.

Domaine Comte Péraldi
20167 Mezzavia
A large estate just outside Ajaccio which produces exemplary wines. The best is the red Clos du Cardinal which is aged for eight to nine months in new casks. The outside wall of the cellar is decorated with colourful pictures.

Domaine Martini
20117 Ocana-Cauro
Famous for its red wine from Sciacarello and Nielluccio.

Domaine de Paviglia
20166 Pisciatella
Shares the same owner as Clos Capitoro.

PATRIMONIO

Domaine Antoine Arena
20253 Patrimonio
Very successful dry whites from Malvoisie, and interesting reds.

Domaine Napoléon Brizi
20217 St-Florent

Domaine de Catarelli
20253 Farinole
Recommended for its rosé and white wines.

Domaine de Catarelli
20253 Patrimonio

Clos de Bernardi 20253 Patrimonio
Superb Muscat du Cap Corse.

Clos Grégoire 20253 Patrimonio

Clos Marfisi 20253 Patrimonio
One of Patrimonio's great names. The red wine (100% Nielluccio) is excellent and the white and Rosé d'une Nuit also show class.

Clos Montemagni
20253 Patrimonio
Red and rosé wines are the stars at this estate.

Domaine Gentile
20217 St-Florent
Gentile father and son produce some delicious white, red and rosé wines using the latest equipment.

Domaine Lazzarini
20253 Patrimonio

Domaine Leccia
20232 Poggio-d'Oletta
Very modern equipment.

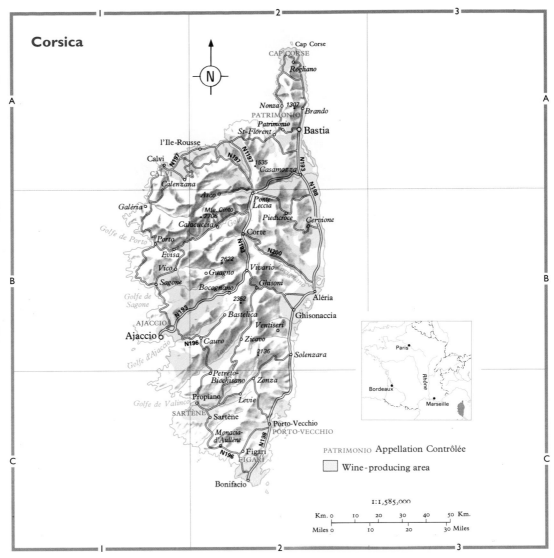

Corsica

PATRIMONIO Appellation Contrôlée

☐ Wine-producing area

1:1,585,000

Km. 0   10   20   30   40   50 Km.
Miles 0   10   20   30 Miles

Domaine Orenga de Gaffory
20253 Patrimonio
The Cuvée des Gourmets, which includes red and white wines, stands for top quality. A rich Muscat du Cap Corse is also produced.

Domaine Pastricciola
20253 Patrimonio
The tasting room is entered through a colonnaded terrace. Wines produced by Patrimonio's mayor Guy Maestracci include a decent fruity rosé and a succulent white wine, a pleasant red and beautiful Muscat.

Domaine San Quilico 20253 Patrimonio

VIN DE CORSE
Union des Vignerons Associés du Levant (Uval)
20290 Borgo
This group of cooperatives has been a driving force behind the revival of the wine industry on the Eastern Plain. It produces reliable, delicious wines among which are an attractive fruity pure Nielluccio; a refreshing, pure Vermentino and branded wines

including Corsican and varietal wines from Chardonnay, Cabernet Sauvignon, Merlot and Pinot Noir among other varieties. The group also represents several domaines including Corsica's largest estate, Domaine Santa Maria (300 hectares), Domaine de Lischetto, Domaine De Saline and Domaine de Tarrezza.

Union des Vignerons de l'Île de Beauté 20270 Aléria
Active cooperative producing a range of successful wines including the red Réserve du Président. The company also offers domaine wines such as Domaine de Ste Juliette.

Domaine Vico 20218 Ponte-Leccia
Decent wines from the mountains.

VIN DE CORSE-CALVI
Domaine d'Alzipratu
20214 Calenzana
Isolated estate producing a meaty, deep-red wine as well as a pleasant dry rosé.

Clos Landry 20260 Calvi
One of the most reliable and best producers of the AC wines. The rosé

is a real treat on a summer's day, the red a fine accompaniment to grilled meat and the white perfect with a salad.

Clos Reginu 20225 Feliceto
Absolutely delicious white, red and rosé wines including the rosé E Prove.

Domaine Culombu 20260 Lumio
The red Cuvée Prestige with its black label bearing the name Clos Culombu is particularly worthwhile.

Domaine de la Figarella
20260 Calvi

Domaine La Signoria 20260 Calvi
The same owner as Domaine de la Figarella: Achille Acquaviva.

VIN DE CORSE-COTEAUX DU CAP CORSE
Clos Nicrosi 20247 Rogliano
The whites produced here are perhaps the most famous in Corsica. The Muscat is also magnificent.

Domaine de Gioielli
20248 Macinaggio

Domaine Pieretti
20228 Sante-Severa
Produces both white and red wines.

VIN DE CORSE-FIGARI
Cave Coopérative Omu di Cagna 20131 Pianottoli

VIN DE CORSE-SARTÈNE
Domaine Fiumicicoli
20100 Sartène
Domaine de San-Michèle
20100 Sartène
Successful white and rosé wines.

VIN DE CORSE-PORTO-VECCHIO
Domaine de Torraccia
20137 Lecci-de-Porto-Vecchio
Christian Imbert is one of the most dynamic and expert wine-growers on the island. He makes firm, well balanced red wines, an aromatic white and a pleasant rosé.

WINE INFORMATION

Groupement Interprofessionnel des Vins de l'Île de Corse (GIVIC) Maison Verte, 13 boulevard du Fangu, 20200 Bastia
Tel (0)495 31 37 36 or (0)495 32 36 57
The Comité Régional d'Expansion et de Promotion Agricole de la Corse (CREPAC)
2 avenue Noël Franchini
20178 Ajaccio; Tel (0)495 29 42 63

HOTELS

Cala di Sole route des Sanguinaires 20000 Ajaccio Tel (0)495 52 01 36
Pleasant, modern rooms with sea views. Large swimming pool, tennis court. Half-board obligatory. Unfortunately, the quality of the food is not always first class.
Dolce Vita route des Sanguinaires 20000 Ajaccio Tel (0)495 52 00 93
This hotel-restaurant situated on the Gulf of Ajaccio offers excellent food as well as comfortable, modern rooms. It also has a swimming pool. In high season half-board is obligatory.

Eden Roc route des Sanguinaires 20000 Ajaccio Tel (0)495 52 01 47
Luxury hotel by the sea. All rooms have a terrace. Swimming pool. Sophisticated cuisine.
Fesch 7 rue Cardinal-Fesch 20000 Ajaccio Tel (0)495 21 50 52
Reasonably comfortable hotel in the centre of town. No restaurant.
Napoléon 4 rue Lorenzo Vero 20000 Ajaccio Tel (0)495 51 54 00
Rather featureless but adequate.
Posta Vecchia 3 rue Posta Vecchia 20200 Bastia Tel (0)495 32 32 38
Business-type hotel near the old town centre, right behind the quay.
La Signoria 20260 Calvi
Tel (0)495 65 23 73
Set in a beautiful park this quiet, pretty hotel manages to avoid the summer crowds. Swimming pool and tennis courts. The restaurant offers first-class cuisine.
Castel Brando 20222 Erbalunga
Tel (0)495 30 10 30
Charming hotel in a 19th-century country house. Rooms and suites are available. Erbalunga is by the sea not far north of Bastia and is very picturesque. No restaurant.
Dolce Notte 20217 St-Florent
Tel (0)495 370 665
Hotel without restaurant, situated near the beach. Very peaceful. Functional rooms.
Hôtel de la Corniche
20200 San Martino di Lota
Tel (0)495 31 40 98
High in the hills, 15 minutes' drive from Bastia, this fairly small hotel (20 rooms) has a good restaurant, a swimming pool and pleasant views.

RESTAURANTS

Corsican cuisine is closely akin to Italian, so many restaurants serve a rich variety of pastas (*pâtes*). The local charcuterie is tasty and one of the most common pâtés is made from blackbirds. The meat of young goats

and lambs is often served and the interior produces a good deal of game including wild boar. Naturally fish from the sea and from the mountain streams features frequently on menus and tomatoes, peppers, garlic, olive oil and fennel are used as flavourings. Much of the ewes'-milk cheese is sent to the mainland to be made into Roquefort.

À la Funtana 9 rue Notre-Dame 20000 Ajaccio Tel (0)495 21 78 04
Situated close to the cathedral, it offers excellent fish dishes prepared with love and talent.
Le Point U 59 bis
rue Cardinal-Fesch 20000 Ajaccio
Tel (0)495 21 59 92
Family-orientated cooking but also sumptuous dishes, country atmosphere and reasonable prices.
Le Bistrot du Port
quai des Martyrs 20200 Bastia
Tel (0)495 32 19 83
Fine fish dishes. Terrace.
Lavezzi 8 rue St-Jean, 20200 Bastia
Tel (0)495 31 05 73
The menu offers a wide choice of original, succulent dishes, prepared with fresh fish and shellfish.
La Caravelle 20169 Bonifacio
Tel (0)495 73 00 03
A converted Romanesque chapel with terrace, this is the best restaurant in town. Situated along the harbour, it specialises in Corsican-Italian fish dishes. There is also a luxury hotel with very pleasant, air-conditioned rooms.
U'Spuntu 20260 Calvi
Tel (0)495 65 07 06
Traditional country cooking in a country atmosphere.
La Ferme Campo di Monte
20239 Murato Tel (0)495 37 64 39
Here you can sample such irresistible Corsican specialities as charcuterie, marinated aubergines, braised lamb and cheeses. This farm-restaurant nestles on a hill slope above Murato,

some 30 minutes' drive from Bastia. Book in advance since it is very popular with the Corsicans themselves. Restricted opening times.
Le Bistrot du Port 20137 Porto-Vecchio Tel (0)495 70 22 96
Perfect for enjoying pleasant pasta and fish dishes on the terrace overlooking the harbour.
Le Lucullus 20137 Porto-Vecchio
Tel (0)495 70 10 17
The simple dishes are the best in this more expensive restaurant: grilled or roast lamb or goat, charcuterie and oven-baked fish dishes. Country decor.
La Chaumière 20100 Sartène
Tel (0)495 77 07 13
Pleasant for lunch: simple, delicious cuisine without fuss.

PLACES OF INTEREST

Corsica is an arid, rocky island, but it offers far more than that description suggests. Its coast is spectacular, with many sandy beaches and coves. The mountains and forests are superb walking country and there are many fascinating towns and villages with reminders of the island's warlike past.

Ajaccio Napoleon Bonaparte, born here in 1769, is still very much present. The main street is called the cours Napoléon and his name appears in many other places. The house where he was born (rue St-Charles) is a museum and the town hall houses a museum devoted to his life, the Musée Napoléonien. In the place Maréchal-Foch, the square in front of the town hall, a white marble statue of Napoleon as first consul stands above a fountain with four lions, and other statues of him are dotted about the town. Many members of the Bonaparte family are buried in the Chapelle Impériale (rue Cardinal-Fesch). The Musée Fesch beside the chapel has an admirable collection of Italian primitive art, and a

The Îles Sanguinaires contribute the island's ancient fortified defences.

Ajaccio bears many reminders of its favourite son, Napoleon Bonaparte.

collection of Corsican paintings is housed in the Musée du Capitellu opposite the Citadel (the Citadel is closed to visitors). The 16th-century Ajaccio cathedral where Napoleon was baptised is built in Venetian Renaissance style; the great man's last words are chiselled on a column to the left of the entrance.

About 12km north-west of Ajaccio is the imposing 19th-century Château de la Punta which is open to visitors. Behind the façade with its two rows of columns there are richly decorated rooms and an enormous fireplace.

Aléria Founded by the Phoenicians around 565BC, Aléria was later inhabited by the Etruscans, Romans and others. The Jérôme-Carcopino museum in the Matra fort exhibits local archeological finds. Among the most remarkable items are drinking vessels from 480BC in the form of a dog's and a donkey's head. The excavations are also open to visitors. In a nearby lake, whole islets of empty oyster shells have been found, tipped there by the Romans.

Aregno A village in the Balange with a church built from multicoloured stones and containing splendid 15th-century frescoes.

Bastia The island's largest commercial centre and port. The district around the old harbour has a great deal of atmosphere and the terraces along the 300-m open space opposite the new harbour can be convivial in the summer. Above Bastia there is a 14th-century Genoese fortification, the bastion from which the town's name is derived. Within its walls are the former cathedral of Ste-Marie (which houses an Assumption of the Virgin in silver); the chapel of Ste-Cros and the Musée Ethnographe de Corse (a governor's palace with vaulted rooms full of local history).

Bonifacio A fortress town on a spectacular site at the southern end of the island. Ramparts, a church and cobbled streets under arches survive from medieval times.

Calenzana The Couvent d'Alzipratu is at the foot of Monto Grosso. A former religious house, it was founded in 1509 and is partly in ruins but frescos and an impressive library can still be seen.

Calvi Columbus was born here in 1441 (a wall plaque in the rue Columbo commemorates the fact) and the French Foreign Legion has barracks here, but Calvi is first and foremost a holiday resort with a harbour for pleasure craft and fishing boats. The enormous citadel above the town contains, among other things, a museum of religious art (Oratoire St-Antoine) and the church of St-Jean-Baptiste (13th and 16th century). At the foot of the citadel, by

The steep vineyards of Domaine de Torraccia lie near the popular east-coast resort of Porto-Vecchio.

the harbour and the colourful La Marine district, there is an old round *tour du sel*, or salt store.

Cap Corse The island's northern tip is a rugged peninsula jutting into the Mediterranean. It offers dramatic scenery, fine beaches and fascinating hill villages. The area has its own wine, AC Coteaux de Cap Corse.

Corte Once the island's capital, now the largest inland town. The Foreign Legion garrisons the citadel which dates from medieval times. The old streets and shady courts are charming. Corte is a good centre from which to explore the island's wild interior.

Evisa Mountain village and a centre for fine walks in the hills and forests, including the three-hour descent of the Gorges de Spelunca.

Figari North-west of this wine village, Mount l'Omo de Cagna has a rock shaped like a man.

Filitosa Prehistoric religious and cultural monuments have been found here, including carved menhirs. Filitosa also has a museum.

l'Île Rousse Resort with a casino on the west coast.

Macinaggio In this Cap Corse village, 19th-century wine warehouses have been converted into a museum for Roman archeological finds which include a great deal of pottery.

Mariana The remains of a Roman harbour, a little to the south of Bastia. A Romanesque cathedral dating from 1119 stands next to the excavations.

Murato This hill-top village south-west of Bastia boasts a remarkable Italianate Romanesque church.

Patrimonio The photogenic 16th-century church of St-Martin stands amid the vineyards.

Porto-Vecchio Just north of this busy resort to the right of the N198 is the hamlet of Torre. It has given its name to a people who lived on the island around 1500BC and left behind many monuments. Torre itself has a burial site and just a little farther south, across the N189, is Castello d'Arraggio, the remains of a primitive fortification.

Propriano This little port at the mouth of a gulf in the south-west of the island dates from classical times. It is now a thriving seaside resort.

Roccapina On the road from Sartène to Bonifacio you can see the Rocher du Lion, a rock whose shape is reminiscent of a recumbent lion. Beside it stands a Genoese watch-tower.

Rogliano One of the prettiest villages of Cap Corse with many old houses, a ruined castle and the church of St-Agnel, whose chancel balustrade was donated by the Empress Eugénie.

St-Florent Resort and old harbour town in the north of the island, close to Cap Corse. Nearby is a 12th-century cathedral, all that remains of a city destroyed by the Saracen pirates.

Sartène The town centre is medieval and pure Corsican. A former prison now serves as a museum of prehistory. As in many places in Corsica, the Holy Week celebrations include a spectacular procession.

Index and Gazetteer

Entries in this combined index and gazetteer include wine areas, vineyards, châteaux, producers, grape varieties and places of interest. Alphabetisation is in word-by-word order, ignoring de, du, la and les etc. The words 'Château' and 'Domaine' are abbreviated in the index to Ch and Dom respectively. Châteaux and Domaines appear under the next element in their names, so Château Lafite-Rothschild, for example, is indexed as Lafite-Rothschild, Ch.

References in italic type indicate map pages and grid reference.

261

Picture Credits

AKG London 189
Robert Harding Picture Library: David Hughes 26–7
Scope: Jean-Luc Barde 4–5, 14, 16, 21, 25, 46 right, 83, 92, 100, 102, 103, 105, 106, 108, 111, 146, 148 left, 154, 166, 168, 169, 170 top, 173, 182, 184–5, 188, 190, 191, 194, 195, 196, 197, 198, 199, 200, 201, 202, 203, 231, 232, 234, 235, 236, 239, 241, 243 right, 245, 247 right; **Philippe Blondel** 226; **Charles Bowman** 192; **Daniel Czap** 151; **Michel Gotin** 40; **Jacques Guillard** 6, 15, 19, 22, 32, 34, 35, 37, 38 right, 42, 43, 44, 46 left, 48–9, 51, 54, 55, 57, 58–9, 61, 64, 65, 69, 70, 72–3, 74, 80, 84, 85, 88, 89, 95, 96, 98, 112, 114, 204–5, 206, 209, 211, 214, 215, 216, 217, 218, 220, 221, 222–3, 225, 233 bottom, 237, 248 left, 249; **Michel Guillard** 2–3, 24, 38 left, 56, 116–7, 118, 120, 121, 122, 124, 125, 126, 128, 129, 130, 132, 133, 134, 136, 137, 138, 140, 141, 142, 145, 148 right, 150, 152, 156, 157, 160, 162, 163, 164, 165, 170 bottom, 172, 174, 175, 176, 178, 179, 180, 183; **Noël Hautemanière** 30 top left, 47, 228–9, 233 top, 237 top, 242, 243 left, 246, 247 left; **Ph Beuzen: Îles Images** 244–5; **Francis Jalain** 36; **Michel Plassart** 13, 17, 28, 30 bottom, 30 top right, 76, 78, 97; **Guy Thouvenin** 212, 246, 248 right **VMF/Galeron** 71